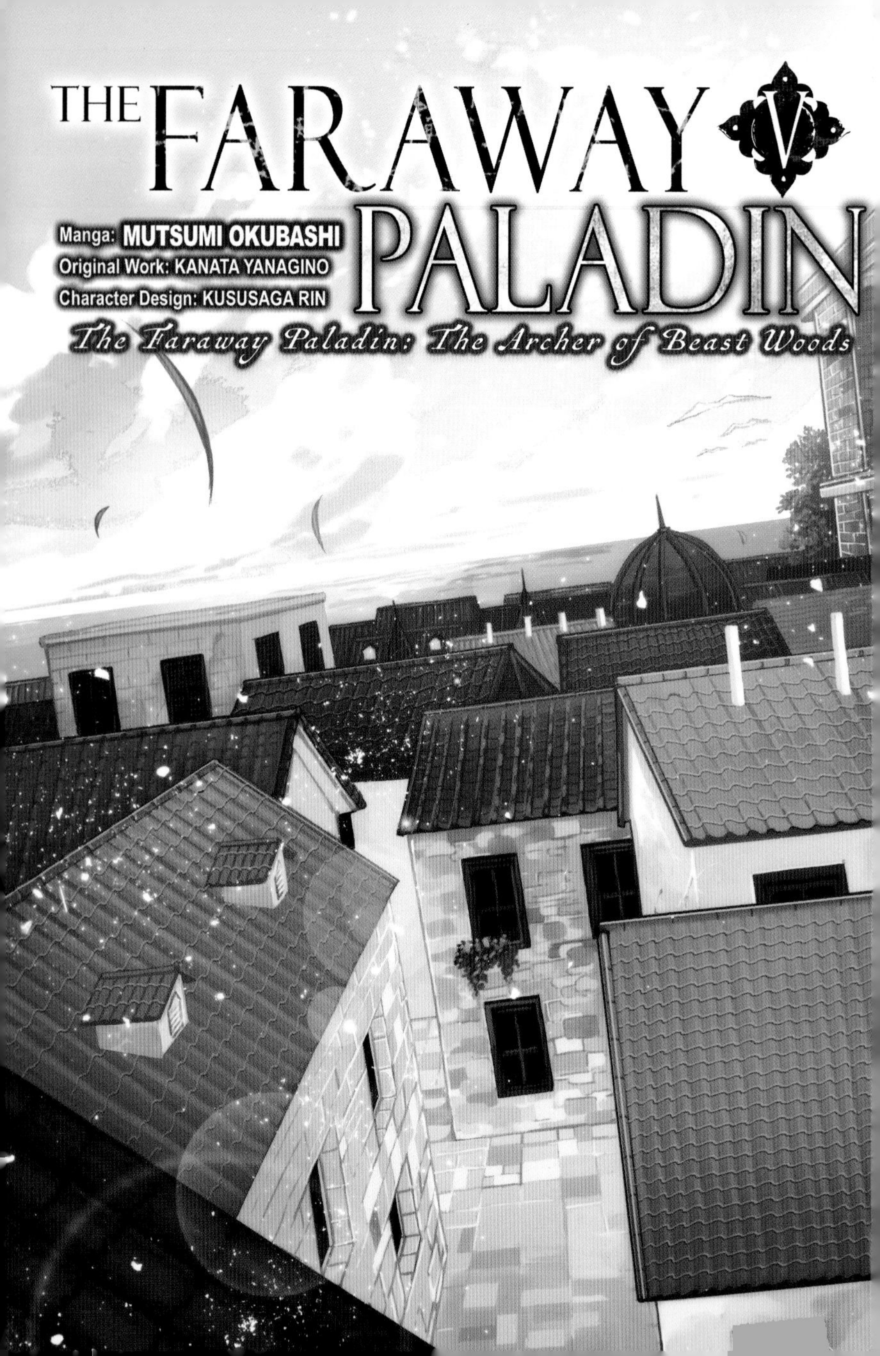
THE FARAWAY PALADIN V
Manga: MUTSUMI OKUBASHI
Original Work: KANATA YANAGINO
Character Design: KUSUSAGA RIN
The Faraway Paladin: The Archer of Beast Woods

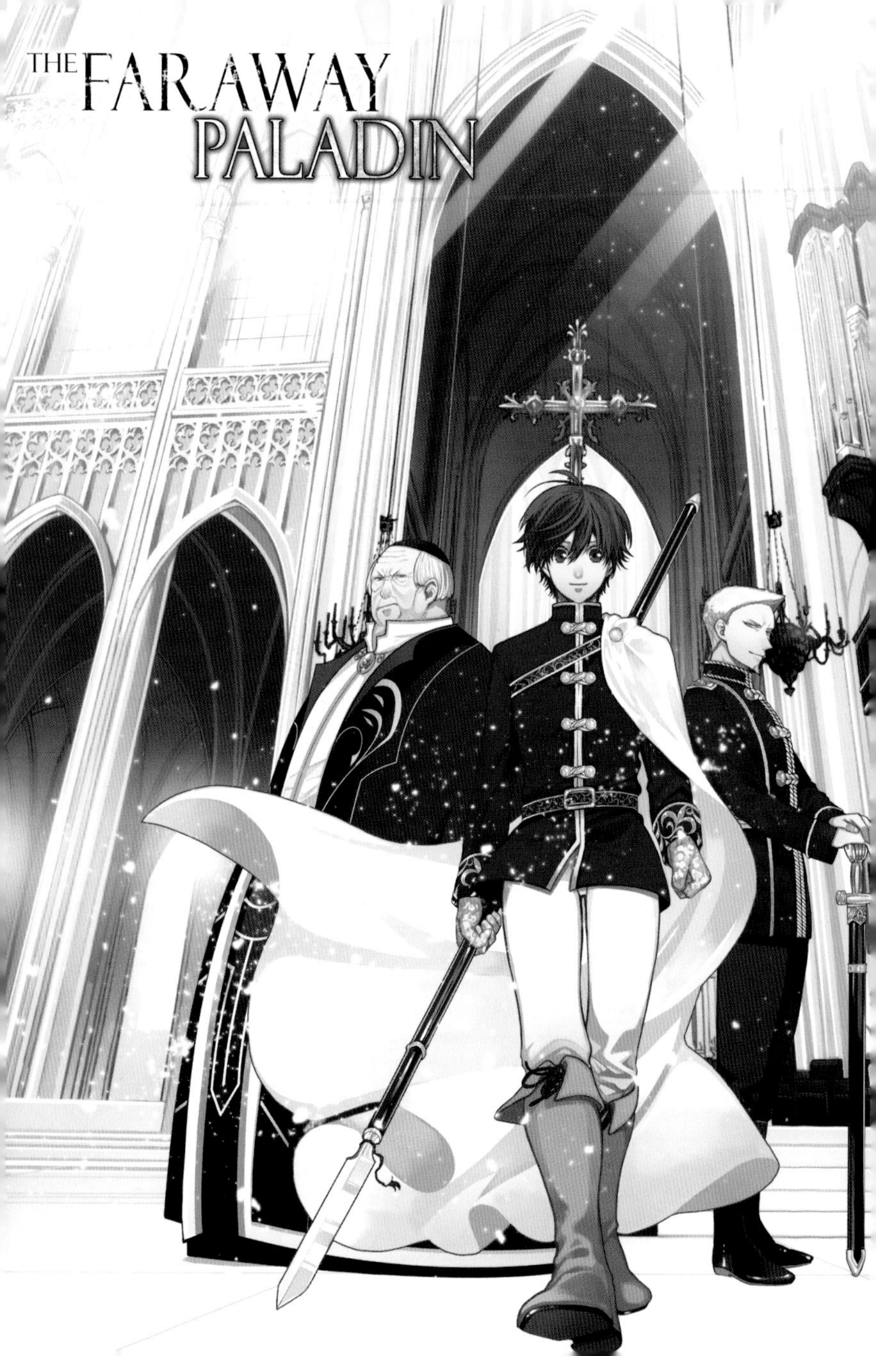
THE FARAWAY
PALADIN

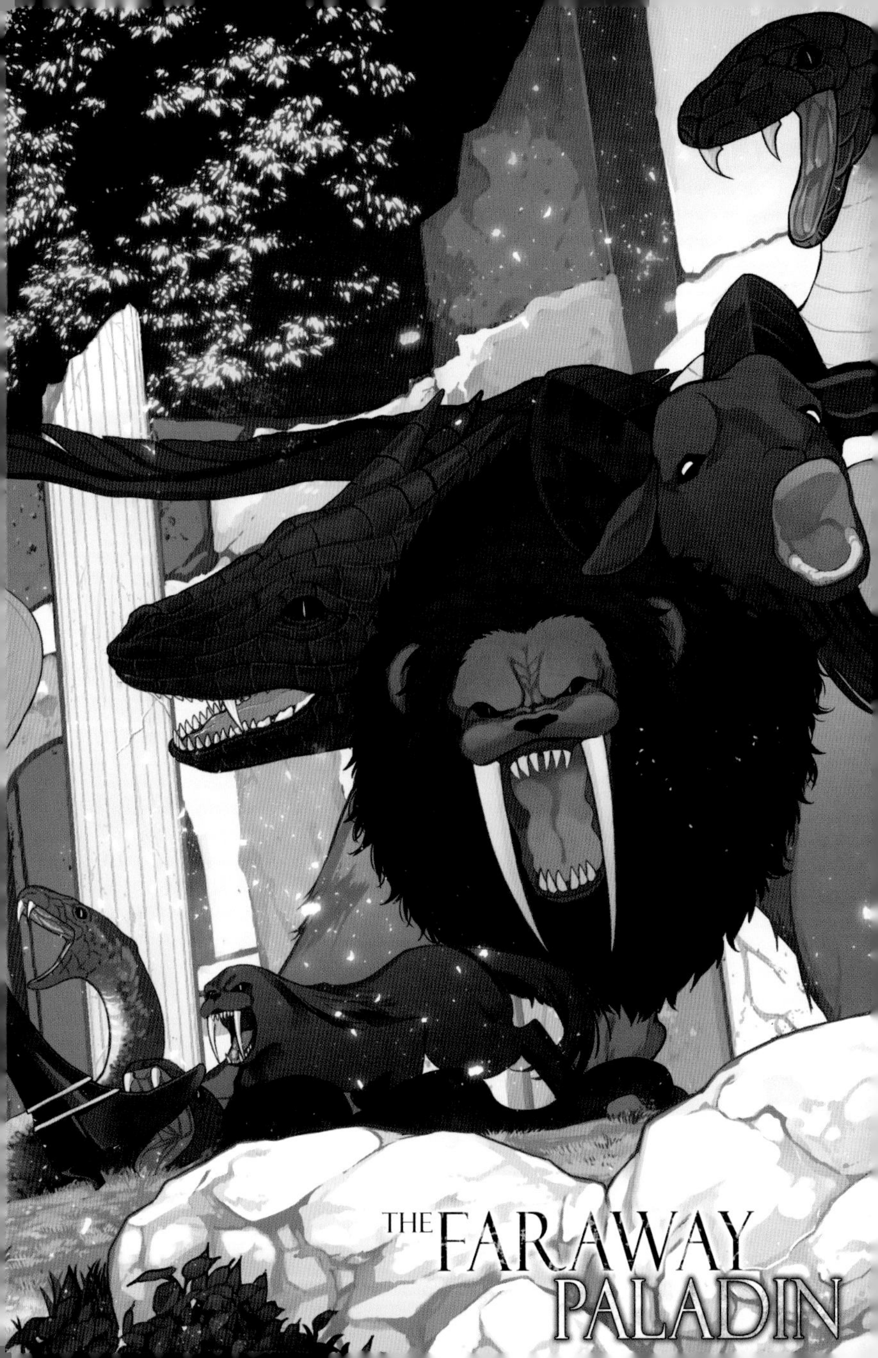
THE FARAWAY PALADIN

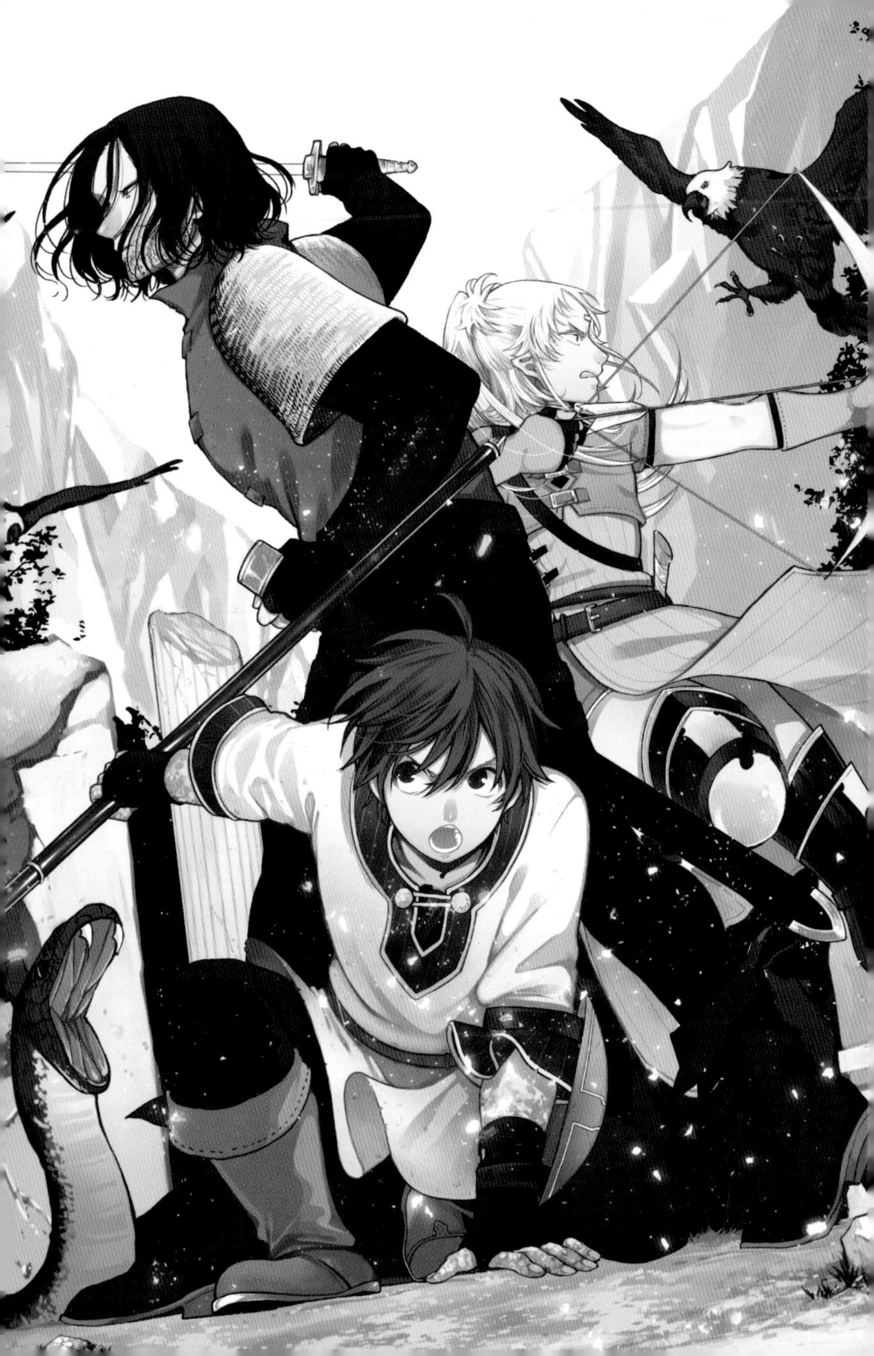

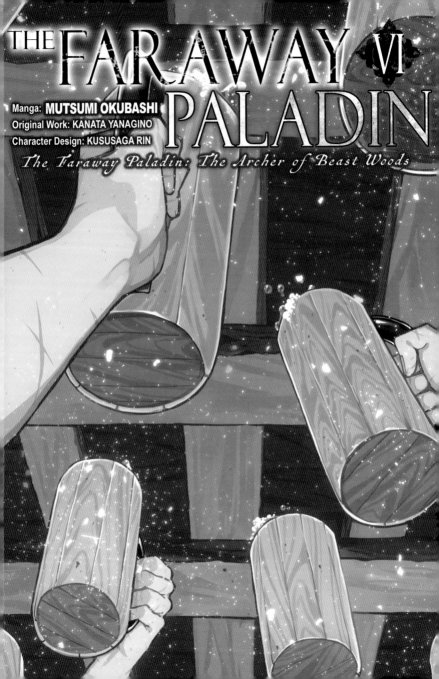

THE FARAWAY PALADIN VI

Manga: MUTSUMI OKUBASHI
Original Work: KANATA YANAGINO
Character Design: KUSUSAGA RIN

The Faraway Paladin: The Archer of Beast Woods

The Faraway Paladin
contents

The Faraway Paladin
contents

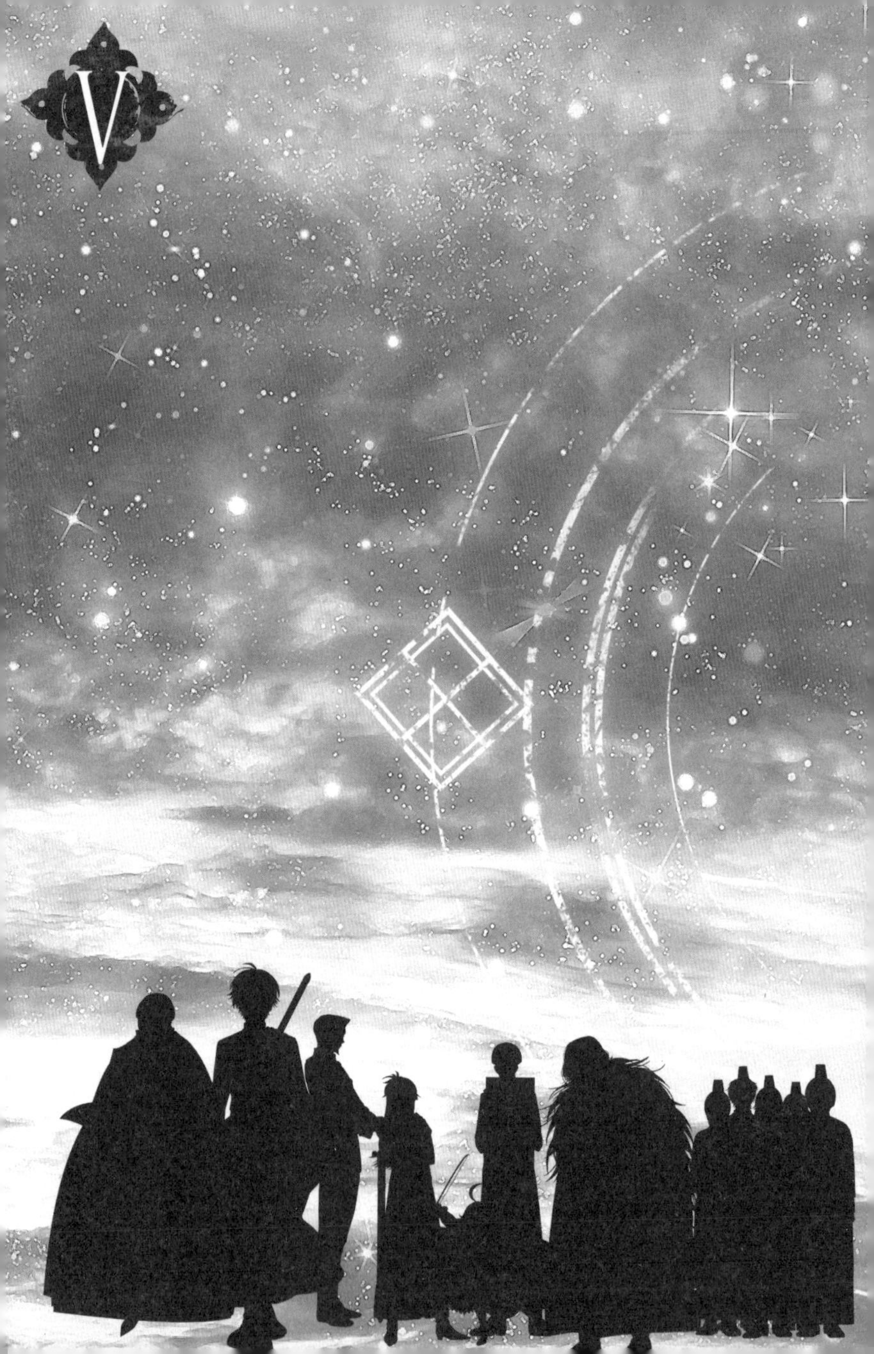
V

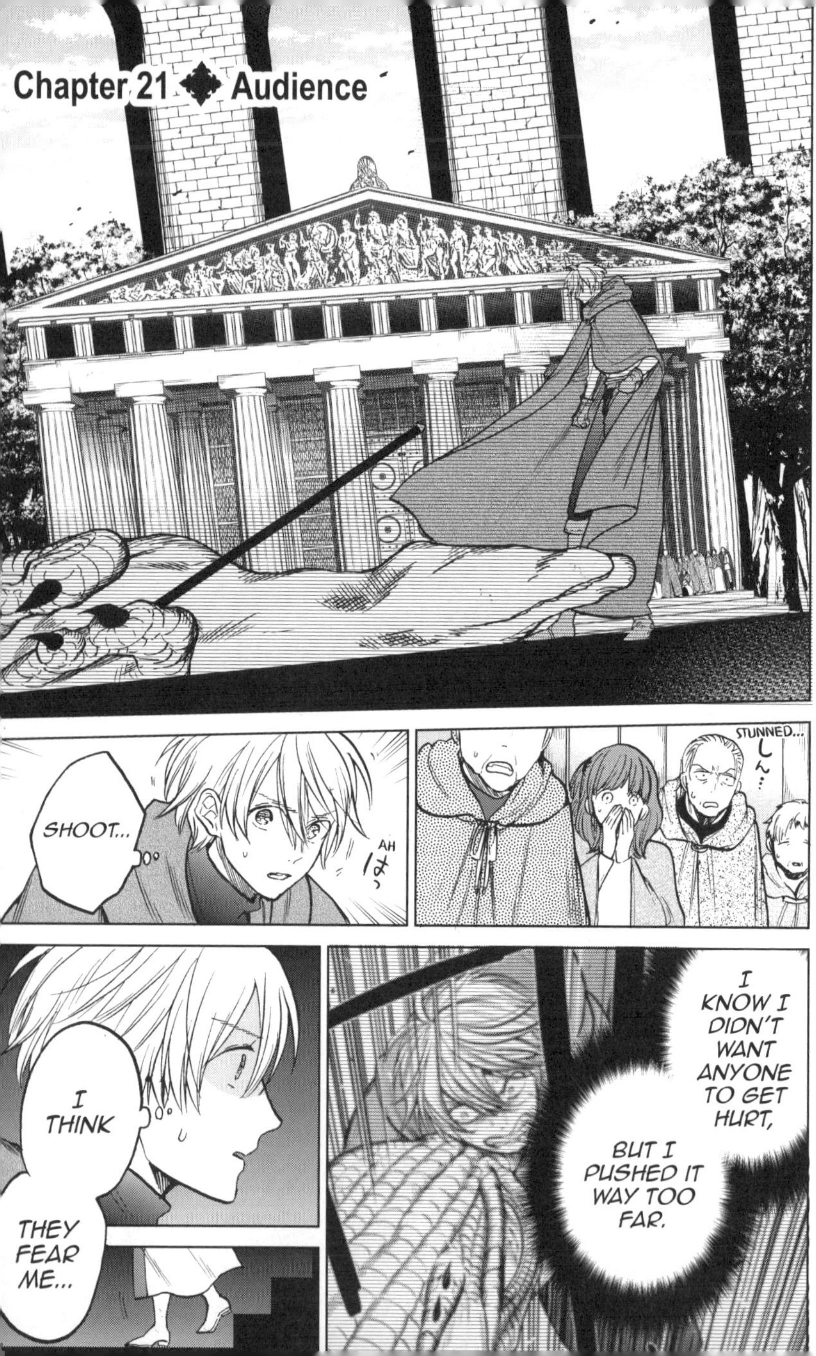
Chapter 21 Audience
STUNNED...
しん...
SHOOT...
AH
はっ
I KNOW I DIDN'T WANT ANYONE TO GET HURT,
BUT I PUSHED IT WAY TOO FAR.
I THINK
THEY FEAR ME...

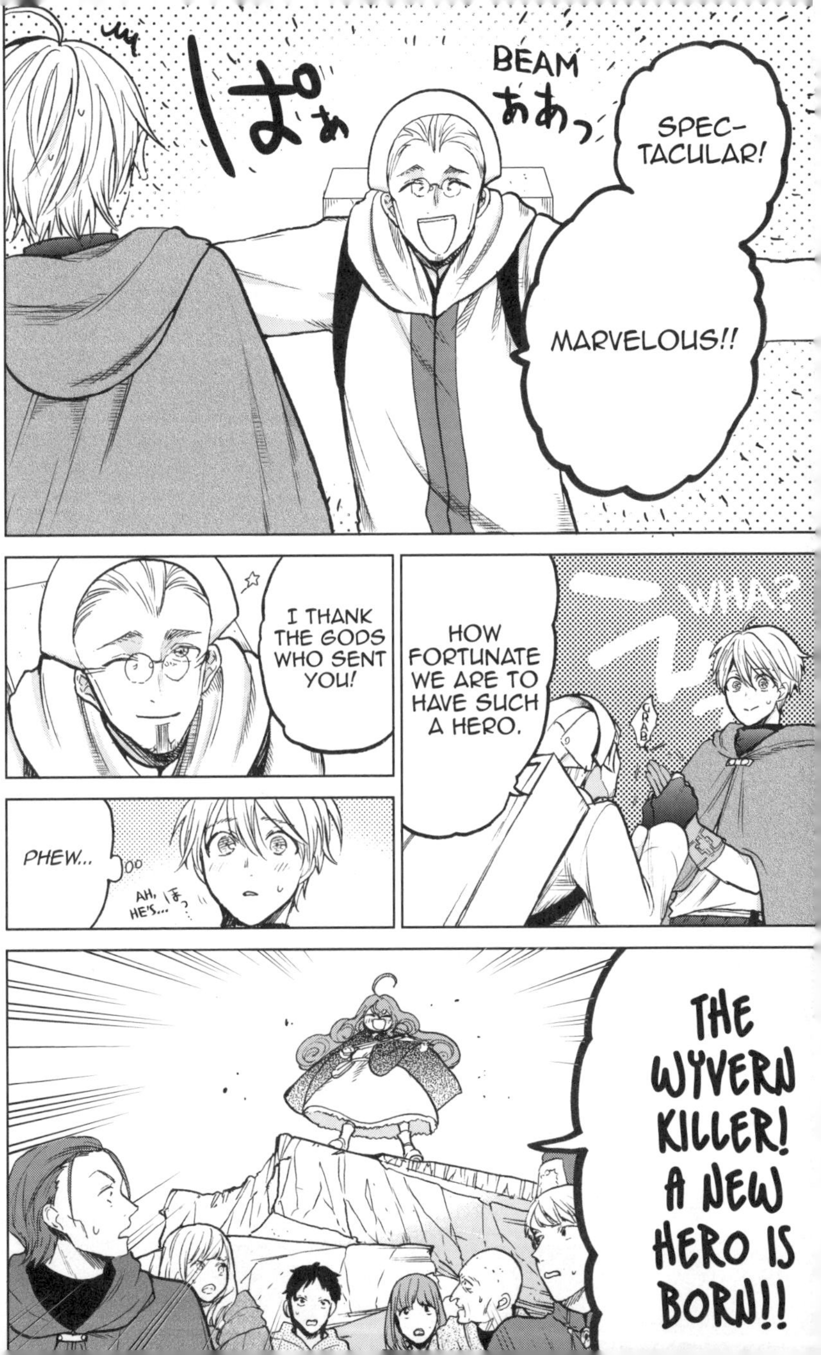
SPEC-TACULAR!
MARVELOUS!!
BEAM
ああっ
ぱぁ
HOW FORTUNATE WE ARE TO HAVE SUCH A HERO.
WHA?
GRAB
I THANK THE GODS WHO SENT YOU!
PHEW...
AH, HE'S...
ほっ
THE WYVERN KILLER! A NEW HERO IS BORN!!

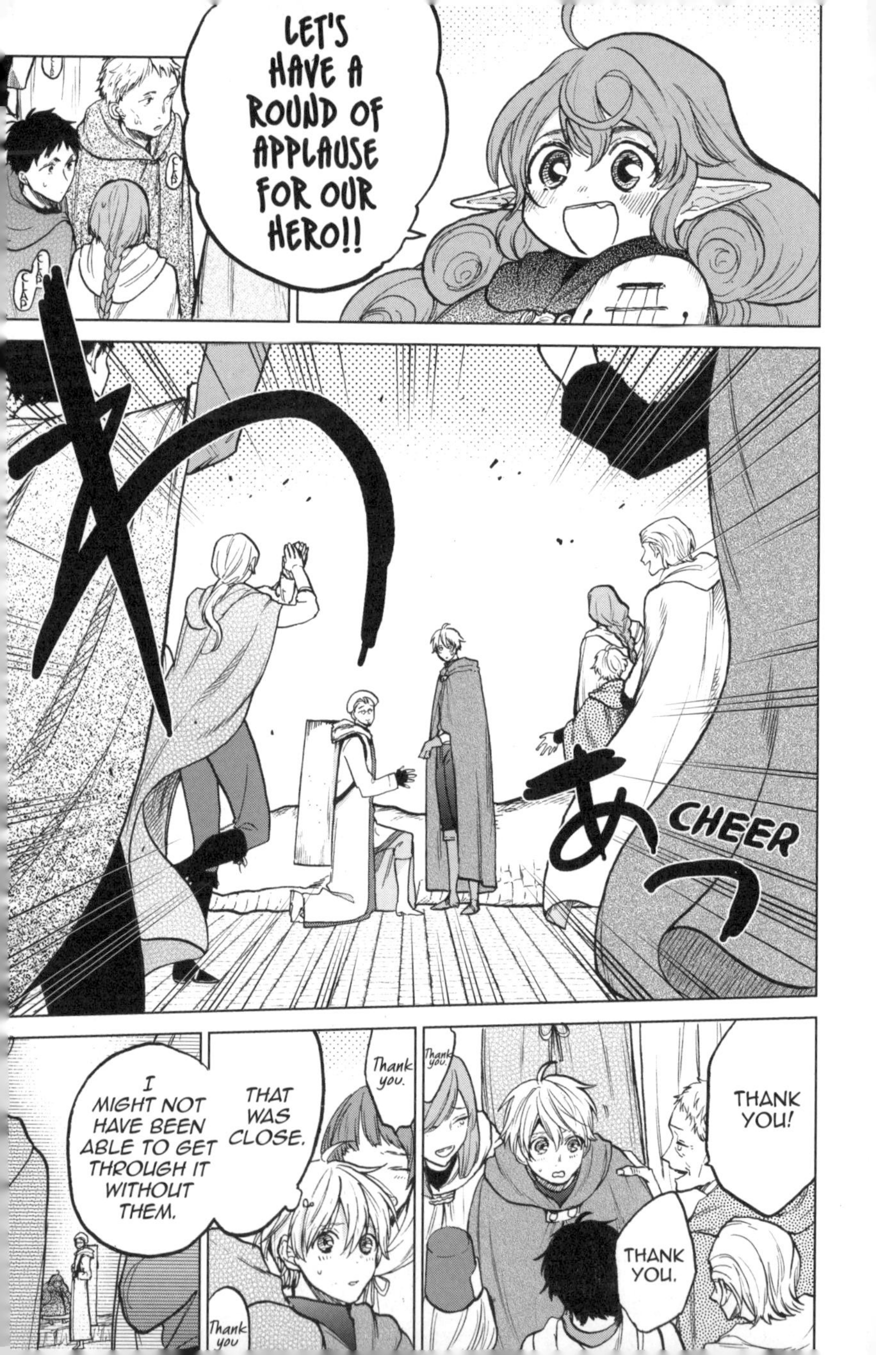

LET'S HAVE A ROUND OF APPLAUSE FOR OUR HERO!!
CLAP
CLAP
CLAP
わあっ
CHEER
THANK YOU!
Thank you.
THANK YOU.
Thank you.
THAT WAS CLOSE.
I MIGHT NOT HAVE BEEN ABLE TO GET THROUGH IT WITHOUT THEM.
Thank you

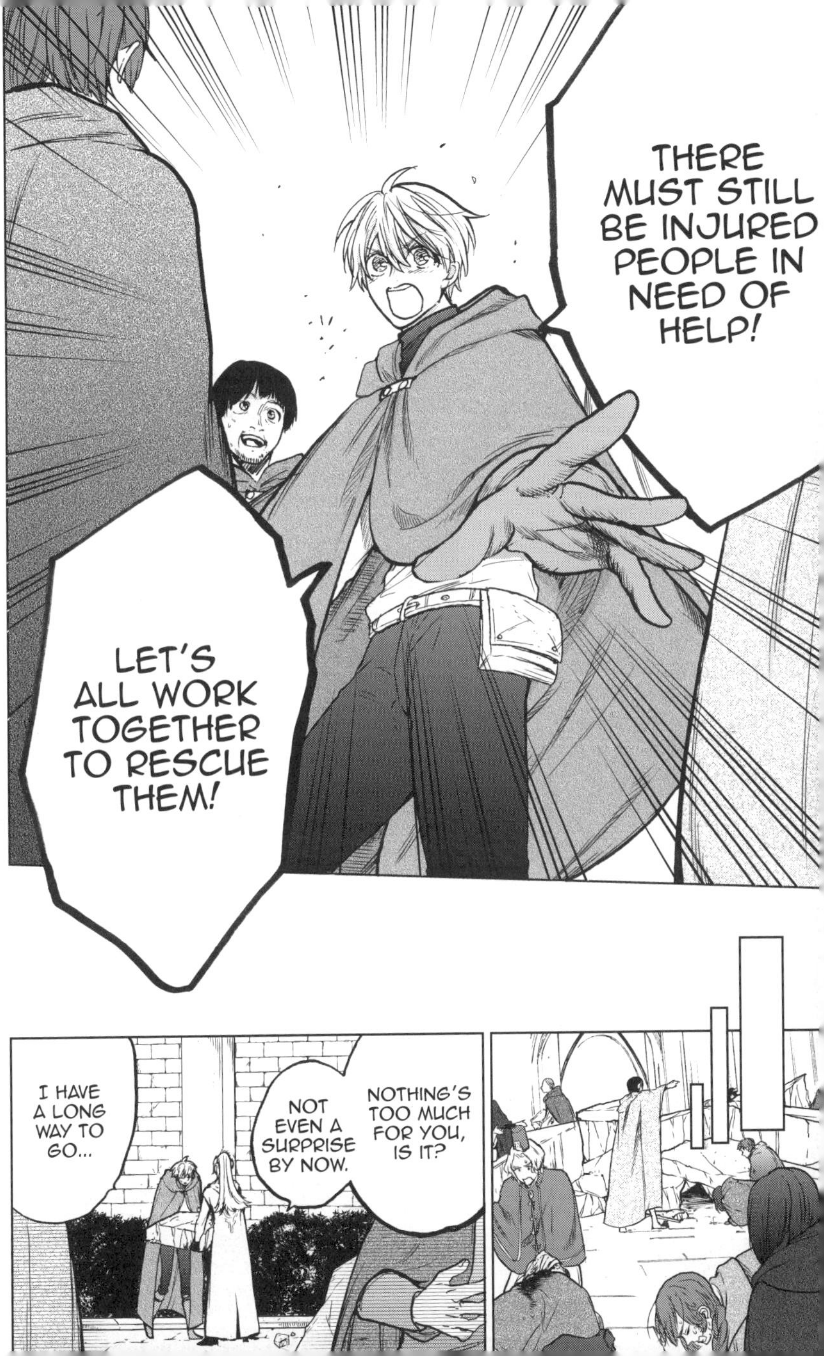
THERE MUST STILL BE INJURED PEOPLE IN NEED OF HELP!
LET'S ALL WORK TOGETHER TO RESCUE THEM!
NOTHING'S TOO MUCH FOR YOU, IS IT?
NOT EVEN A SURPRISE BY NOW.
I HAVE A LONG WAY TO GO...

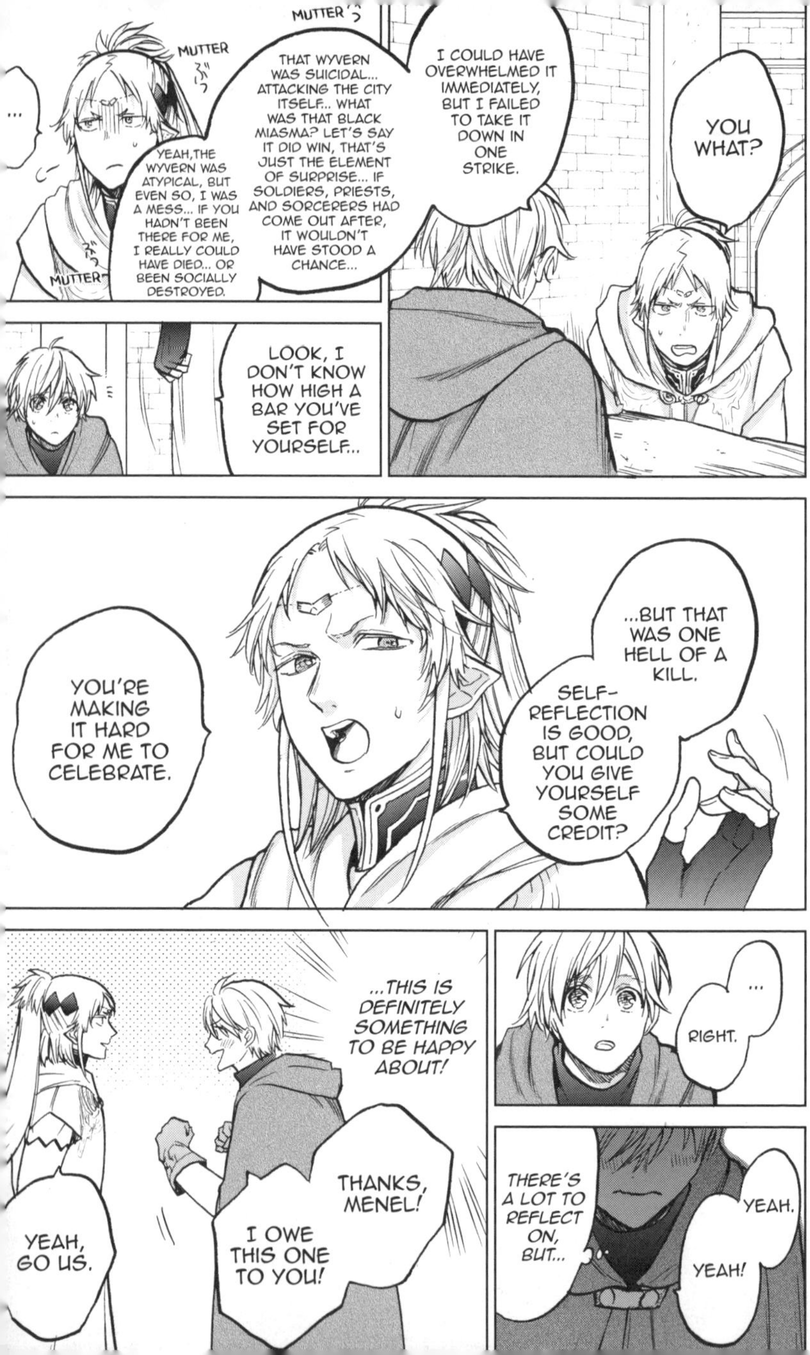
I COULD HAVE OVERWHELMED IT IMMEDIATELY, BUT I FAILED TO TAKE IT DOWN IN ONE STRIKE.
YOU WHAT?
MUTTER
THAT WYVERN WAS SUICIDAL... ATTACKING THE CITY ITSELF... WHAT WAS THAT BLACK MIASMA? LET'S SAY IT DID WIN, THAT'S JUST THE ELEMENT OF SURPRISE... IF SOLDIERS, PRIESTS, AND SORCERERS HAD COME OUT AFTER, IT WOULDN'T HAVE STOOD A CHANCE...
MUTTER
YEAH, THE WYVERN WAS ATYPICAL, BUT EVEN SO, I WAS A MESS... IF YOU HADN'T BEEN THERE FOR ME, I REALLY COULD HAVE DIED... OR BEEN SOCIALLY DESTROYED.
MUTTER
...
LOOK, I DON'T KNOW HOW HIGH A BAR YOU'VE SET FOR YOURSELF...
...BUT THAT WAS ONE HELL OF A KILL.
SELF-REFLECTION IS GOOD, BUT COULD YOU GIVE YOURSELF SOME CREDIT?
YOU'RE MAKING IT HARD FOR ME TO CELEBRATE.
...
RIGHT.
THERE'S A LOT TO REFLECT ON, BUT...
YEAH.
YEAH!
...THIS IS DEFINITELY SOMETHING TO BE HAPPY ABOUT!
THANKS, MENEL!
I OWE THIS ONE TO YOU!
YEAH, GO US.

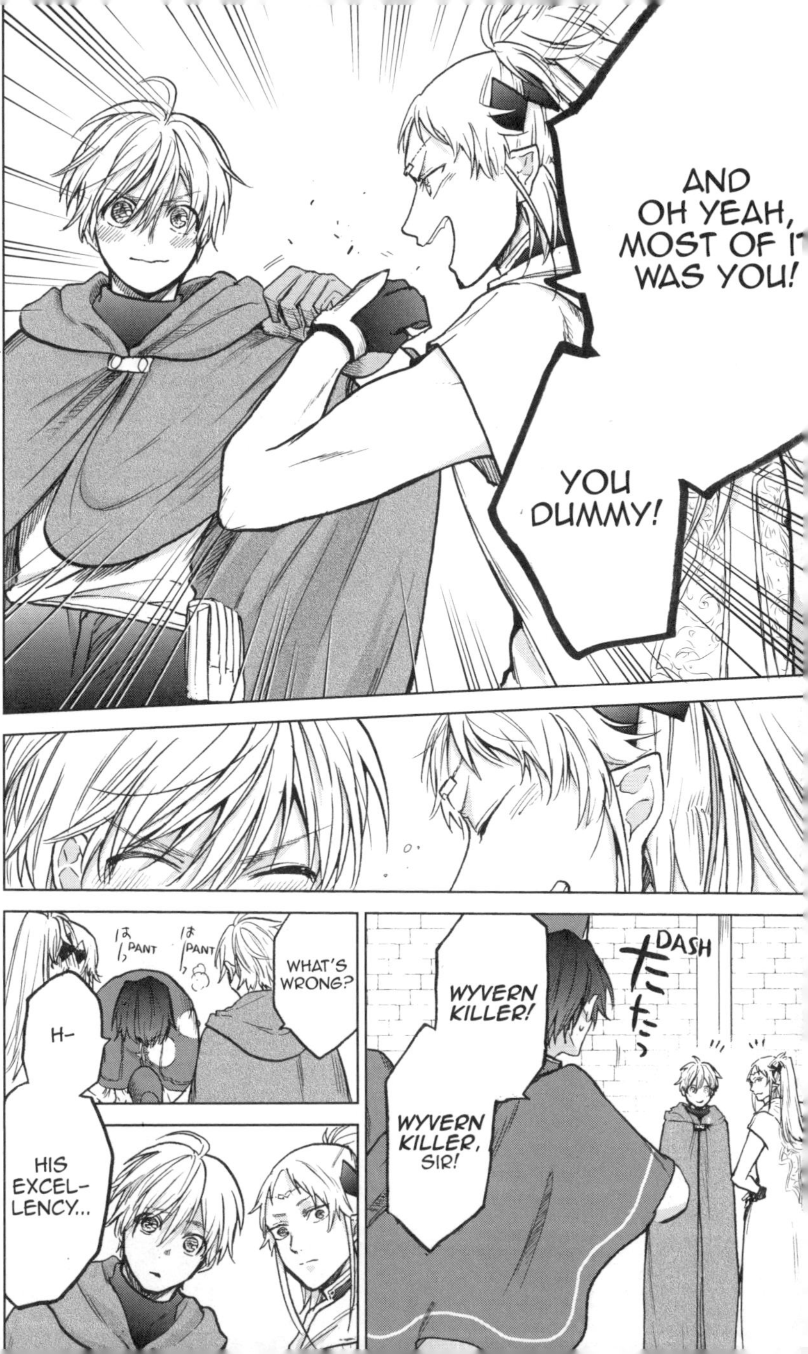
AND OH YEAH, MOST OF IT WAS YOU!
YOU DUMMY!
DASH
WYVERN KILLER!
WYVERN KILLER, SIR!
WHAT'S WRONG?
PANT
PANT
H-
HIS EXCELLENCY...

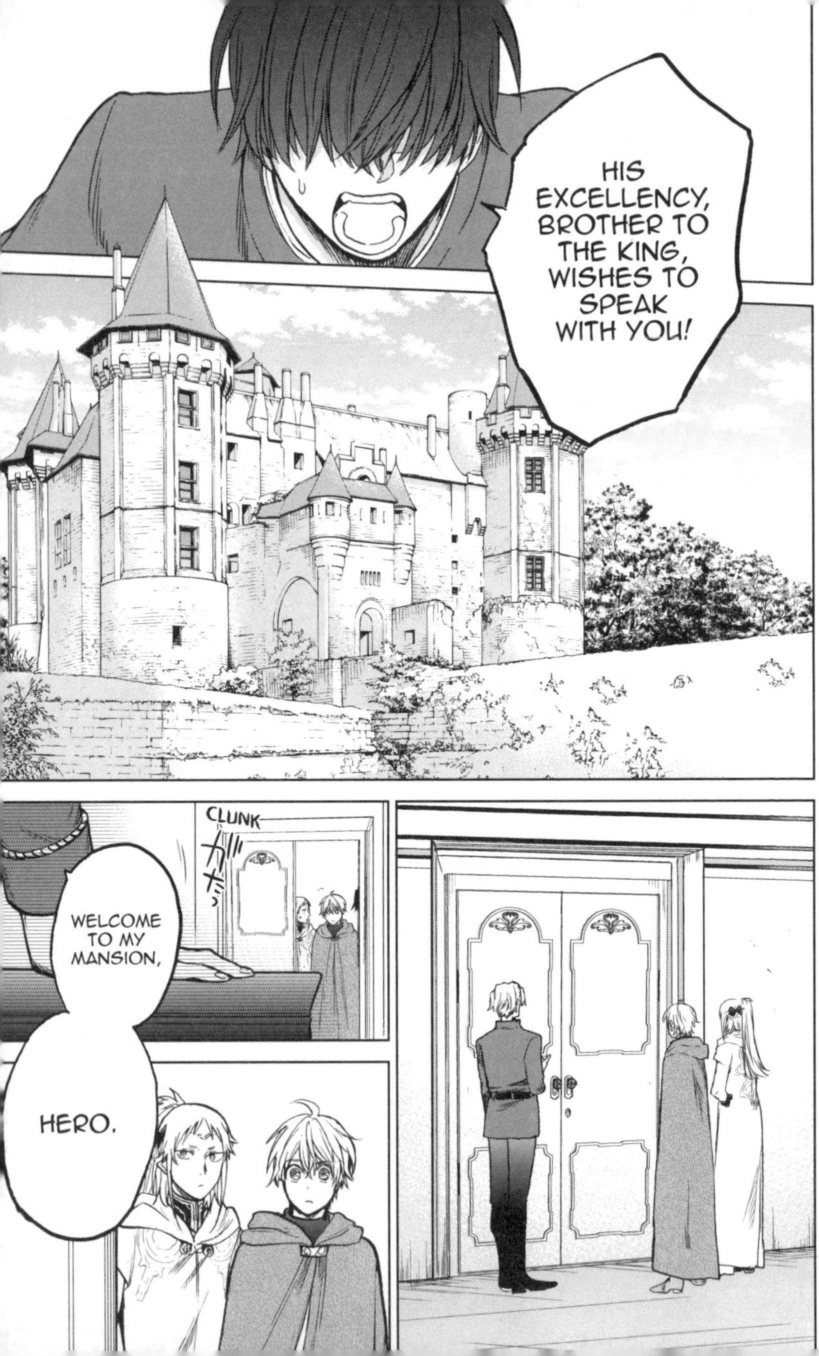
HIS EXCELLENCY, BROTHER TO THE KING, WISHES TO SPEAK WITH YOU!
CLUNK
WELCOME TO MY MANSION,
HERO.

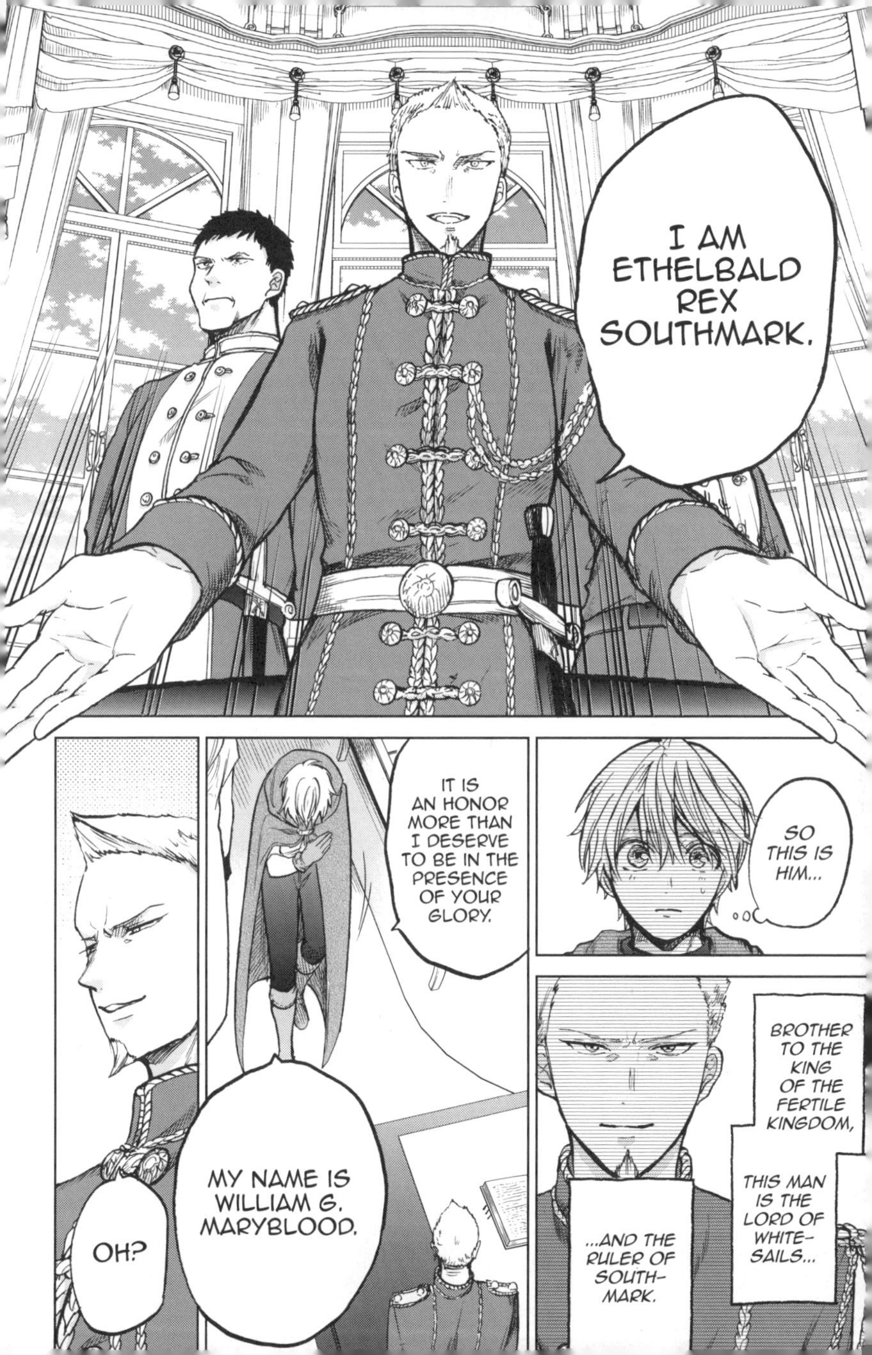
I AM ETHELBALD REX SOUTHMARK.
SO THIS IS HIM...
BROTHER TO THE KING OF THE FERTILE KINGDOM,
THIS MAN IS THE LORD OF WHITE-SAILS...
...AND THE RULER OF SOUTH-MARK.
IT IS AN HONOR MORE THAN I DESERVE TO BE IN THE PRESENCE OF YOUR GLORY.
MY NAME IS WILLIAM G. MARYBLOOD.
OH?

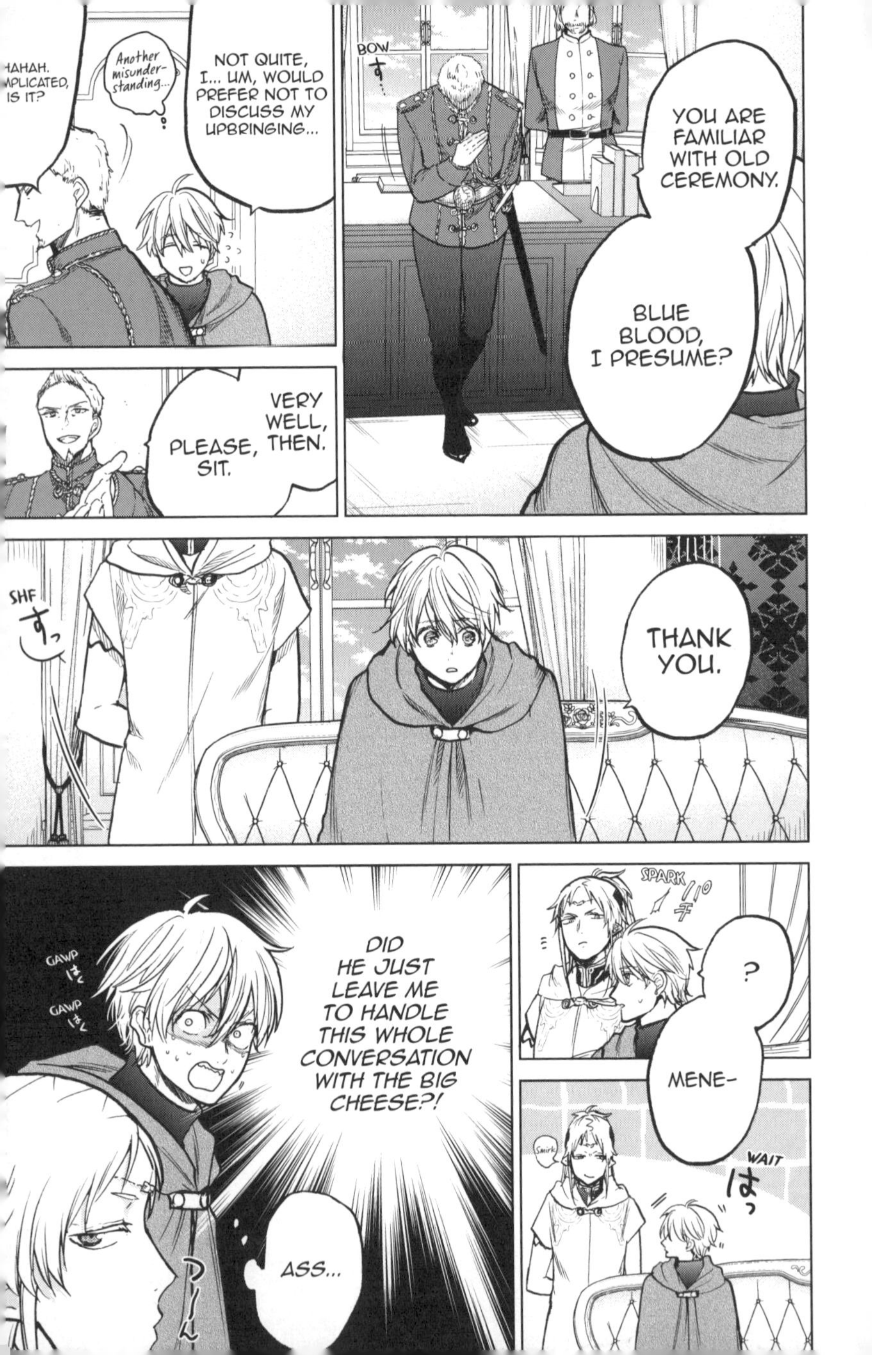
BOW
す…
YOU ARE FAMILIAR WITH OLD CEREMONY.
BLUE BLOOD, I PRESUME?
HAHAH. MPLICATED, IS IT?
Another misunder-standing...
NOT QUITE, I... UM, WOULD PREFER NOT TO DISCUSS MY UPBRINGING...
VERY WELL, THEN. PLEASE, SIT.
THANK YOU.
SHF
すっ
SPARK
パチ
?
MENE-
WAIT
はっ
Smirk
DID HE JUST LEAVE ME TO HANDLE THIS WHOLE CONVERSATION WITH THE BIG CHEESE?!
GAWP
はく
GAWP
はく
ASS...

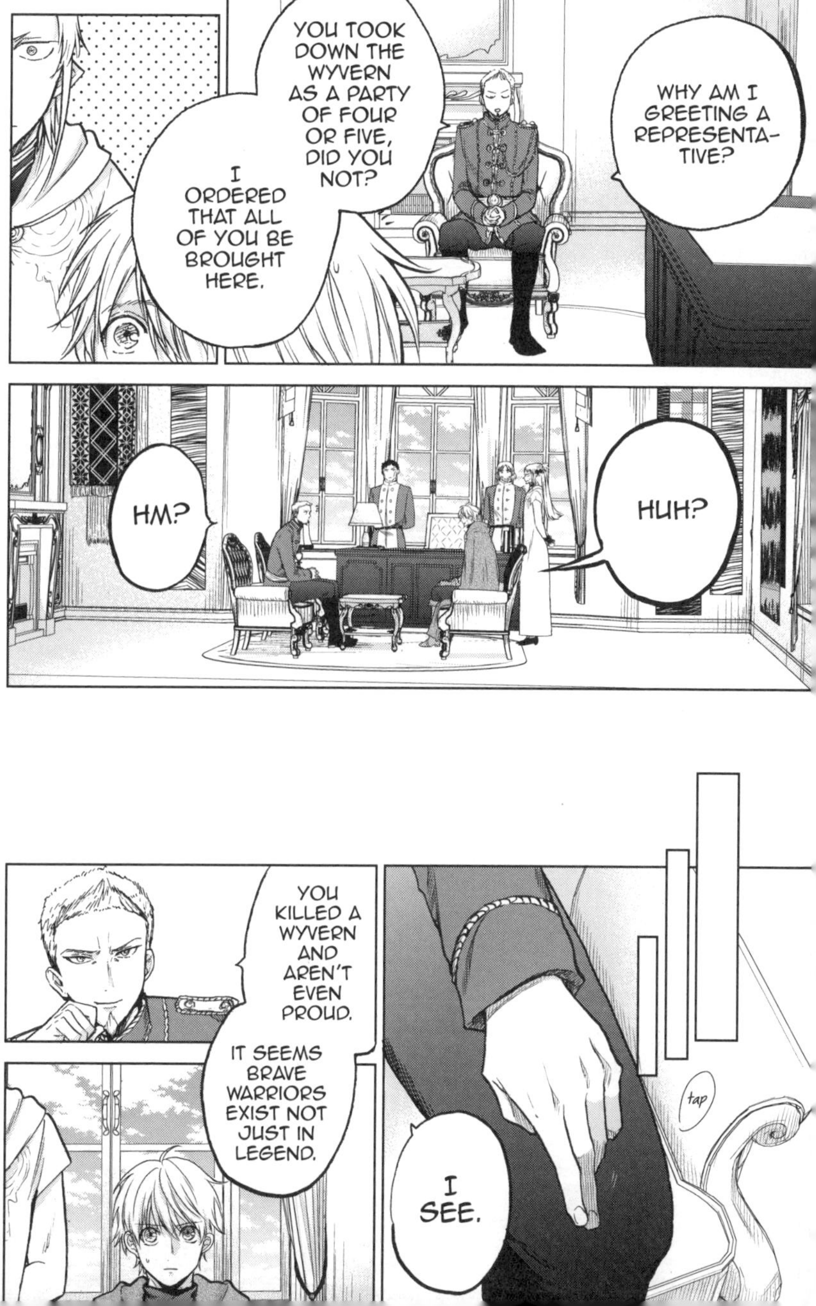
WHY AM I GREETING A REPRESENTA-TIVE?
YOU TOOK DOWN THE WYVERN AS A PARTY OF FOUR OR FIVE, DID YOU NOT?
I ORDERED THAT ALL OF YOU BE BROUGHT HERE.
HUH?
HM?
tap
I SEE.
YOU KILLED A WYVERN AND AREN'T EVEN PROUD.
IT SEEMS BRAVE WARRIORS EXIST NOT JUST IN LEGEND.

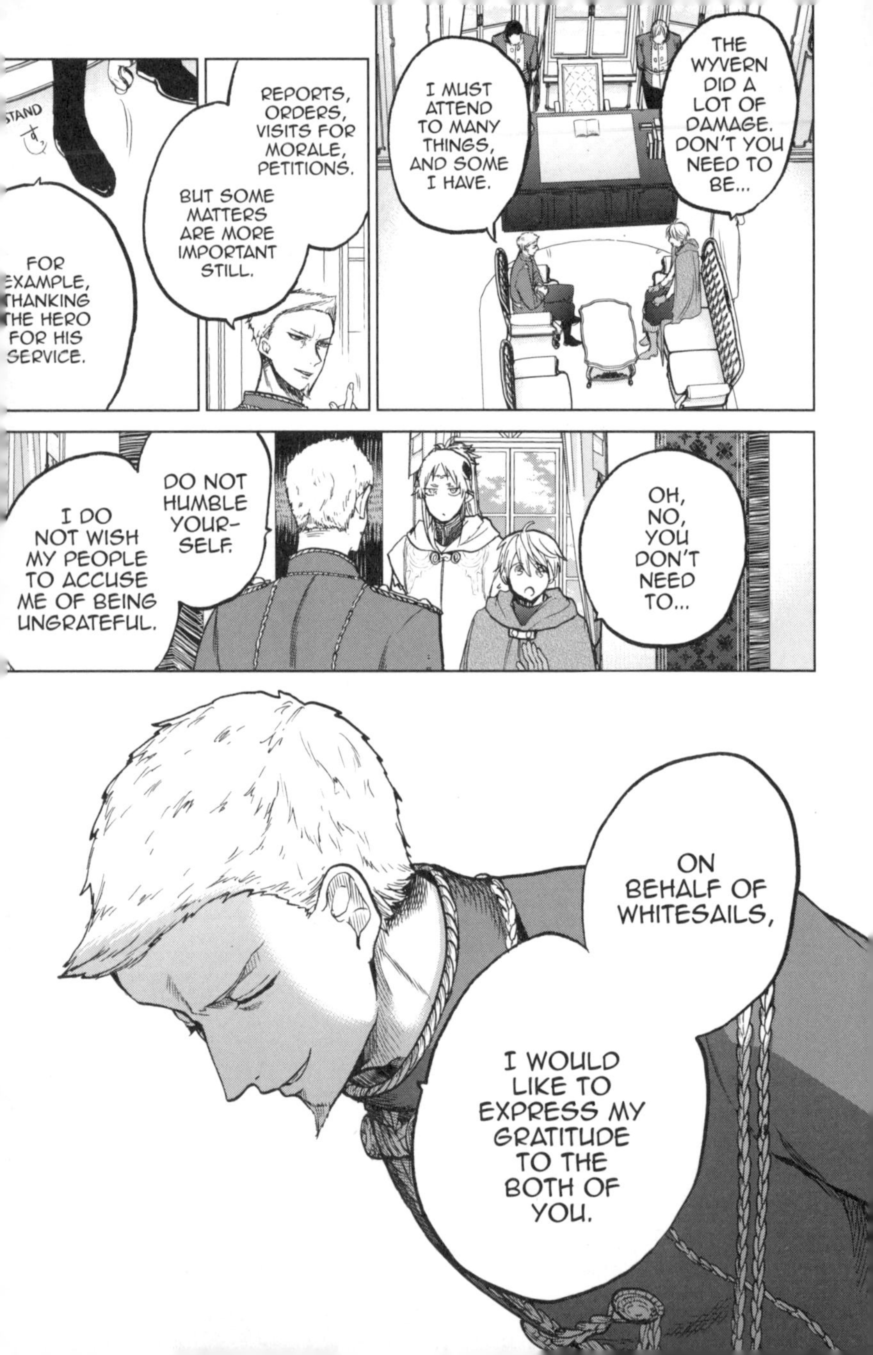
THE WYVERN DID A LOT OF DAMAGE. DON'T YOU NEED TO BE...
I MUST ATTEND TO MANY THINGS, AND SOME I HAVE.
REPORTS, ORDERS, VISITS FOR MORALE, PETITIONS.
BUT SOME MATTERS ARE MORE IMPORTANT STILL.
STAND
FOR EXAMPLE, THANKING THE HERO FOR HIS SERVICE.
OH, NO, YOU DON'T NEED TO...
DO NOT HUMBLE YOURSELF.
I DO NOT WISH MY PEOPLE TO ACCUSE ME OF BEING UNGRATEFUL.
ON BEHALF OF WHITESAILS,
I WOULD LIKE TO EXPRESS MY GRATITUDE TO THE BOTH OF YOU.

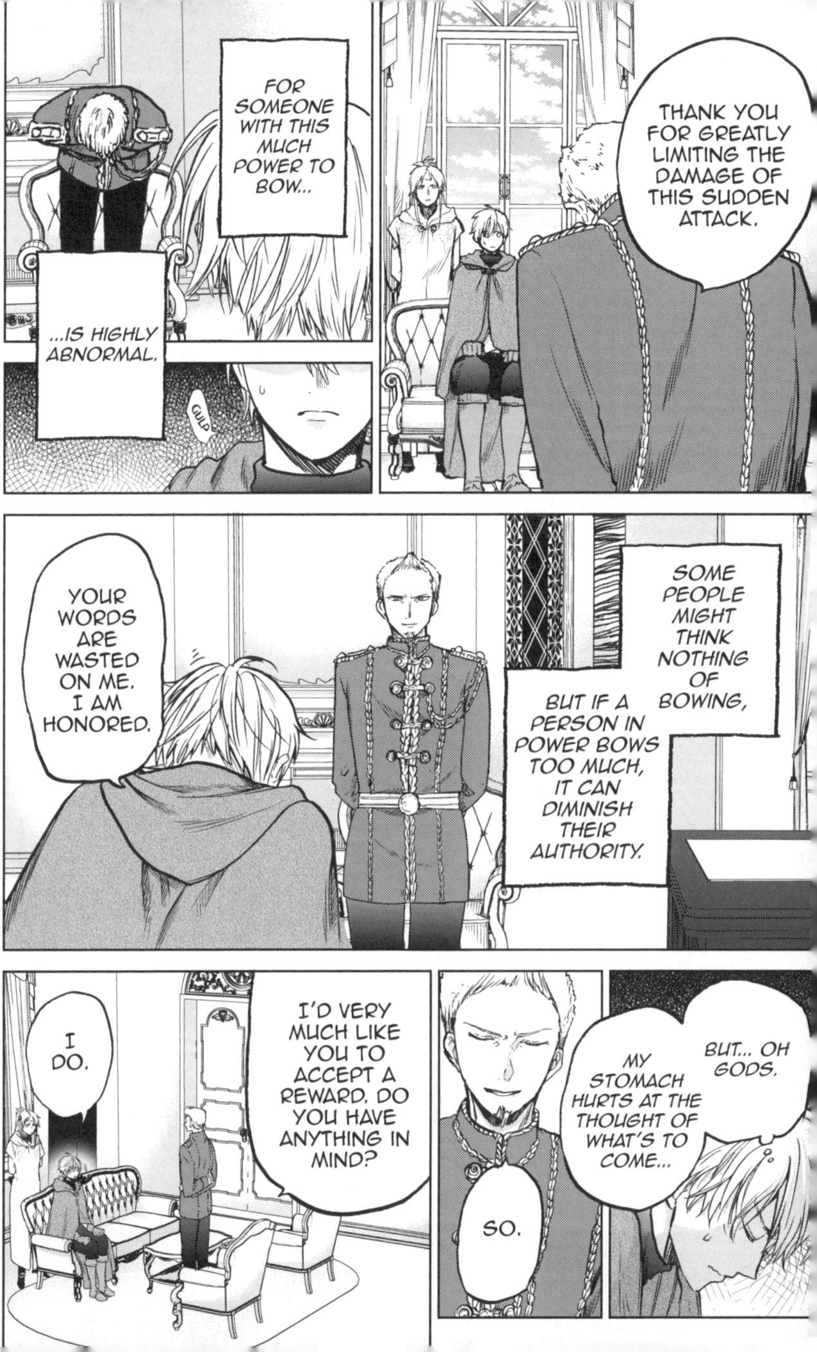
THANK YOU FOR GREATLY LIMITING THE DAMAGE OF THIS SUDDEN ATTACK.
FOR SOMEONE WITH THIS MUCH POWER TO BOW...
...IS HIGHLY ABNORMAL.
GULP
SOME PEOPLE MIGHT THINK NOTHING OF BOWING,
BUT IF A PERSON IN POWER BOWS TOO MUCH, IT CAN DIMINISH THEIR AUTHORITY.
YOUR WORDS ARE WASTED ON ME. I AM HONORED.
BUT... OH GODS.
MY STOMACH HURTS AT THE THOUGHT OF WHAT'S TO COME...
SO.
I'D VERY MUCH LIKE YOU TO ACCEPT A REWARD. DO YOU HAVE ANYTHING IN MIND?
I DO.

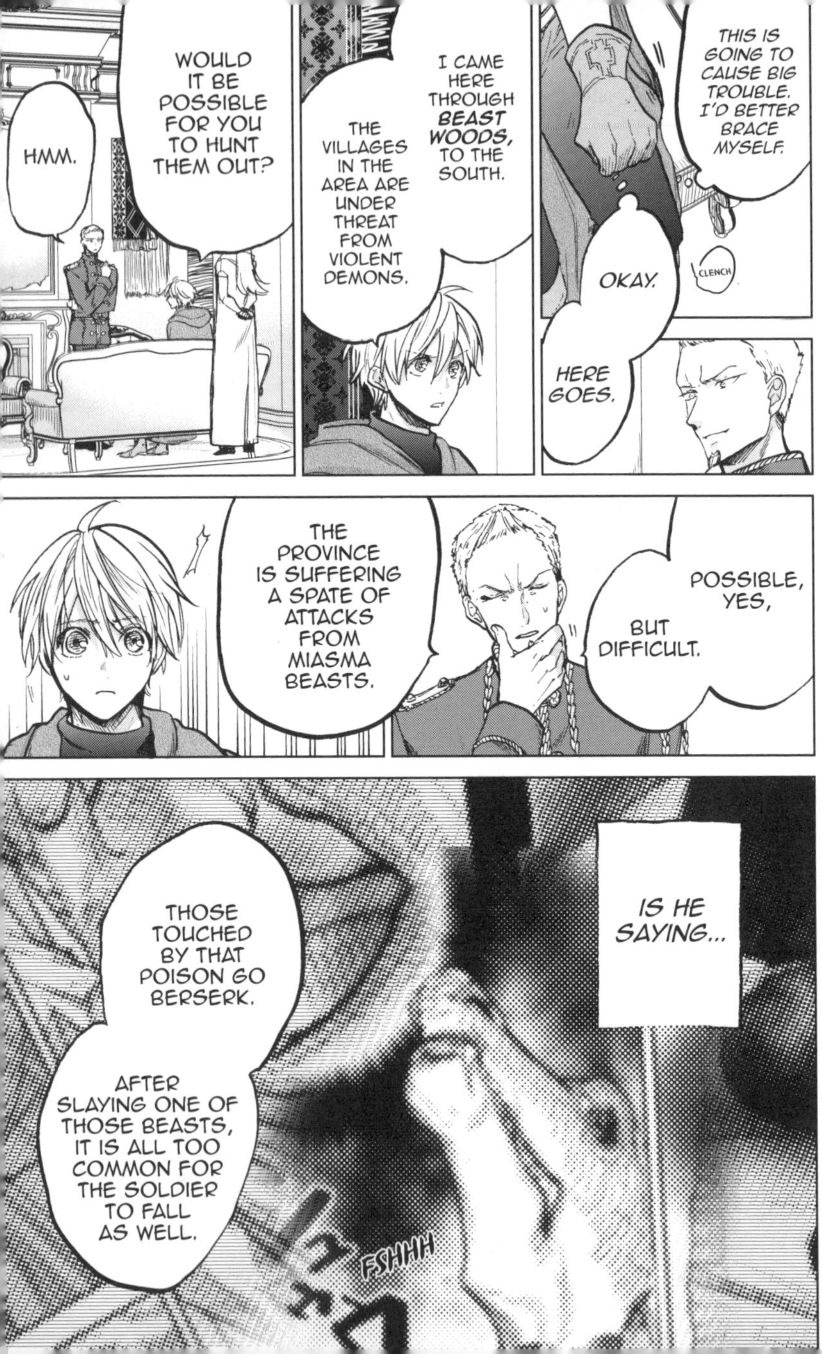
THIS IS GOING TO CAUSE BIG TROUBLE. I'D BETTER BRACE MYSELF.
OKAY.
CLENCH
HERE GOES.
I CAME HERE THROUGH BEAST WOODS, TO THE SOUTH.
THE VILLAGES IN THE AREA ARE UNDER THREAT FROM VIOLENT DEMONS.
WOULD IT BE POSSIBLE FOR YOU TO HUNT THEM OUT?
HMM.
POSSIBLE, YES,
BUT DIFFICULT.
THE PROVINCE IS SUFFERING A SPATE OF ATTACKS FROM MIASMA BEASTS.
IS HE SAYING...
THOSE TOUCHED BY THAT POISON GO BERSERK.
AFTER SLAYING ONE OF THOSE BEASTS, IT IS ALL TOO COMMON FOR THE SOLDIER TO FALL AS WELL.
FSHHH

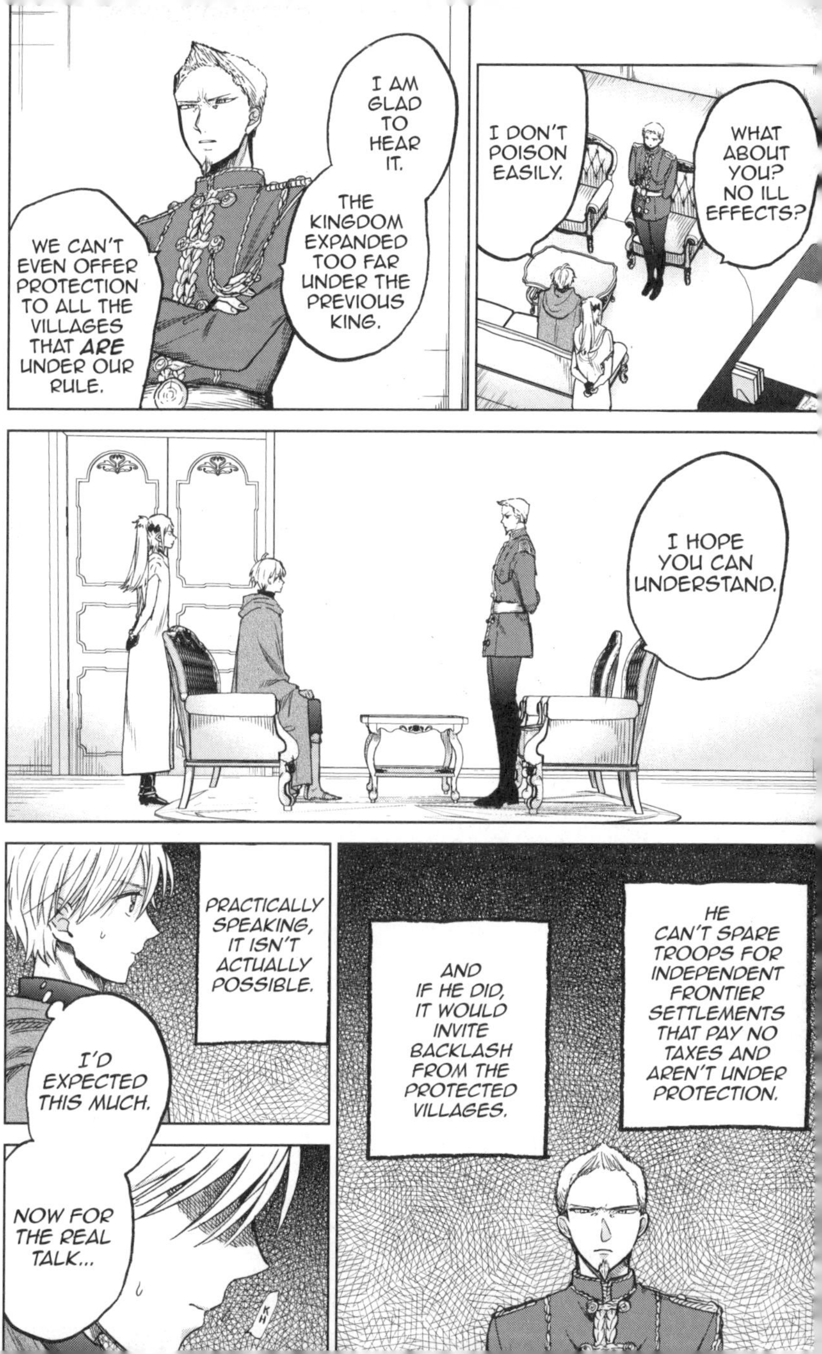
WHAT ABOUT YOU? NO ILL EFFECTS?
I DON'T POISON EASILY.
I AM GLAD TO HEAR IT.
THE KINGDOM EXPANDED TOO FAR UNDER THE PREVIOUS KING.
WE CAN'T EVEN OFFER PROTECTION TO ALL THE VILLAGES THAT ARE UNDER OUR RULE.
I HOPE YOU CAN UNDERSTAND.
HE CAN'T SPARE TROOPS FOR INDEPENDENT FRONTIER SETTLEMENTS THAT PAY NO TAXES AND AREN'T UNDER PROTECTION.
AND IF HE DID, IT WOULD INVITE BACKLASH FROM THE PROTECTED VILLAGES.
PRACTICALLY SPEAKING, IT ISN'T ACTUALLY POSSIBLE.
I'D EXPECTED THIS MUCH.
NOW FOR THE REAL TALK...
KH

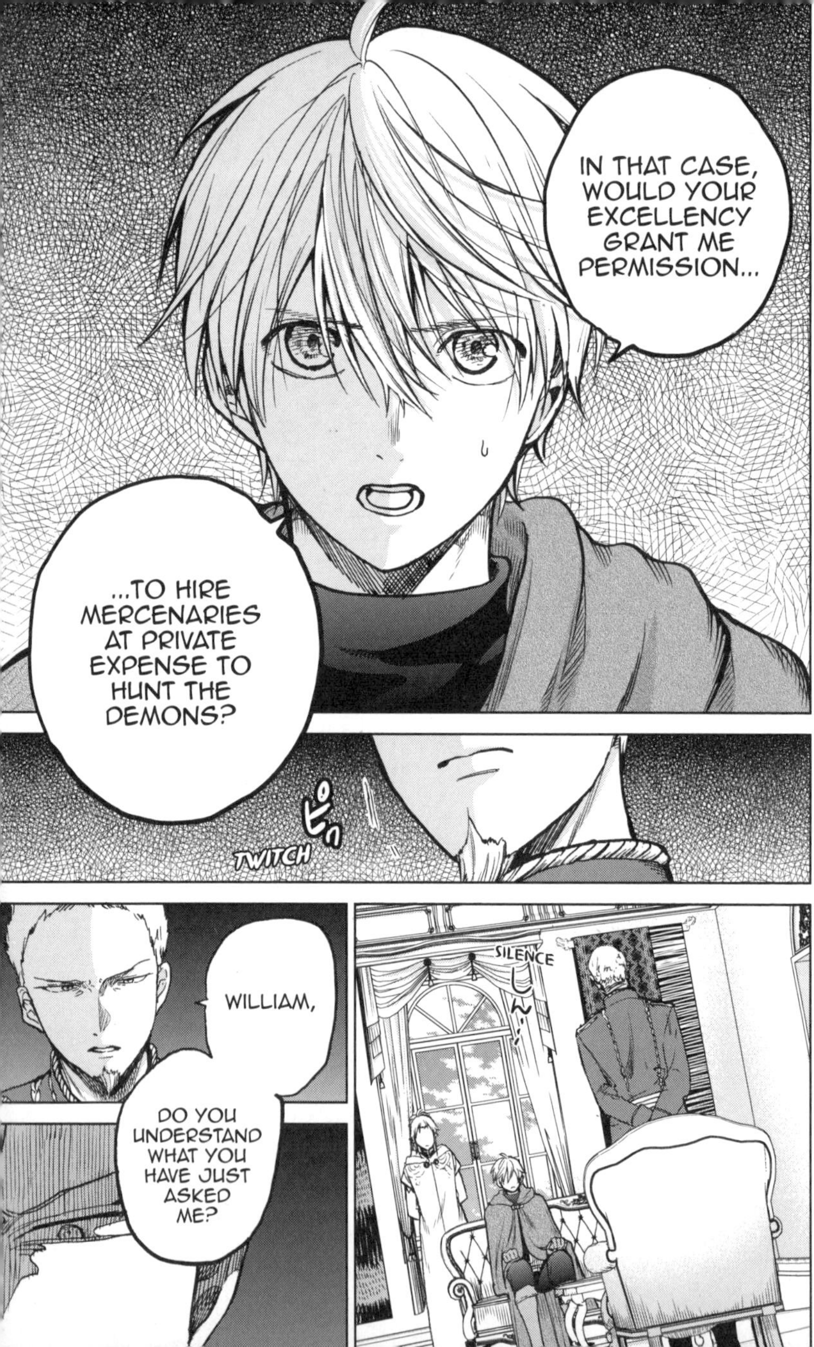
IN THAT CASE, WOULD YOUR EXCELLENCY GRANT ME PERMISSION...
...TO HIRE MERCENARIES AT PRIVATE EXPENSE TO HUNT THE DEMONS?
TWITCH
SILENCE
WILLIAM,
DO YOU UNDERSTAND WHAT YOU HAVE JUST ASKED ME?

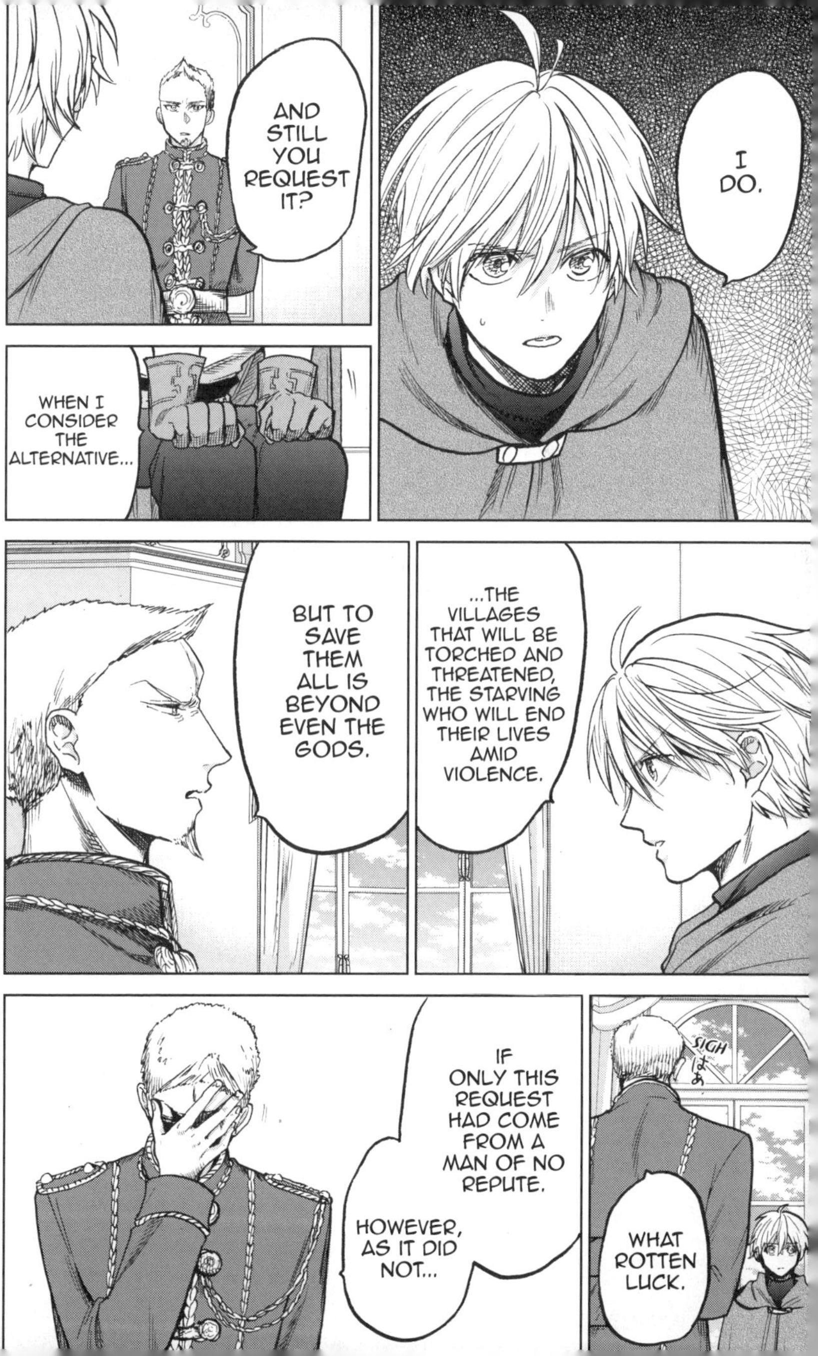
I DO.
AND STILL YOU REQUEST IT?
WHEN I CONSIDER THE ALTERNATIVE...
...THE VILLAGES THAT WILL BE TORCHED AND THREATENED, THE STARVING WHO WILL END THEIR LIVES AMID VIOLENCE.
BUT TO SAVE THEM ALL IS BEYOND EVEN THE GODS.
SIGH
はあ
WHAT ROTTEN LUCK.
IF ONLY THIS REQUEST HAD COME FROM A MAN OF NO REPUTE.
HOWEVER, AS IT DID NOT...

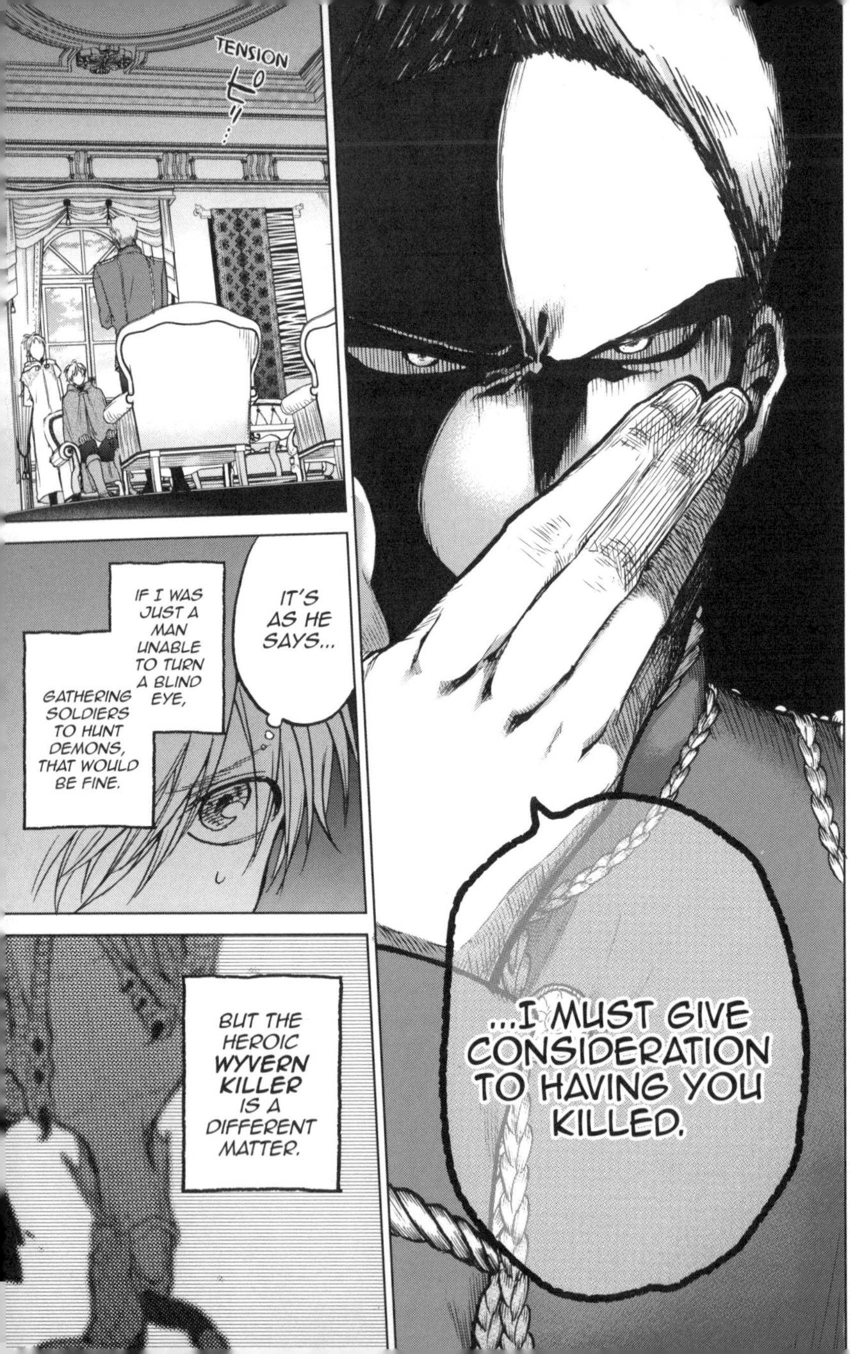
...I MUST GIVE CONSIDERATION TO HAVING YOU KILLED.
TENSION
IT'S AS HE SAYS...
IF I WAS JUST A MAN UNABLE TO TURN A BLIND EYE,
GATHERING SOLDIERS TO HUNT DEMONS, THAT WOULD BE FINE.
BUT THE HEROIC WYVERN KILLER IS A DIFFERENT MATTER.

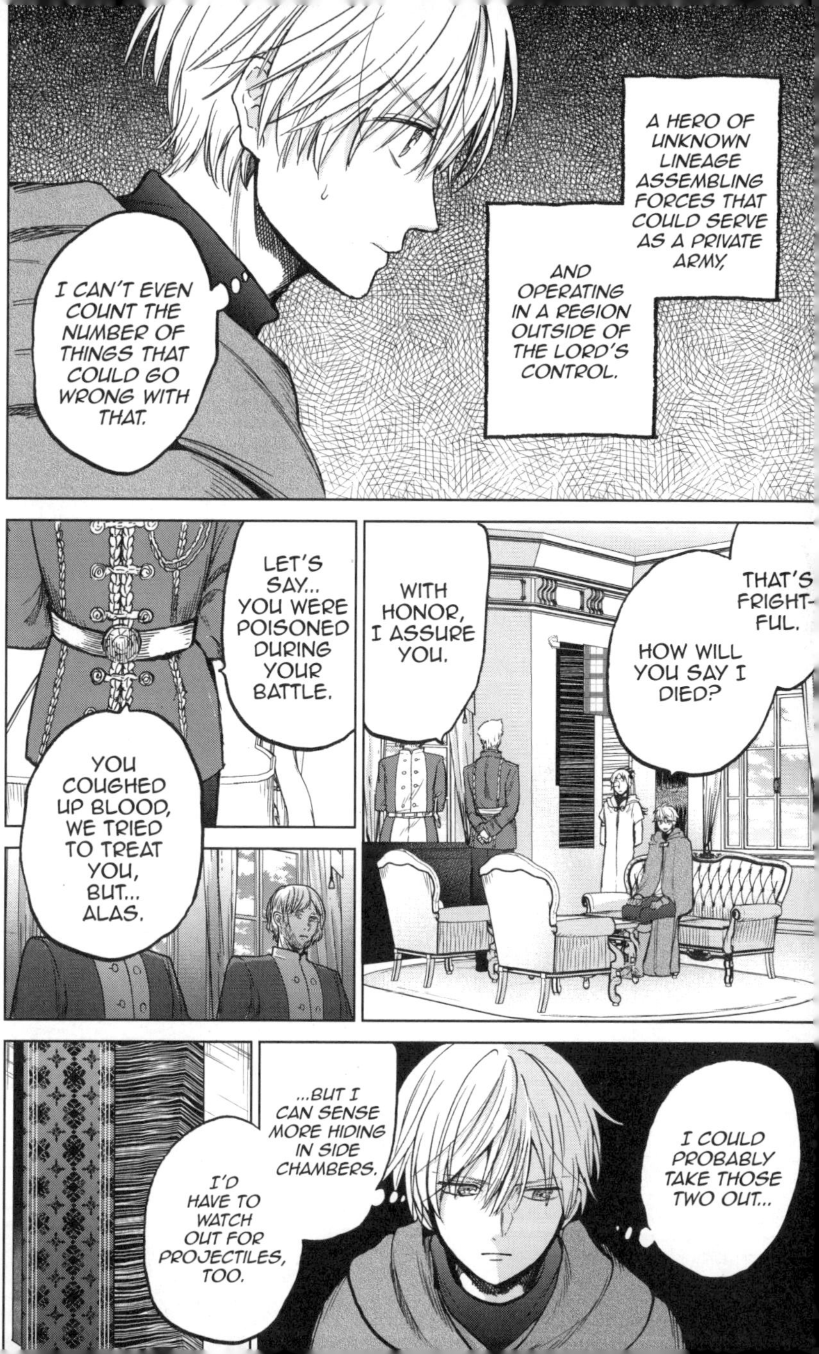
A HERO OF UNKNOWN LINEAGE ASSEMBLING FORCES THAT COULD SERVE AS A PRIVATE ARMY,
AND OPERATING IN A REGION OUTSIDE OF THE LORD'S CONTROL.
I CAN'T EVEN COUNT THE NUMBER OF THINGS THAT COULD GO WRONG WITH THAT.
THAT'S FRIGHTFUL.
HOW WILL YOU SAY I DIED?
WITH HONOR, I ASSURE YOU.
LET'S SAY... YOU WERE POISONED DURING YOUR BATTLE.
YOU COUGHED UP BLOOD, WE TRIED TO TREAT YOU, BUT... ALAS.
I COULD PROBABLY TAKE THOSE TWO OUT...
...BUT I CAN SENSE MORE HIDING IN SIDE CHAMBERS.
I'D HAVE TO WATCH OUT FOR PROJECTILES, TOO.

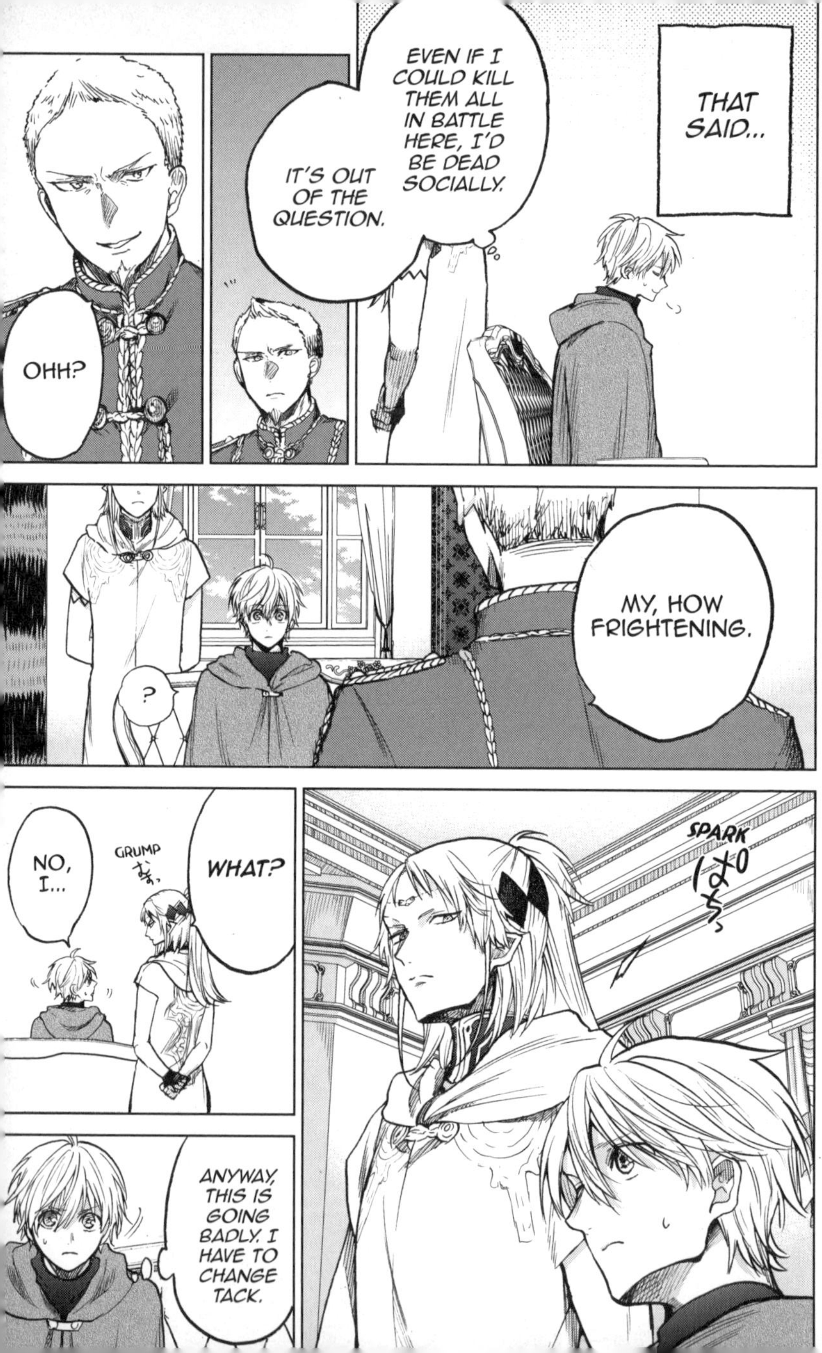
THAT SAID...
EVEN IF I COULD KILL THEM ALL IN BATTLE HERE, I'D BE DEAD SOCIALLY.
IT'S OUT OF THE QUESTION.
OHH?
MY, HOW FRIGHTENING.
?
SPARK
WHAT?
GRUMP
NO, I...
ANYWAY, THIS IS GOING BADLY. I HAVE TO CHANGE TACK.

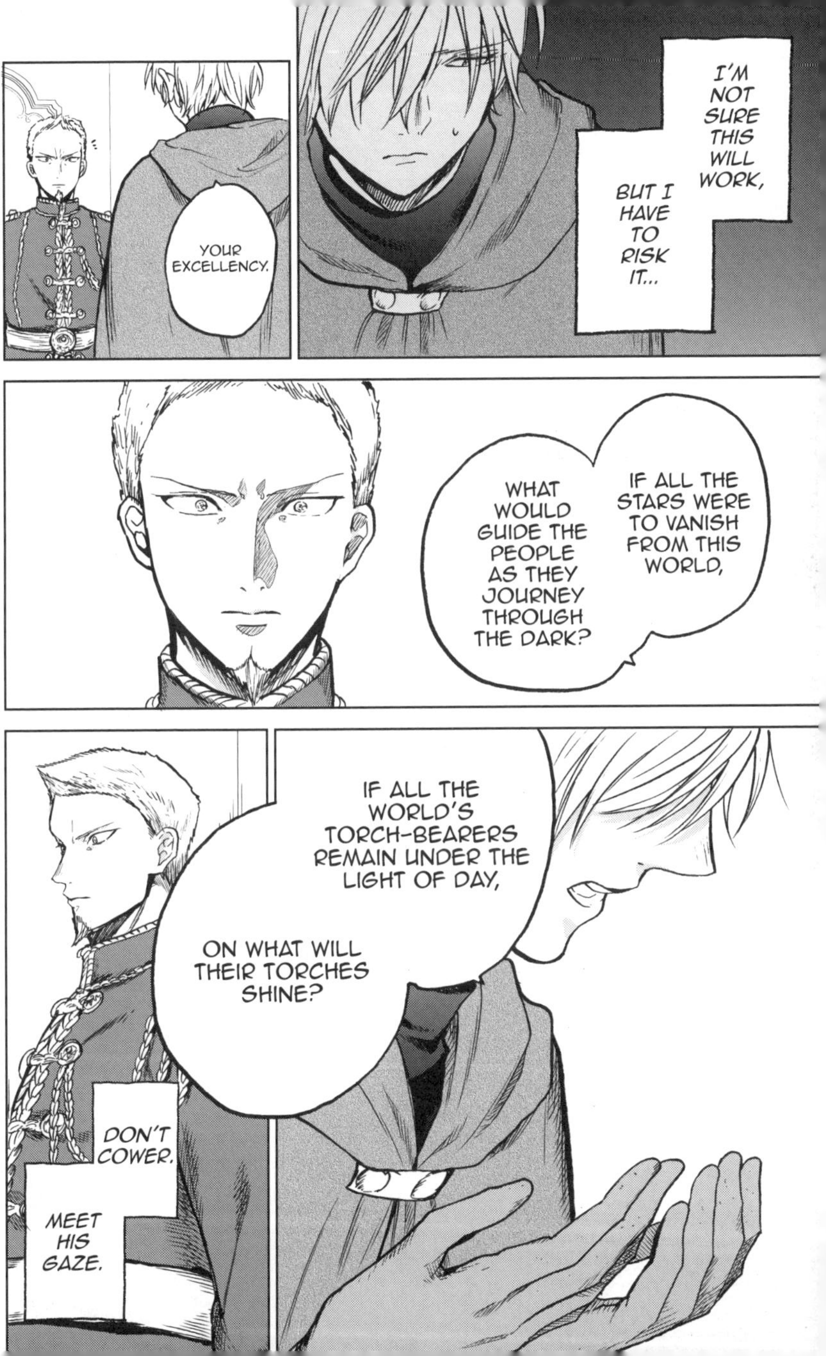
I'M NOT SURE THIS WILL WORK,
BUT I HAVE TO RISK IT...
YOUR EXCELLENCY.
IF ALL THE STARS WERE TO VANISH FROM THIS WORLD,
WHAT WOULD GUIDE THE PEOPLE AS THEY JOURNEY THROUGH THE DARK?
IF ALL THE WORLD'S TORCH-BEARERS REMAIN UNDER THE LIGHT OF DAY,
ON WHAT WILL THEIR TORCHES SHINE?
DON'T COWER.
MEET HIS GAZE.

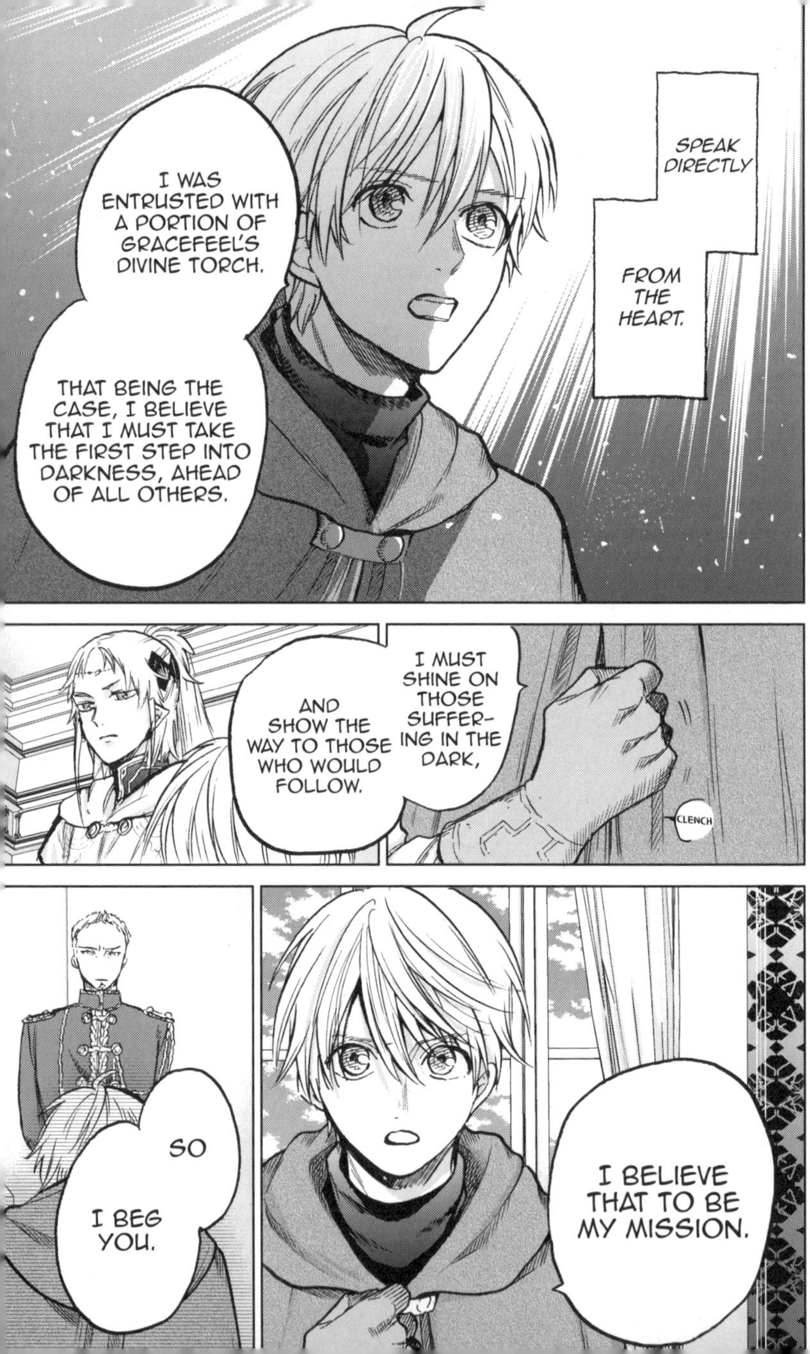
SPEAK DIRECTLY
FROM THE HEART.
I WAS ENTRUSTED WITH A PORTION OF GRACEFEEL'S DIVINE TORCH.
THAT BEING THE CASE, I BELIEVE THAT I MUST TAKE THE FIRST STEP INTO DARKNESS, AHEAD OF ALL OTHERS.
I MUST SHINE ON THOSE SUFFER-ING IN THE DARK,
AND SHOW THE WAY TO THOSE WHO WOULD FOLLOW.
CLENCH
I BELIEVE THAT TO BE MY MISSION.
SO
I BEG YOU.

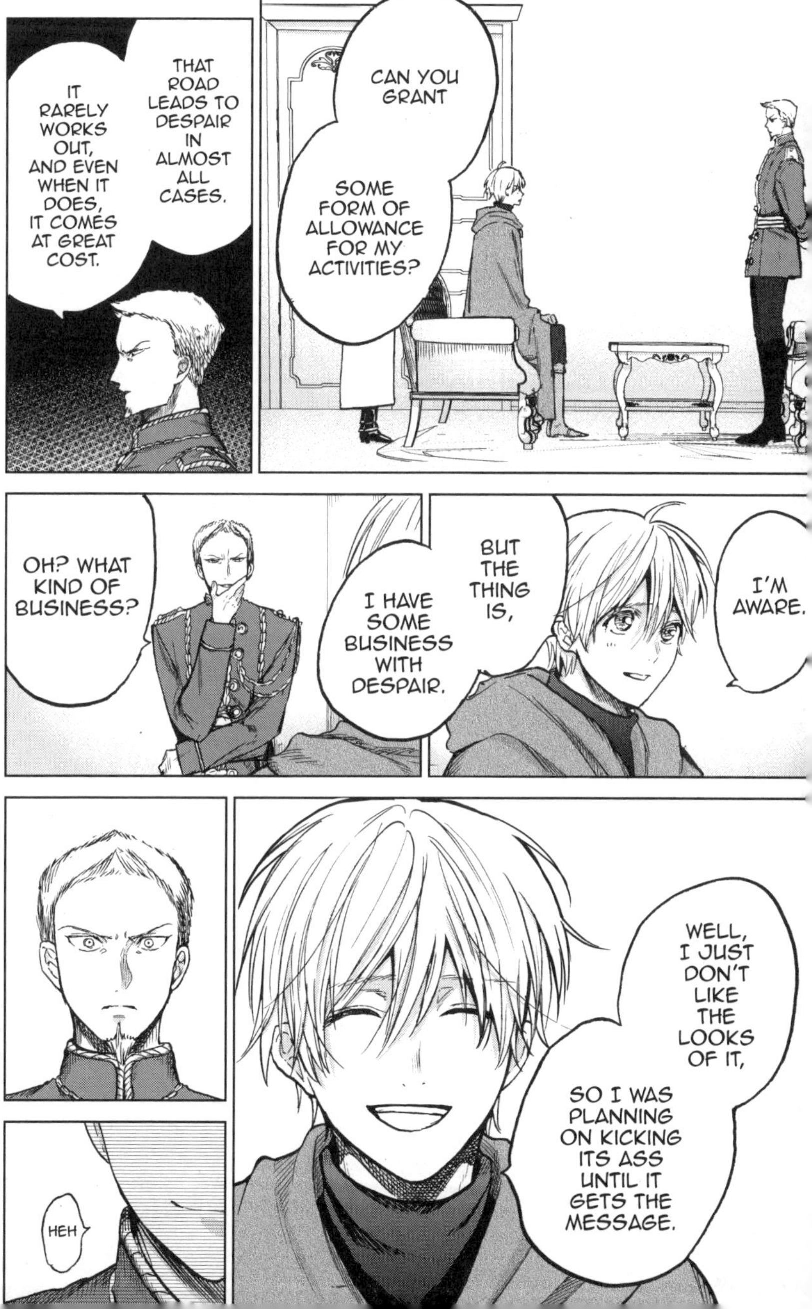
CAN YOU GRANT
SOME FORM OF ALLOWANCE FOR MY ACTIVITIES?
THAT ROAD LEADS TO DESPAIR IN ALMOST ALL CASES.
IT RARELY WORKS OUT, AND EVEN WHEN IT DOES, IT COMES AT GREAT COST.
I'M AWARE.
BUT THE THING IS,
I HAVE SOME BUSINESS WITH DESPAIR.
OH? WHAT KIND OF BUSINESS?
WELL, I JUST DON'T LIKE THE LOOKS OF IT,
SO I WAS PLANNING ON KICKING ITS ASS UNTIL IT GETS THE MESSAGE.
HEH

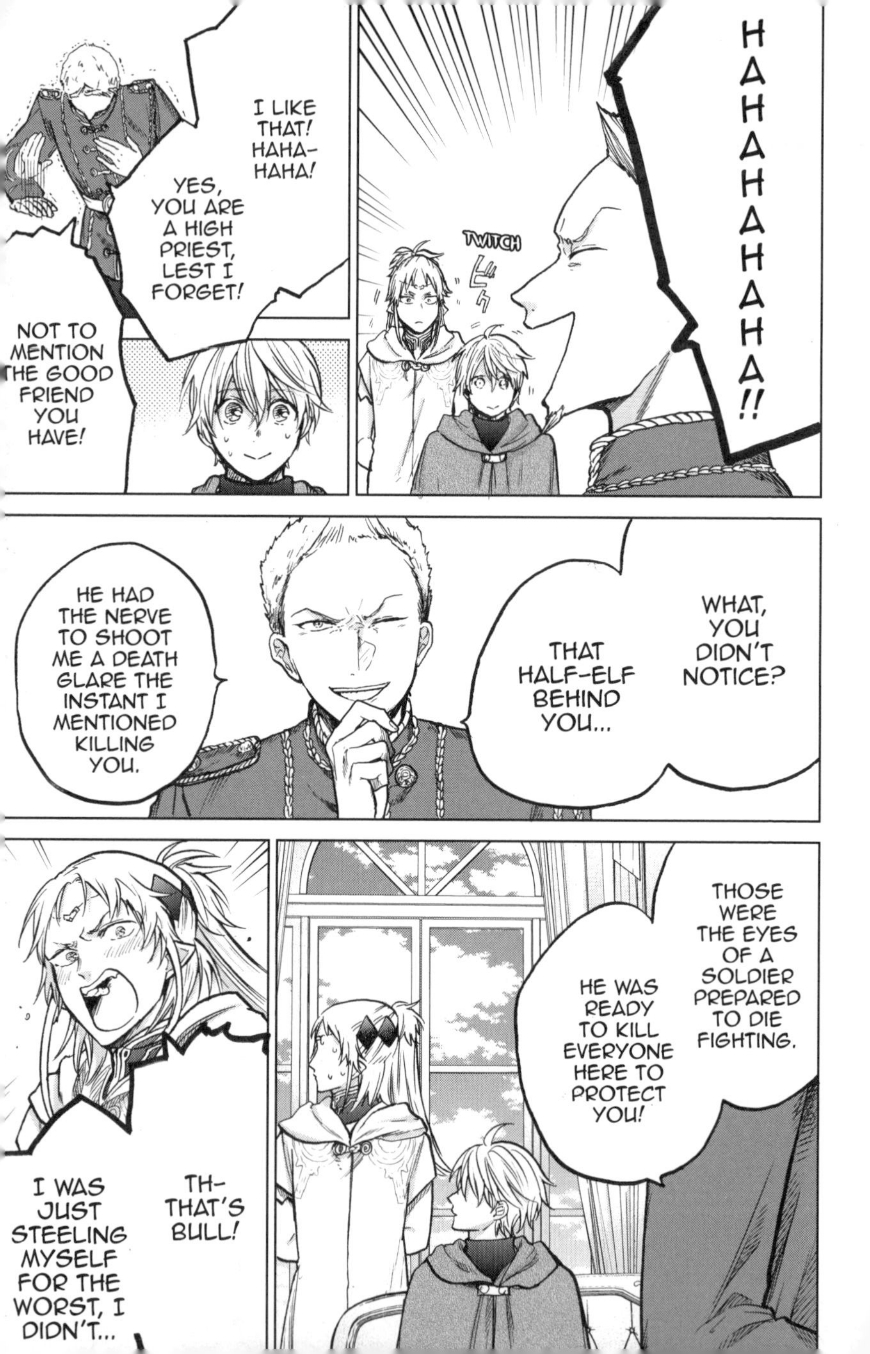
HAHAHAHAHAHAHA!!
TWITCH
I LIKE THAT! HAHA-HAHA!
YES, YOU ARE A HIGH PRIEST, LEST I FORGET!
NOT TO MENTION THE GOOD FRIEND YOU HAVE!
WHAT, YOU DIDN'T NOTICE?
THAT HALF-ELF BEHIND YOU...
HE HAD THE NERVE TO SHOOT ME A DEATH GLARE THE INSTANT I MENTIONED KILLING YOU.
THOSE WERE THE EYES OF A SOLDIER PREPARED TO DIE FIGHTING.
HE WAS READY TO KILL EVERYONE HERE TO PROTECT YOU!
TH- THAT'S BULL!
I WAS JUST STEELING MYSELF FOR THE WORST, I DIDN'T...

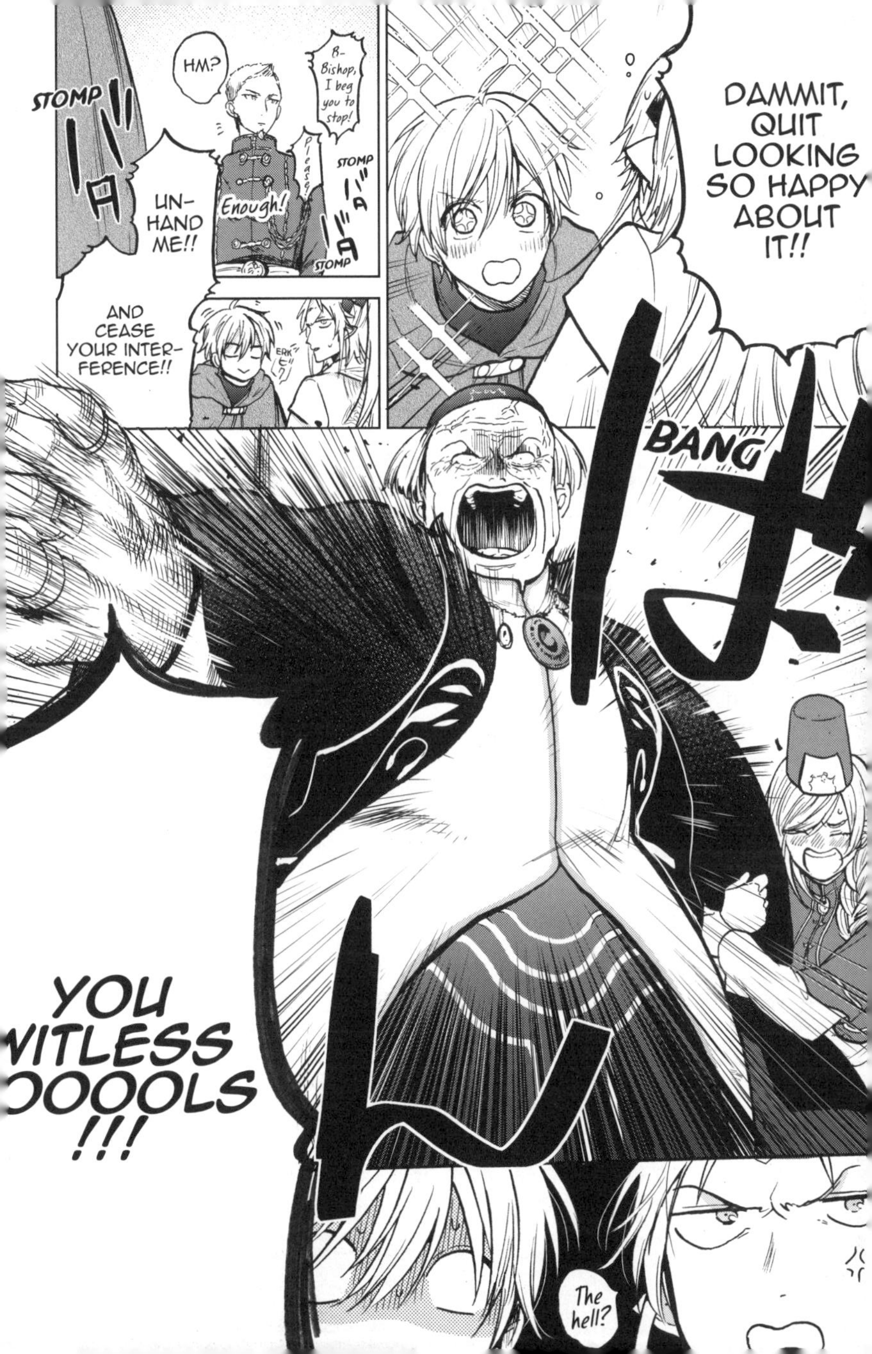
DAMMIT, QUIT LOOKING SO HAPPY ABOUT IT!!
B-Bishop, I beg you to stop!
HM?
STOMP
STOMP
STOMP
Please!
Enough!
UN-HAND ME!!
AND CEASE YOUR INTER-FERENCE!!
ERK
BANG
YOU VITLESS OOOOLS !!!
The hell?

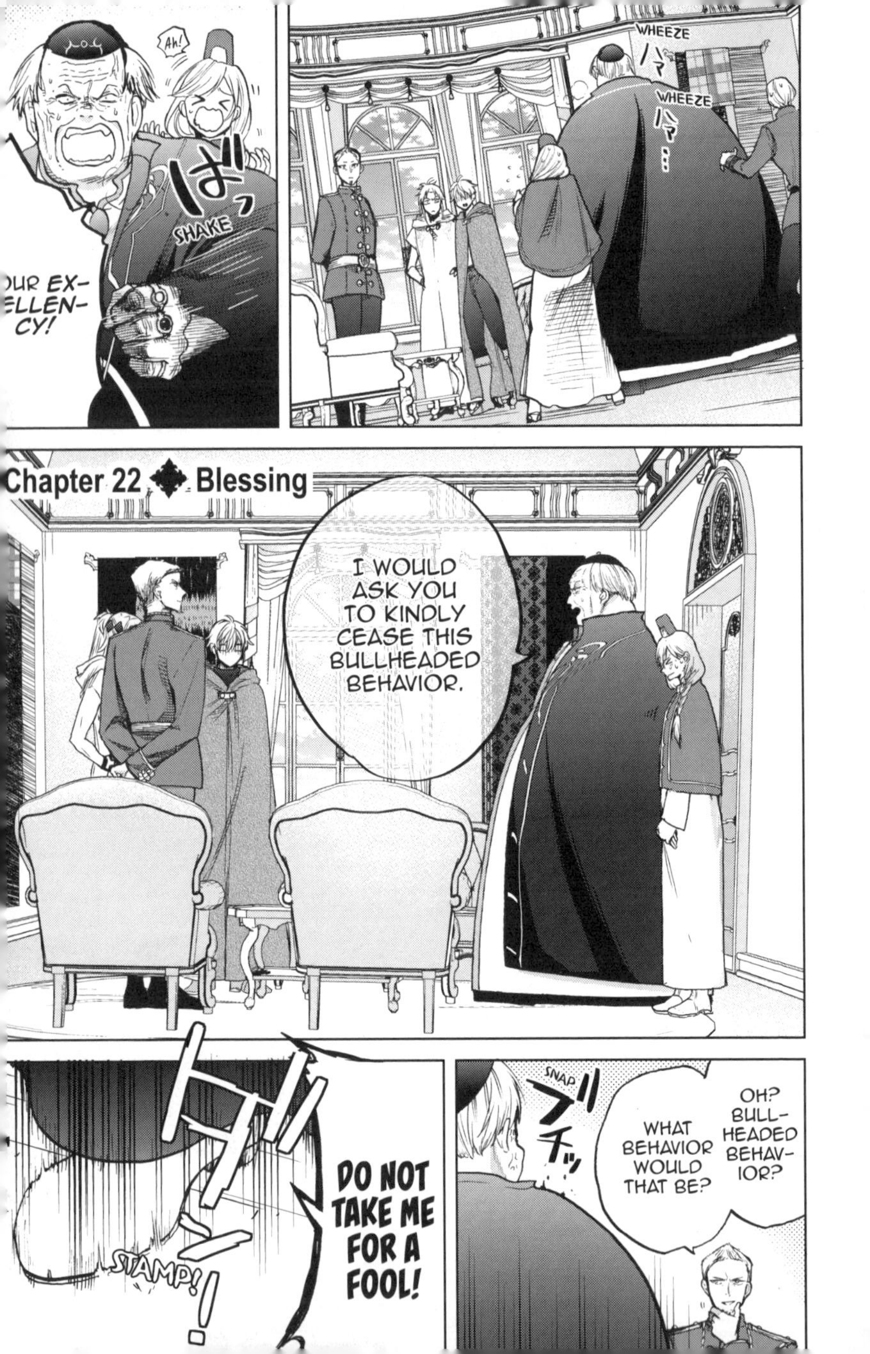
WHEEZE
WHEEZE
Ah!
SHAKE
OUR EX-ELLEN-CY!
Chapter 22 Blessing
I WOULD ASK YOU TO KINDLY CEASE THIS BULLHEADED BEHAVIOR.
SNAP
OH? BULL-HEADED BEHAV-IOR?
WHAT BEHAVIOR WOULD THAT BE?
DO NOT TAKE ME FOR A FOOL!
STAMP!

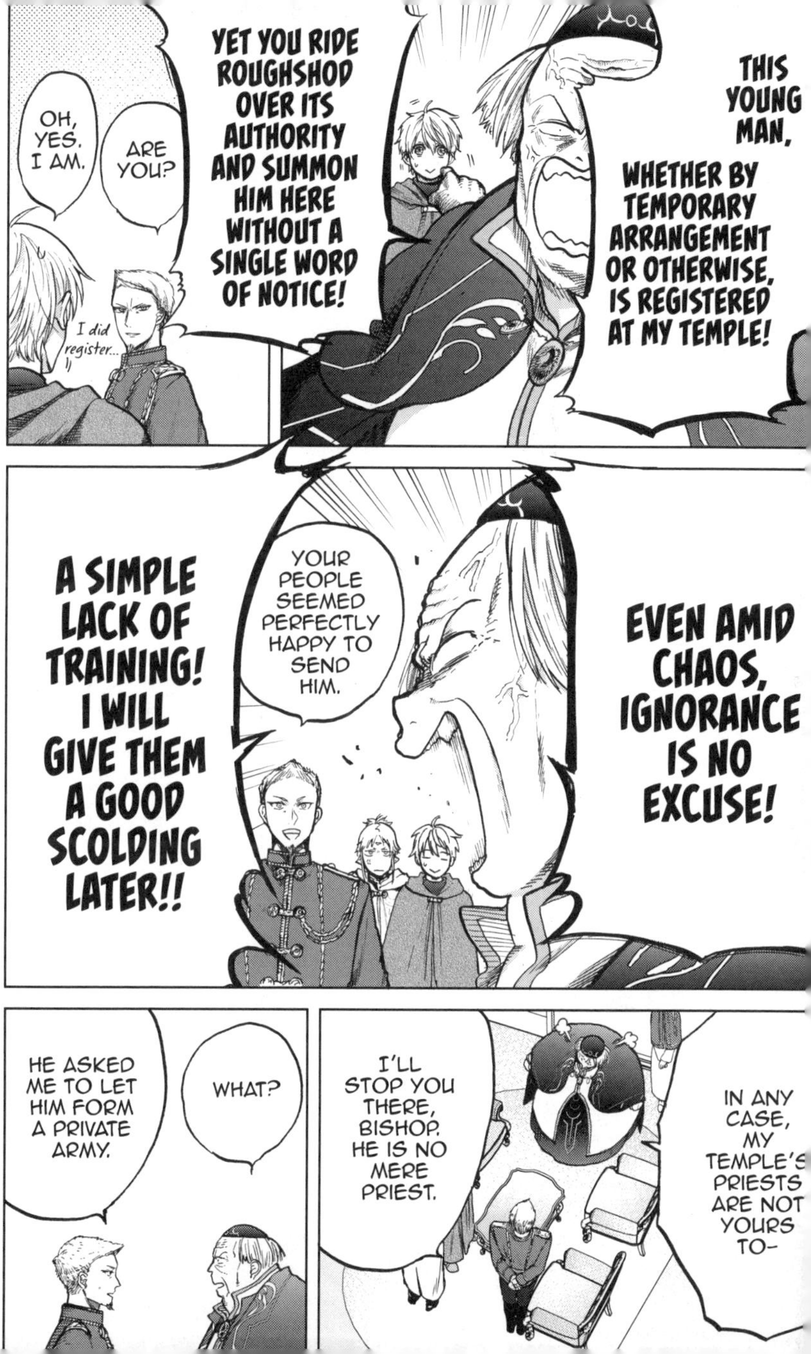
THIS YOUNG MAN, WHETHER BY TEMPORARY ARRANGEMENT OR OTHERWISE, IS REGISTERED AT MY TEMPLE!
YET YOU RIDE ROUGHSHOD OVER ITS AUTHORITY AND SUMMON HIM HERE WITHOUT A SINGLE WORD OF NOTICE!
ARE YOU?
OH, YES. I AM.
I did register...
EVEN AMID CHAOS, IGNORANCE IS NO EXCUSE!
YOUR PEOPLE SEEMED PERFECTLY HAPPY TO SEND HIM.
A SIMPLE LACK OF TRAINING! I WILL GIVE THEM A GOOD SCOLDING LATER!!
IN ANY CASE, MY TEMPLE'S PRIESTS ARE NOT YOURS TO–
I'LL STOP YOU THERE, BISHOP. HE IS NO MERE PRIEST.
WHAT?
HE ASKED ME TO LET HIM FORM A PRIVATE ARMY.

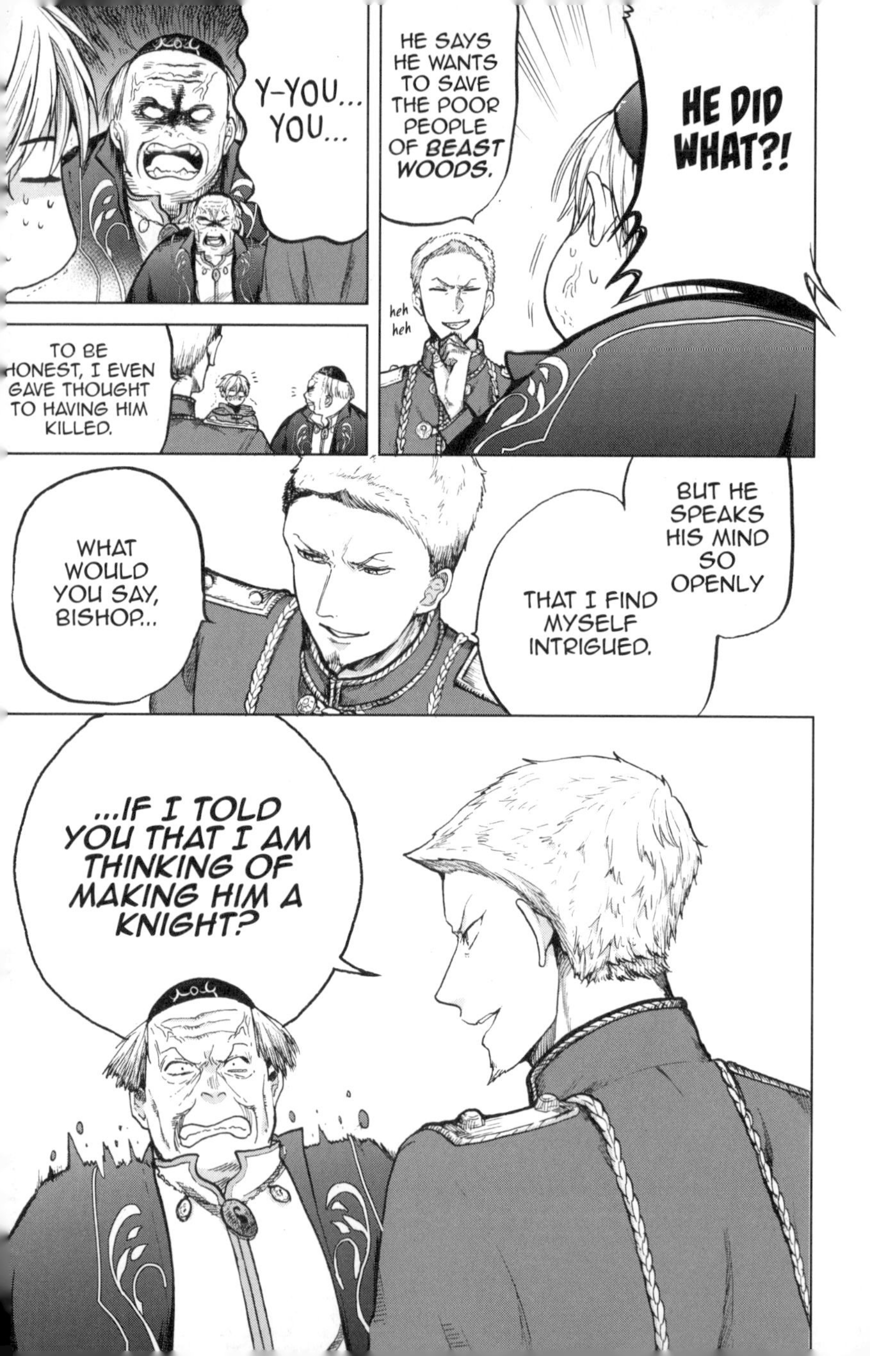
HE DID WHAT?!
HE SAYS HE WANTS TO SAVE THE POOR PEOPLE OF *BEAST WOODS.*
heh heh
Y-YOU... YOU...
TO BE HONEST, I EVEN GAVE THOUGHT TO HAVING HIM KILLED.
BUT HE SPEAKS HIS MIND SO OPENLY
THAT I FIND MYSELF INTRIGUED.
WHAT WOULD YOU SAY, BISHOP...
...IF I TOLD YOU THAT I AM THINKING OF MAKING HIM A KNIGHT?

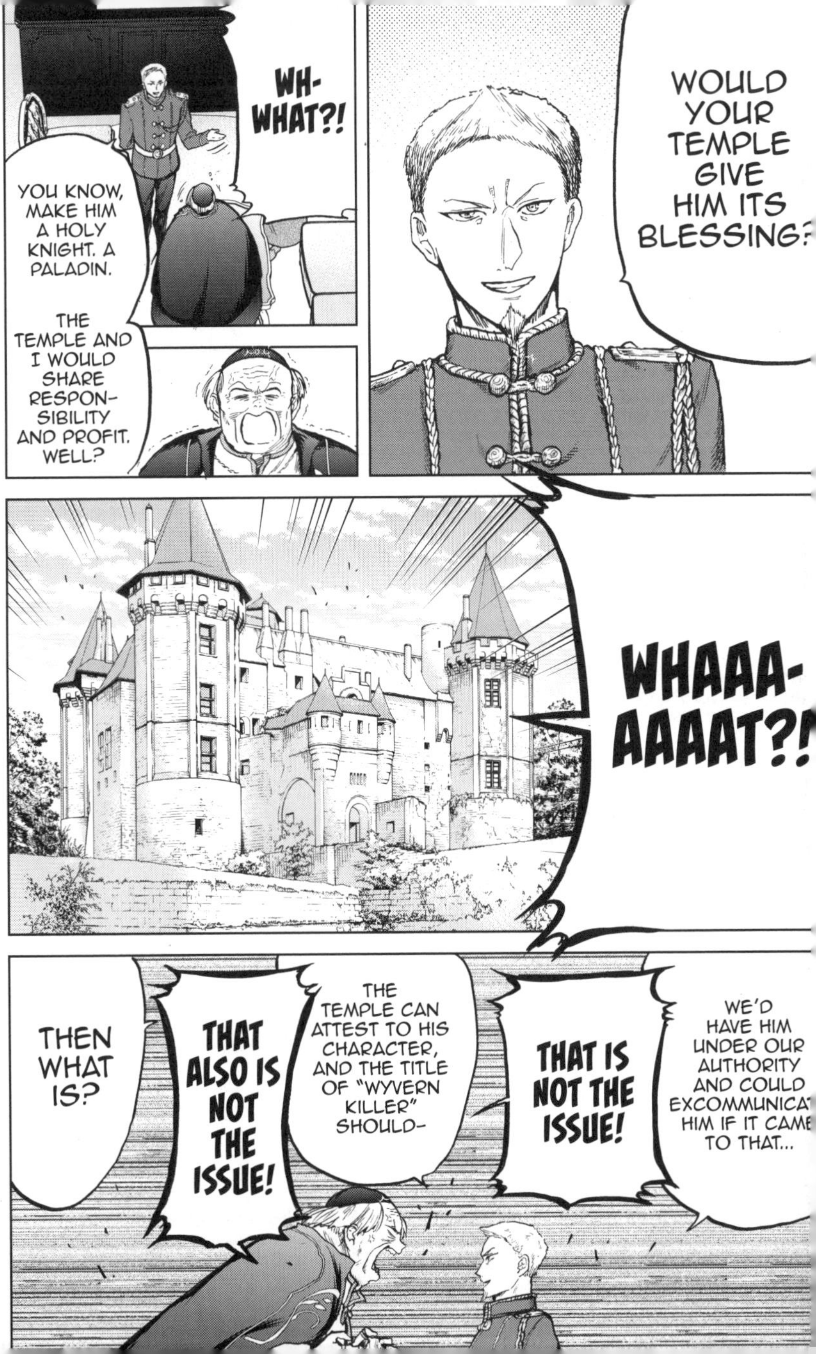
WOULD YOUR TEMPLE GIVE HIM ITS BLESSING?
WH-WHAT?!
YOU KNOW, MAKE HIM A HOLY KNIGHT. A PALADIN.
THE TEMPLE AND I WOULD SHARE RESPON-SIBILITY AND PROFIT. WELL?
WHAAAA-AAAAT?!
WE'D HAVE HIM UNDER OUR AUTHORITY AND COULD EXCOMMUNICAT HIM IF IT CAME TO THAT...
THAT IS NOT THE ISSUE!
THE TEMPLE CAN ATTEST TO HIS CHARACTER, AND THE TITLE OF "WYVERN KILLER" SHOULD-
THAT ALSO IS NOT THE ISSUE!
THEN WHAT IS?

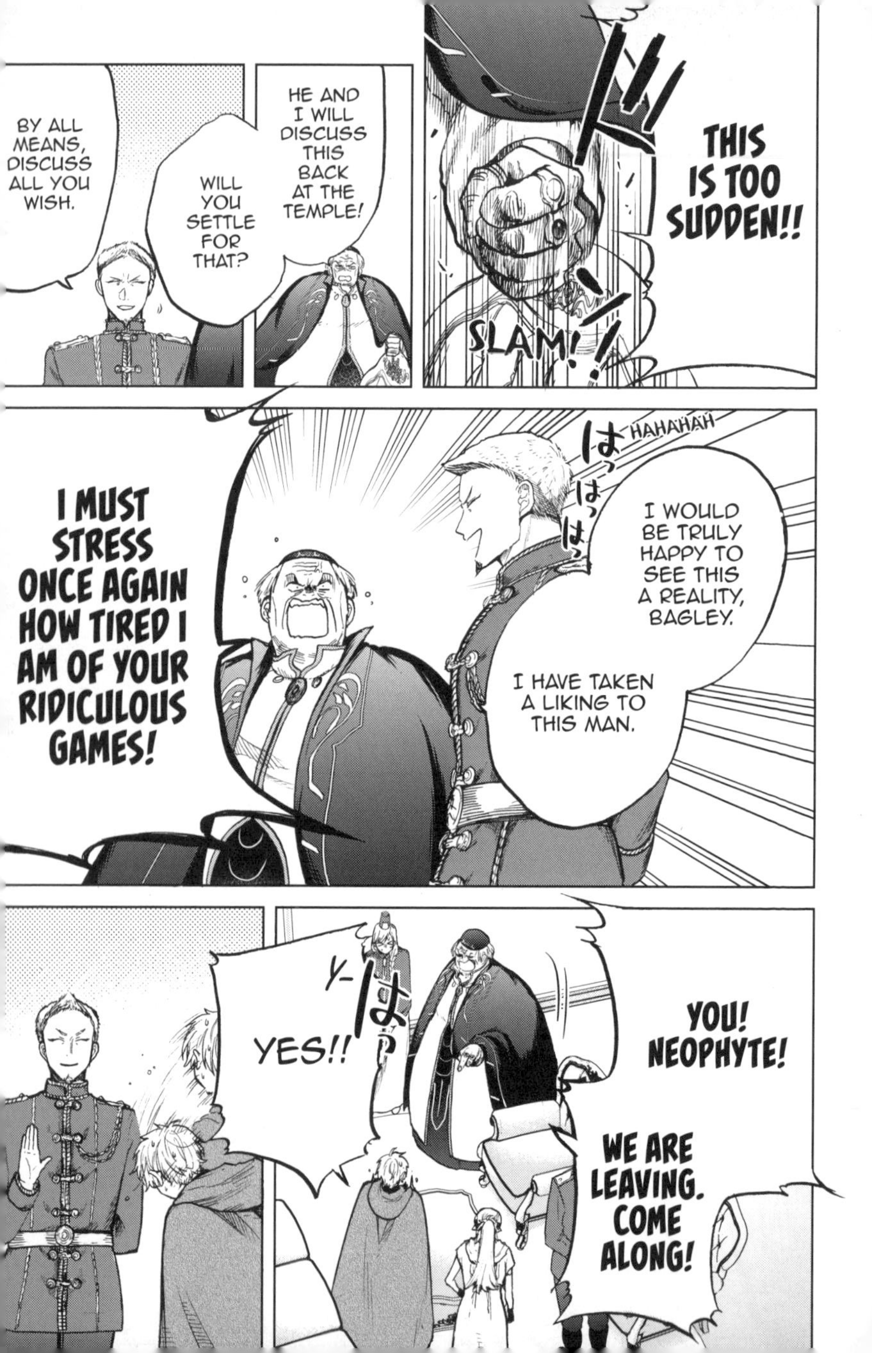

THIS IS TOO SUDDEN!!
SLAM!!
HE AND I WILL DISCUSS THIS BACK AT THE TEMPLE!
WILL YOU SETTLE FOR THAT?
BY ALL MEANS, DISCUSS ALL YOU WISH.
はっはっはっ
HAHAHAH
I WOULD BE TRULY HAPPY TO SEE THIS A REALITY, BAGLEY.
I HAVE TAKEN A LIKING TO THIS MAN.
I MUST STRESS ONCE AGAIN HOW TIRED I AM OF YOUR RIDICULOUS GAMES!
YOU! NEOPHYTE!
WE ARE LEAVING. COME ALONG!
Y-
はっ
YES!!

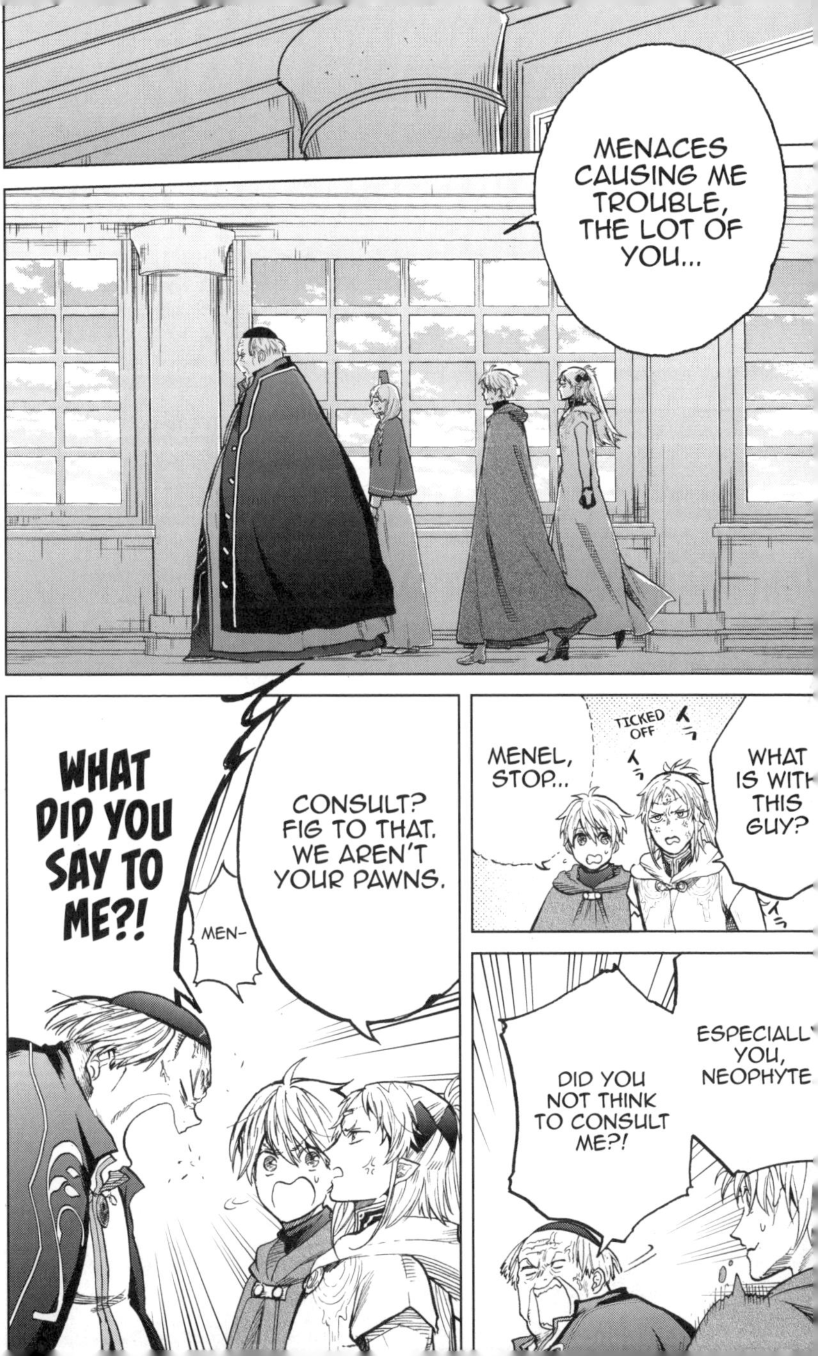
MENACES CAUSING ME TROUBLE, THE LOT OF YOU...
WHAT IS WITH THIS GUY?
TICKED OFF
MENEL, STOP...
ESPECIALLY YOU, NEOPHYTE
DID YOU NOT THINK TO CONSULT ME?!
CONSULT? FIG TO THAT. WE AREN'T YOUR PAWNS.
MEN-
WHAT DID YOU SAY TO ME?!

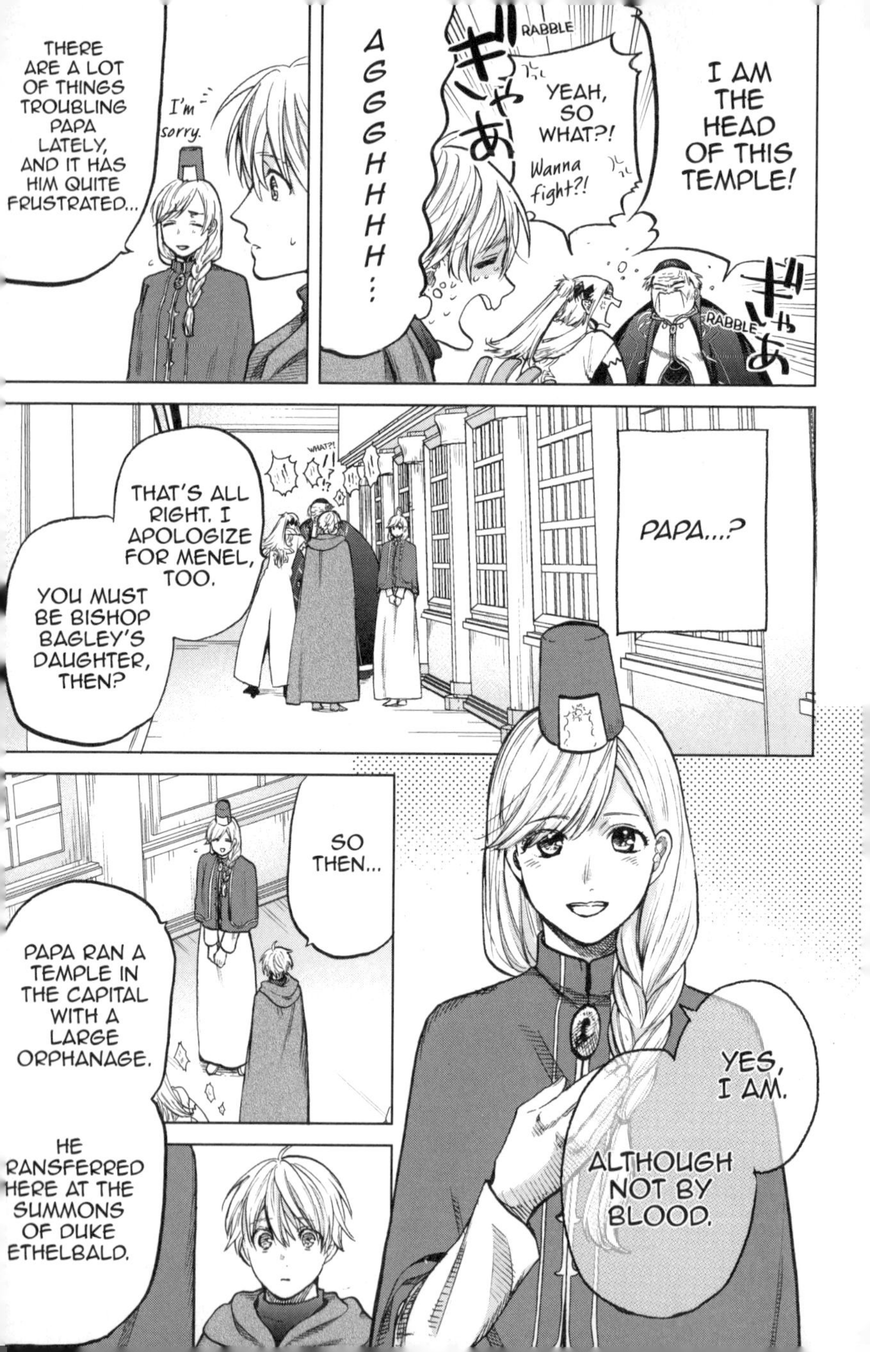
I AM THE HEAD OF THIS TEMPLE!
ギャあ
RABBLE
ギャあ
RABBLE
YEAH, SO WHAT?!
Wanna fight?!
AGGGHHHHH...
I'm sorry.
THERE ARE A LOT OF THINGS TROUBLING PAPA LATELY, AND IT HAS HIM QUITE FRUSTRATED...
PAPA...?
WHAT?!
THAT'S ALL RIGHT. I APOLOGIZE FOR MENEL, TOO.
YOU MUST BE BISHOP BAGLEY'S DAUGHTER, THEN?
YES, I AM.
ALTHOUGH NOT BY BLOOD.
SO THEN...
PAPA RAN A TEMPLE IN THE CAPITAL WITH A LARGE ORPHANAGE.
HE RANSFERRED HERE AT THE SUMMONS OF DUKE ETHELBALD.

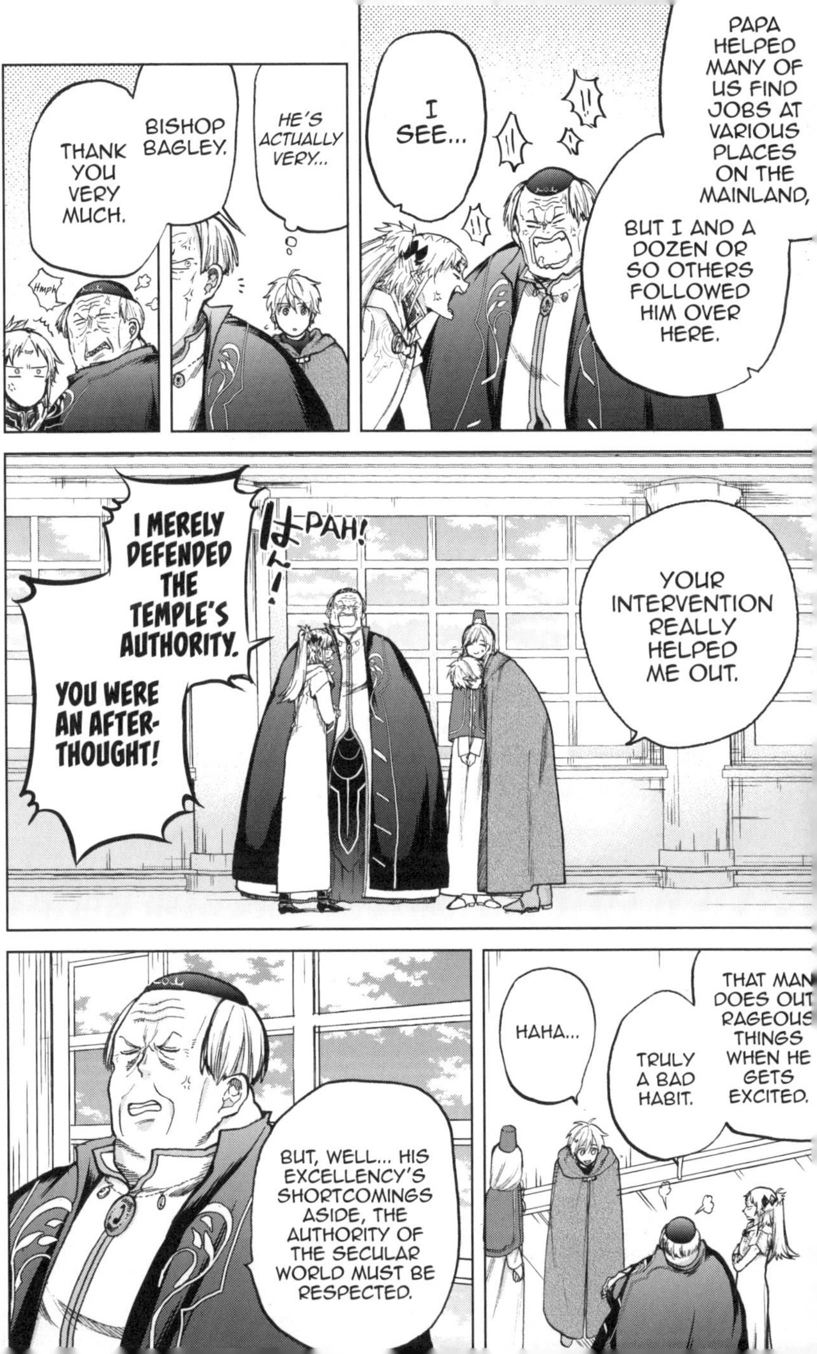
PAPA HELPED MANY OF US FIND JOBS AT VARIOUS PLACES ON THE MAINLAND,
BUT I AND A DOZEN OR SO OTHERS FOLLOWED HIM OVER HERE.
!!
I SEE...
HE'S ACTUALLY VERY...
BISHOP BAGLEY.
THANK YOU VERY MUCH.
Hmph
YOUR INTERVENTION REALLY HELPED ME OUT.
PAH!
I MERELY DEFENDED THE TEMPLE'S AUTHORITY.
YOU WERE AN AFTER-THOUGHT!
THAT MAN DOES OUTRAGEOUS THINGS WHEN HE GETS EXCITED.
TRULY A BAD HABIT.
HAHA...
BUT, WELL... HIS EXCELLENCY'S SHORTCOMINGS ASIDE, THE AUTHORITY OF THE SECULAR WORLD MUST BE RESPECTED.

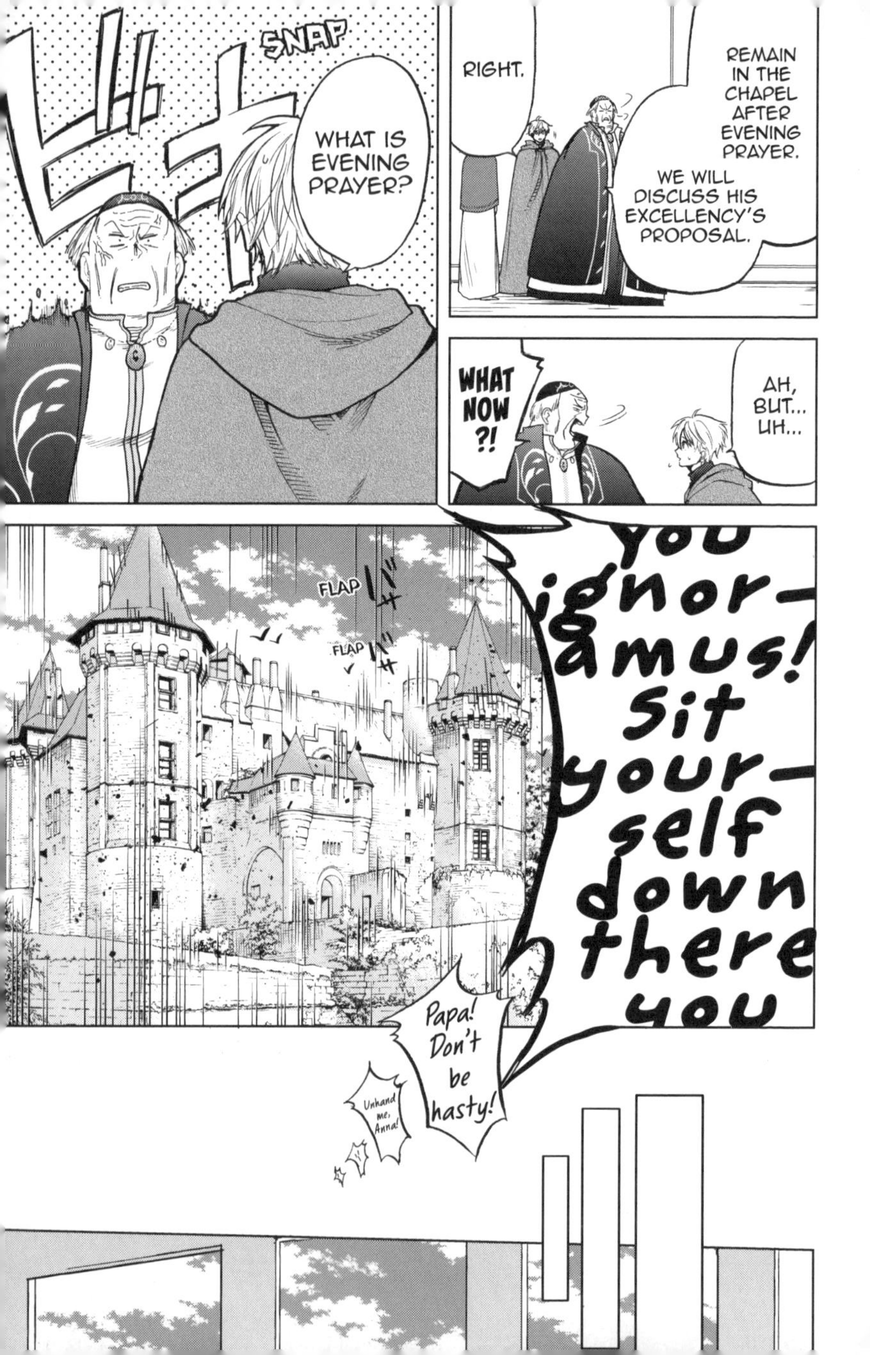
REMAIN IN THE CHAPEL AFTER EVENING PRAYER.
WE WILL DISCUSS HIS EXCELLENCY'S PROPOSAL.
RIGHT.
AH, BUT... UH...
WHAT NOW?!
SNAP
WHAT IS EVENING PRAYER?
you ignor-amus! Sit your-self down there you
FLAP
FLAP
Papa! Don't be hasty!
Unhand me, Anna!

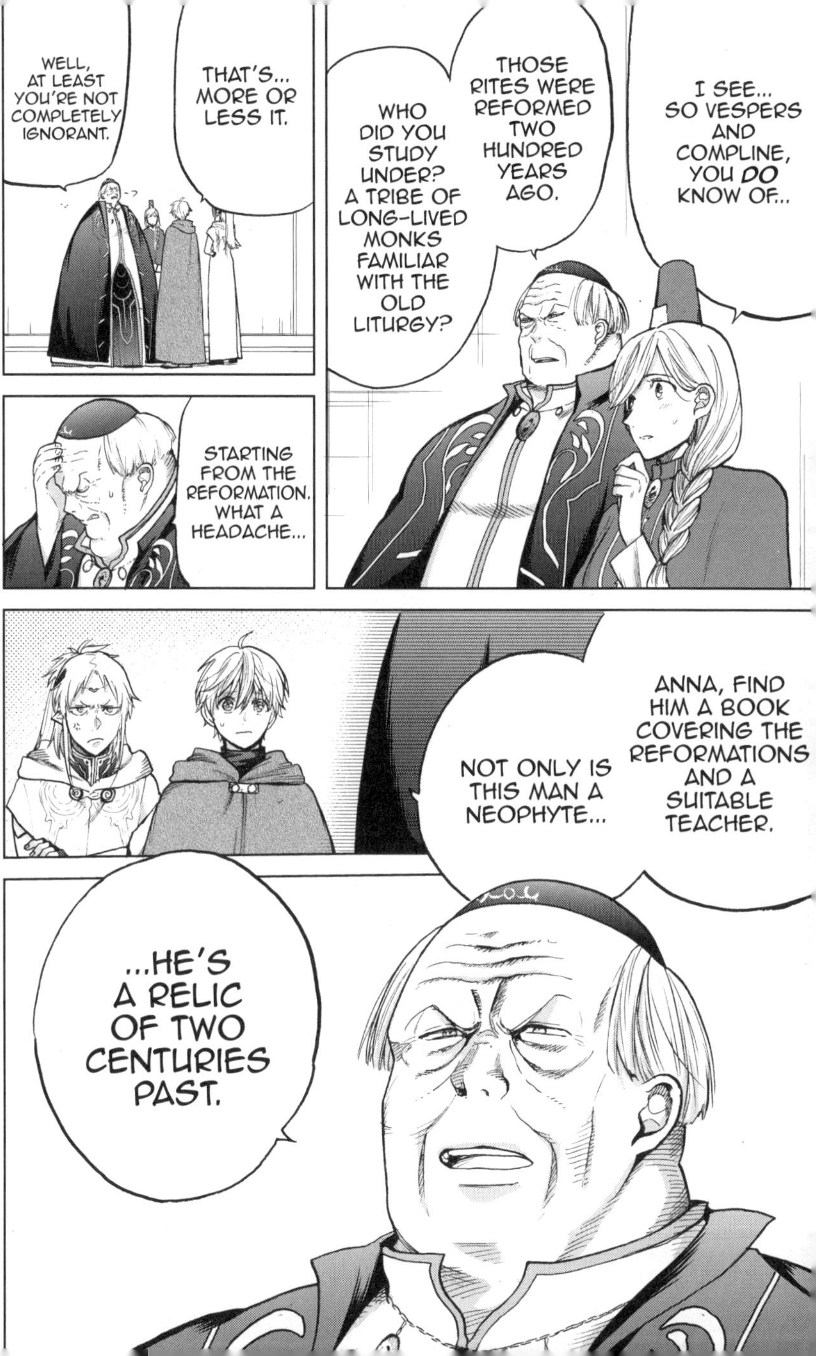
I SEE... SO VESPERS AND COMPLINE, YOU DO KNOW OF...
THOSE RITES WERE REFORMED TWO HUNDRED YEARS AGO.
WHO DID YOU STUDY UNDER? A TRIBE OF LONG-LIVED MONKS FAMILIAR WITH THE OLD LITURGY?
THAT'S... MORE OR LESS IT.
WELL, AT LEAST YOU'RE NOT COMPLETELY IGNORANT.
STARTING FROM THE REFORMATION. WHAT A HEADACHE...
ANNA, FIND HIM A BOOK COVERING THE REFORMATIONS AND A SUITABLE TEACHER.
NOT ONLY IS THIS MAN A NEOPHYTE...
...HE'S A RELIC OF TWO CENTURIES PAST.

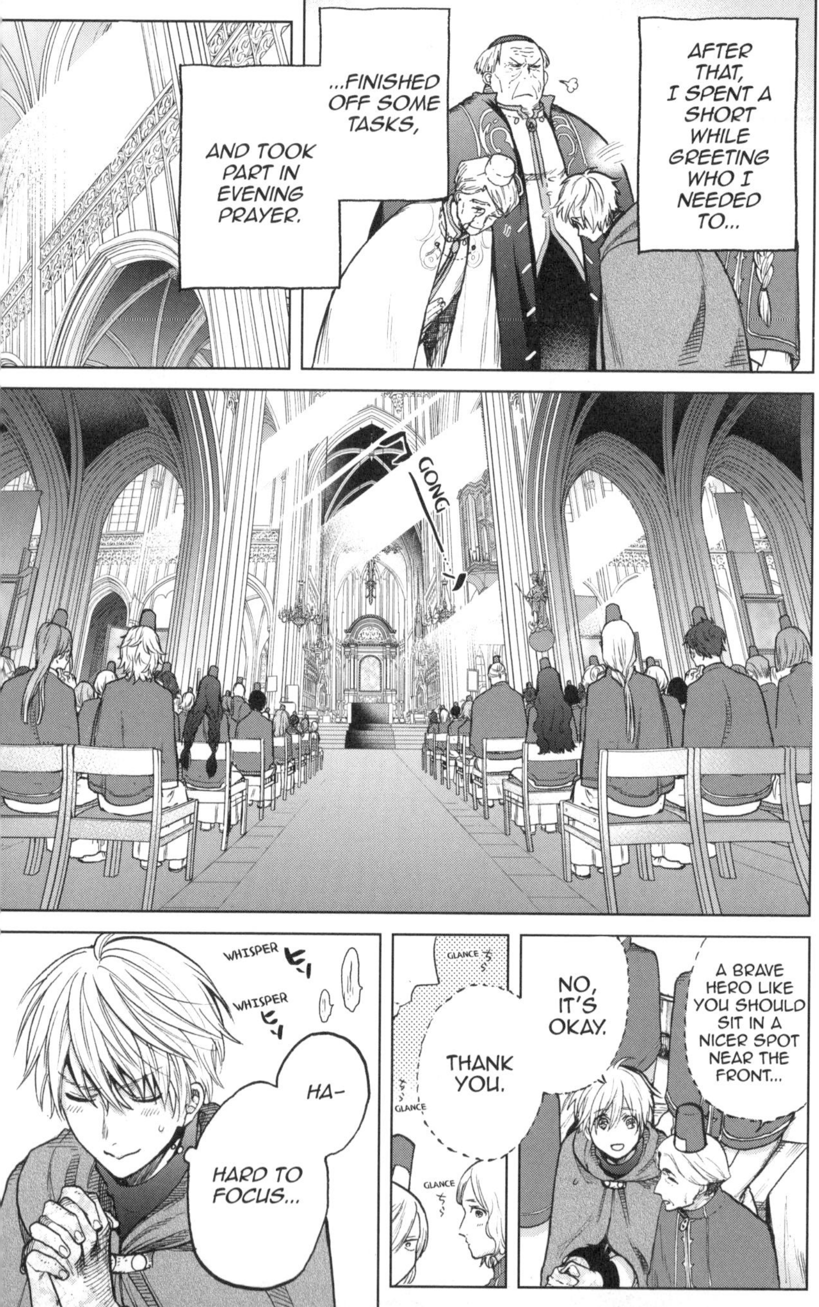
AFTER THAT, I SPENT A SHORT WHILE GREETING WHO I NEEDED TO...
...FINISHED OFF SOME TASKS,
AND TOOK PART IN EVENING PRAYER.
GONG
A BRAVE HERO LIKE YOU SHOULD SIT IN A NICER SPOT NEAR THE FRONT...
NO, IT'S OKAY.
THANK YOU.
GLANCE
GLANCE
GLANCE
WHISPER
WHISPER
HA-
HARD TO FOCUS...

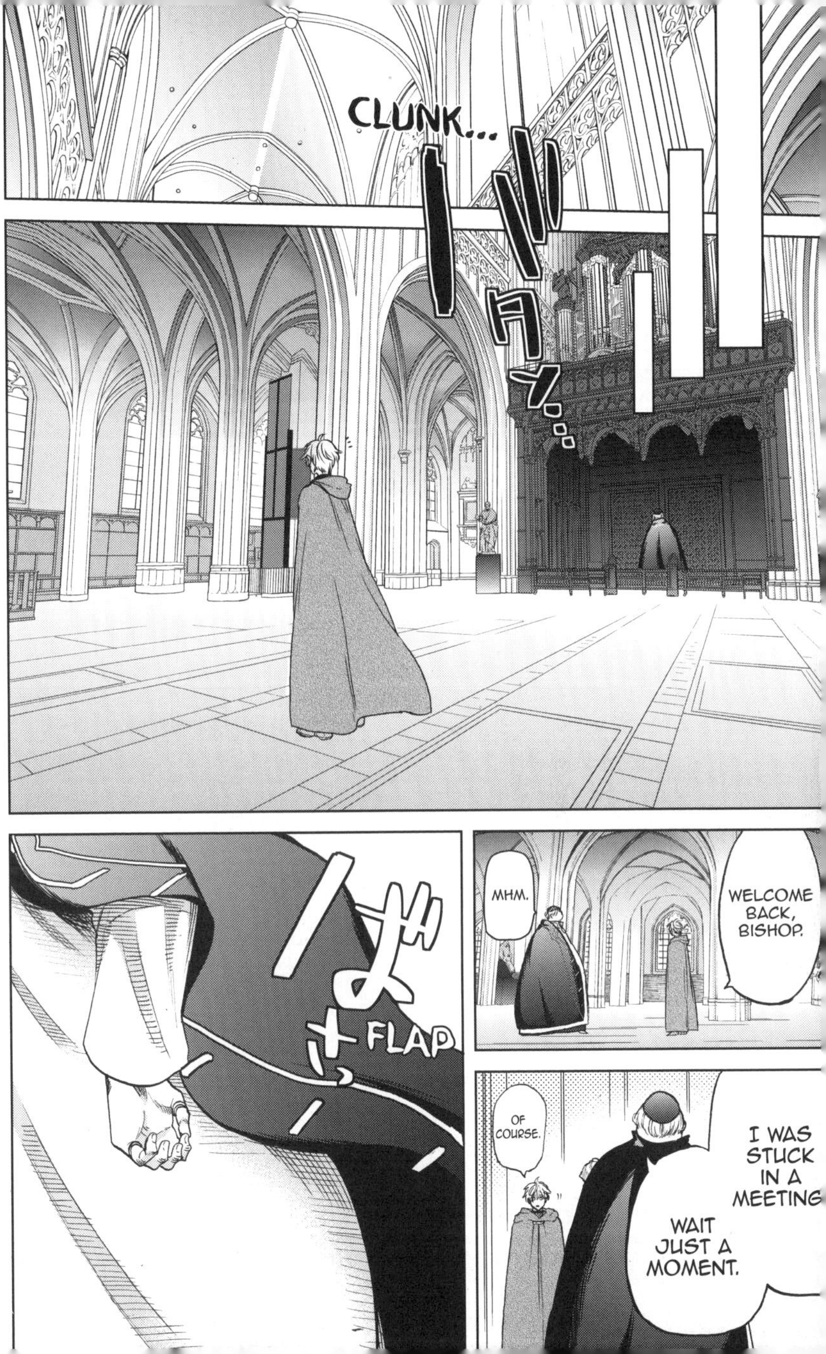
CLUNK...
WELCOME BACK, BISHOP.
MHM.
I WAS STUCK IN A MEETING
WAIT JUST A MOMENT.
OF COURSE.
FLAP

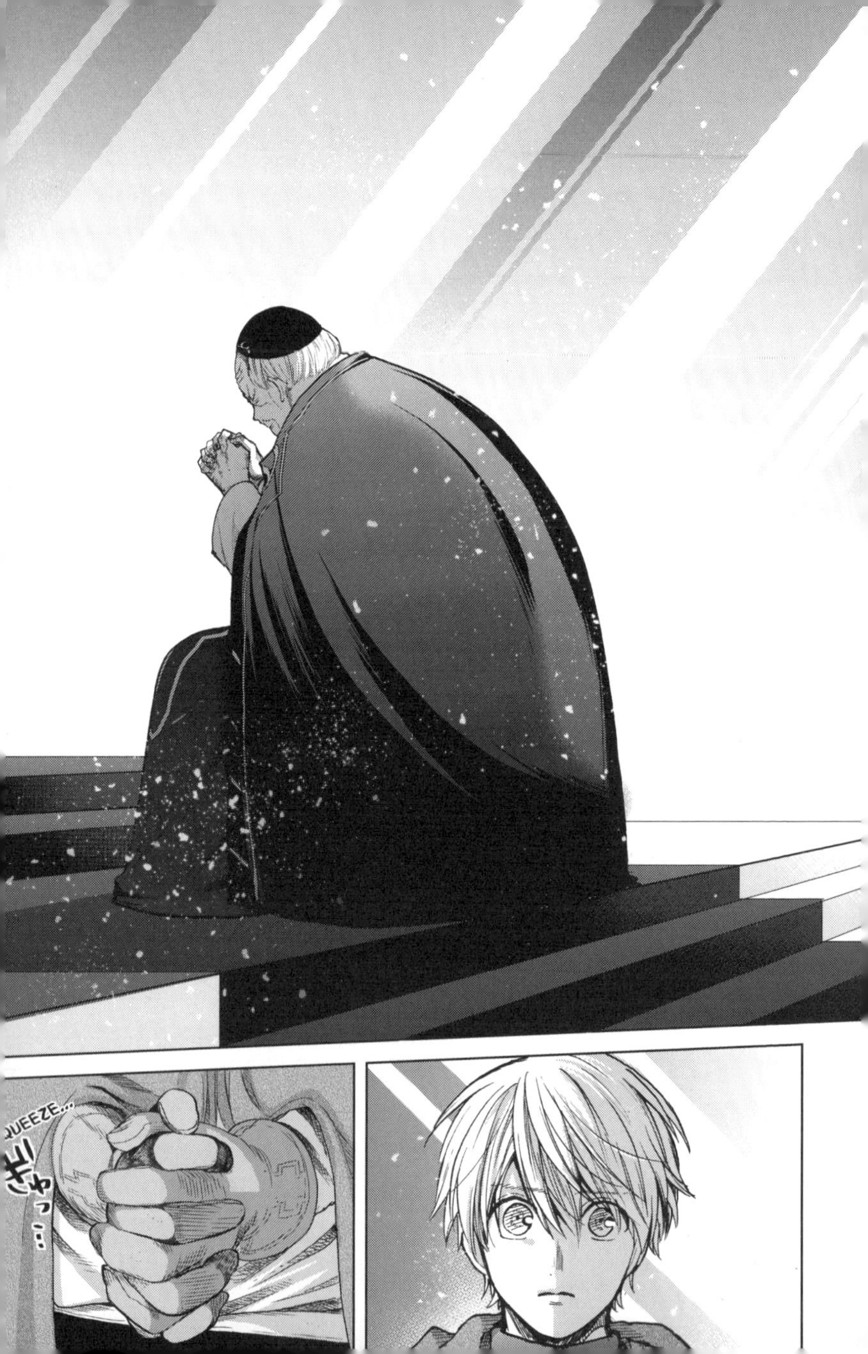
QUEEZE...
ぎりゅっ…

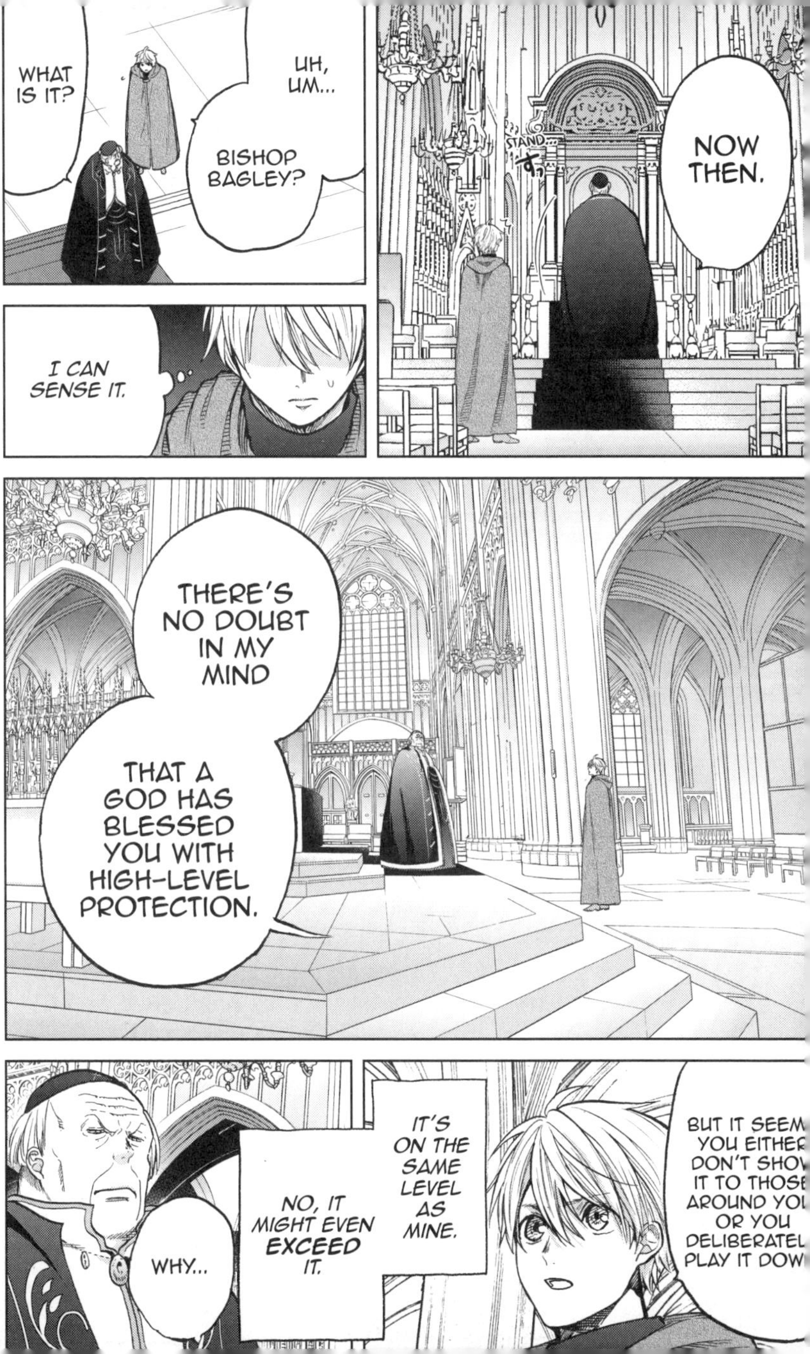
NOW THEN.
STAND
す
UH, UM...
BISHOP BAGLEY?
WHAT IS IT?
I CAN SENSE IT.
THERE'S NO DOUBT IN MY MIND
THAT A GOD HAS BLESSED YOU WITH HIGH-LEVEL PROTECTION.
BUT IT SEEM YOU EITHER DON'T SHOV IT TO THOSE AROUND YO OR YOU DELIBERATEL PLAY IT DOW
IT'S ON THE SAME LEVEL AS MINE.
NO, IT MIGHT EVEN **EXCEED** IT.
WHY...

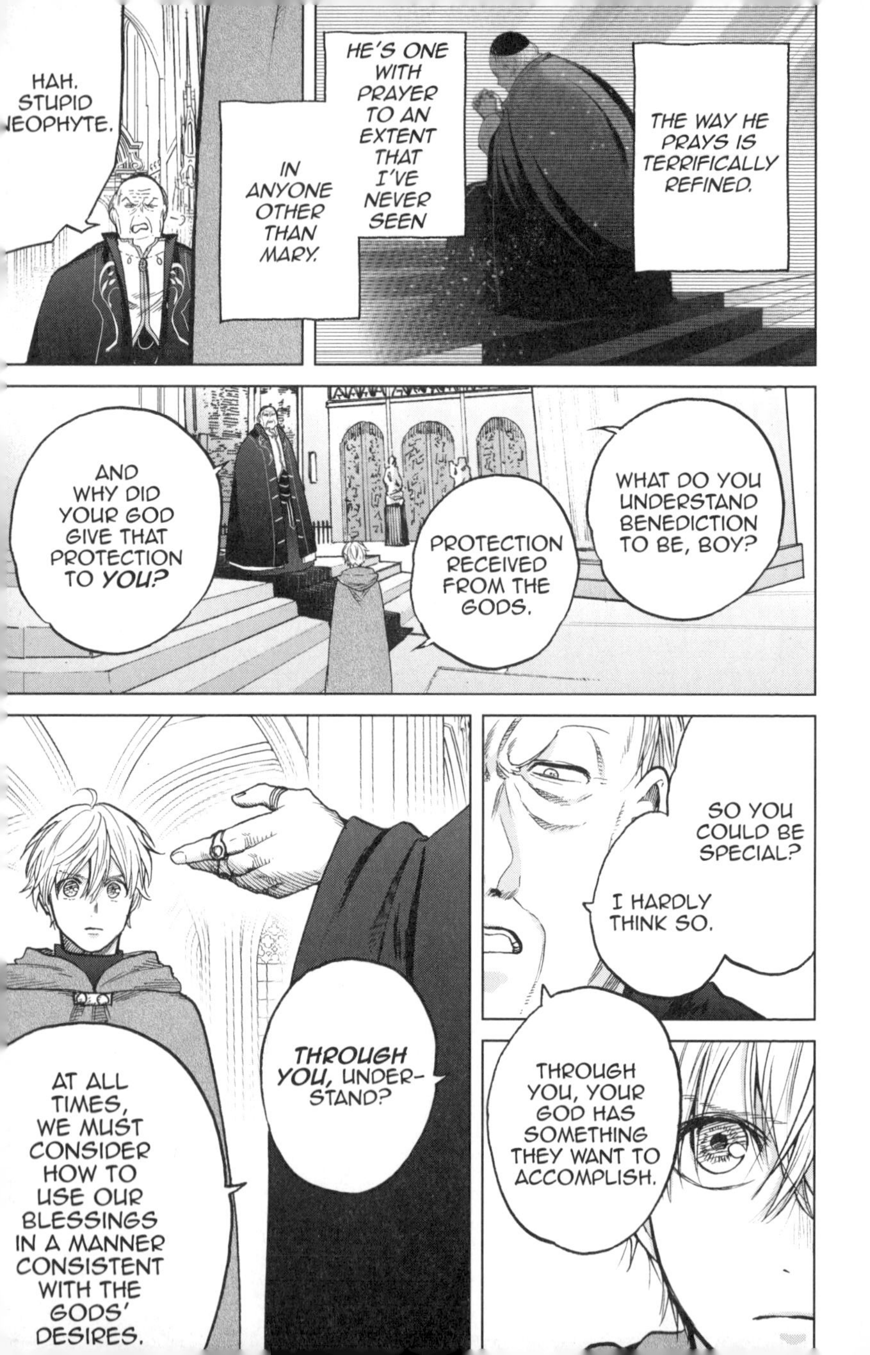
THE WAY HE PRAYS IS TERRIFICALLY REFINED.
HE'S ONE WITH PRAYER TO AN EXTENT THAT I'VE NEVER SEEN
IN ANYONE OTHER THAN MARY.
HAH. STUPID NEOPHYTE.
WHAT DO YOU UNDERSTAND BENEDICTION TO BE, BOY?
PROTECTION RECEIVED FROM THE GODS.
AND WHY DID YOUR GOD GIVE THAT PROTECTION TO *YOU?*
SO YOU COULD BE SPECIAL?
I HARDLY THINK SO.
THROUGH YOU, YOUR GOD HAS SOMETHING THEY WANT TO ACCOMPLISH.
THROUGH YOU, UNDERSTAND?
AT ALL TIMES, WE MUST CONSIDER HOW TO USE OUR BLESSINGS IN A MANNER CONSISTENT WITH THE GODS' DESIRES.

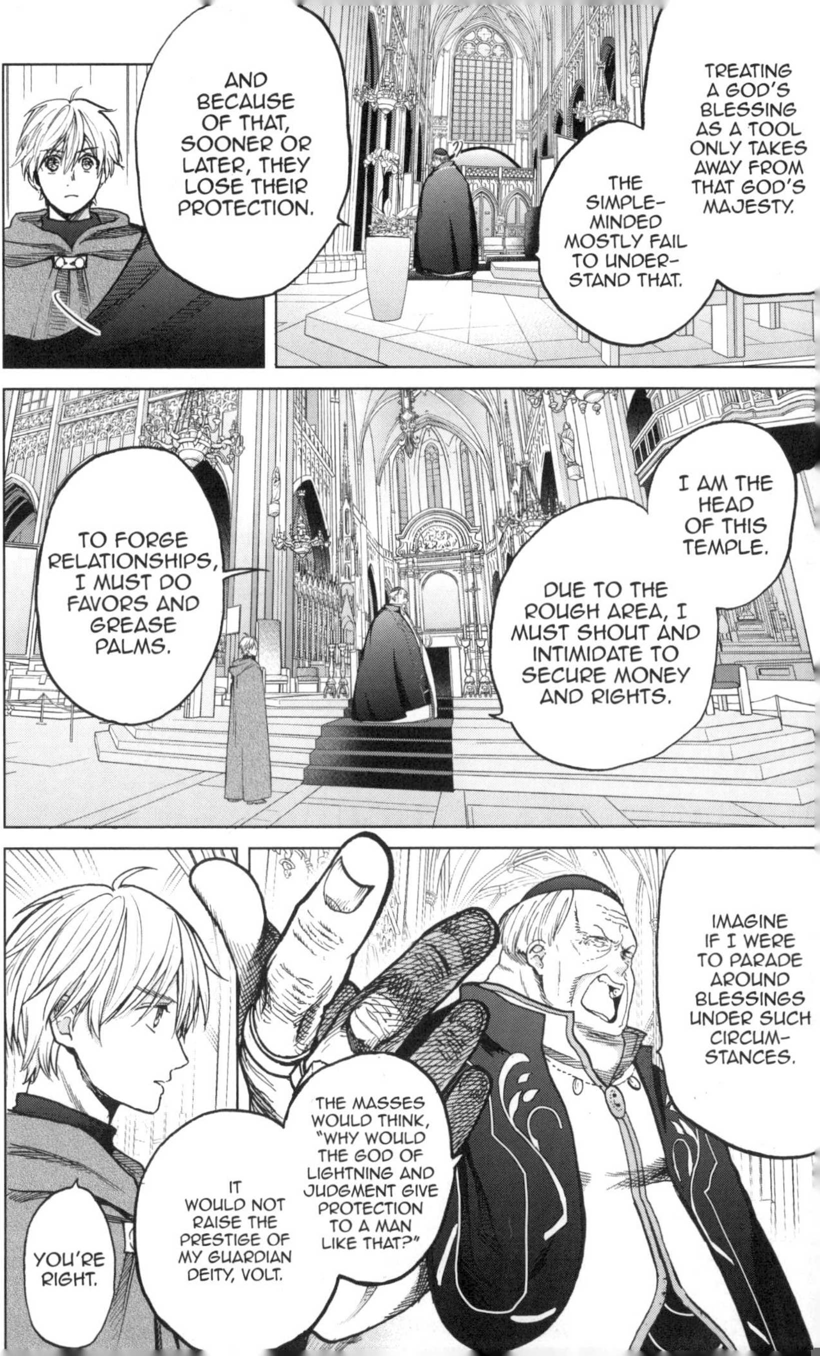
TREATING A GOD'S BLESSING AS A TOOL ONLY TAKES AWAY FROM THAT GOD'S MAJESTY.
THE SIMPLE-MINDED MOSTLY FAIL TO UNDER-STAND THAT.
AND BECAUSE OF THAT, SOONER OR LATER, THEY LOSE THEIR PROTECTION.
I AM THE HEAD OF THIS TEMPLE.
DUE TO THE ROUGH AREA, I MUST SHOUT AND INTIMIDATE TO SECURE MONEY AND RIGHTS.
TO FORGE RELATIONSHIPS, I MUST DO FAVORS AND GREASE PALMS.
IMAGINE IF I WERE TO PARADE AROUND BLESSINGS UNDER SUCH CIRCUM-STANCES.
THE MASSES WOULD THINK, "WHY WOULD THE GOD OF LIGHTNING AND JUDGMENT GIVE PROTECTION TO A MAN LIKE THAT?"
IT WOULD NOT RAISE THE PRESTIGE OF MY GUARDIAN DEITY, VOLT.
YOU'RE RIGHT.

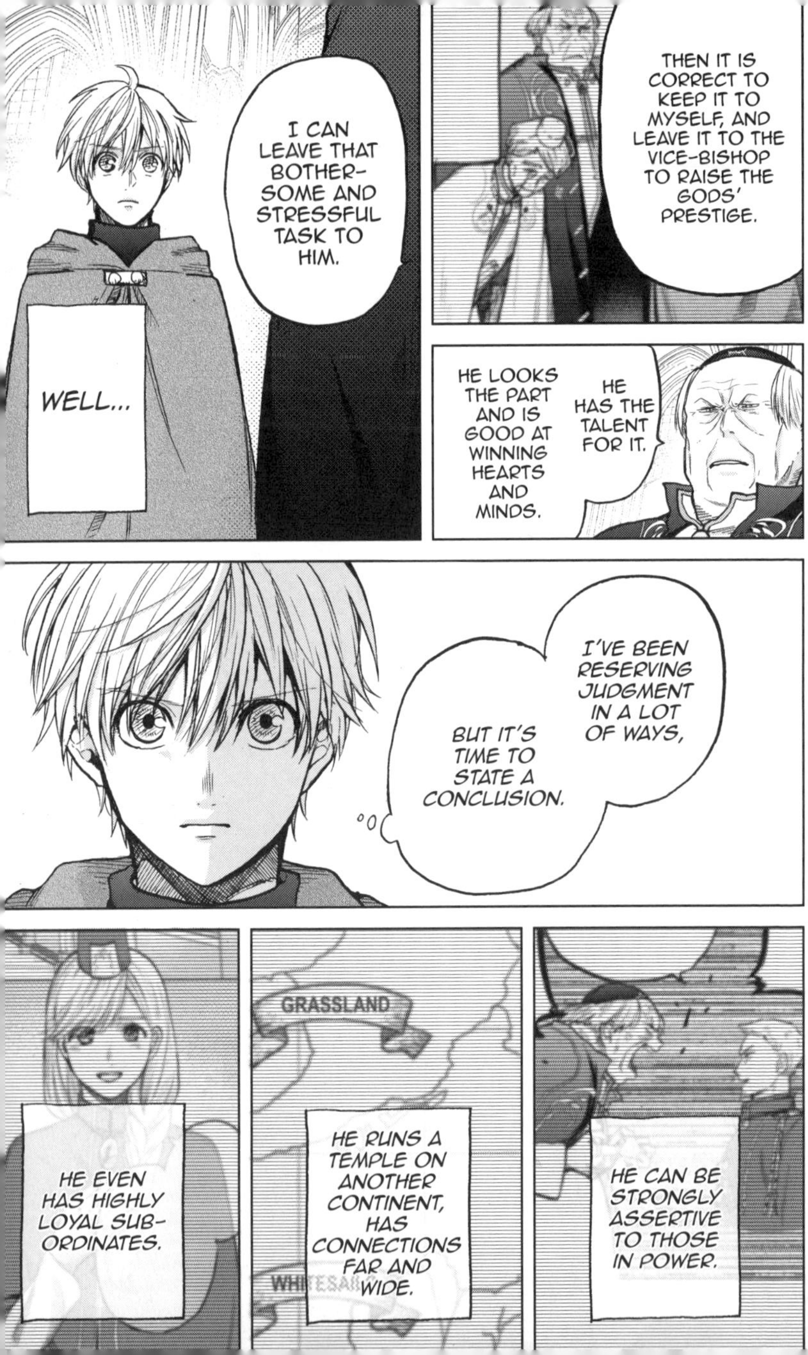
THEN IT IS CORRECT TO KEEP IT TO MYSELF, AND LEAVE IT TO THE VICE-BISHOP TO RAISE THE GODS' PRESTIGE.
HE HAS THE TALENT FOR IT.
HE LOOKS THE PART AND IS GOOD AT WINNING HEARTS AND MINDS.
I CAN LEAVE THAT BOTHER-SOME AND STRESSFUL TASK TO HIM.
WELL...
I'VE BEEN RESERVING JUDGMENT IN A LOT OF WAYS,
BUT IT'S TIME TO STATE A CONCLUSION.
HE CAN BE STRONGLY ASSERTIVE TO THOSE IN POWER.
GRASSLAND
HE RUNS A TEMPLE ON ANOTHER CONTINENT, HAS CONNECTIONS FAR AND WIDE.
HE EVEN HAS HIGHLY LOYAL SUB-ORDINATES.

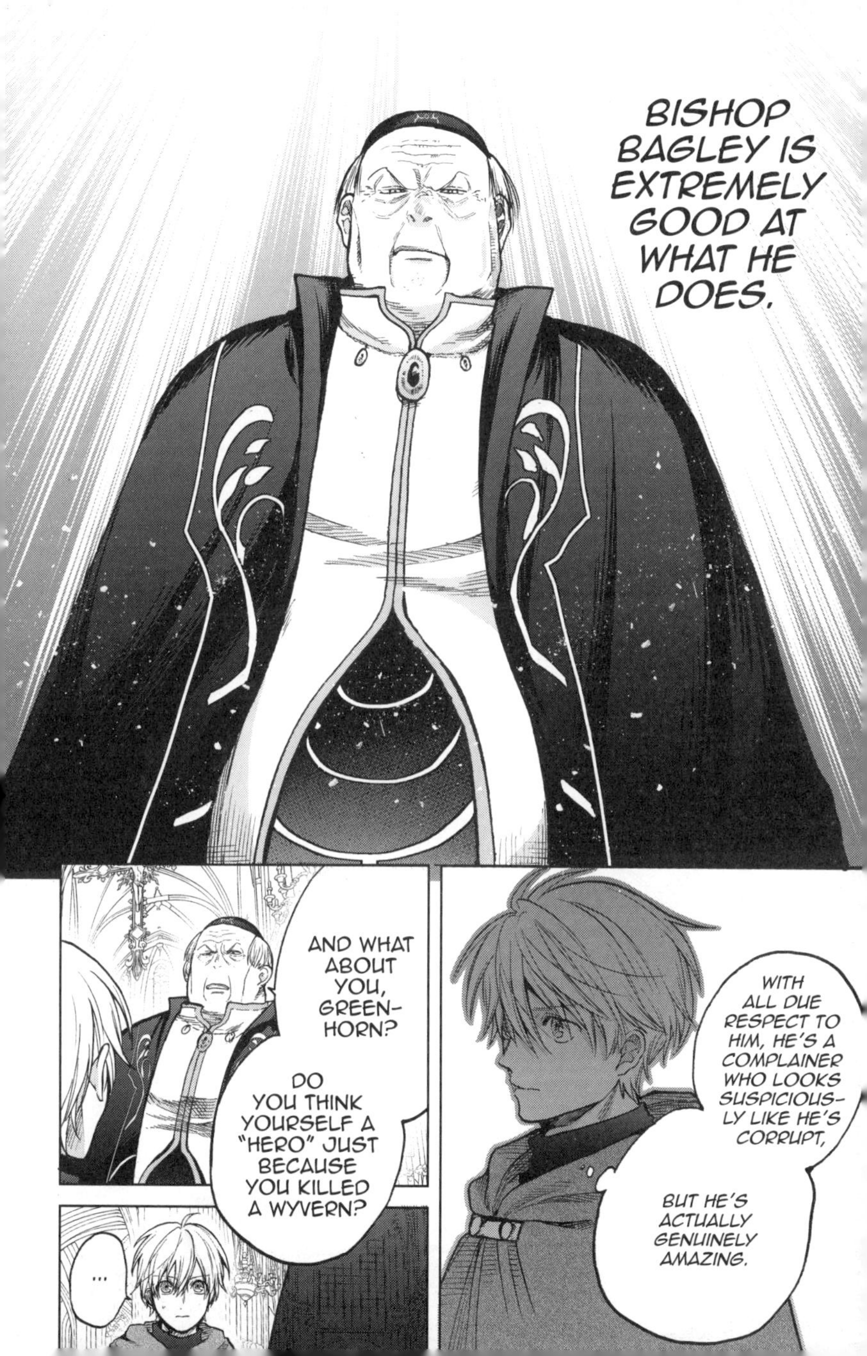
BISHOP BAGLEY IS EXTREMELY GOOD AT WHAT HE DOES.
WITH ALL DUE RESPECT TO HIM, HE'S A COMPLAINER WHO LOOKS SUSPICIOUS-LY LIKE HE'S CORRUPT,
BUT HE'S ACTUALLY GENUINELY AMAZING.
AND WHAT ABOUT YOU, GREEN-HORN?
DO YOU THINK YOURSELF A "HERO" JUST BECAUSE YOU KILLED A WYVERN?
...

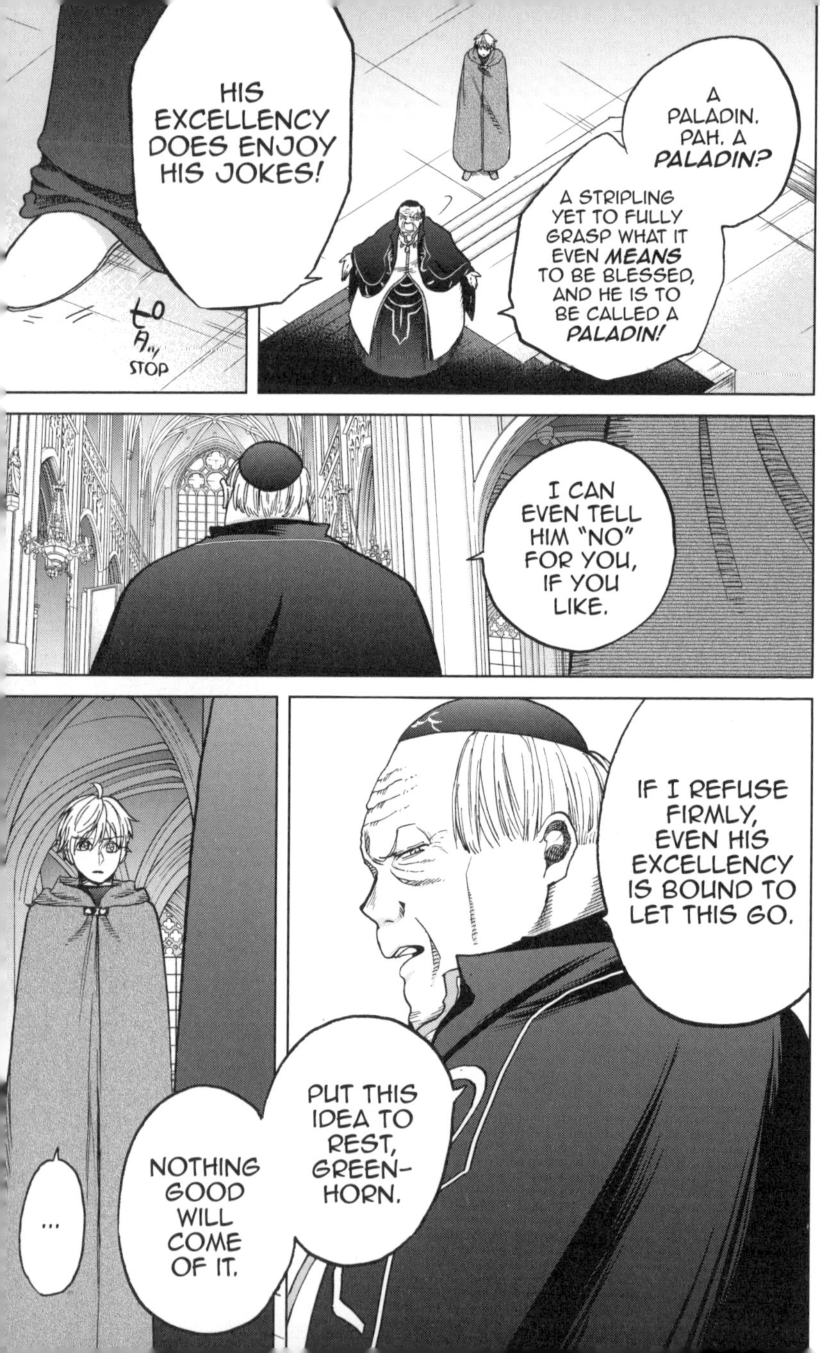
A PALADIN. PAH. A *PALADIN?*
A STRIPLING YET TO FULLY GRASP WHAT IT EVEN *MEANS* TO BE BLESSED, AND HE IS TO BE CALLED A *PALADIN!*
HIS EXCELLENCY DOES ENJOY HIS JOKES!
STOP
I CAN EVEN TELL HIM "NO" FOR YOU, IF YOU LIKE.
IF I REFUSE FIRMLY, EVEN HIS EXCELLENCY IS BOUND TO LET THIS GO.
PUT THIS IDEA TO REST, GREEN-HORN.
NOTHING GOOD WILL COME OF IT.
...

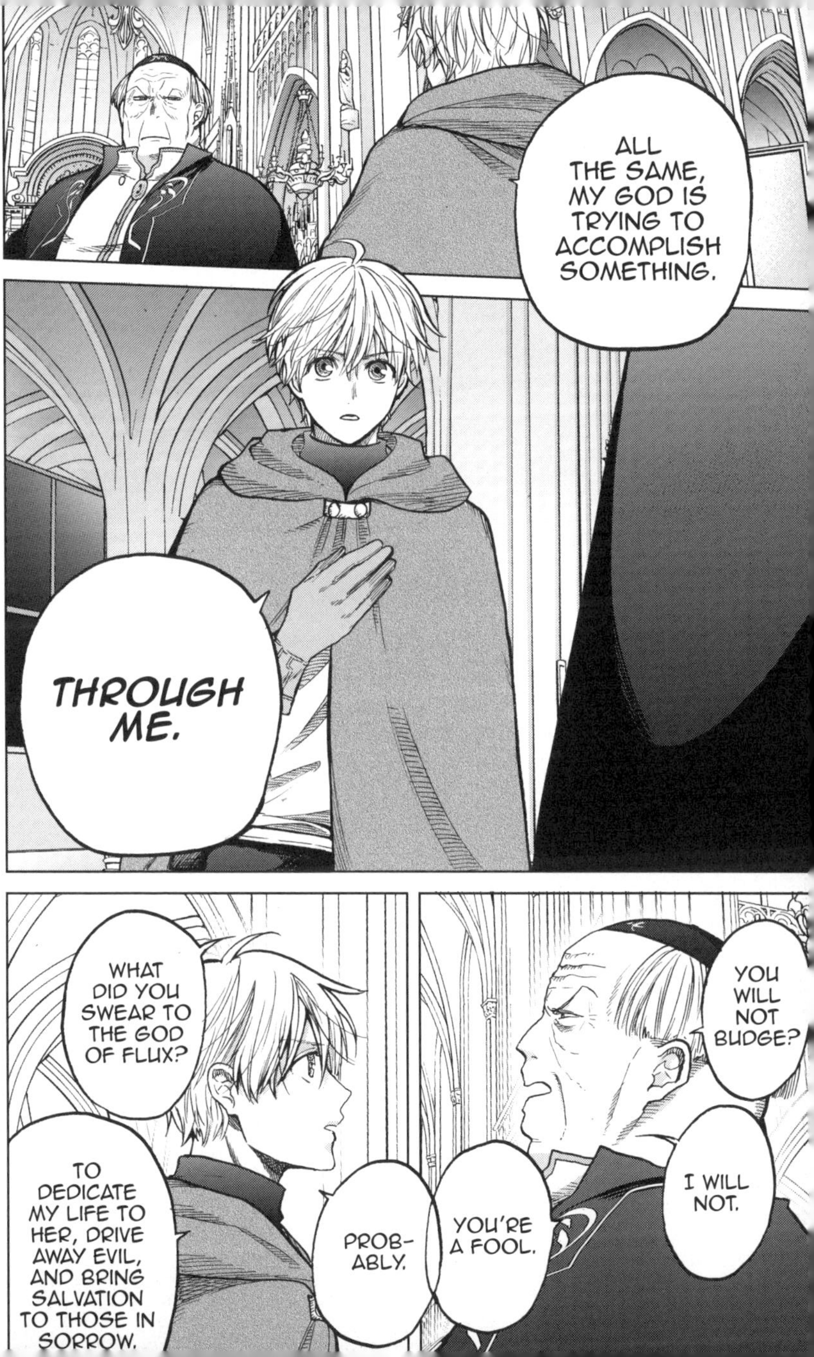
ALL THE SAME, MY GOD IS TRYING TO ACCOMPLISH SOMETHING.
THROUGH ME.
YOU WILL NOT BUDGE?
I WILL NOT.
YOU'RE A FOOL.
PROB-ABLY.
WHAT DID YOU SWEAR TO THE GOD OF FLUX?
TO DEDICATE MY LIFE TO HER, DRIVE AWAY EVIL, AND BRING SALVATION TO THOSE IN SORROW.

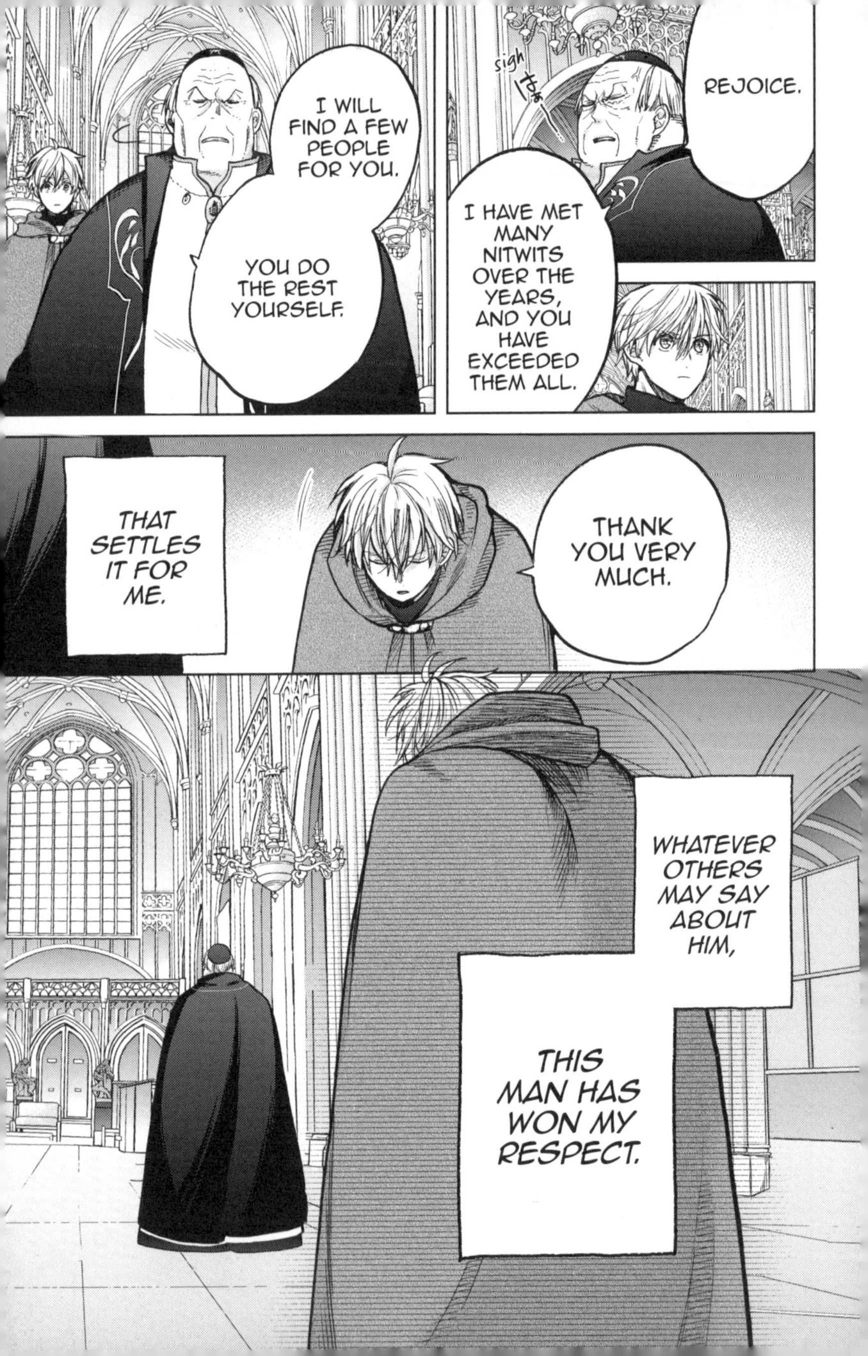
REJOICE.
sigh
はぁ
I HAVE MET MANY NITWITS OVER THE YEARS, AND YOU HAVE EXCEEDED THEM ALL.
I WILL FIND A FEW PEOPLE FOR YOU.
YOU DO THE REST YOURSELF.
THANK YOU VERY MUCH.
THAT SETTLES IT FOR ME.
WHATEVER OTHERS MAY SAY ABOUT HIM,
THIS MAN HAS WON MY RESPECT.

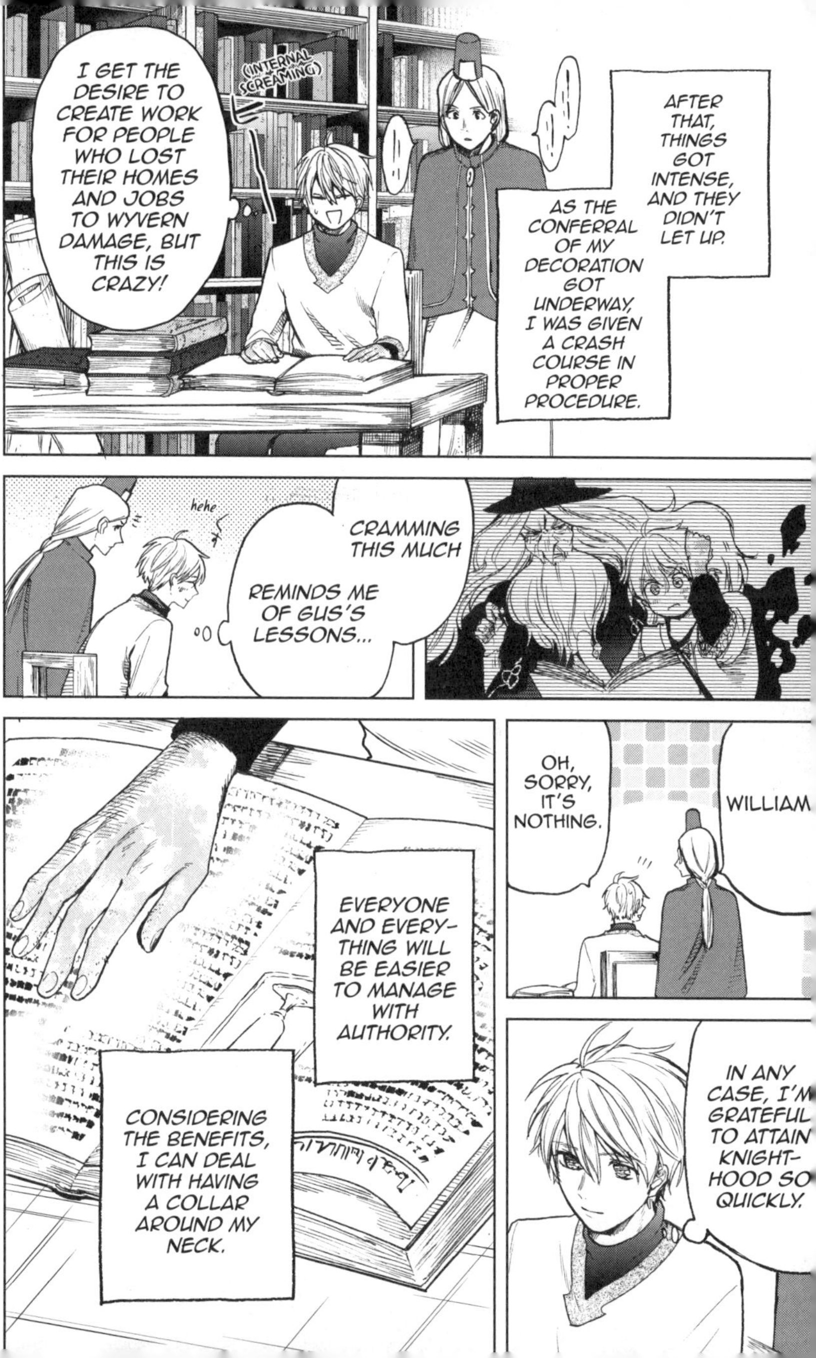
AFTER THAT, THINGS GOT INTENSE, AND THEY DIDN'T LET UP.
AS THE CONFERRAL OF MY DECORATION GOT UNDERWAY, I WAS GIVEN A CRASH COURSE IN PROPER PROCEDURE.
(INTERNAL SCREAMING)
I GET THE DESIRE TO CREATE WORK FOR PEOPLE WHO LOST THEIR HOMES AND JOBS TO WYVERN DAMAGE, BUT THIS IS CRAZY!
hehe
CRAMMING THIS MUCH
REMINDS ME OF GUS'S LESSONS...
WILLIAM
OH, SORRY, IT'S NOTHING.
IN ANY CASE, I'M GRATEFUL TO ATTAIN KNIGHT-HOOD SO QUICKLY.
EVERYONE AND EVERY-THING WILL BE EASIER TO MANAGE WITH AUTHORITY.
CONSIDERING THE BENEFITS, I CAN DEAL WITH HAVING A COLLAR AROUND MY NECK.

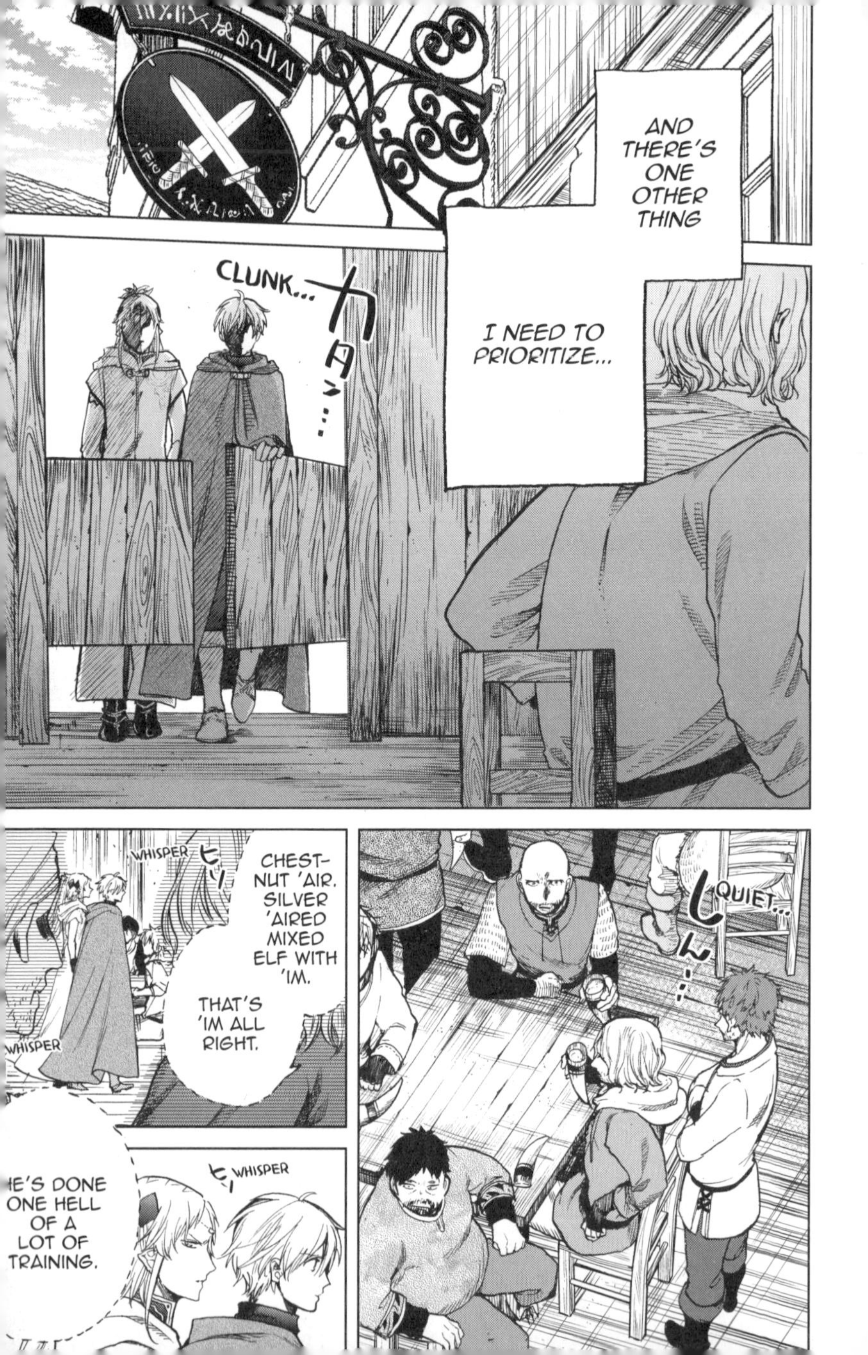
AND THERE'S ONE OTHER THING
CLUNK...
カタン...
I NEED TO PRIORITIZE...
QUIET...
WHISPER
CHEST-NUT 'AIR. SILVER 'AIRED MIXED ELF WITH 'IM.
THAT'S 'IM ALL RIGHT.
WHISPER
WHISPER
HE'S DONE ONE HELL OF A LOT OF TRAINING.

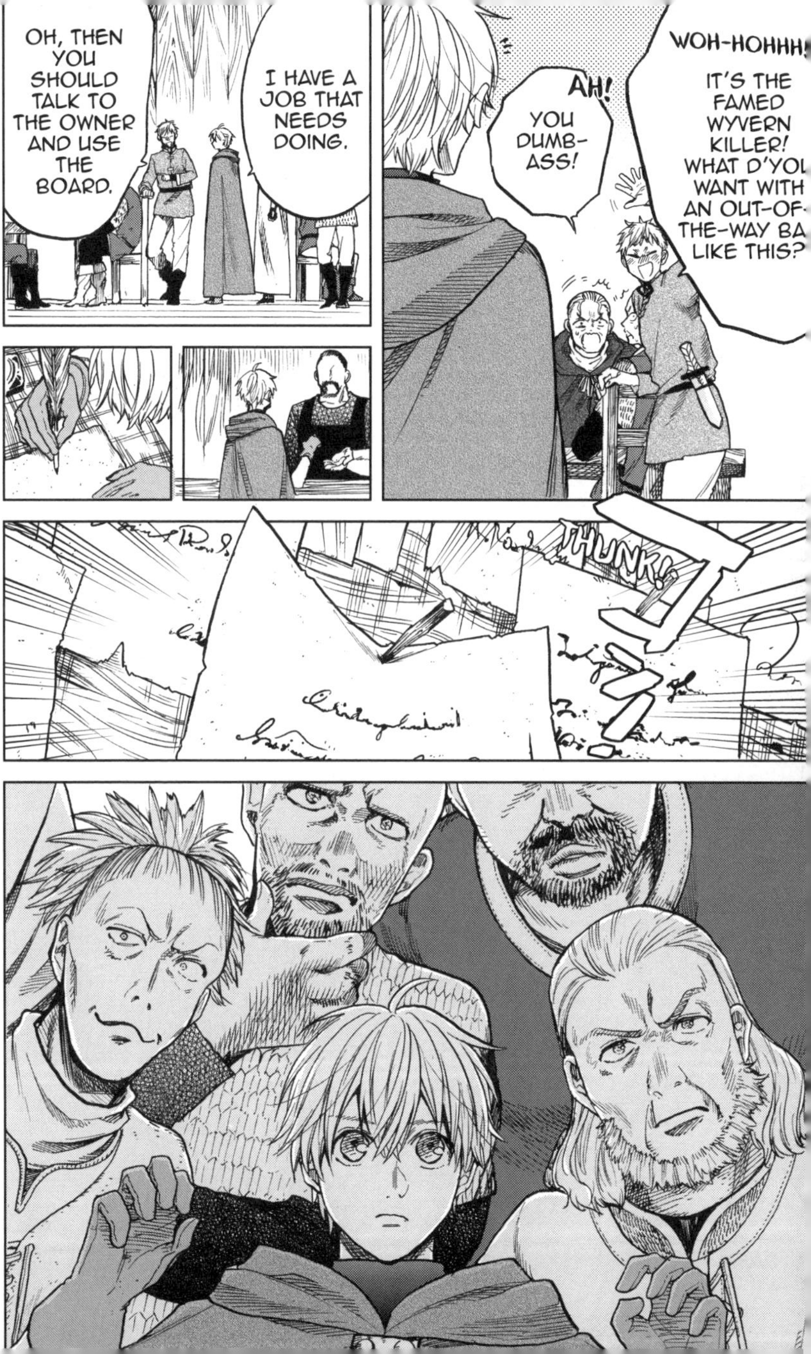
WOH-HOHHH!
IT'S THE FAMED WYVERN KILLER! WHAT D'YOU WANT WITH AN OUT-OF-THE-WAY BA LIKE THIS?
AH!
YOU DUMB-ASS!
I HAVE A JOB THAT NEEDS DOING.
OH, THEN YOU SHOULD TALK TO THE OWNER AND USE THE BOARD.
THUNK!!

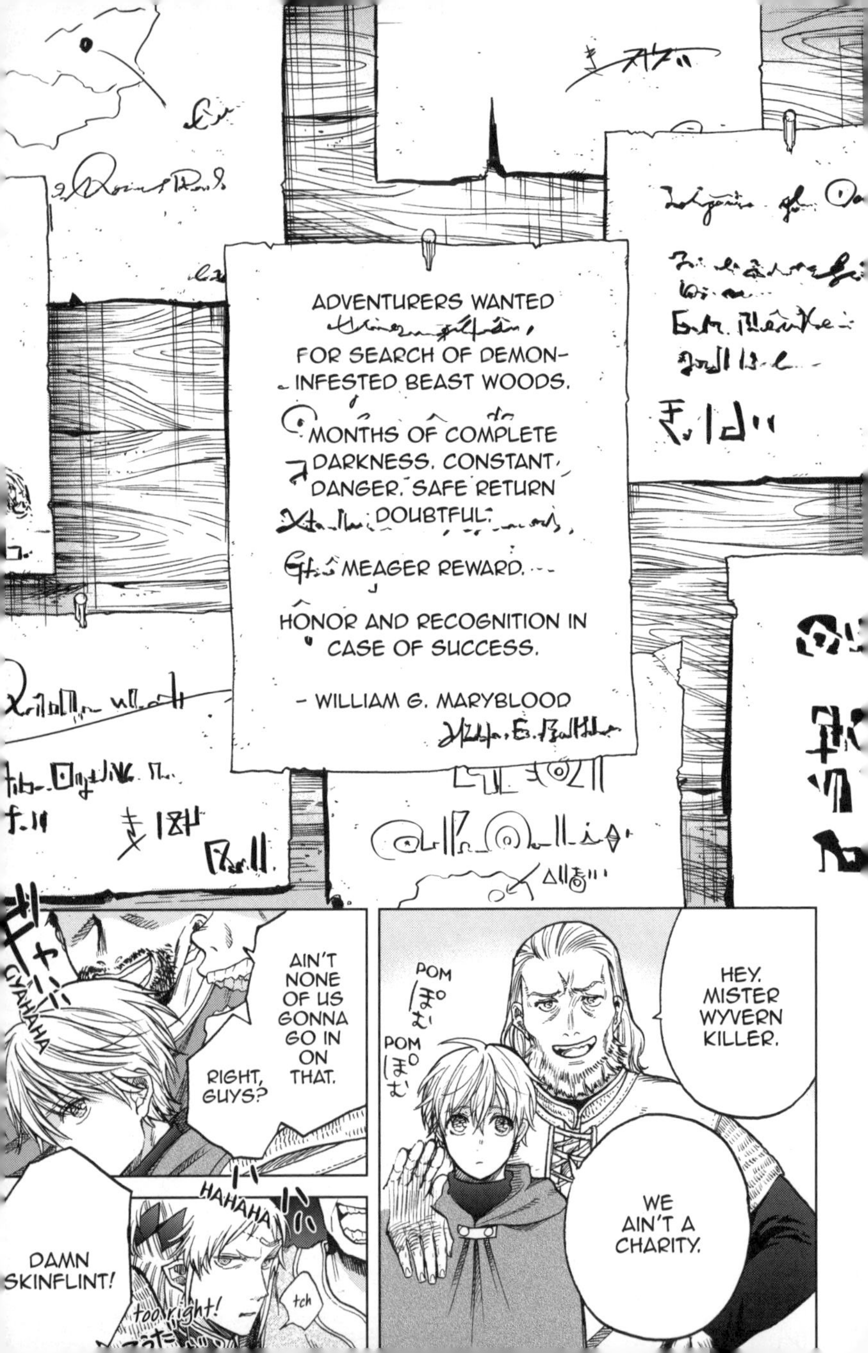

ADVENTURERS WANTED
FOR SEARCH OF DEMON-INFESTED BEAST WOODS.
MONTHS OF COMPLETE DARKNESS. CONSTANT DANGER. SAFE RETURN DOUBTFUL.
MEAGER REWARD.
HONOR AND RECOGNITION IN CASE OF SUCCESS.
- WILLIAM G. MARYBLOOD
HEY. MISTER WYVERN KILLER.
POM ぽむ
POM ぽむ
WE AIN'T A CHARITY.
AIN'T NONE OF US GONNA GO IN ON THAT.
RIGHT, GUYS?
GYAHAHA
HAHAHA
tch
DAMN SKINFLINT!
too right!

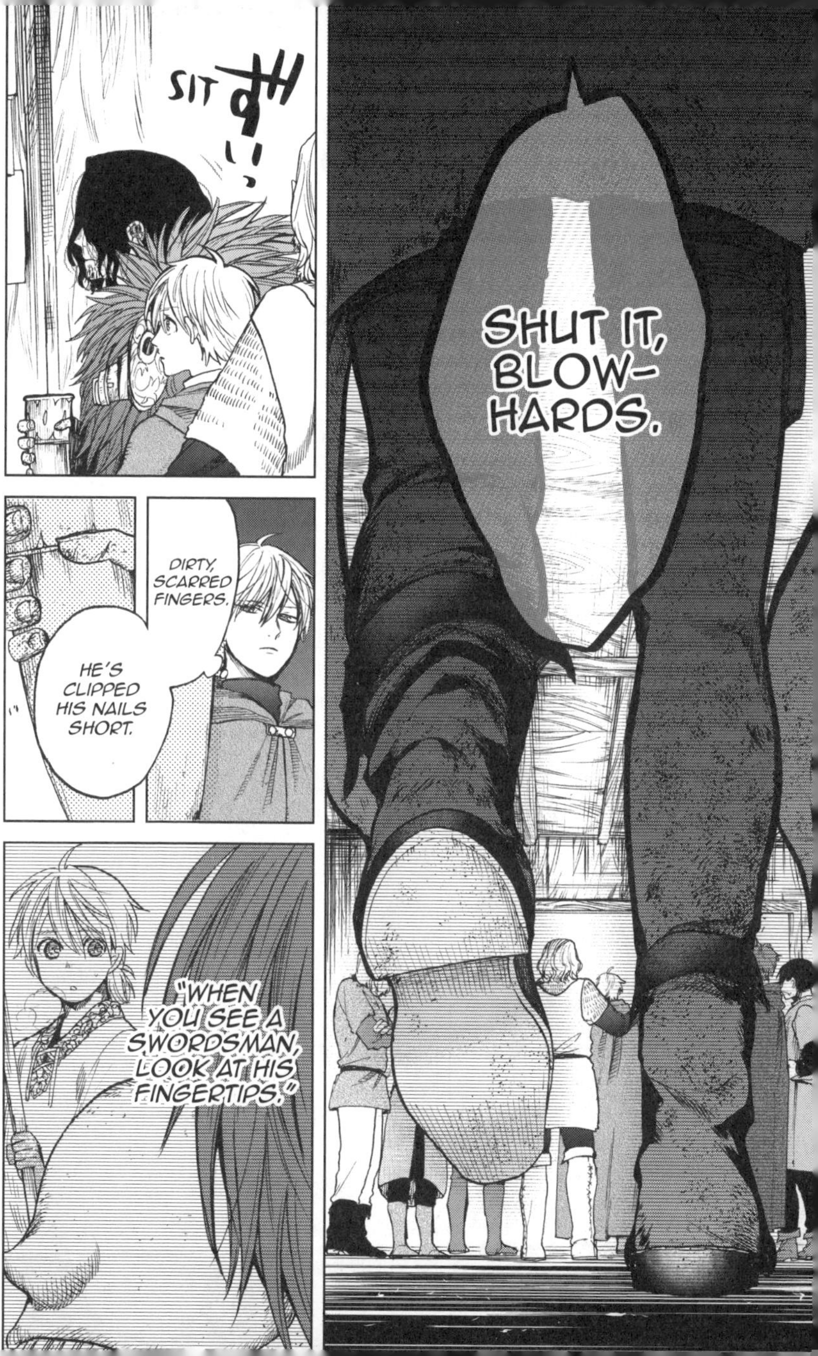
SHUT IT, BLOW-HARDS.
SIT
DIRTY, SCARRED FINGERS.
HE'S CLIPPED HIS NAILS SHORT.
"WHEN YOU SEE A SWORDSMAN, LOOK AT HIS FINGERTIPS."

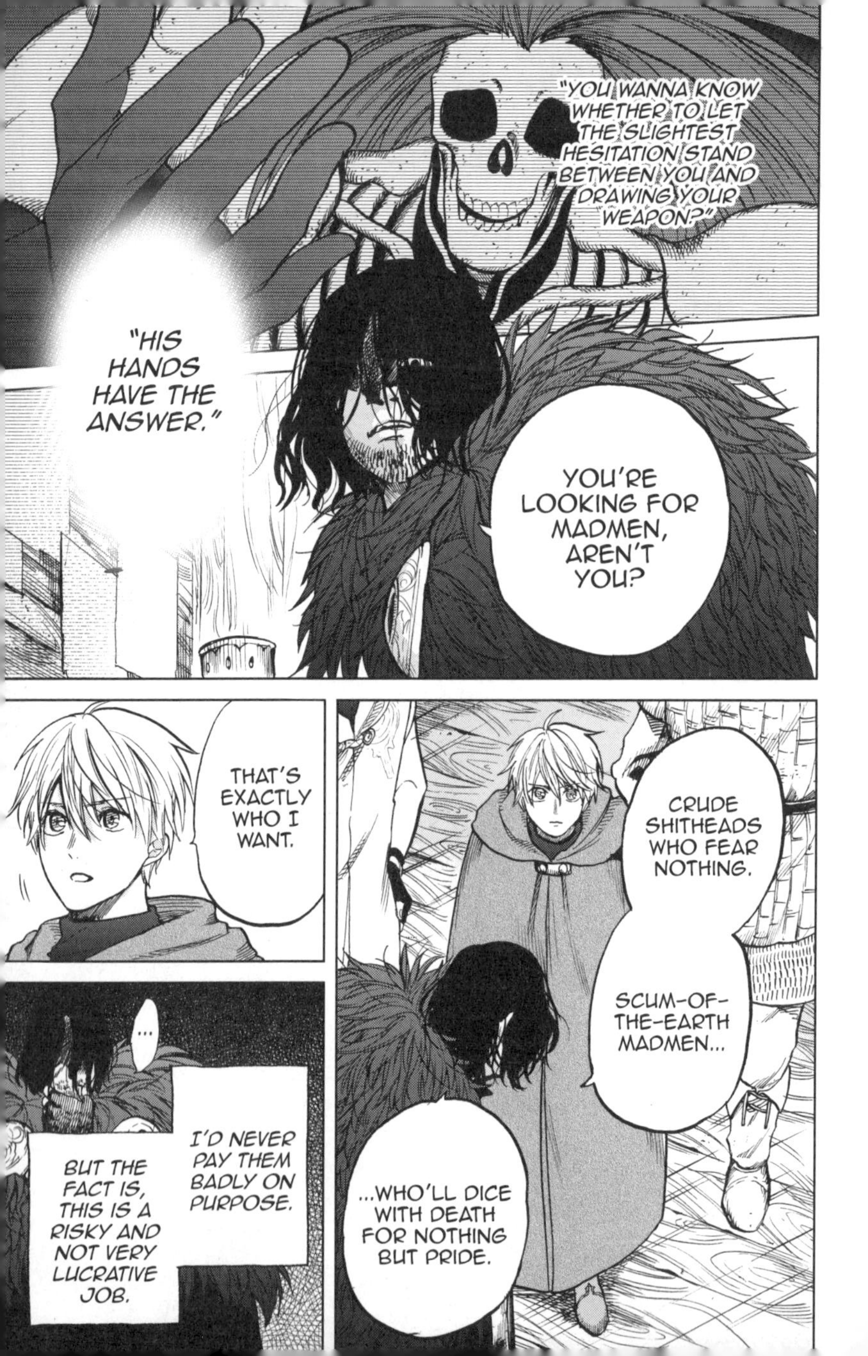
"YOU WANNA KNOW WHETHER TO LET THE SLIGHTEST HESITATION STAND BETWEEN YOU AND DRAWING YOUR WEAPON?"
"HIS HANDS HAVE THE ANSWER."
YOU'RE LOOKING FOR MADMEN, AREN'T YOU?
CRUDE SHITHEADS WHO FEAR NOTHING.
SCUM-OF-THE-EARTH MADMEN...
...WHO'LL DICE WITH DEATH FOR NOTHING BUT PRIDE.
THAT'S EXACTLY WHO I WANT.
...
I'D NEVER PAY THEM BADLY ON PURPOSE.
BUT THE FACT IS, THIS IS A RISKY AND NOT VERY LUCRATIVE JOB.

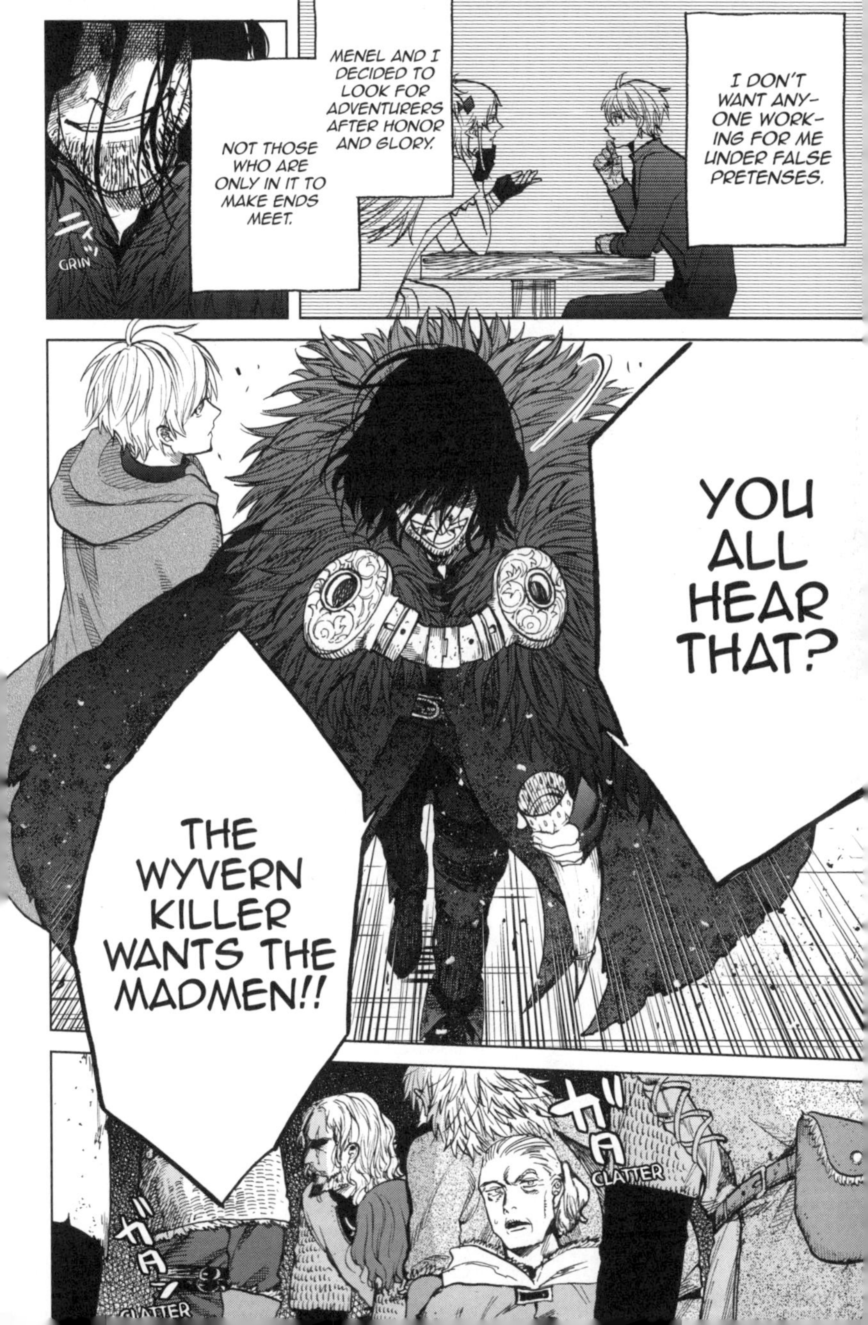
I DON'T WANT ANY-ONE WORKING FOR ME UNDER FALSE PRETENSES.
MENEL AND I DECIDED TO LOOK FOR ADVENTURERS AFTER HONOR AND GLORY.
NOT THOSE WHO ARE ONLY IN IT TO MAKE ENDS MEET.
GRIN
YOU ALL HEAR THAT?
THE WYVERN KILLER WANTS THE MADMEN!!
CLATTER
CLATTER

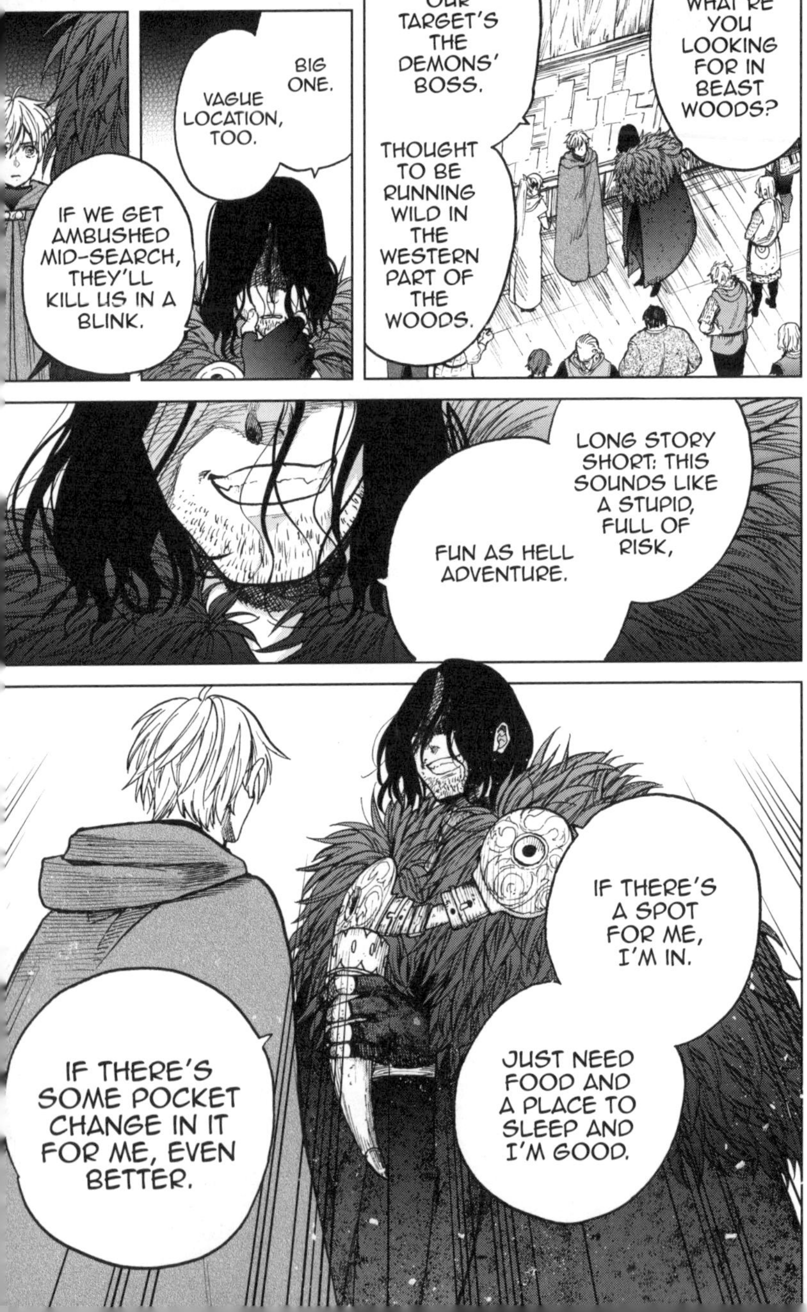
WHAT'RE YOU LOOKING FOR IN BEAST WOODS?
OUR TARGET'S THE DEMONS' BOSS.
THOUGHT TO BE RUNNING WILD IN THE WESTERN PART OF THE WOODS.
BIG ONE.
VAGUE LOCATION, TOO.
IF WE GET AMBUSHED MID-SEARCH, THEY'LL KILL US IN A BLINK.
LONG STORY SHORT: THIS SOUNDS LIKE A STUPID, FULL OF RISK,
FUN AS HELL ADVENTURE.
IF THERE'S A SPOT FOR ME, I'M IN.
JUST NEED FOOD AND A PLACE TO SLEEP AND I'M GOOD.
IF THERE'S SOME POCKET CHANGE IN IT FOR ME, EVEN BETTER.

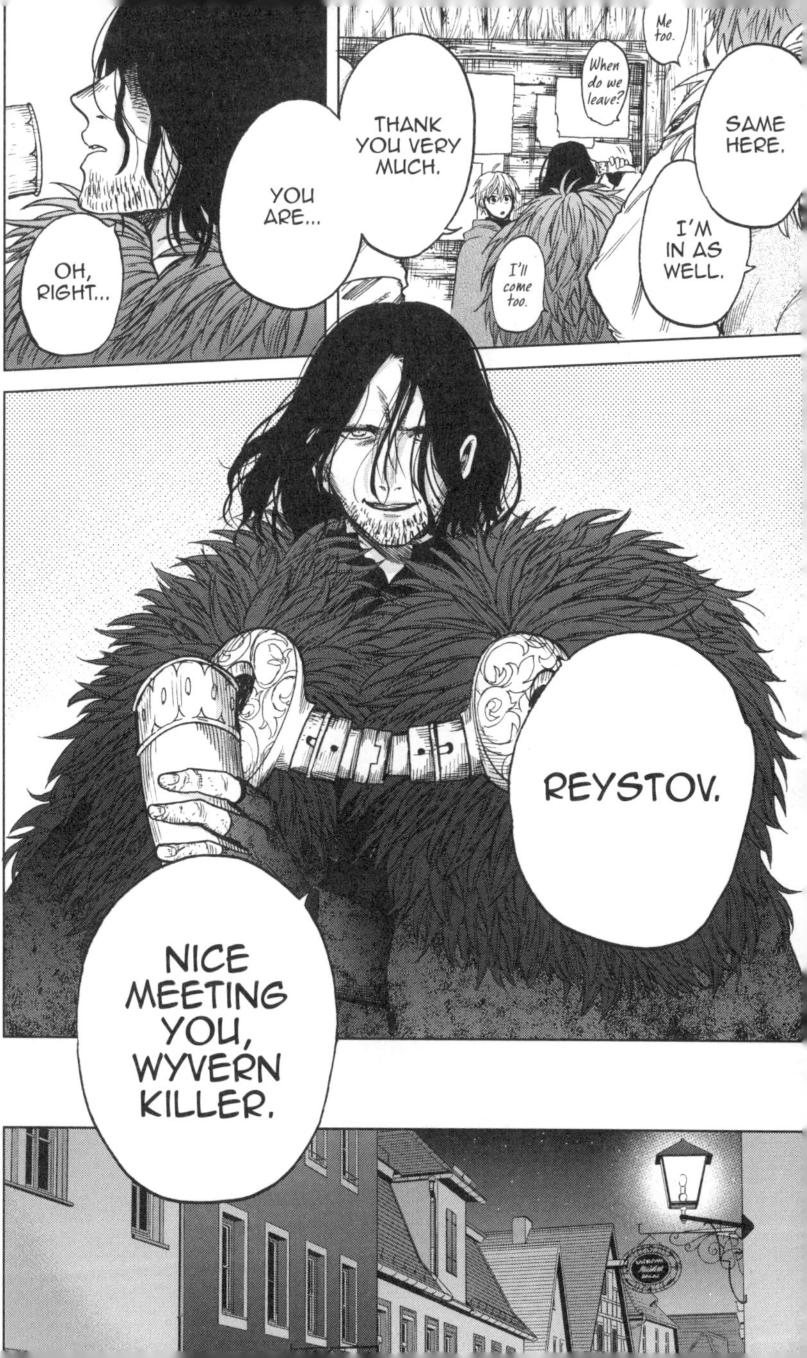
Me too.
When do we leave?
SAME HERE.
I'M IN AS WELL.
I'll come too.
THANK YOU VERY MUCH.
YOU ARE...
OH, RIGHT...
REYSTOV.
NICE MEETING YOU, WYVERN KILLER.

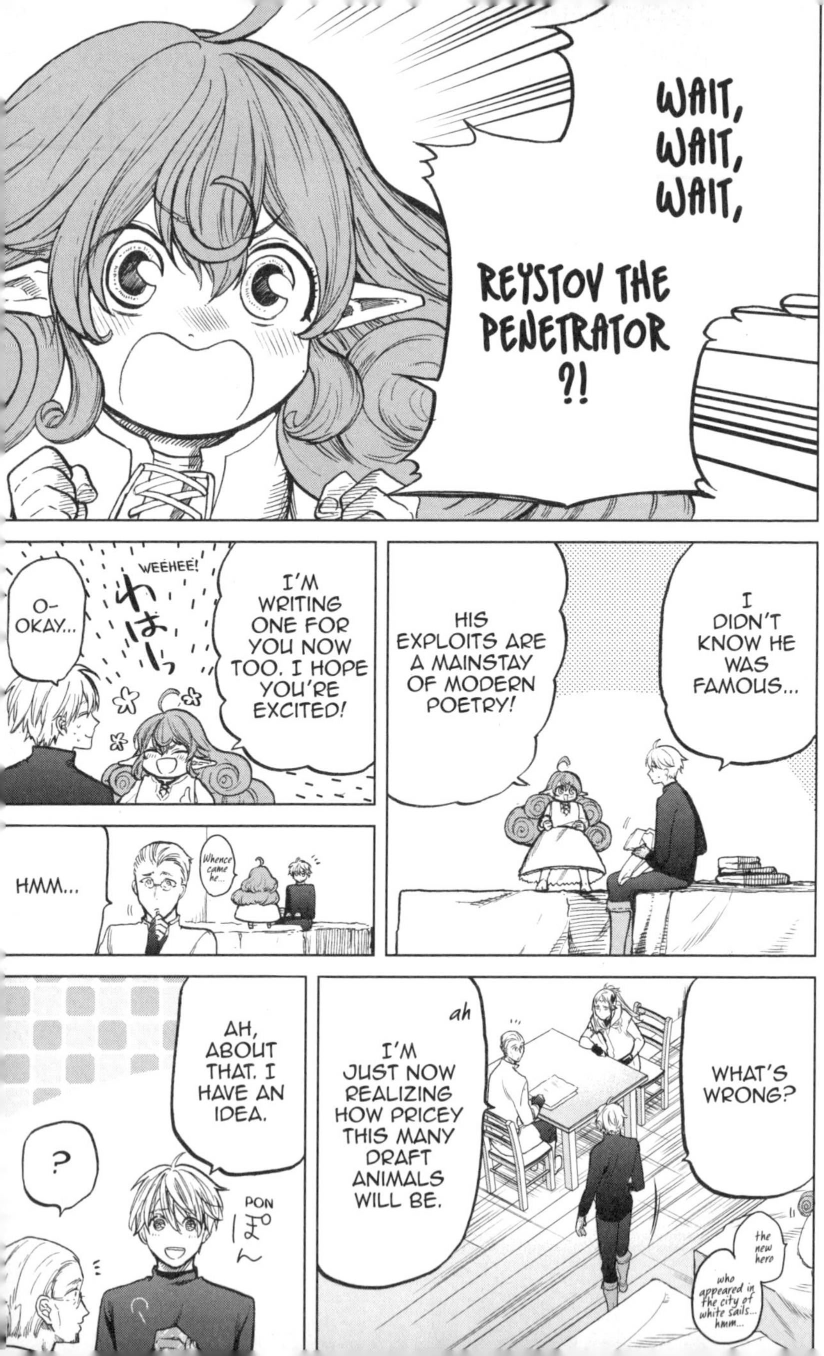
WAIT, WAIT, WAIT,
REYSTOV THE PENETRATOR ?!
I DIDN'T KNOW HE WAS FAMOUS...
HIS EXPLOITS ARE A MAINSTAY OF MODERN POETRY!
I'M WRITING ONE FOR YOU NOW TOO. I HOPE YOU'RE EXCITED!
WEEHEE!
わはーっ
O-OKAY...
Whence came he...
HMM...
WHAT'S WRONG?
the new hero who appeared in the city of white sails... hmm...
ah
I'M JUST NOW REALIZING HOW PRICEY THIS MANY DRAFT ANIMALS WILL BE.
AH, ABOUT THAT. I HAVE AN IDEA.
PON
ぽん
?

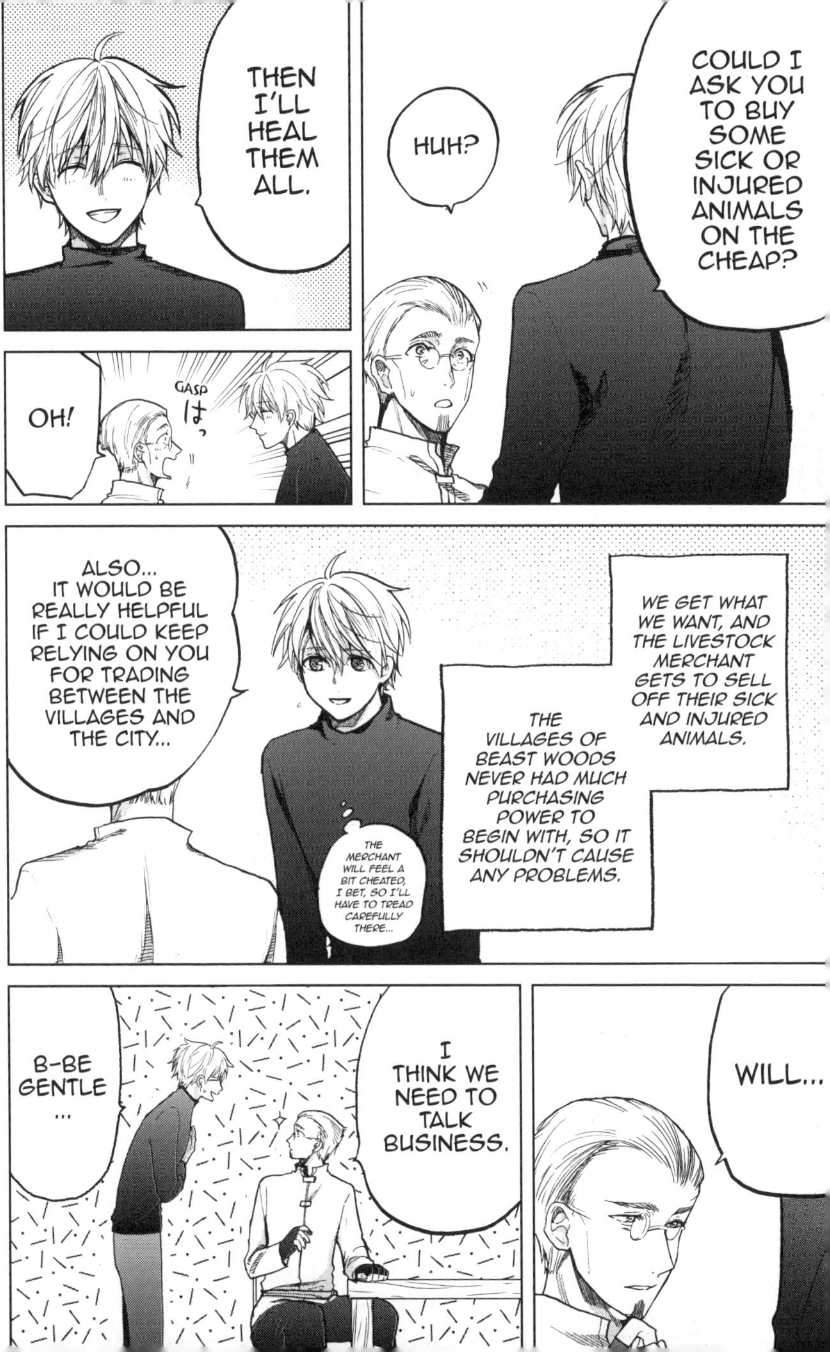
COULD I ASK YOU TO BUY SOME SICK OR INJURED ANIMALS ON THE CHEAP?
HUH?
THEN I'LL HEAL THEM ALL.
OH!
GASP
は,
WE GET WHAT WE WANT, AND THE LIVESTOCK MERCHANT GETS TO SELL OFF THEIR SICK AND INJURED ANIMALS.
THE VILLAGES OF BEAST WOODS NEVER HAD MUCH PURCHASING POWER TO BEGIN WITH, SO IT SHOULDN'T CAUSE ANY PROBLEMS.
ALSO... IT WOULD BE REALLY HELPFUL IF I COULD KEEP RELYING ON YOU FOR TRADING BETWEEN THE VILLAGES AND THE CITY...
THE MERCHANT WILL FEEL A BIT CHEATED, I BET, SO I'LL HAVE TO TREAD CAREFULLY THERE...
WILL...
I THINK WE NEED TO TALK BUSINESS.
B-BE GENTLE ...

THE DAYS IN WHITESAILS ROLLED BY,

AND BEFORE LONG—

I, ETHELBALD REX SOUTHMARK, DUKE OF SOUTHMARK, CONFER THE HONOR OF KNIGHTHOOD UPON THEE.

TO YOU, THE ONE WHO WILL NOW BECOME A KNIGHT—

YOU MUST DEFEND THE TEACHINGS OF THE GOOD GODS

AND PROTECT ALL THOSE WHO WORK IN ADNEST

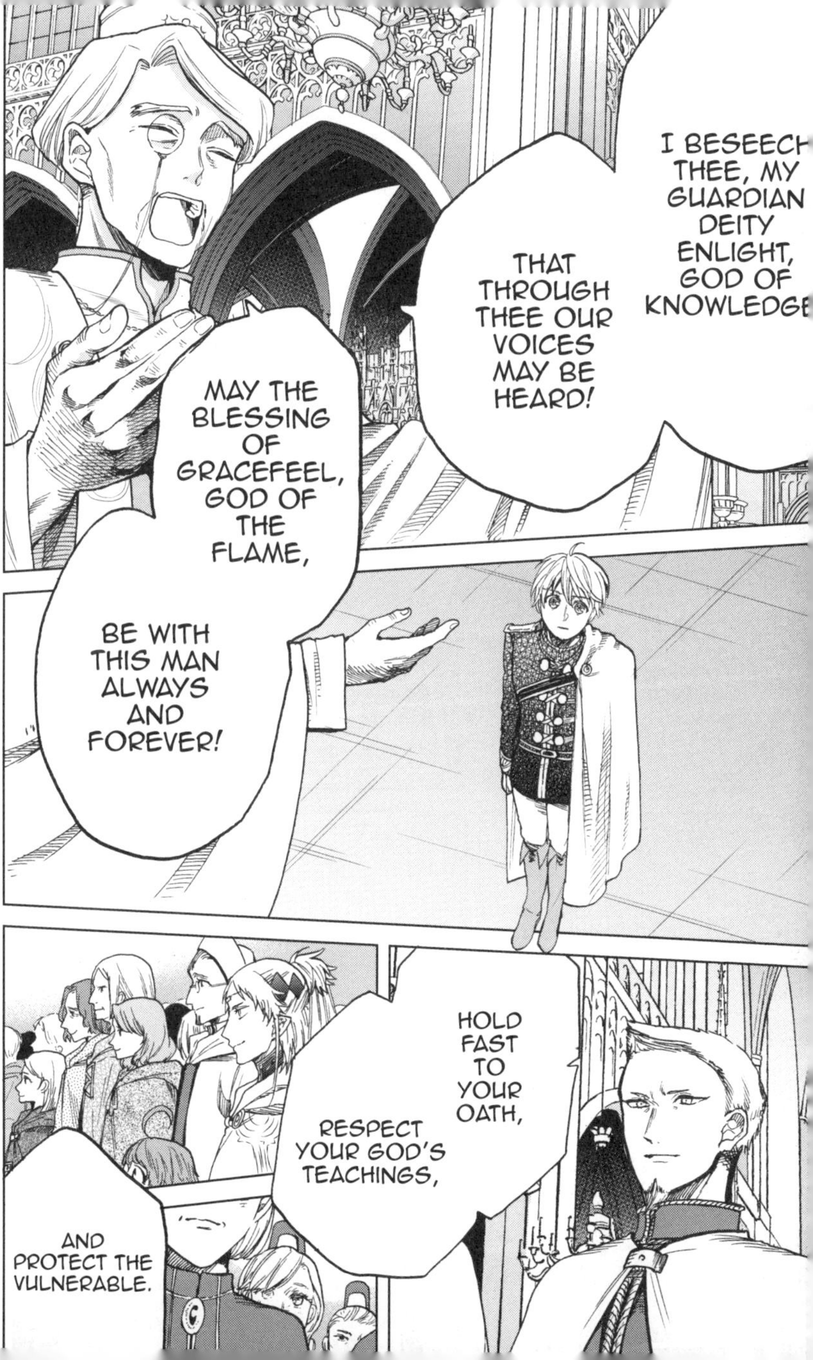
I BESEECH THEE, MY GUARDIAN DEITY ENLIGHT, GOD OF KNOWLEDGE
THAT THROUGH THEE OUR VOICES MAY BE HEARD!
MAY THE BLESSING OF GRACEFEEL, GOD OF THE FLAME,
BE WITH THIS MAN ALWAYS AND FOREVER!
HOLD FAST TO YOUR OATH,
RESPECT YOUR GOD'S TEACHINGS,
AND PROTECT THE VULNERABLE.

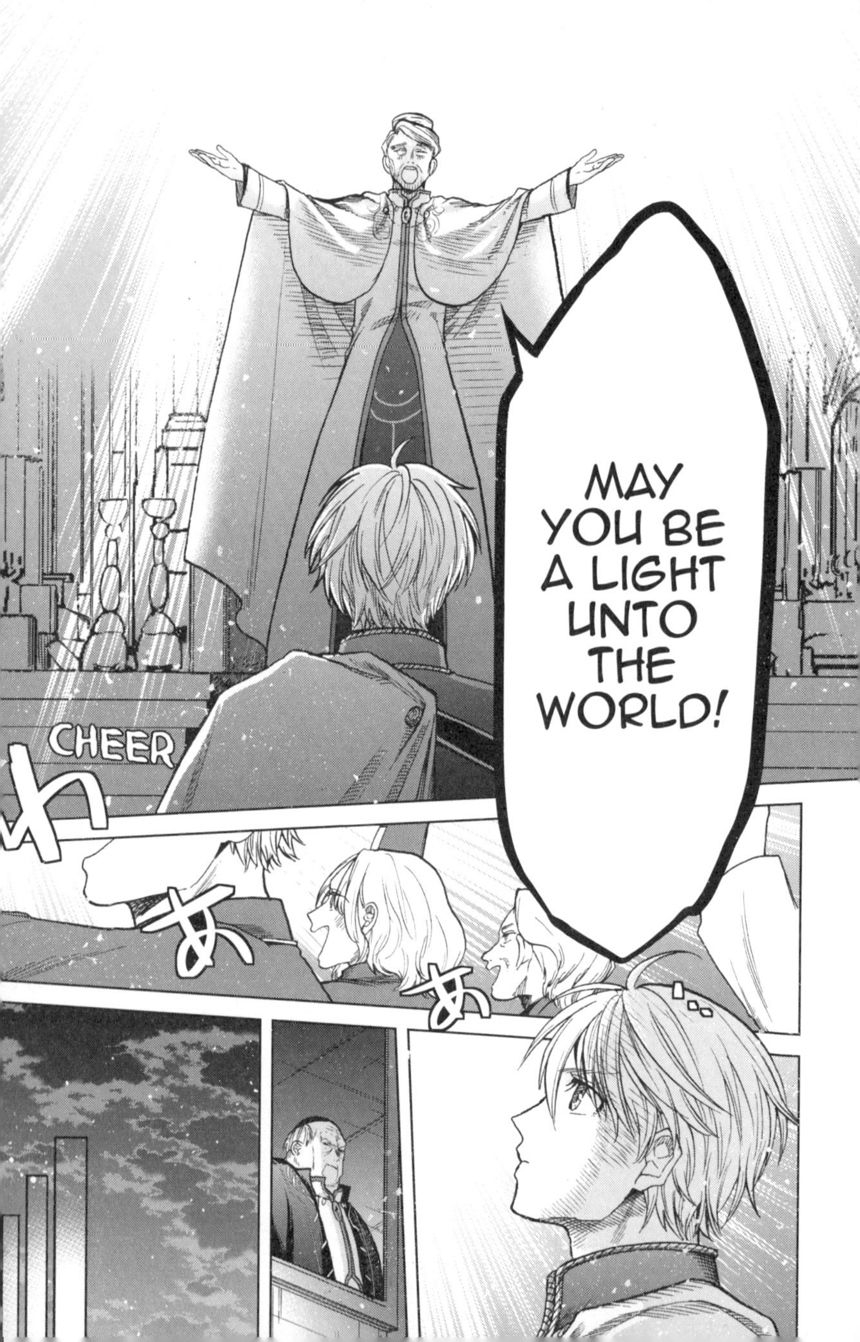
MAY YOU BE A LIGHT UNTO THE WORLD!
CHEER
わ
あ
あ

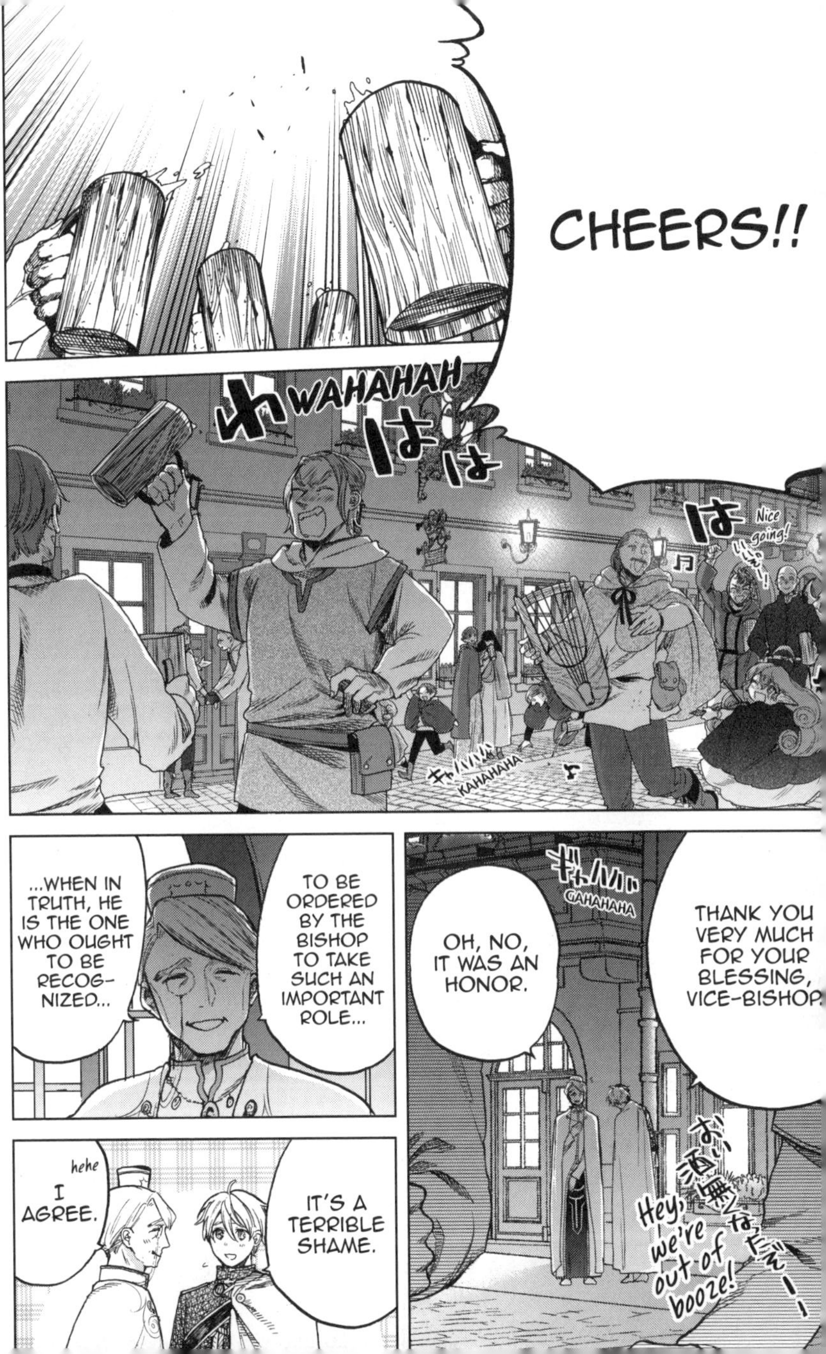

CHEERS!!
WAHAHAH
はは
は
Nice going!
いいぞー!
KAHAHAHA
GAHAHAHA
THANK YOU VERY MUCH FOR YOUR BLESSING, VICE-BISHOP.
OH, NO, IT WAS AN HONOR.
Hey, we're out of booze!
お酒無くなったぞーー
TO BE ORDERED BY THE BISHOP TO TAKE SUCH AN IMPORTANT ROLE...
...WHEN IN TRUTH, HE IS THE ONE WHO OUGHT TO BE RECOG-NIZED...
IT'S A TERRIBLE SHAME.
hehe
I AGREE.

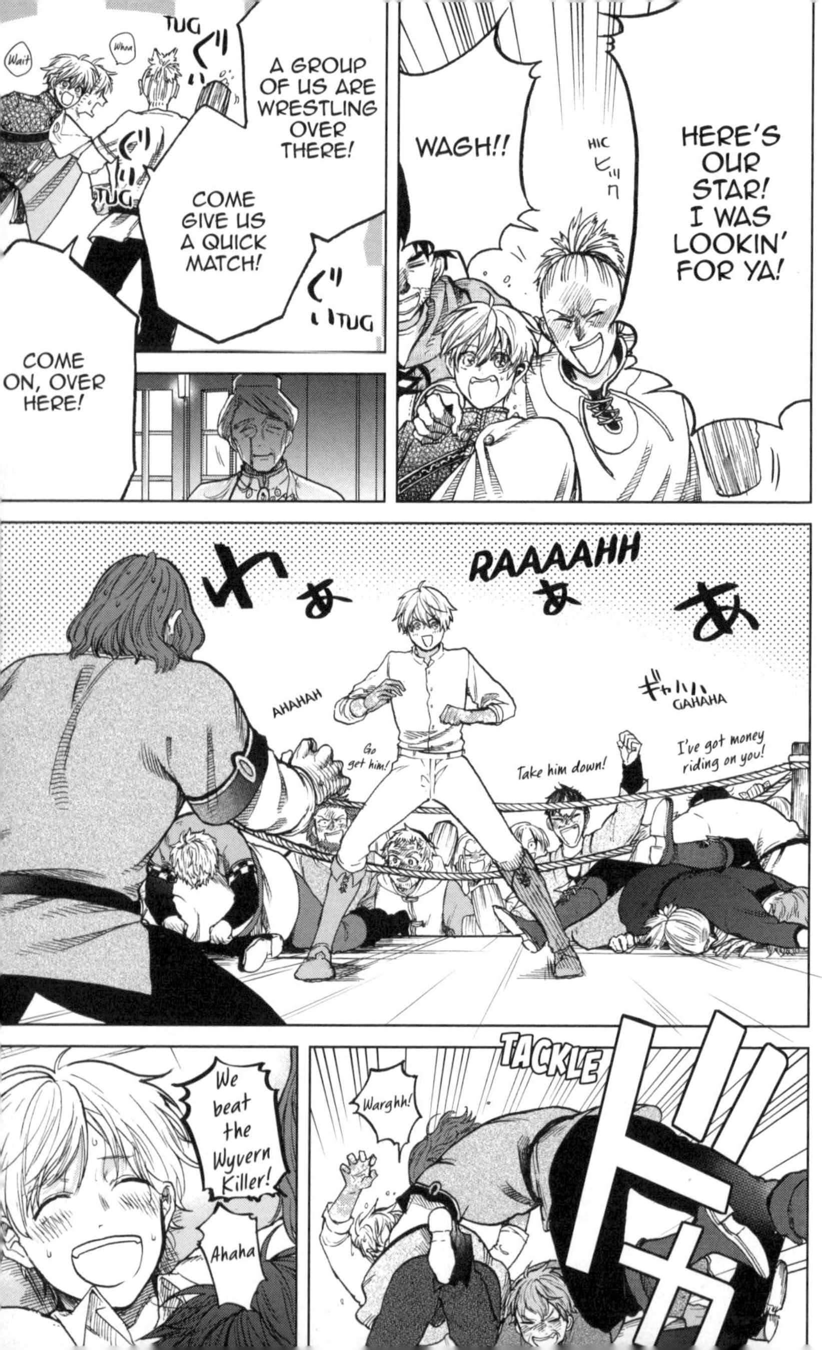
HERE'S OUR STAR! I WAS LOOKIN' FOR YA!
HIC ヒック
WAGH!!
A GROUP OF US ARE WRESTLING OVER THERE!
TUG ぐい
Whoa
Wait
ぐい TUG
COME GIVE US A QUICK MATCH!
ぐい TUG
COME ON, OVER HERE!
わぁぁぁ RAAAAHH
ギャハハ GAHAHA
I've got money riding on you!
Take him down!
Go get him!
AHAHAH
TACKLE ドカ
Warghh!
We beat the Wyvern Killer!
Ahaha

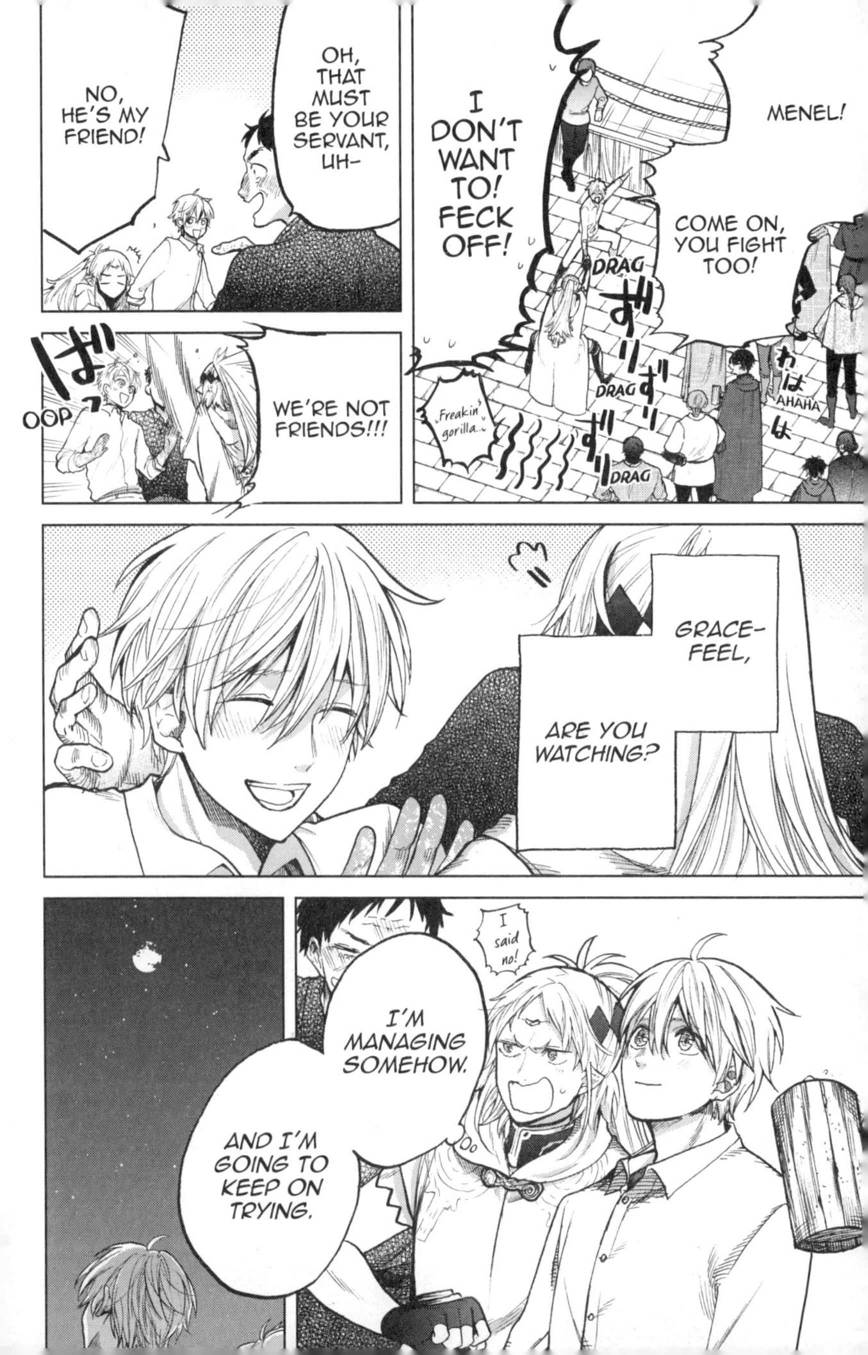
MENEL!
COME ON, YOU FIGHT TOO!
I DON'T WANT TO! FECK OFF!
わはは AHAHA
DRAG ずりずりずり DRAG DRAG
Freakin' gorilla...
OH, THAT MUST BE YOUR SERVANT, UH-
NO, HE'S MY FRIEND!
WE'RE NOT FRIENDS!!!
ばっ OOP
GRACE-FEEL,
ARE YOU WATCHING?
I said no!
I'M MANAGING SOMEHOW.
AND I'M GOING TO KEEP ON TRYING.

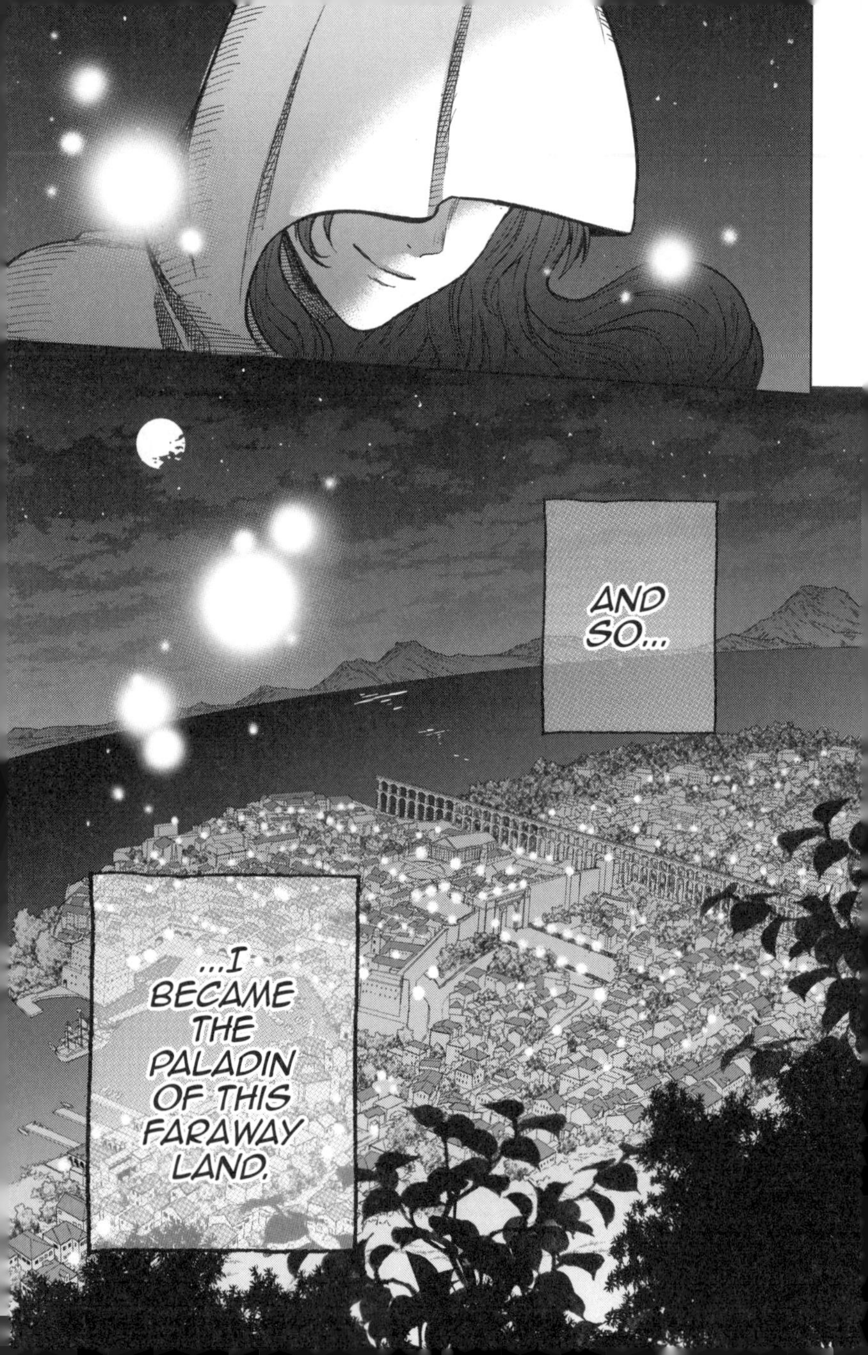
AND SO...
...I BECAME THE PALADIN OF THIS FARAWAY LAND.

THE FARAWAY
PALADIN

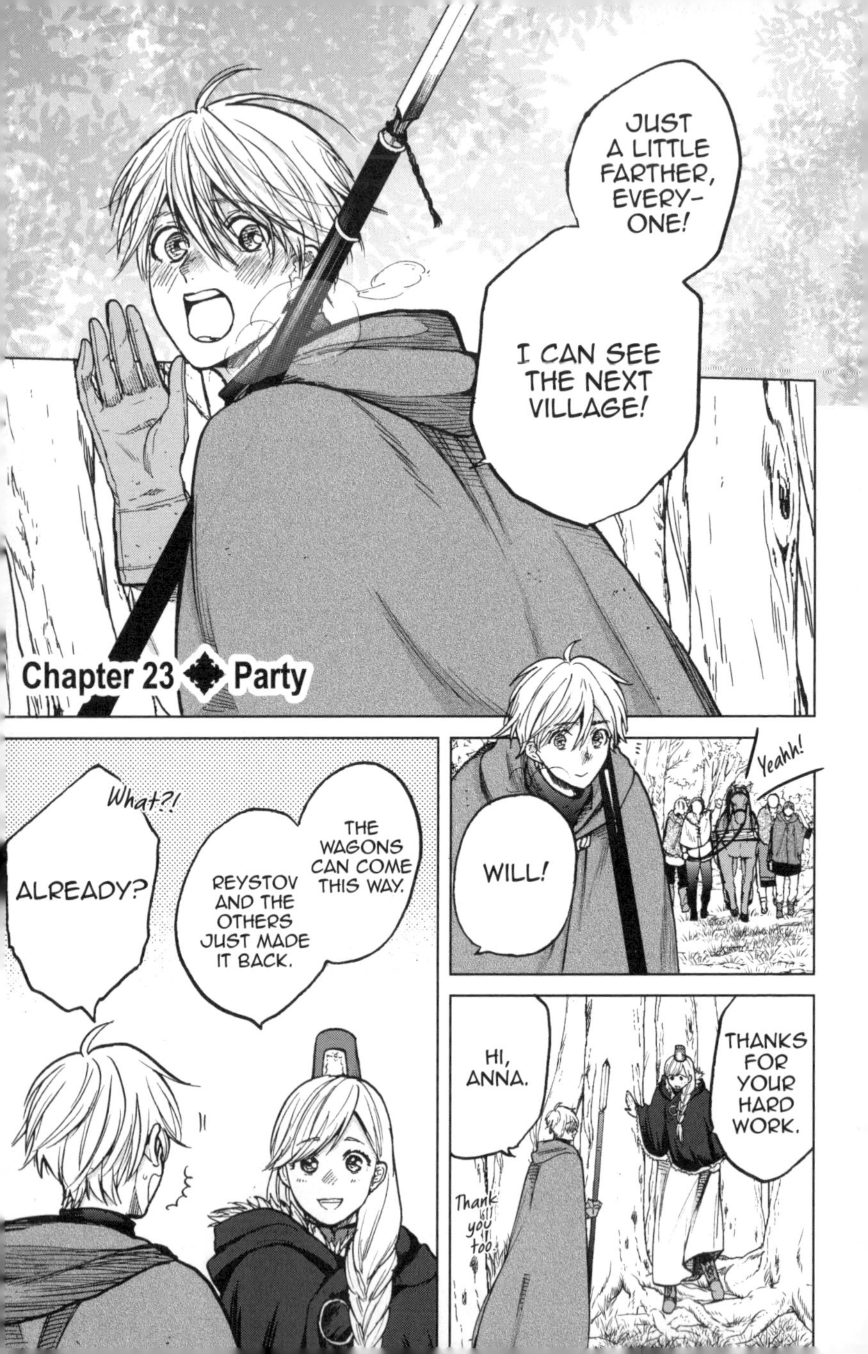
JUST A LITTLE FARTHER, EVERY-ONE!
I CAN SEE THE NEXT VILLAGE!
Chapter 23 ◆ Party
Yeahh!
WILL!
THANKS FOR YOUR HARD WORK.
HI, ANNA.
Thank you too.
THE WAGONS CAN COME THIS WAY.
REYSTOV AND THE OTHERS JUST MADE IT BACK.
What?!
ALREADY?

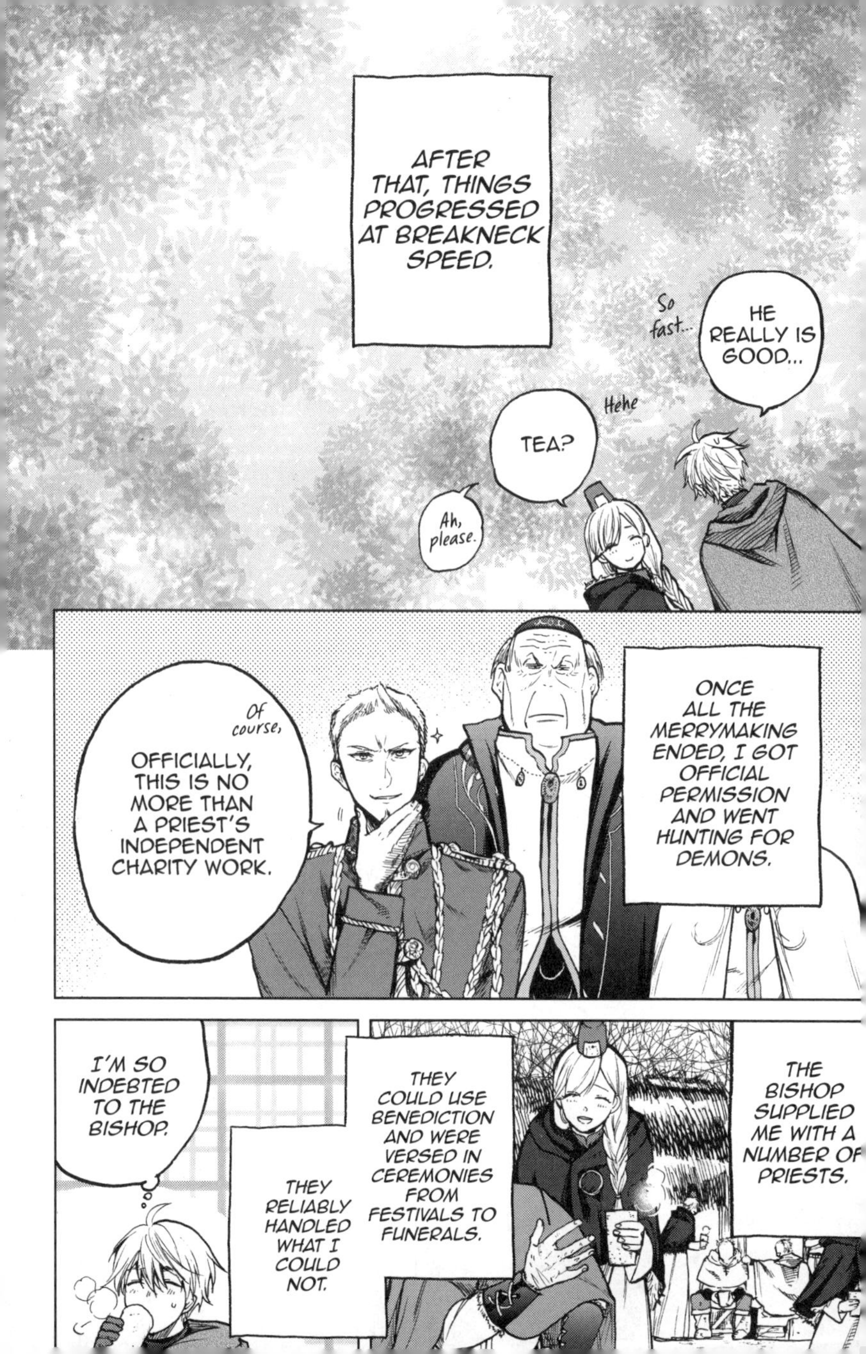
AFTER THAT, THINGS PROGRESSED AT BREAKNECK SPEED.
So fast...
HE REALLY IS GOOD...
Hehe
TEA?
Ah, please.
ONCE ALL THE MERRYMAKING ENDED, I GOT OFFICIAL PERMISSION AND WENT HUNTING FOR DEMONS.
Of course,
OFFICIALLY, THIS IS NO MORE THAN A PRIEST'S INDEPENDENT CHARITY WORK.
THE BISHOP SUPPLIED ME WITH A NUMBER OF PRIESTS.
THEY COULD USE BENEDICTION AND WERE VERSED IN CEREMONIES FROM FESTIVALS TO FUNERALS.
THEY RELIABLY HANDLED WHAT I COULD NOT.
I'M SO INDEBTED TO THE BISHOP.

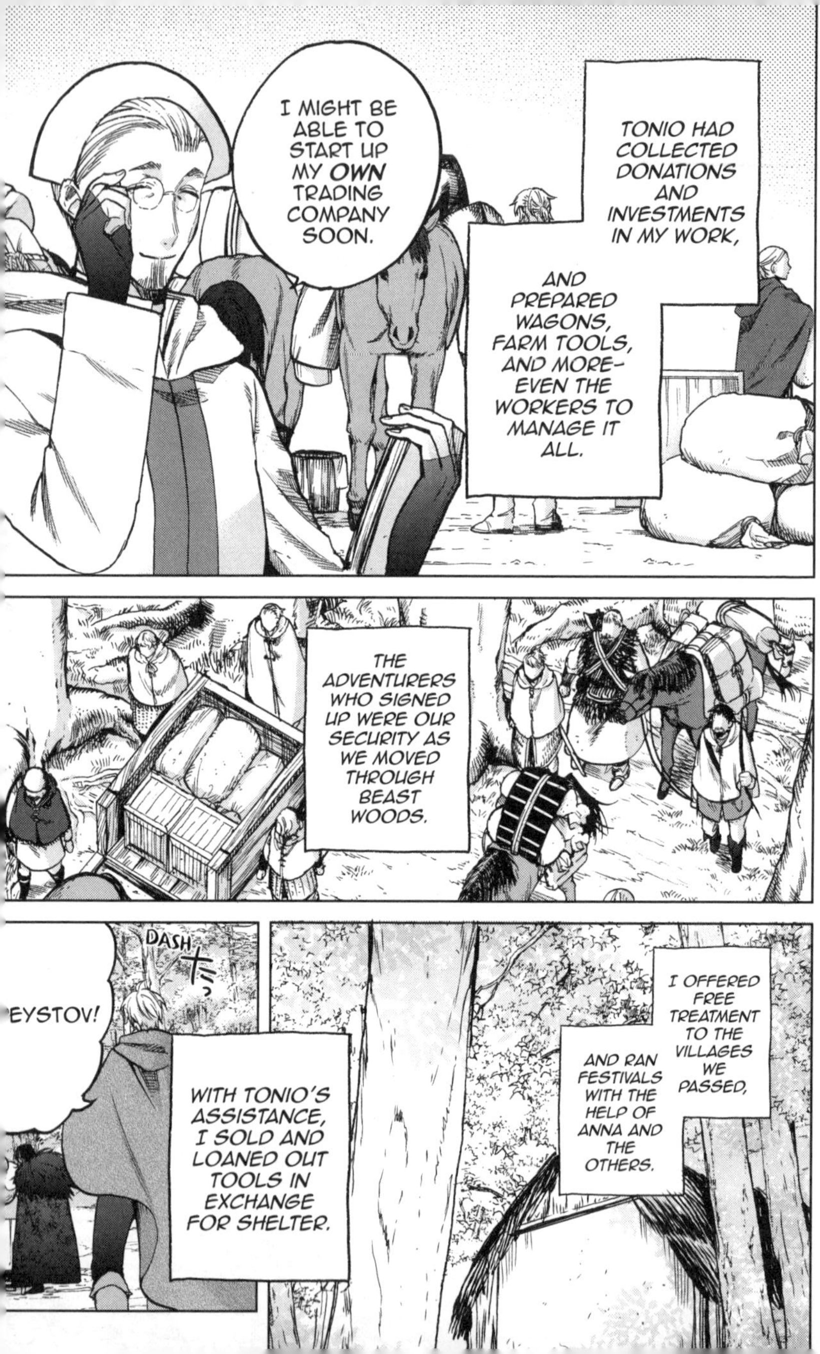
TONIO HAD COLLECTED DONATIONS AND INVESTMENTS IN MY WORK,
AND PREPARED WAGONS, FARM TOOLS, AND MORE- EVEN THE WORKERS TO MANAGE IT ALL.
I MIGHT BE ABLE TO START UP MY **OWN** TRADING COMPANY SOON.
THE ADVENTURERS WHO SIGNED UP WERE OUR SECURITY AS WE MOVED THROUGH BEAST WOODS.
I OFFERED FREE TREATMENT TO THE VILLAGES WE PASSED,
AND RAN FESTIVALS WITH THE HELP OF ANNA AND THE OTHERS.
DASH
EYSTOV!
WITH TONIO'S ASSISTANCE, I SOLD AND LOANED OUT TOOLS IN EXCHANGE FOR SHELTER.

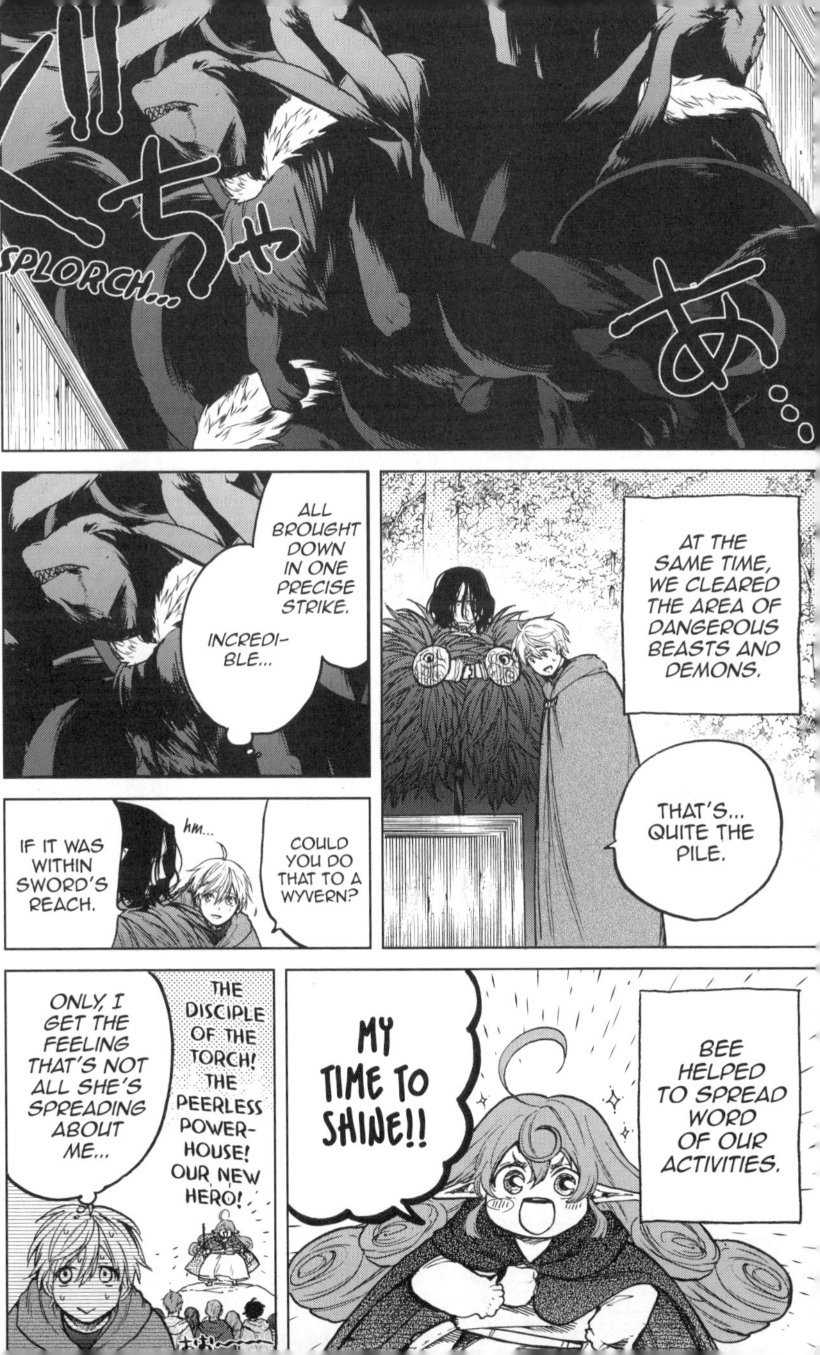
くちゃ
SPLORCH...
あ...
AT THE SAME TIME, WE CLEARED THE AREA OF DANGEROUS BEASTS AND DEMONS.
THAT'S... QUITE THE PILE.
ALL BROUGHT DOWN IN ONE PRECISE STRIKE.
INCREDIBLE...
COULD YOU DO THAT TO A WYVERN?
hm...
IF IT WAS WITHIN SWORD'S REACH.
BEE HELPED TO SPREAD WORD OF OUR ACTIVITIES.
MY TIME TO SHINE!!
THE DISCIPLE OF THE TORCH! THE PEERLESS POWER-HOUSE! OUR NEW HERO!
ONLY, I GET THE FEELING THAT'S NOT ALL SHE'S SPREADING ABOUT ME...

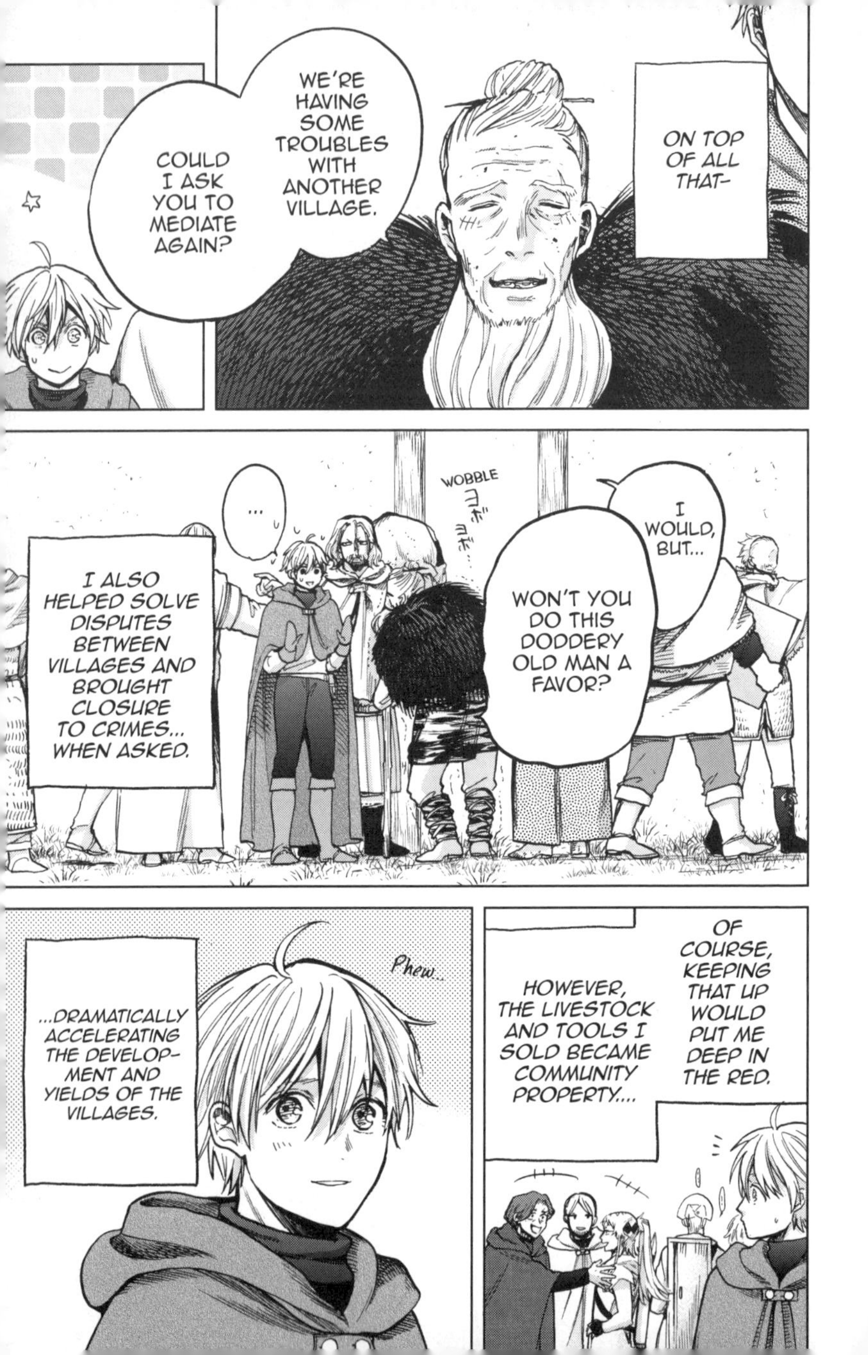
ON TOP OF ALL THAT-
WE'RE HAVING SOME TROUBLES WITH ANOTHER VILLAGE.
COULD I ASK YOU TO MEDIATE AGAIN?
I WOULD, BUT...
WON'T YOU DO THIS DODDERY OLD MAN A FAVOR?
WOBBLE ヨボ ヨボ...
...
I ALSO HELPED SOLVE DISPUTES BETWEEN VILLAGES AND BROUGHT CLOSURE TO CRIMES... WHEN ASKED.
OF COURSE, KEEPING THAT UP WOULD PUT ME DEEP IN THE RED.
HOWEVER, THE LIVESTOCK AND TOOLS I SOLD BECAME COMMUNITY PROPERTY....
Phew...
...DRAMATICALLY ACCELERATING THE DEVELOPMENT AND YIELDS OF THE VILLAGES.

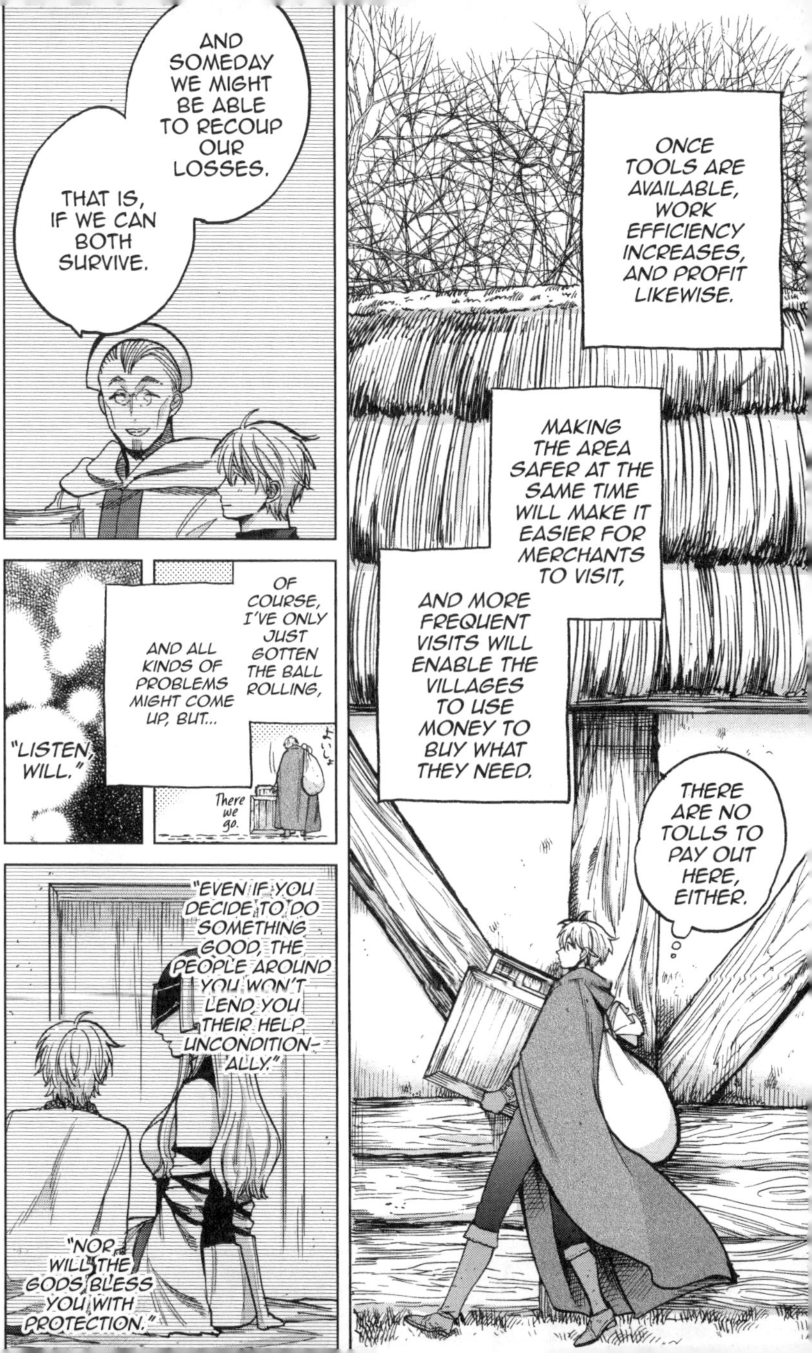
ONCE TOOLS ARE AVAILABLE, WORK EFFICIENCY INCREASES, AND PROFIT LIKEWISE.
MAKING THE AREA SAFER AT THE SAME TIME WILL MAKE IT EASIER FOR MERCHANTS TO VISIT,
AND MORE FREQUENT VISITS WILL ENABLE THE VILLAGES TO USE MONEY TO BUY WHAT THEY NEED.
THERE ARE NO TOLLS TO PAY OUT HERE, EITHER.
AND SOMEDAY WE MIGHT BE ABLE TO RECOUP OUR LOSSES.
THAT IS, IF WE CAN BOTH SURVIVE.
OF COURSE, I'VE ONLY JUST GOTTEN THE BALL ROLLING,
There we go.
AND ALL KINDS OF PROBLEMS MIGHT COME UP, BUT...
"LISTEN, WILL."
"EVEN IF YOU DECIDE TO DO SOMETHING GOOD, THE PEOPLE AROUND YOU WON'T LEND YOU THEIR HELP UNCONDITION-ALLY."
"NOR WILL THE GODS BLESS YOU WITH PROTECTION."

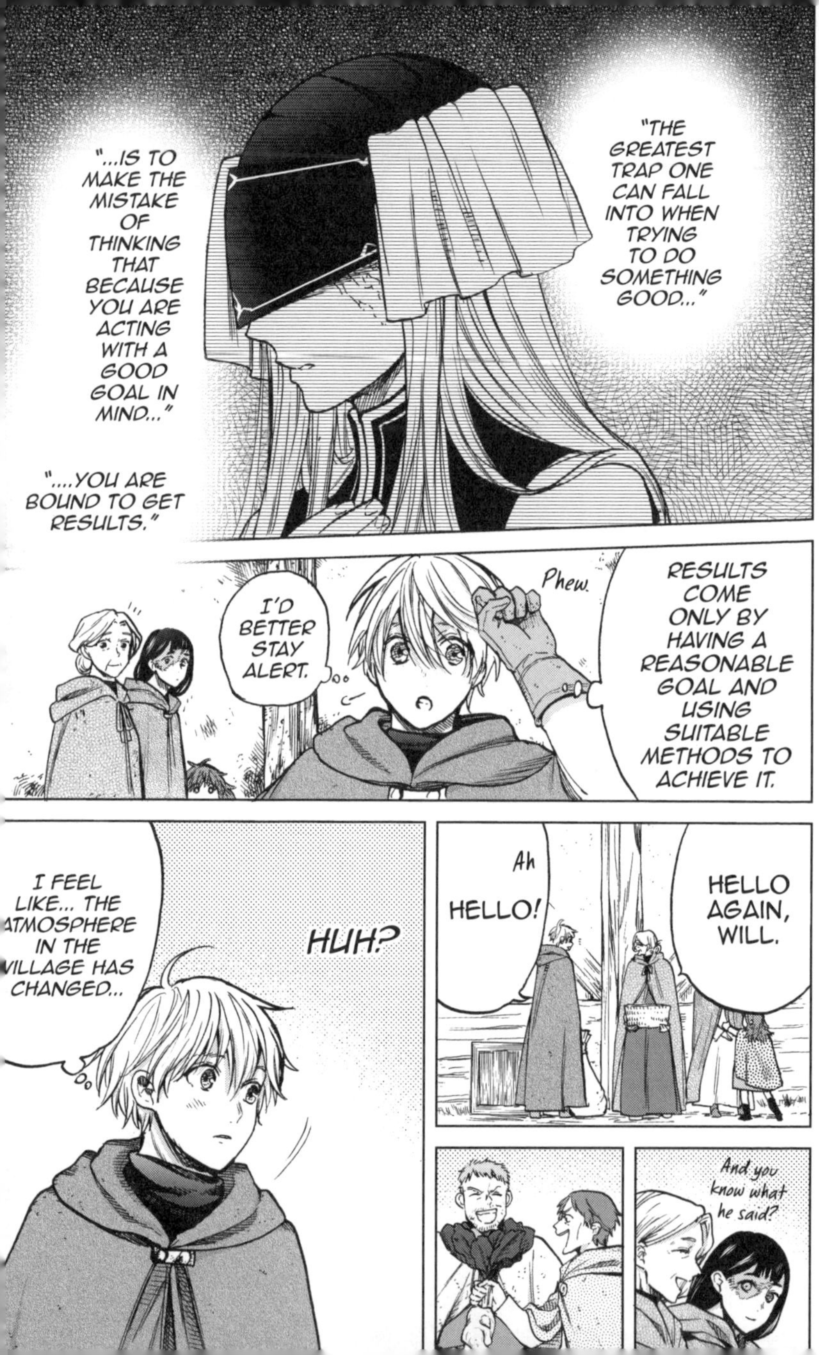
"THE GREATEST TRAP ONE CAN FALL INTO WHEN TRYING TO DO SOMETHING GOOD..."
"...IS TO MAKE THE MISTAKE OF THINKING THAT BECAUSE YOU ARE ACTING WITH A GOOD GOAL IN MIND..."
"....YOU ARE BOUND TO GET RESULTS."
RESULTS COME ONLY BY HAVING A REASONABLE GOAL AND USING SUITABLE METHODS TO ACHIEVE IT.
Phew.
I'D BETTER STAY ALERT.
HELLO AGAIN, WILL.
Ah
HELLO!
And you know what he said?
HUH?
I FEEL LIKE... THE ATMOSPHERE IN THE VILLAGE HAS CHANGED...

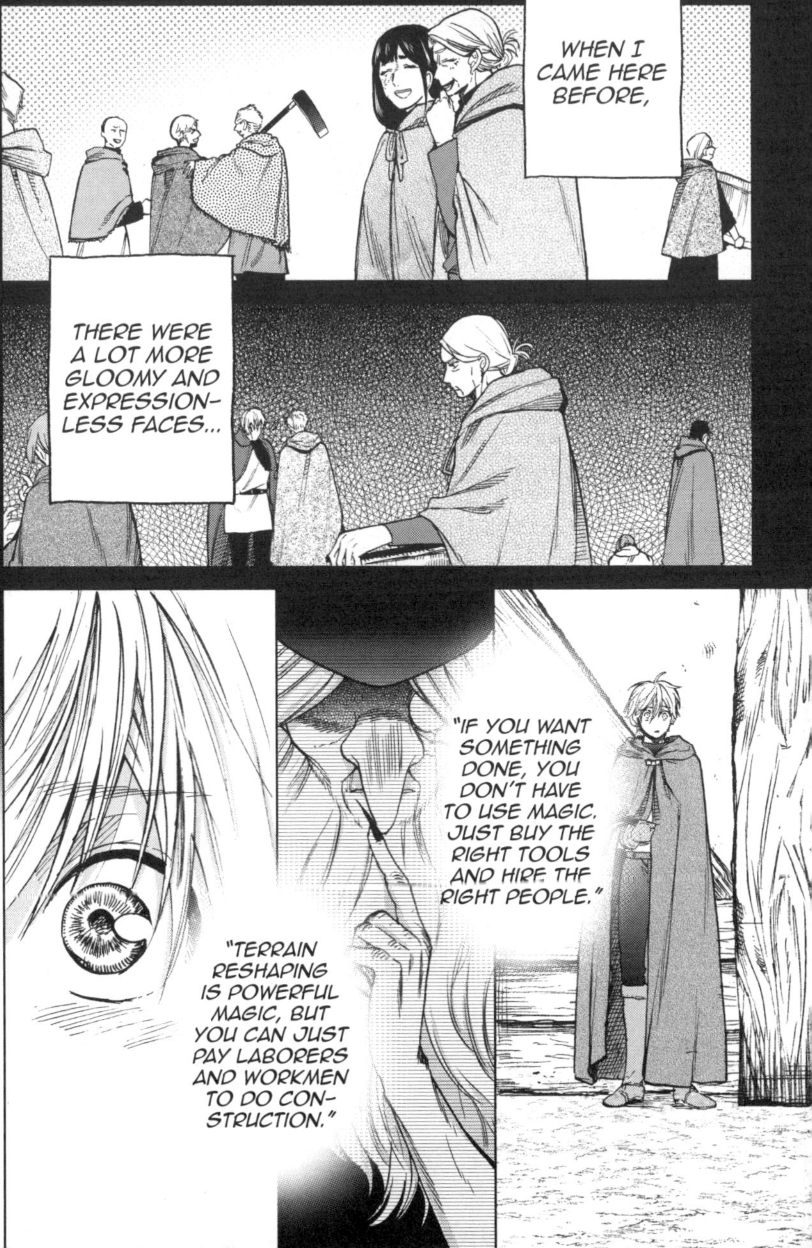
WHEN I CAME HERE BEFORE,
THERE WERE A LOT MORE GLOOMY AND EXPRESSION-LESS FACES...
"IF YOU WANT SOMETHING DONE, YOU DON'T HAVE TO USE MAGIC. JUST BUY THE RIGHT TOOLS AND HIRE THE RIGHT PEOPLE."
"TERRAIN RESHAPING IS POWERFUL MAGIC, BUT YOU CAN JUST PAY LABORERS AND WORKMEN TO DO CON-STRUCTION."

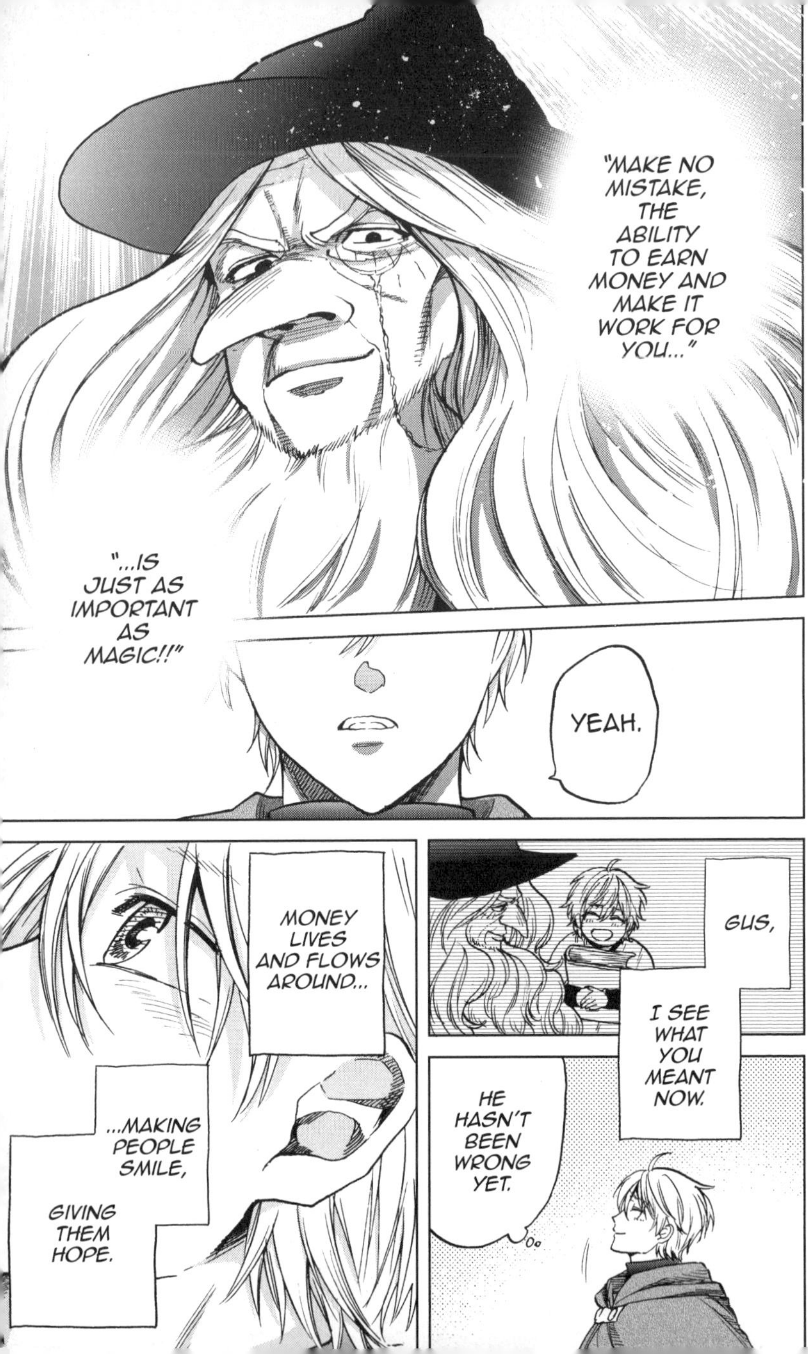
"MAKE NO MISTAKE, THE ABILITY TO EARN MONEY AND MAKE IT WORK FOR YOU..."
"...IS JUST AS IMPORTANT AS MAGIC!!"
YEAH.
GUS,
I SEE WHAT YOU MEANT NOW.
HE HASN'T BEEN WRONG YET.
MONEY LIVES AND FLOWS AROUND...
...MAKING PEOPLE SMILE,
GIVING THEM HOPE.

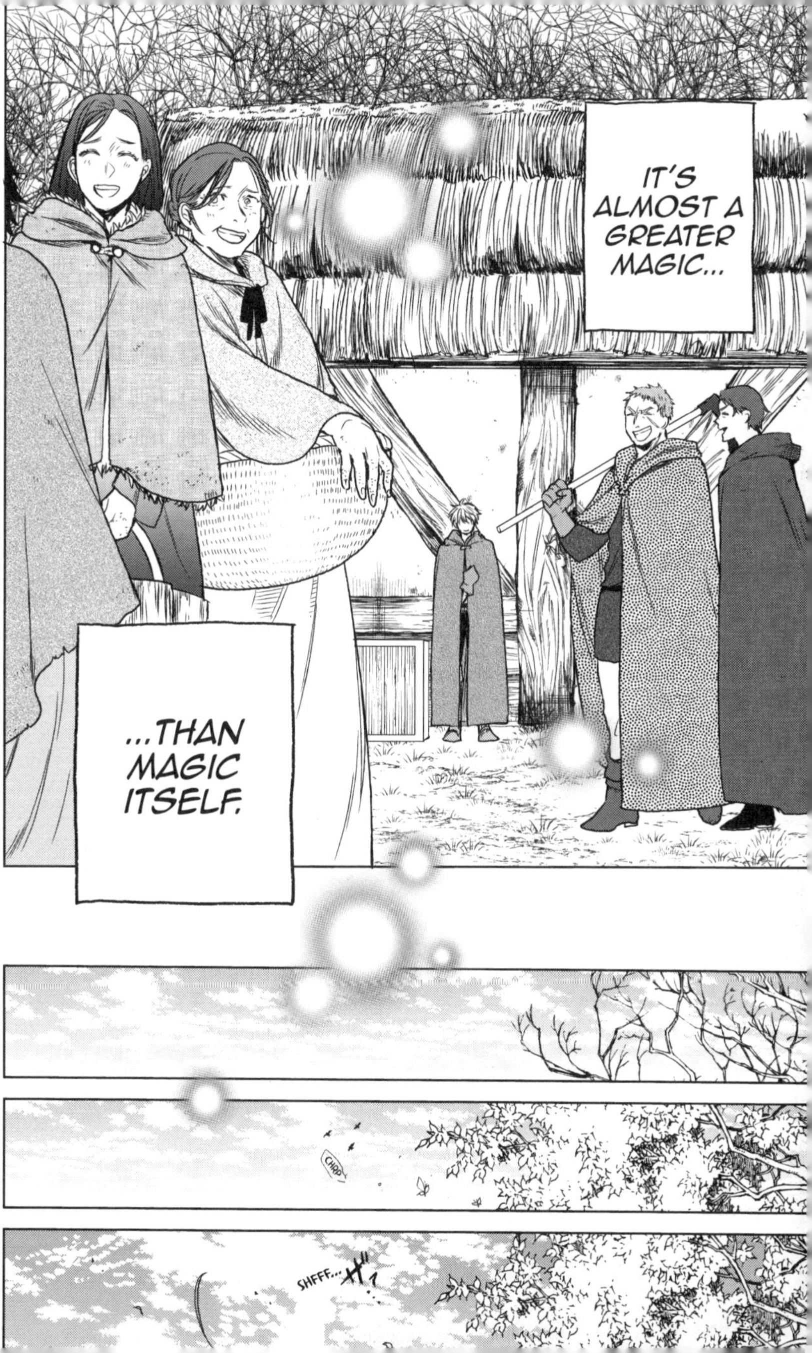
IT'S ALMOST A GREATER MAGIC...
...THAN MAGIC ITSELF.
CHIRP
SHFFF...

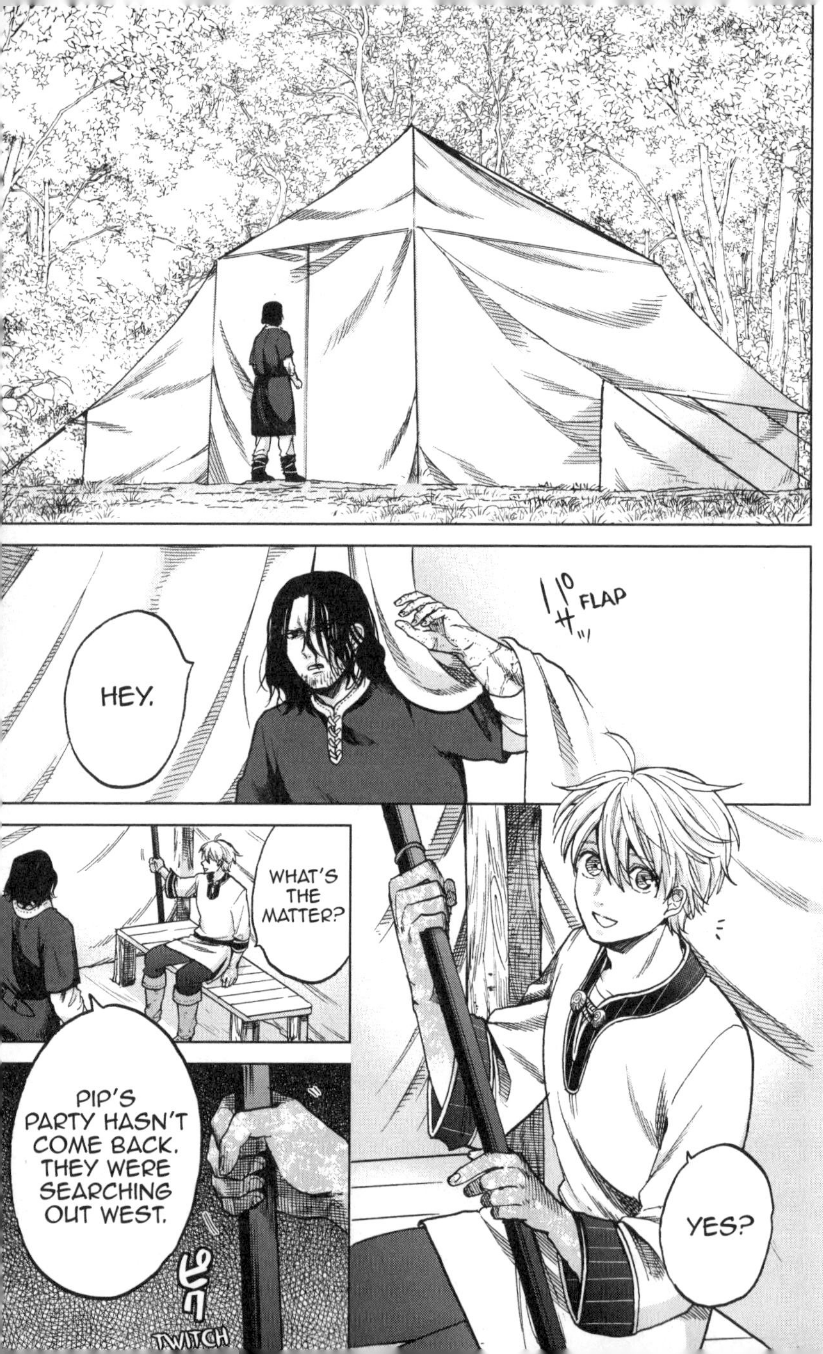

FLAP
HEY.
YES?
WHAT'S THE MATTER?
PIP'S PARTY HASN'T COME BACK. THEY WERE SEARCHING OUT WEST.
TWITCH

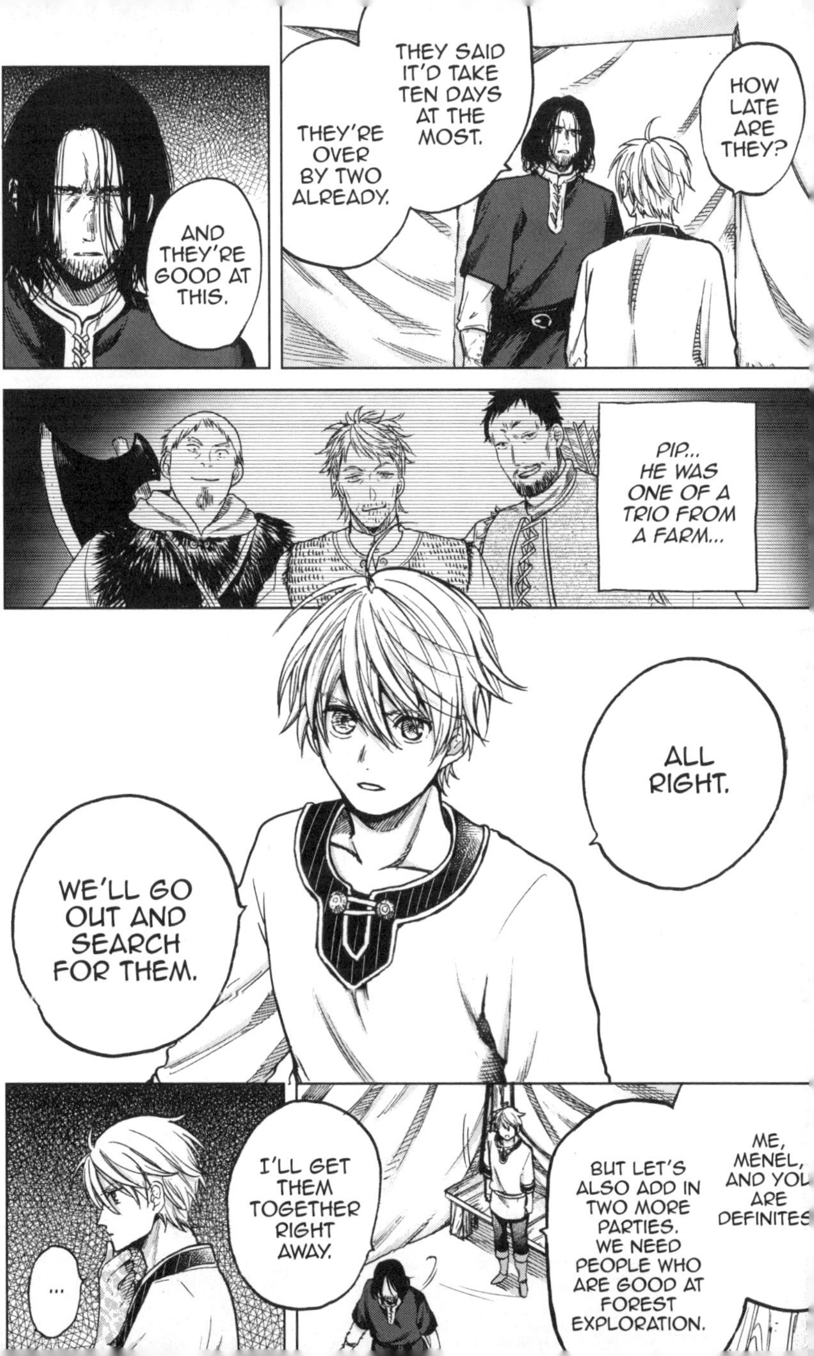
HOW LATE ARE THEY?
THEY SAID IT'D TAKE TEN DAYS AT THE MOST.
THEY'RE OVER BY TWO ALREADY.
AND THEY'RE GOOD AT THIS.
PIP... HE WAS ONE OF A TRIO FROM A FARM...
ALL RIGHT.
WE'LL GO OUT AND SEARCH FOR THEM.
ME, MENEL, AND YO ARE DEFINITES
BUT LET'S ALSO ADD IN TWO MORE PARTIES. WE NEED PEOPLE WHO ARE GOOD AT FOREST EXPLORATION.
I'LL GET THEM TOGETHER RIGHT AWAY.
...

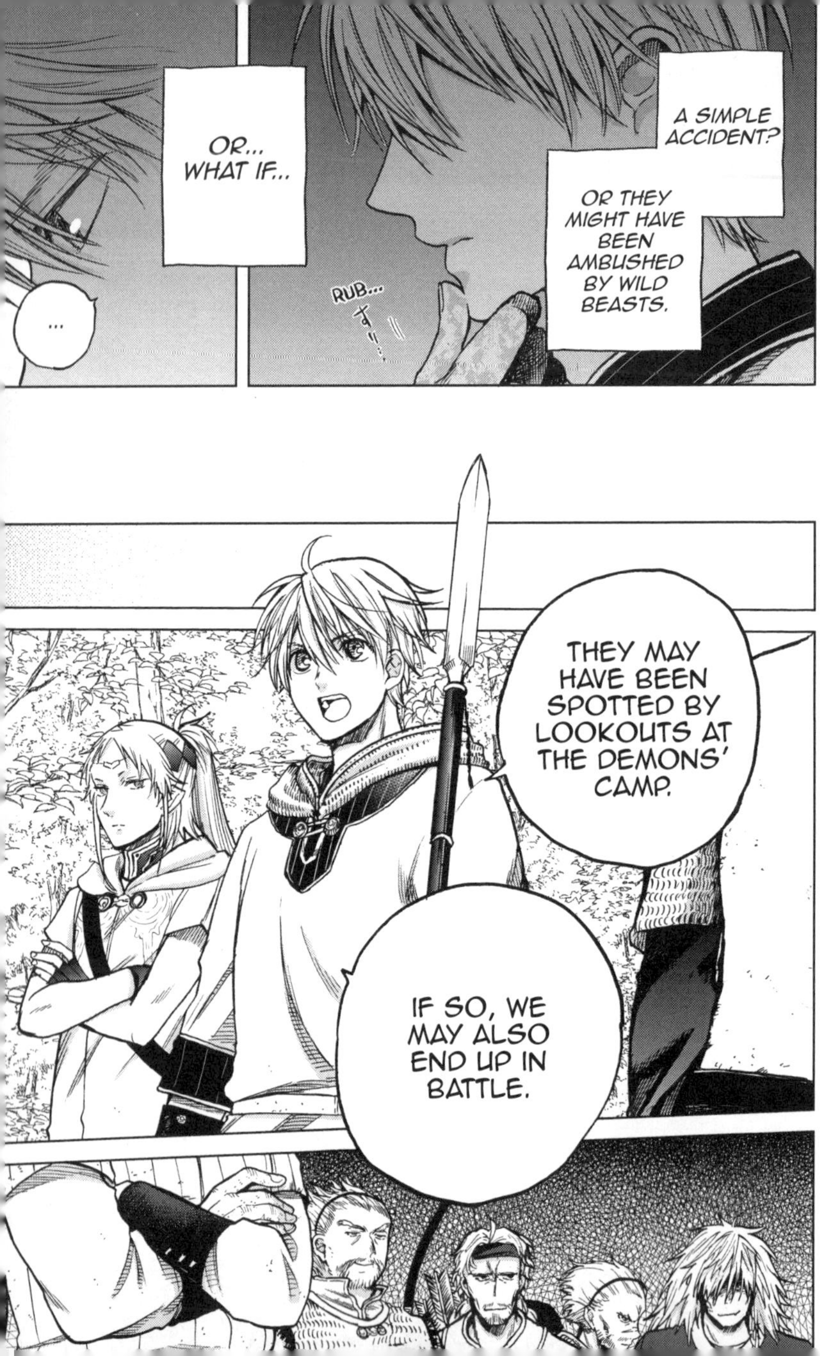
A SIMPLE ACCIDENT?
OR THEY MIGHT HAVE BEEN AMBUSHED BY WILD BEASTS.
RUB...
すり…
OR... WHAT IF...
...
THEY MAY HAVE BEEN SPOTTED BY LOOKOUTS AT THE DEMONS' CAMP.
IF SO, WE MAY ALSO END UP IN BATTLE.

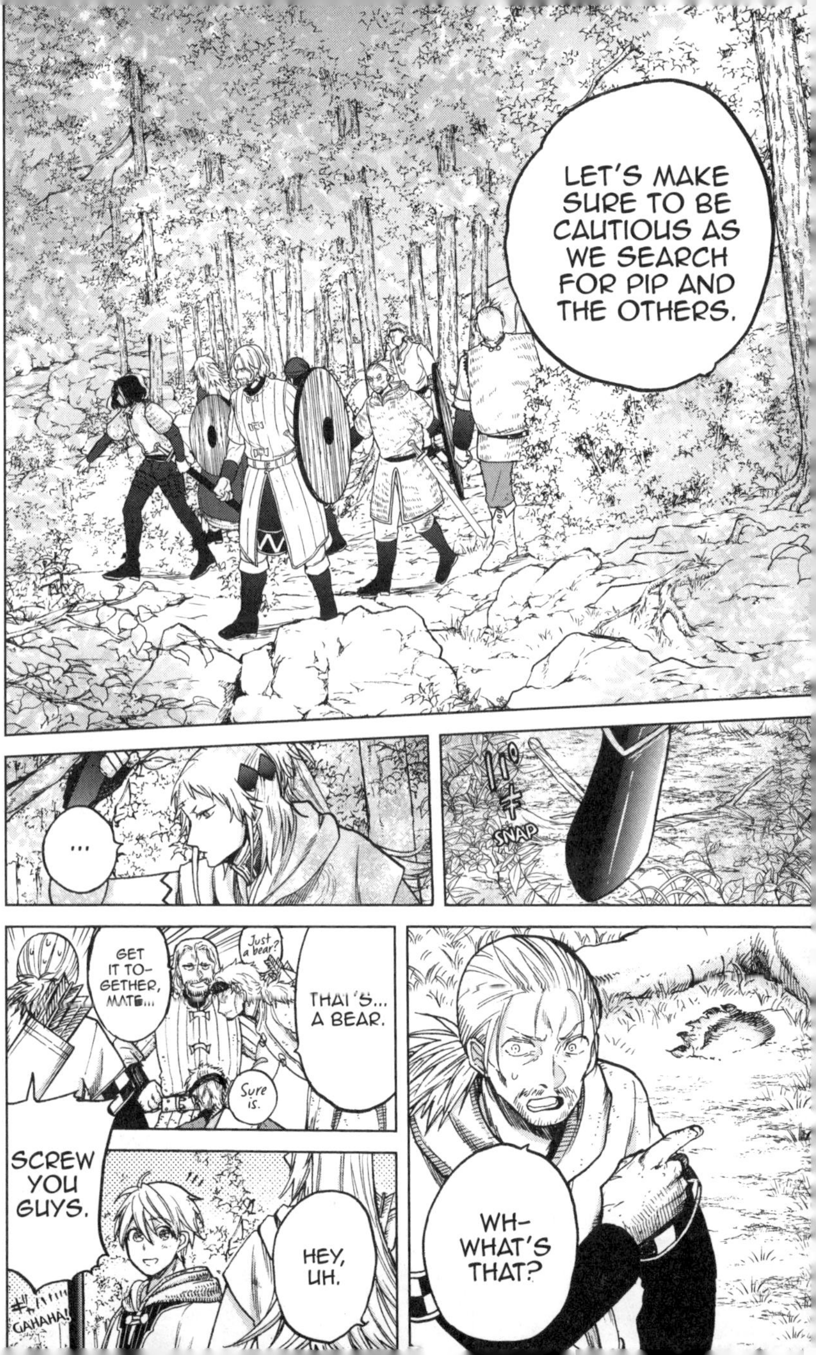

LET'S MAKE SURE TO BE CAUTIOUS AS WE SEARCH FOR PIP AND THE OTHERS.
パキ
SNAP
...
WH-WHAT'S THAT?
THAT'S... A BEAR.
Just a bear?
Sure is.
GET IT TO-GETHER, MATE...
HEY, UH.
SCREW YOU GUYS.
GAHAHA!

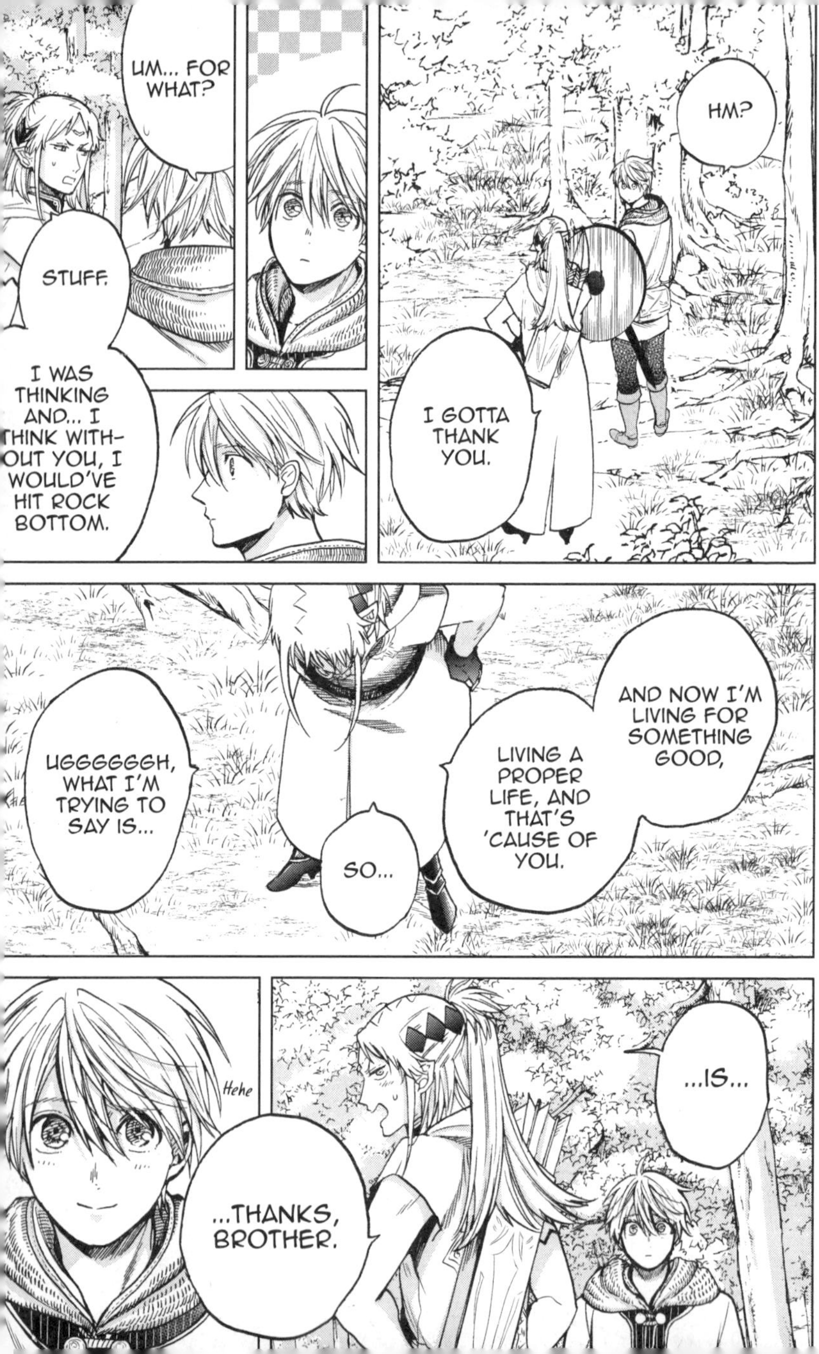
HM?
I GOTTA THANK YOU.
UM... FOR WHAT?
STUFF.
I WAS THINKING AND... I THINK WITH-OUT YOU, I WOULD'VE HIT ROCK BOTTOM.
AND NOW I'M LIVING FOR SOMETHING GOOD,
LIVING A PROPER LIFE, AND THAT'S 'CAUSE OF YOU.
SO...
UGGGGGGH, WHAT I'M TRYING TO SAY IS...
...IS...
...THANKS, BROTHER.
Hehe

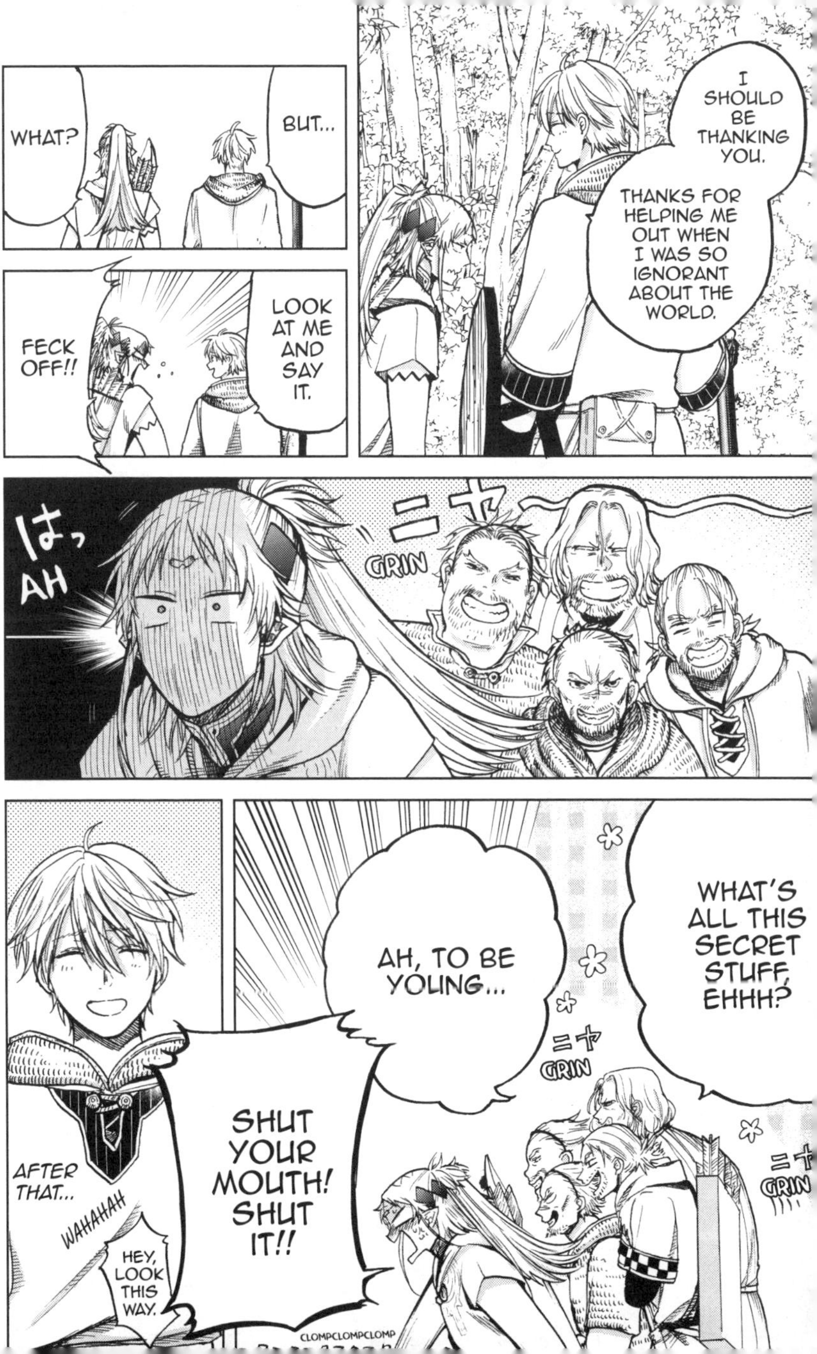
I SHOULD BE THANKING YOU.
THANKS FOR HELPING ME OUT WHEN I WAS SO IGNORANT ABOUT THE WORLD.
BUT...
WHAT?
LOOK AT ME AND SAY IT.
FECK OFF!!
ニヤ
GRIN
はっ
AH
WHAT'S ALL THIS SECRET STUFF, EHHH?
ニヤ
GRIN
AH, TO BE YOUNG...
ニヤ
GRIN
SHUT YOUR MOUTH! SHUT IT!!
CLOMPCLOMPCLOMP
AFTER THAT...
WAHAHAH
HEY, LOOK THIS WAY.

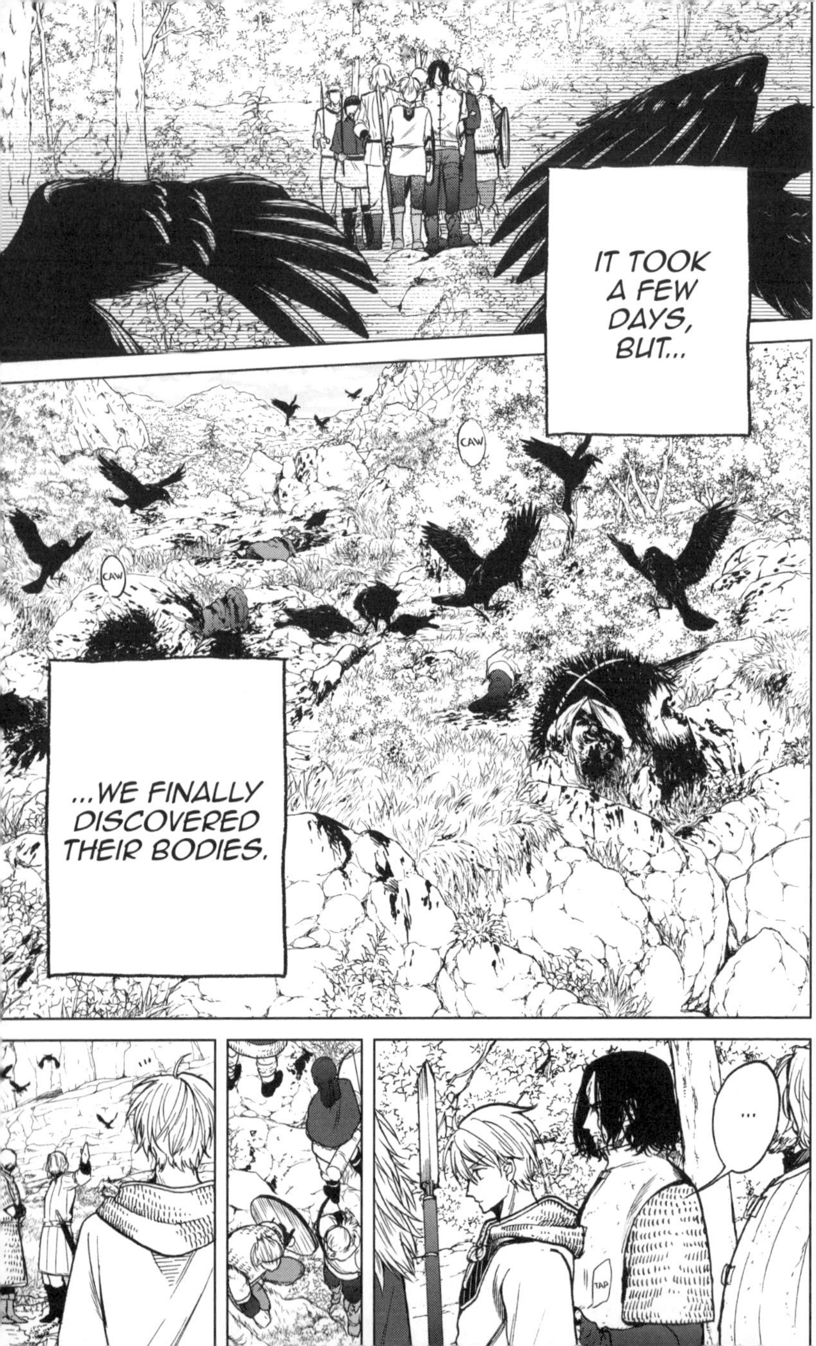
IT TOOK A FEW DAYS, BUT...
CAW
CAW
...WE FINALLY DISCOVERED THEIR BODIES.
...
TAP
...

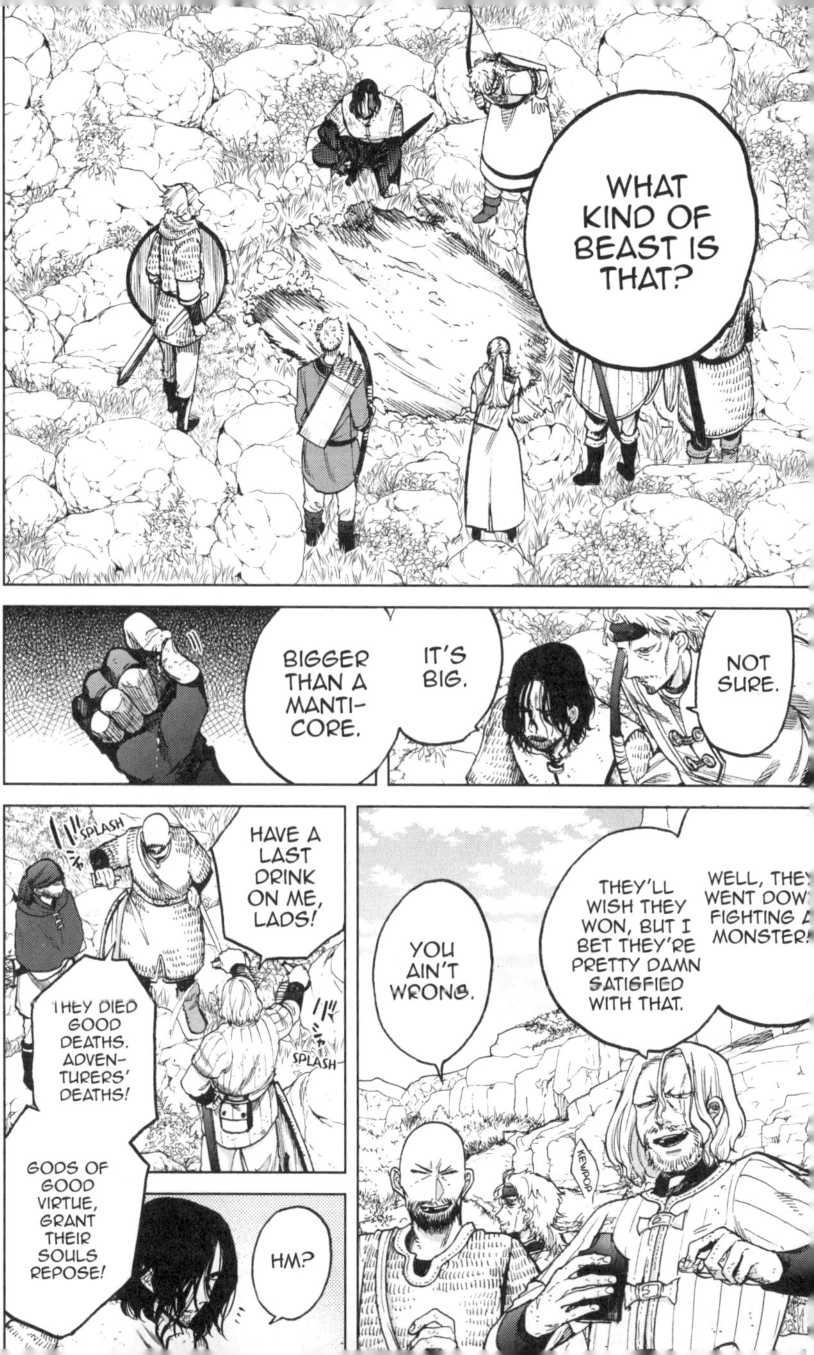
WHAT KIND OF BEAST IS THAT?
NOT SURE.
IT'S BIG.
BIGGER THAN A MANTI-CORE.
WELL, THEY WENT DOWN FIGHTING A MONSTER!
THEY'LL WISH THEY WON, BUT I BET THEY'RE PRETTY DAMN SATISFIED WITH THAT.
YOU AIN'T WRONG.
HAVE A LAST DRINK ON ME, LADS!
SPLASH
SPLASH
THEY DIED GOOD DEATHS. ADVEN-TURERS' DEATHS!
GODS OF GOOD VIRTUE, GRANT THEIR SOULS REPOSE!
HM?

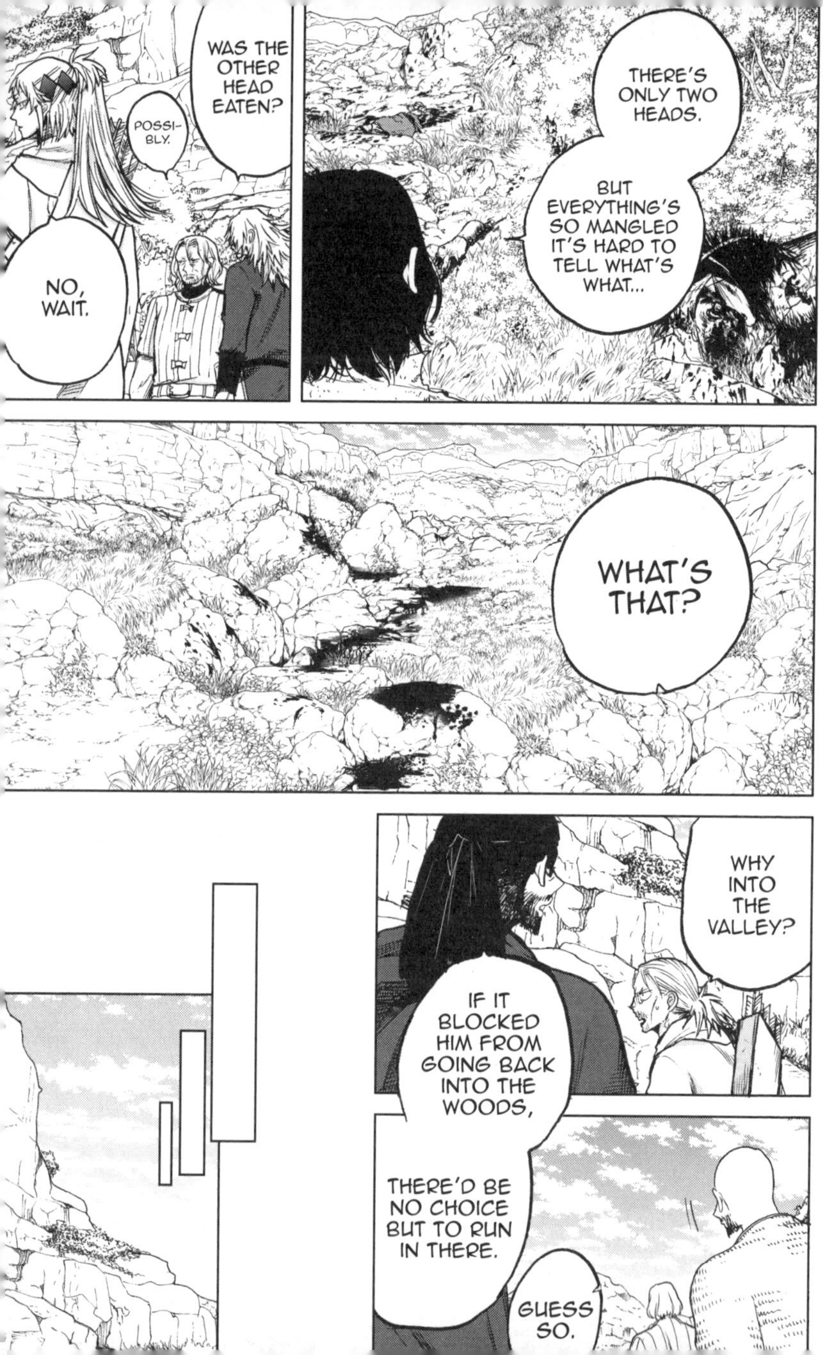
THERE'S ONLY TWO HEADS.
BUT EVERYTHING'S SO MANGLED IT'S HARD TO TELL WHAT'S WHAT...
WAS THE OTHER HEAD EATEN?
POSSIBLY.
NO, WAIT.
WHAT'S THAT?
WHY INTO THE VALLEY?
IF IT BLOCKED HIM FROM GOING BACK INTO THE WOODS,
THERE'D BE NO CHOICE BUT TO RUN IN THERE.
GUESS SO.

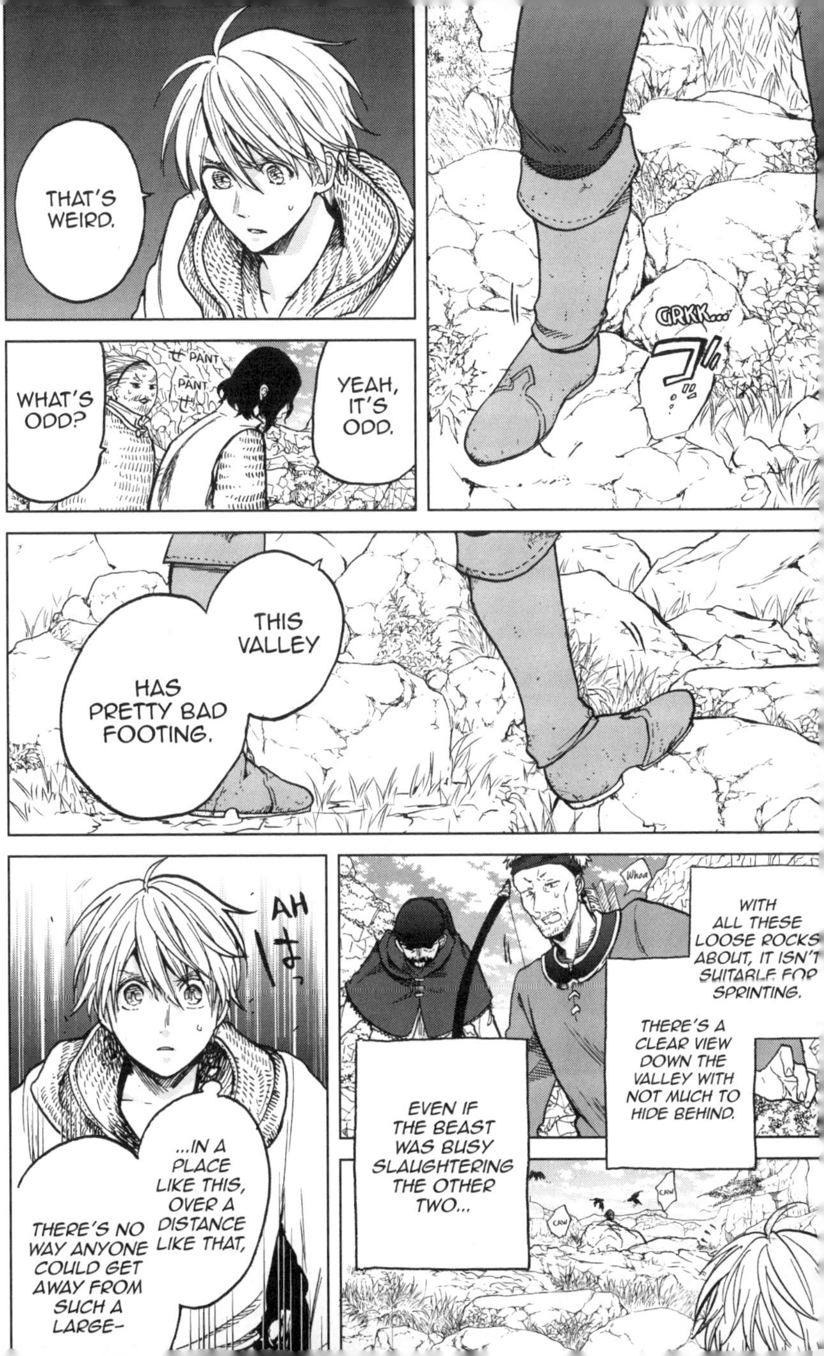
GRKK...
THAT'S WEIRD.
YEAH, IT'S ODD.
PANT
PANT
WHAT'S ODD?
THIS VALLEY
HAS PRETTY BAD FOOTING.
Whoa
WITH ALL THESE LOOSE ROCKS ABOUT, IT ISN'T SUITABLE FOR SPRINTING.
THERE'S A CLEAR VIEW DOWN THE VALLEY WITH NOT MUCH TO HIDE BEHIND.
CAW
CAW
EVEN IF THE BEAST WAS BUSY SLAUGHTERING THE OTHER TWO...
AH
...IN A PLACE LIKE THIS, OVER A DISTANCE LIKE THAT,
THERE'S NO WAY ANYONE COULD GET AWAY FROM SUCH A LARGE-

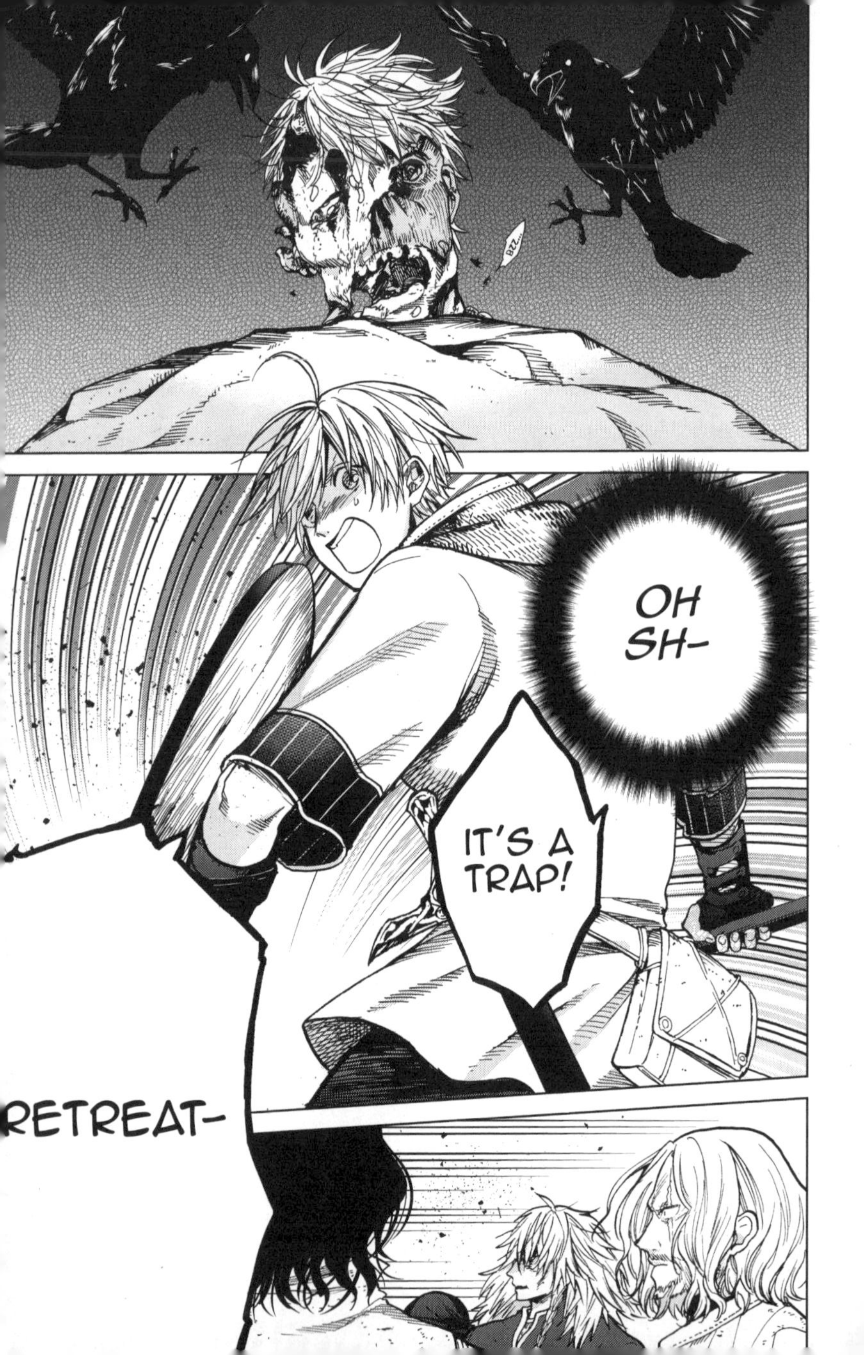
BZZ...
OH SH-
IT'S A TRAP!
RETREAT-

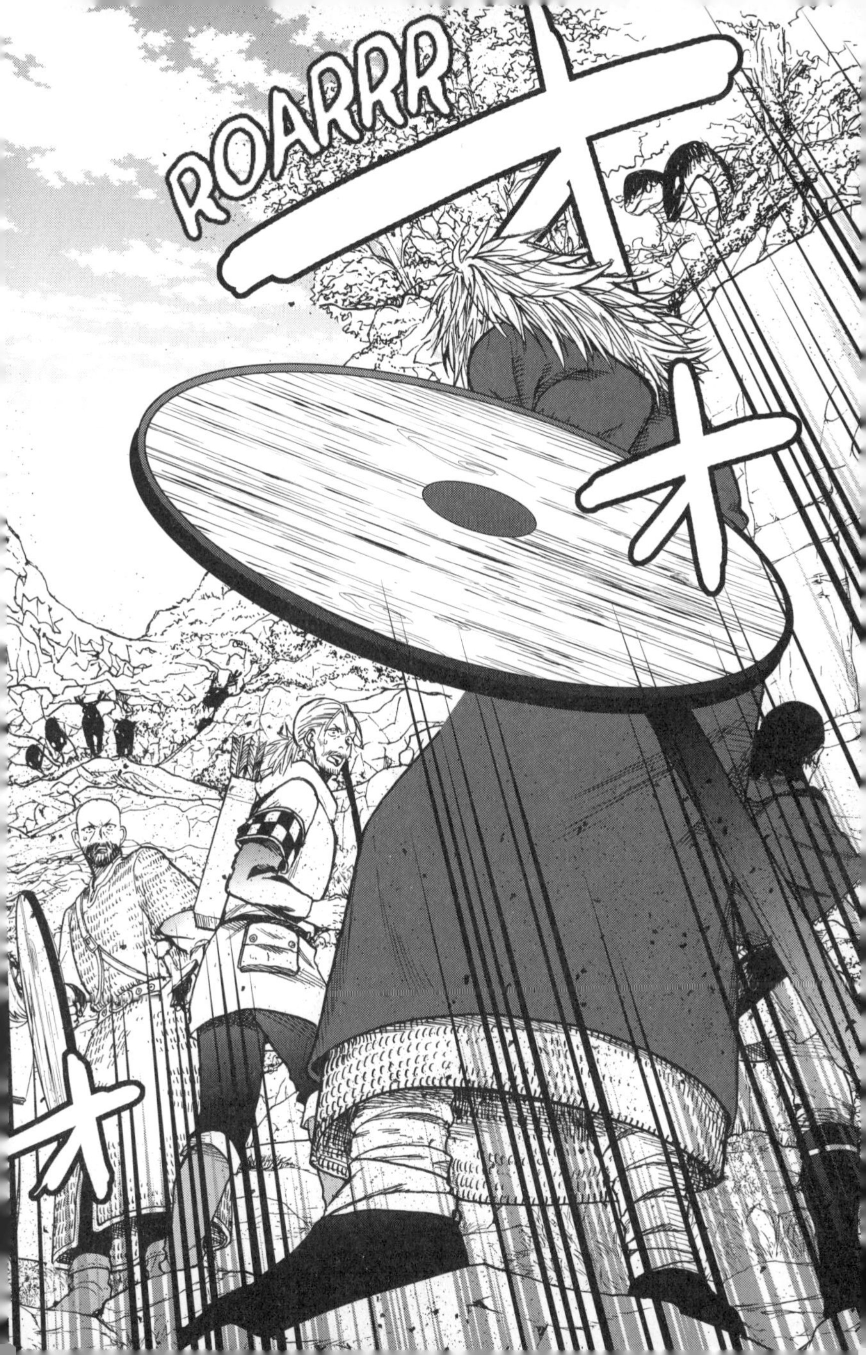
ROARRR

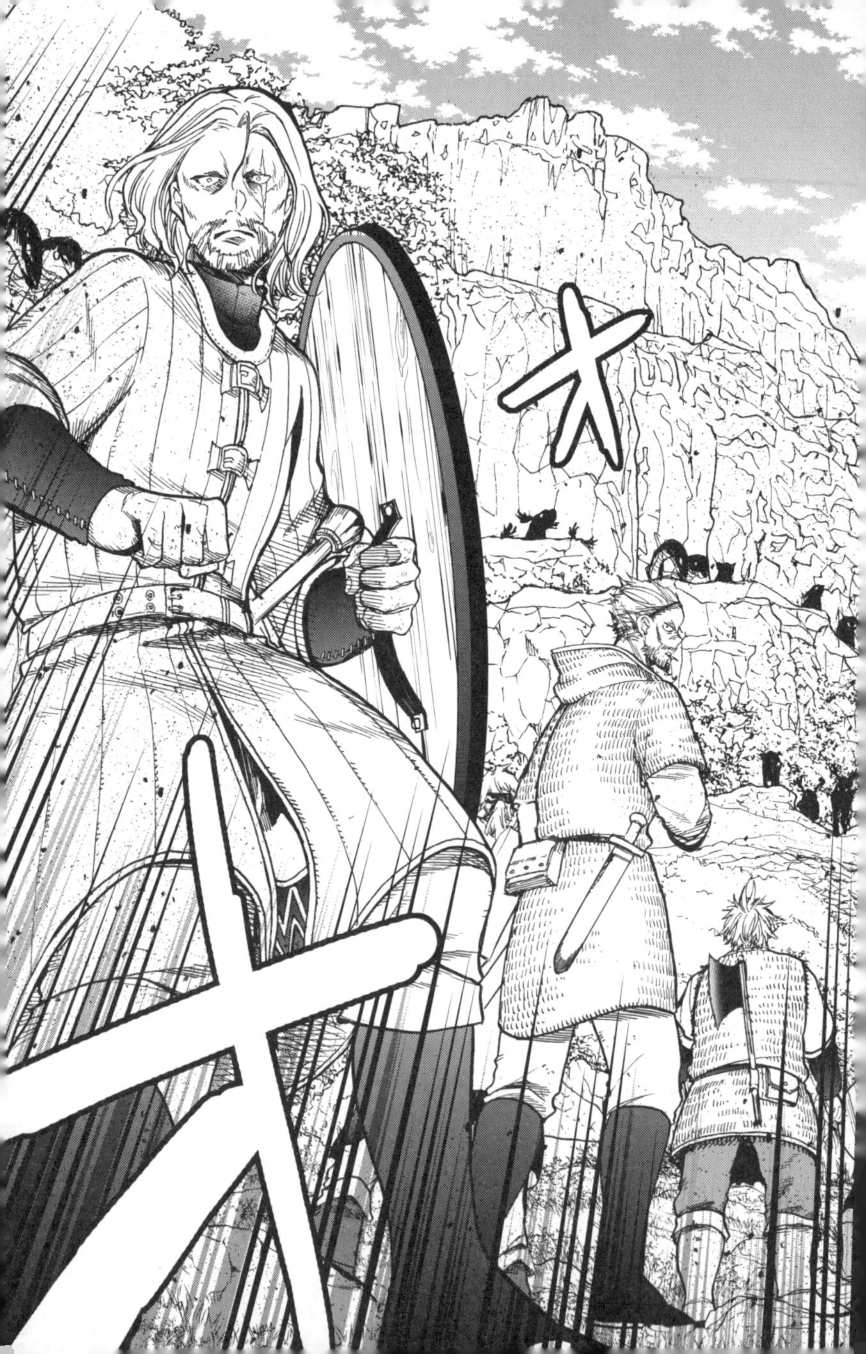

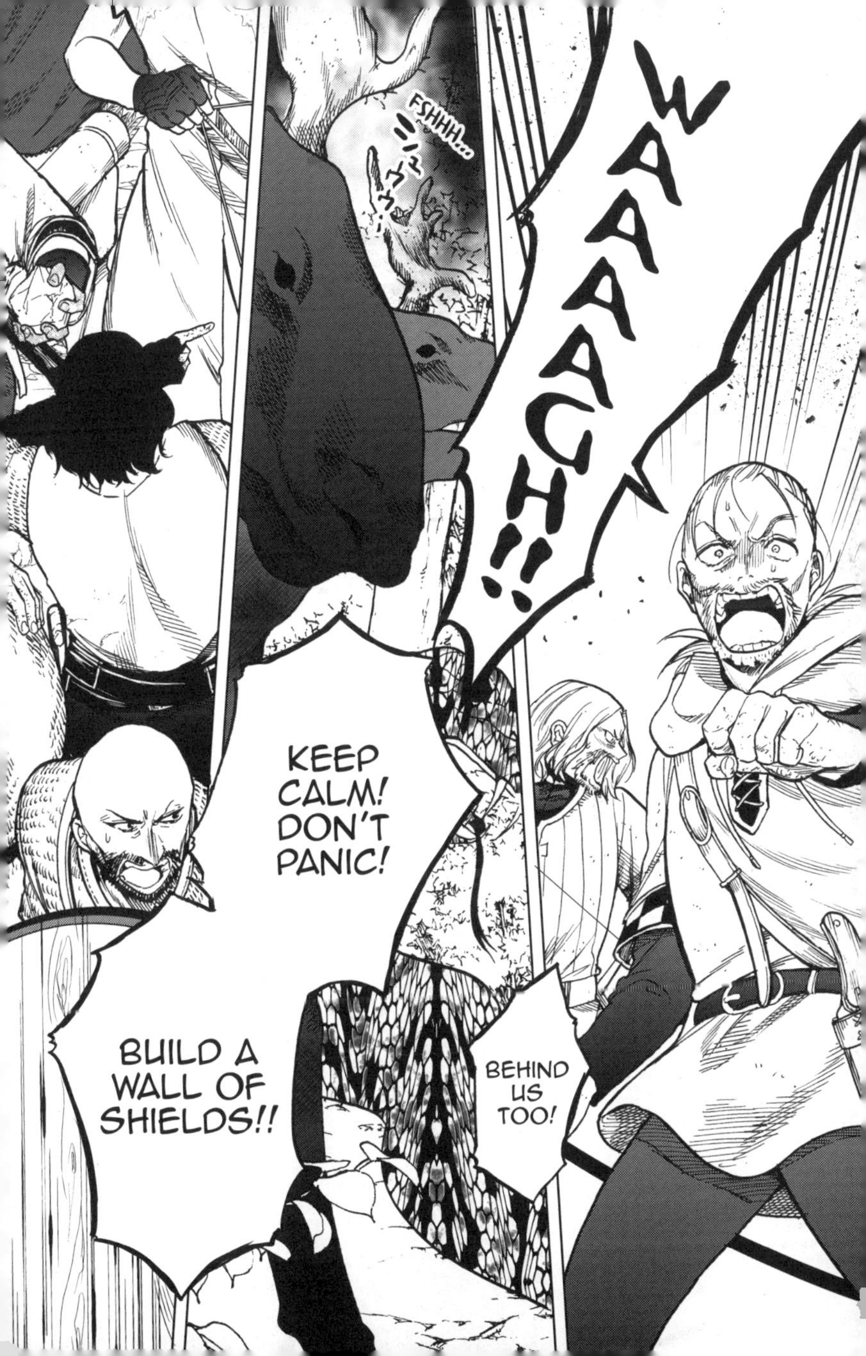
WAAAAGH!!
BEHIND US TOO!
FSHHH...
KEEP CALM! DON'T PANIC!
BUILD A WALL OF SHIELDS!!

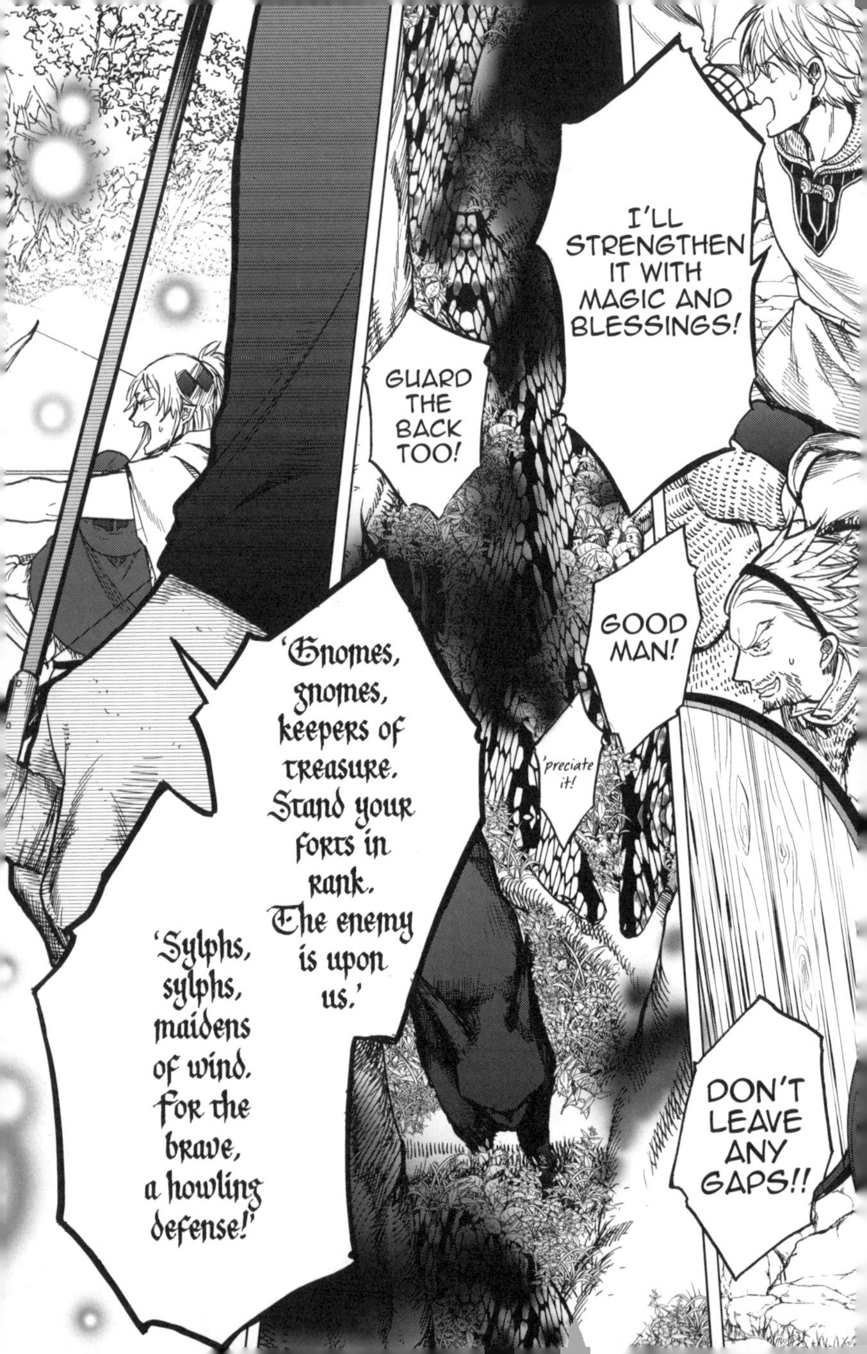
I'LL STRENGTHEN IT WITH MAGIC AND BLESSINGS!
GUARD THE BACK TOO!
GOOD MAN!
'preciate it!
DON'T LEAVE ANY GAPS!!
'Gnomes, gnomes, keepers of treasure. Stand your forts in rank. The enemy is upon us.'
'Sylphs, sylphs, maidens of wind. For the brave, a howling defense!'

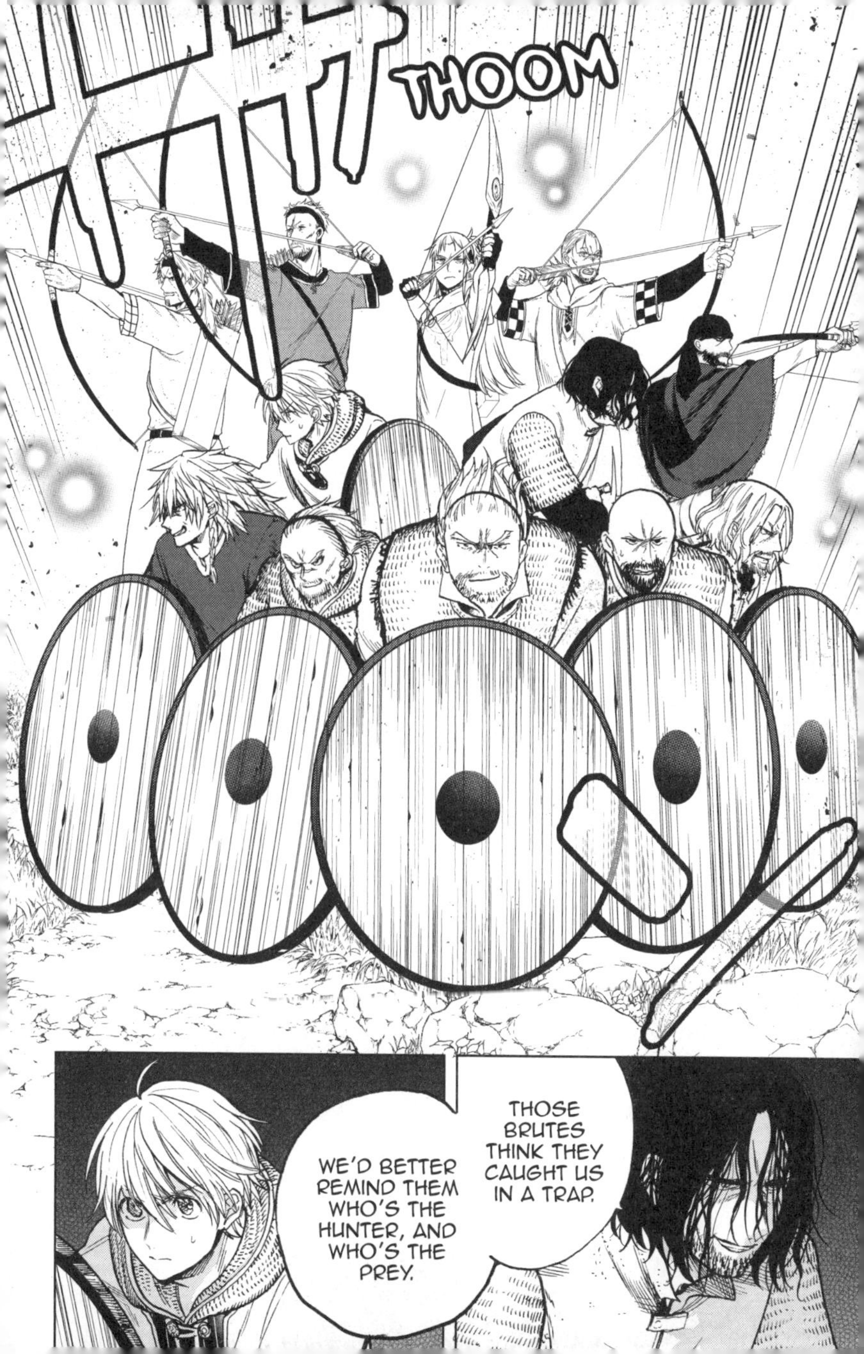
THOOM
THOSE BRUTES THINK THEY CAUGHT US IN A TRAP.
WE'D BETTER REMIND THEM WHO'S THE HUNTER, AND WHO'S THE PREY.

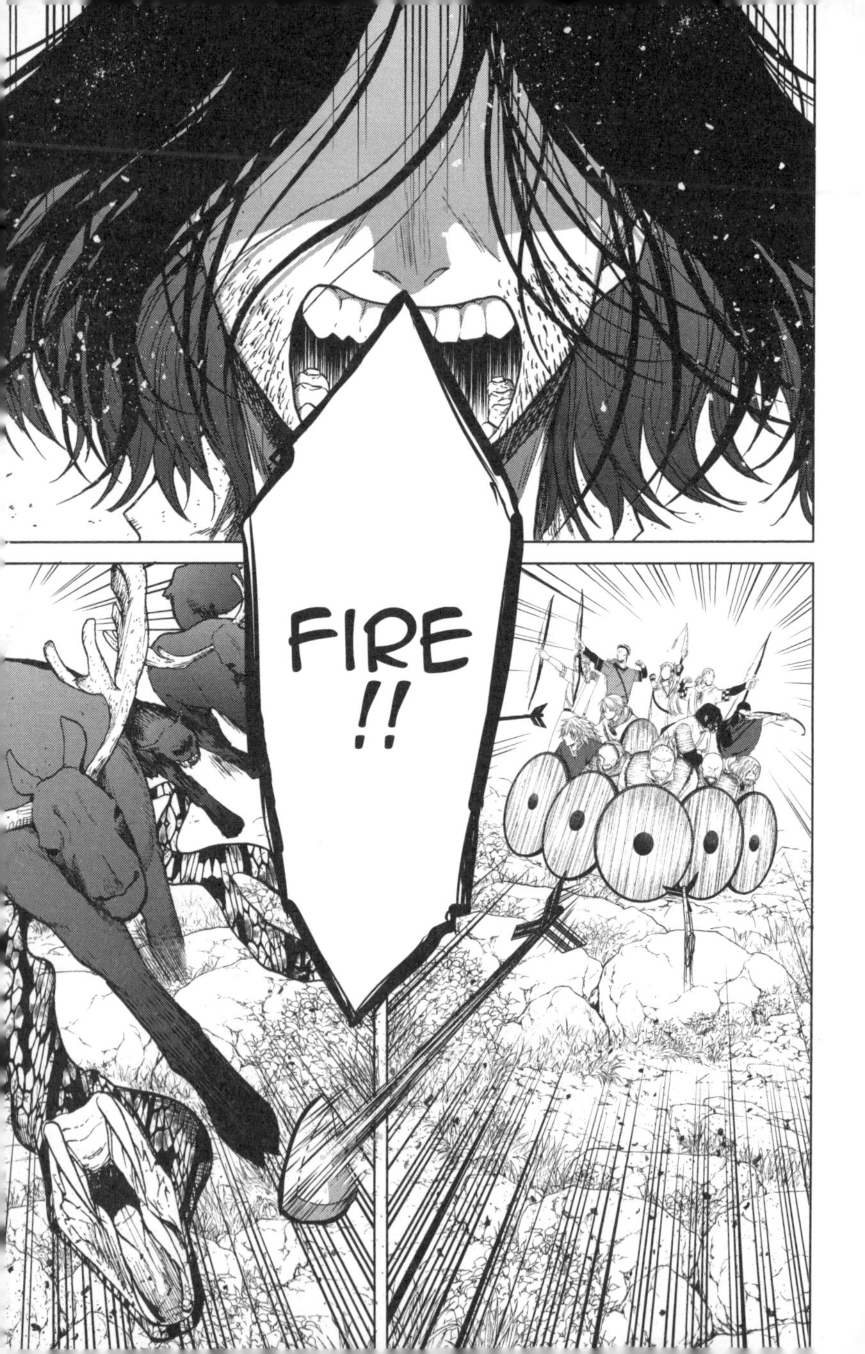
FIRE !!

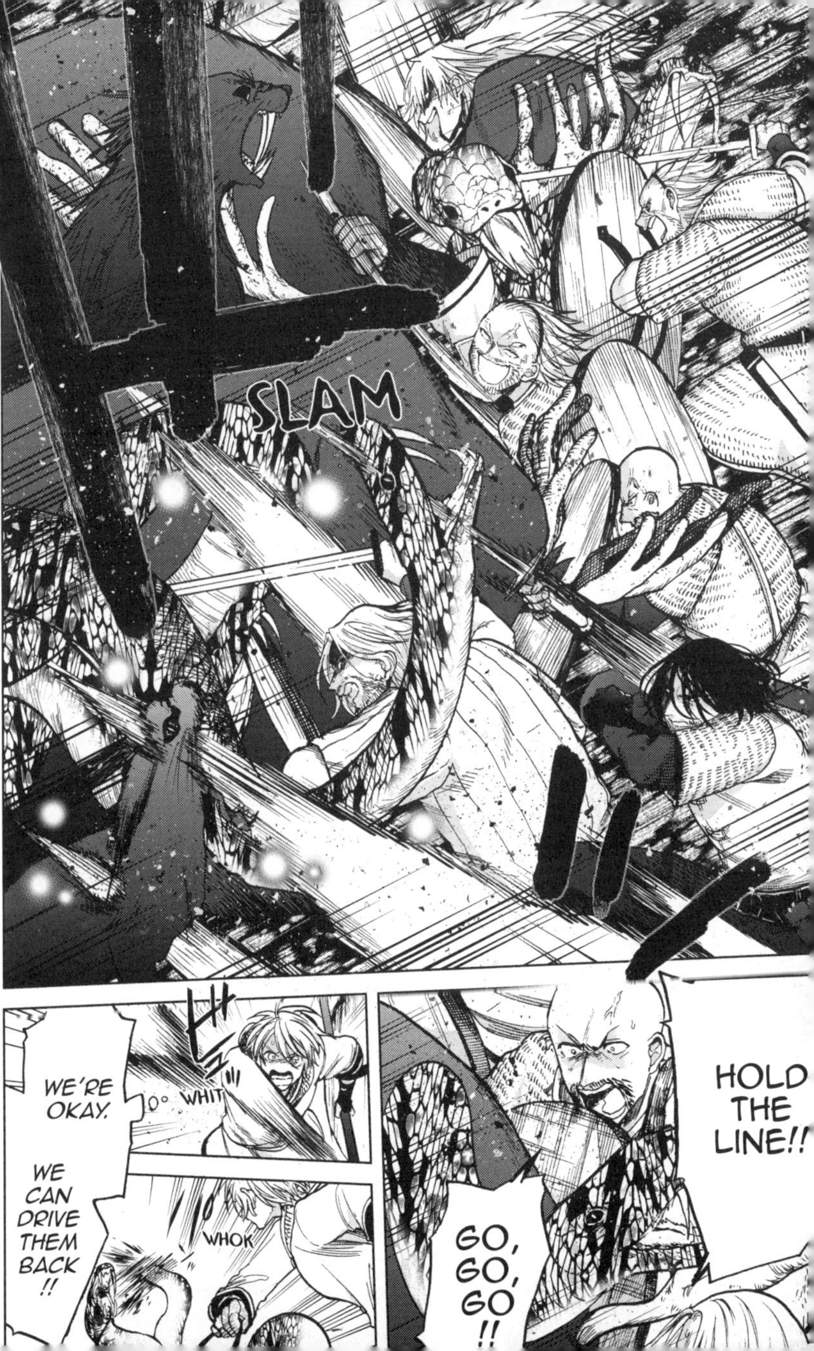
SLAM
HOLD THE LINE!!
GO, GO, GO!!
WE'RE OKAY.
WHIT
WE CAN DRIVE THEM BACK!!
WHOK

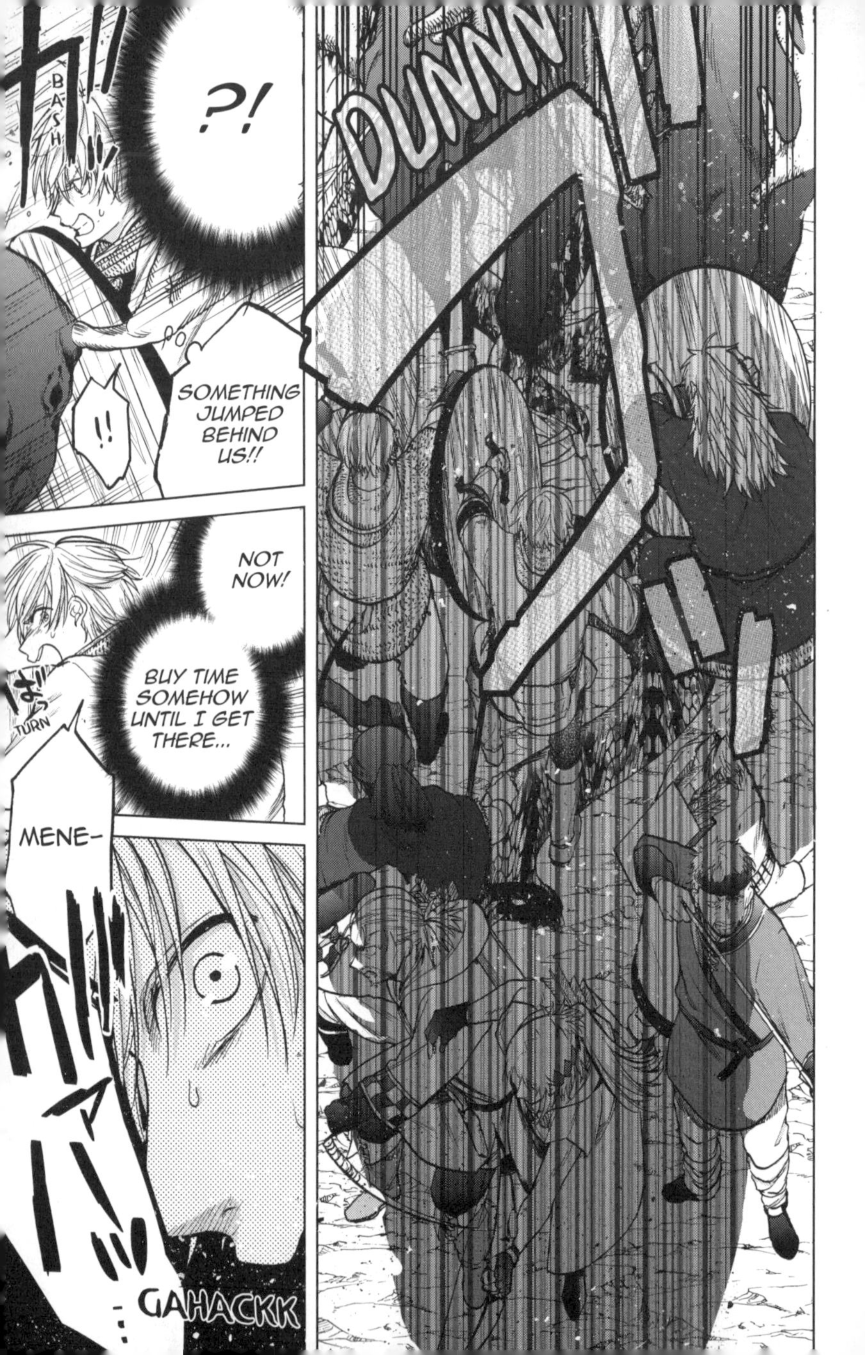
DUNNN
?!
BASH
SOMETHING JUMPED BEHIND US!!
!!
NOT NOW!
BUY TIME SOMEHOW UNTIL I GET THERE...
TURN
MENE-
GAHACKK

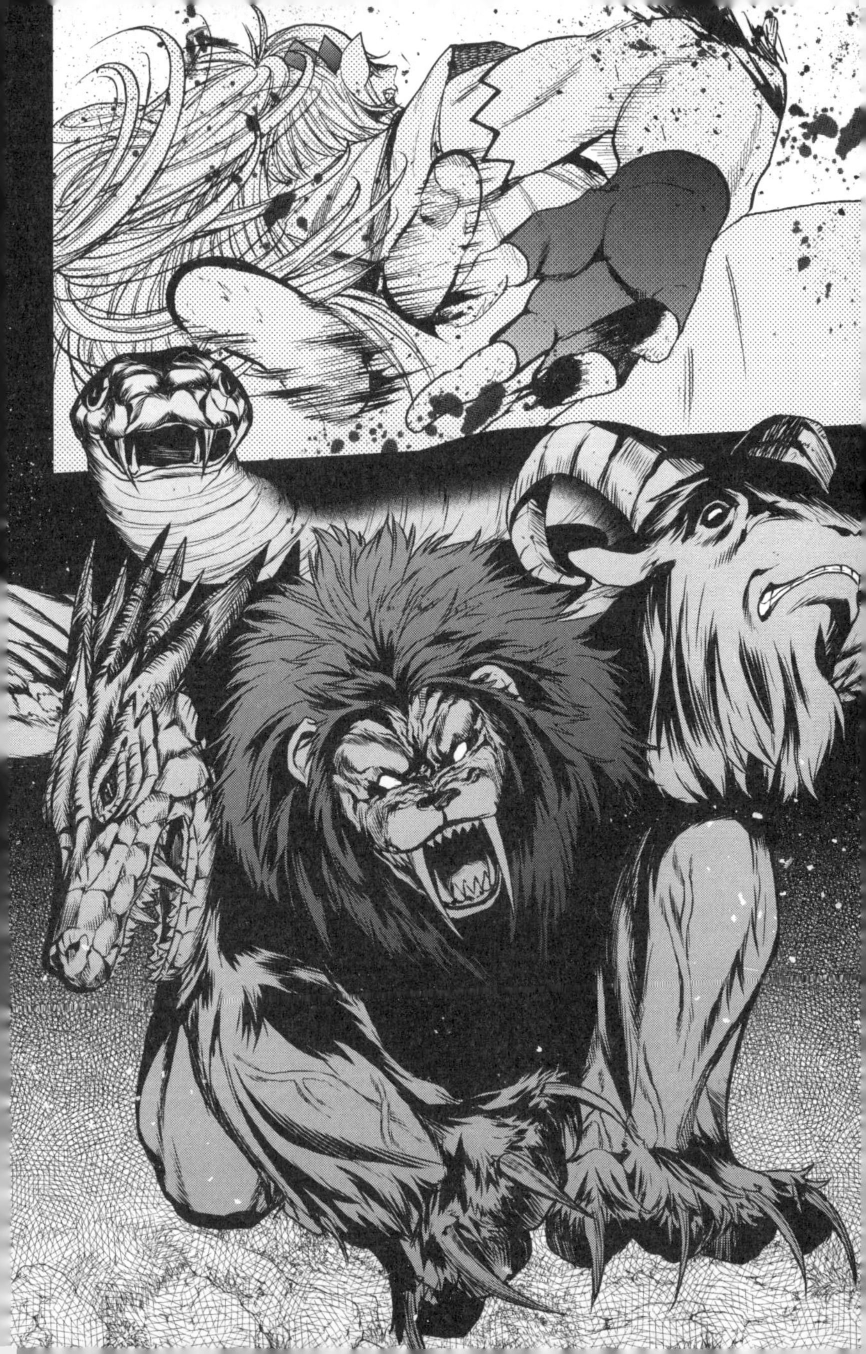

Chapter 24 ◆ Alone

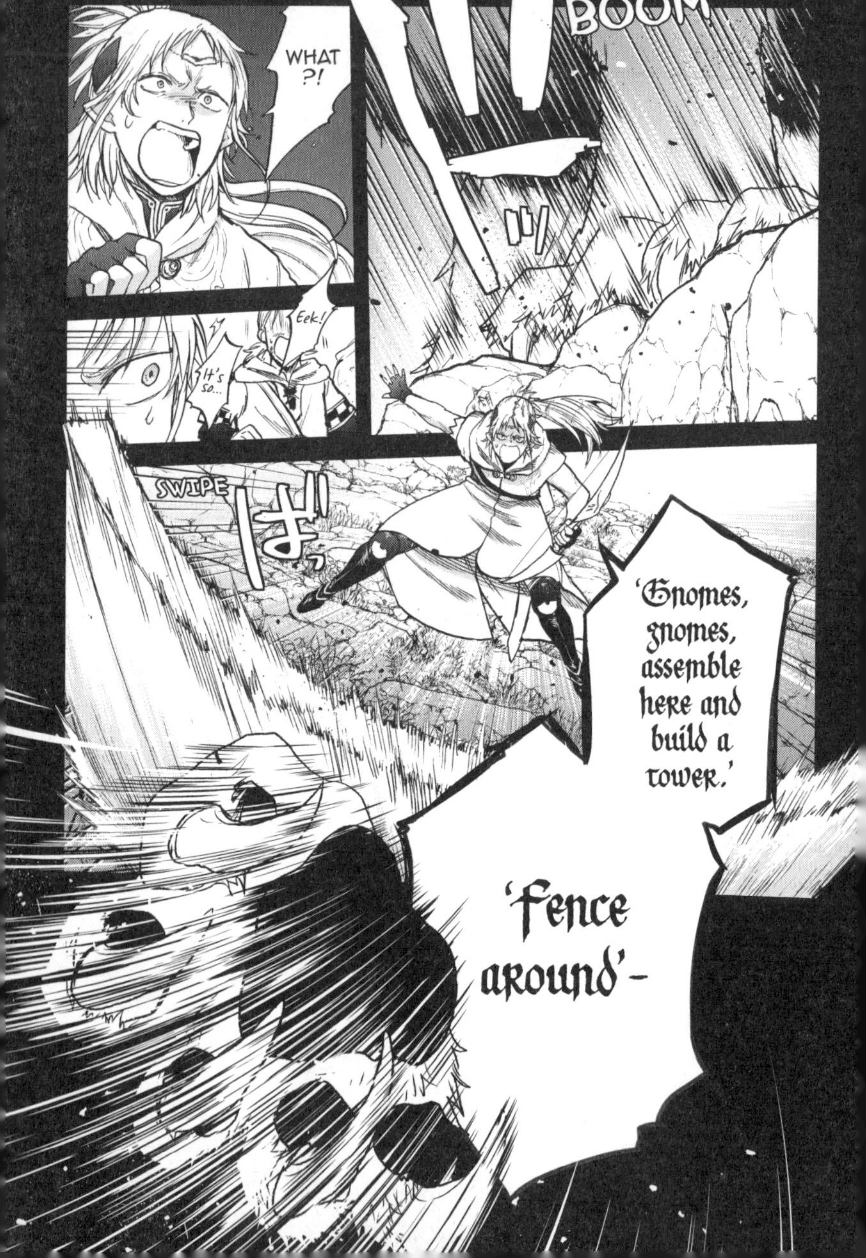
BOOM
WHAT ?!
Eek!
It's so...
SWIPE
'Gnomes, gnomes, assemble here and build a tower.'
'Fence around'-

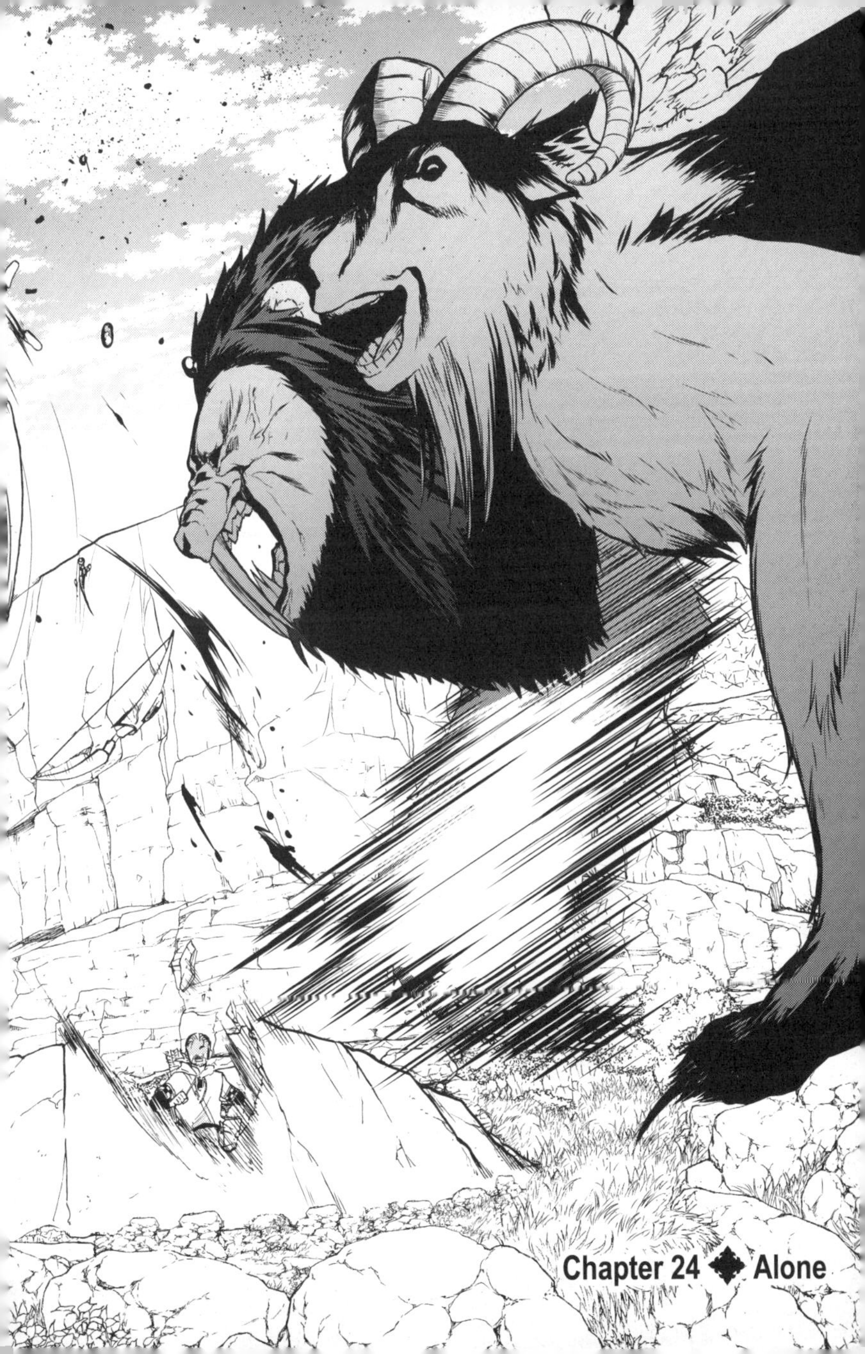
Chapter 24 ◆ Alone

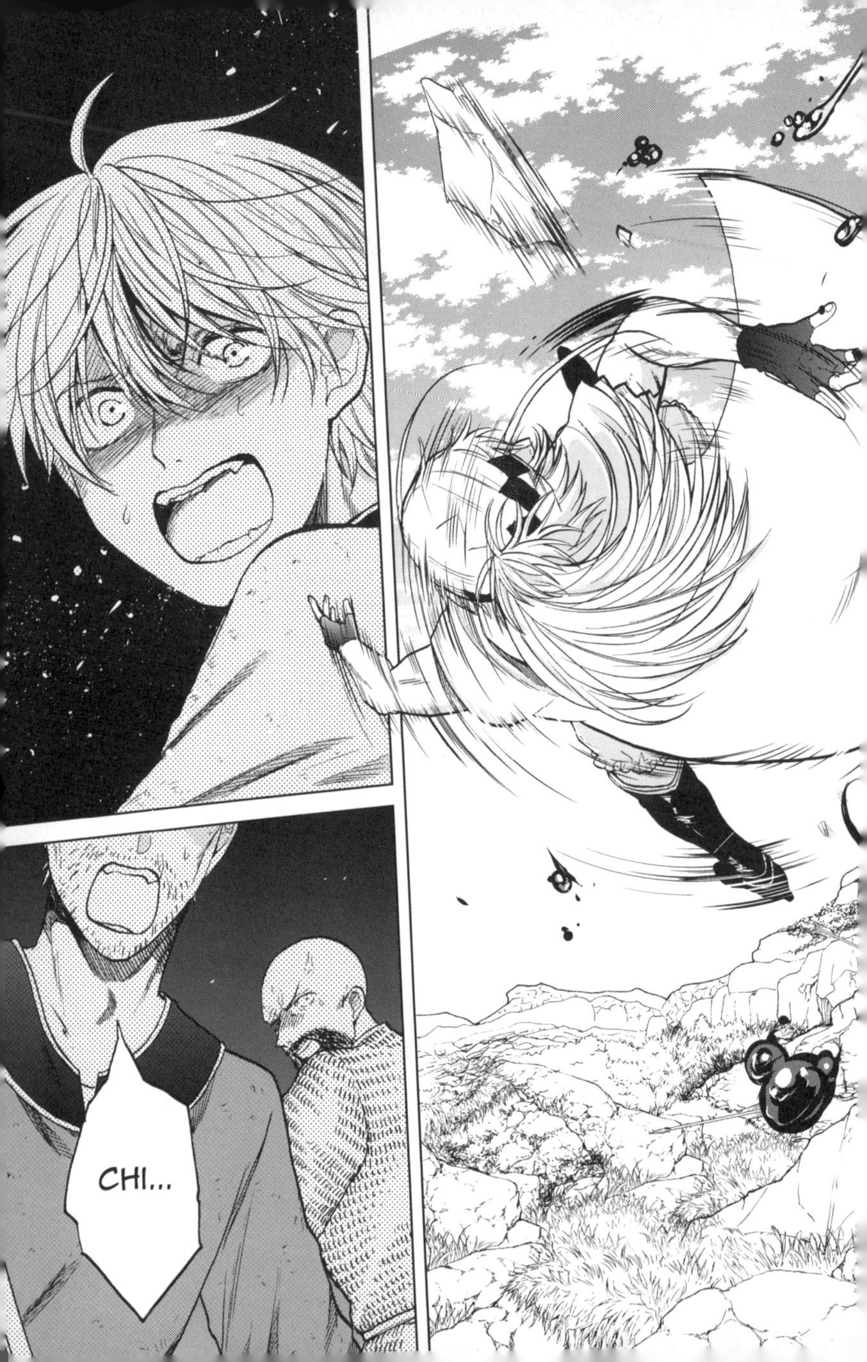
CHI...

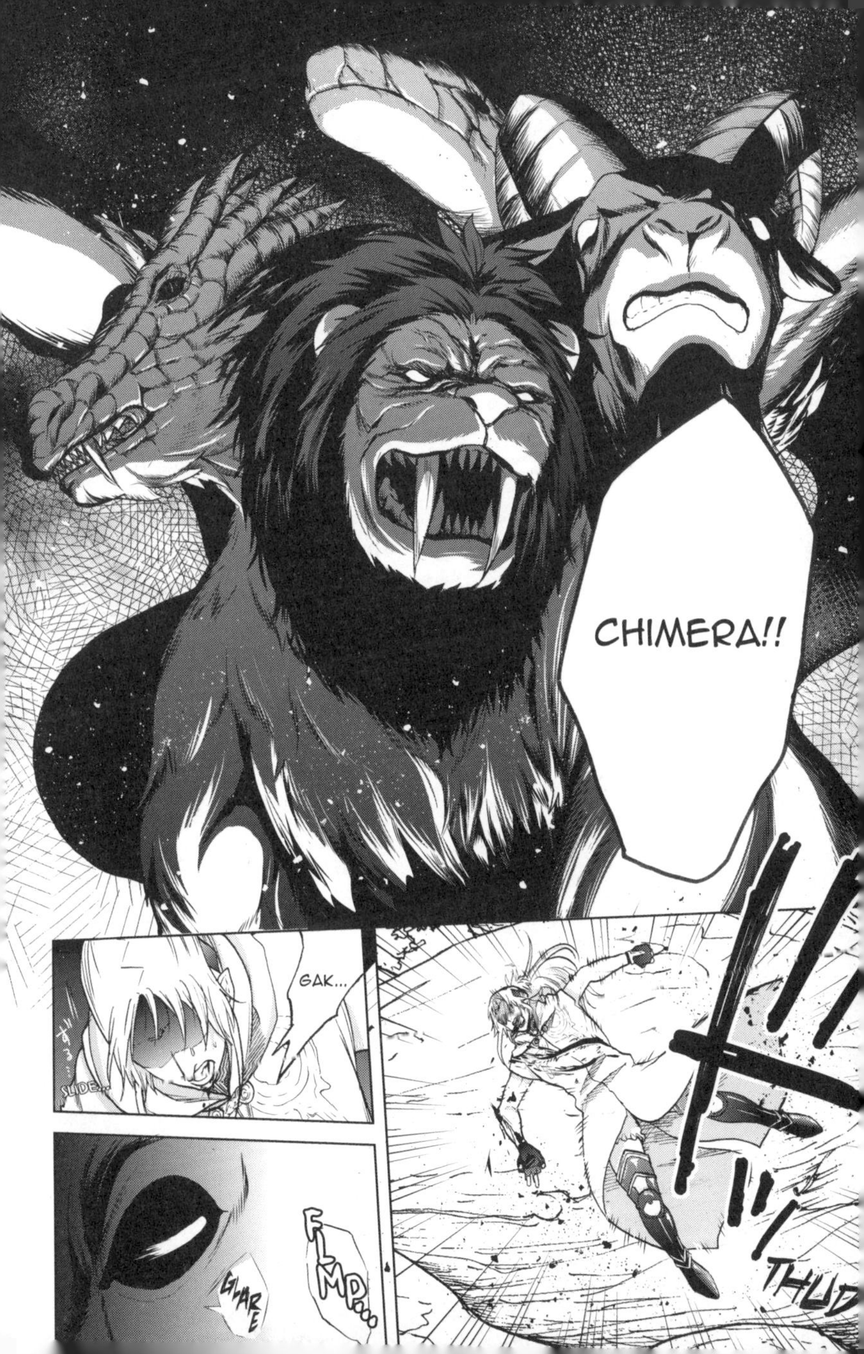
CHIMERA!!
THUD
GAK...
SLIDE...
FLMP...
GLARE

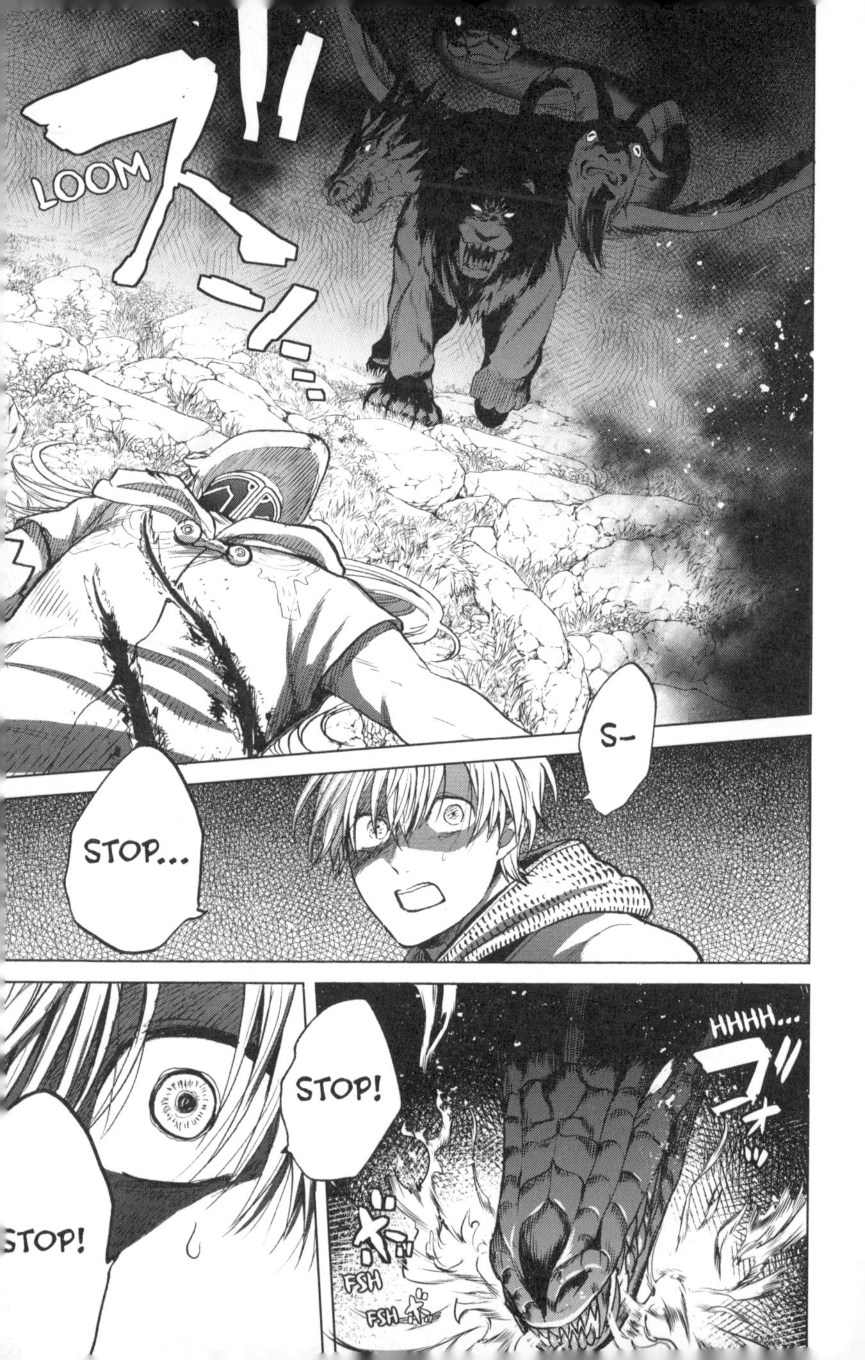
LOOM
S-
STOP...
HHHH...
FSH
FSH
STOP!
STOP!

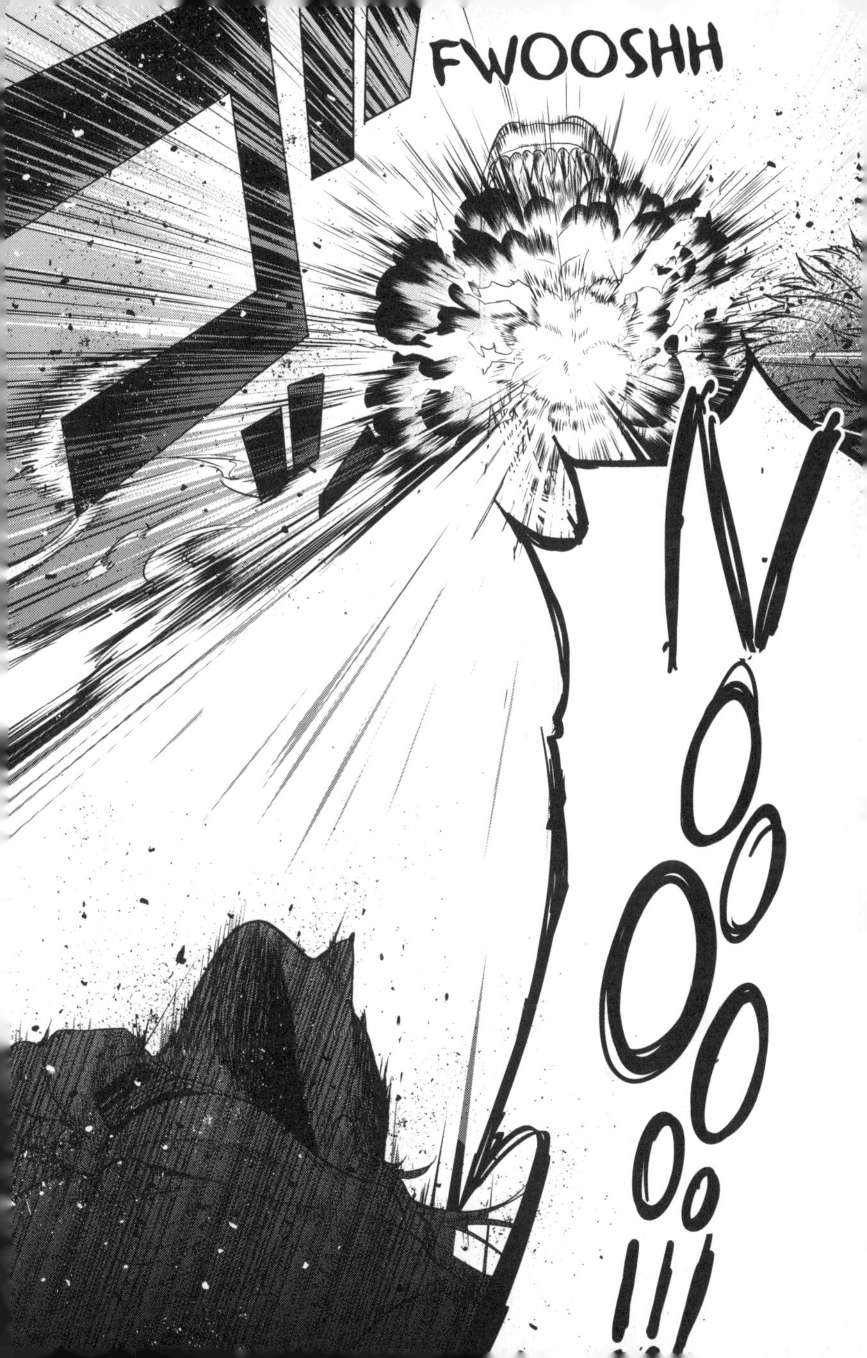
FWOOSHH
NOOOOOOOO!!!

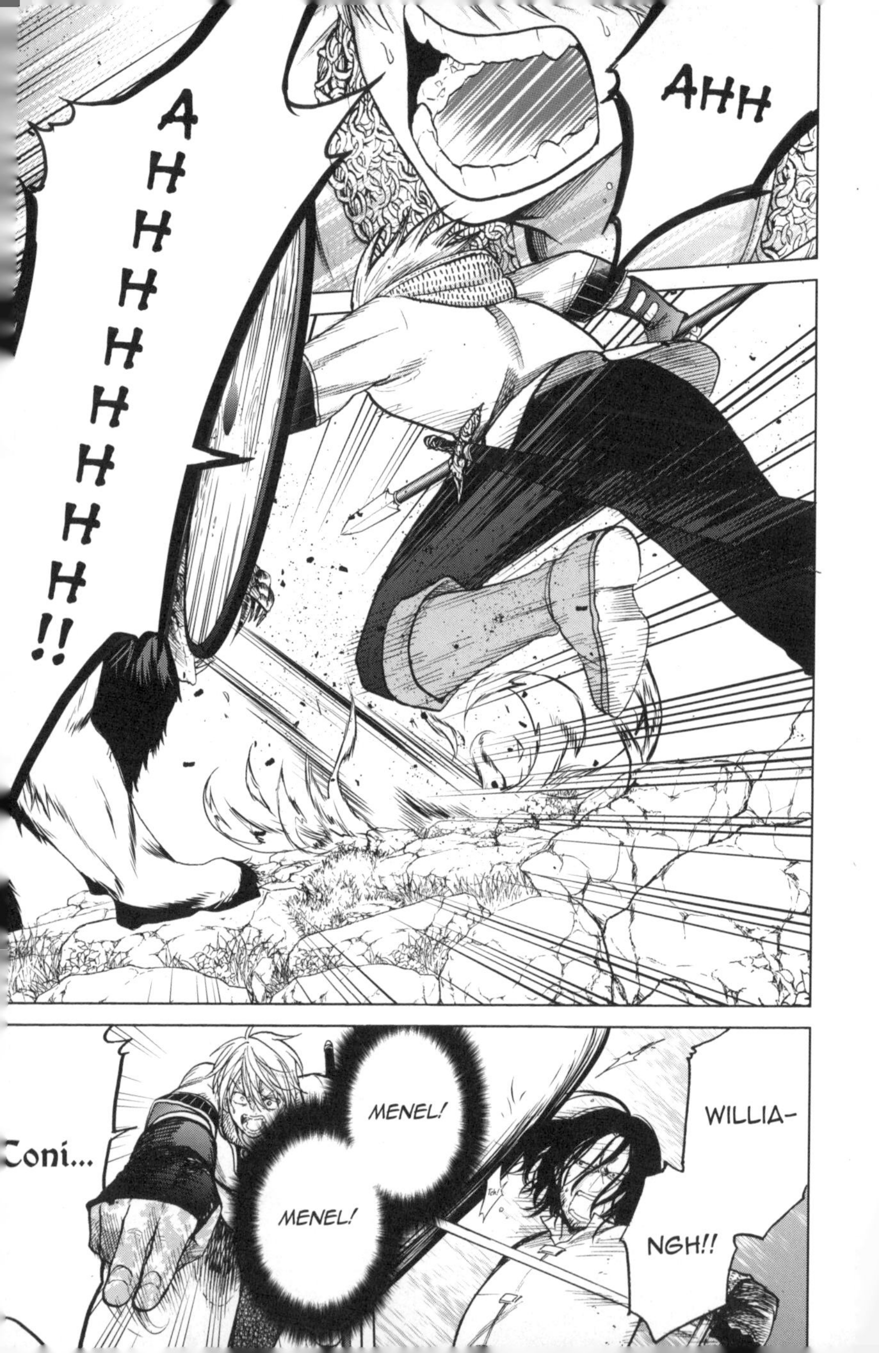
AHH
AHHHHHHHH!!
WILLIA-
NGH!!
Tch!
MENEL!
MENEL!
Coni...

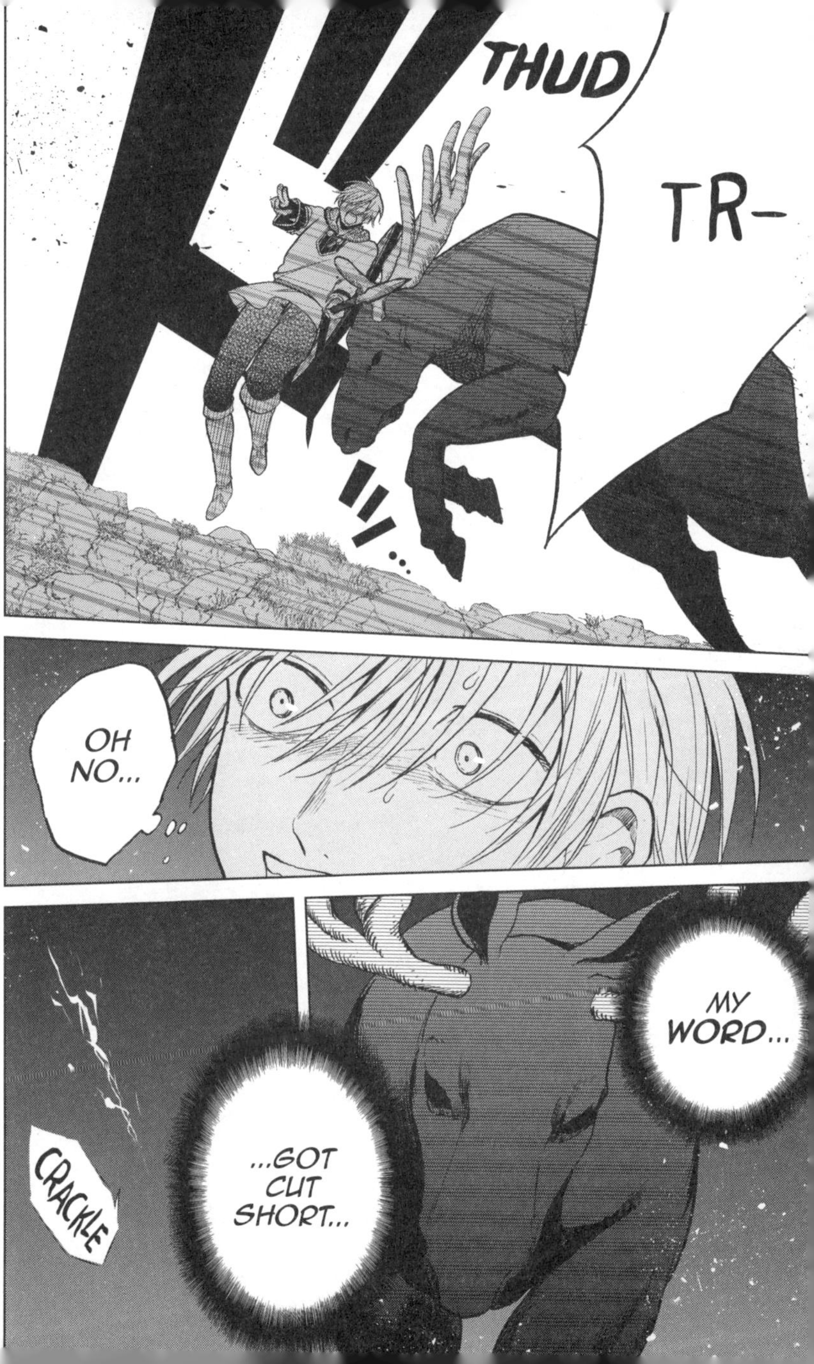
TR-
THUD
OH NO...
MY WORD...
...GOT CUT SHORT...
CRACKLE

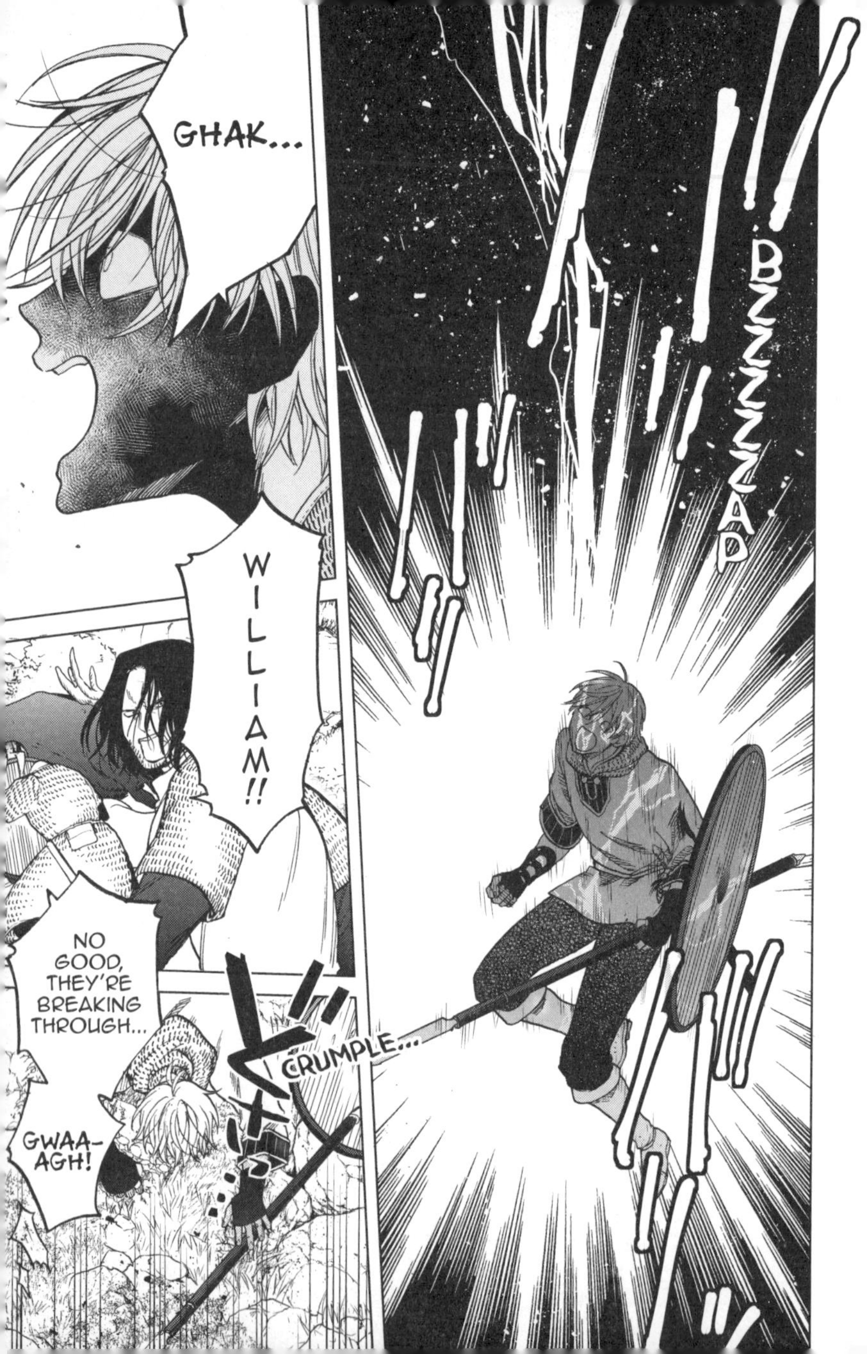
BZZZZZAP
GHAK...
WILLIAM!!
NO GOOD, THEY'RE BREAKING THROUGH...
CRUMPLE...
GWAA-AGH!

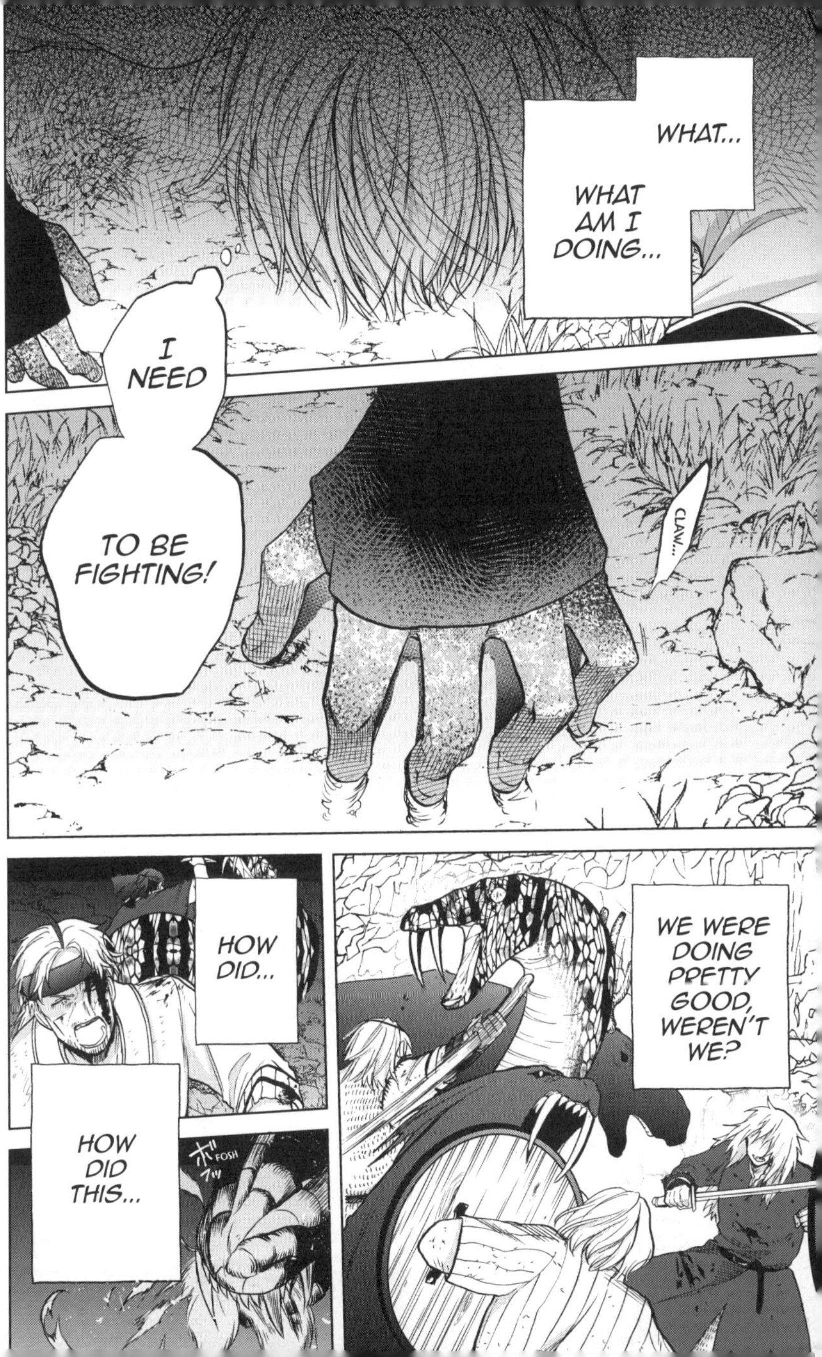
WHAT...
WHAT AM I DOING...
I NEED
TO BE FIGHTING!
CLAW...
WE WERE DOING PRETTY GOOD, WEREN'T WE?
HOW DID...
HOW DID THIS...
FOSH

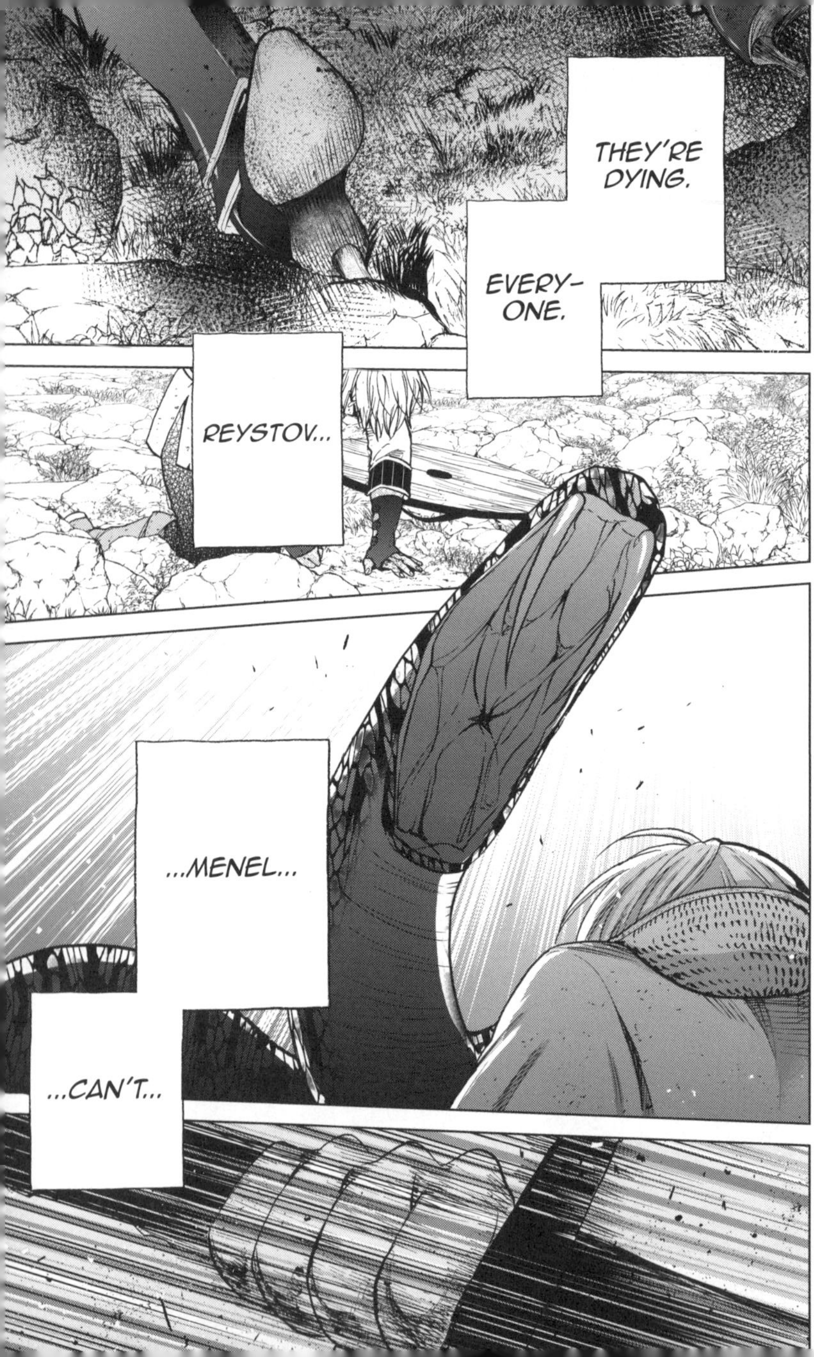
THEY'RE DYING.
EVERY-ONE.
REYSTOV...
...MENEL...
...CAN'T...

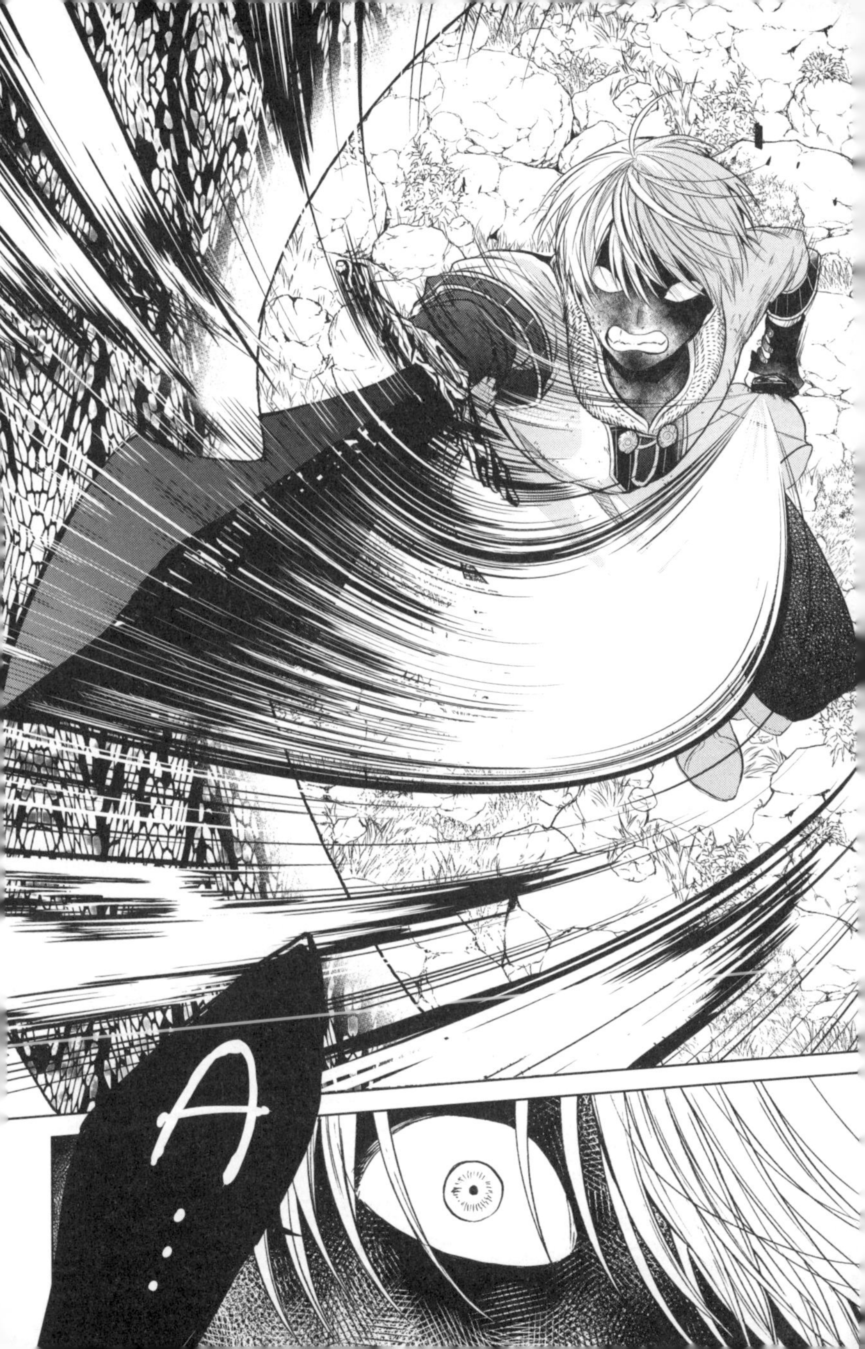
A...

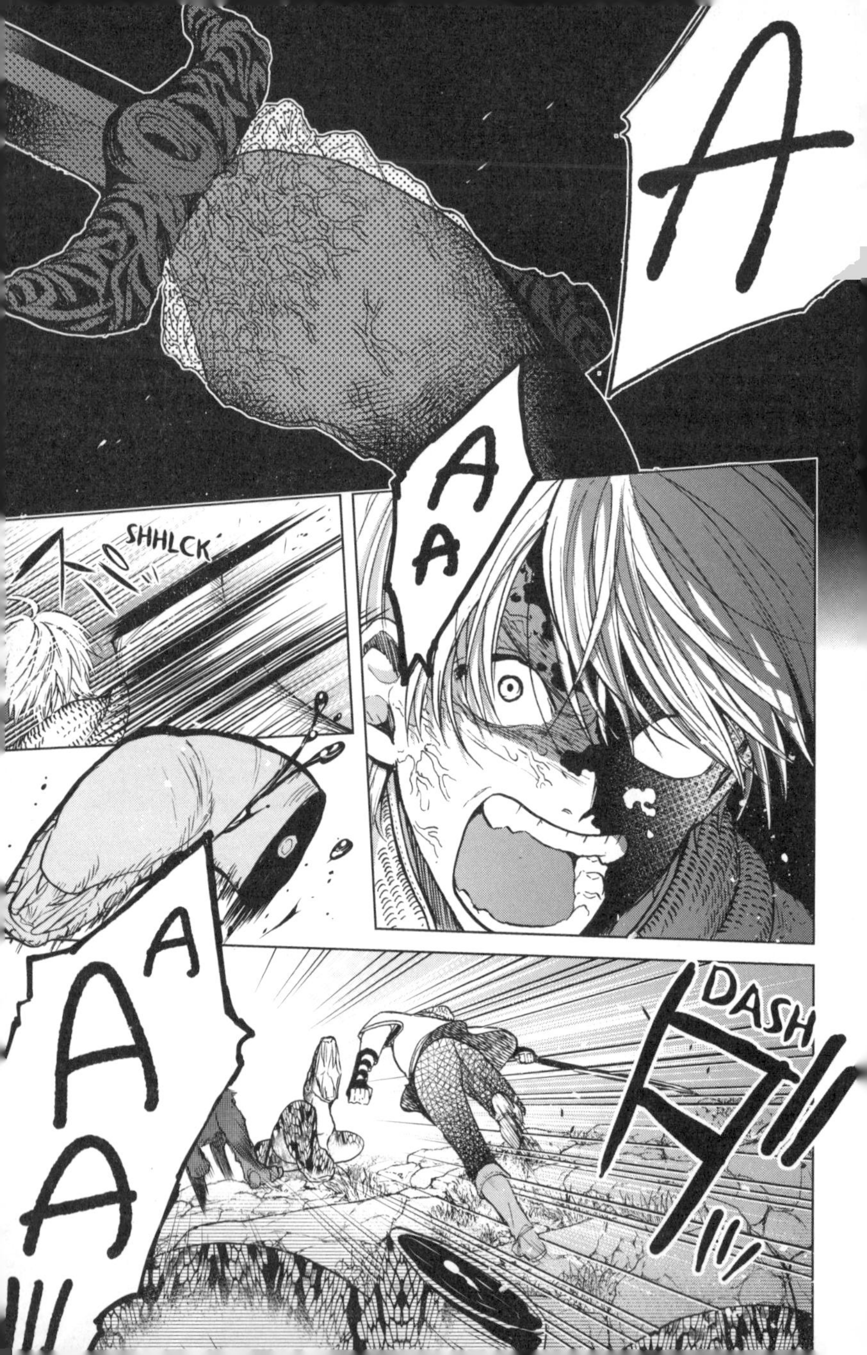

A
AA
SHHLCK
AAA
DASH

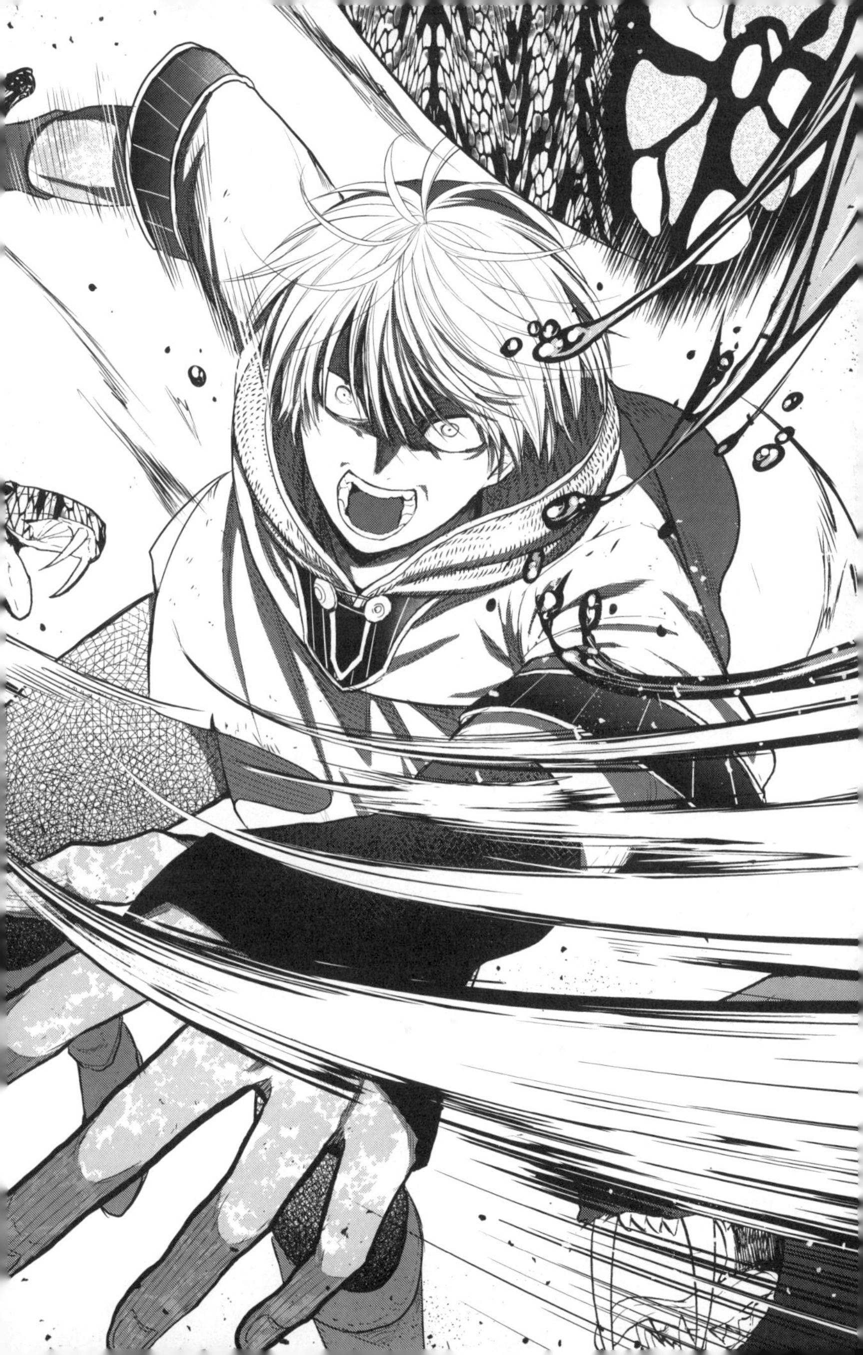

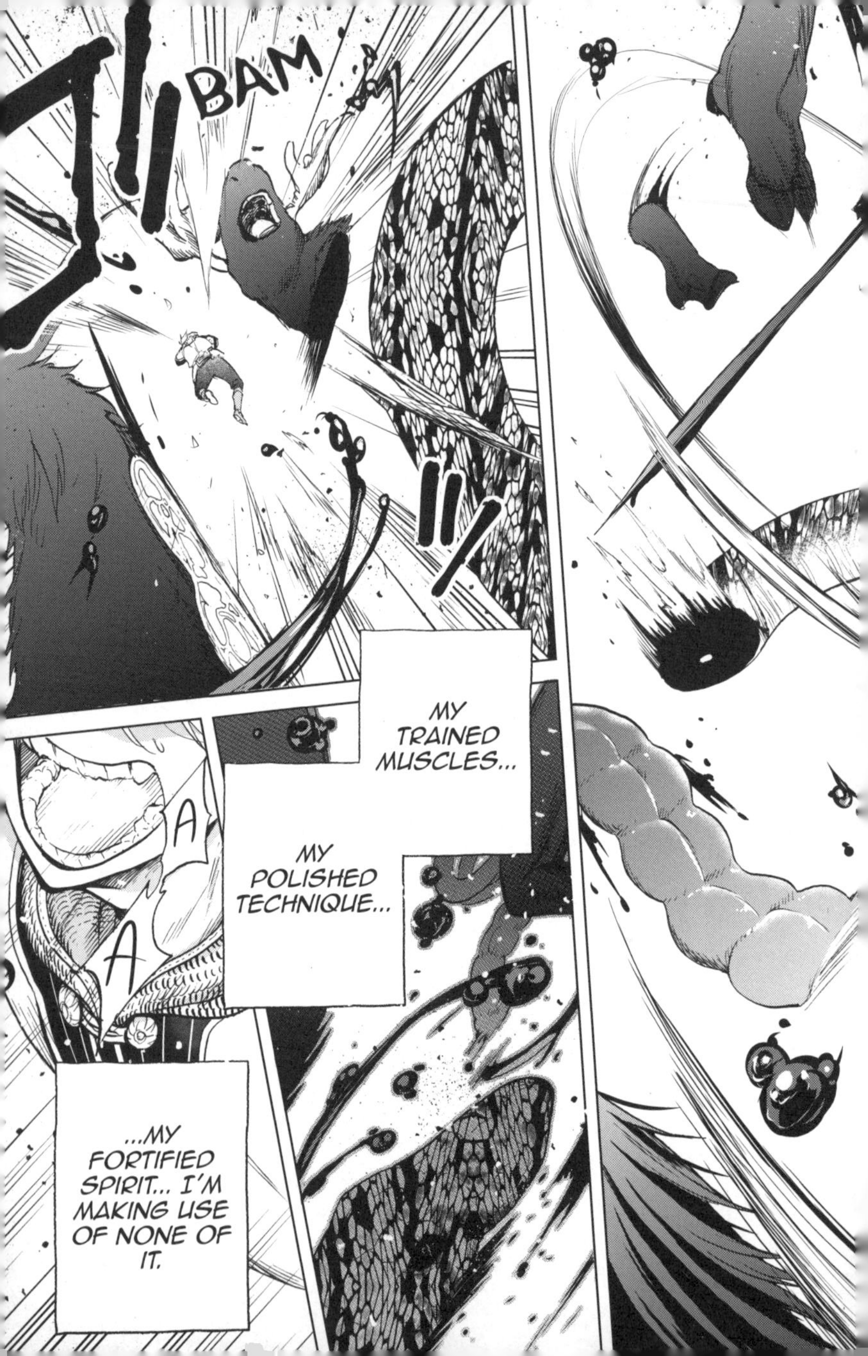
BAM
MY TRAINED MUSCLES...
MY POLISHED TECHNIQUE...
A
A
...MY FORTIFIED SPIRIT... I'M MAKING USE OF NONE OF IT.

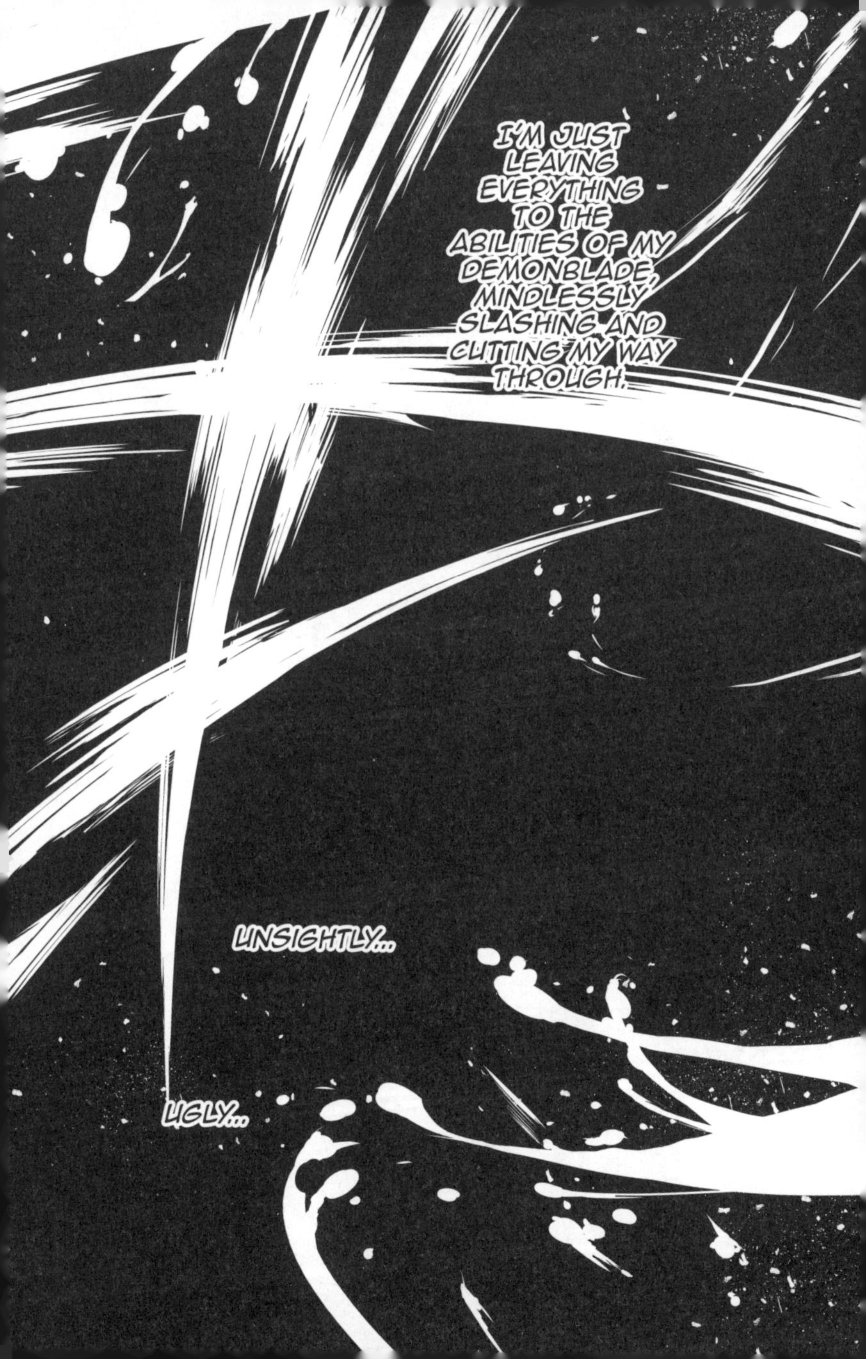
I'M JUST LEAVING EVERYTHING TO THE ABILITIES OF MY DEMONBLADE, MINDLESSLY SLASHING AND CUTTING MY WAY THROUGH.
UNSIGHTLY...
UGLY...

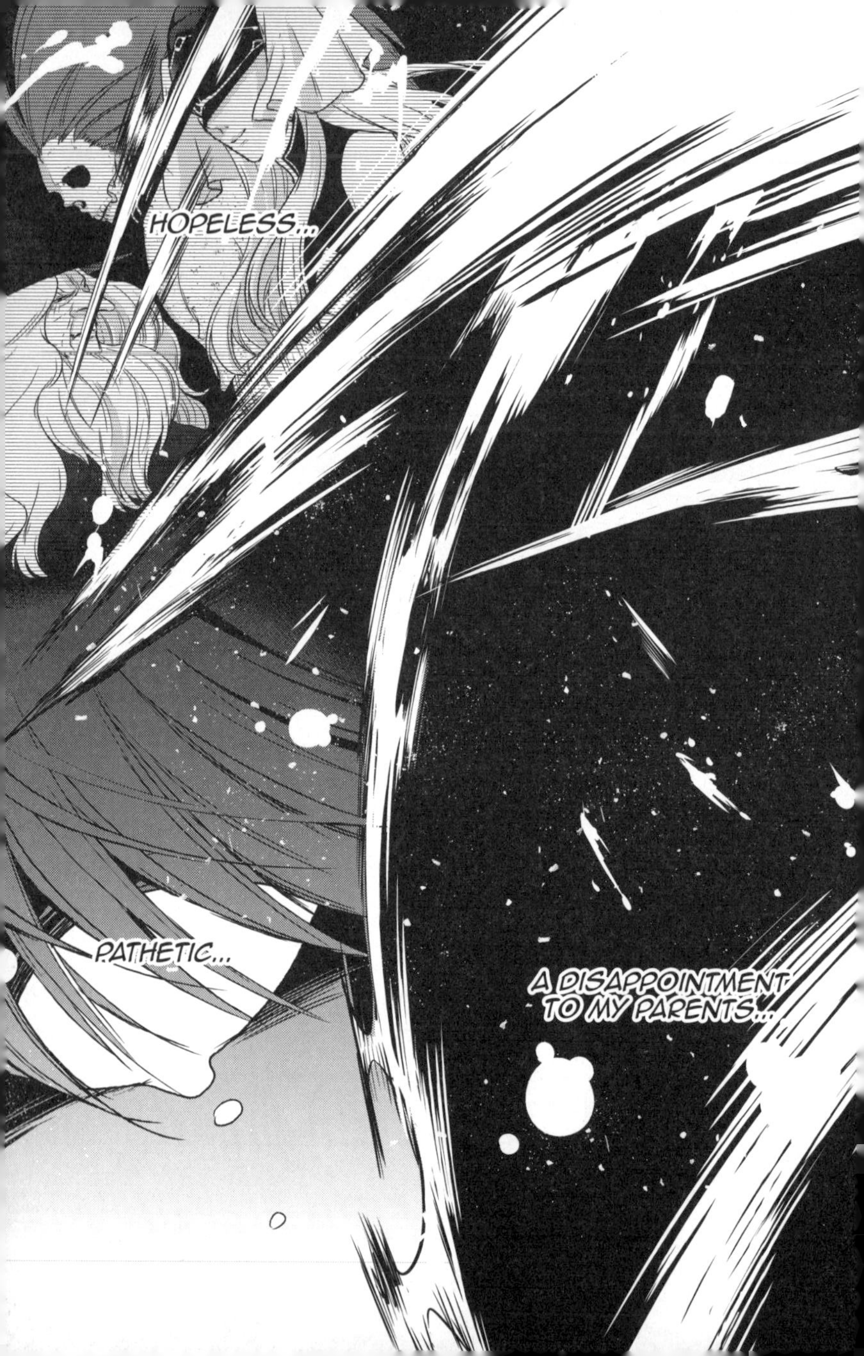
HOPELESS...
A DISAPPOINTMENT TO MY PARENTS...
PATHETIC...

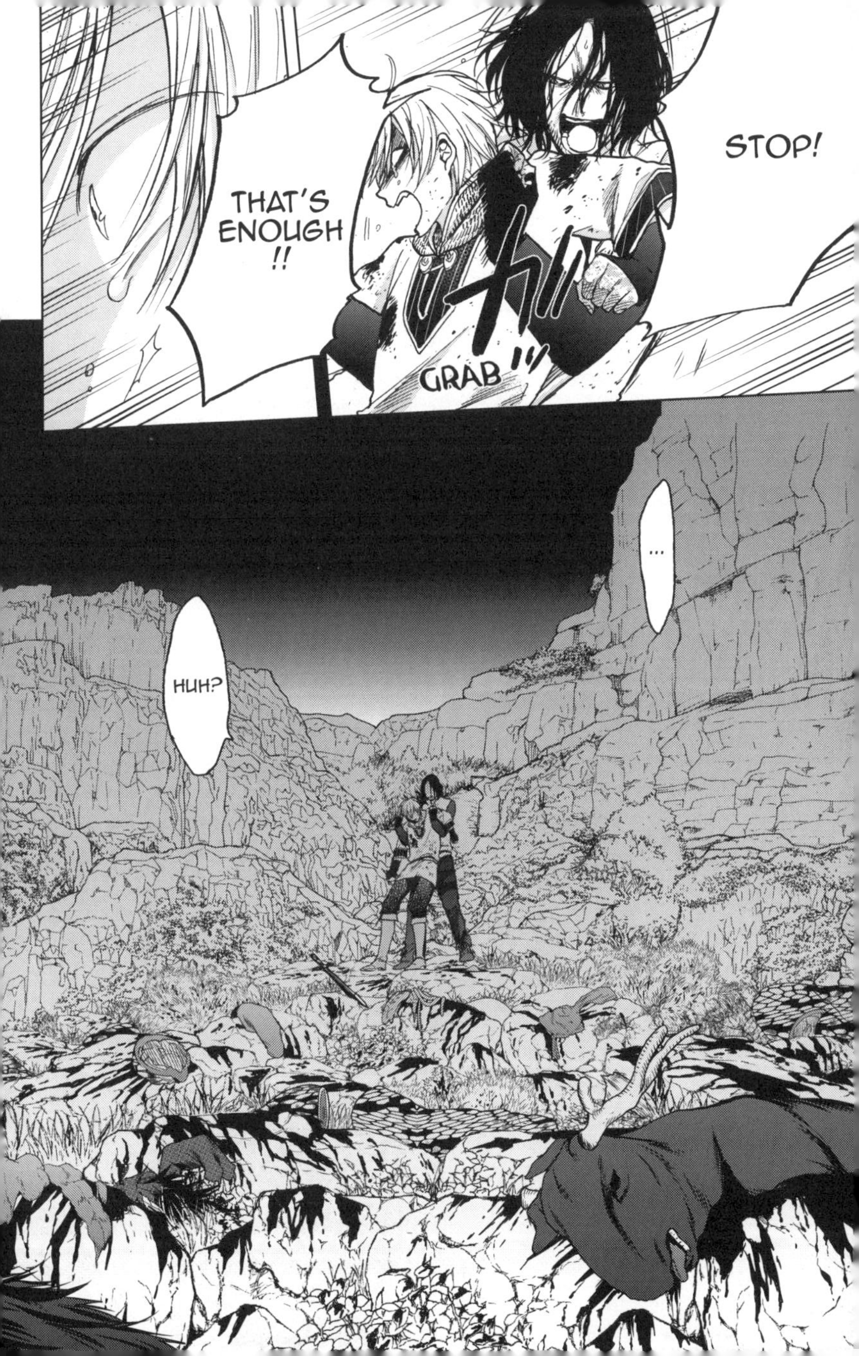
STOP!
THAT'S ENOUGH !!
GRAB
...
HUH?

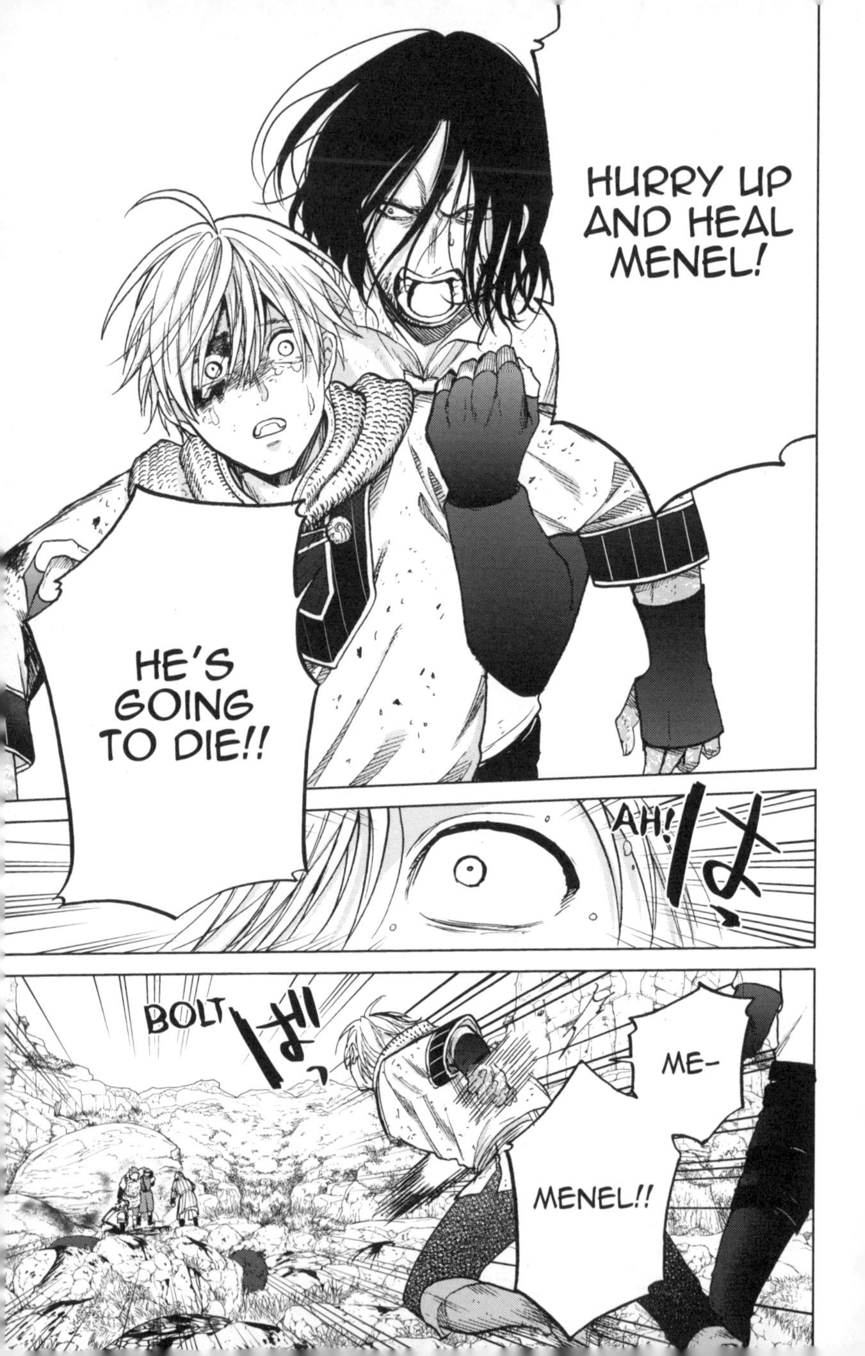
HURRY UP AND HEAL MENEL!
HE'S GOING TO DIE!!
AH!
は
ME-
MENEL!!
BOLT
ば

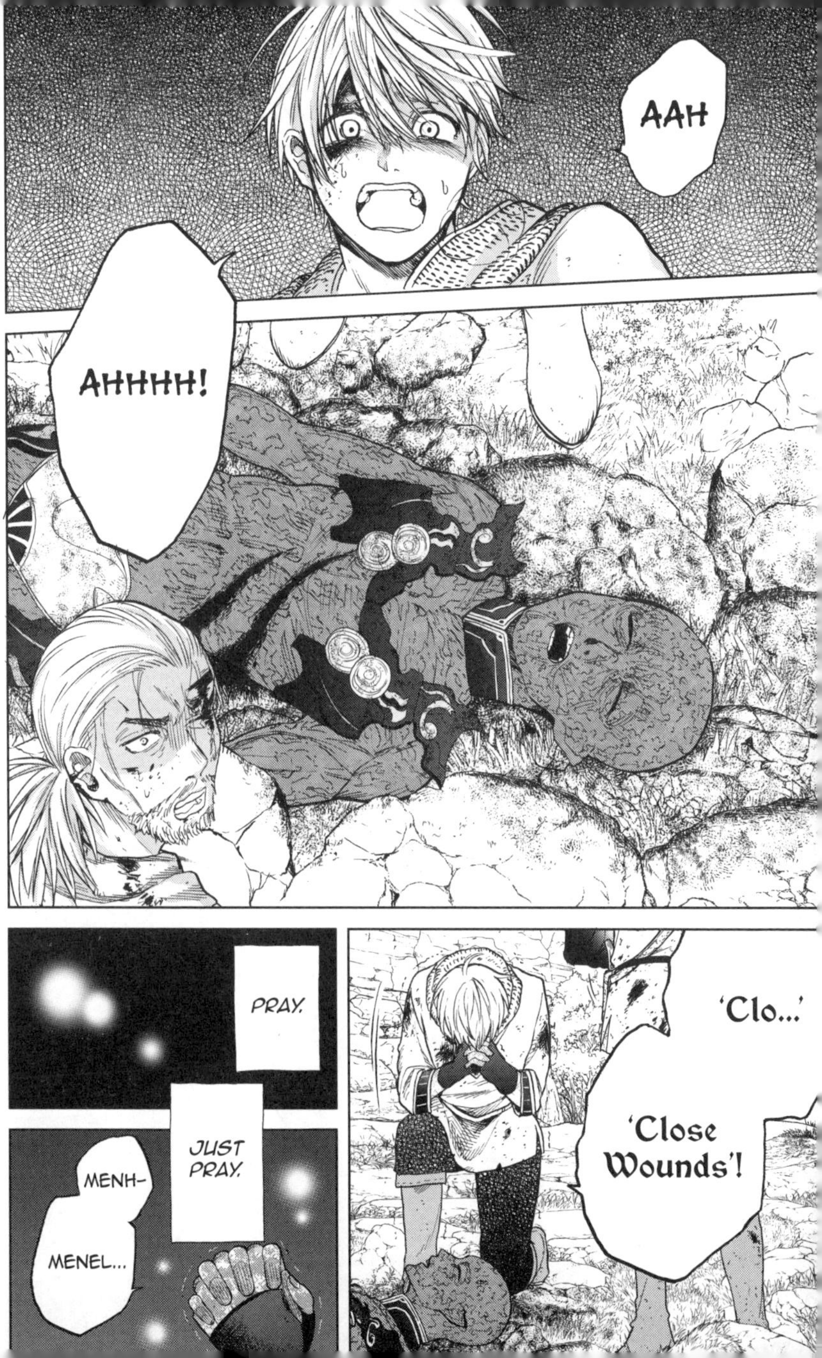
AAH
AHHHH!
'Clo...'
'Close Wounds'!
PRAY.
JUST PRAY.
MENH-
MENEL...

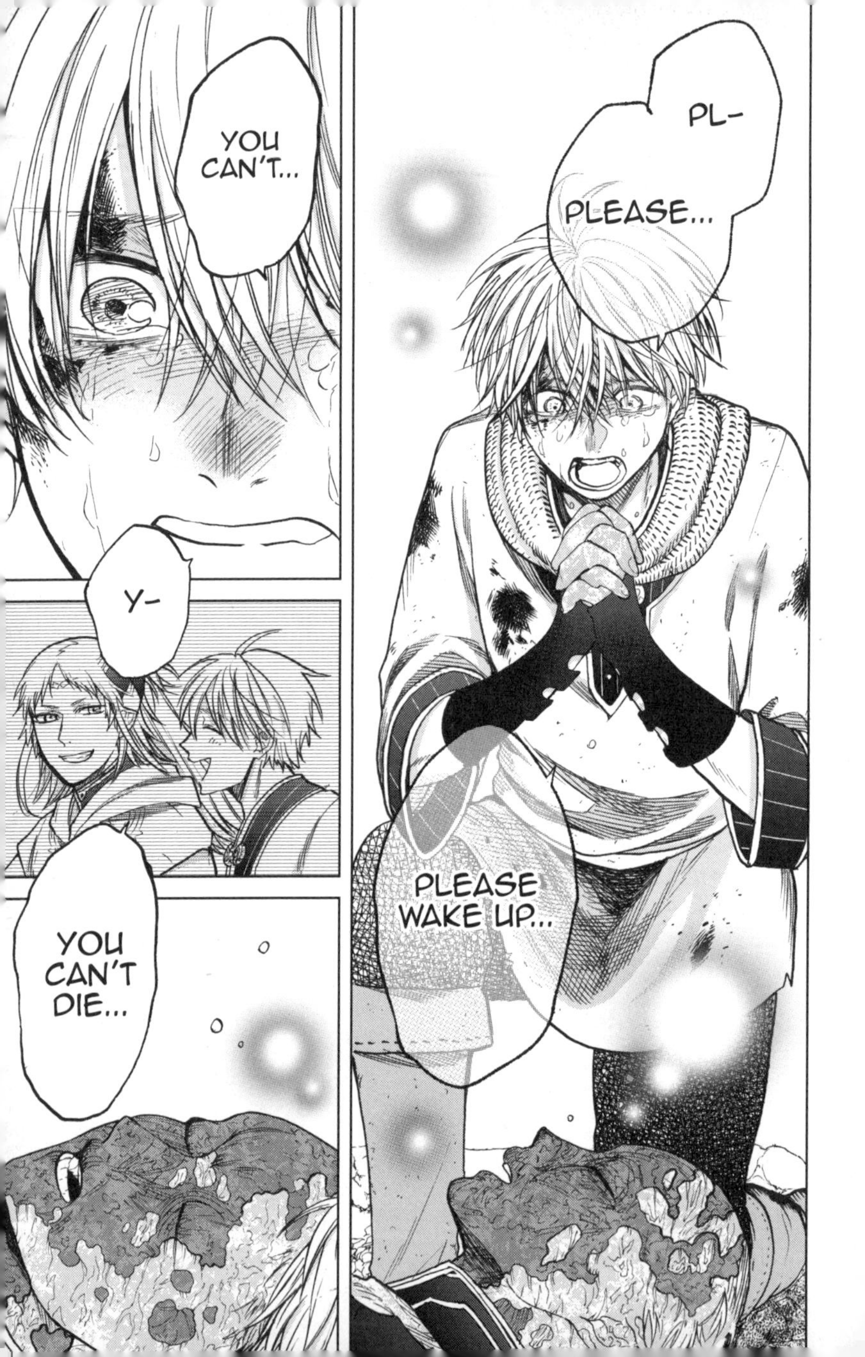
PL-
PLEASE...
PLEASE WAKE UP...
YOU CAN'T...
Y-
YOU CAN'T DIE...

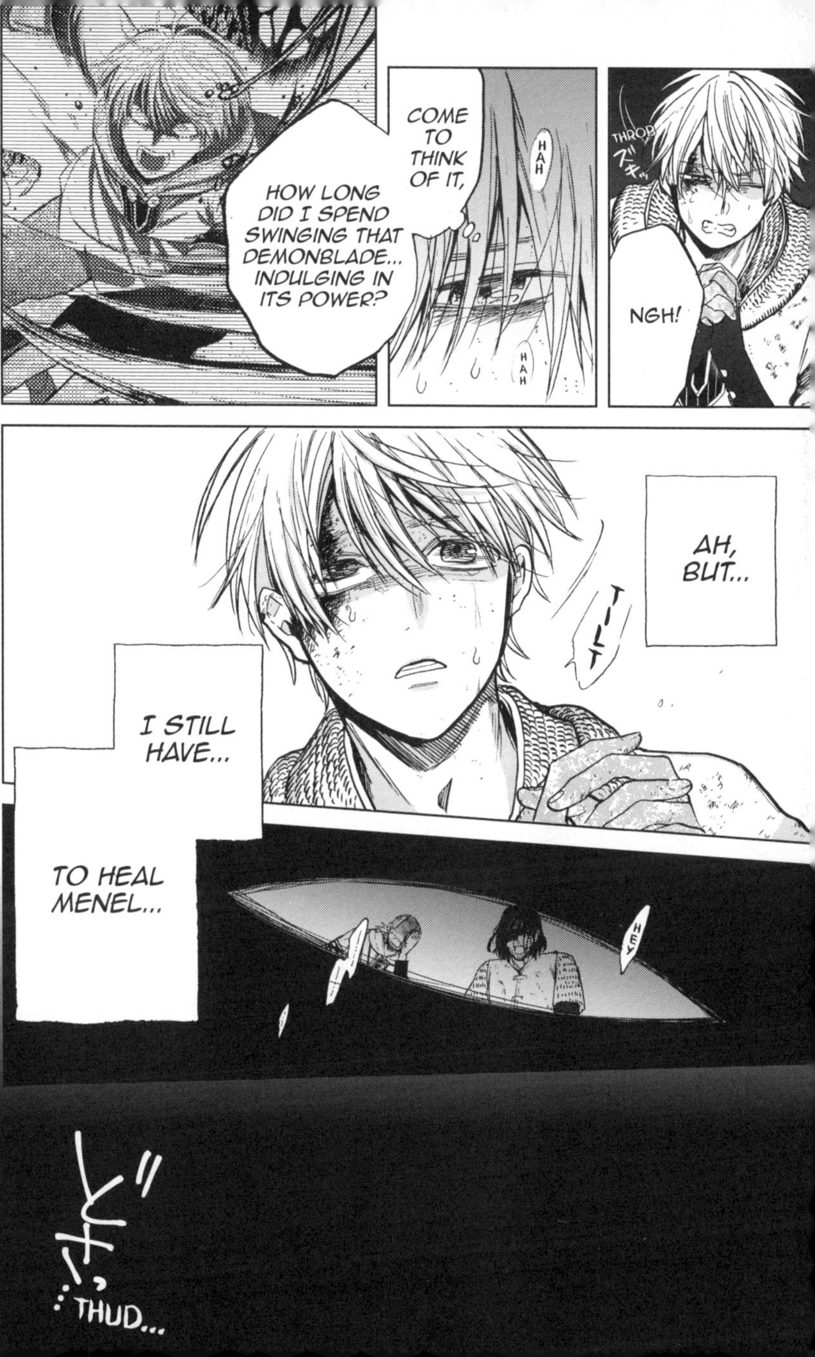
THROB
NGH!
HAH
COME TO THINK OF IT,
HOW LONG DID I SPEND SWINGING THAT DEMONBLADE... INDULGING IN ITS POWER?
HAH
AH, BUT...
TILT
I STILL HAVE...
TO HEAL MENEL...
HEY
THUD...

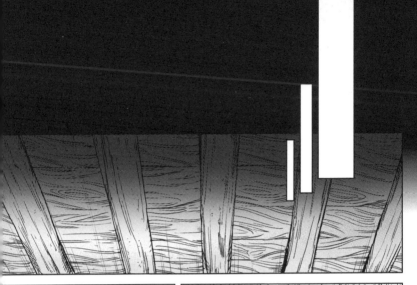

THIS IS...

...

!

ACCORDING TO REYSTOV...

YOU'RE AWAKE.

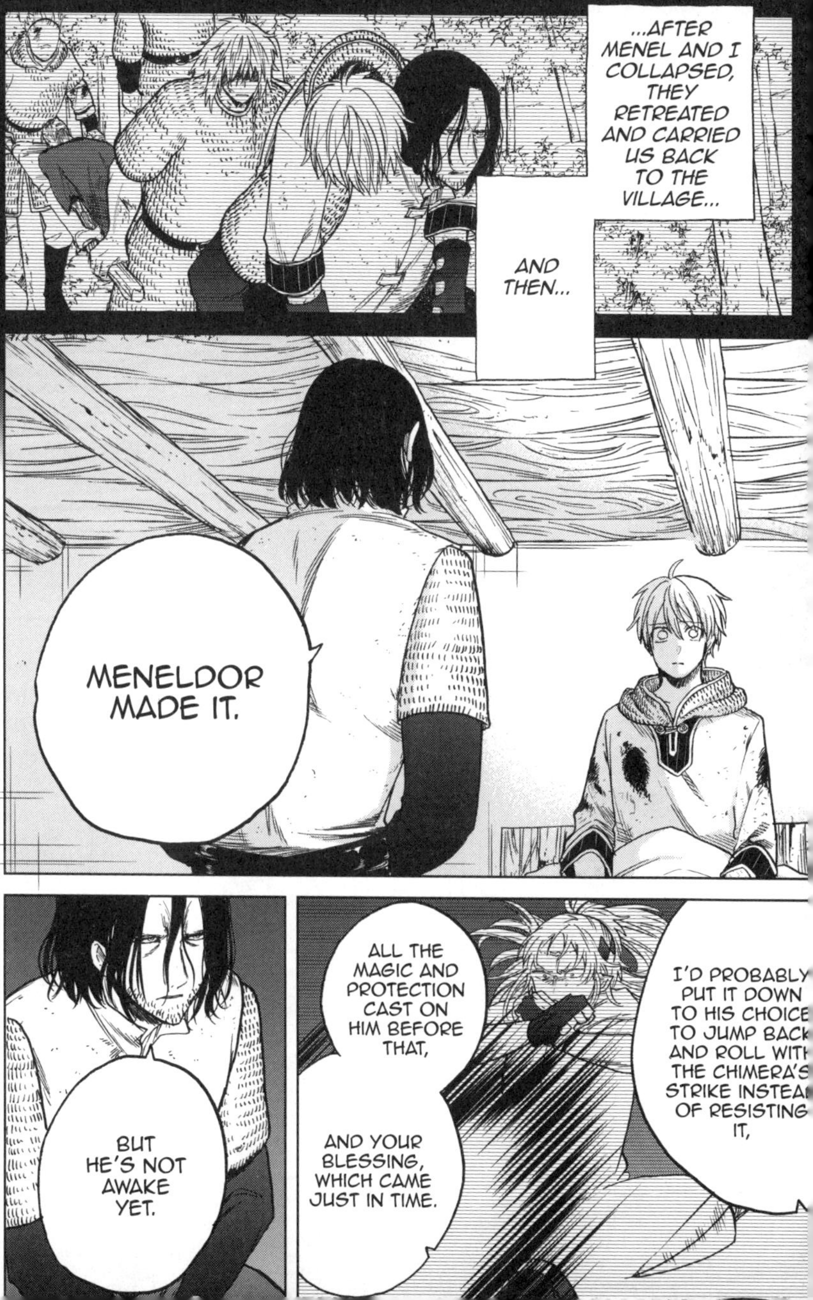
...AFTER MENEL AND I COLLAPSED, THEY RETREATED AND CARRIED US BACK TO THE VILLAGE...
AND THEN...
MENELDOR MADE IT.
I'D PROBABLY PUT IT DOWN TO HIS CHOICE TO JUMP BACK AND ROLL WITH THE CHIMERA'S STRIKE INSTEA OF RESISTING IT,
ALL THE MAGIC AND PROTECTION CAST ON HIM BEFORE THAT,
AND YOUR BLESSING, WHICH CAME JUST IN TIME.
BUT HE'S NOT AWAKE YET.

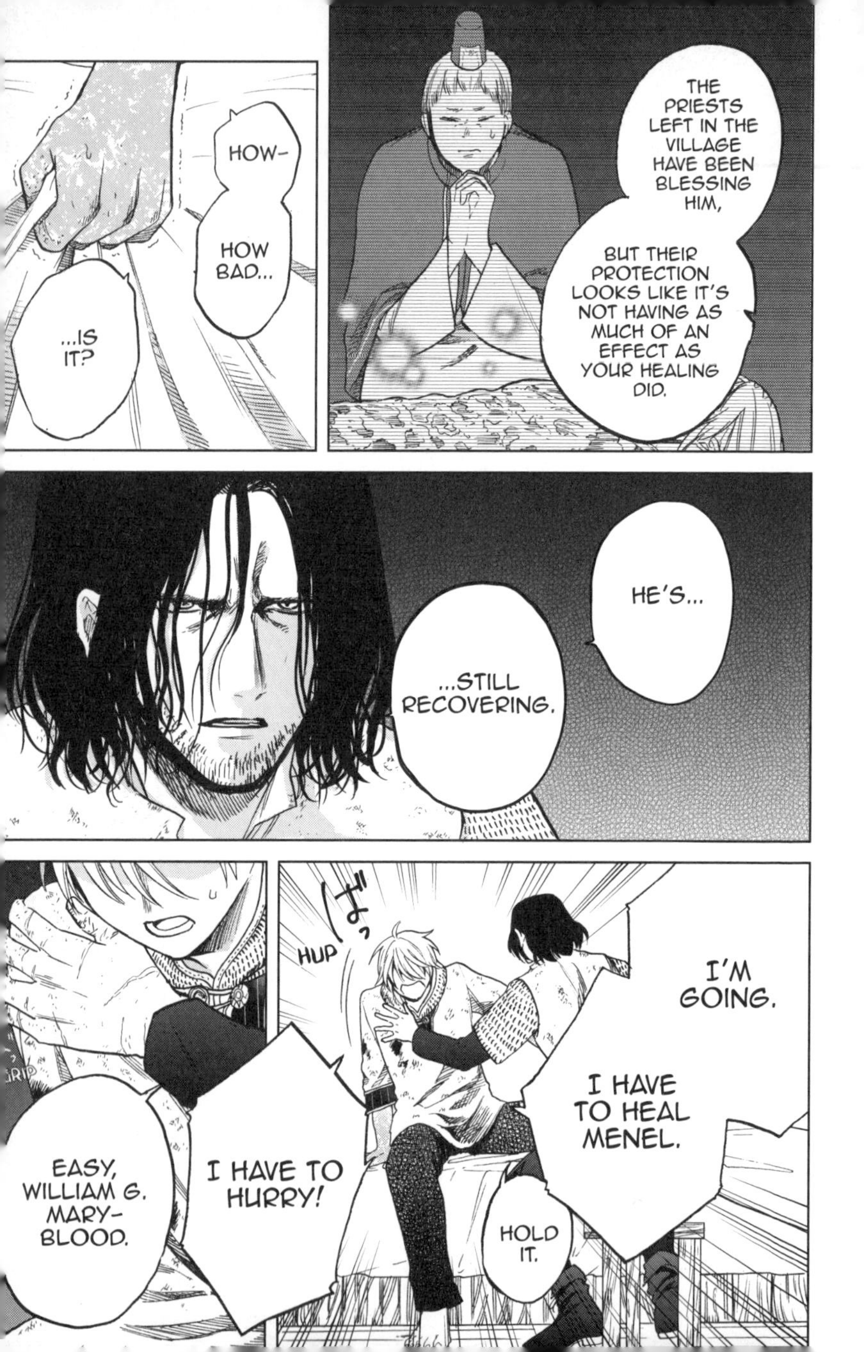
THE PRIESTS LEFT IN THE VILLAGE HAVE BEEN BLESSING HIM,
BUT THEIR PROTECTION LOOKS LIKE IT'S NOT HAVING AS MUCH OF AN EFFECT AS YOUR HEALING DID.
HOW-
HOW BAD...
...IS IT?
HE'S...
...STILL RECOVERING.
I'M GOING.
I HAVE TO HEAL MENEL.
HUP
HOLD IT.
I HAVE TO HURRY!
EASY, WILLIAM G. MARY-BLOOD.

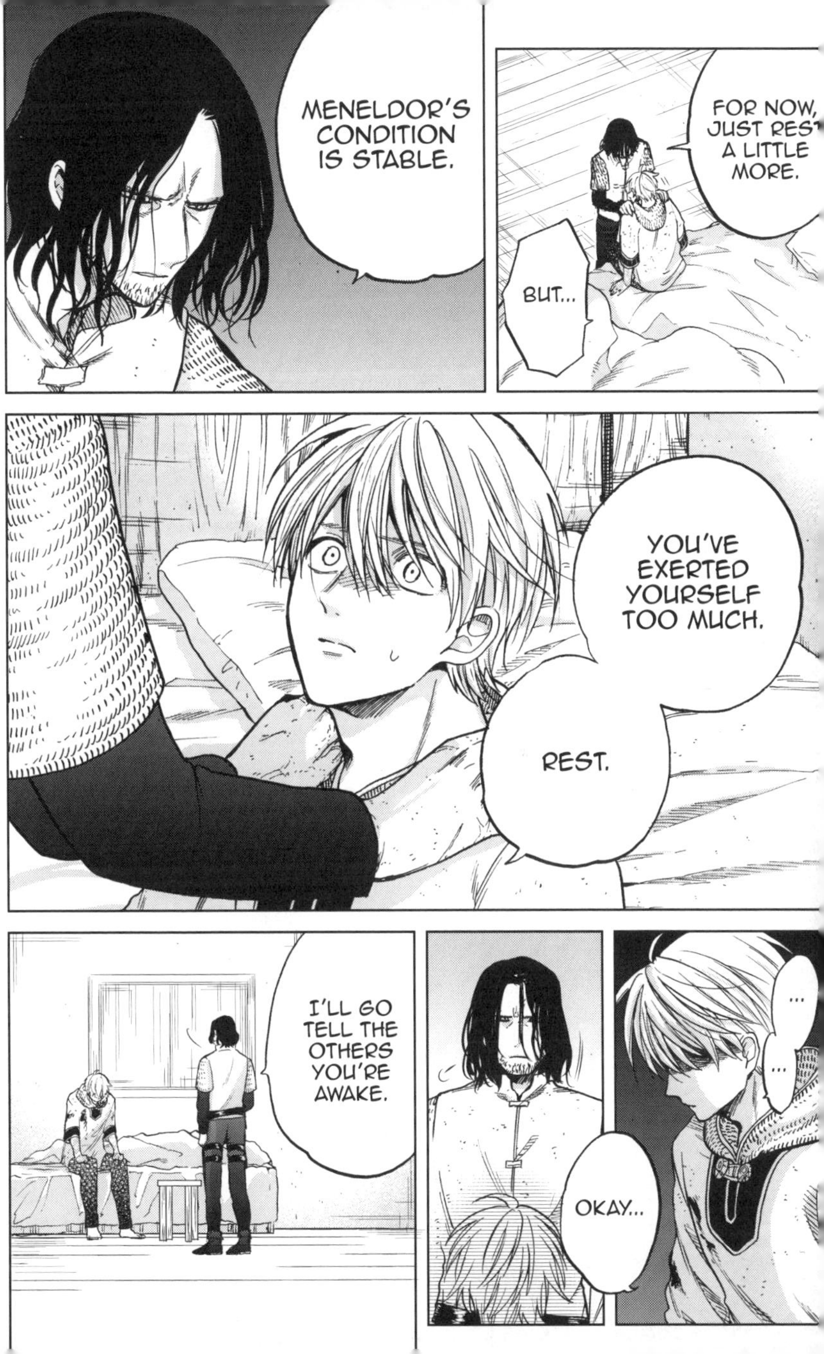
FOR NOW, JUST REST A LITTLE MORE.
BUT...
MENELDOR'S CONDITION IS STABLE.
YOU'VE EXERTED YOURSELF TOO MUCH.
REST.
...
...
OKAY...
I'LL GO TELL THE OTHERS YOU'RE AWAKE.

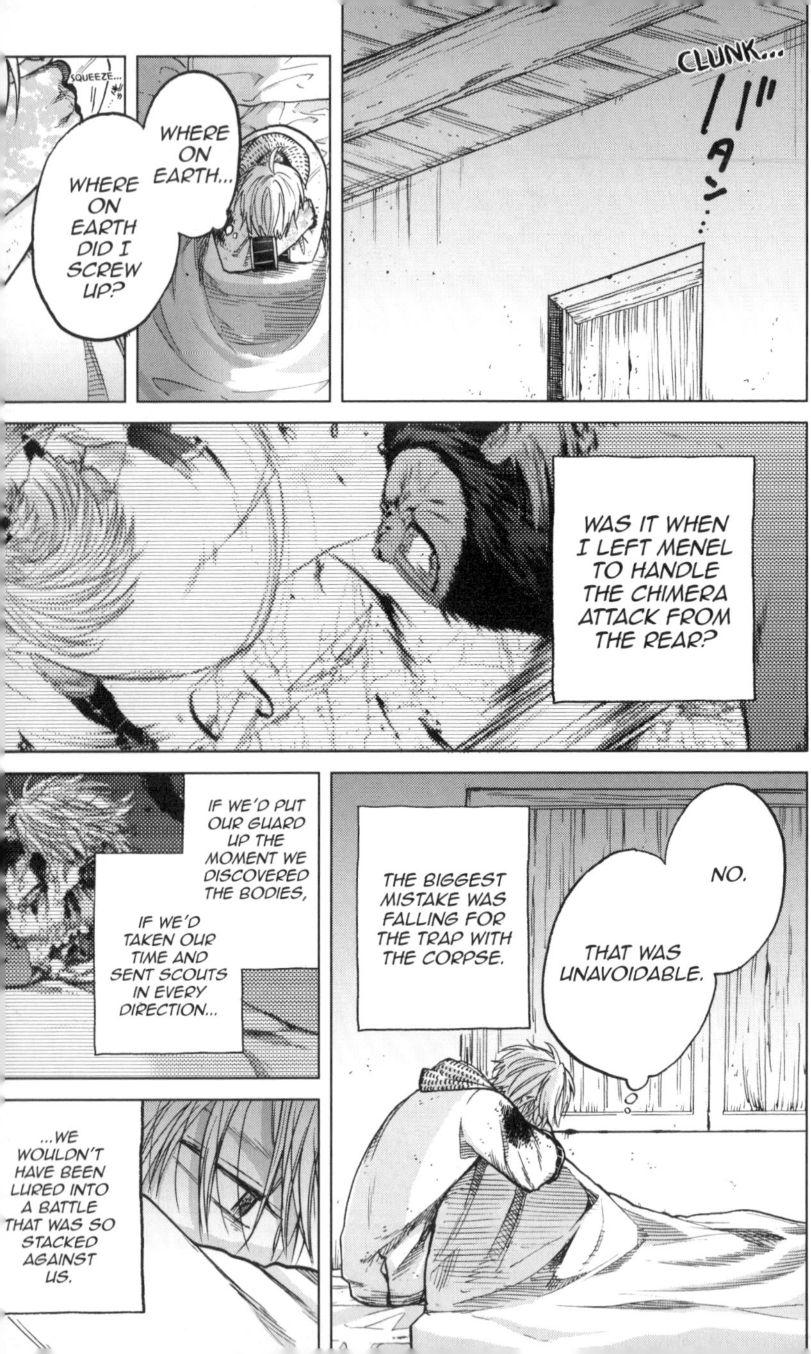
CLUNK...
バタン…
WHERE ON EARTH...
WHERE ON EARTH DID I SCREW UP?
SQUEEZE...
WAS IT WHEN I LEFT MENEL TO HANDLE THE CHIMERA ATTACK FROM THE REAR?
NO.
THAT WAS UNAVOIDABLE.
THE BIGGEST MISTAKE WAS FALLING FOR THE TRAP WITH THE CORPSE.
IF WE'D PUT OUR GUARD UP THE MOMENT WE DISCOVERED THE BODIES,
IF WE'D TAKEN OUR TIME AND SENT SCOUTS IN EVERY DIRECTION...
...WE WOULDN'T HAVE BEEN LURED INTO A BATTLE THAT WAS SO STACKED AGAINST US.

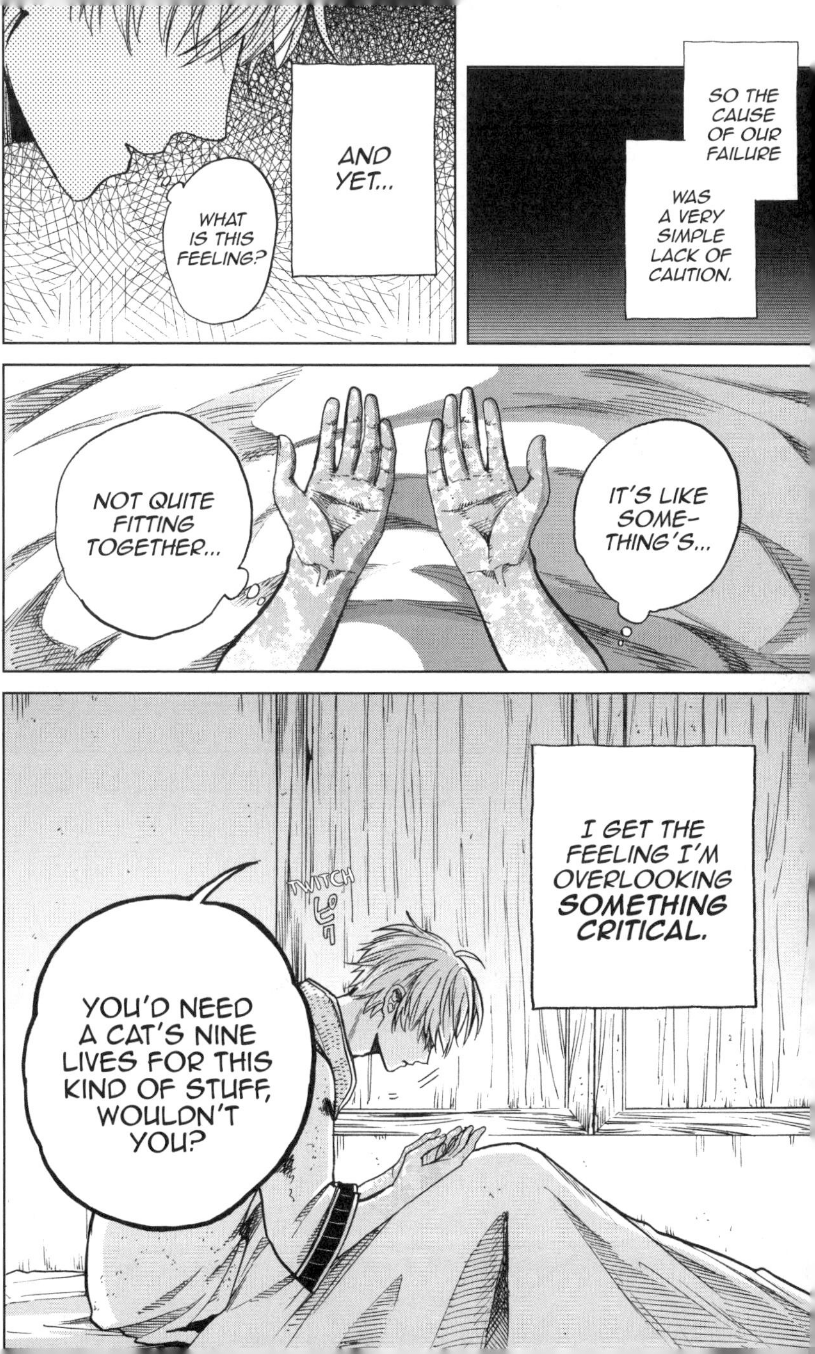
SO THE CAUSE OF OUR FAILURE
WAS A VERY SIMPLE LACK OF CAUTION.
AND YET...
WHAT IS THIS FEELING?
IT'S LIKE SOME-THING'S...
NOT QUITE FITTING TOGETHER...
I GET THE FEELING I'M OVERLOOKING SOMETHING CRITICAL.
TWITCH
YOU'D NEED A CAT'S NINE LIVES FOR THIS KIND OF STUFF, WOULDN'T YOU?

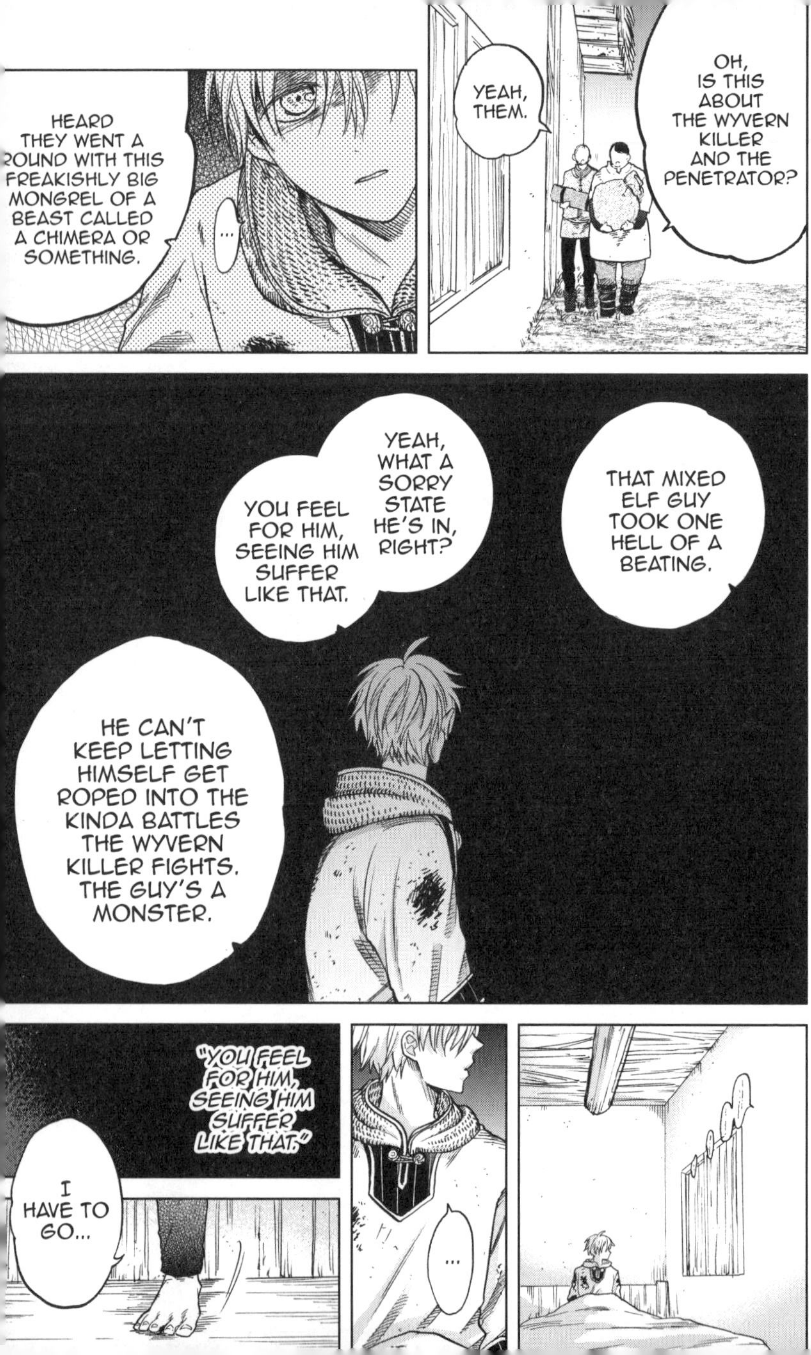
OH, IS THIS ABOUT THE WYVERN KILLER AND THE PENETRATOR?
YEAH, THEM.
HEARD THEY WENT A ROUND WITH THIS FREAKISHLY BIG MONGREL OF A BEAST CALLED A CHIMERA OR SOMETHING.
...
THAT MIXED ELF GUY TOOK ONE HELL OF A BEATING.
YEAH, WHAT A SORRY STATE HE'S IN, RIGHT?
YOU FEEL FOR HIM, SEEING HIM SUFFER LIKE THAT.
HE CAN'T KEEP LETTING HIMSELF GET ROPED INTO THE KINDA BATTLES THE WYVERN KILLER FIGHTS. THE GUY'S A MONSTER.
...
"YOU FEEL FOR HIM, SEEING HIM SUFFER LIKE THAT."
I HAVE TO GO...

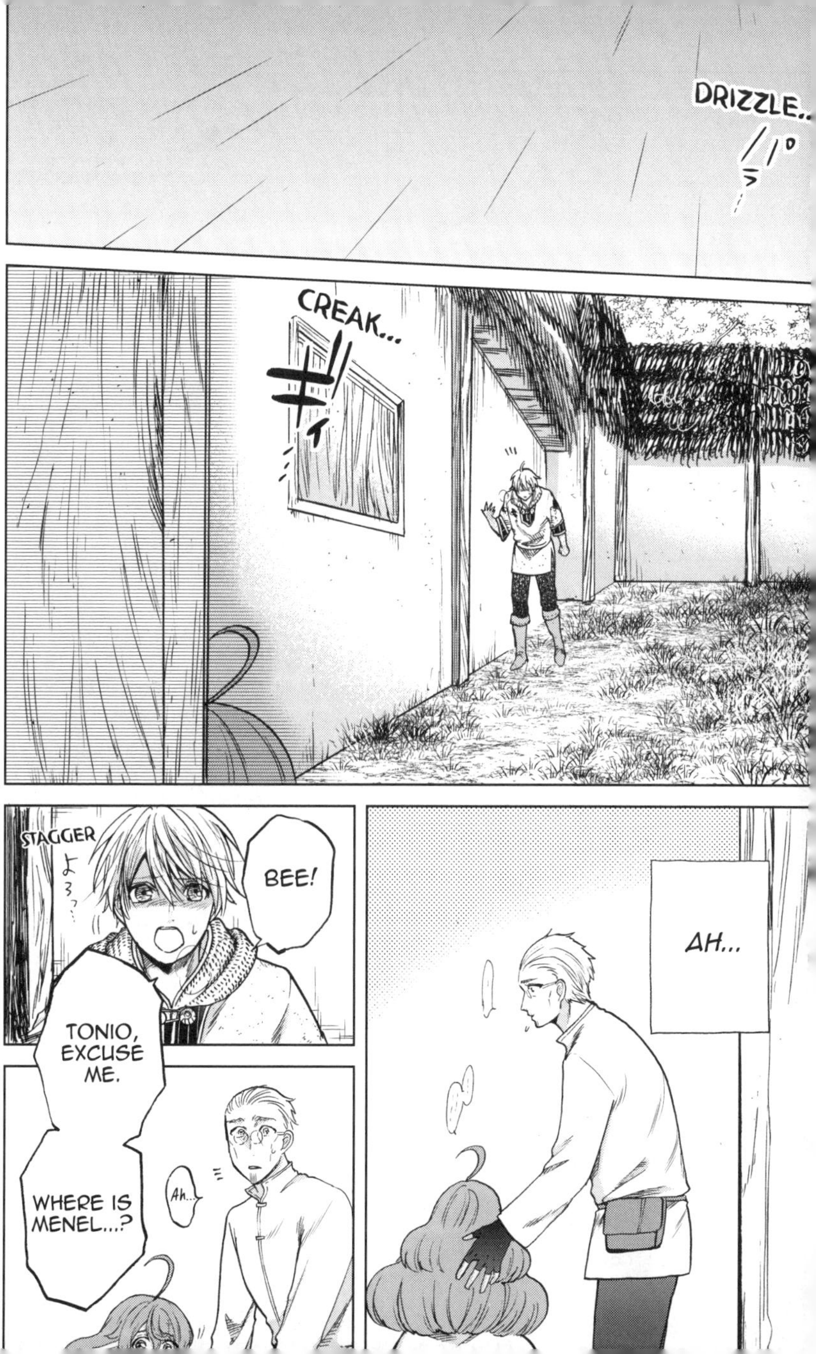

DRIZZLE...
パラ
CREAK...
ギィ
AH...
STAGGER
よろっ
BEE!
TONIO, EXCUSE ME.
WHERE IS MENEL...?
Ah...

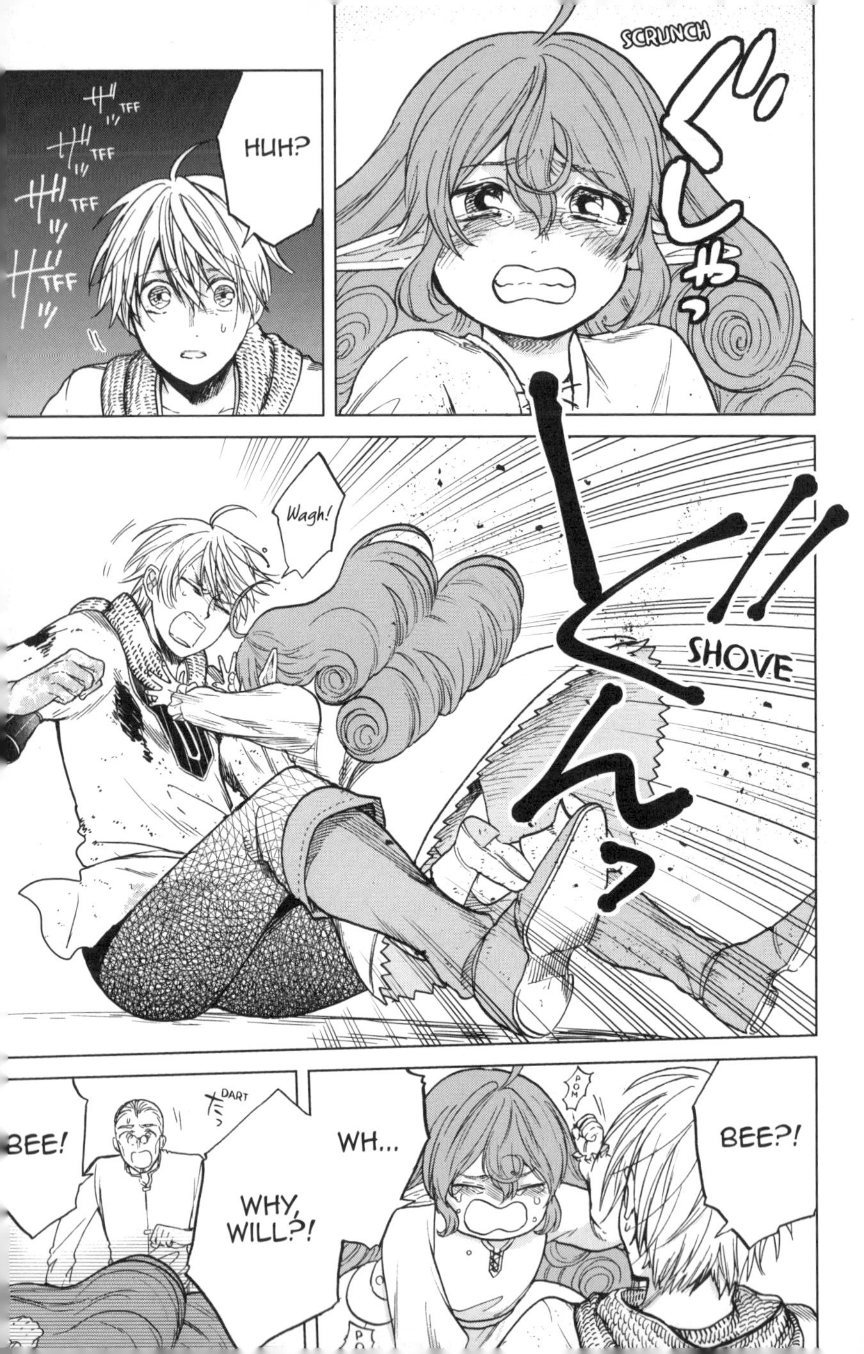
SCRUNCH
TFF
TFF
TFF
TFF
HUH?
SHOVE
Wagh!
BEE?!
POM
WH...
WHY, WILL?!
DART
BEE!

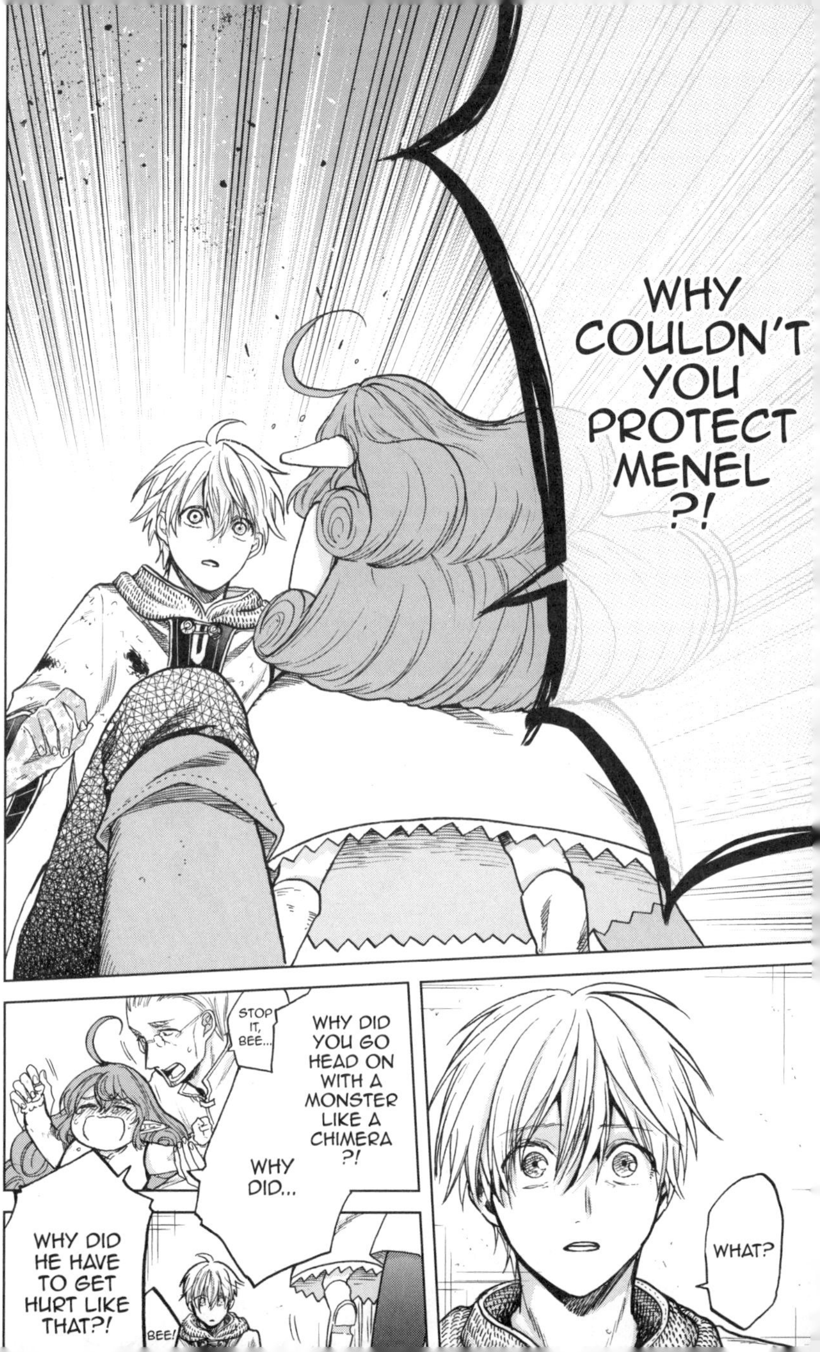
WHY COULDN'T YOU PROTECT MENEL?!
WHAT?
WHY DID YOU GO HEAD ON WITH A MONSTER LIKE A CHIMERA?!
STOP IT, BEE...
WHY DID...
WHY DID HE HAVE TO GET HURT LIKE THAT?!
BEE!

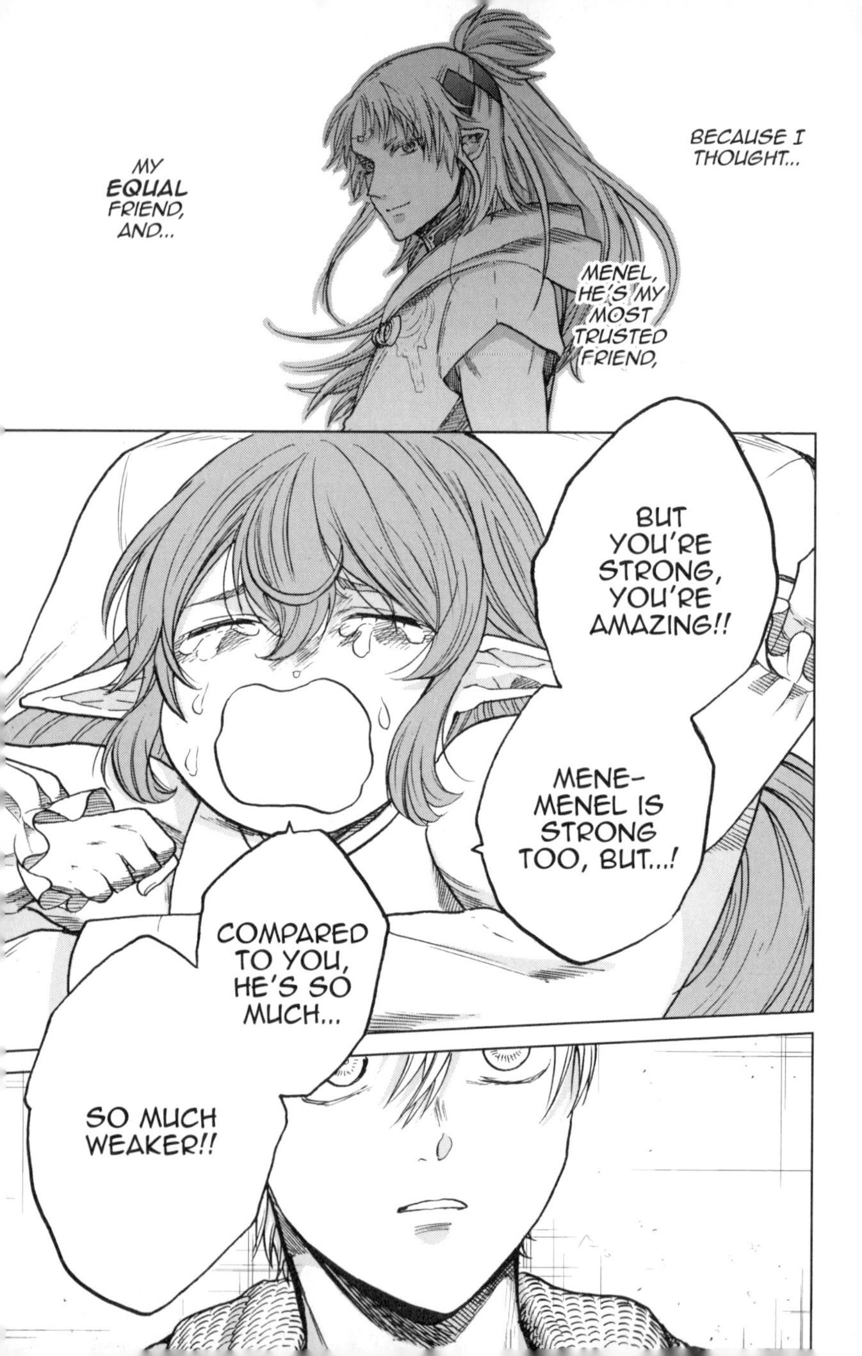
BECAUSE I THOUGHT...
MENEL, HE'S MY MOST TRUSTED FRIEND,
MY **EQUAL** FRIEND, AND...
BUT YOU'RE STRONG, YOU'RE AMAZING!!
MENE-MENEL IS STRONG TOO, BUT...!
COMPARED TO YOU, HE'S SO MUCH...
SO MUCH WEAKER!!

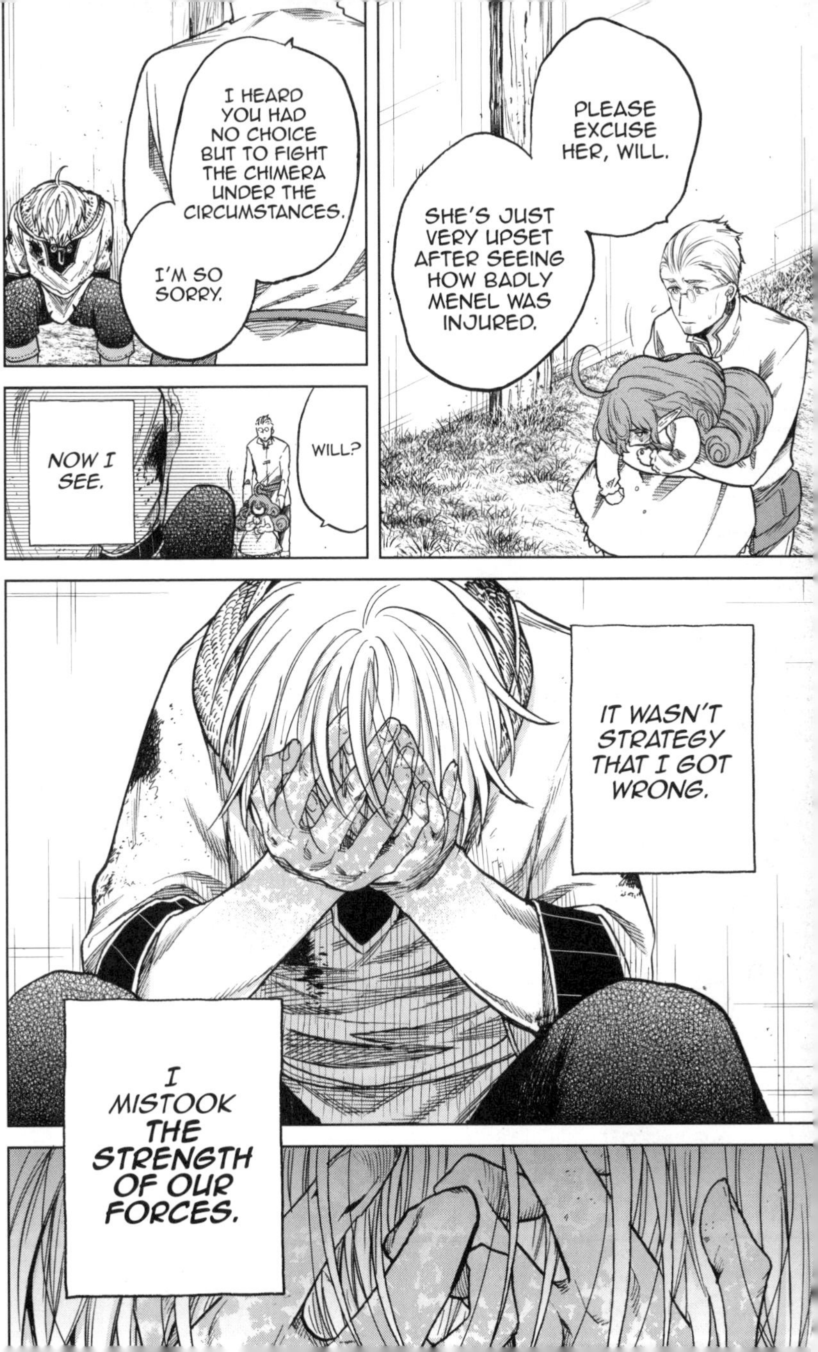
PLEASE EXCUSE HER, WILL.
SHE'S JUST VERY UPSET AFTER SEEING HOW BADLY MENEL WAS INJURED.
I HEARD YOU HAD NO CHOICE BUT TO FIGHT THE CHIMERA UNDER THE CIRCUMSTANCES.
I'M SO SORRY.
WILL?
NOW I SEE.
IT WASN'T STRATEGY THAT I GOT WRONG.
I MISTOOK THE STRENGTH OF OUR FORCES.

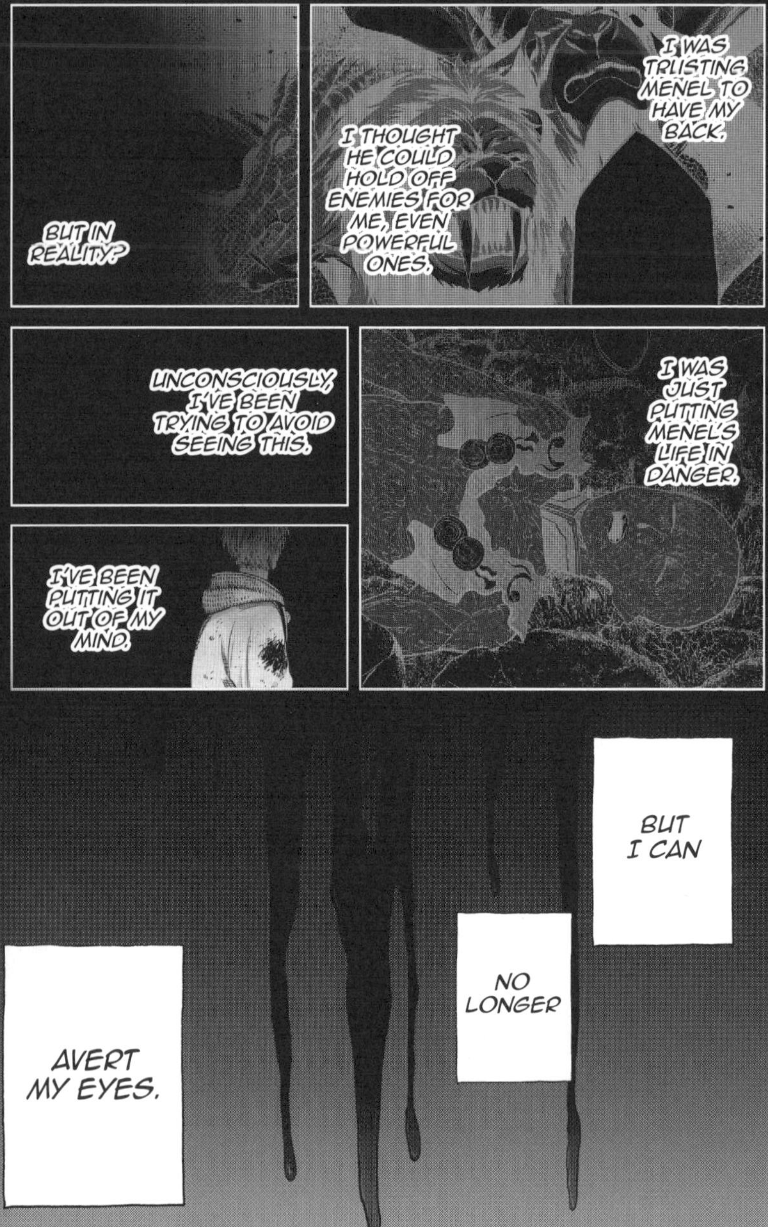
I WAS TRUSTING MENEL TO HAVE MY BACK.
I THOUGHT HE COULD HOLD OFF ENEMIES FOR ME, EVEN POWERFUL ONES.
BUT IN REALITY?
I WAS JUST PUTTING MENEL'S LIFE IN DANGER.
UNCONSCIOUSLY, I'VE BEEN TRYING TO AVOID SEEING THIS.
I'VE BEEN PUTTING IT OUT OF MY MIND.
BUT I CAN
NO LONGER
AVERT MY EYES.

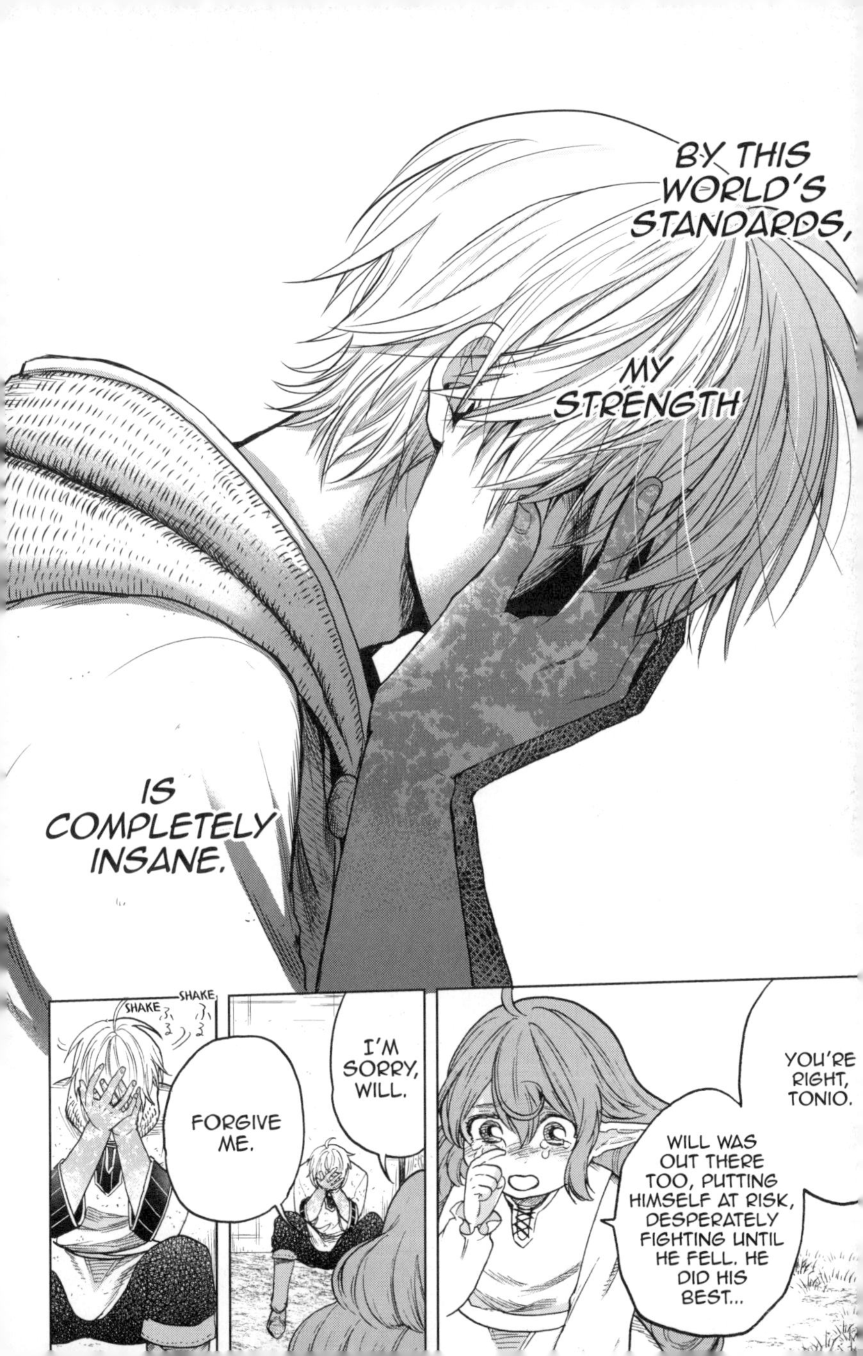
BY THIS WORLD'S STANDARDS,
MY STRENGTH
IS COMPLETELY INSANE.
YOU'RE RIGHT, TONIO.
WILL WAS OUT THERE TOO, PUTTING HIMSELF AT RISK, DESPERATELY FIGHTING UNTIL HE FELL. HE DID HIS BEST...
I'M SORRY, WILL.
SHAKE
SHAKE
FORGIVE ME.

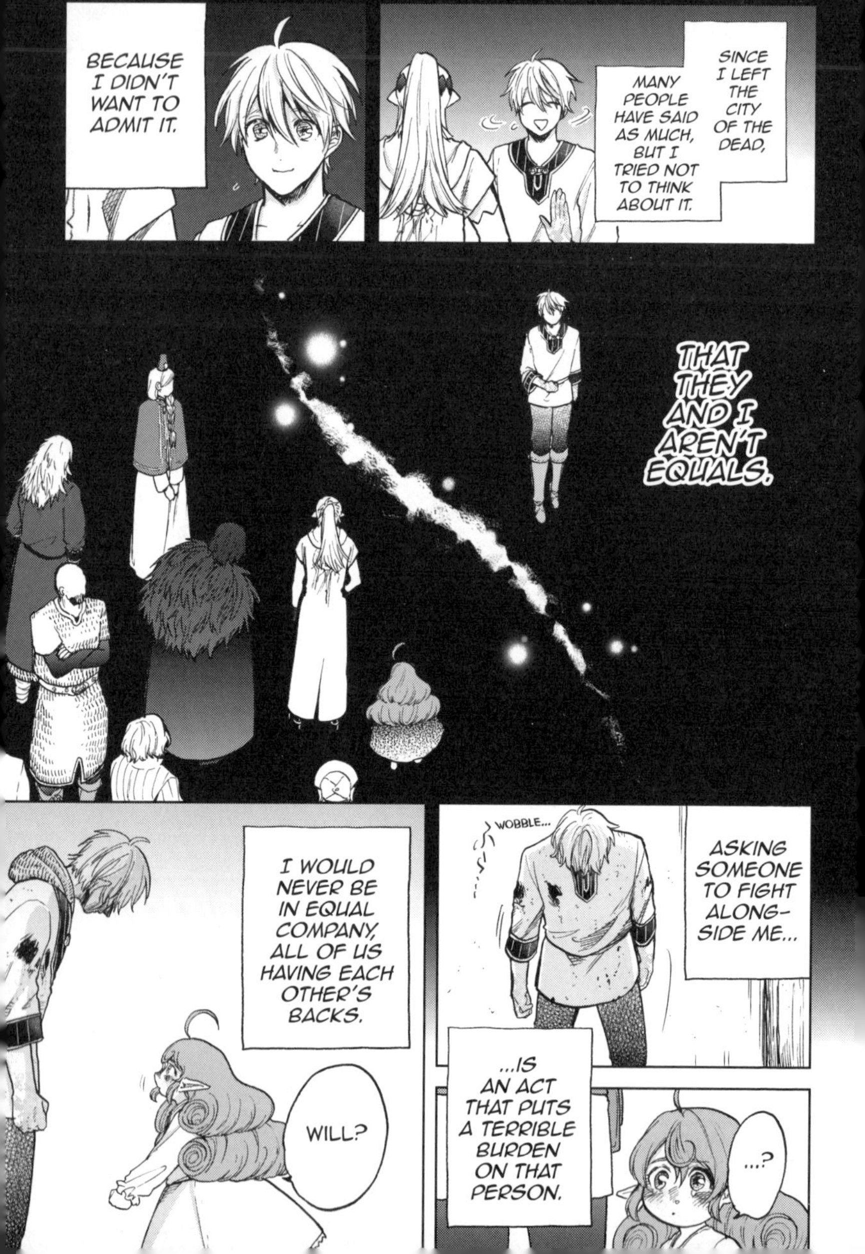
SINCE I LEFT THE CITY OF THE DEAD,
MANY PEOPLE HAVE SAID AS MUCH, BUT I TRIED NOT TO THINK ABOUT IT.
BECAUSE I DIDN'T WANT TO ADMIT IT.
THAT THEY AND I AREN'T EQUALS.
WOBBLE...
ASKING SOMEONE TO FIGHT ALONG-SIDE ME...
...IS AN ACT THAT PUTS A TERRIBLE BURDEN ON THAT PERSON.
...?
I WOULD NEVER BE IN EQUAL COMPANY, ALL OF US HAVING EACH OTHER'S BACKS.
WILL?

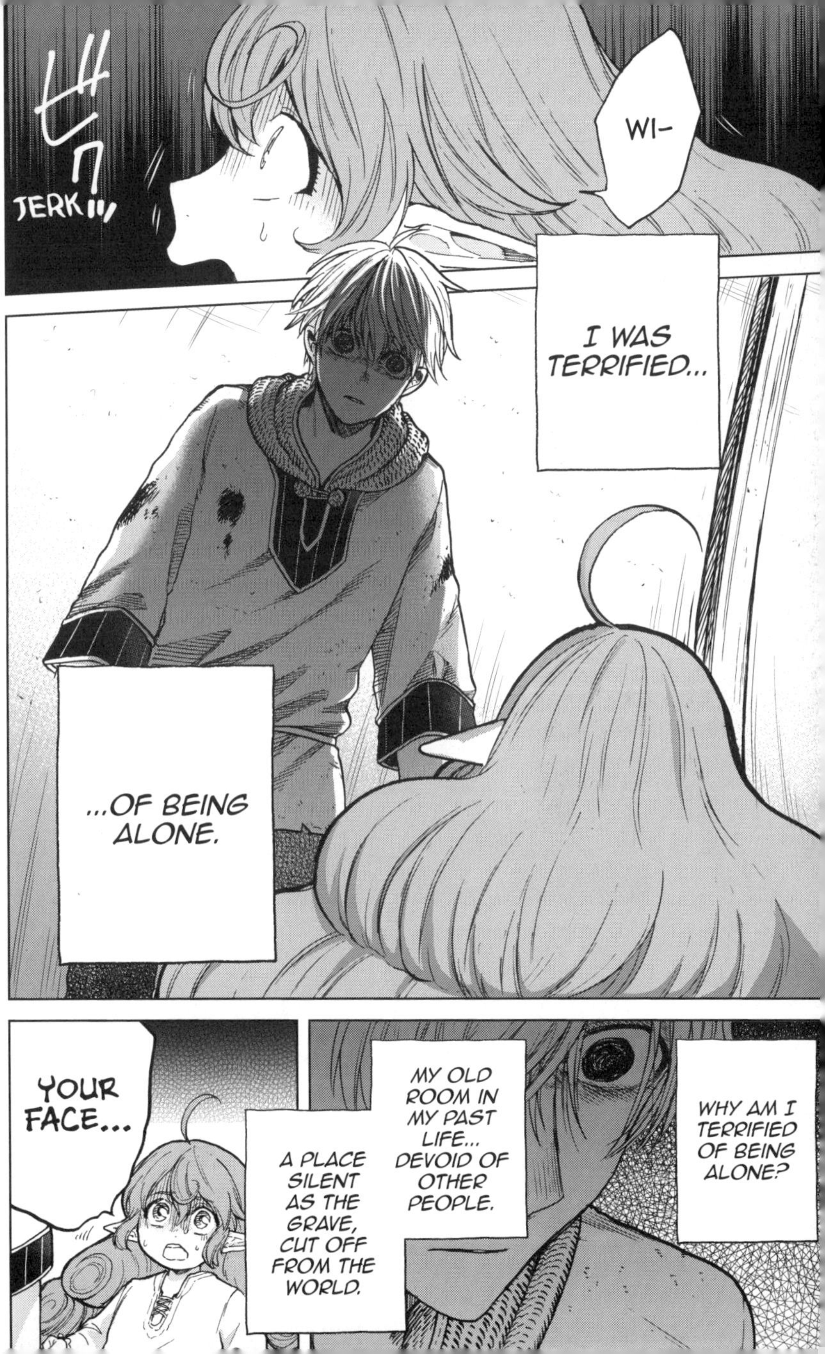
WI-
JERK
I WAS TERRIFIED...
...OF BEING ALONE.
WHY AM I TERRIFIED OF BEING ALONE?
MY OLD ROOM IN MY PAST LIFE... DEVOID OF OTHER PEOPLE.
A PLACE SILENT AS THE GRAVE, CUT OFF FROM THE WORLD.
YOUR FACE...

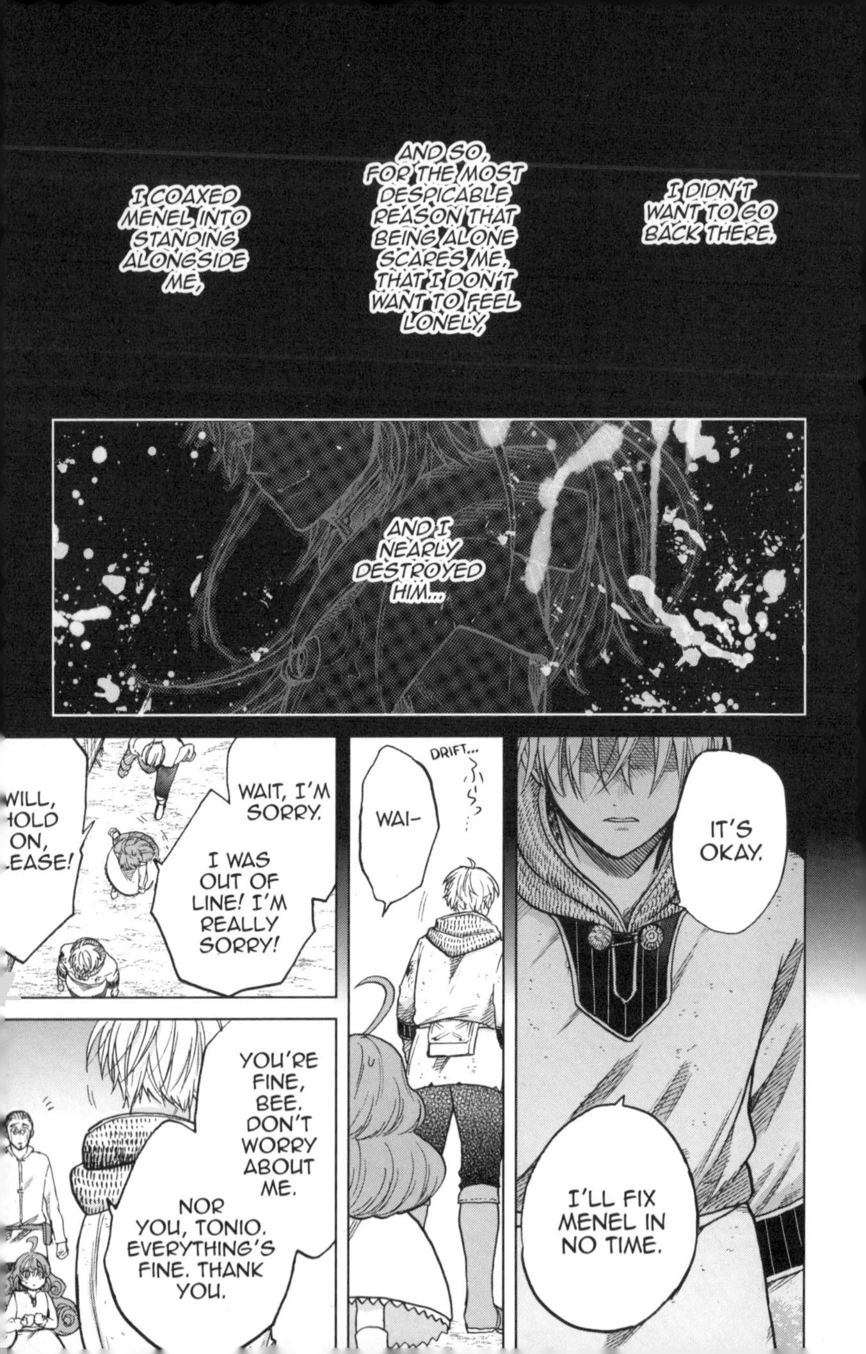
I DIDN'T WANT TO GO BACK THERE.
AND SO, FOR THE MOST DESPICABLE REASON THAT BEING ALONE SCARES ME, THAT I DON'T WANT TO FEEL LONELY,
I COAXED MENEL INTO STANDING ALONGSIDE ME,
AND I NEARLY DESTROYED HIM...
IT'S OKAY.
I'LL FIX MENEL IN NO TIME.
DRIFT...
WAI-
WAIT, I'M SORRY.
I WAS OUT OF LINE! I'M REALLY SORRY!
WILL, HOLD ON,
YOU'RE FINE, BEE. DON'T WORRY ABOUT ME.
NOR YOU, TONIO. EVERYTHING'S FINE. THANK YOU.

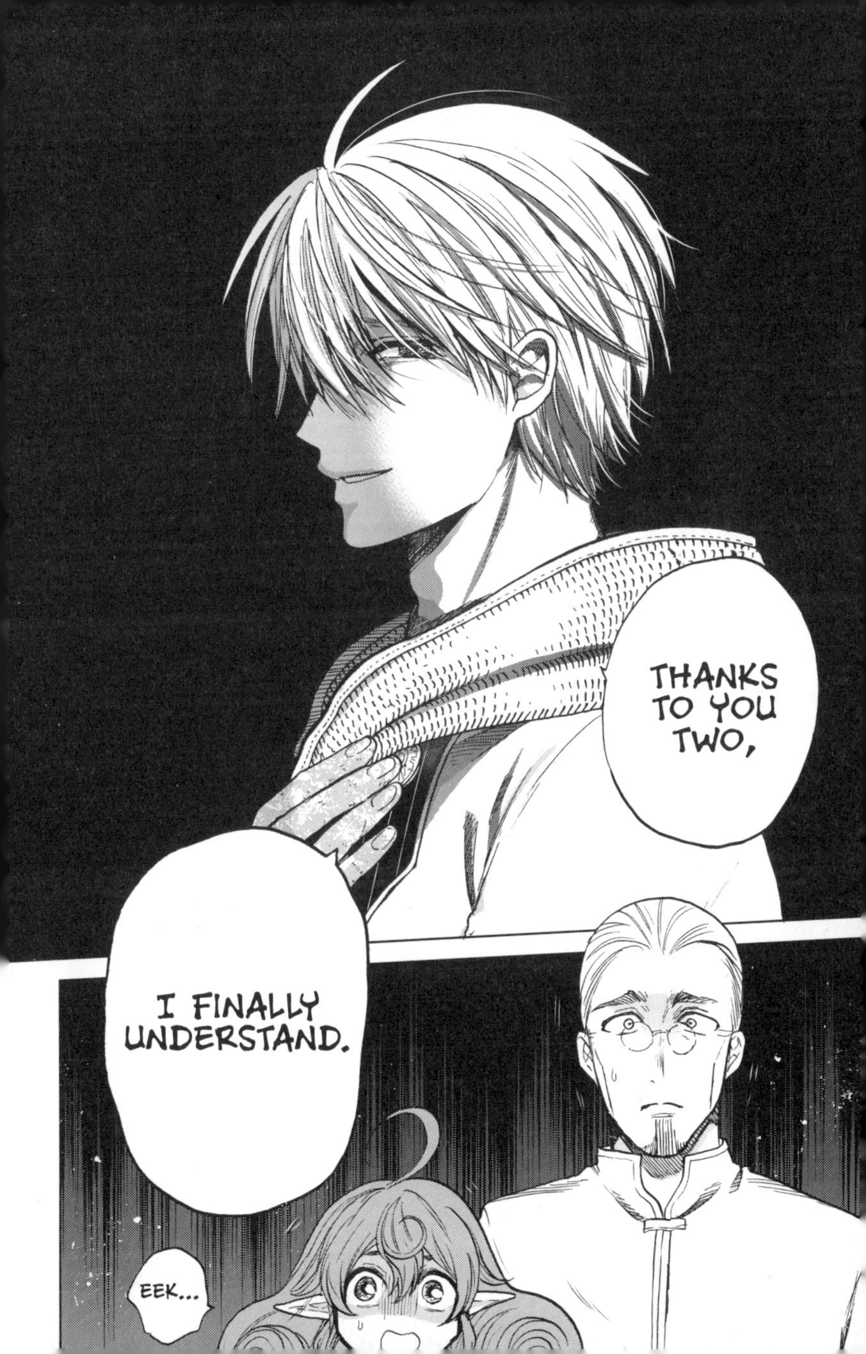
THANKS TO YOU TWO,
I FINALLY UNDERSTAND.
EEK...

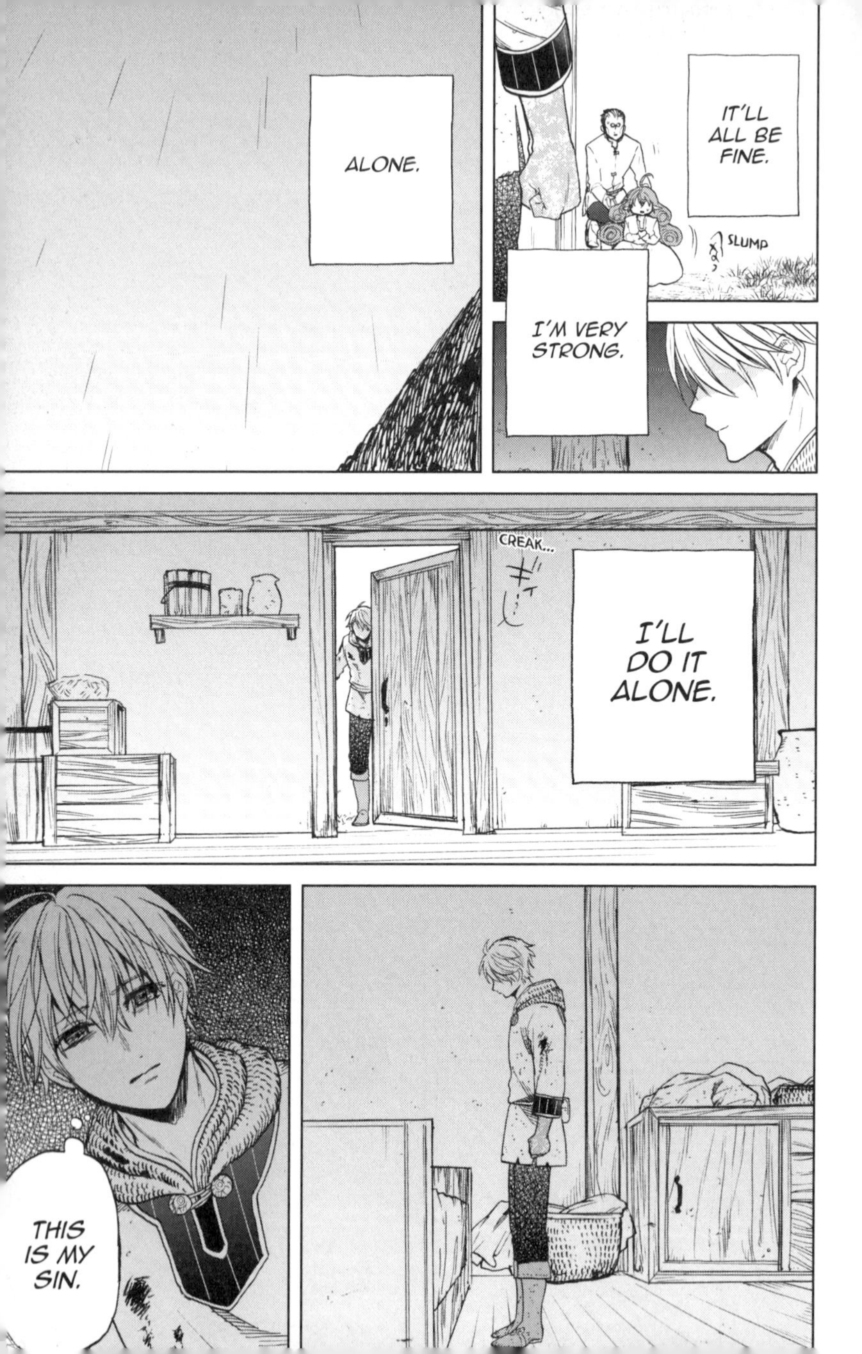
IT'LL ALL BE FINE.
SLUMP
I'M VERY STRONG.
ALONE.
I'LL DO IT ALONE.
CREAK...
THIS IS MY SIN.

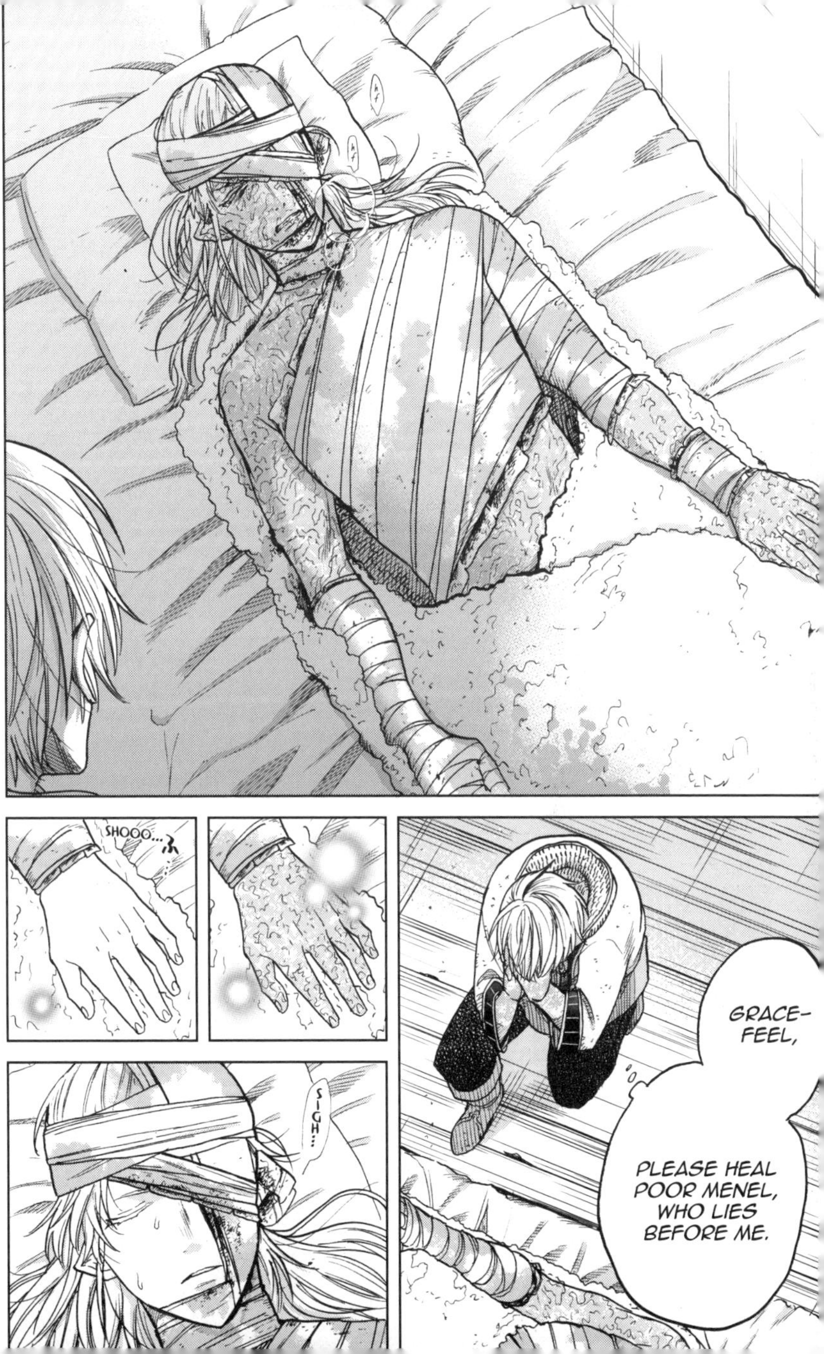
GRACE-
FEEL,
PLEASE HEAL
POOR MENEL,
WHO LIES
BEFORE ME.
SHOOO...ふ
SIGH...

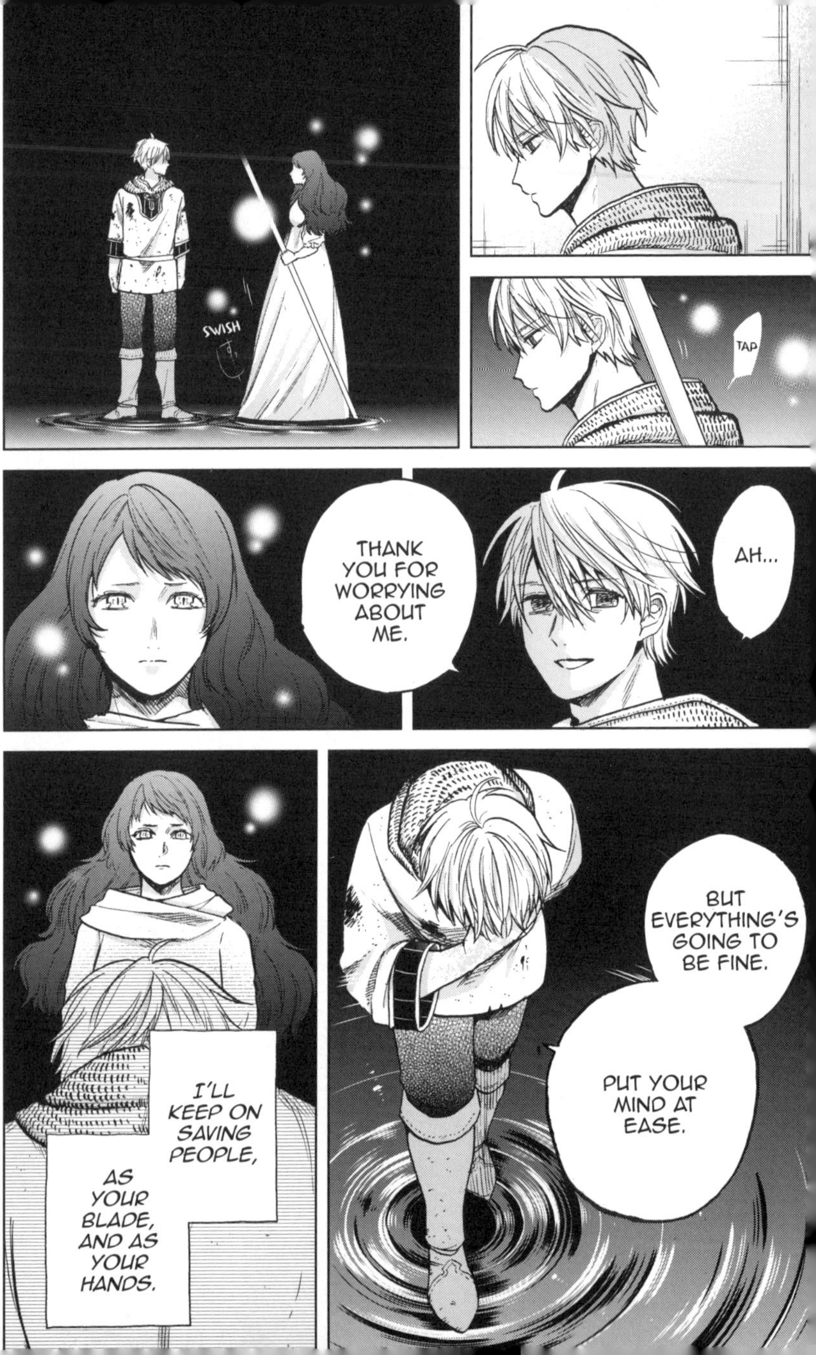
TAP
SWISH
AH...
THANK YOU FOR WORRYING ABOUT ME.
BUT EVERYTHING'S GOING TO BE FINE.
PUT YOUR MIND AT EASE.
I'LL KEEP ON SAVING PEOPLE,
AS YOUR BLADE, AND AS YOUR HANDS.

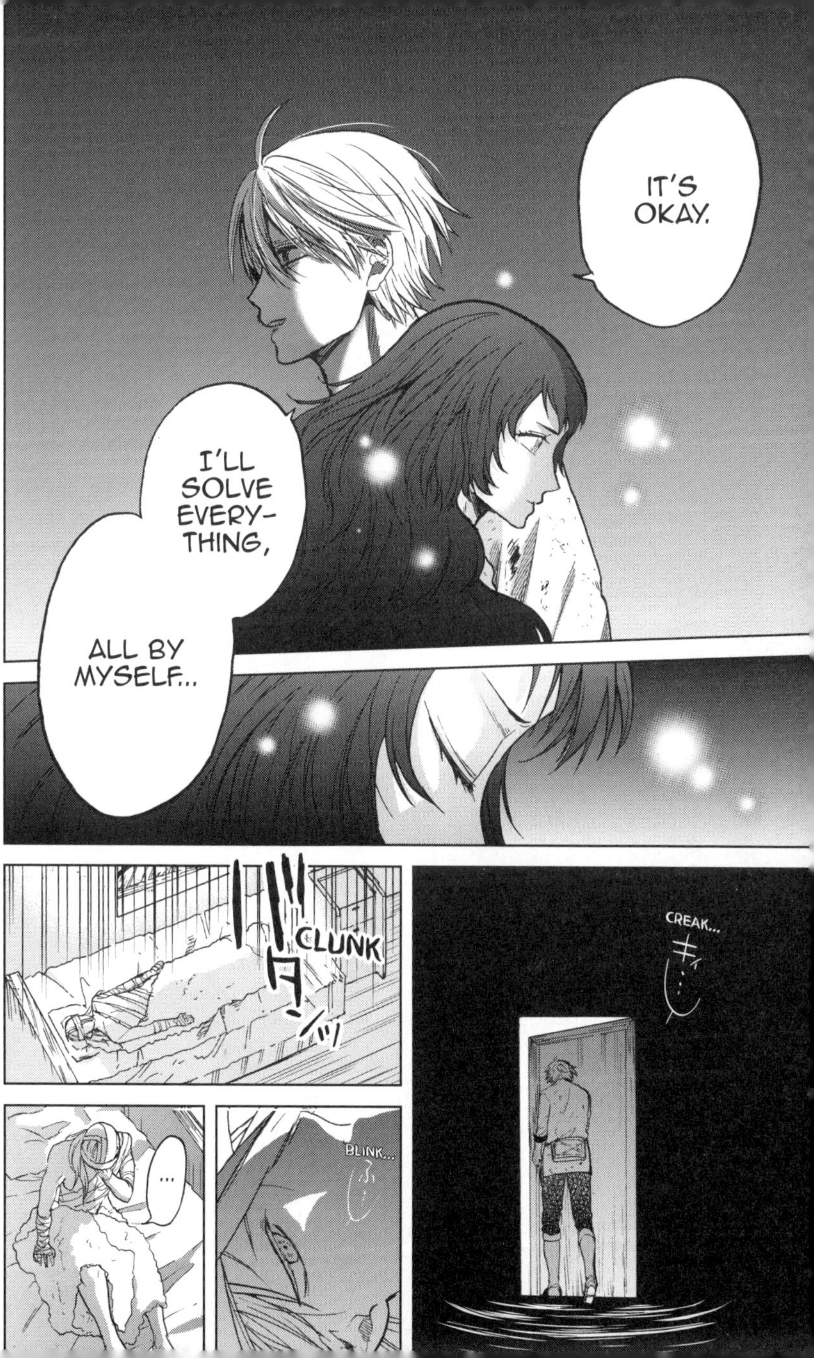
IT'S OKAY.
I'LL SOLVE EVERY-THING,
ALL BY MYSELF...
CREAK...
CLUNK
BLINK...
...

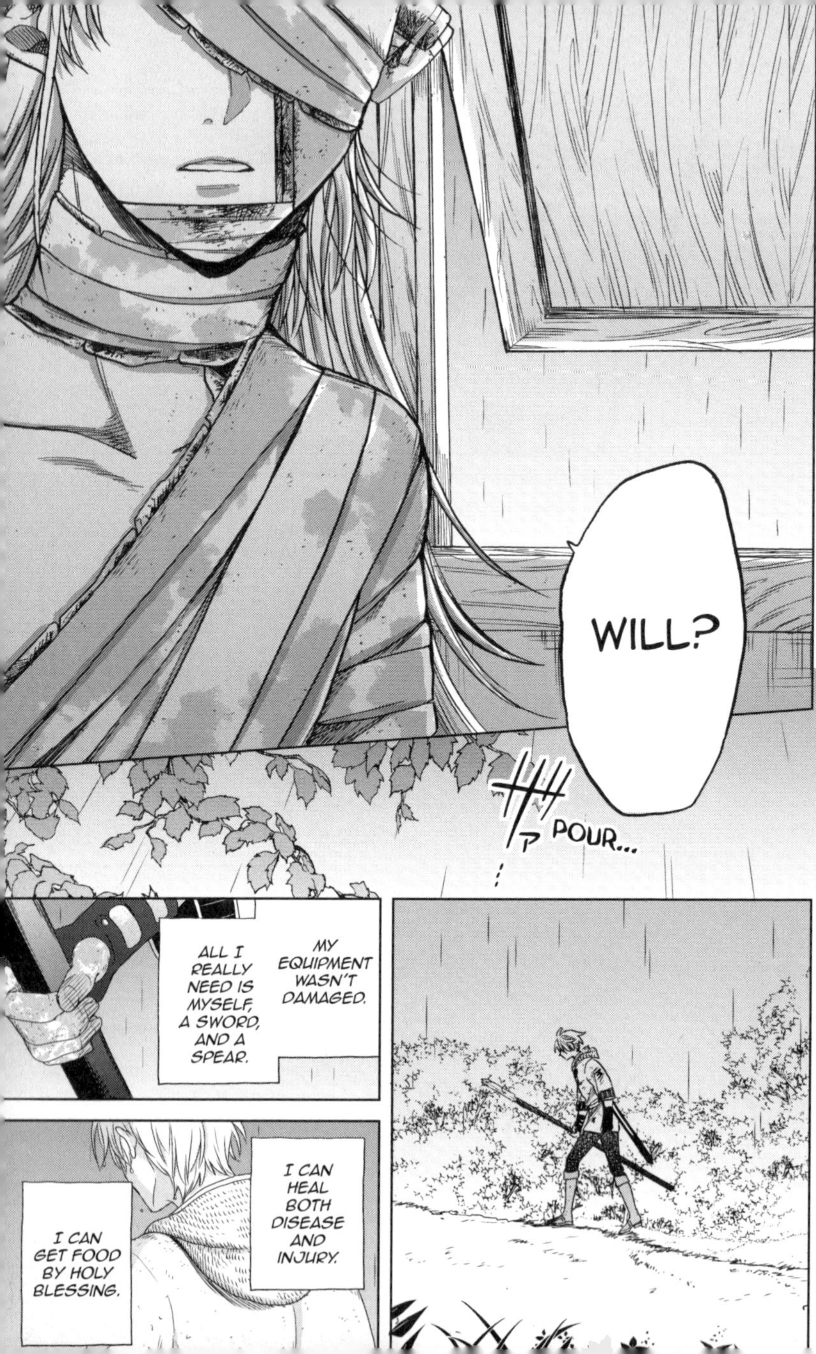
WILL?
POUR...
MY EQUIPMENT WASN'T DAMAGED.
ALL I REALLY NEED IS MYSELF, A SWORD, AND A SPEAR.
I CAN HEAL BOTH DISEASE AND INJURY.
I CAN GET FOOD BY HOLY BLESSING.

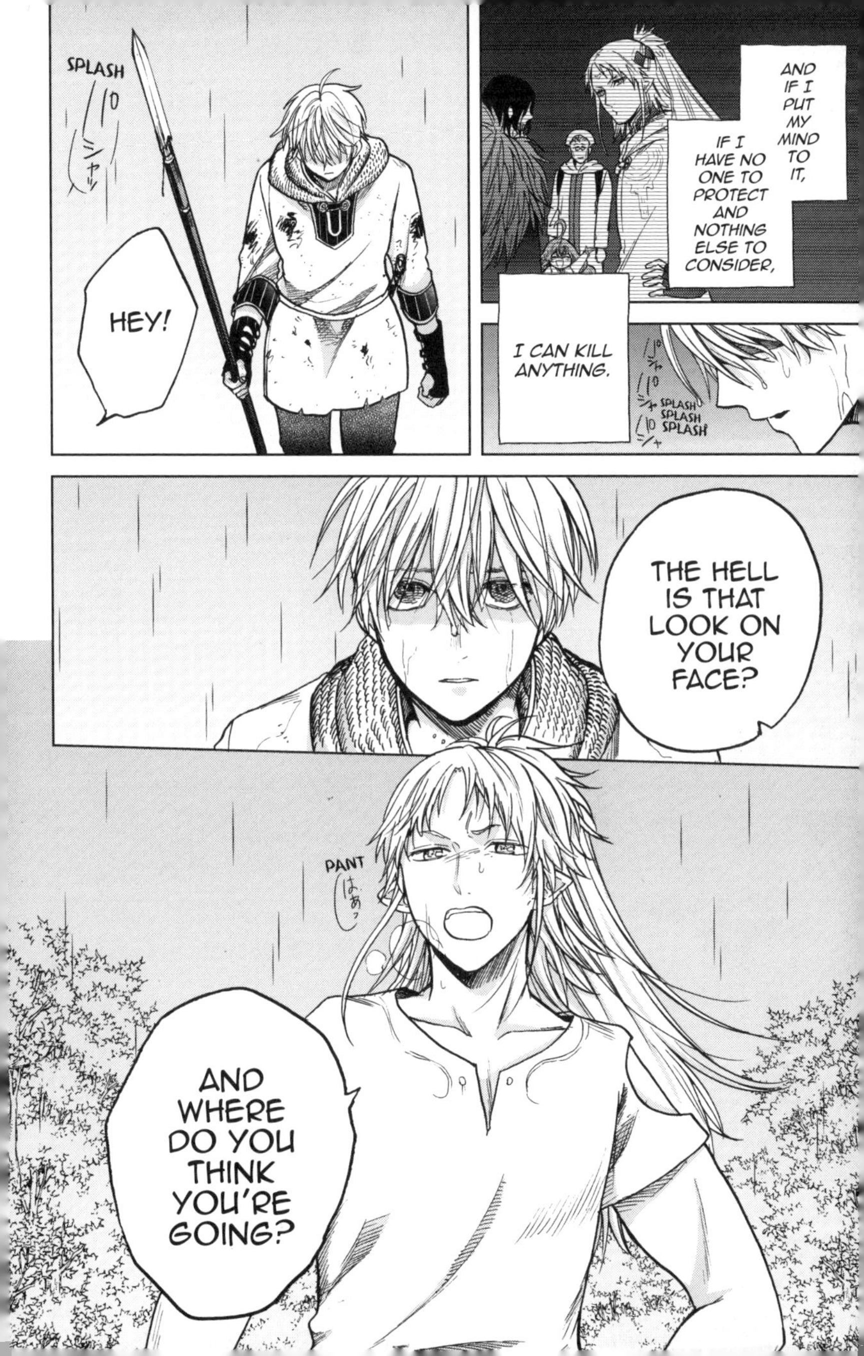
IF I HAVE NO ONE TO PROTECT AND NOTHING ELSE TO CONSIDER,
AND IF I PUT MY MIND TO IT,
I CAN KILL ANYTHING.
SPLASH SPLASH SPLASH
パシャ パシャ パシャ
SPLASH
パシャッ
HEY!
THE HELL IS THAT LOOK ON YOUR FACE?
PANT
はあっ
AND WHERE DO YOU THINK YOU'RE GOING?

Chapter 25 ✦ Friends

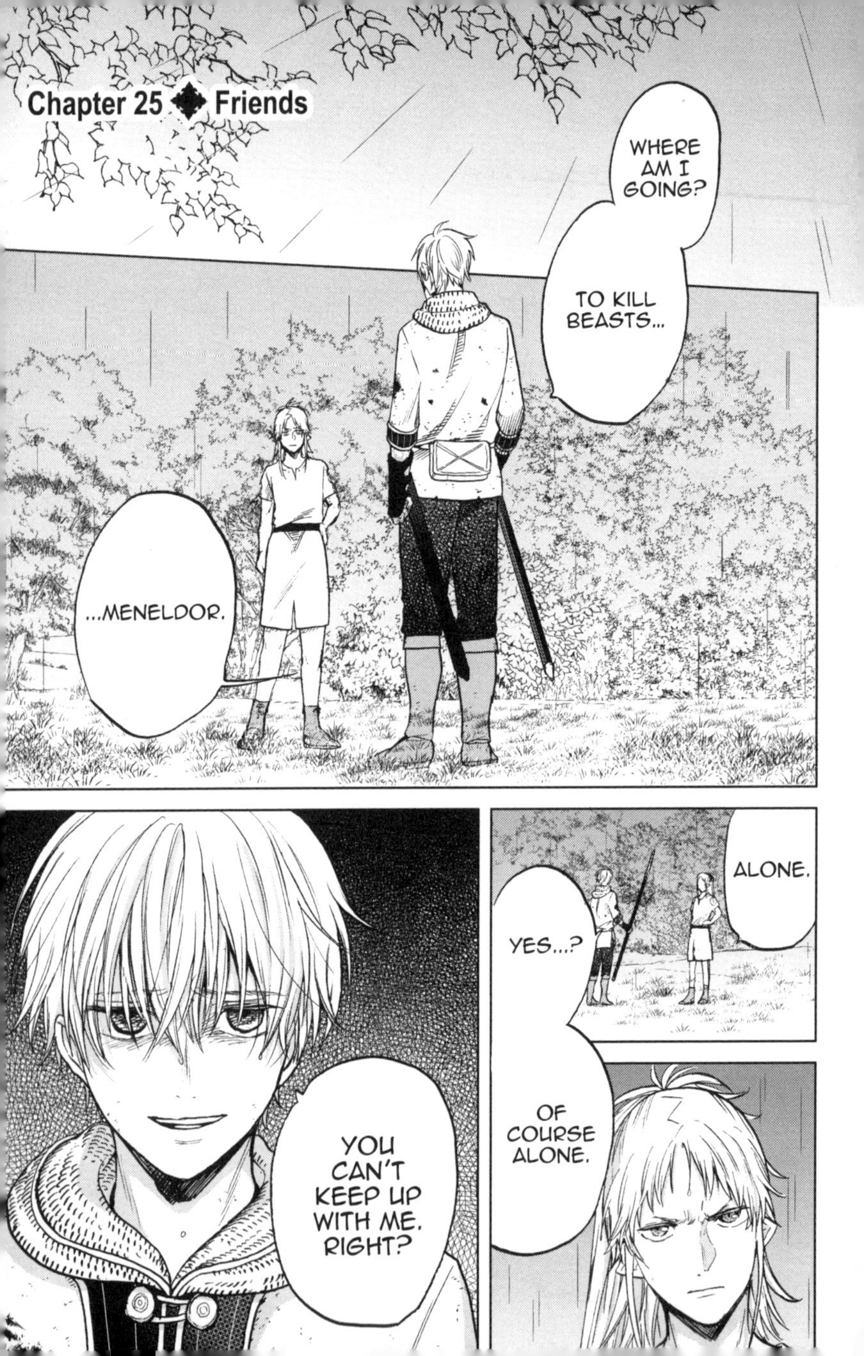
WHERE AM I GOING?
TO KILL BEASTS...
...MENELDOR.
ALONE.
YES...?
OF COURSE ALONE.
YOU CAN'T KEEP UP WITH ME. RIGHT?

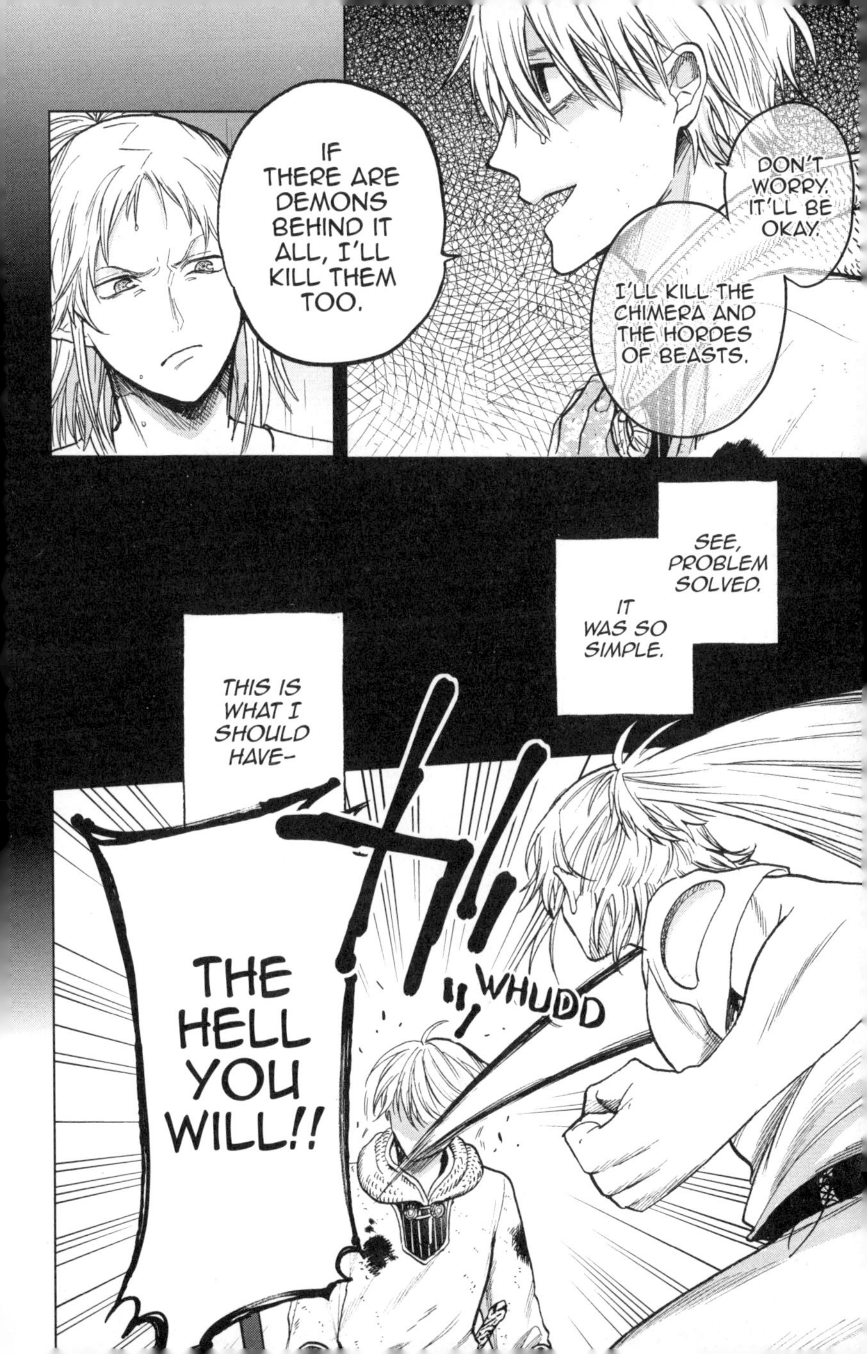
DON'T WORRY. IT'LL BE OKAY.
I'LL KILL THE CHIMERA AND THE HORDES OF BEASTS.
IF THERE ARE DEMONS BEHIND IT ALL, I'LL KILL THEM TOO.
SEE, PROBLEM SOLVED.
IT WAS SO SIMPLE.
THIS IS WHAT I SHOULD HAVE-
THE HELL YOU WILL!!
WHUDD

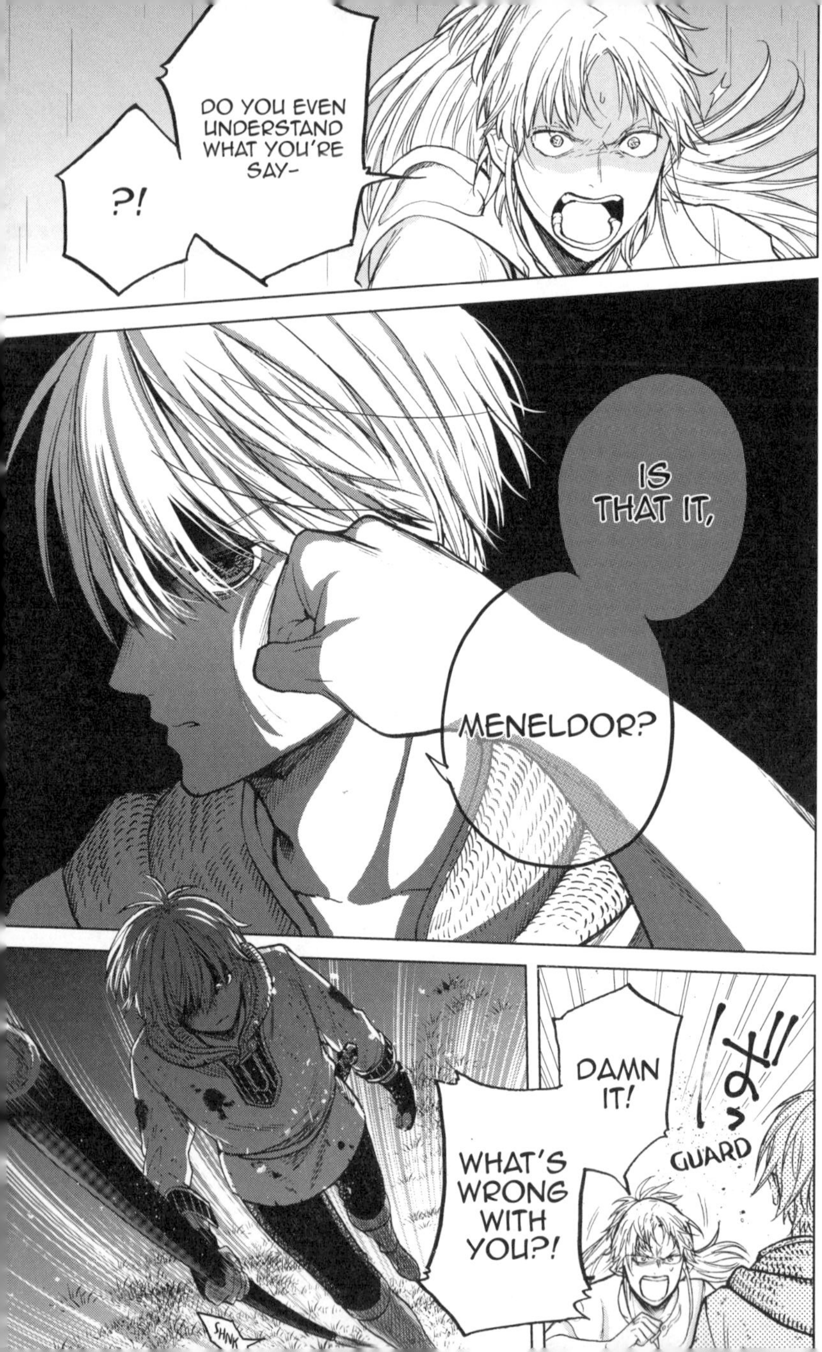
DO YOU EVEN UNDERSTAND WHAT YOU'RE SAY-
?!
IS THAT IT,
MENELDOR?
DAMN IT!
WHAT'S WRONG WITH YOU?!
GUARD
SHNK

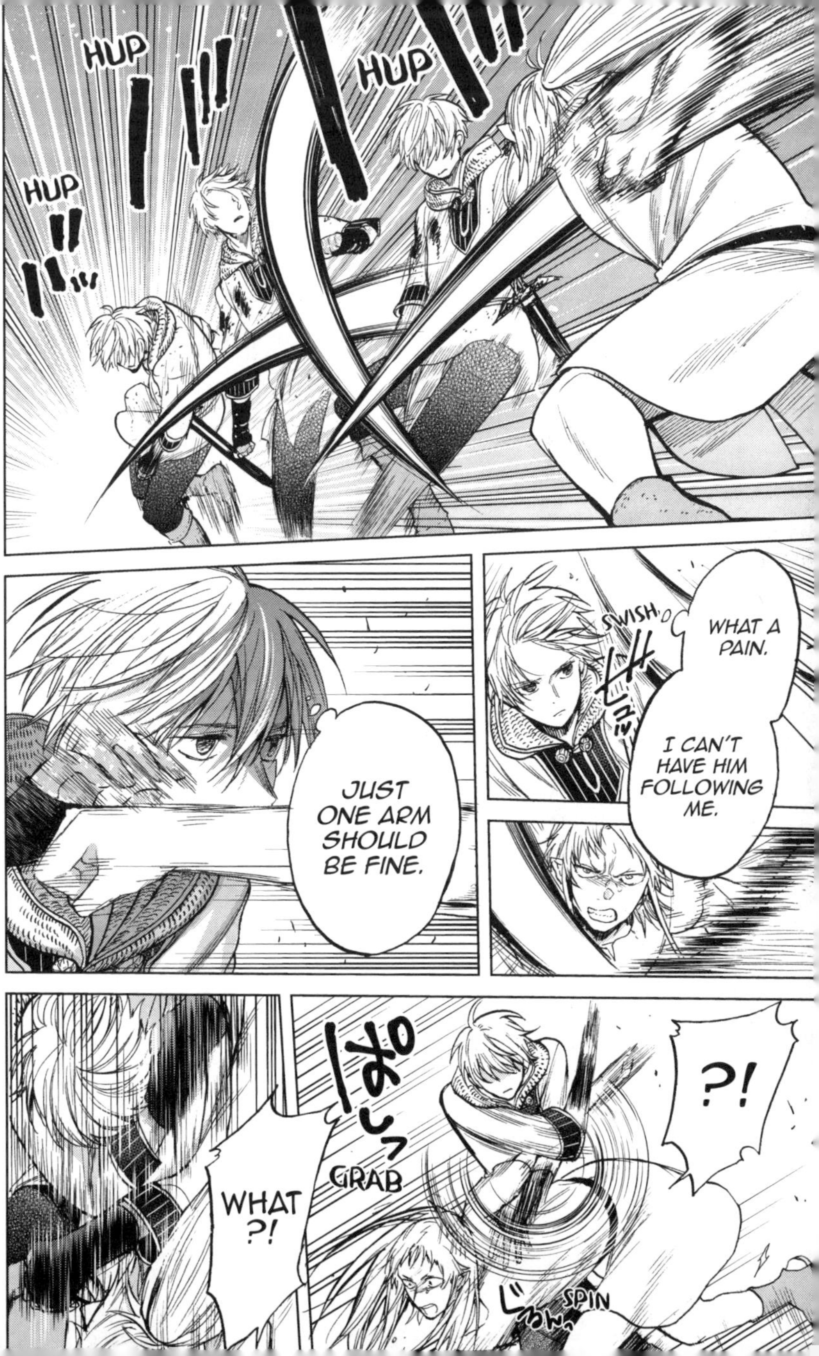
HUP
HUP
HUP
SWISH
WHAT A PAIN.
I CAN'T HAVE HIM FOLLOWING ME.
JUST ONE ARM SHOULD BE FINE.
?!
GRAB
WHAT ?!
SPIN

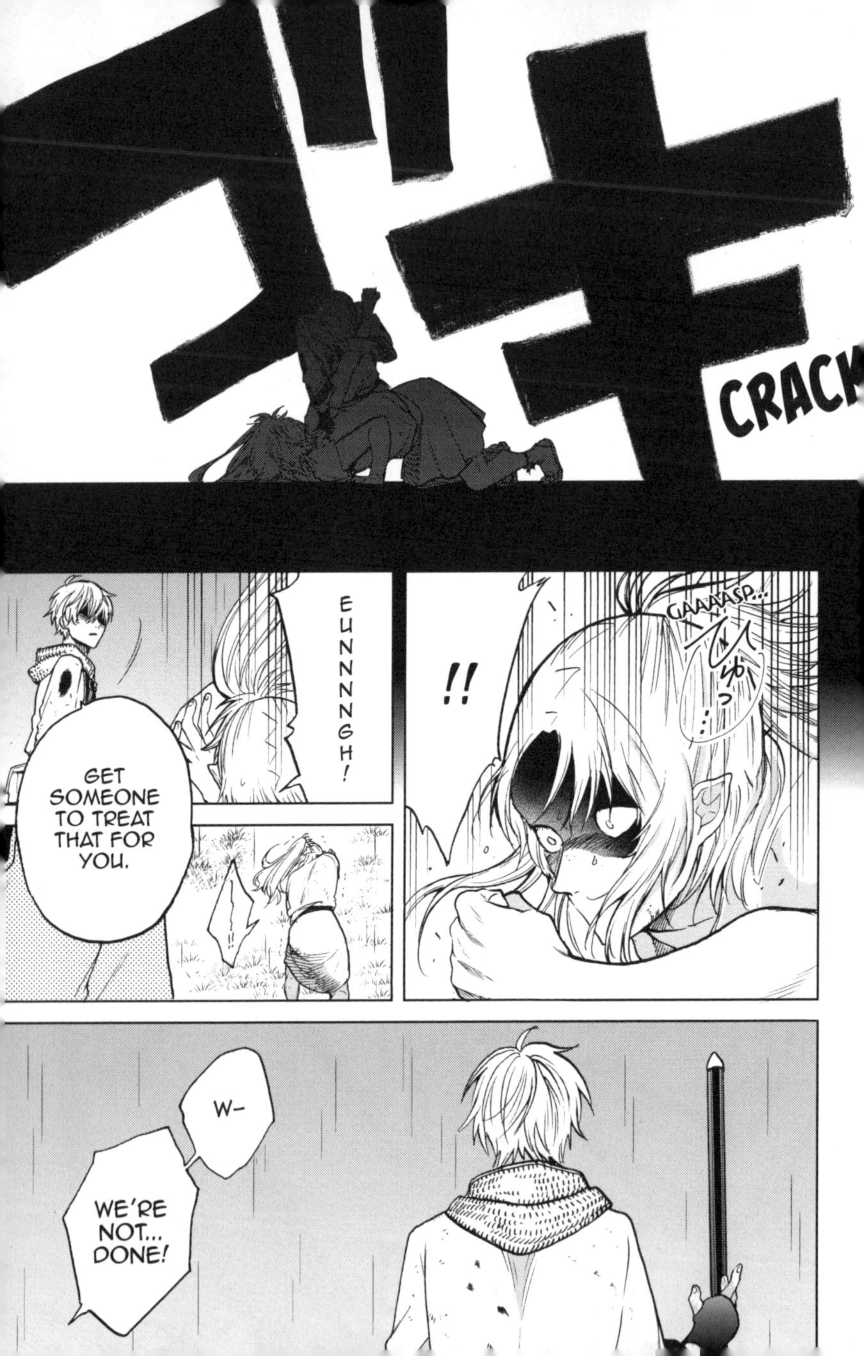
ゴキ
CRACK
GAAAASP...
!!
EUNNNNGH!
GET SOMEONE TO TREAT THAT FOR YOU.
!!
W-
WE'RE NOT... DONE!

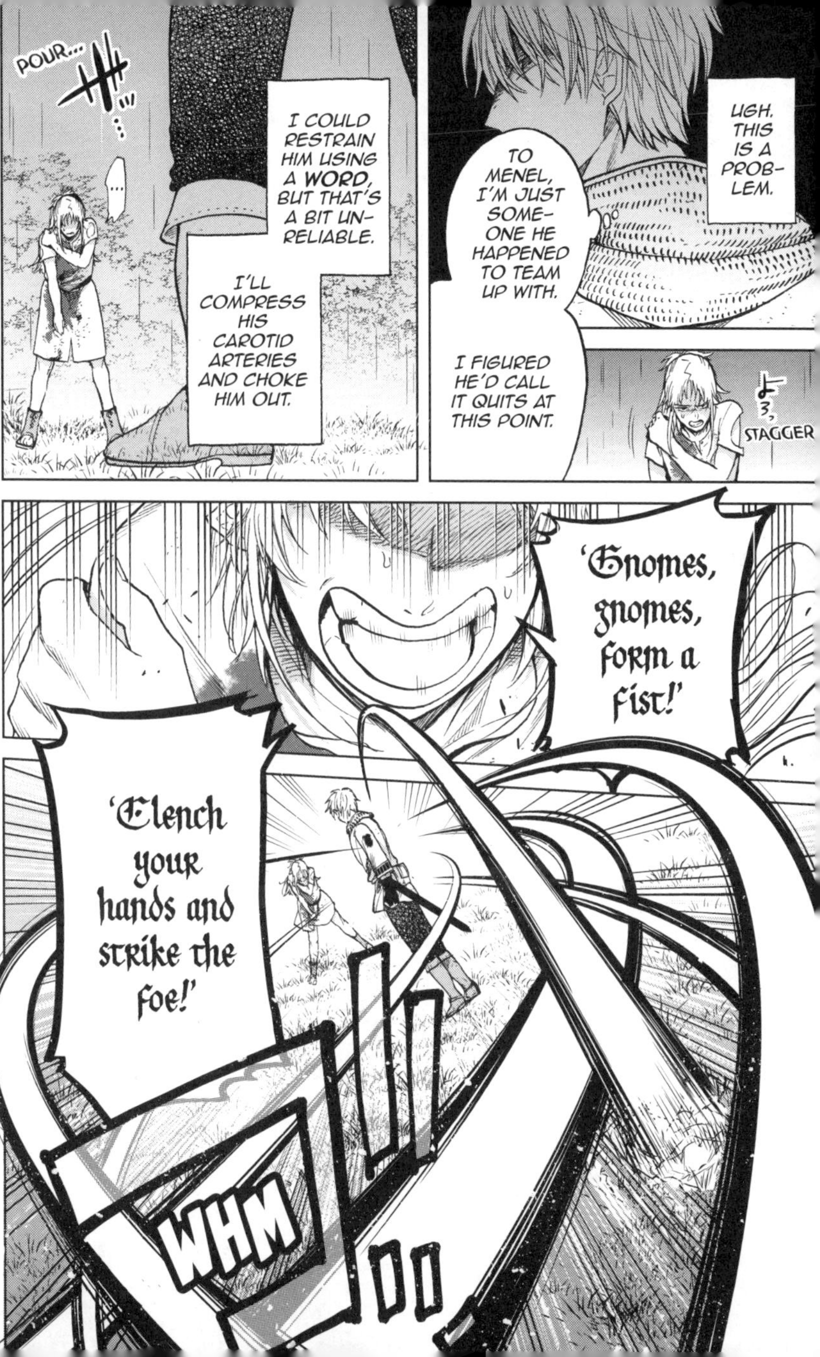

UGH. THIS IS A PROBLEM.
TO MENEL, I'M JUST SOMEONE HE HAPPENED TO TEAM UP WITH.
I FIGURED HE'D CALL IT QUITS AT THIS POINT.
よろ
STAGGER
POUR...
...
I COULD RESTRAIN HIM USING A **WORD**, BUT THAT'S A BIT UNRELIABLE.
I'LL COMPRESS HIS CAROTID ARTERIES AND CHOKE HIM OUT.
'Gnomes, gnomes, form a fist!'
'Clench your hands and strike the foe!'
WHM

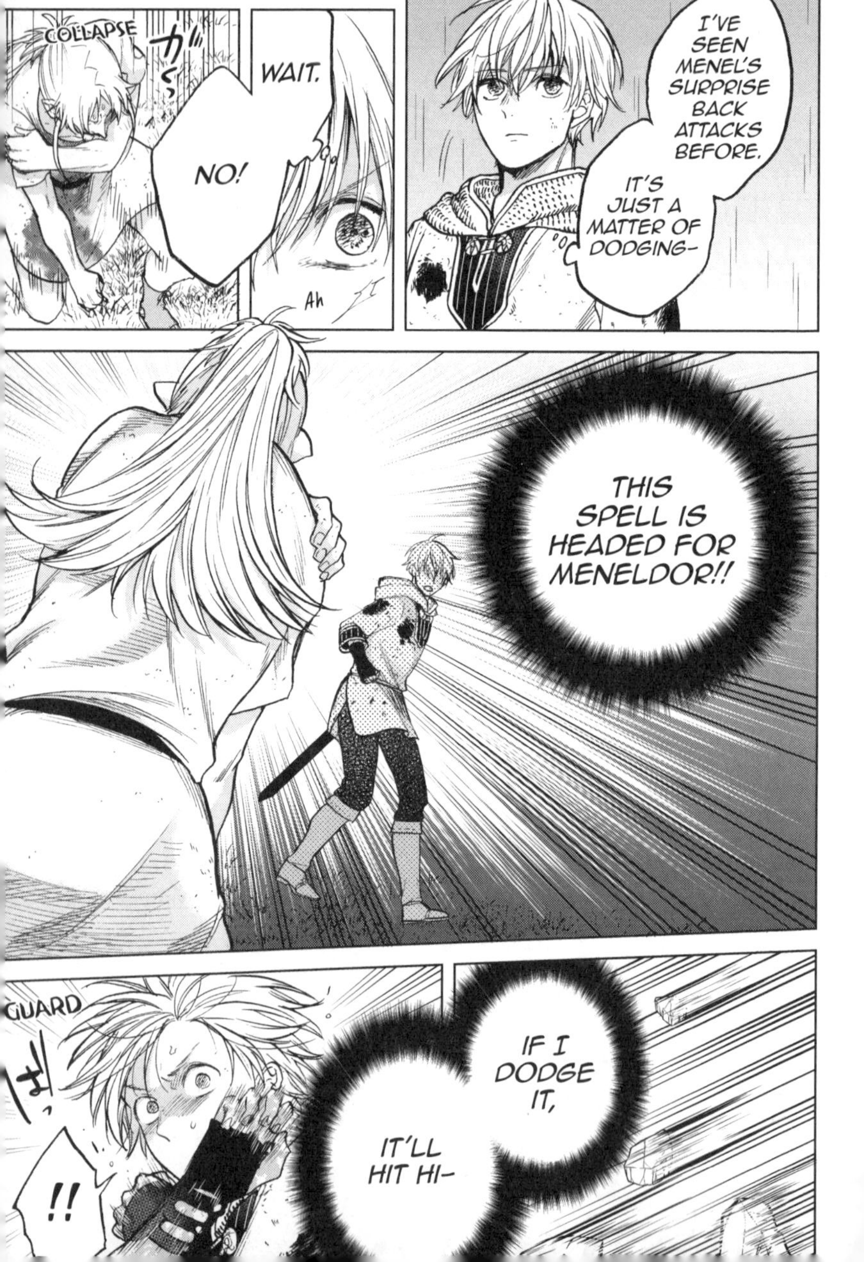
I'VE SEEN MENEL'S SURPRISE BACK ATTACKS BEFORE.
IT'S JUST A MATTER OF DODGING-
WAIT.
NO!
Ah
COLLAPSE
THIS SPELL IS HEADED FOR MENELDOR!!
IF I DODGE IT,
IT'LL HIT HI-
GUARD
!!

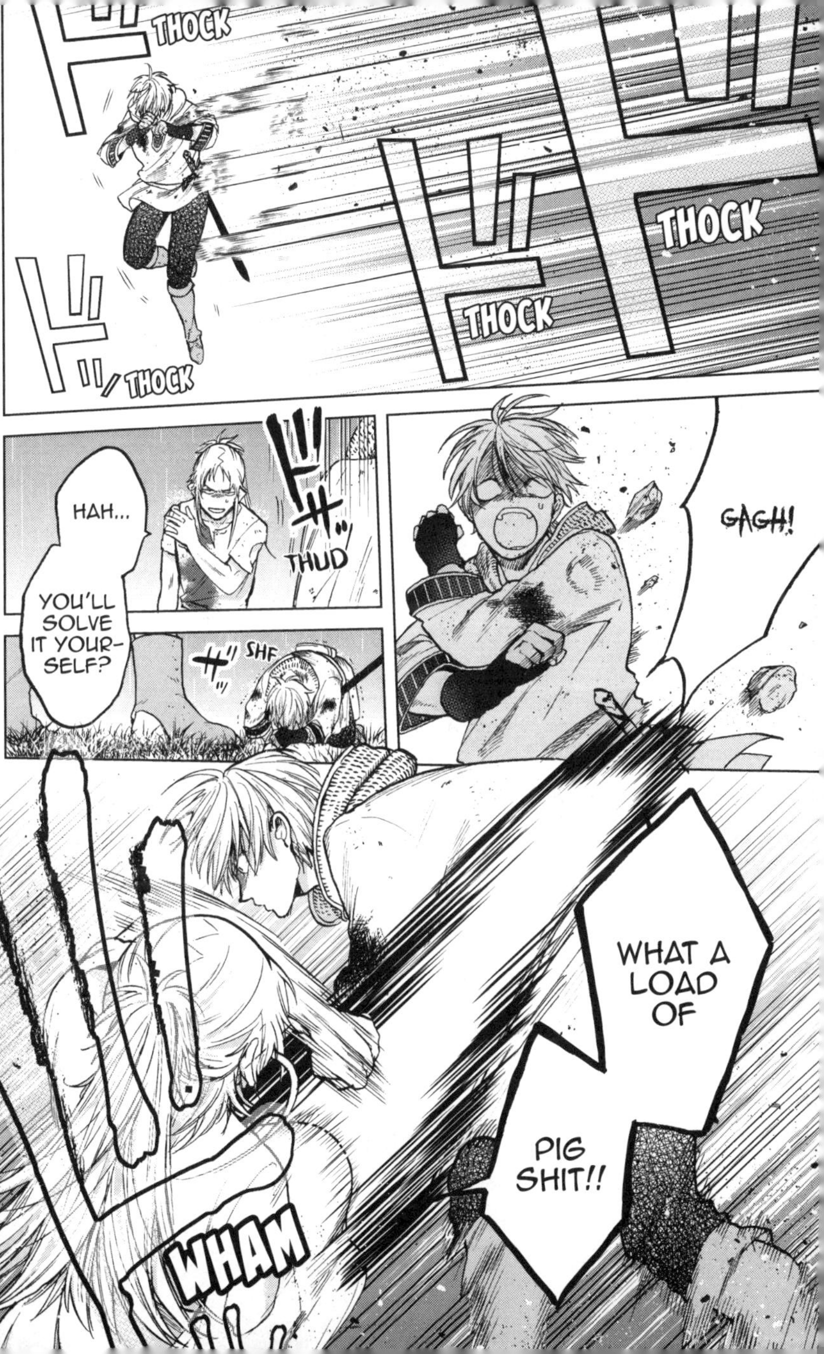
THOCK
THOCK
THOCK
THOCK
GAGH!
THUD
HAH...
YOU'LL SOLVE IT YOUR-SELF?
SHF
WHAT A LOAD OF PIG SHIT!!
WHAM

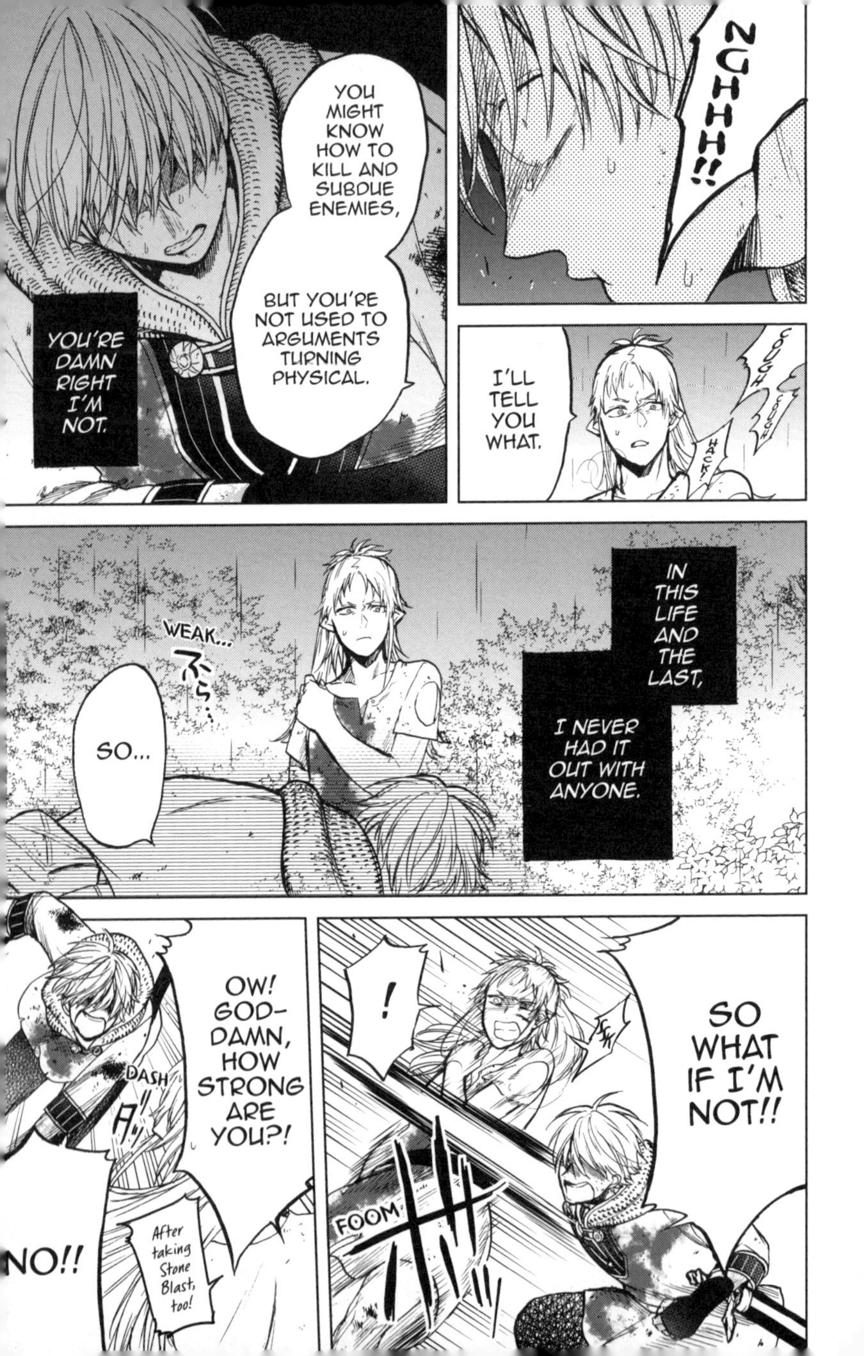
NGHHHH!!
COUGH
COUGH
HACK!
I'LL TELL YOU WHAT.
YOU MIGHT KNOW HOW TO KILL AND SUBDUE ENEMIES,
BUT YOU'RE NOT USED TO ARGUMENTS TURNING PHYSICAL.
YOU'RE DAMN RIGHT I'M NOT.
IN THIS LIFE AND THE LAST,
I NEVER HAD IT OUT WITH ANYONE.
WEAK...
ふら…
SO...
SO WHAT IF I'M NOT!!
!
FOOM
OW! GOD-DAMN, HOW STRONG ARE YOU?!
DASH
ダッ
After taking Stone Blast, too!
NO!!

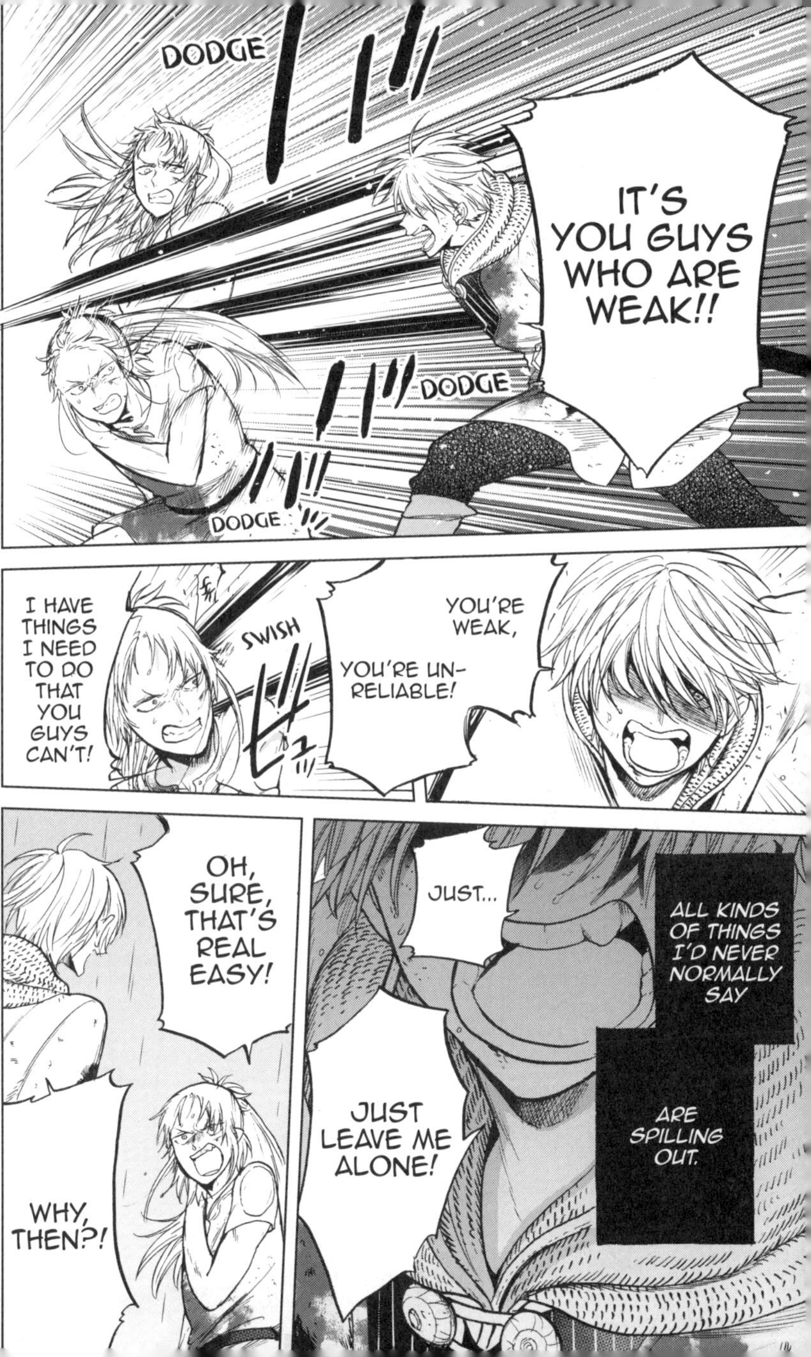
IT'S YOU GUYS WHO ARE WEAK!!
DODGE
DODGE
DODGE
YOU'RE WEAK,
YOU'RE UN-RELIABLE!
SWISH
I HAVE THINGS I NEED TO DO THAT YOU GUYS CAN'T!
ALL KINDS OF THINGS I'D NEVER NORMALLY SAY
JUST...
ARE SPILLING OUT.
JUST LEAVE ME ALONE!
OH, SURE, THAT'S REAL EASY!
WHY, THEN?!

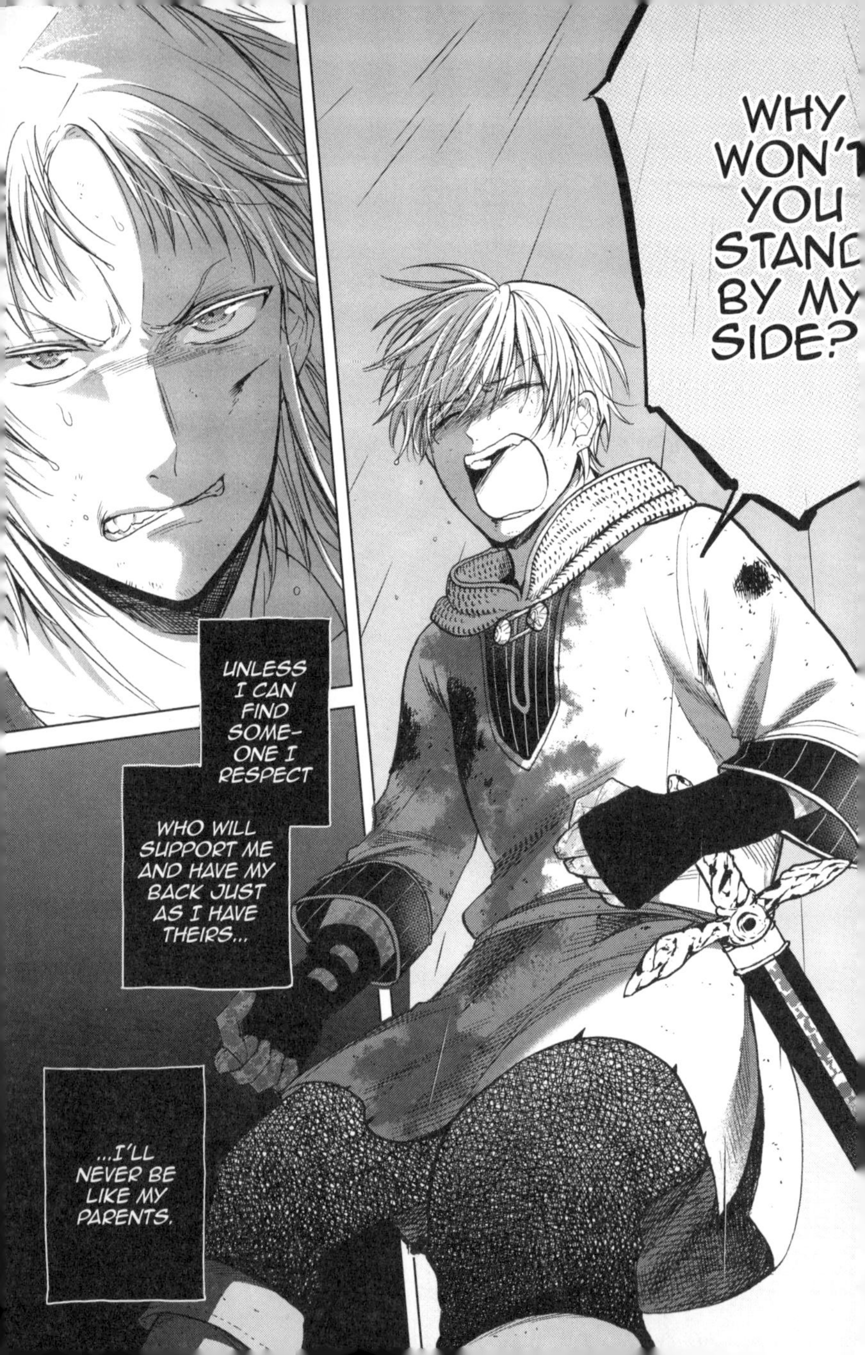
WHY WON'T YOU STAND BY MY SIDE?
UNLESS I CAN FIND SOME-ONE I RESPECT
WHO WILL SUPPORT ME AND HAVE MY BACK JUST AS I HAVE THEIRS...
...I'LL NEVER BE LIKE MY PARENTS.

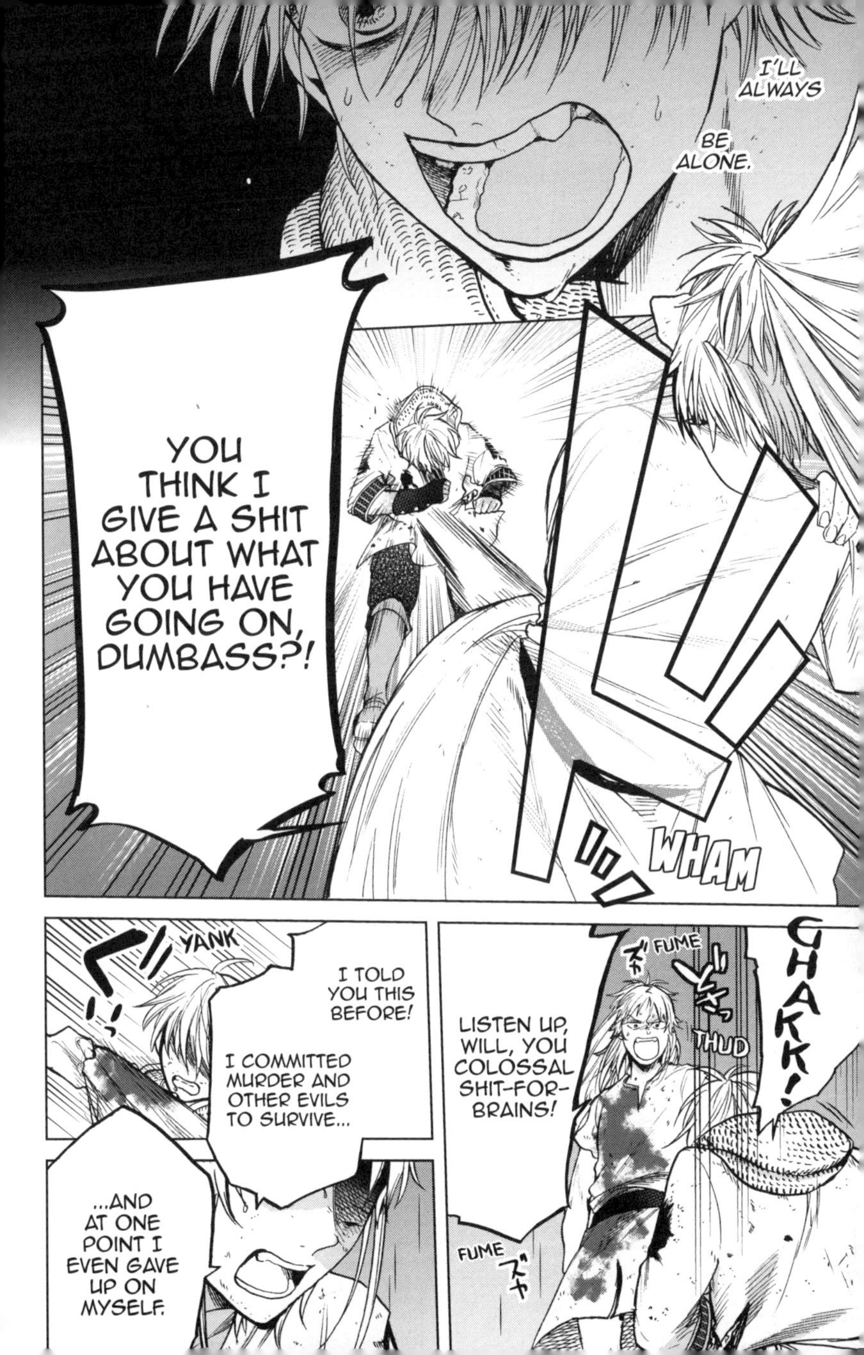
I'LL ALWAYS
BE ALONE.
YOU THINK I GIVE A SHIT ABOUT WHAT YOU HAVE GOING ON, DUMBASS?!
WHAM
CHAK!
FUME
THUD
LISTEN UP, WILL, YOU COLOSSAL SHIT-FOR-BRAINS!
FUME
YANK
I TOLD YOU THIS BEFORE!
I COMMITTED MURDER AND OTHER EVILS TO SURVIVE...
...AND AT ONE POINT I EVEN GAVE UP ON MYSELF.

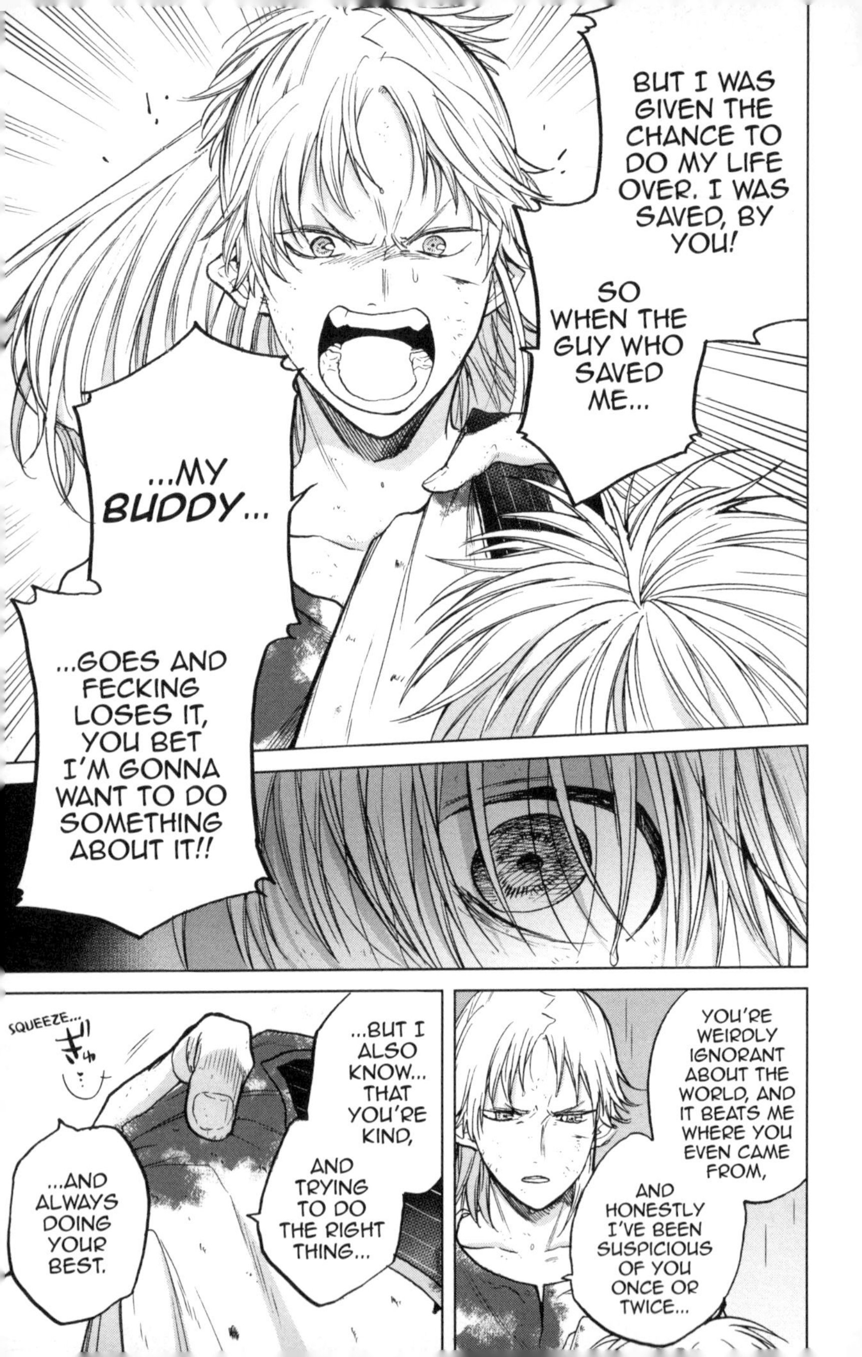
BUT I WAS GIVEN THE CHANCE TO DO MY LIFE OVER. I WAS SAVED, BY YOU!
SO WHEN THE GUY WHO SAVED ME...
...MY BUDDY...
...GOES AND FECKING LOSES IT, YOU BET I'M GONNA WANT TO DO SOMETHING ABOUT IT!!
YOU'RE WEIRDLY IGNORANT ABOUT THE WORLD, AND IT BEATS ME WHERE YOU EVEN CAME FROM,
AND HONESTLY I'VE BEEN SUSPICIOUS OF YOU ONCE OR TWICE...
...BUT I ALSO KNOW... THAT YOU'RE KIND,
AND TRYING TO DO THE RIGHT THING...
SQUEEZE...
...AND ALWAYS DOING YOUR BEST.

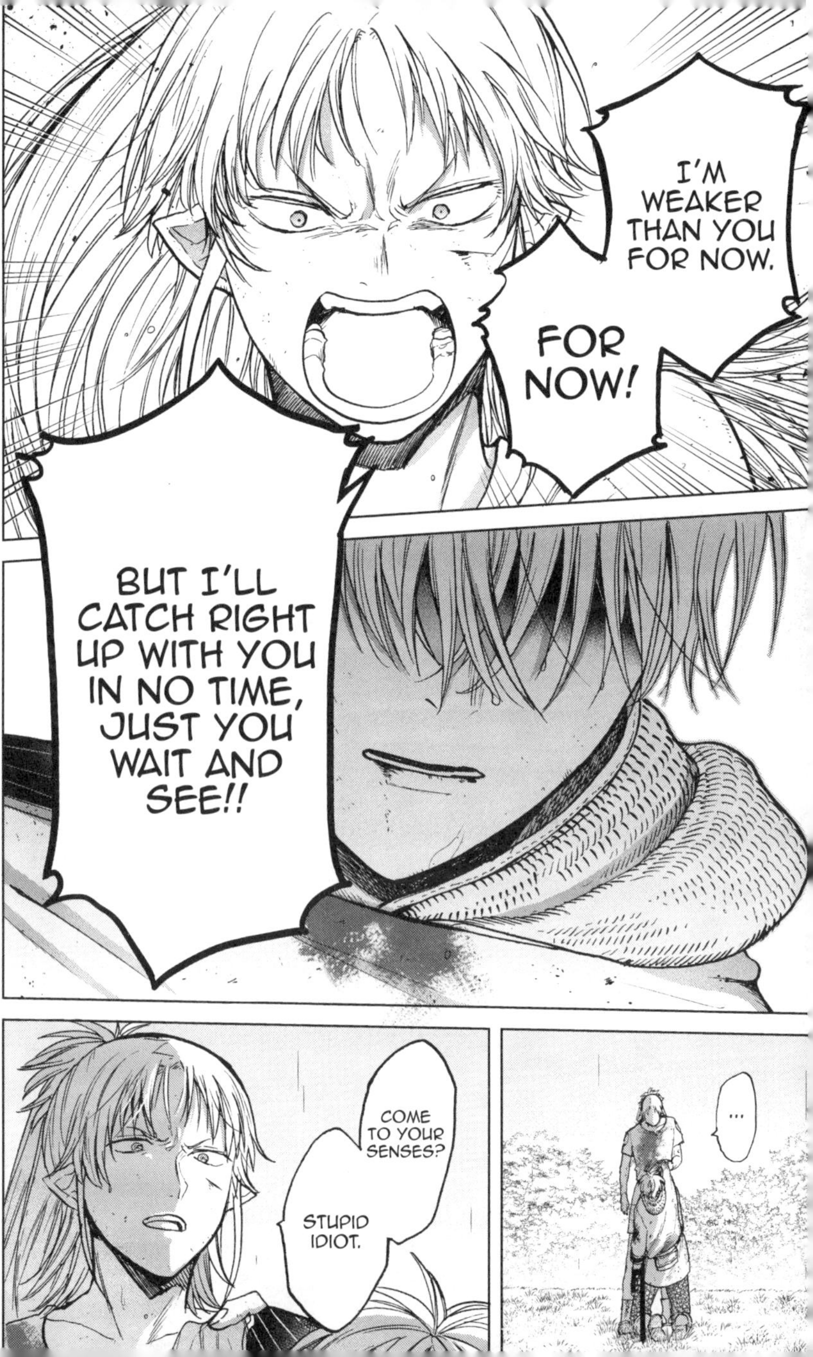
I'M WEAKER THAN YOU FOR NOW.
FOR NOW!
BUT I'LL CATCH RIGHT UP WITH YOU IN NO TIME, JUST YOU WAIT AND SEE!!
...
COME TO YOUR SENSES?
STUPID IDIOT.

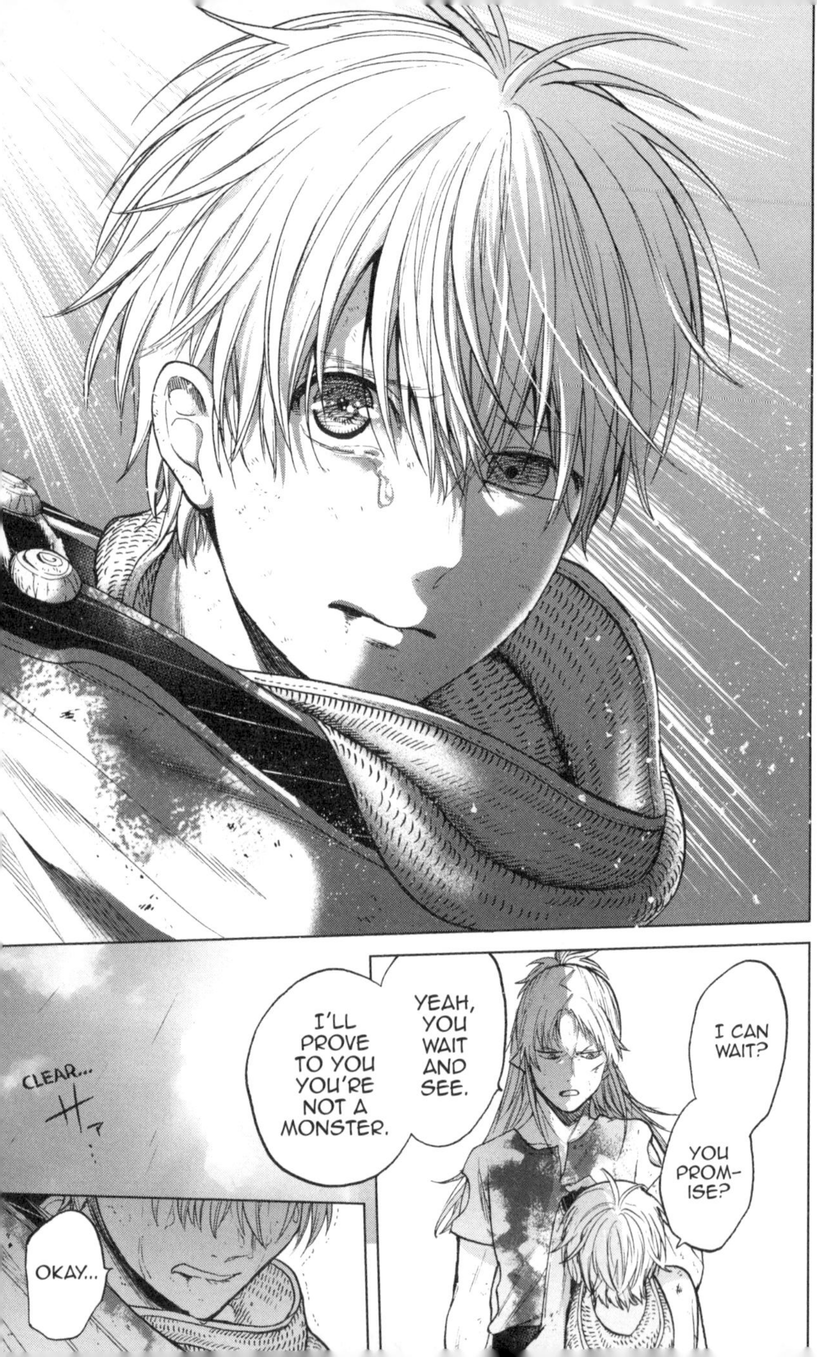
I CAN WAIT?
YOU PROMISE?
YEAH, YOU WAIT AND SEE.
I'LL PROVE TO YOU YOU'RE NOT A MONSTER.
CLEAR...
OKAY...

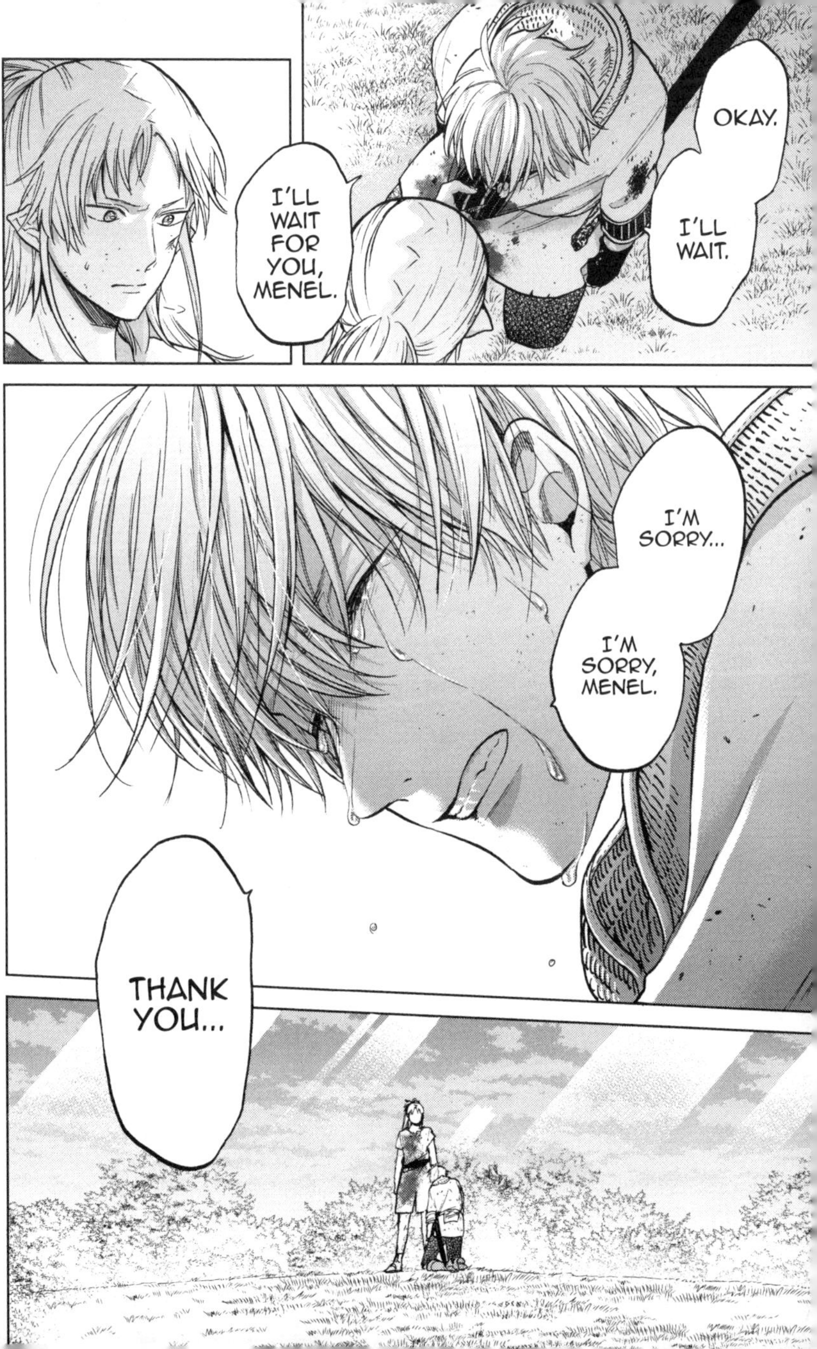
OKAY.
I'LL WAIT.
I'LL WAIT FOR YOU, MENEL.
I'M SORRY...
I'M SORRY, MENEL.
THANK YOU...

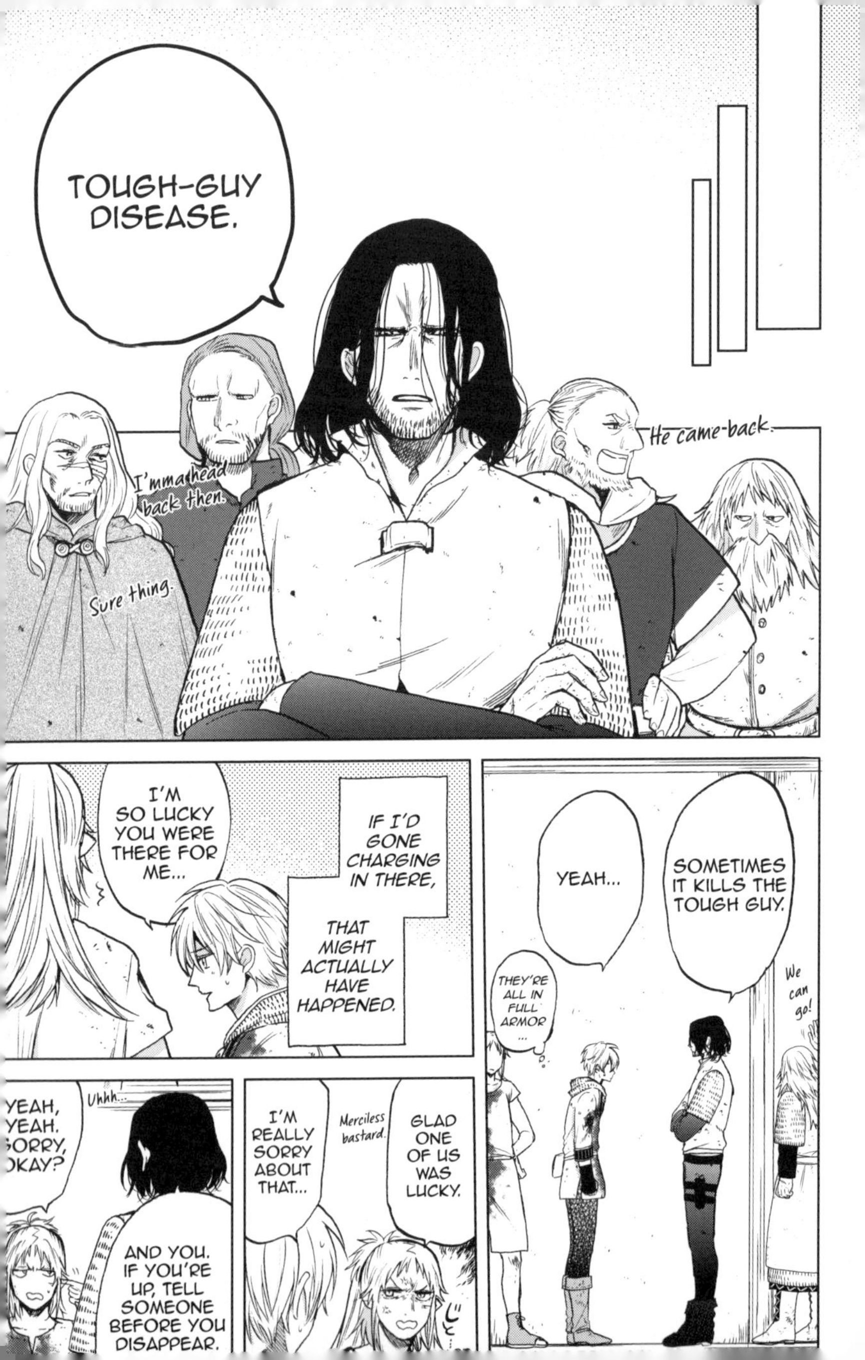
TOUGH-GUY DISEASE.
He came back.
I'mma head back then.
Sure thing.
SOMETIMES IT KILLS THE TOUGH GUY.
YEAH...
We can go!
THEY'RE ALL IN FULL ARMOR...
IF I'D GONE CHARGING IN THERE,
THAT MIGHT ACTUALLY HAVE HAPPENED.
I'M SO LUCKY YOU WERE THERE FOR ME...
GLAD ONE OF US WAS LUCKY.
Merciless bastard.
I'M REALLY SORRY ABOUT THAT...
Uhhh...
YEAH, YEAH. SORRY, OKAY?
AND YOU. IF YOU'RE UP, TELL SOMEONE BEFORE YOU DISAPPEAR.

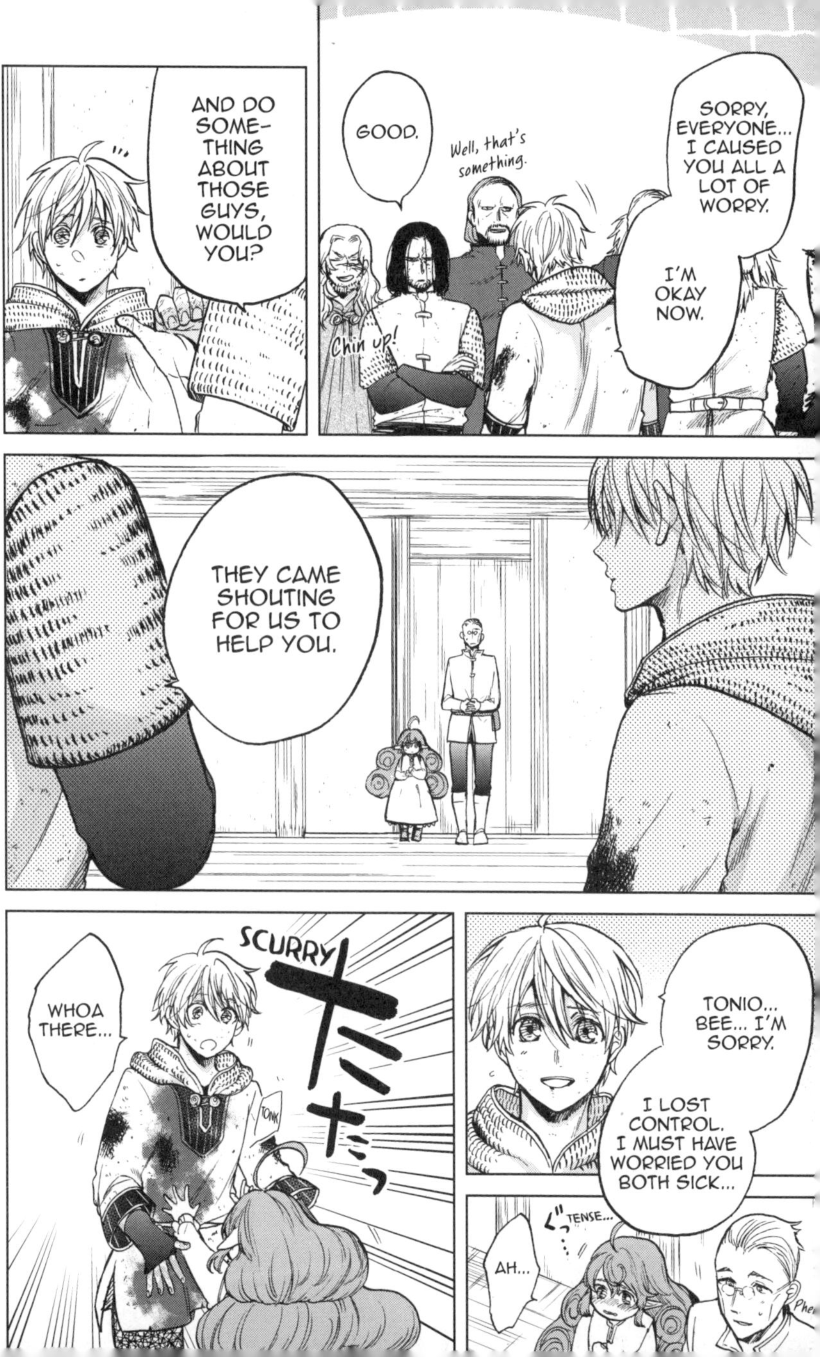
SORRY, EVERYONE... I CAUSED YOU ALL A LOT OF WORRY.
I'M OKAY NOW.
Well, that's something.
GOOD.
Chin up!
AND DO SOME-THING ABOUT THOSE GUYS, WOULD YOU?
THEY CAME SHOUTING FOR US TO HELP YOU.
TONIO... BEE... I'M SORRY.
I LOST CONTROL. I MUST HAVE WORRIED YOU BOTH SICK...
TENSE...
AH...
SCURRY
TONK
WHOA THERE...

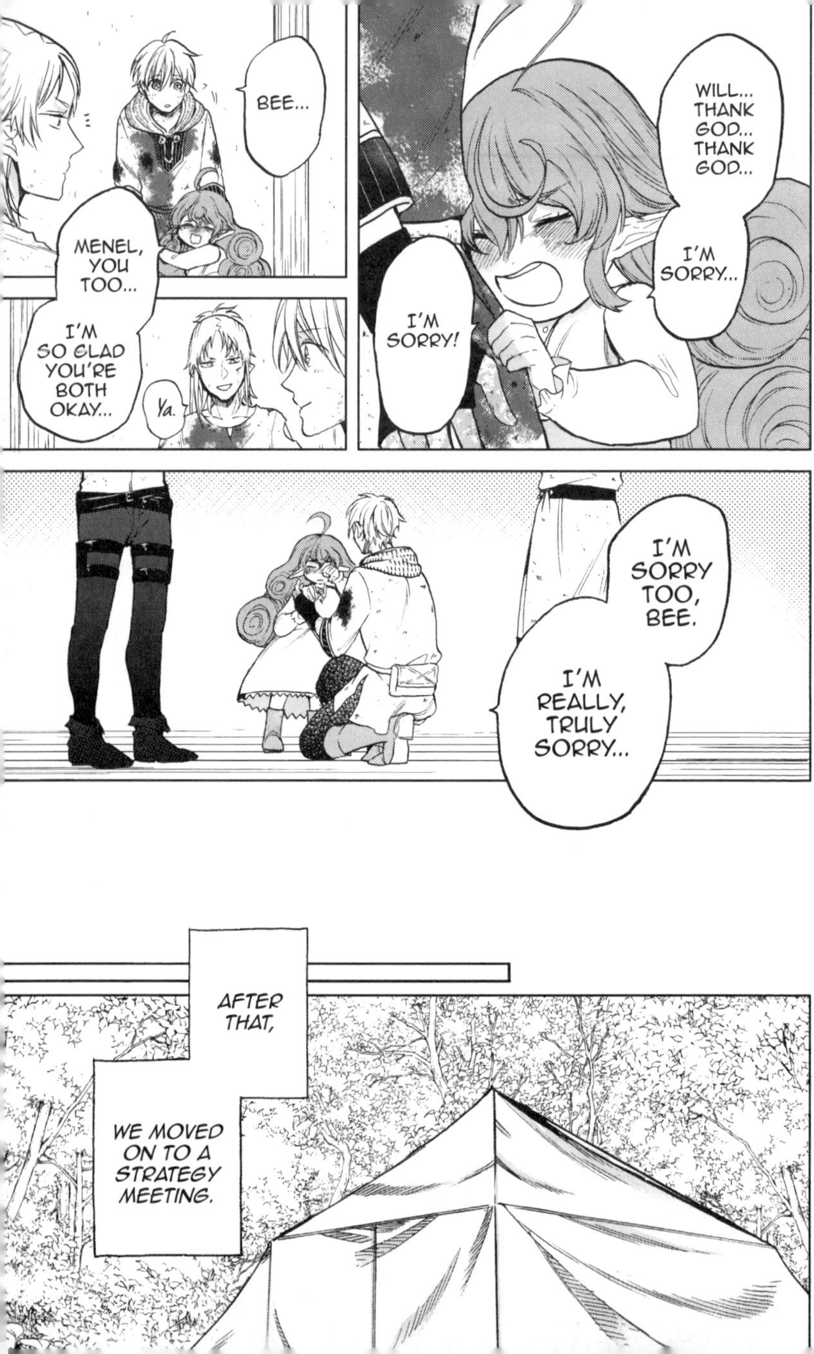
WILL... THANK GOD... THANK GOD...
I'M SORRY...
I'M SORRY!
BEE...
MENEL, YOU TOO...
I'M SO GLAD YOU'RE BOTH OKAY...
Ya.
I'M SORRY TOO, BEE.
I'M REALLY, TRULY SORRY...
AFTER THAT,
WE MOVED ON TO A STRATEGY MEETING.

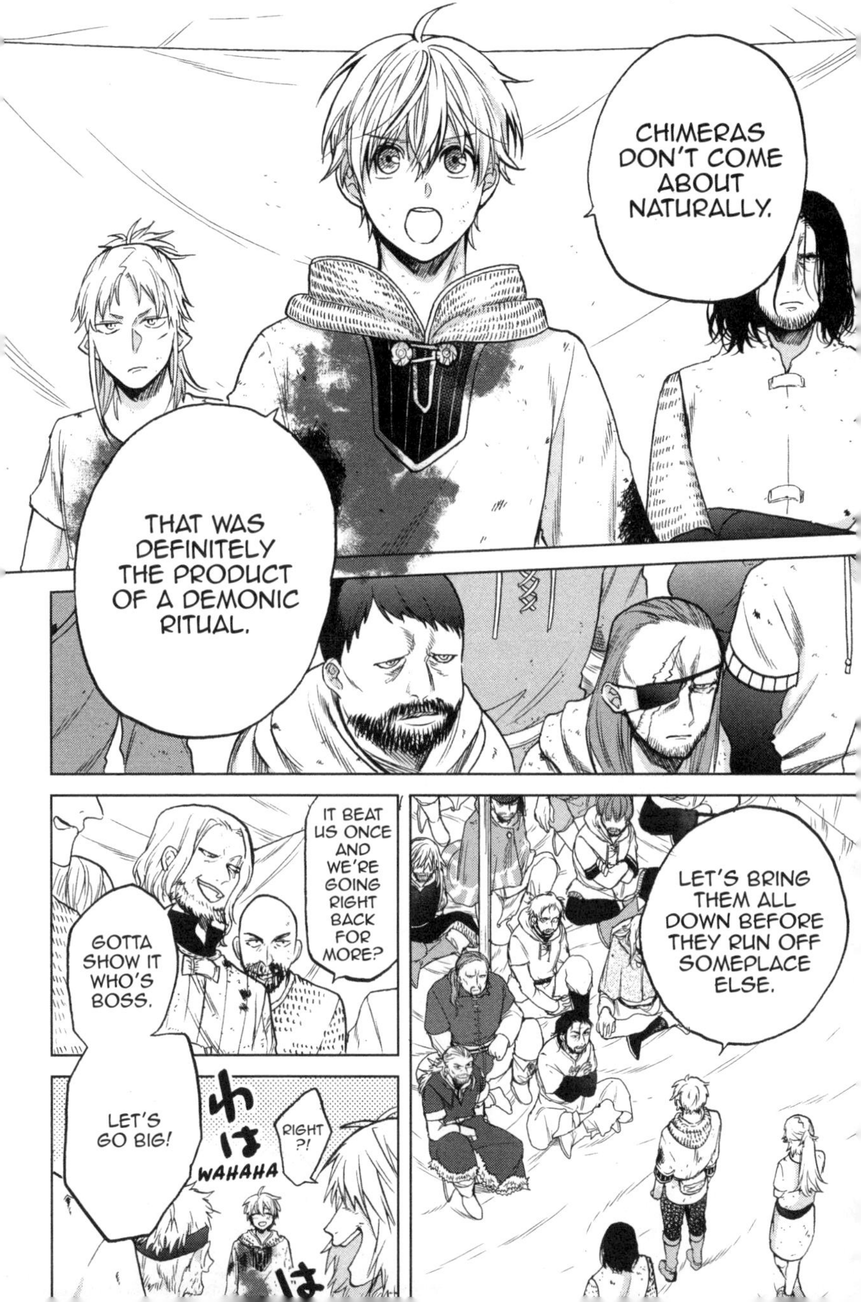
CHIMERAS DON'T COME ABOUT NATURALLY.
THAT WAS DEFINITELY THE PRODUCT OF A DEMONIC RITUAL.
LET'S BRING THEM ALL DOWN BEFORE THEY RUN OFF SOMEPLACE ELSE.
IT BEAT US ONCE AND WE'RE GOING RIGHT BACK FOR MORE?
GOTTA SHOW IT WHO'S BOSS.
RIGHT ?!
わははは
WAHAHA
LET'S GO BIG!

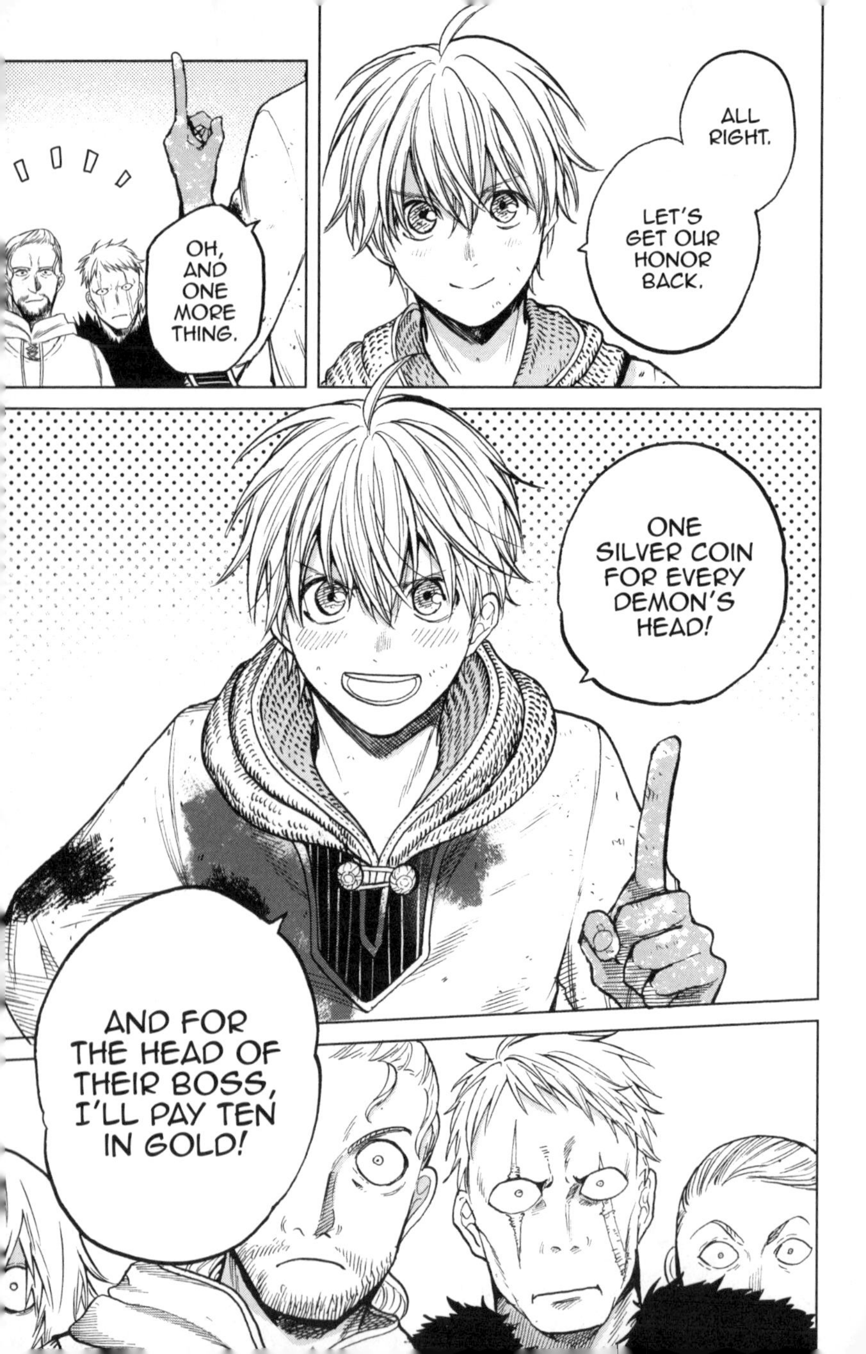
ALL RIGHT.
LET'S GET OUR HONOR BACK.
OH, AND ONE MORE THING.
ONE SILVER COIN FOR EVERY DEMON'S HEAD!
AND FOR THE HEAD OF THEIR BOSS, I'LL PAY TEN IN GOLD!

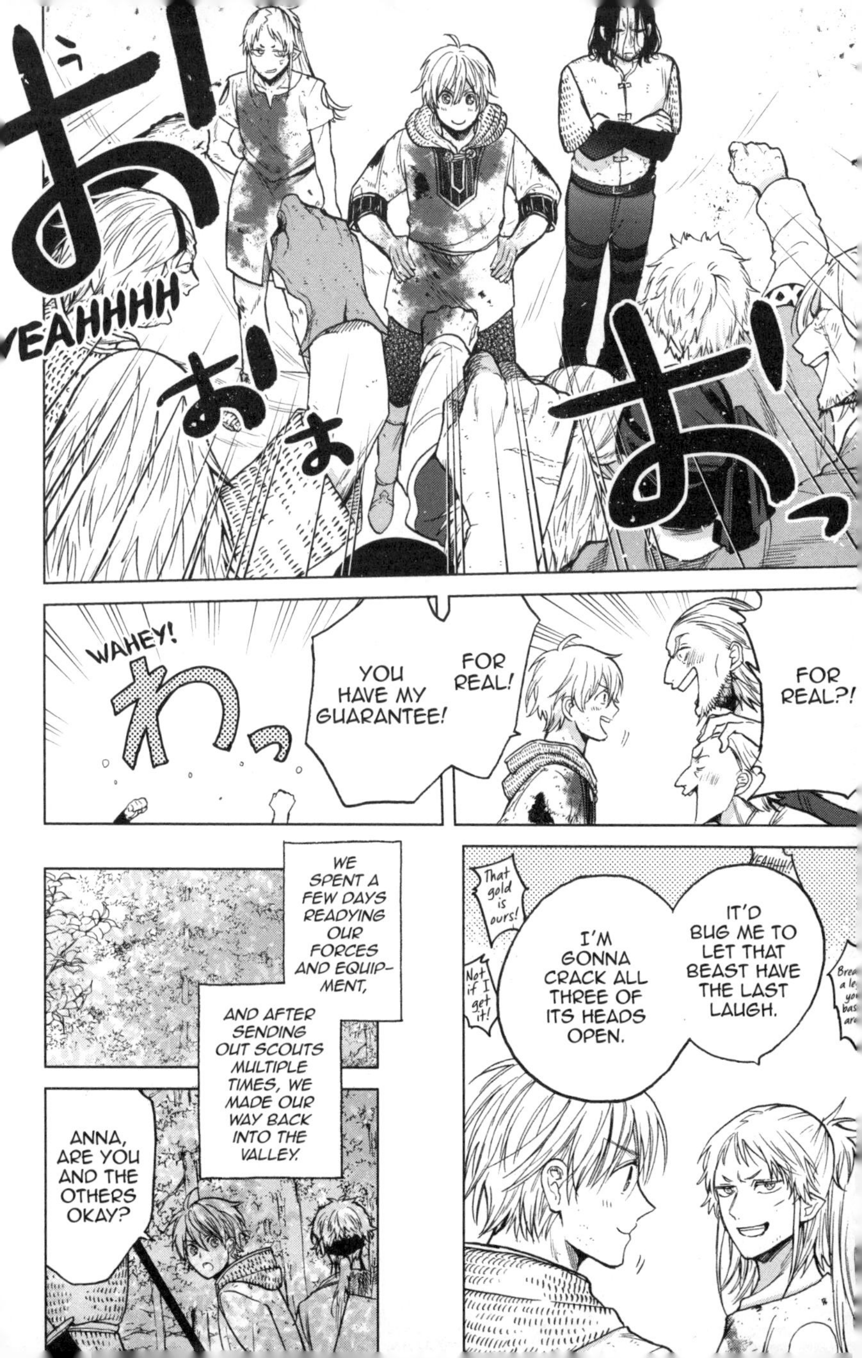
おっ
おぉ
お!
YEAHHHH
FOR REAL?!
FOR REAL!
YOU HAVE MY GUARANTEE!
WAHEY!
わっ
IT'D BUG ME TO LET THAT BEAST HAVE THE LAST LAUGH.
I'M GONNA CRACK ALL THREE OF ITS HEADS OPEN.
That gold is ours!
Not if I get it!
WE SPENT A FEW DAYS READYING OUR FORCES AND EQUIPMENT,
AND AFTER SENDING OUT SCOUTS MULTIPLE TIMES, WE MADE OUR WAY BACK INTO THE VALLEY.
ANNA, ARE YOU AND THE OTHERS OKAY?

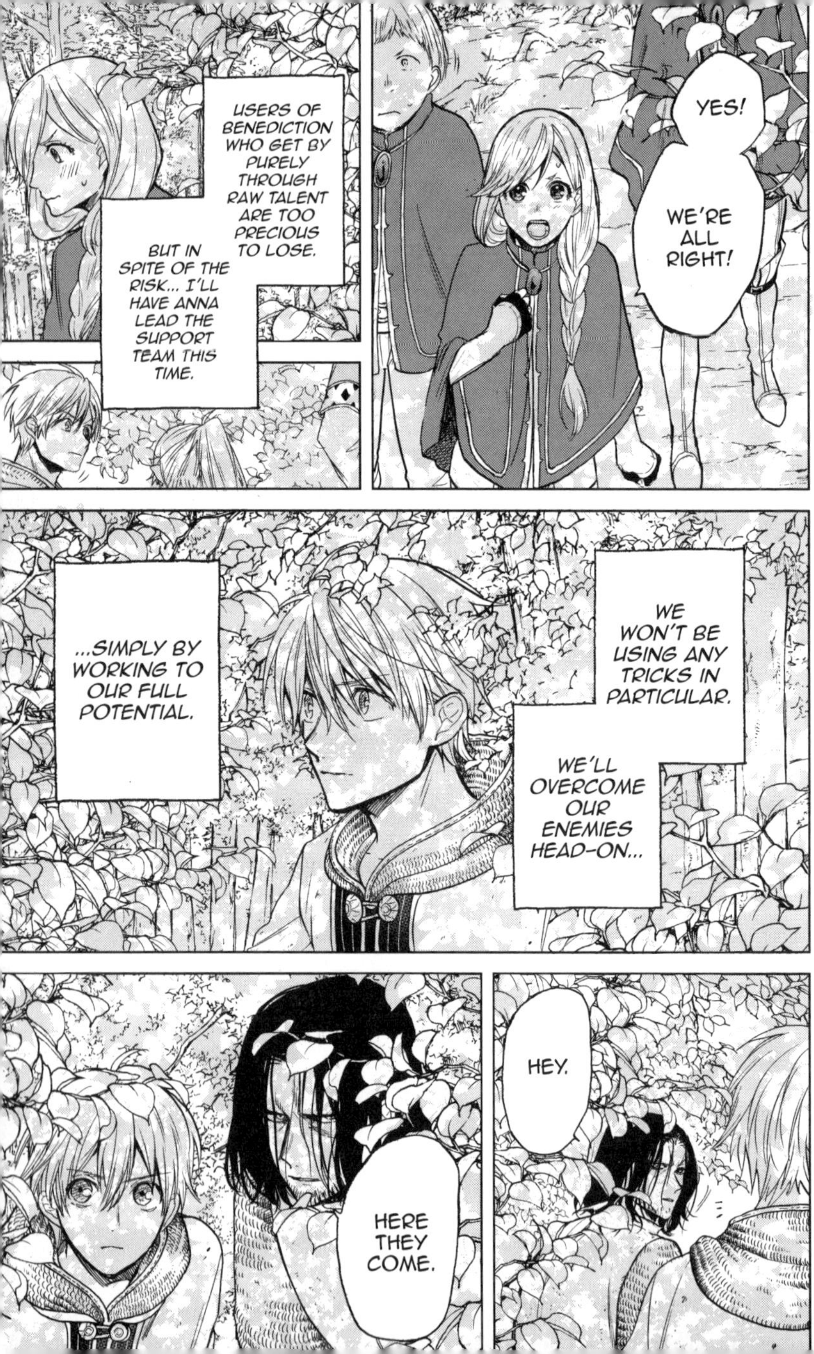
YES!
WE'RE ALL RIGHT!
USERS OF BENEDICTION WHO GET BY PURELY THROUGH RAW TALENT ARE TOO PRECIOUS TO LOSE.
BUT IN SPITE OF THE RISK... I'LL HAVE ANNA LEAD THE SUPPORT TEAM THIS TIME.
WE WON'T BE USING ANY TRICKS IN PARTICULAR.
WE'LL OVERCOME OUR ENEMIES HEAD-ON...
...SIMPLY BY WORKING TO OUR FULL POTENTIAL.
HEY.
HERE THEY COME.

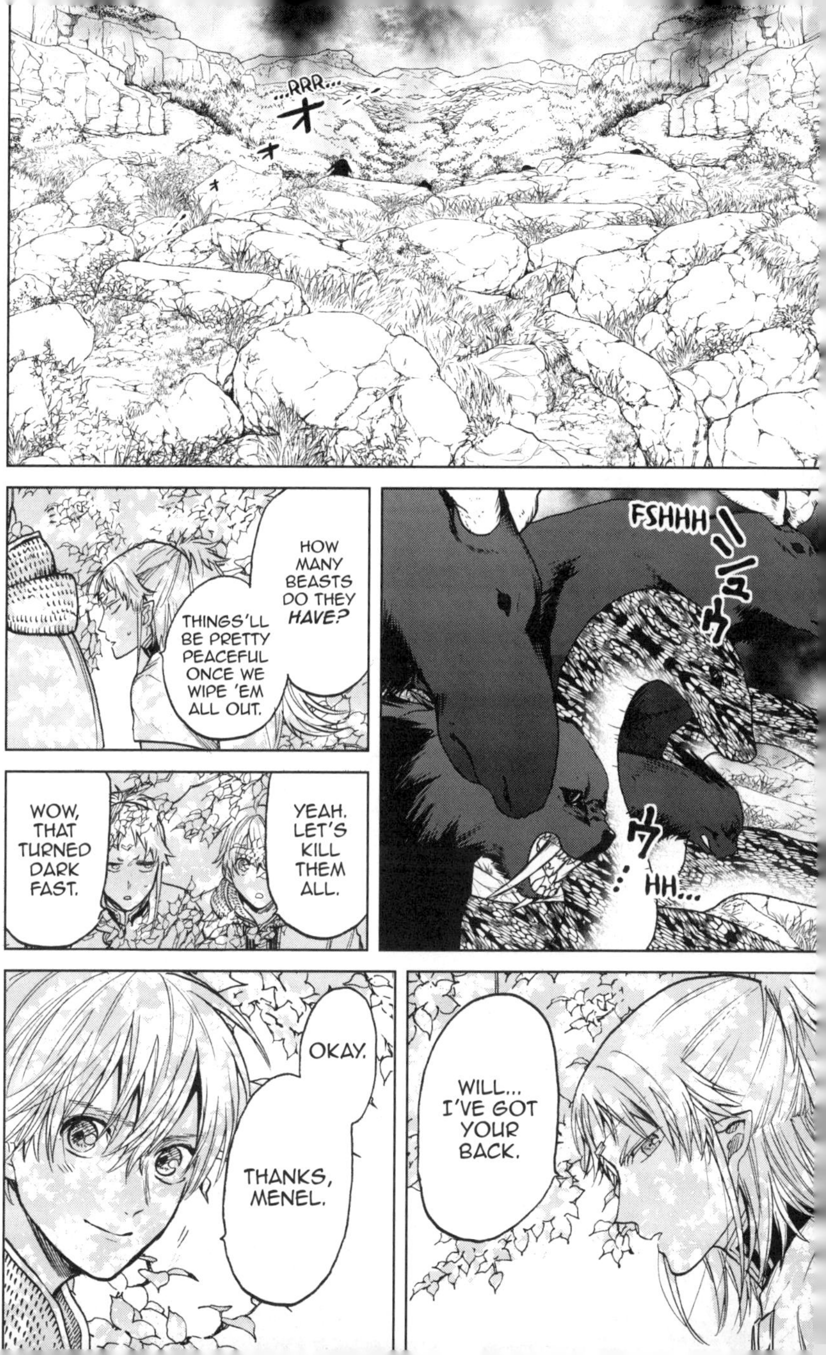

...RRR...
FSHHH
HH...
HOW MANY BEASTS DO THEY *HAVE?*
THINGS'LL BE PRETTY PEACEFUL ONCE WE WIPE 'EM ALL OUT.
YEAH. LET'S KILL THEM ALL.
WOW, THAT TURNED DARK FAST.
WILL... I'VE GOT YOUR BACK.
OKAY.
THANKS, MENEL.

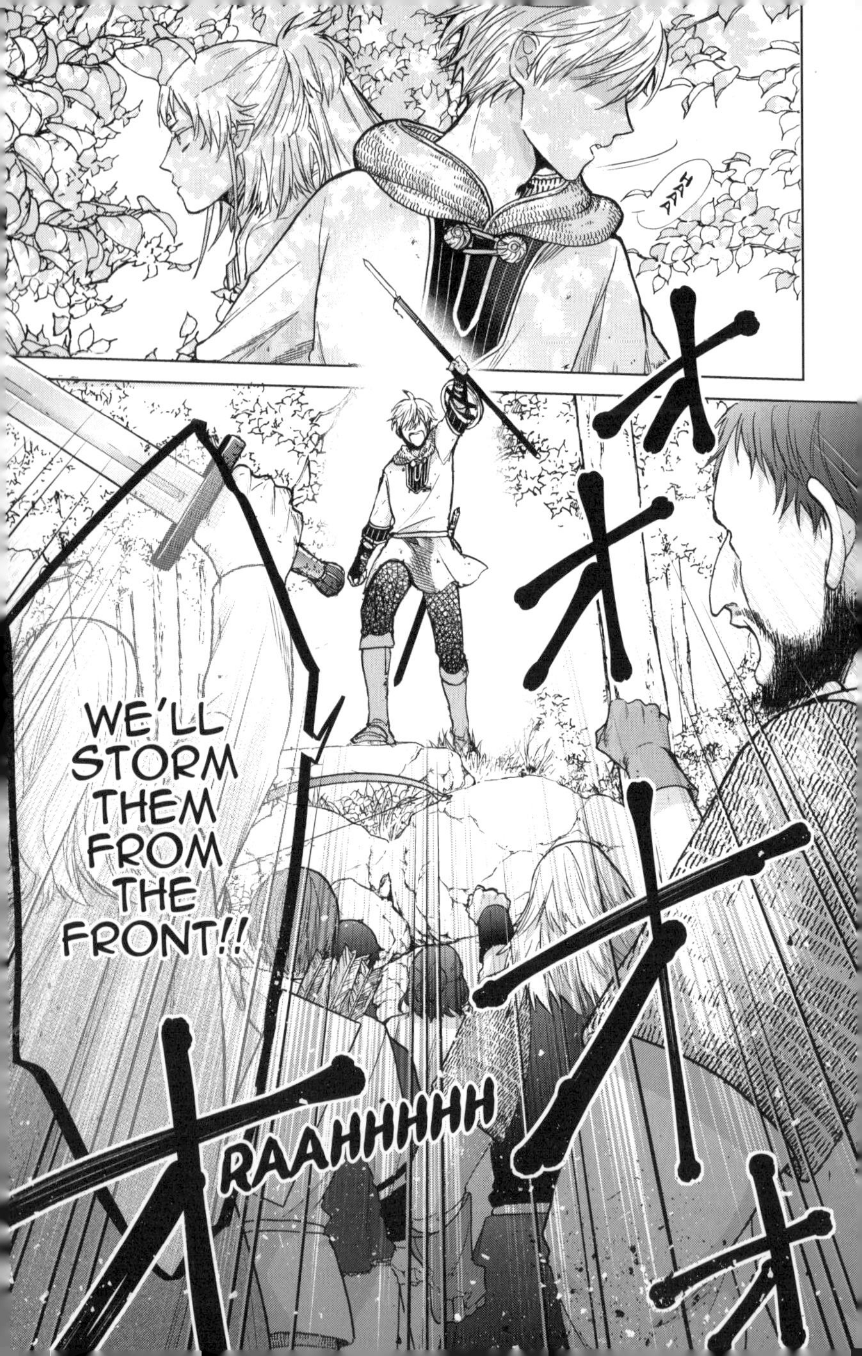
WE'LL STORM THEM FROM THE FRONT!!
RAAHHHHH

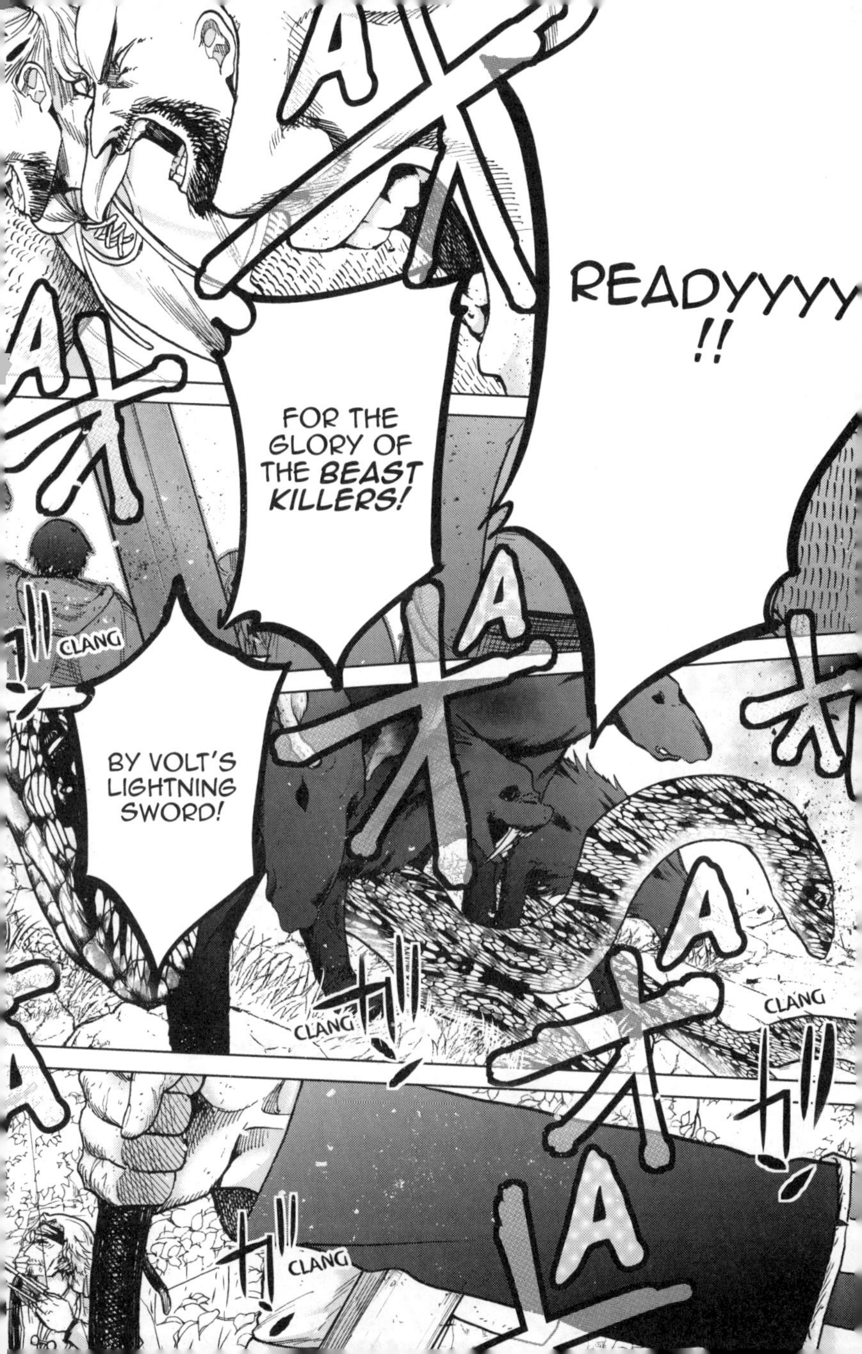
READYYYY!!
FOR THE GLORY OF THE *BEAST KILLERS!*
BY VOLT'S LIGHTNING SWORD!
CLANG
CLANG
CLANG
CLANG

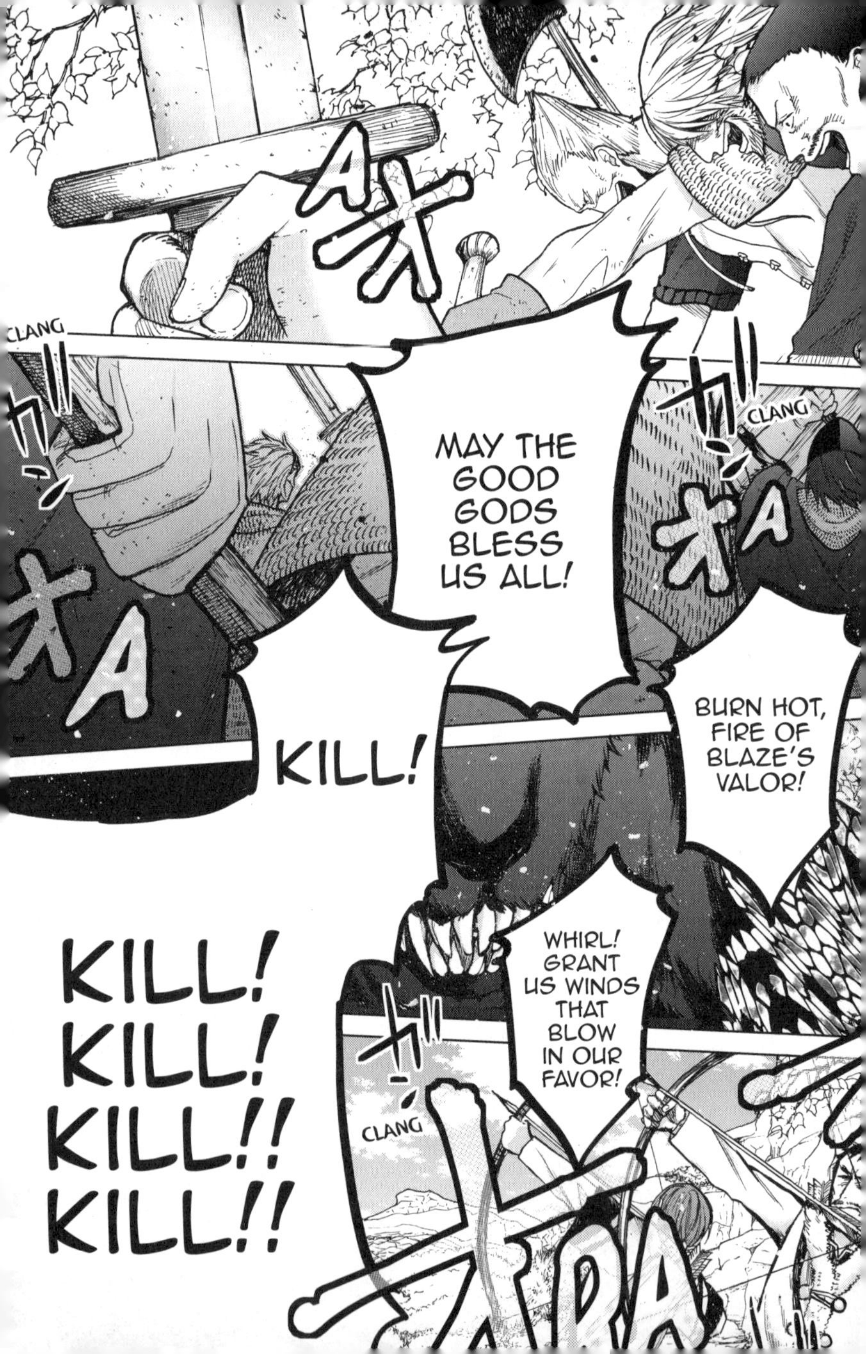

A
CLANG
A
MAY THE GOOD GODS BLESS US ALL!
CLANG
A
BURN HOT, FIRE OF BLAZE'S VALOR!
KILL!
WHIRL! GRANT US WINDS THAT BLOW IN OUR FAVOR!
PA
CLANG
KILL! KILL! KILL!! KILL!!

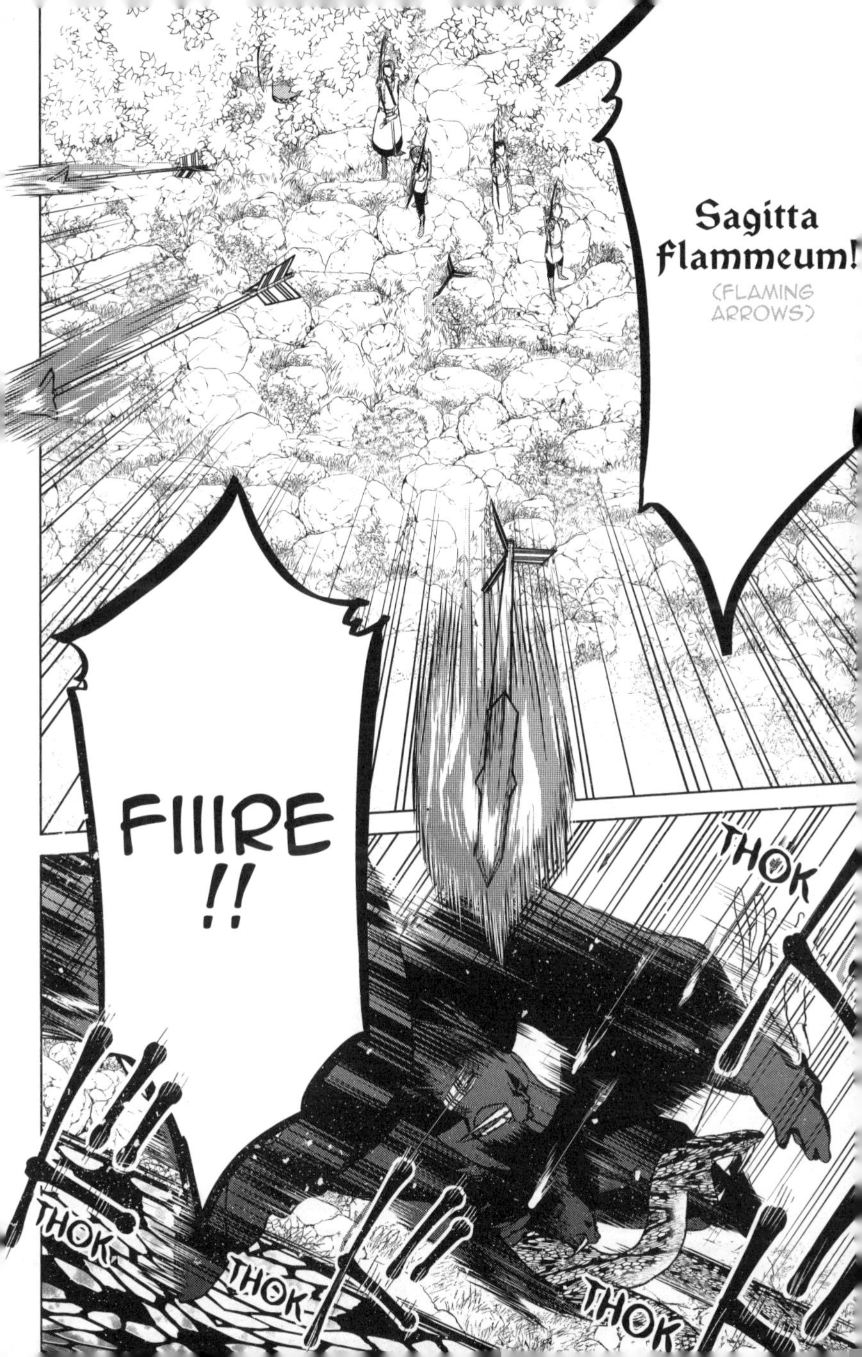
Sagitta Flammeum!
(FLAMING ARROWS)
FIIRE !!
THOK
THOK
THOK-
THOK

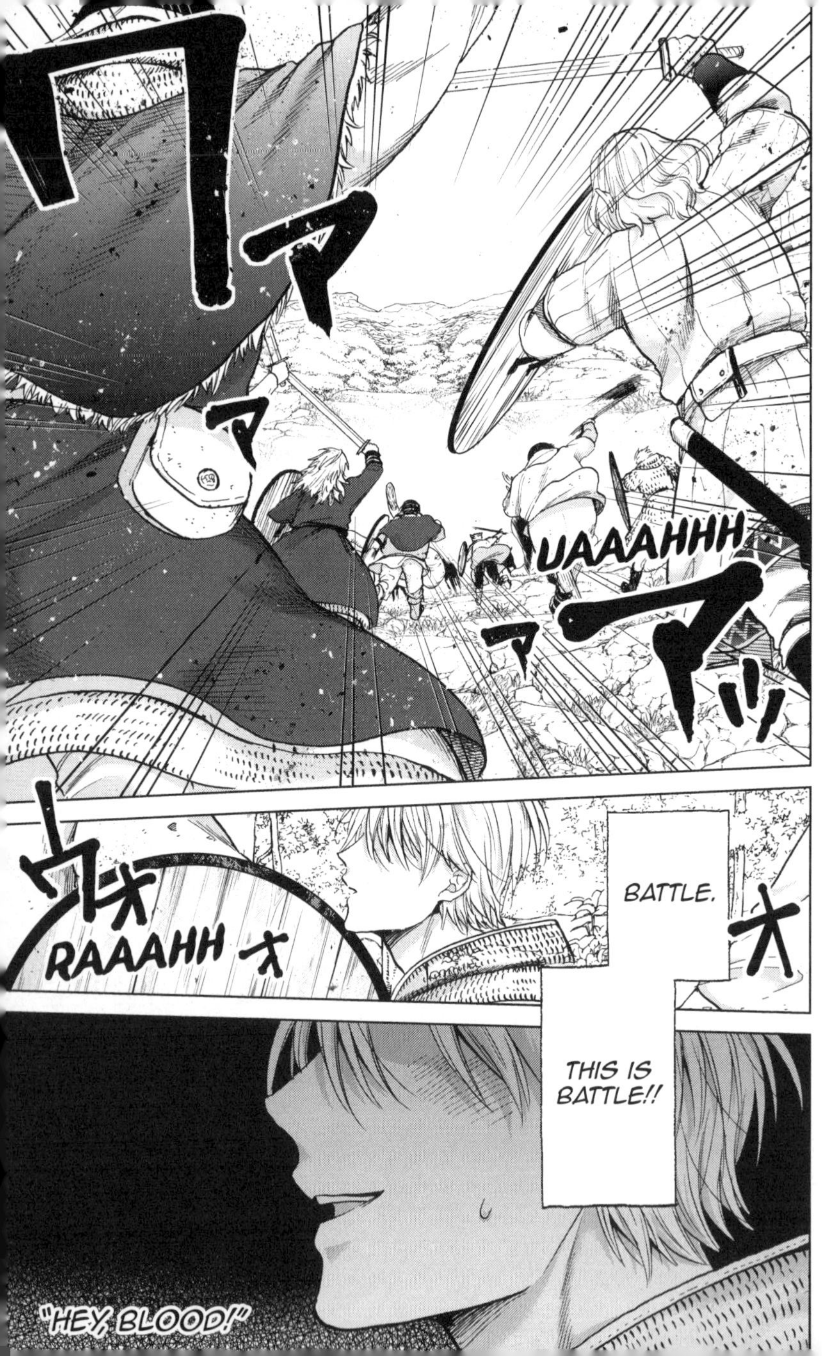

ワァァ
UAAAHHH
ァアッ
BATTLE.
オ
ウオ
RAAAHH
オ
THIS IS BATTLE!!
"HEY, BLOOD!"

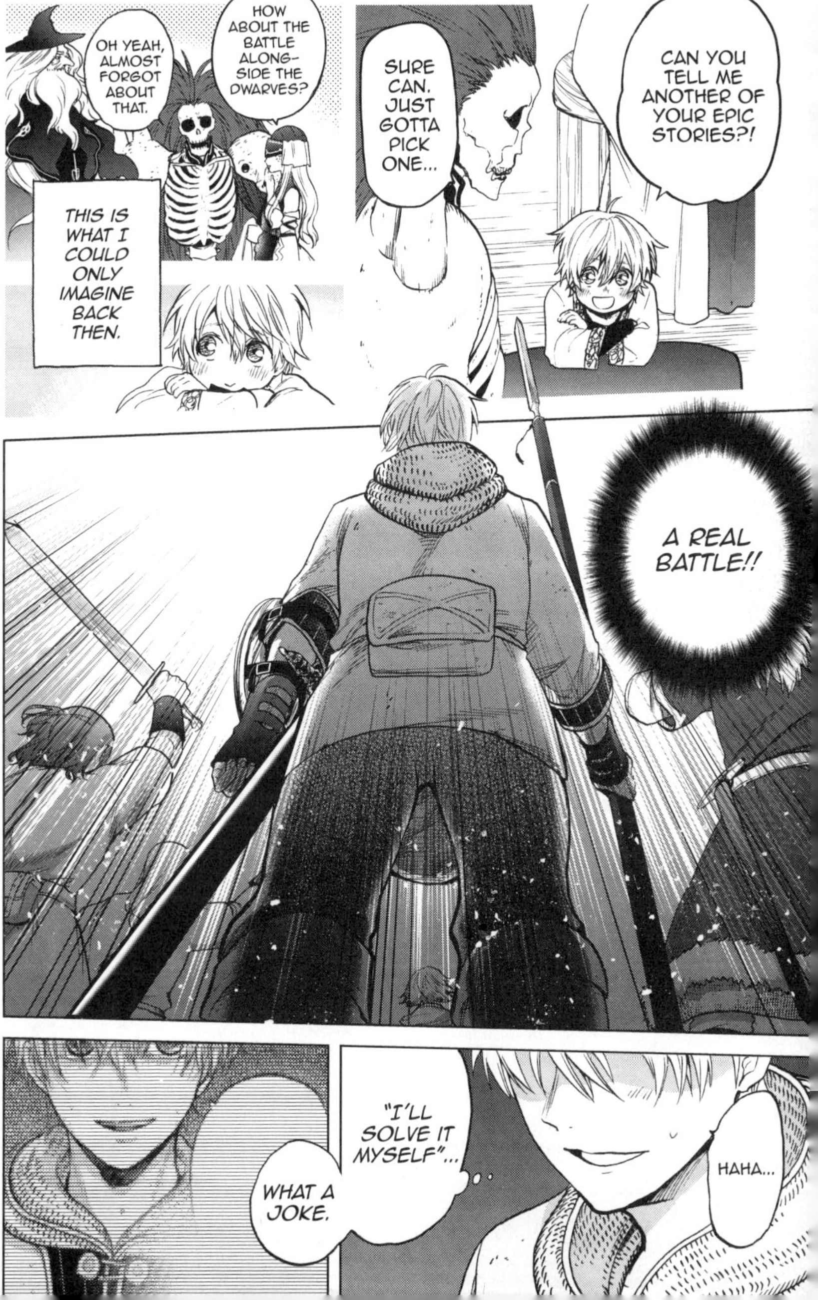
CAN YOU TELL ME ANOTHER OF YOUR EPIC STORIES?!
SURE CAN. JUST GOTTA PICK ONE...
HOW ABOUT THE BATTLE ALONG-SIDE THE DWARVES?
OH YEAH, ALMOST FORGOT ABOUT THAT.
THIS IS WHAT I COULD ONLY IMAGINE BACK THEN.
A REAL BATTLE!!
HAHA...
"I'LL SOLVE IT MYSELF"...
WHAT A JOKE.

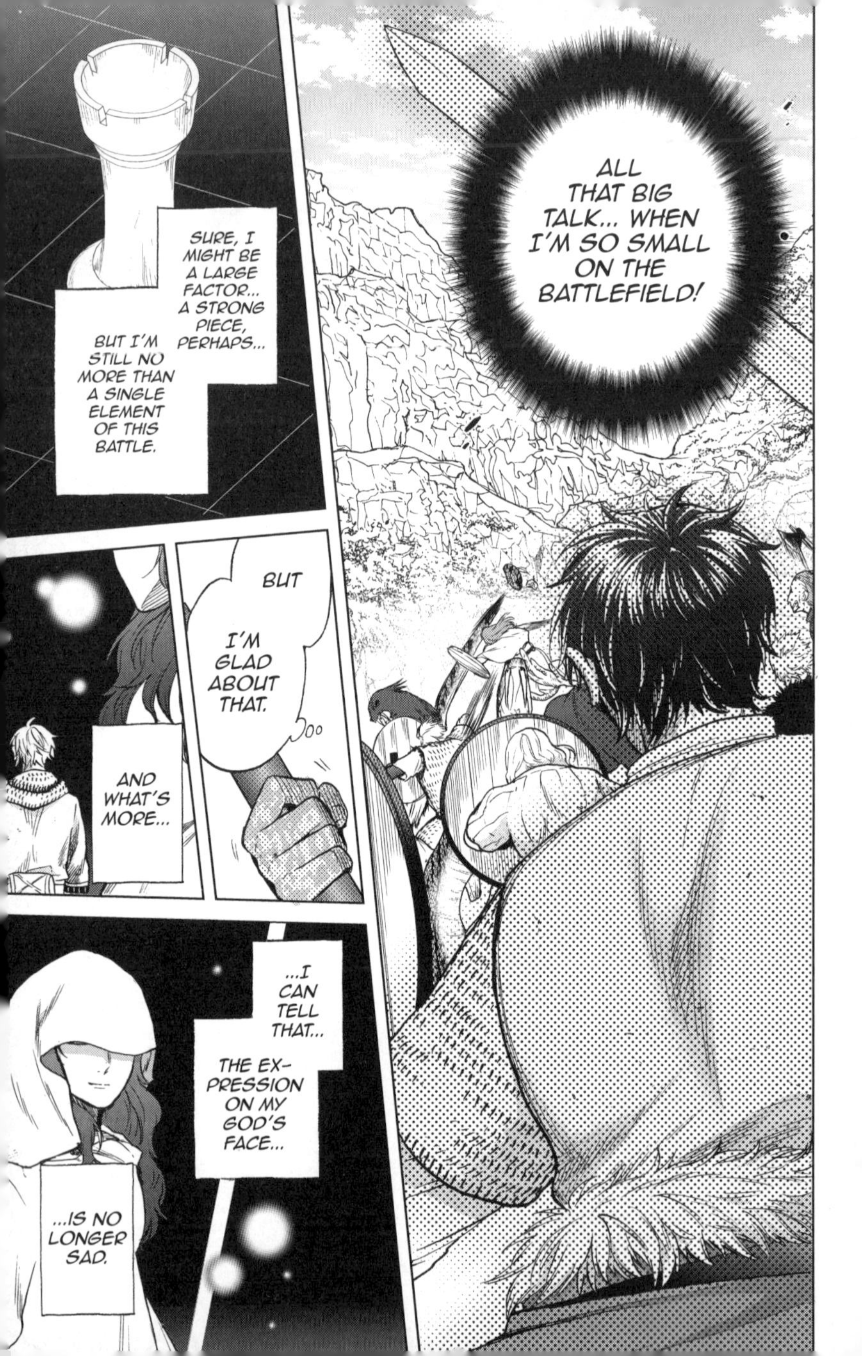
ALL THAT BIG TALK... WHEN I'M SO SMALL ON THE BATTLEFIELD!
SURE, I MIGHT BE A LARGE FACTOR... A STRONG PIECE, PERHAPS...
BUT I'M STILL NO MORE THAN A SINGLE ELEMENT OF THIS BATTLE.
BUT
I'M GLAD ABOUT THAT.
AND WHAT'S MORE...
...I CAN TELL THAT...
THE EX-PRESSION ON MY GOD'S FACE...
...IS NO LONGER SAD.

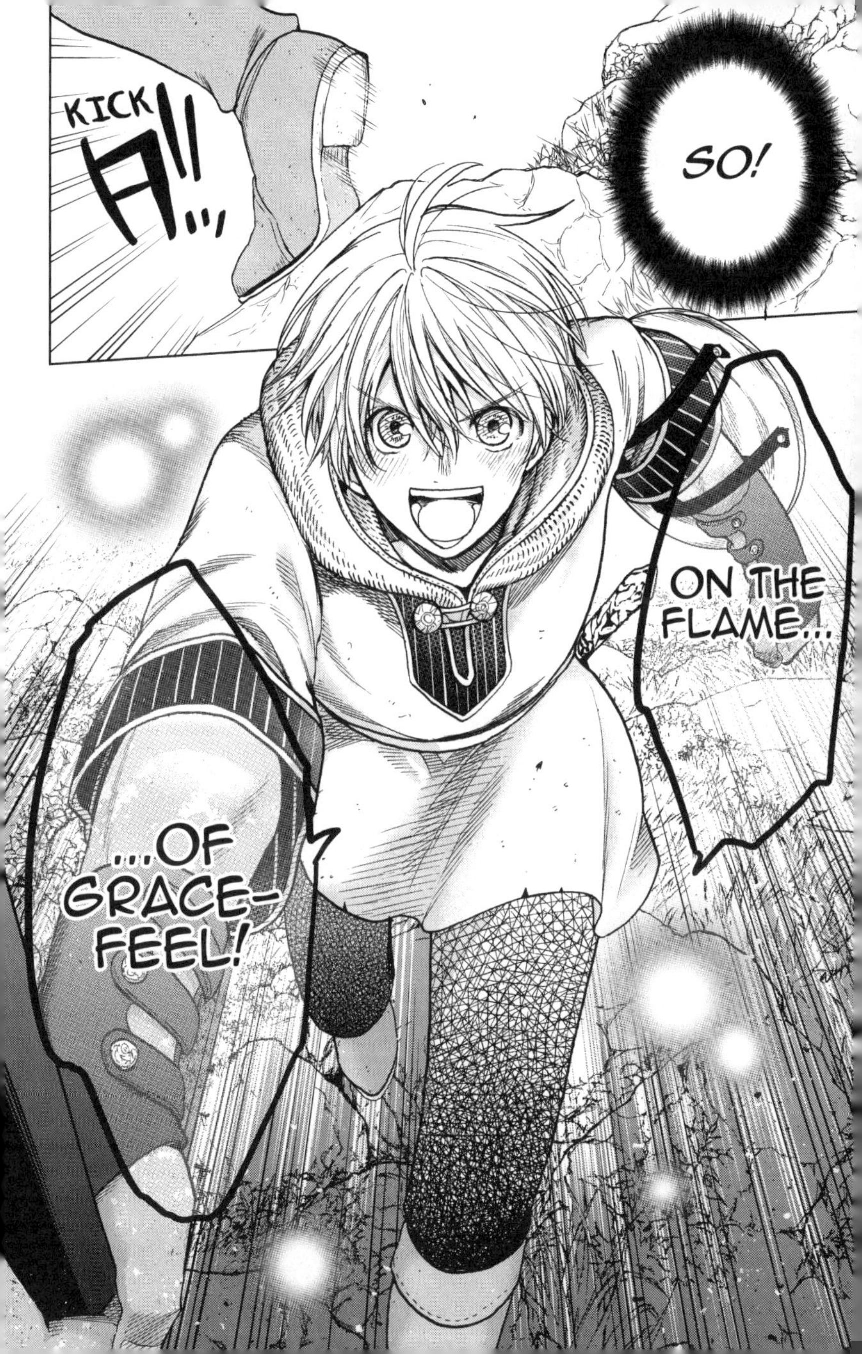
SO!
KICK
ON THE FLAME...
...OF GRACE-FEEL!

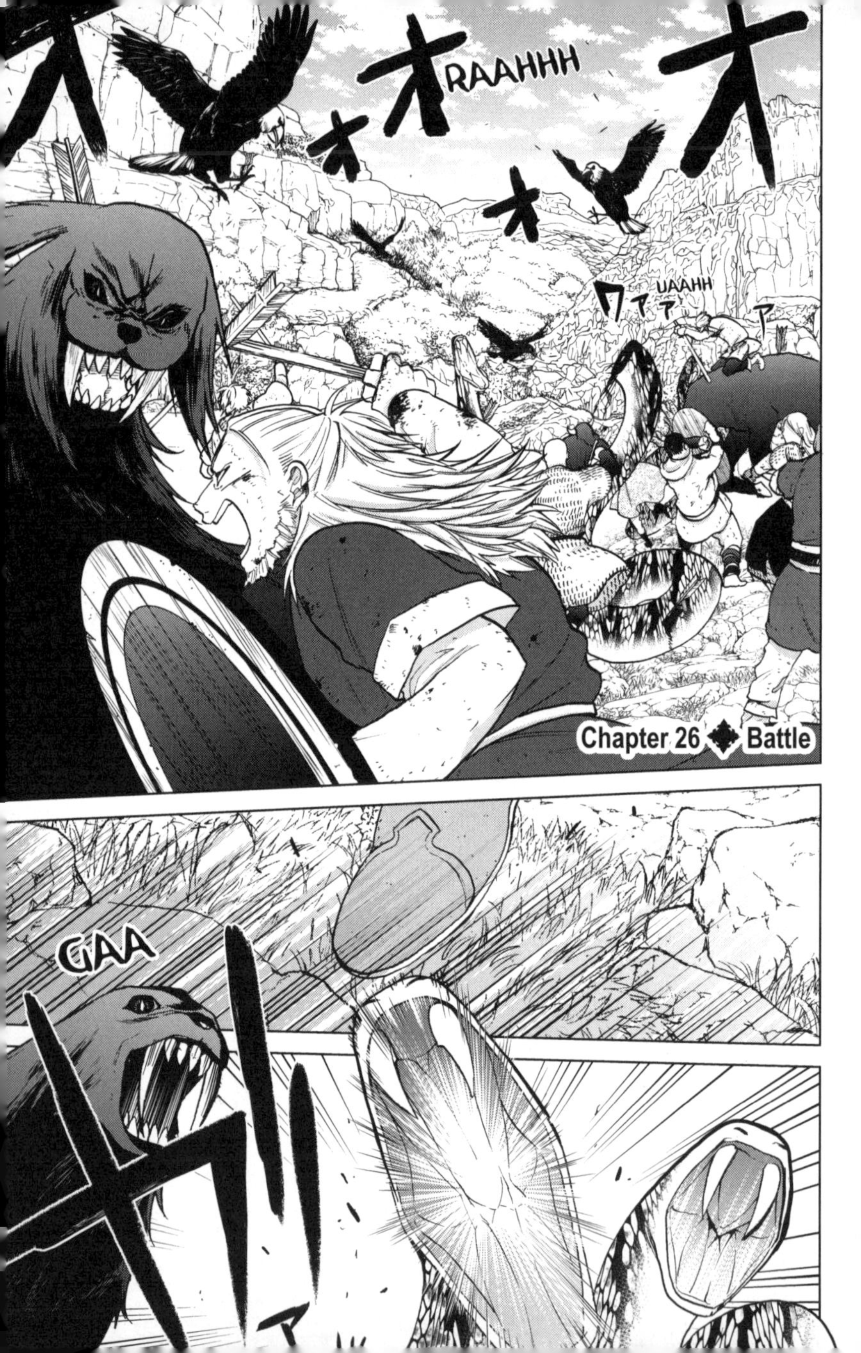
RAAHHH
UAAHH
Chapter 26 ◆ Battle
GAA

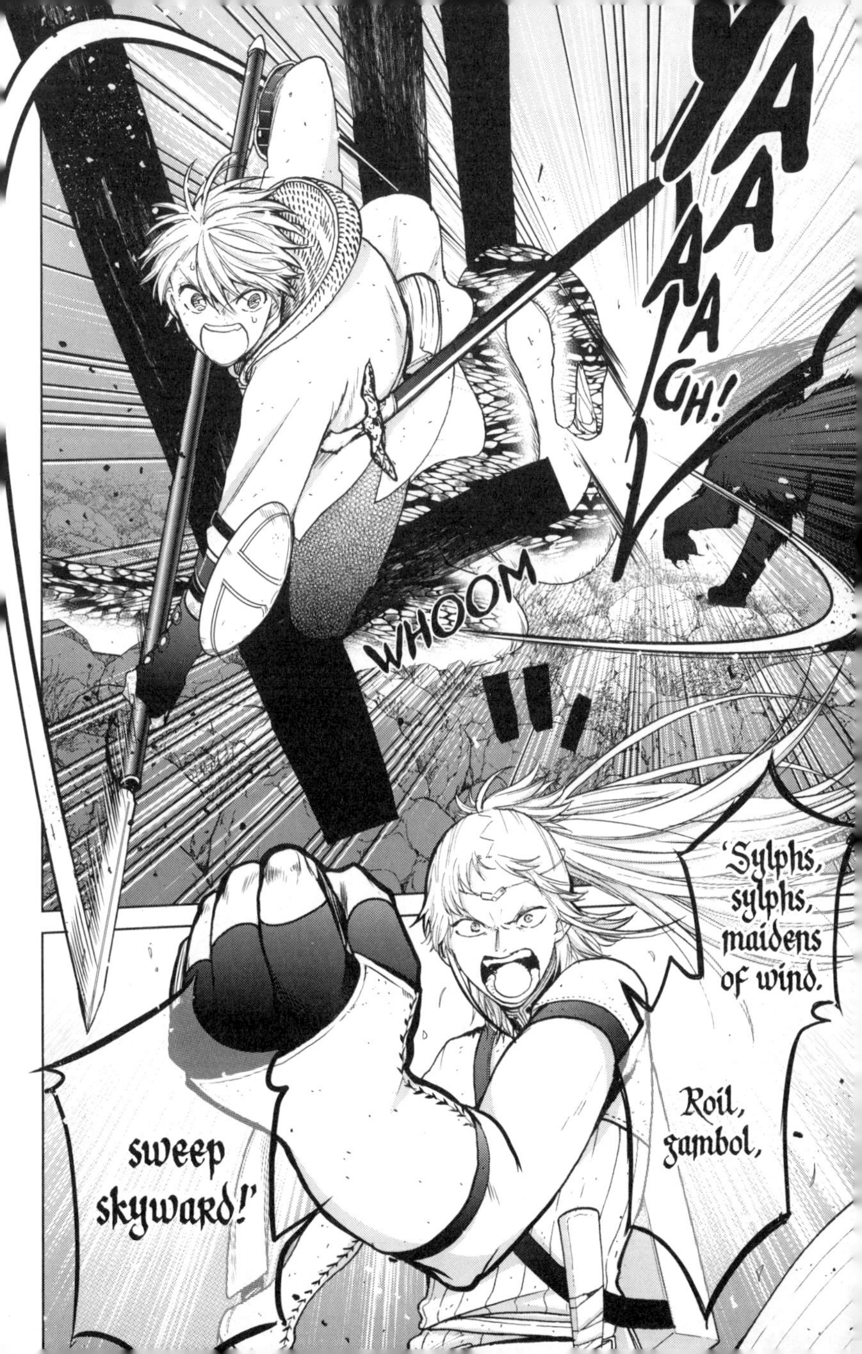
AAAAGH!
WHOOM
'Sylphs, sylphs, maidens of wind.
Roil, gambol,
sweep skyward!'

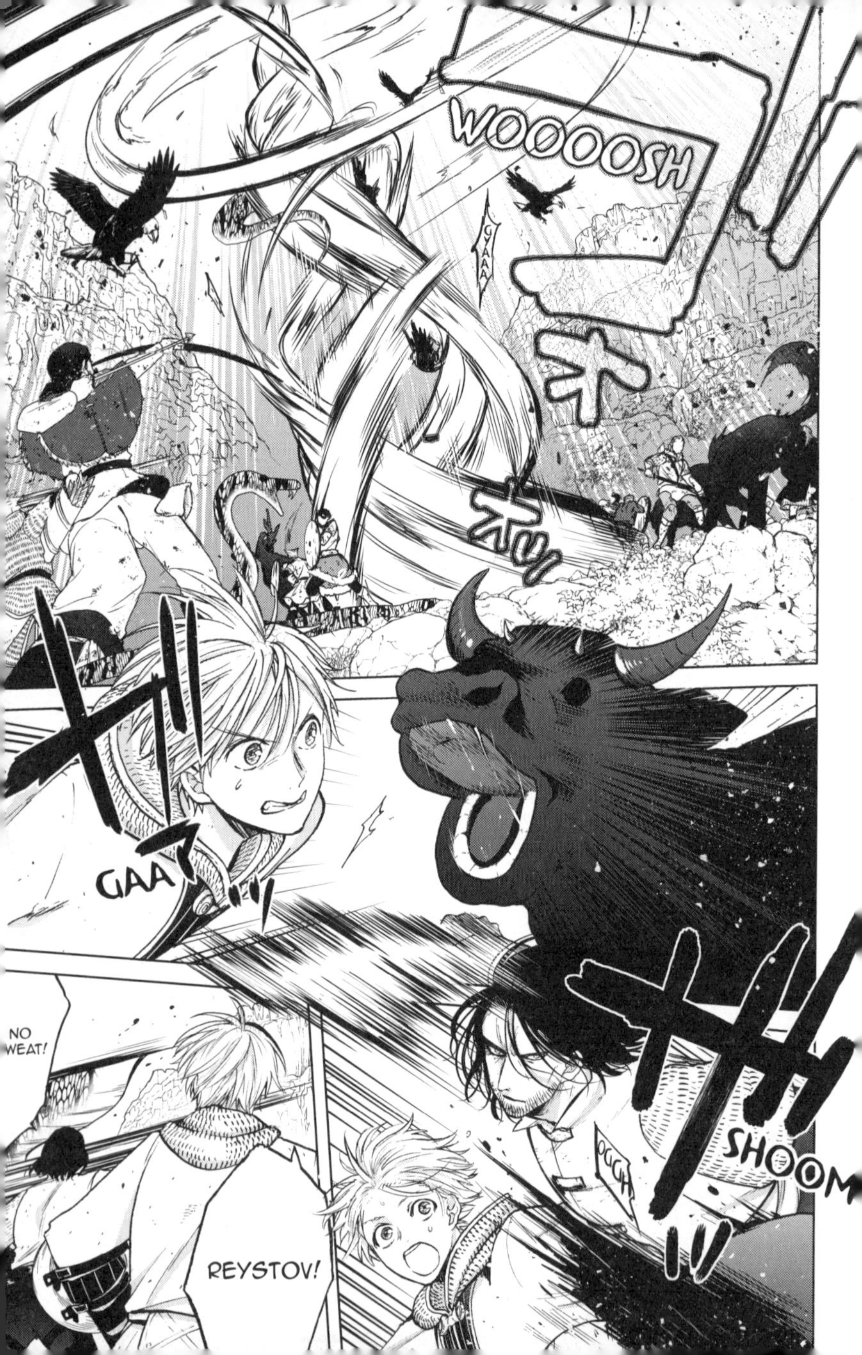
WOOOOSH
GYAAA
GAA
SHOOM
UGGH
NO WEAT!
REYSTOV!

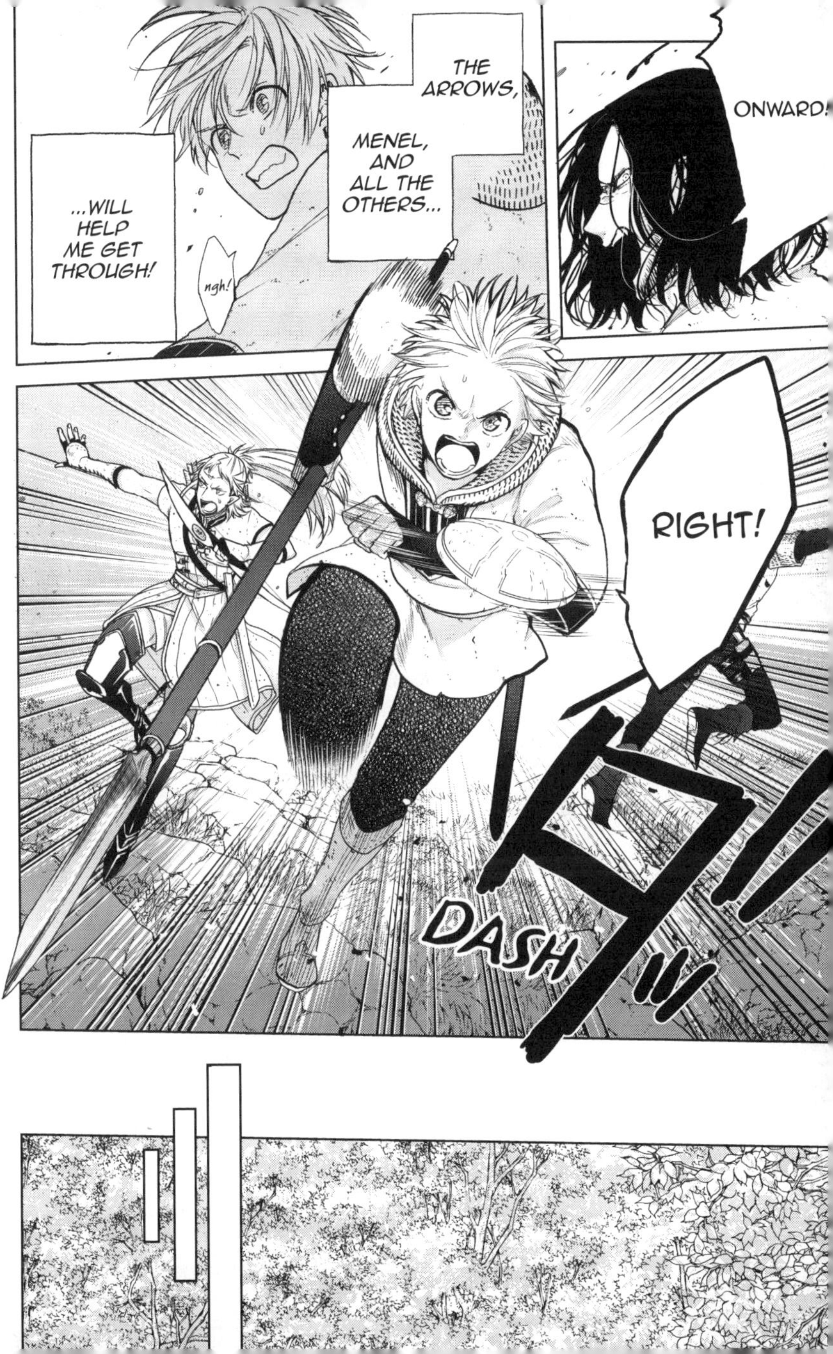
ONWARD!
THE ARROWS,
MENEL, AND ALL THE OTHERS...
ngh!
...WILL HELP ME GET THROUGH!
RIGHT!
DASH

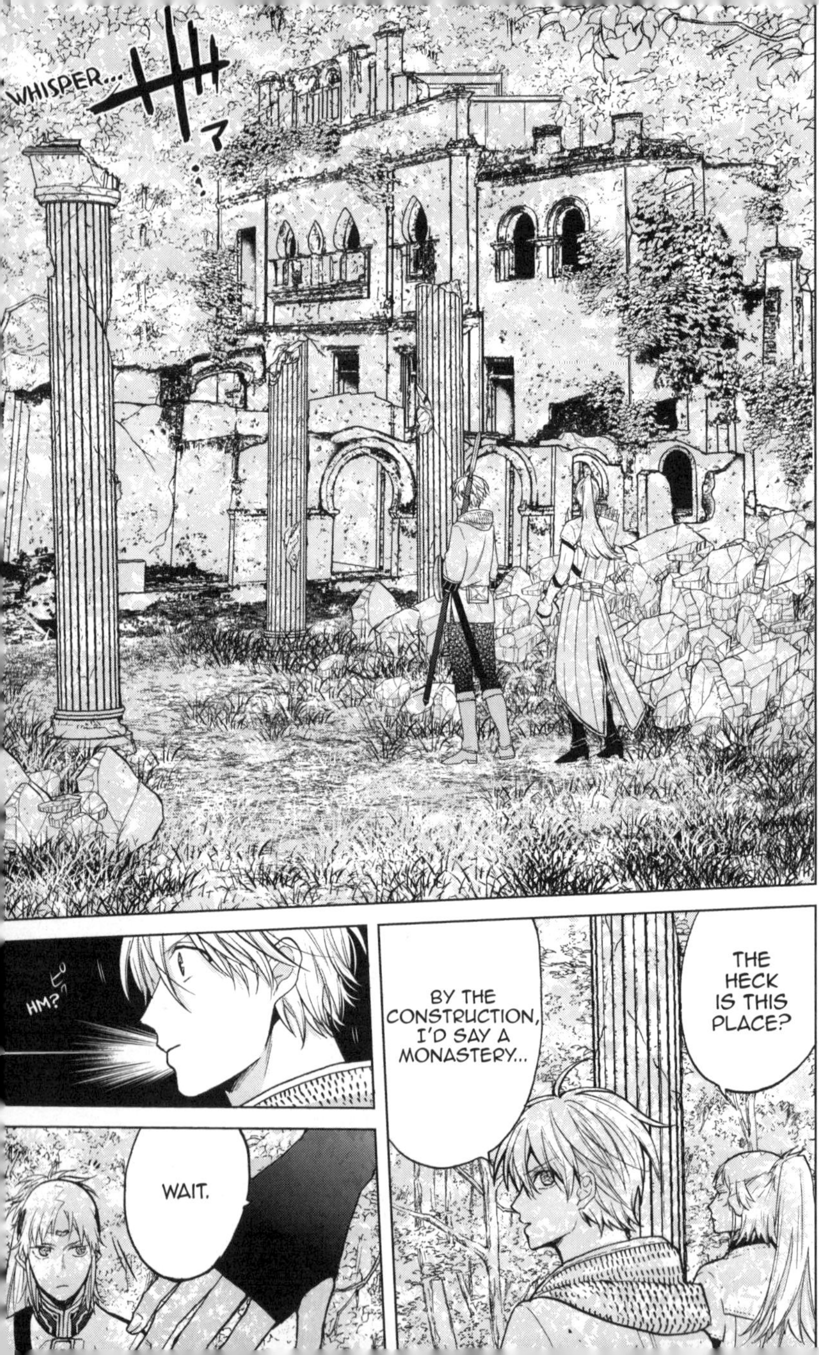
WHISPER...
THE HECK IS THIS PLACE?
BY THE CONSTRUCTION, I'D SAY A MONASTERY...
HM?
WAIT.

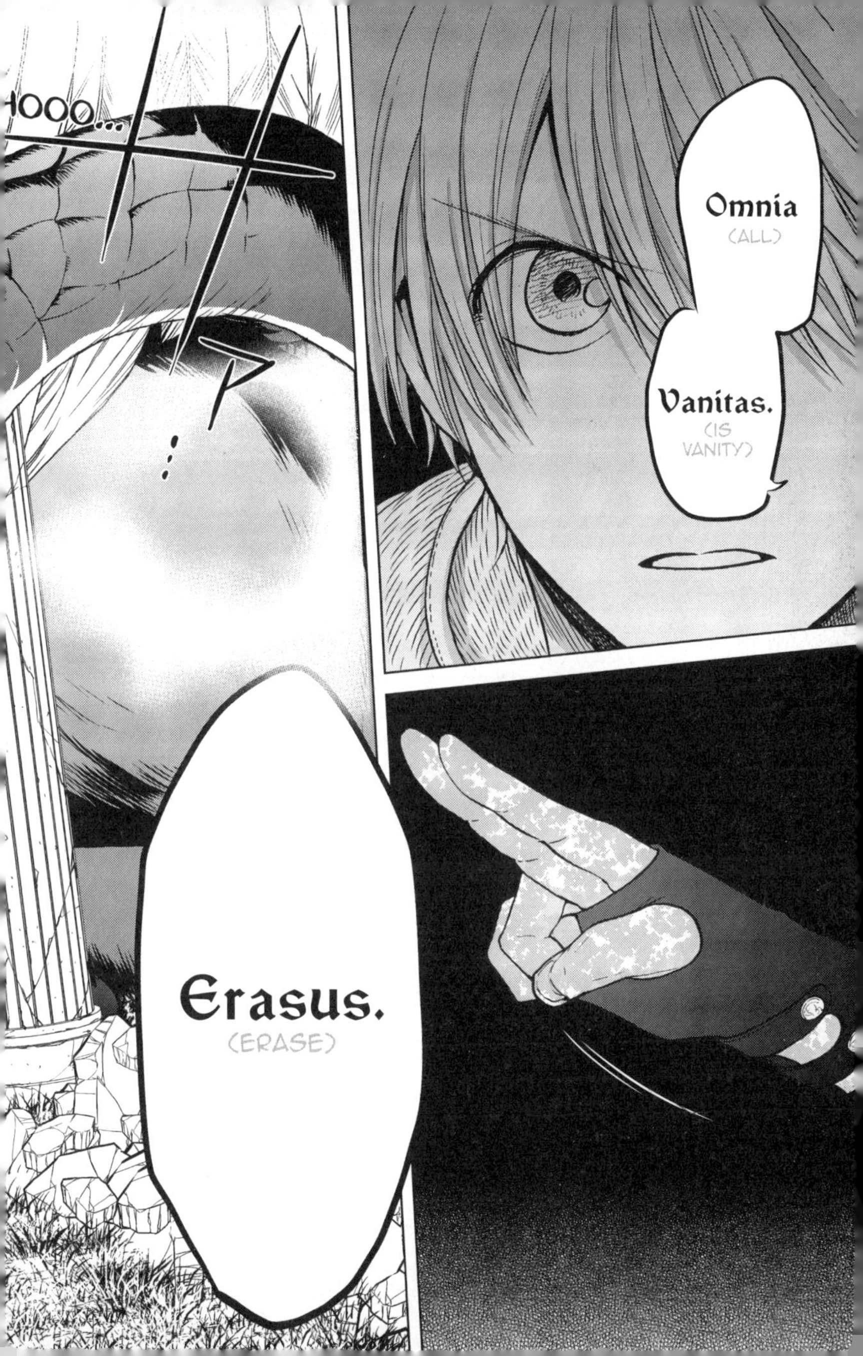

Omnia
(ALL)
Vanitas.
(IS VANITY)
HOOO...
Erasus.
(ERASE)

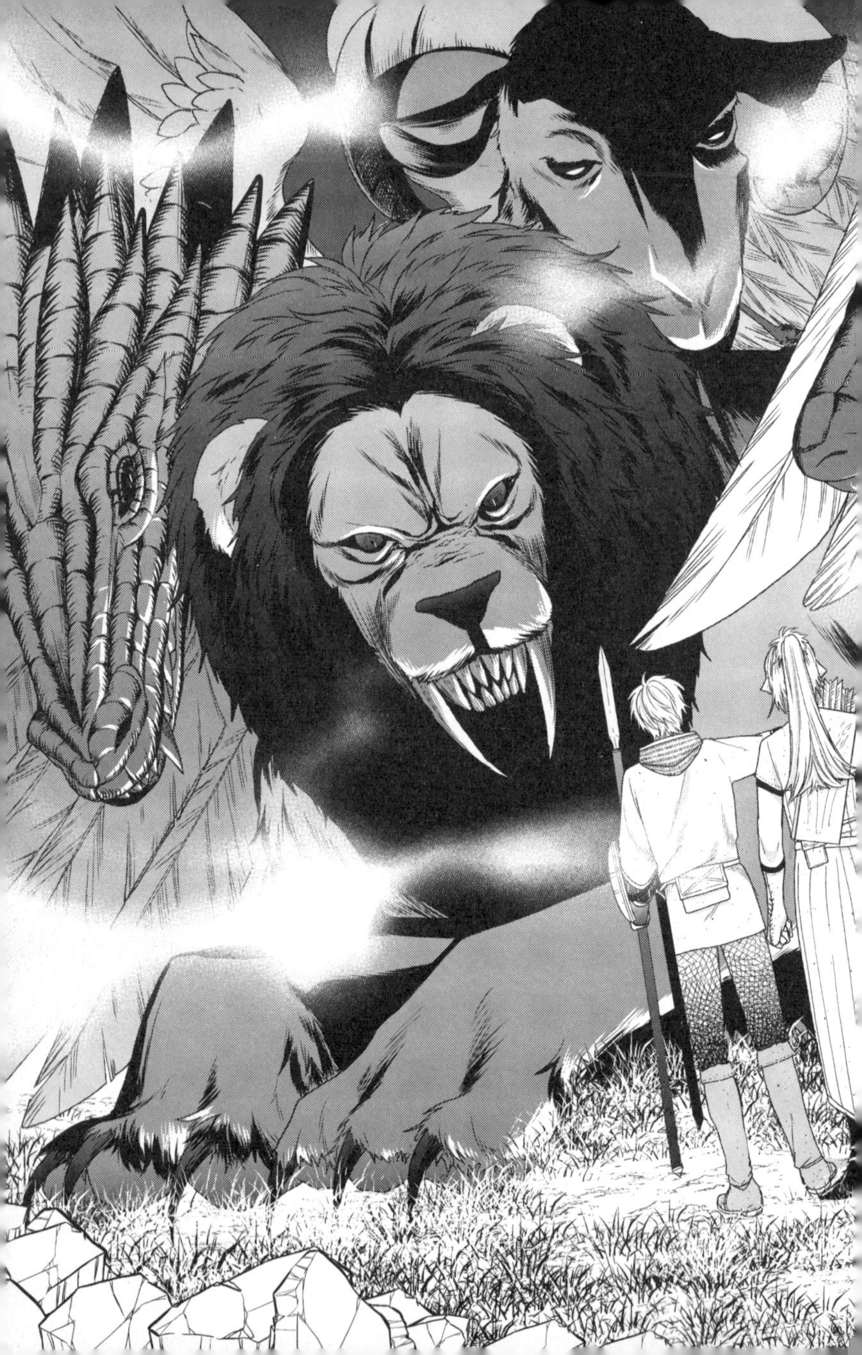

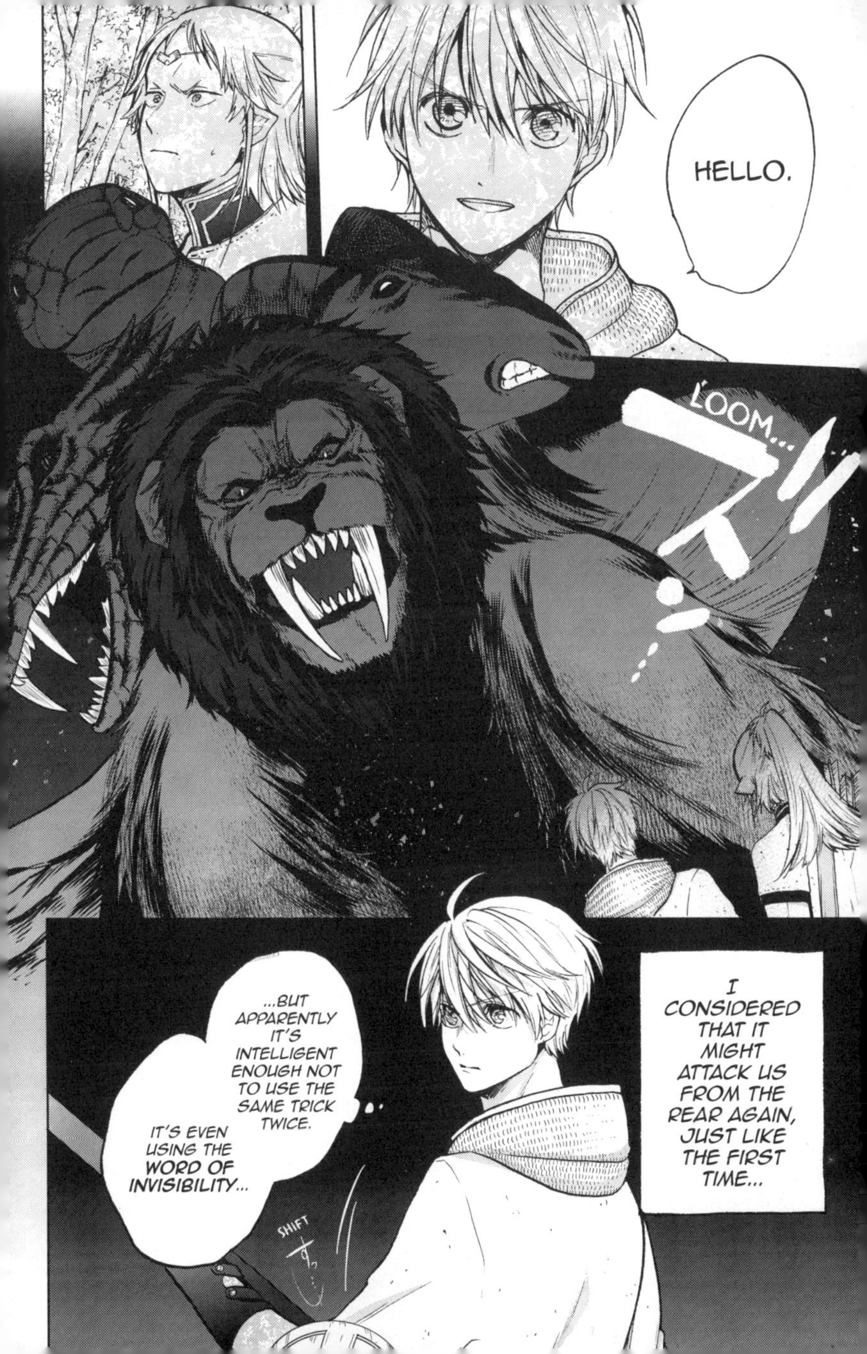
HELLO.
LOOM...
I CONSIDERED THAT IT MIGHT ATTACK US FROM THE REAR AGAIN, JUST LIKE THE FIRST TIME...
...BUT APPARENTLY IT'S INTELLIGENT ENOUGH NOT TO USE THE SAME TRICK TWICE.
IT'S EVEN USING THE WORD OF INVISIBILITY...
SHIFT

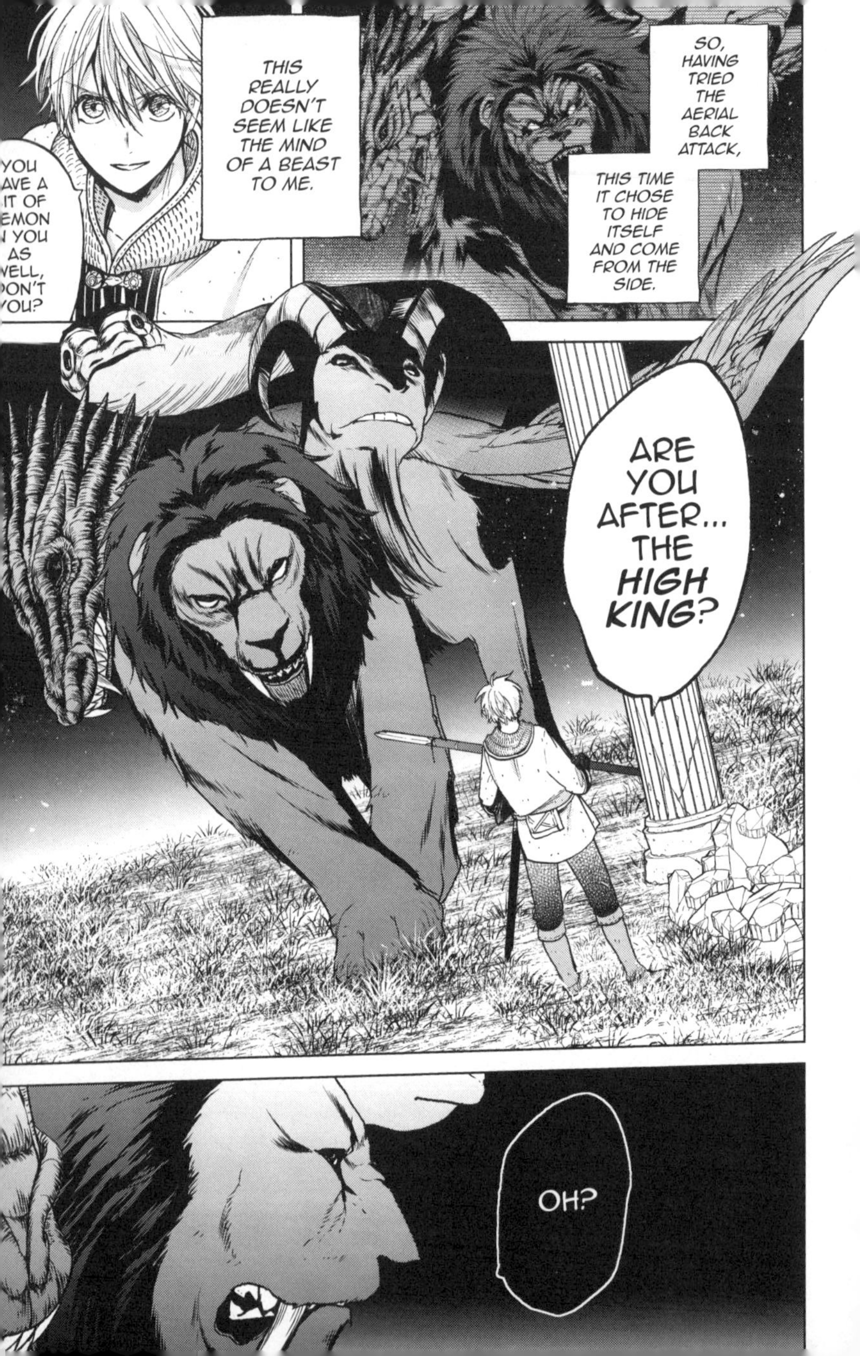
SO, HAVING TRIED THE AERIAL BACK ATTACK,
THIS TIME IT CHOSE TO HIDE ITSELF AND COME FROM THE SIDE.
THIS REALLY DOESN'T SEEM LIKE THE MIND OF A BEAST TO ME.
YOU AVE A IT OF EMON I YOU AS VELL, ON'T OU?
ARE YOU AFTER... THE *HIGH KING*?
OH?

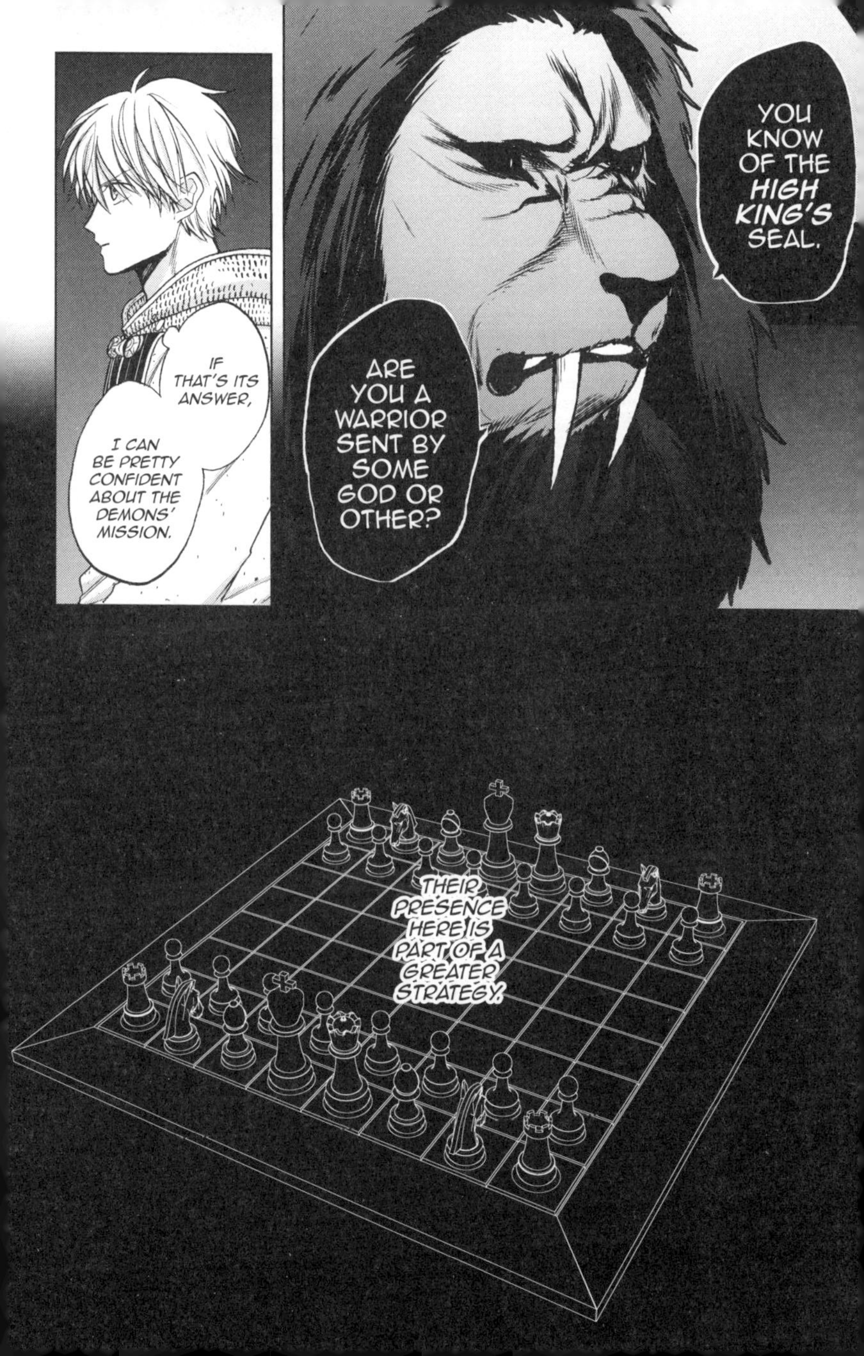
YOU KNOW OF THE HIGH KING'S SEAL.
ARE YOU A WARRIOR SENT BY SOME GOD OR OTHER?
IF THAT'S ITS ANSWER,
I CAN BE PRETTY CONFIDENT ABOUT THE DEMONS' MISSION.
THEIR PRESENCE HERE IS PART OF A GREATER STRATEGY.

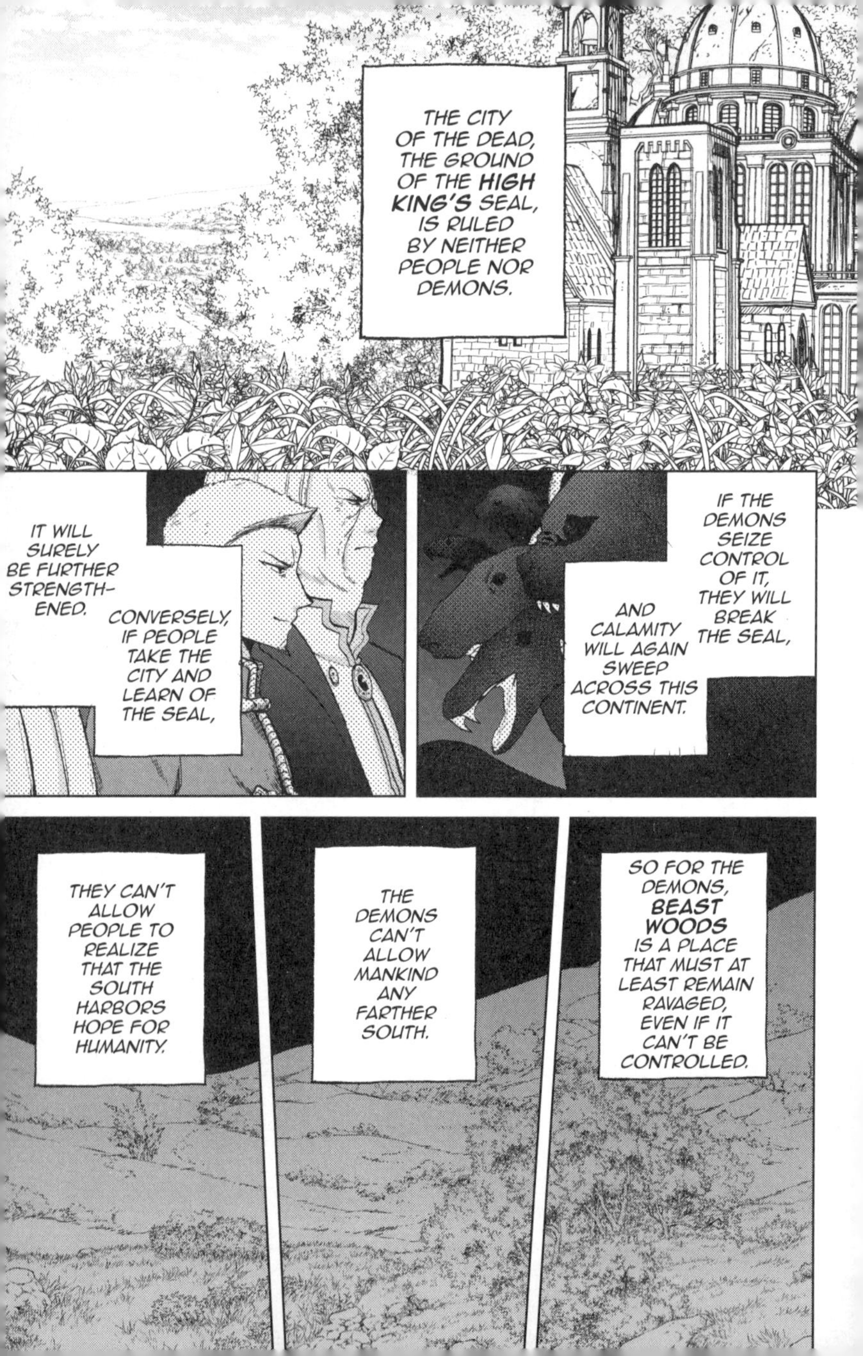
THE CITY OF THE DEAD, THE GROUND OF THE **HIGH KING'S** SEAL, IS RULED BY NEITHER PEOPLE NOR DEMONS.
IF THE DEMONS SEIZE CONTROL OF IT, THEY WILL BREAK THE SEAL,
AND CALAMITY WILL AGAIN SWEEP ACROSS THIS CONTINENT.
CONVERSELY, IF PEOPLE TAKE THE CITY AND LEARN OF THE SEAL,
IT WILL SURELY BE FURTHER STRENGTH-ENED.
SO FOR THE DEMONS, **BEAST WOODS** IS A PLACE THAT MUST AT LEAST REMAIN RAVAGED, EVEN IF IT CAN'T BE CONTROLLED.
THE DEMONS CAN'T ALLOW MANKIND ANY FARTHER SOUTH.
THEY CAN'T ALLOW PEOPLE TO REALIZE THAT THE SOUTH HARBORS HOPE FOR HUMANITY.

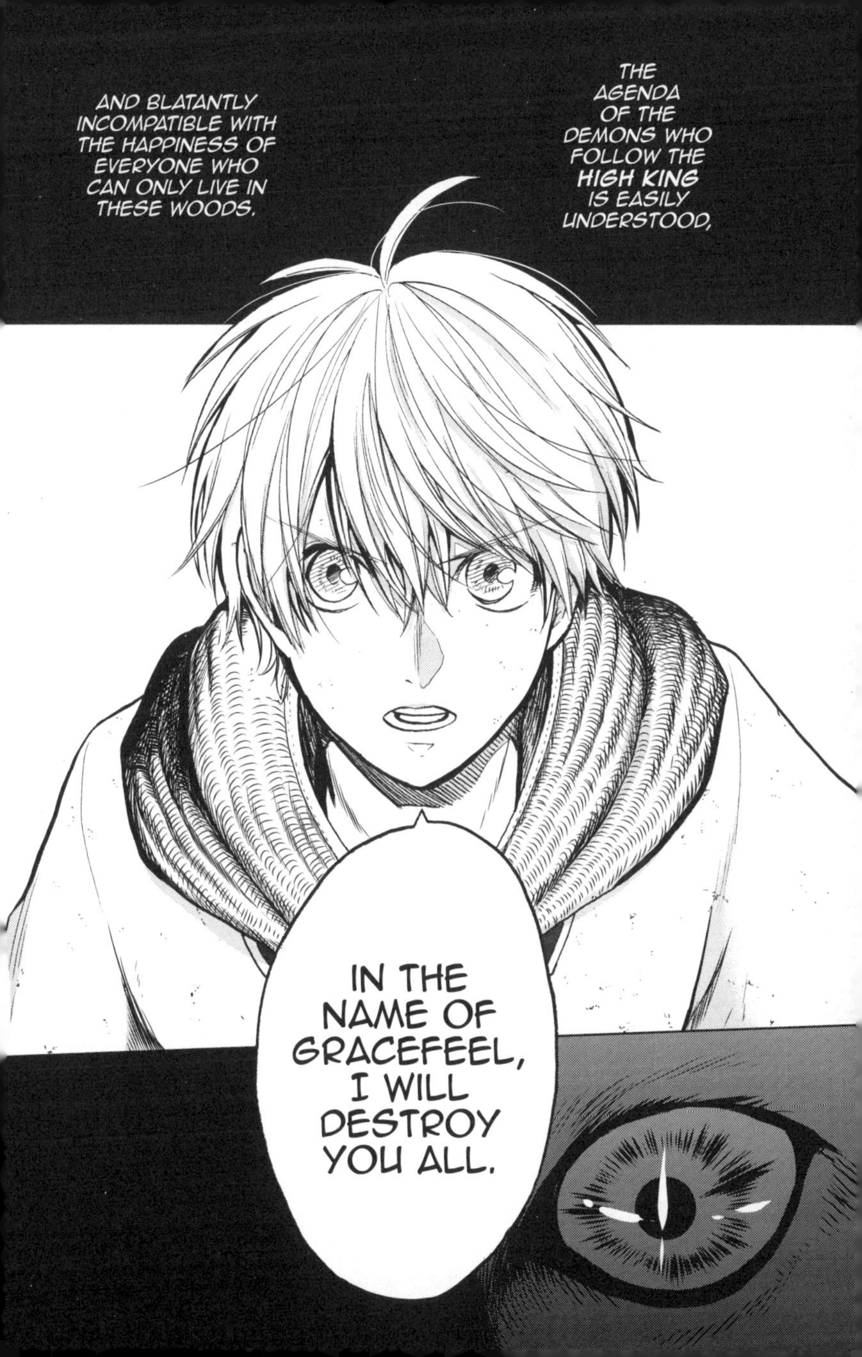
THE AGENDA OF THE DEMONS WHO FOLLOW THE HIGH KING IS EASILY UNDERSTOOD,
AND BLATANTLY INCOMPATIBLE WITH THE HAPPINESS OF EVERYONE WHO CAN ONLY LIVE IN THESE WOODS.
IN THE NAME OF GRACEFEEL, I WILL DESTROY YOU ALL.

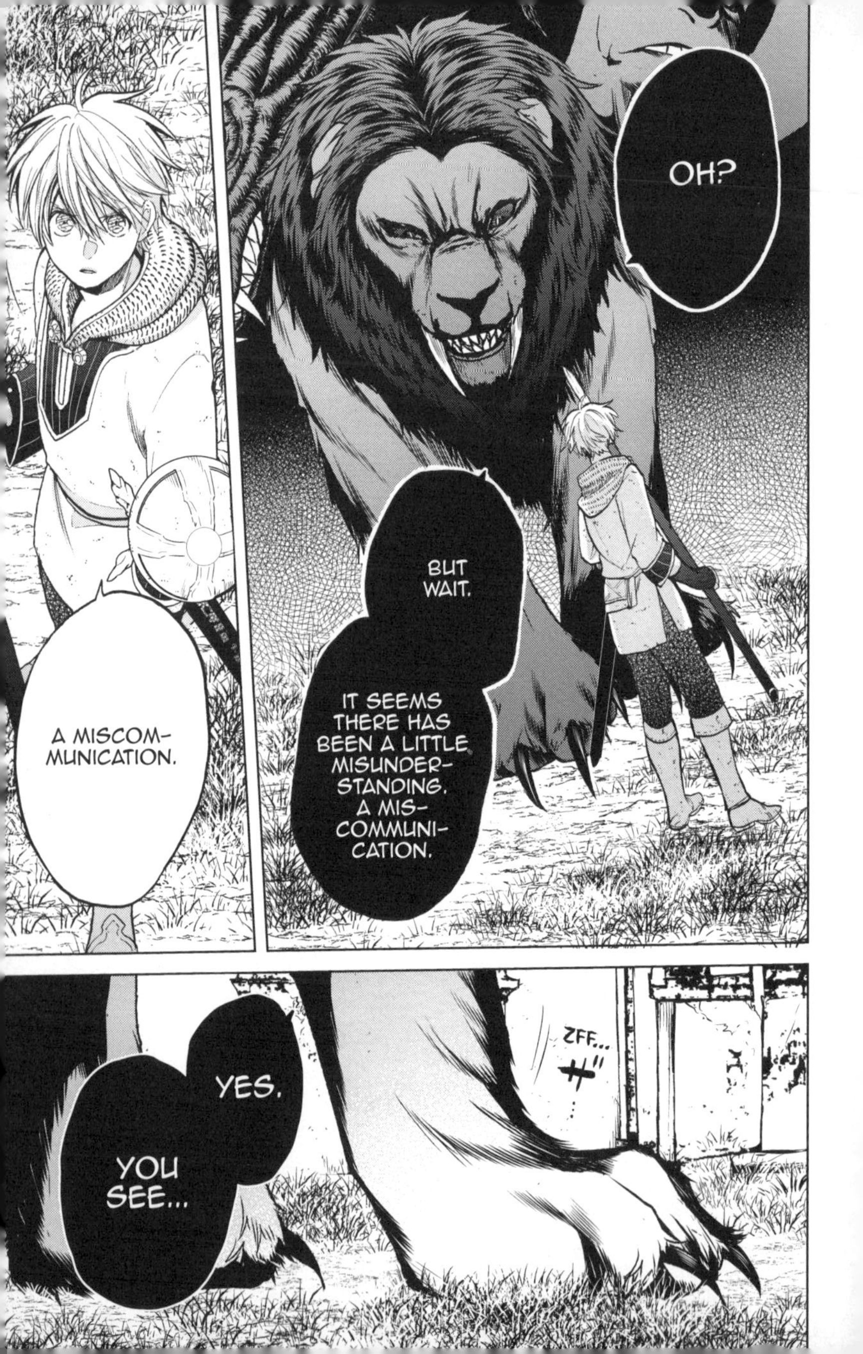
OH?
BUT WAIT.
IT SEEMS THERE HAS BEEN A LITTLE MISUNDER-STANDING. A MIS-COMMUNI-CATION.
A MISCOM-MUNICATION.
ZFF...
YES.
YOU SEE...

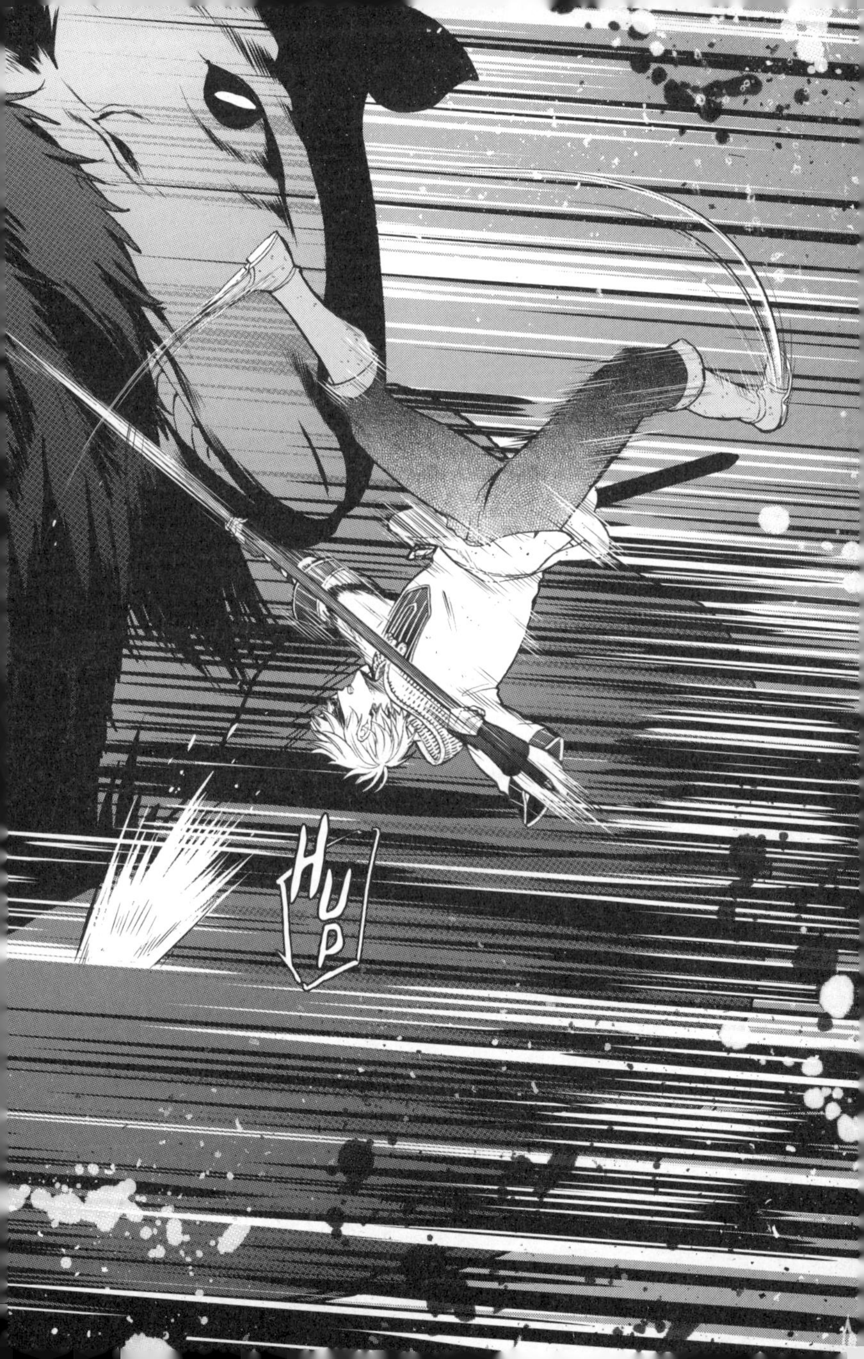
HUP

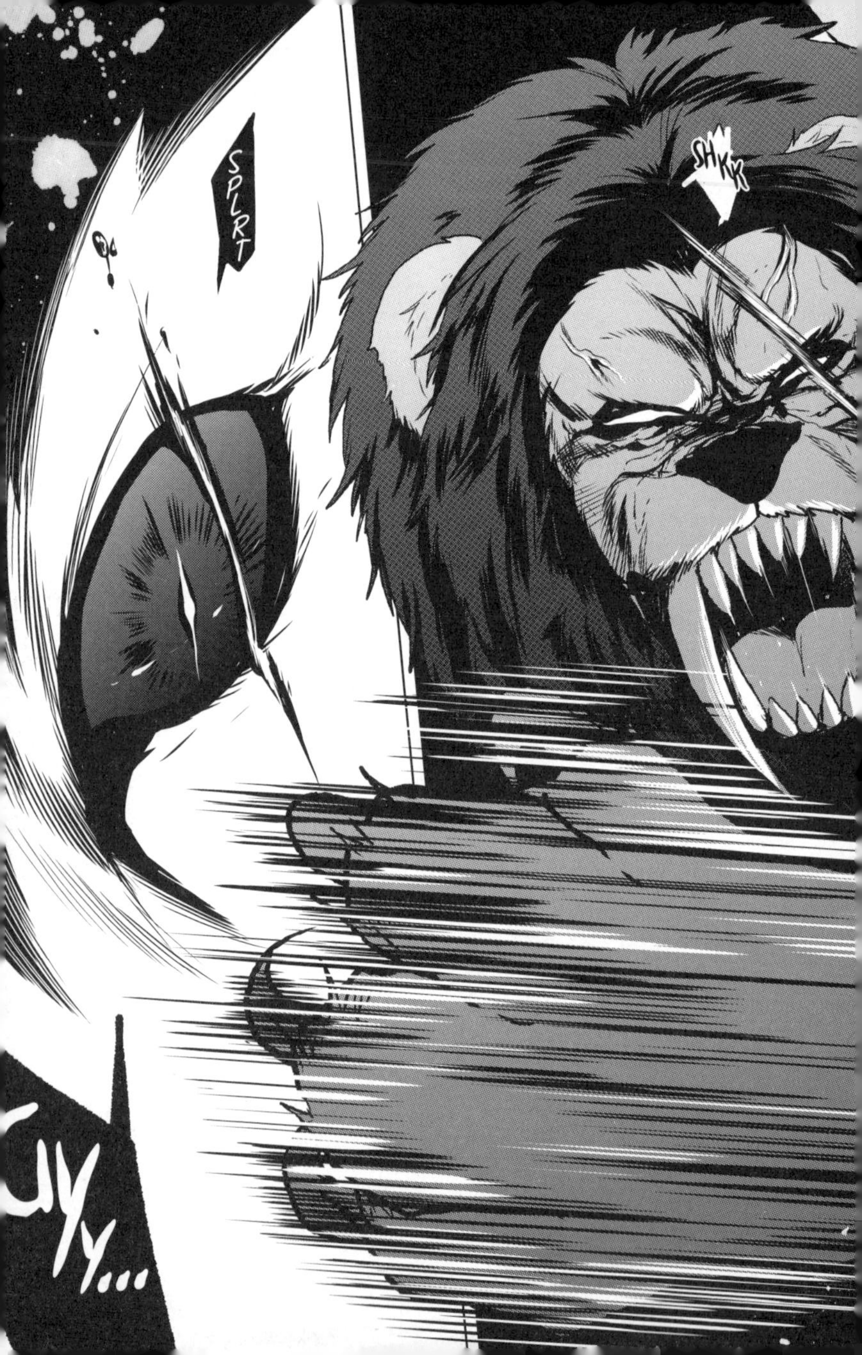
SHKK
SPLRT
Yy...

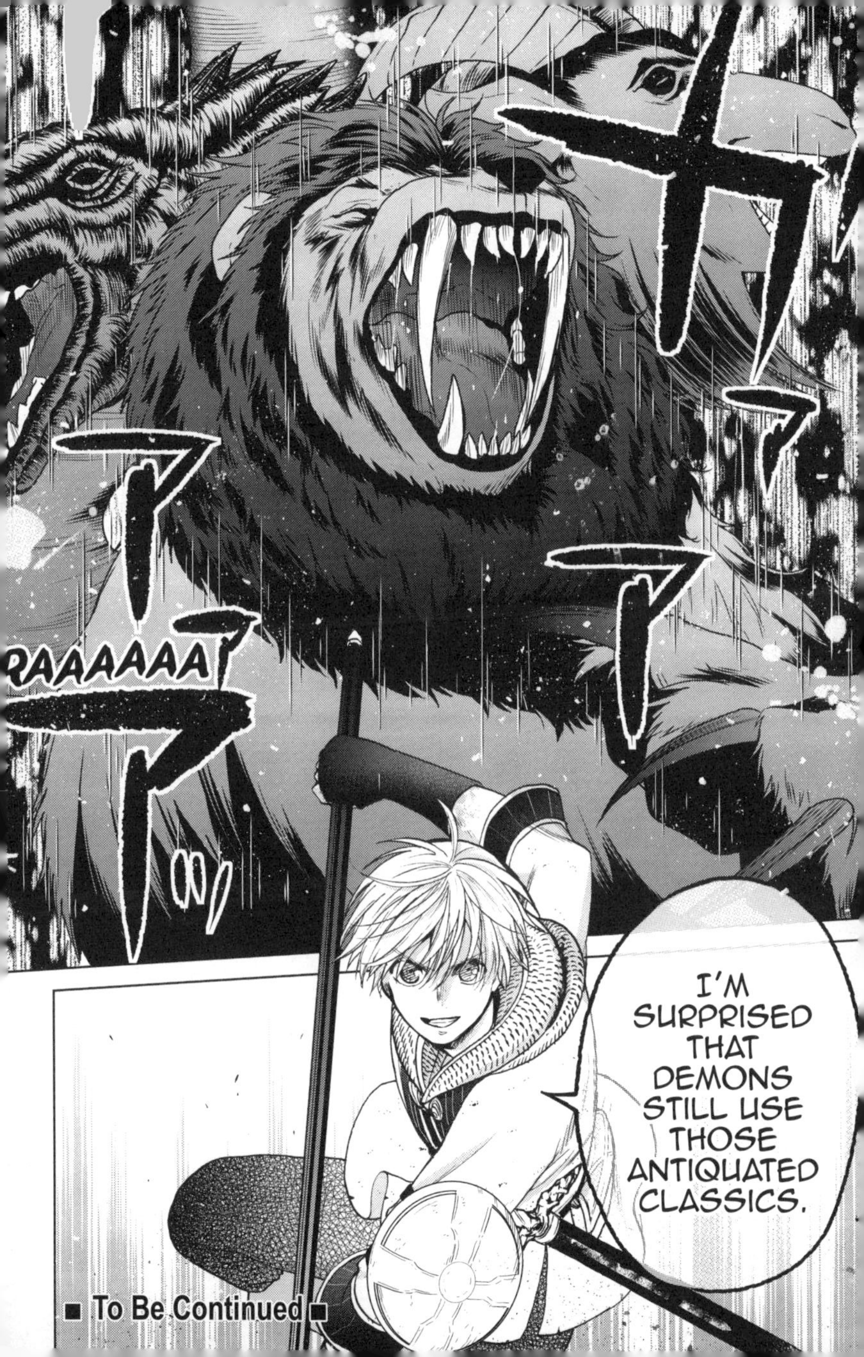
RAAAAAA
I'M SURPRISED THAT DEMONS STILL USE THOSE ANTIQUATED CLASSICS.
■ To Be Continued ■

THE FARAWAY
PALADIN

Afterword

Manga artist: Mutsumi Okubashi

Volume five! This was a challenging volume for depicting Will's emotions as he built new relationships, took his first steps as a paladin, and worried and struggled as a human being. Also, the cool incantations in the battle scenes throughout the volume were provided by Yanagino-sensei. Yanagino-sensei, thank you very much!

Original work: Kanata Yanagino

The comic adaptation reaches its fifth volume at last! To Okubashi-sensei, everyone involved in the publishing process, and you, the one reading this right now: my heartfelt thanks to you all.

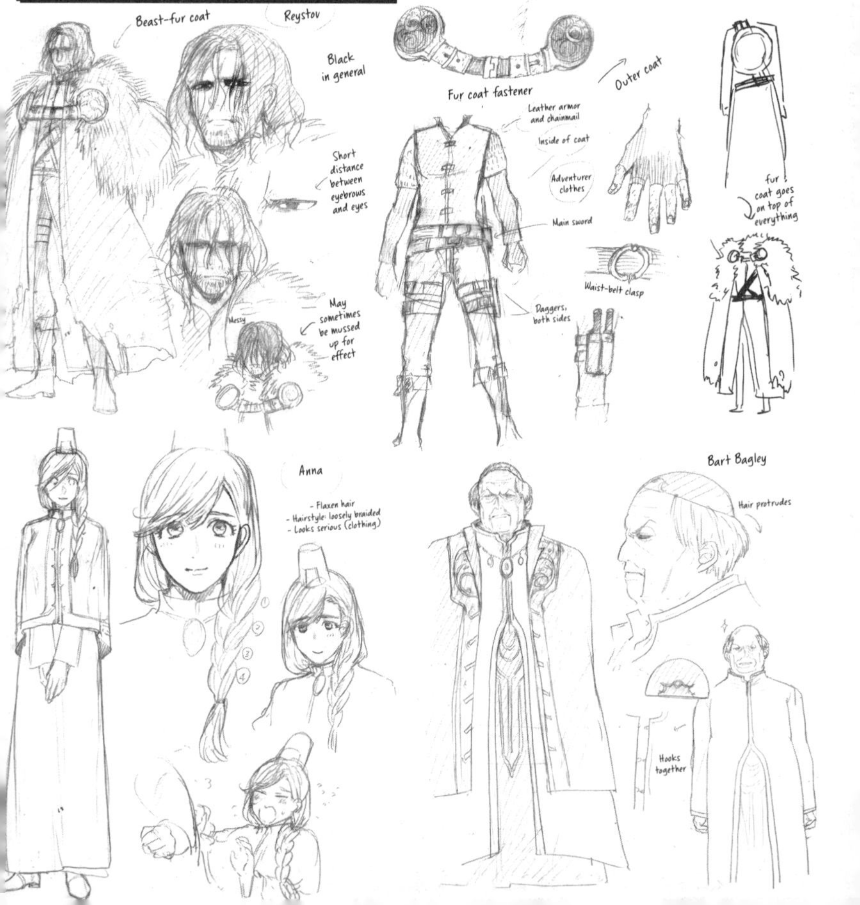

Beast-fur coat
Reystov
Black in general
Short distance between eyebrows and eyes
Messy
May sometimes be mussed up for effect
Fur coat fastener
Outer coat
Leather armor and chainmail
Inside of coat
Adventurer clothes
Main sword
Waist-belt clasp
Daggers, both sides
fur coat goes on top of everything
Anna
- Flaxen hair
- Hairstyle: loosely braided
- Looks serious (clothing)
Bart Bagley
Hair protrudes
Hooks together

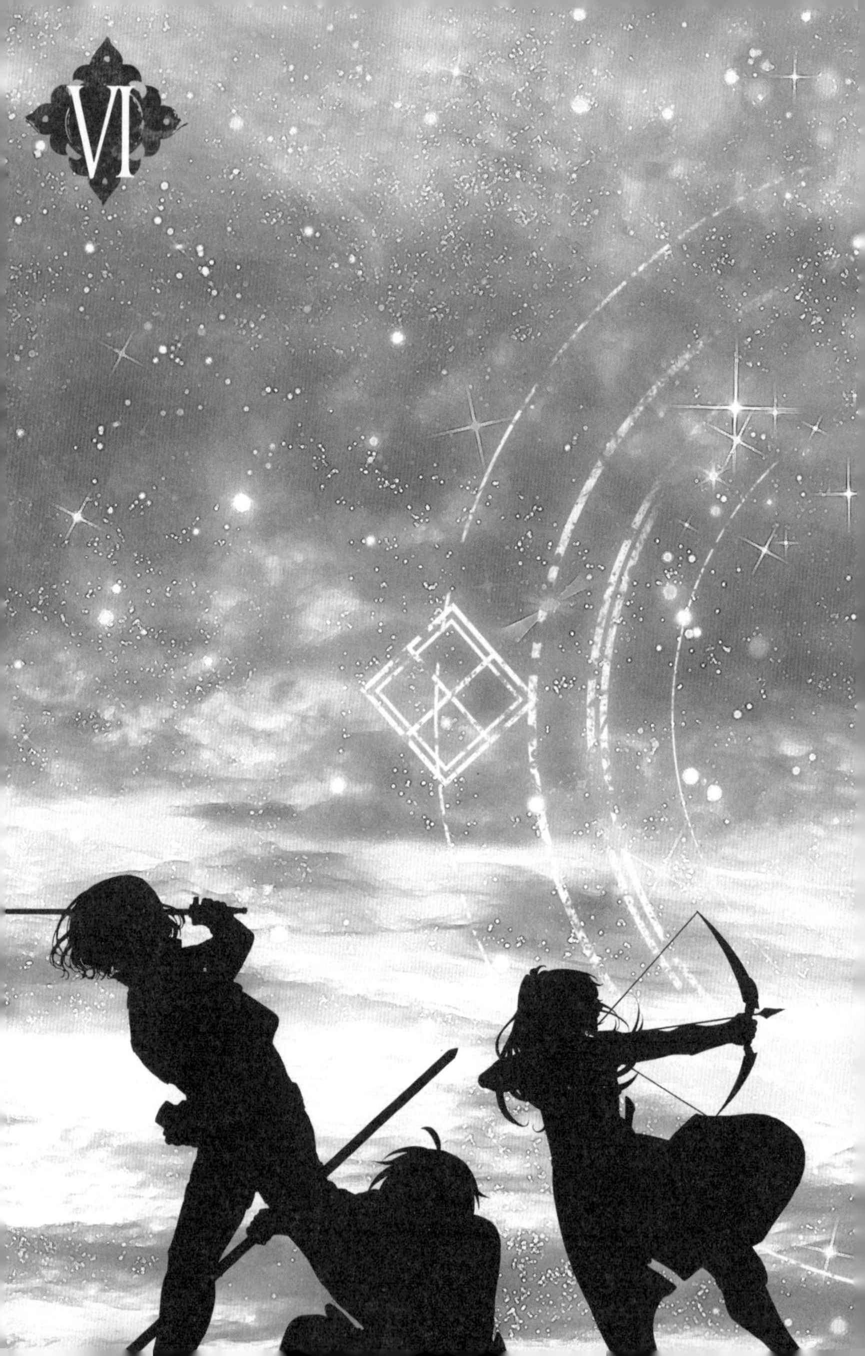
VI

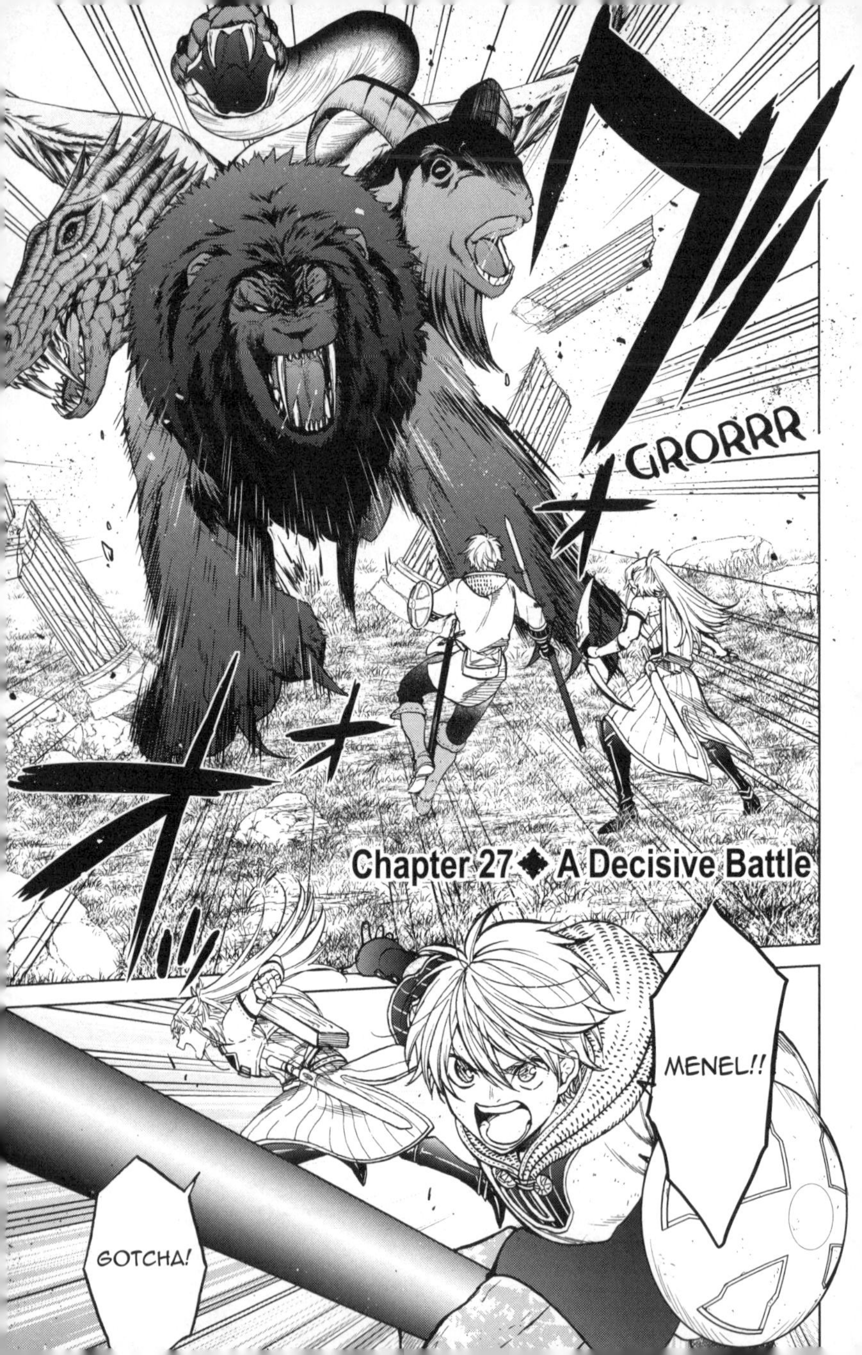
GRORRR
Chapter 27 ◆ A Decisive Battle
MENEL!!
GOTCHA!

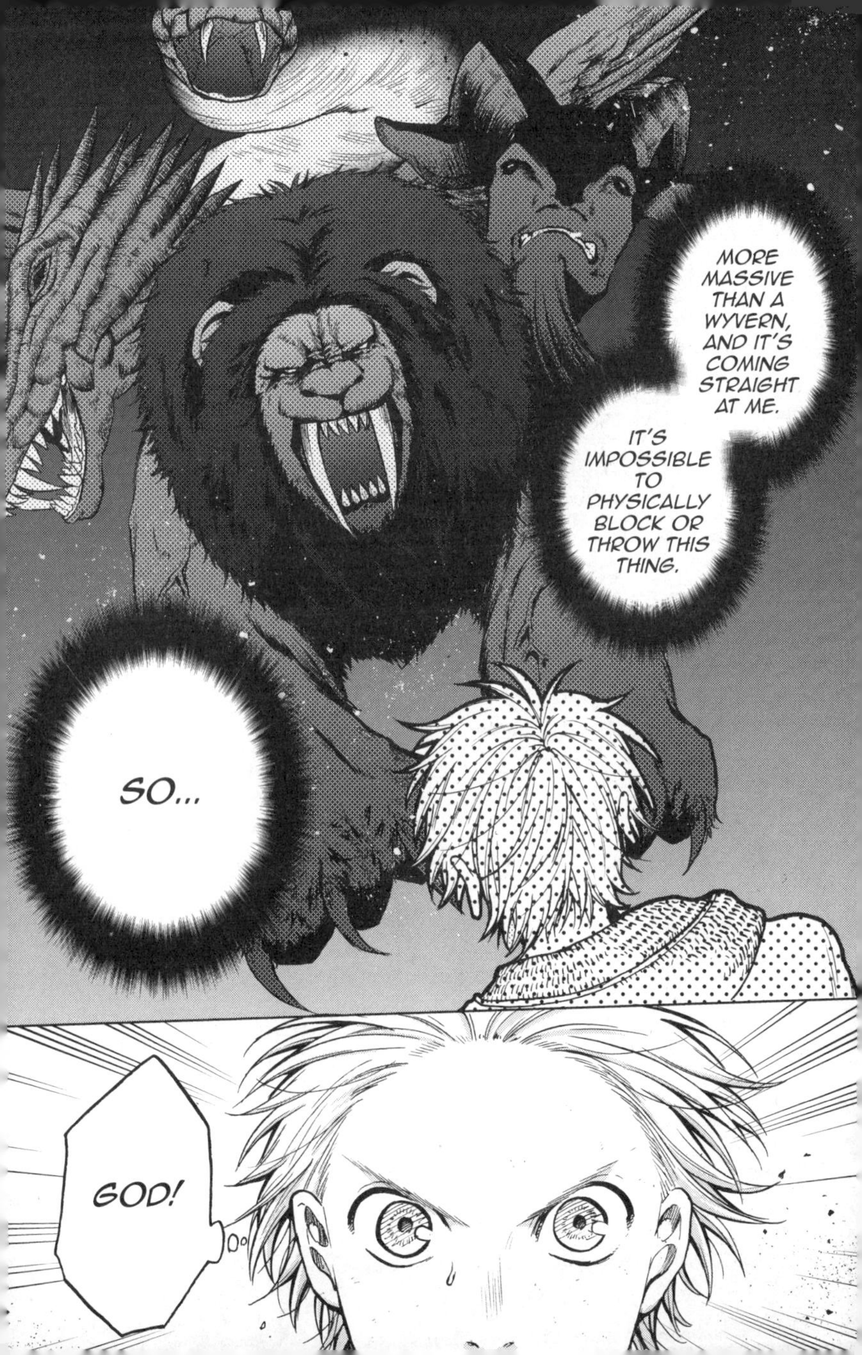
MORE MASSIVE THAN A WYVERN, AND IT'S COMING STRAIGHT AT ME.
IT'S IMPOSSIBLE TO PHYSICALLY BLOCK OR THROW THIS THING.
SO...
GOD!

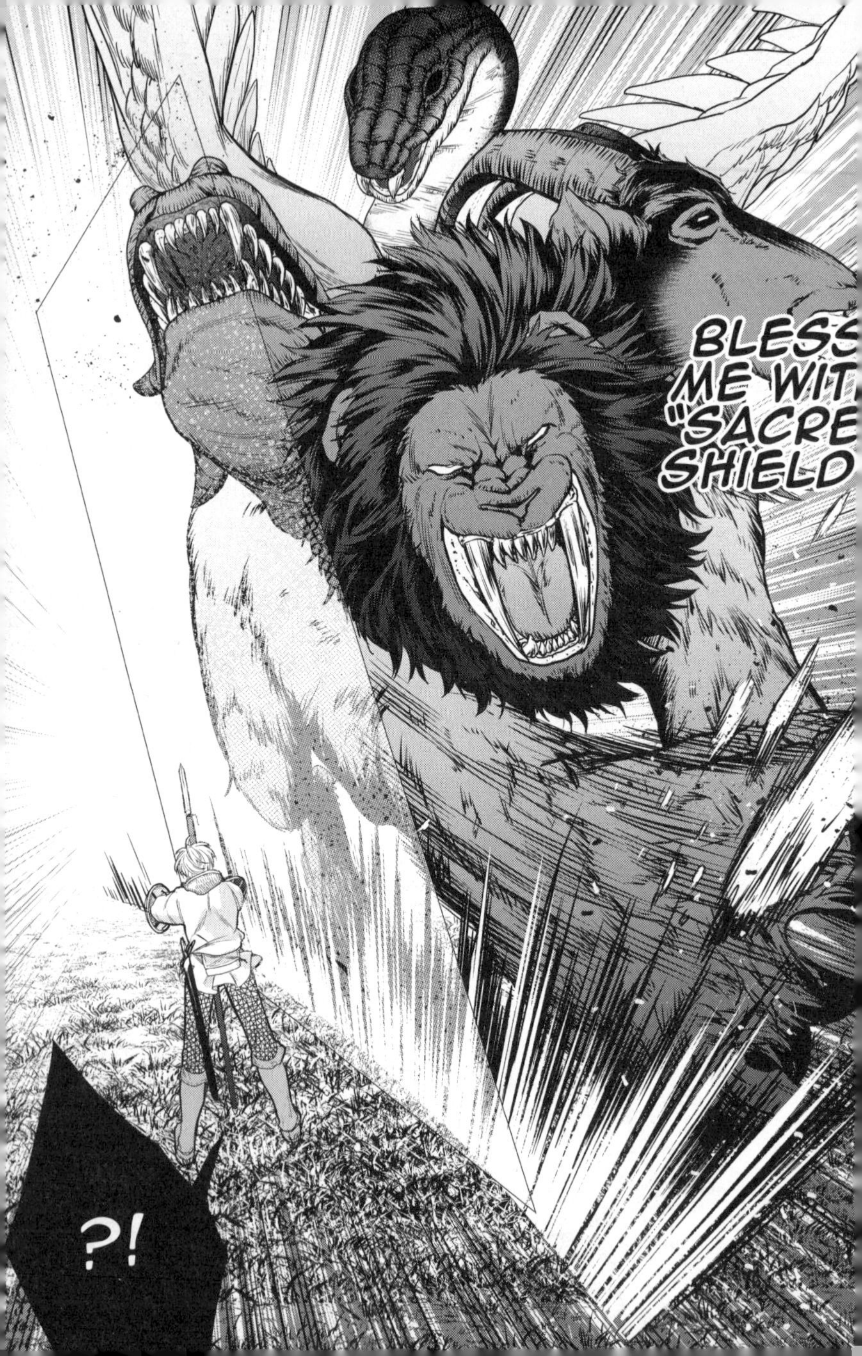
BLESS ME WIT "SACRE SHIELD
?!

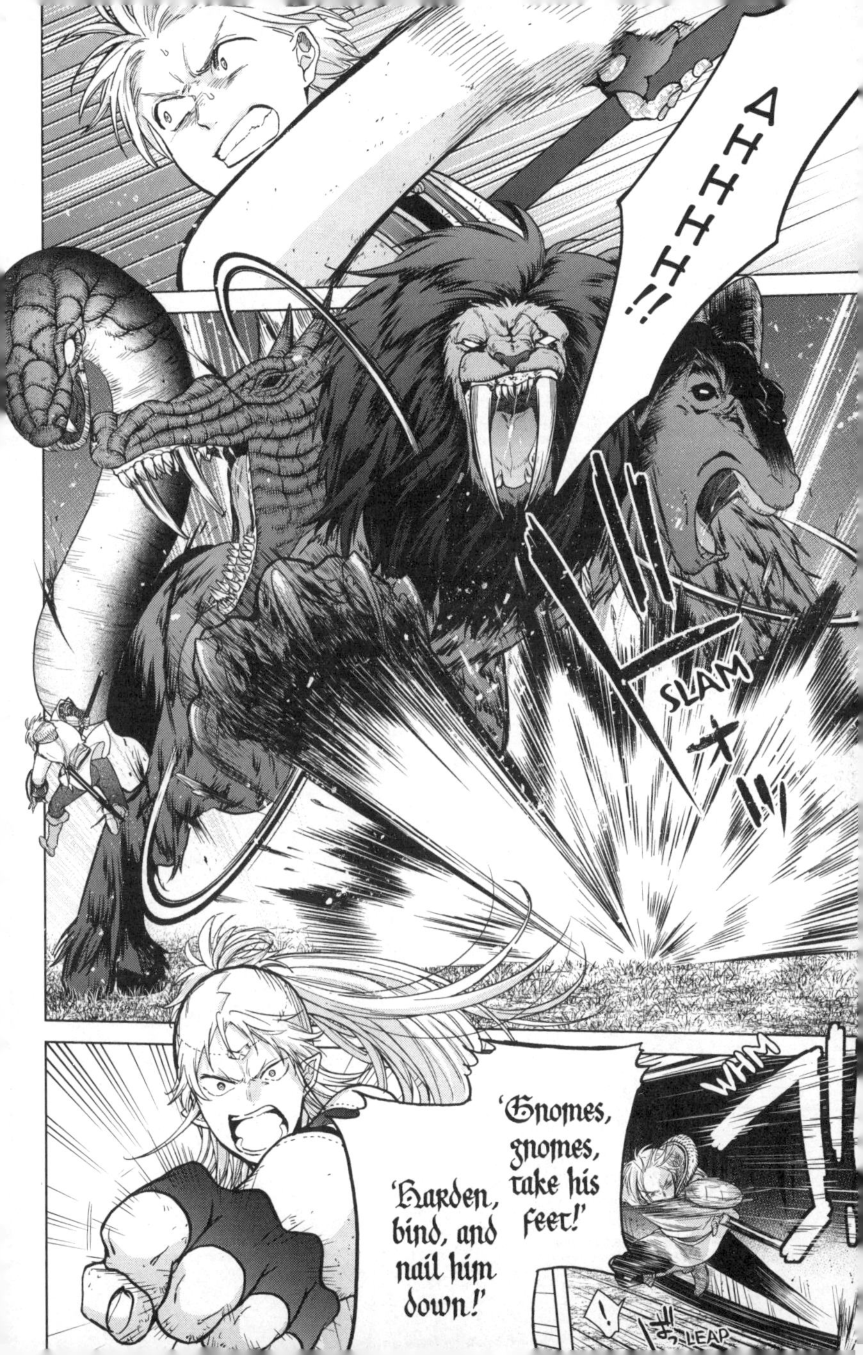
AHHHH!!
SLAM
WHM
!
LEAP
'Gnomes, gnomes, take his feet!'
'Harden, bind, and nail him down!'

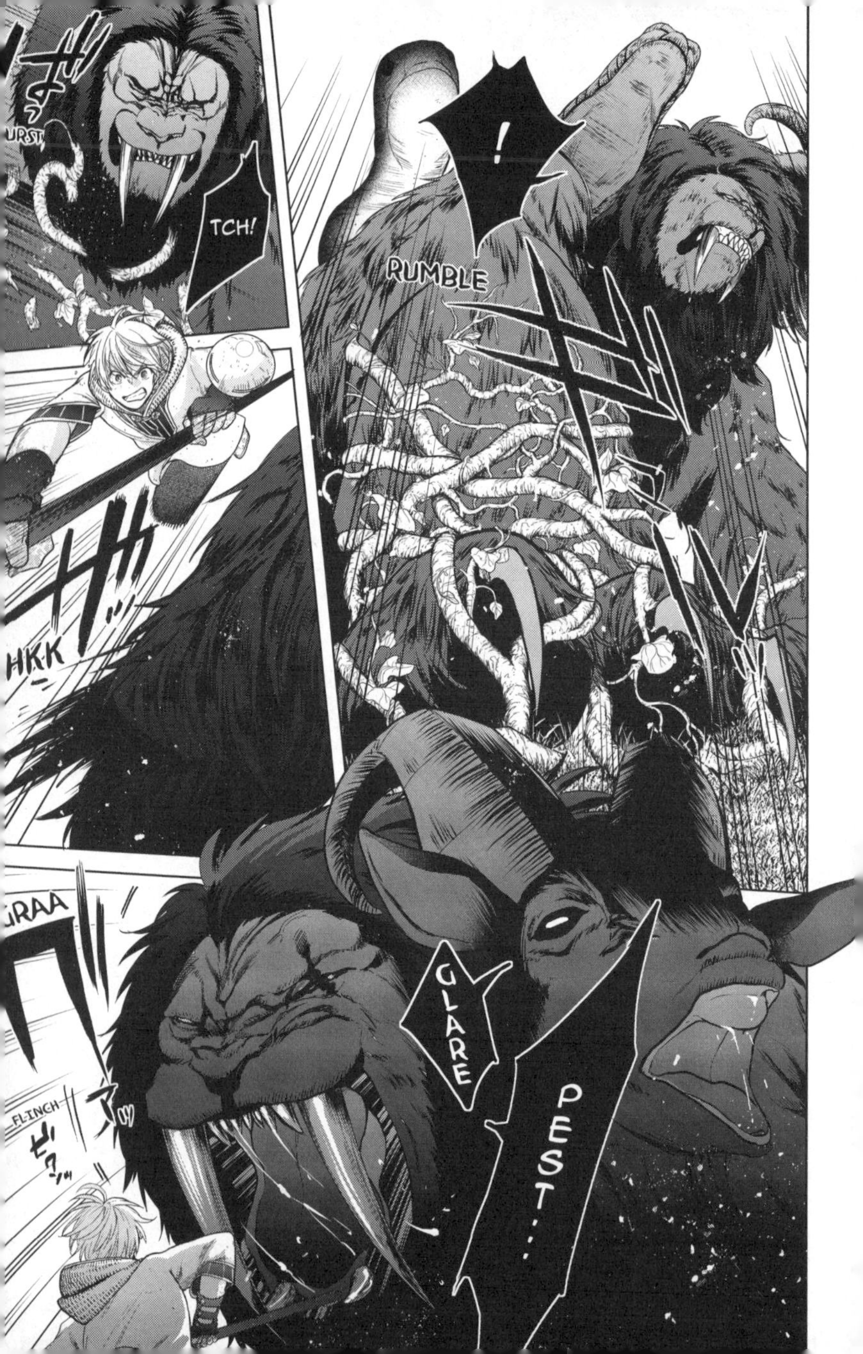
!
RUMBLE
URST
TCH!
HK-K
GLARE
PEST...
RAA
FLINCH

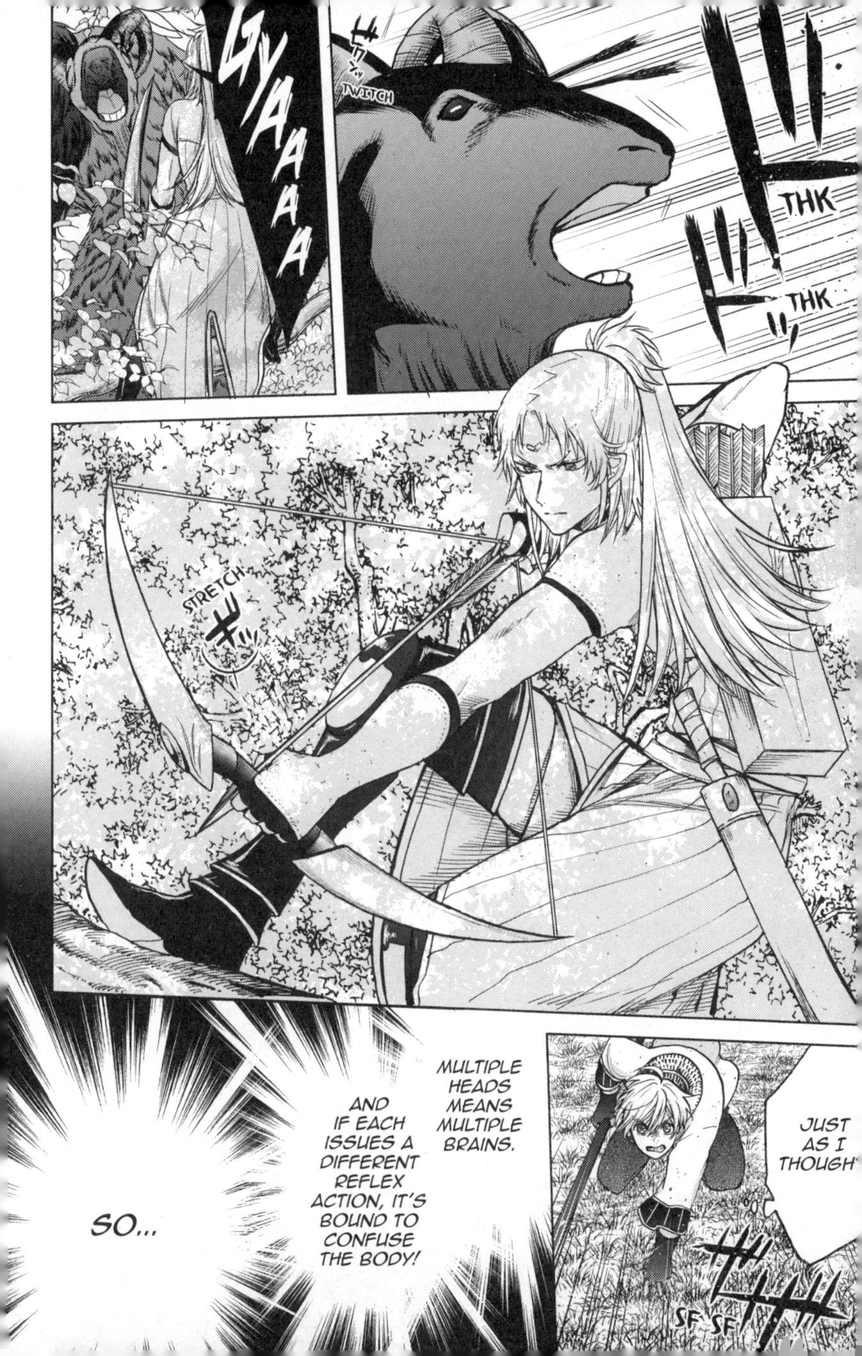
THK
THK
TWITCH
GYAAAAAA
STRETCH
JUST AS I THOUGH
SF SF
MULTIPLE HEADS MEANS MULTIPLE BRAINS.
AND IF EACH ISSUES A DIFFERENT REFLEX ACTION, IT'S BOUND TO CONFUSE THE BODY!
SO...

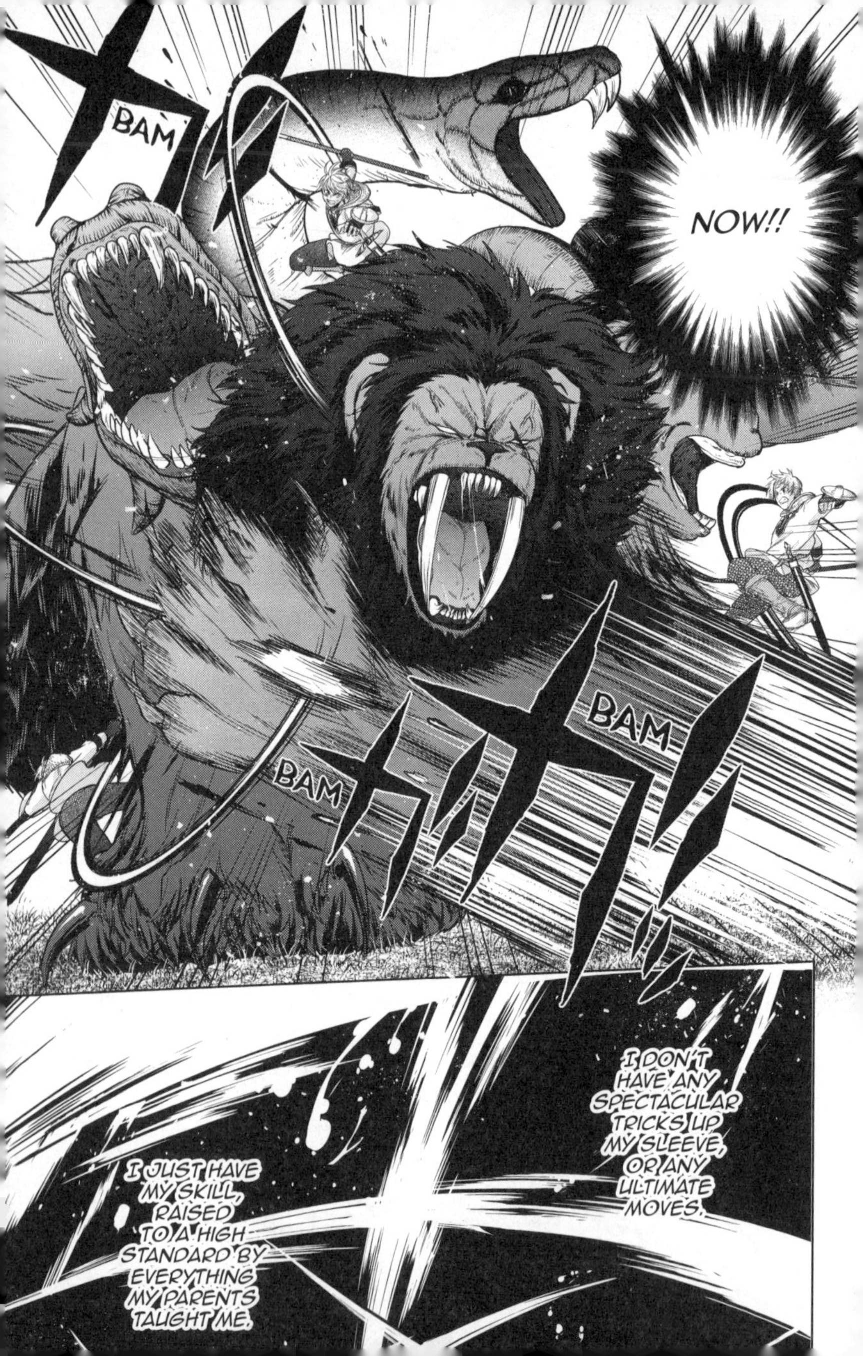
NOW!!
BAM
BAM
BAM
I DON'T HAVE ANY SPECTACULAR TRICKS UP MY SLEEVE, OR ANY ULTIMATE MOVES.
I JUST HAVE MY SKILL, RAISED TO A HIGH STANDARD BY EVERYTHING MY PARENTS TAUGHT ME.

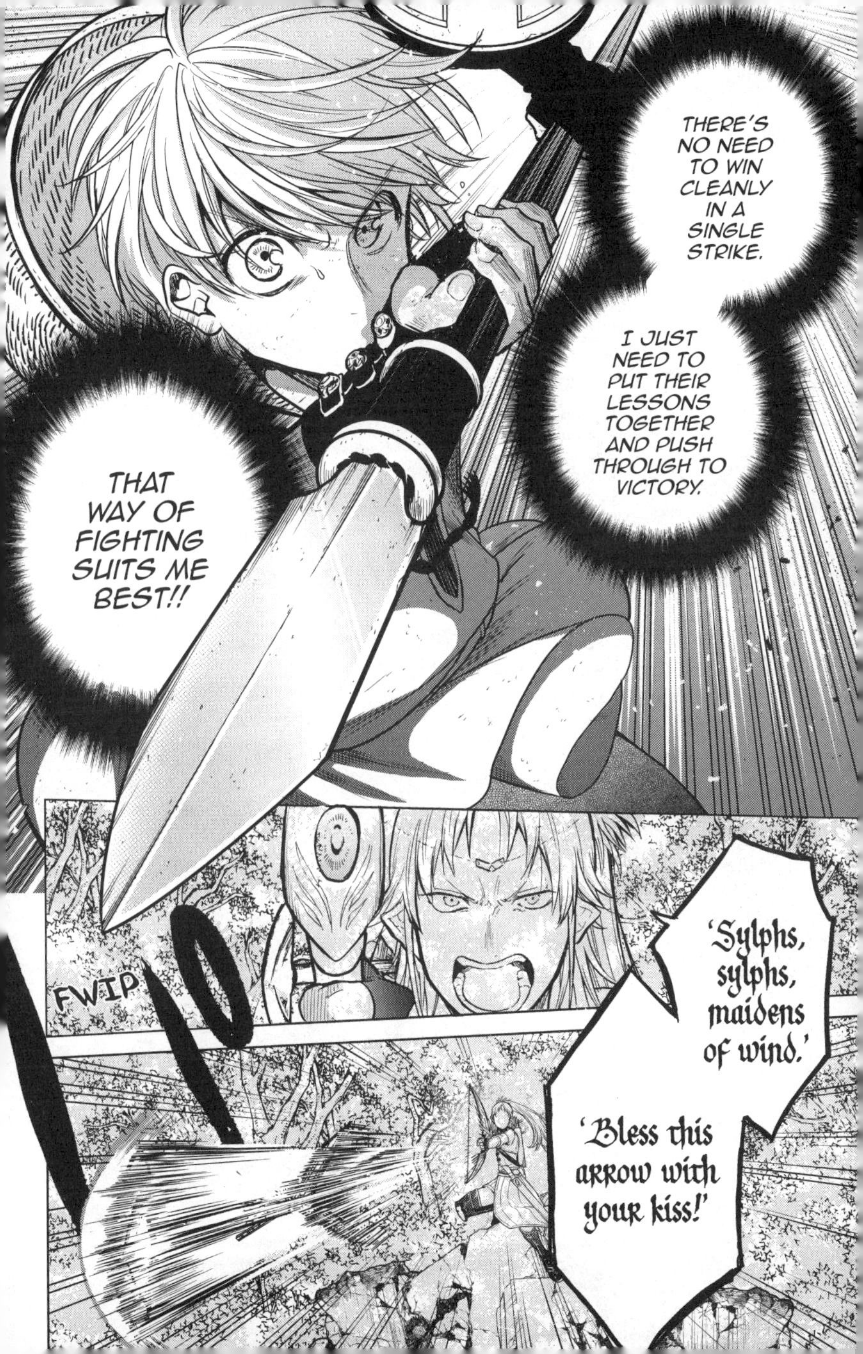
THERE'S NO NEED TO WIN CLEANLY IN A SINGLE STRIKE.
I JUST NEED TO PUT THEIR LESSONS TOGETHER AND PUSH THROUGH TO VICTORY.
THAT WAY OF FIGHTING SUITS ME BEST!!
'Sylphs, sylphs, maidens of wind.'
FWIP
'Bless this arrow with your kiss!'

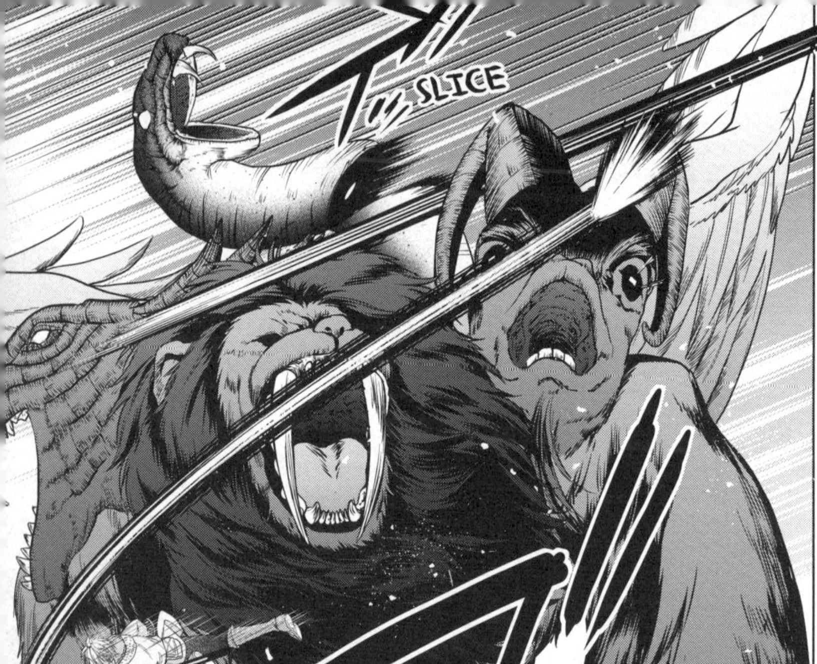
SLICE
WHM

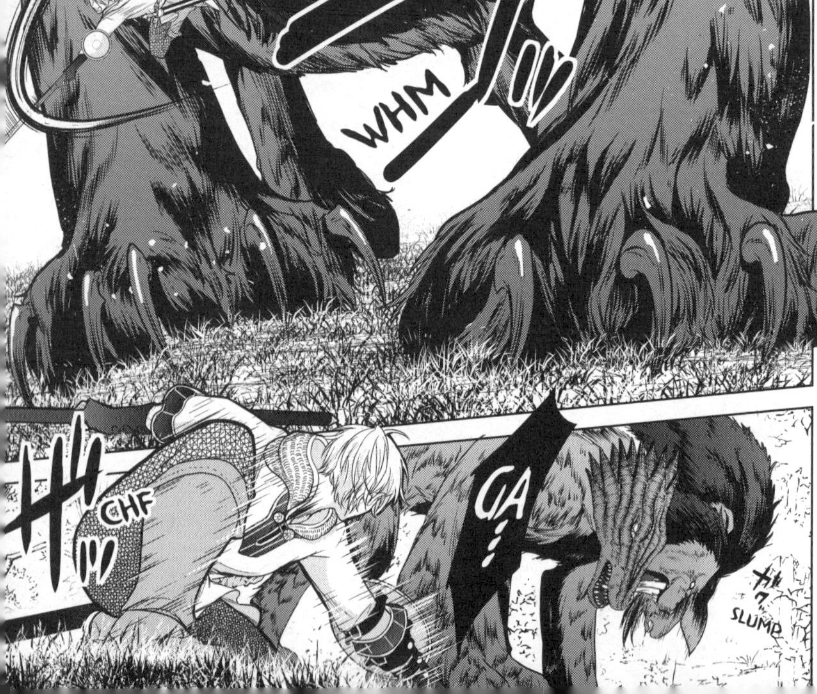
GA...
SLUMP
CHF

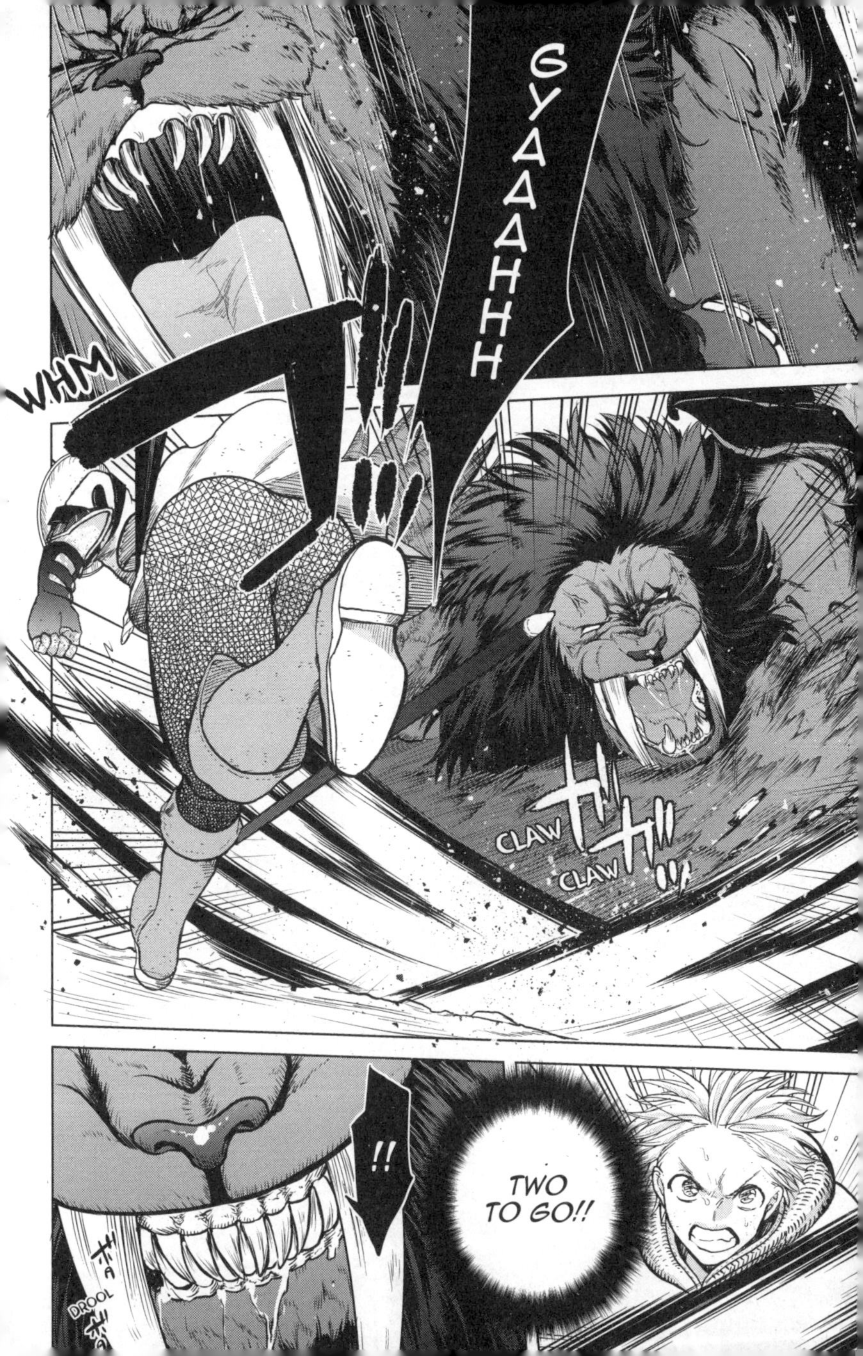
GYAAAHHH
WHM
CLAW
CLAW
TWO TO GO!!
!!
DROOL

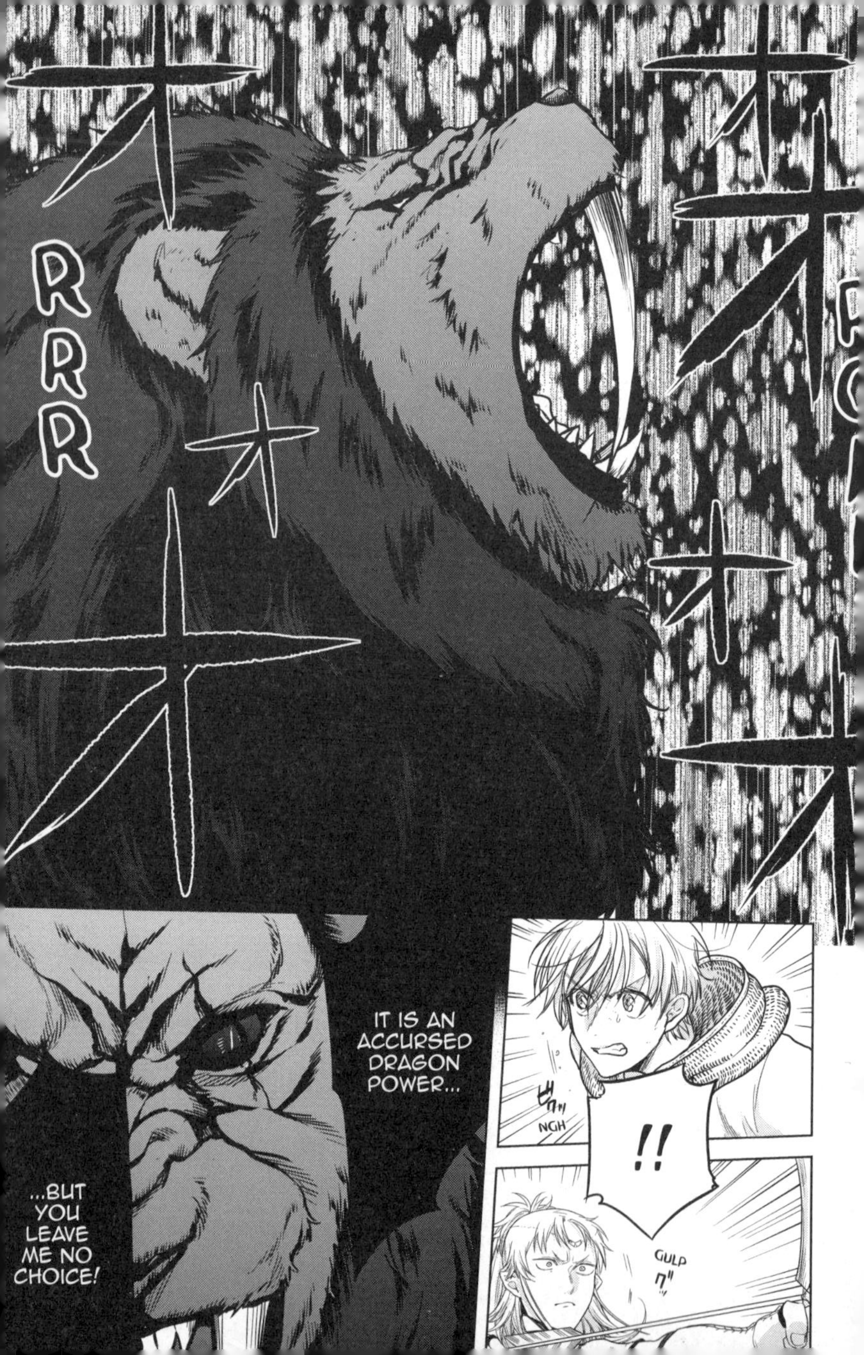
RRR
NGH
!!
GULP
IT IS AN ACCURSED DRAGON POWER...
...BUT YOU LEAVE ME NO CHOICE!

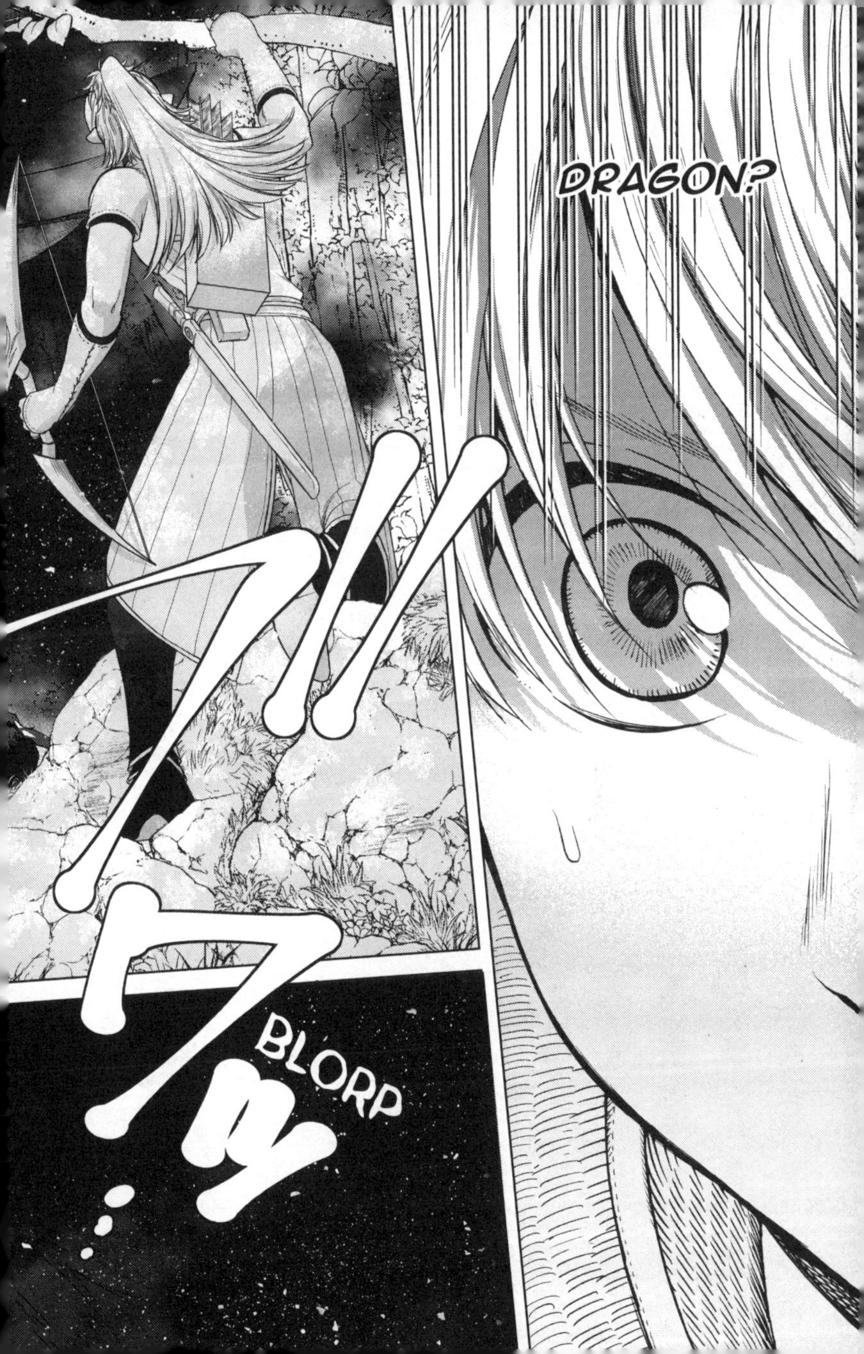
DRAGON?
BLORP

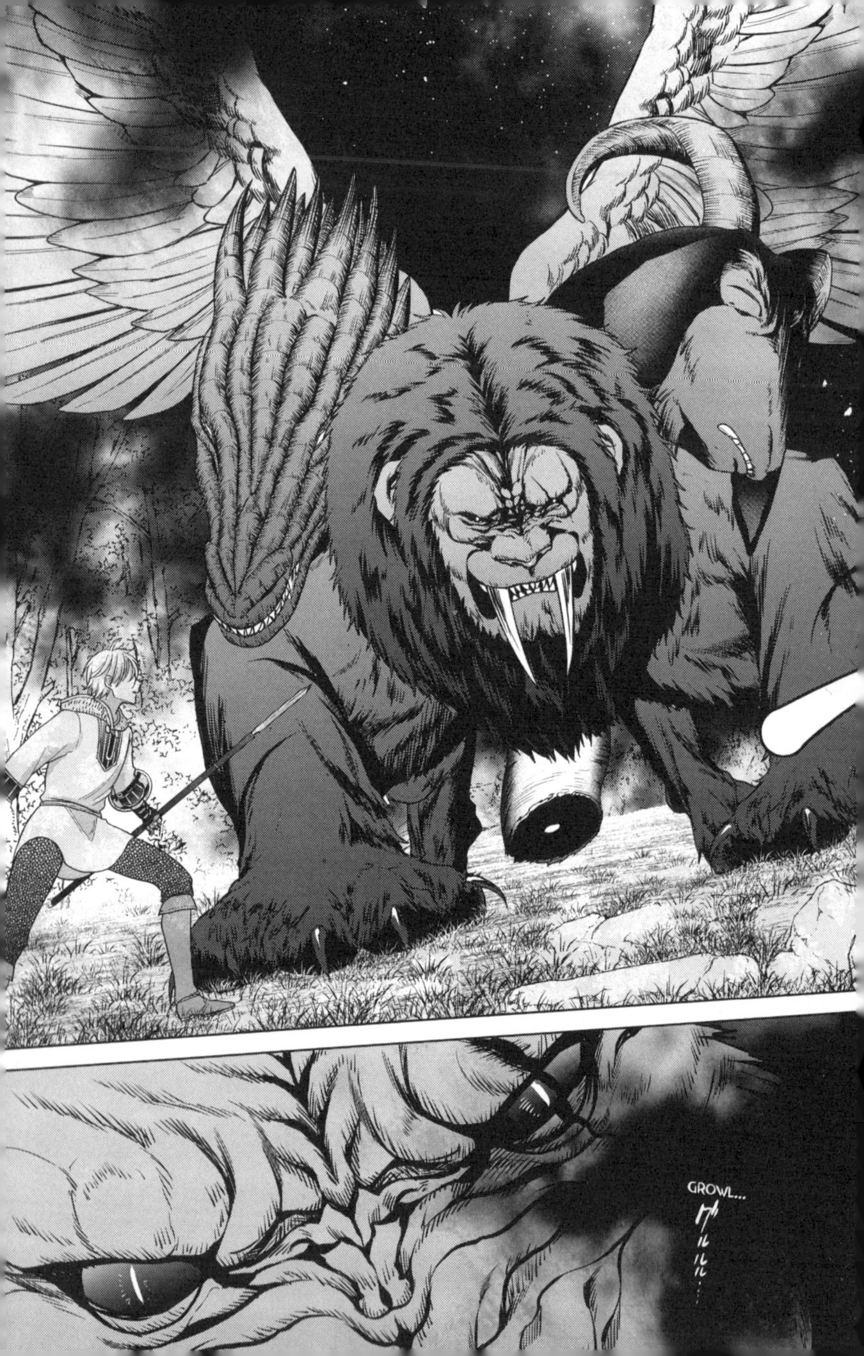
GROWL...
グルルル…

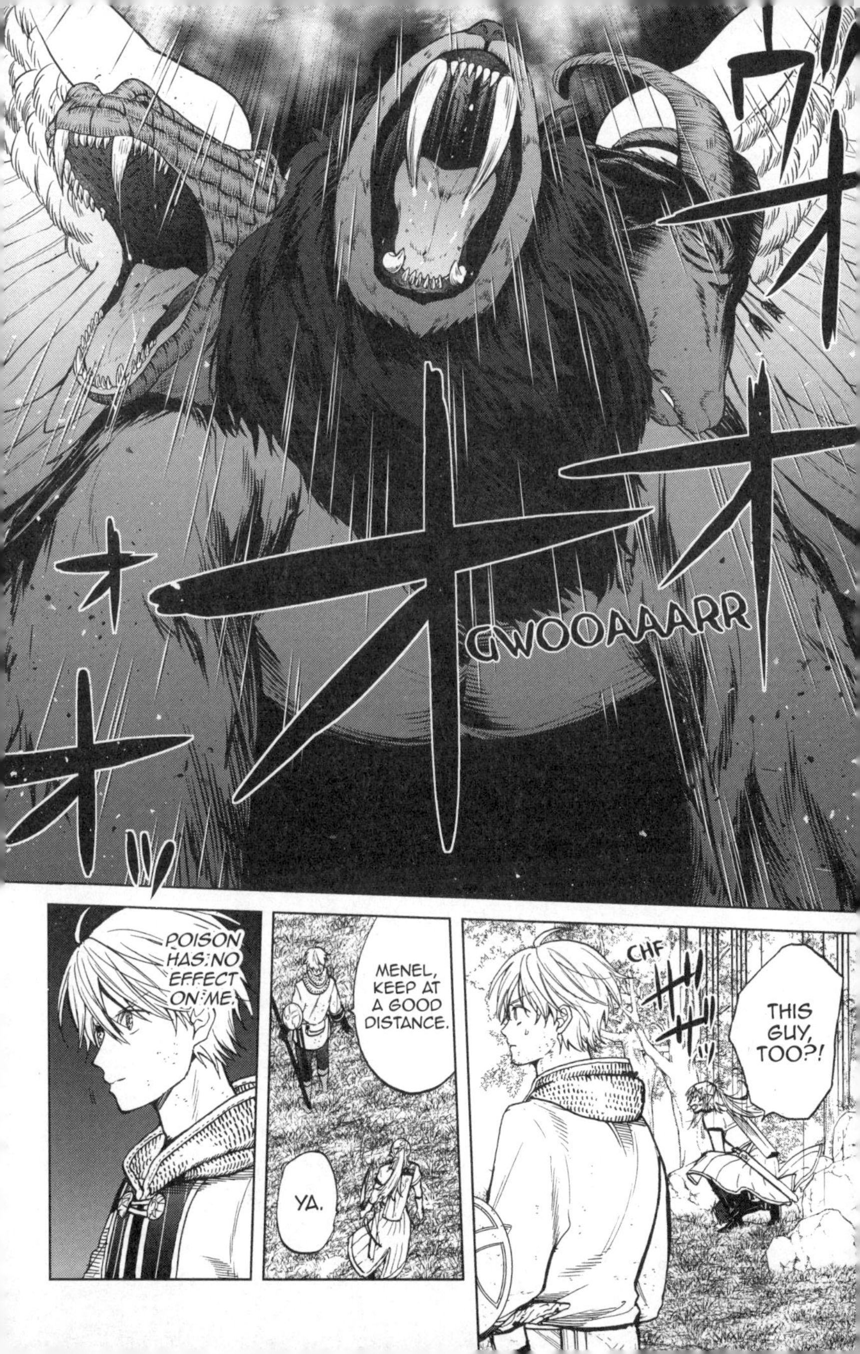
GWOOAAARR
CHF
THIS GUY, TOO?!
MENEL, KEEP AT A GOOD DISTANCE.
YA.
POISON HAS NO EFFECT ON ME.

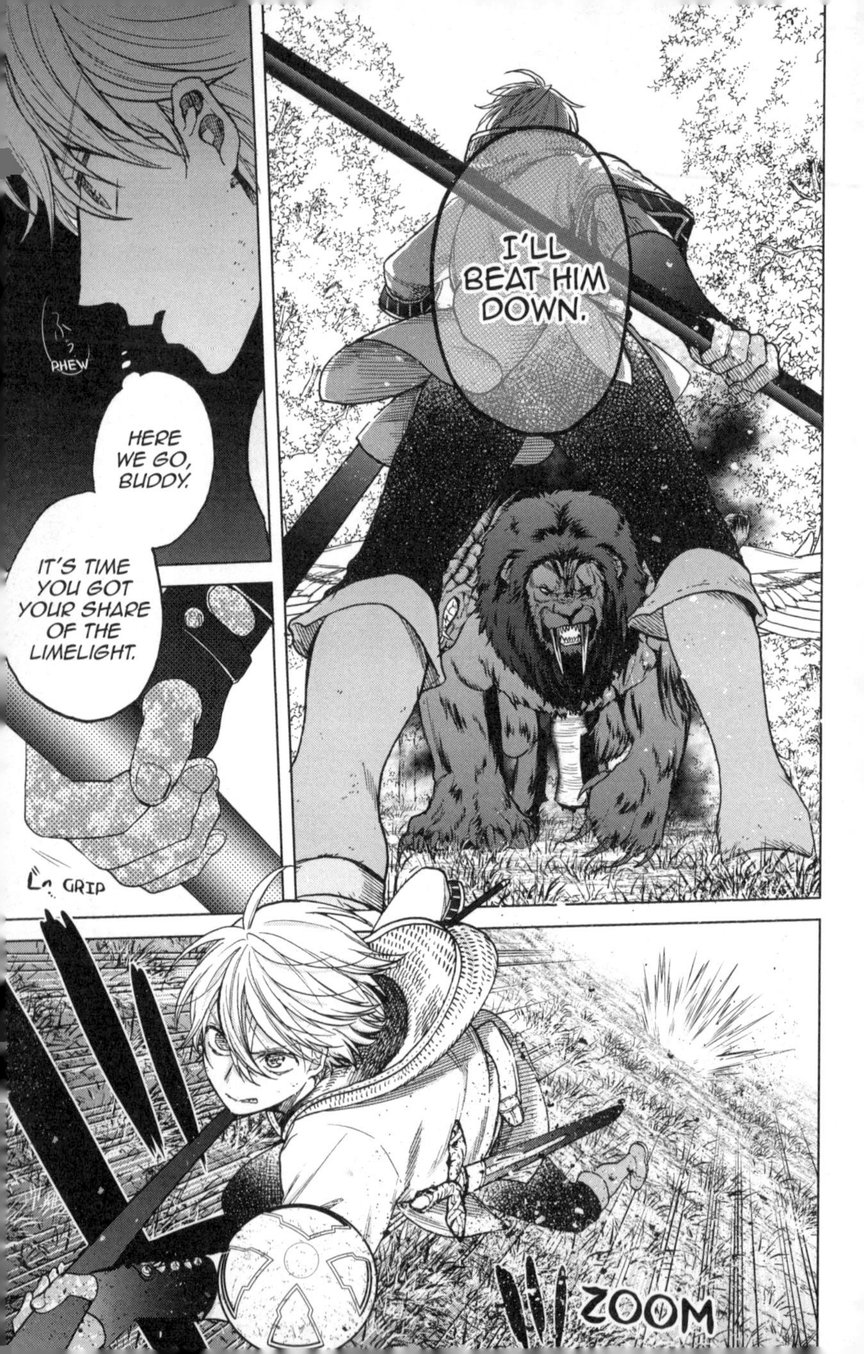
I'LL BEAT HIM DOWN.
PHEW
HERE WE GO, BUDDY.
IT'S TIME YOU GOT YOUR SHARE OF THE LIMELIGHT.
GRIP
ZOOM

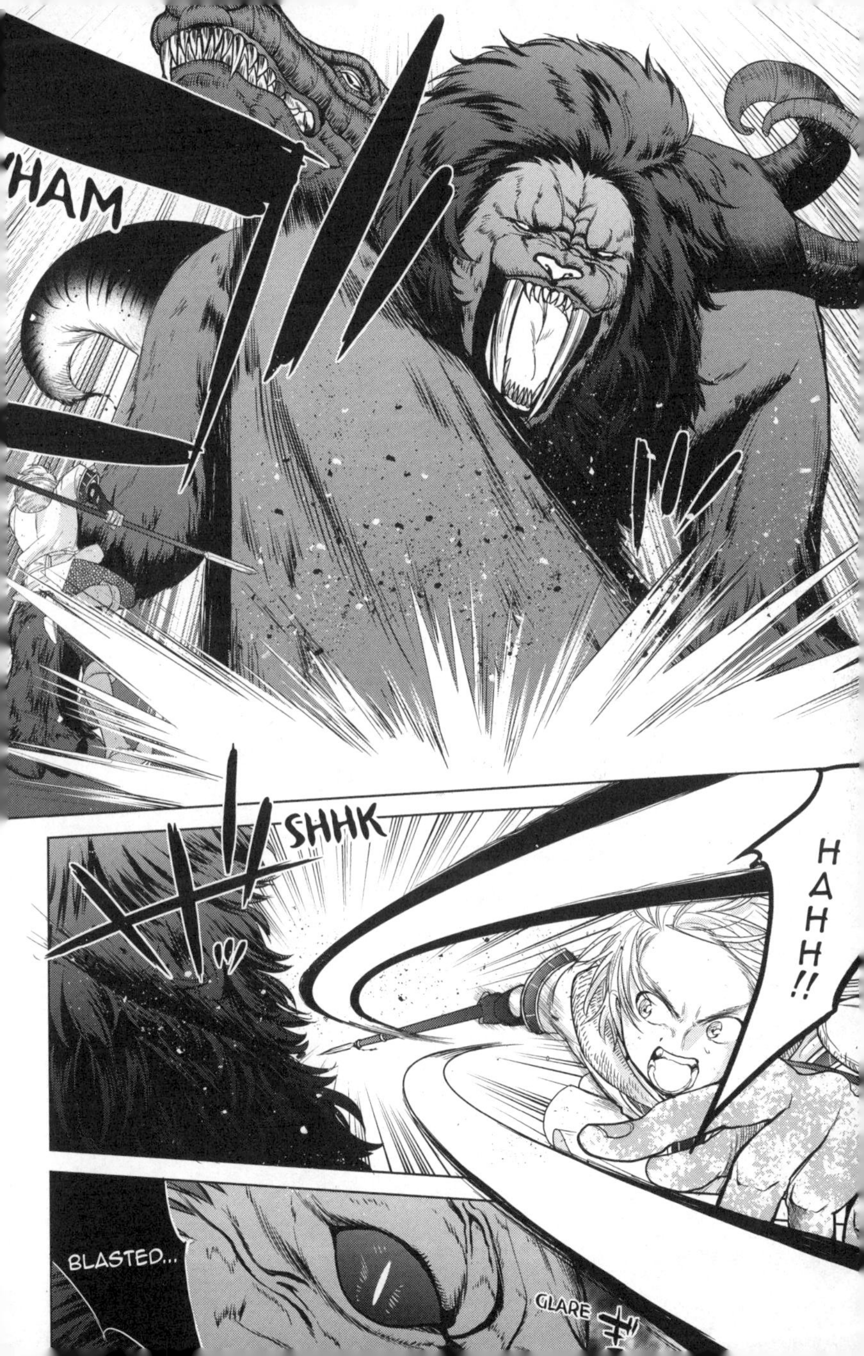
HAM
HAHHH!!
SHHK
BLASTED...
GLARE

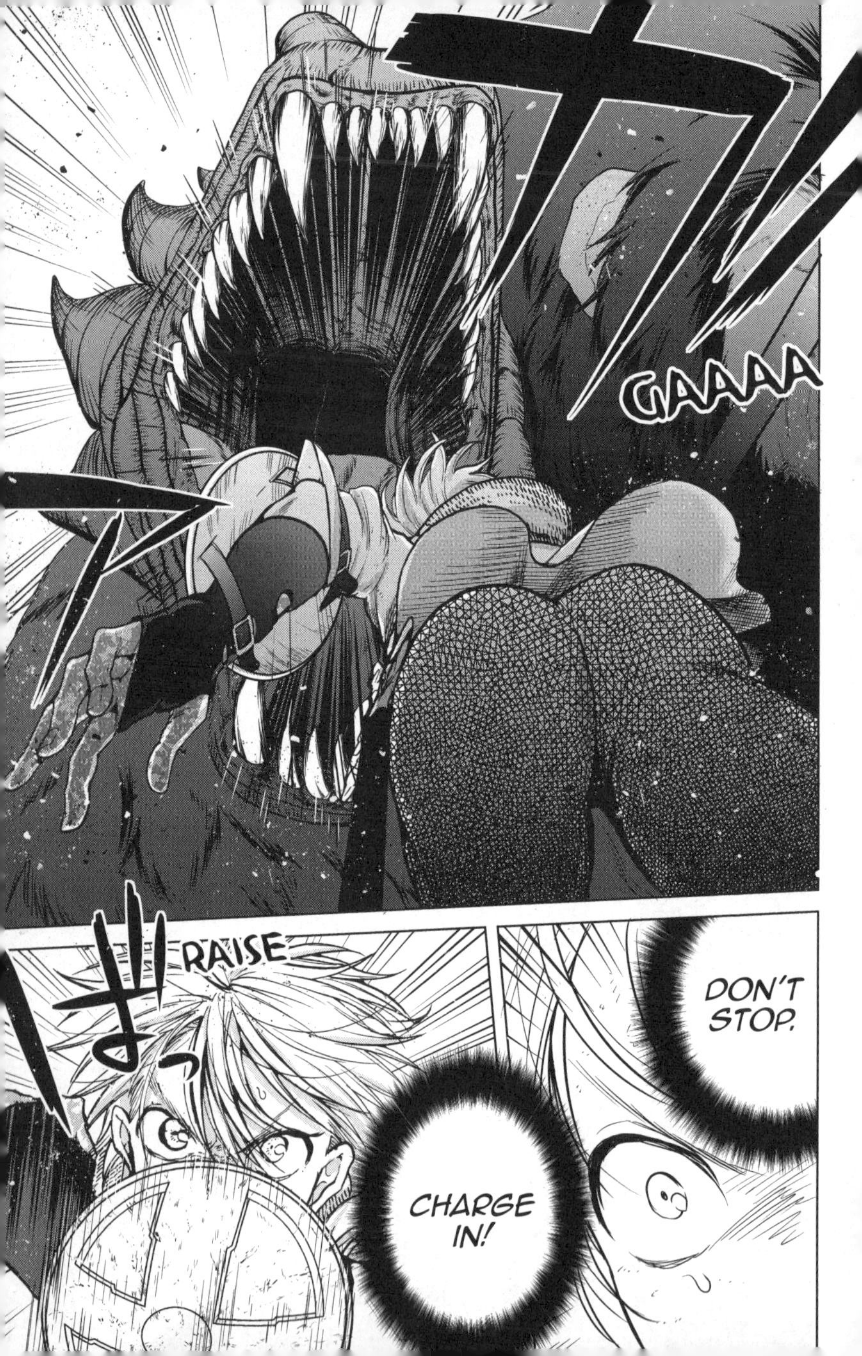
GAAAA
DON'T STOP.
CHARGE IN!
RAISE

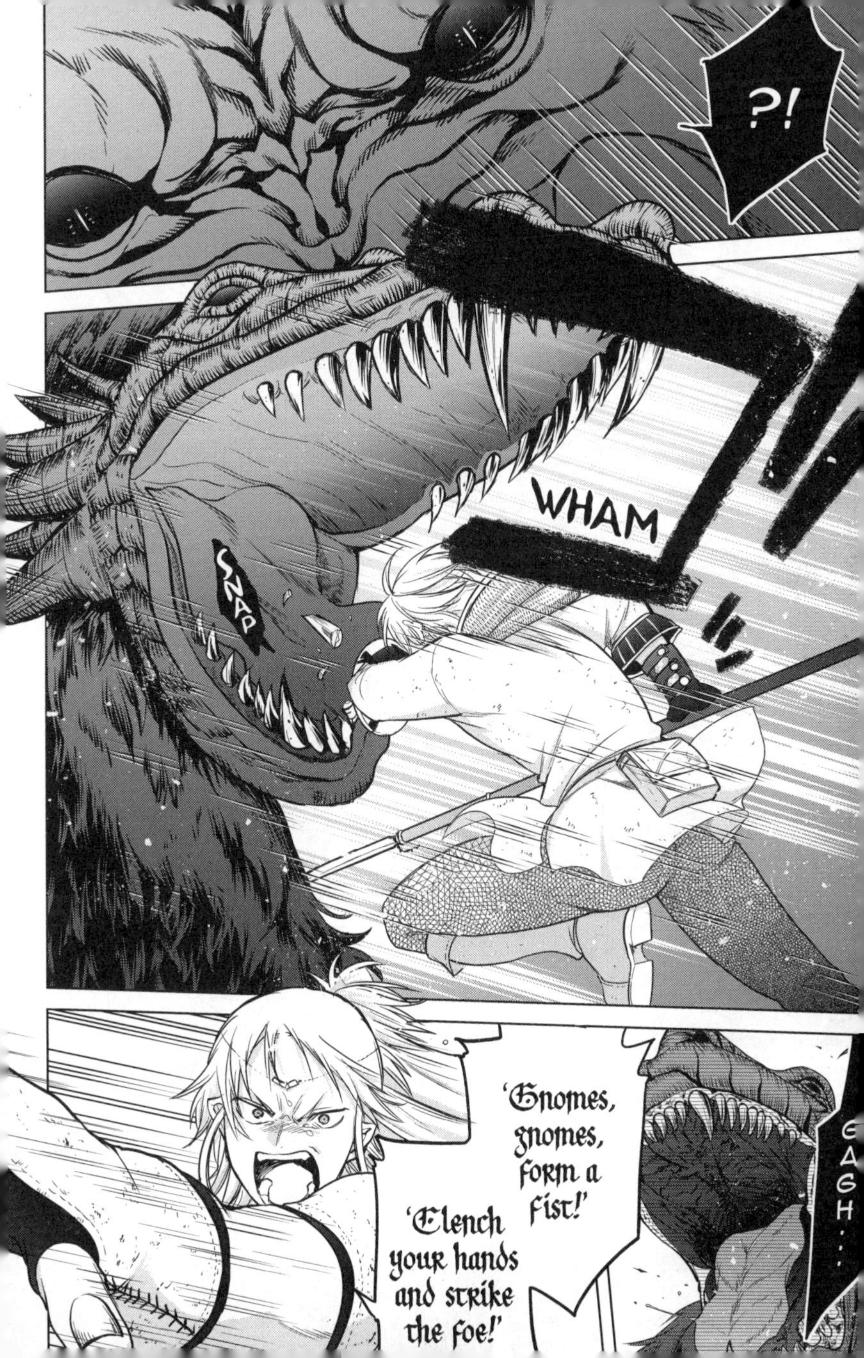
?!
WHAM
SNAP
EAGH...
'Gnomes, gnomes, form a fist!'
'Clench your hands and strike the foe!'

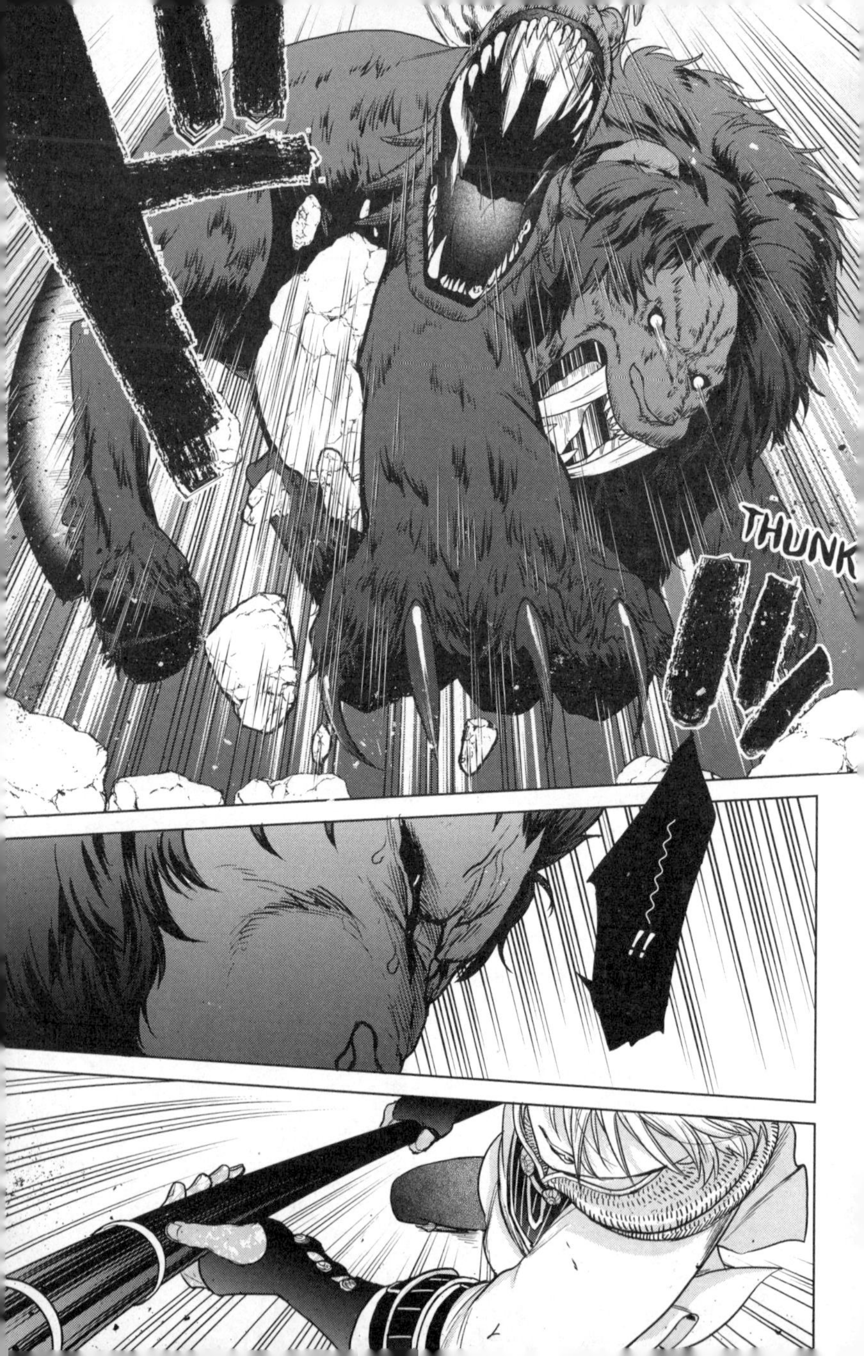
THUNK
!!

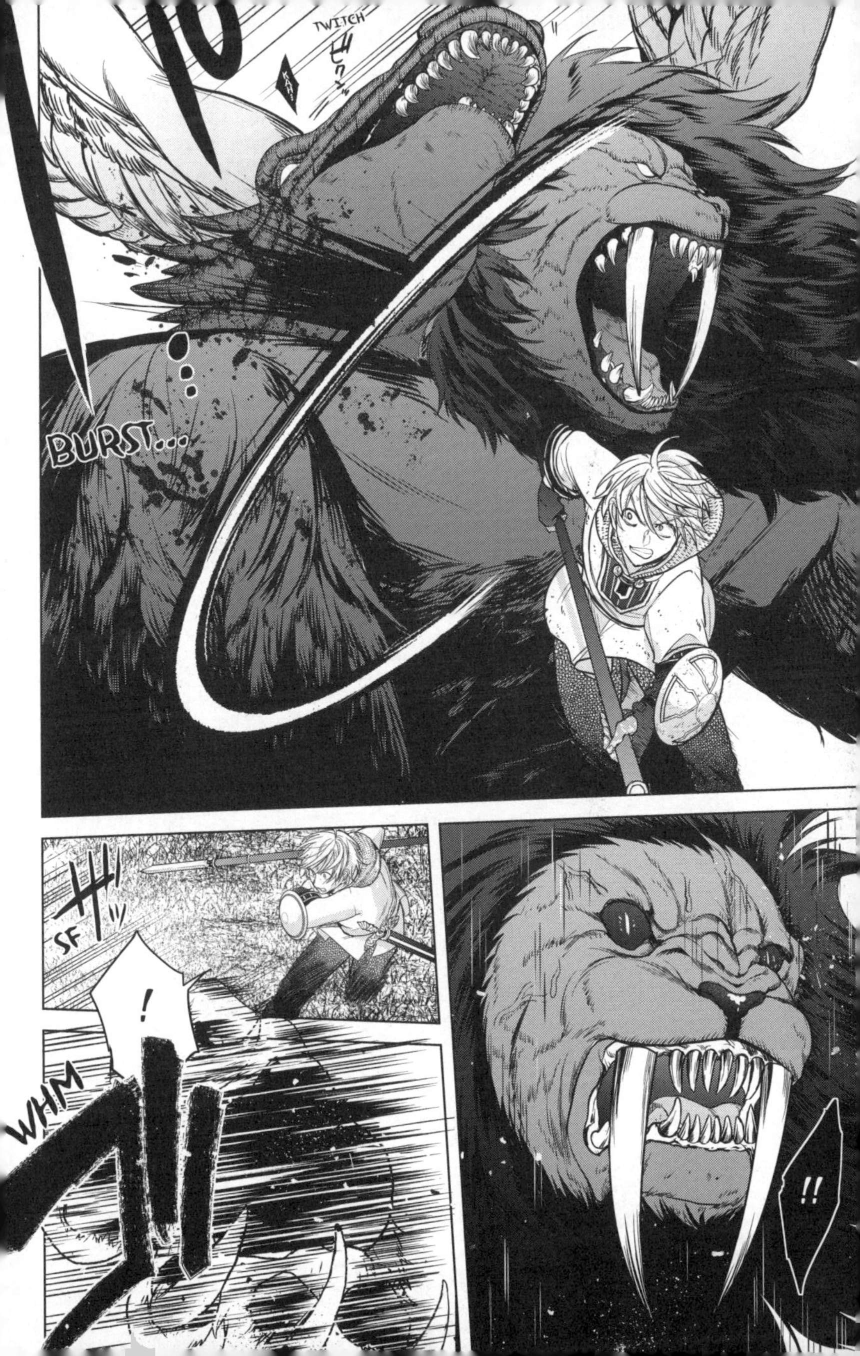
TWITCH
KAH!
BURST...
!!
SF
!
WHM

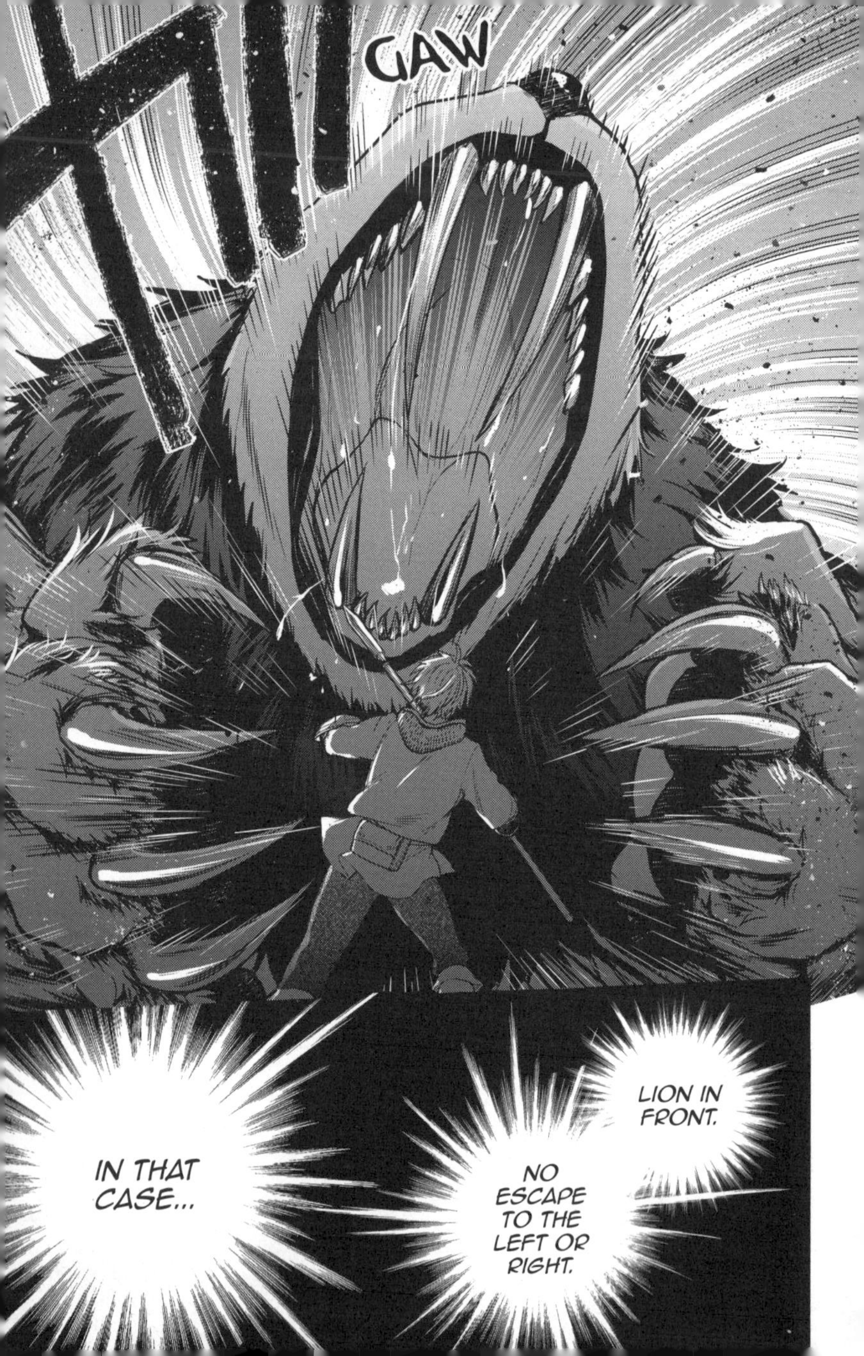
GAW
LION IN FRONT.
NO ESCAPE TO THE LEFT OR RIGHT.
IN THAT CASE...

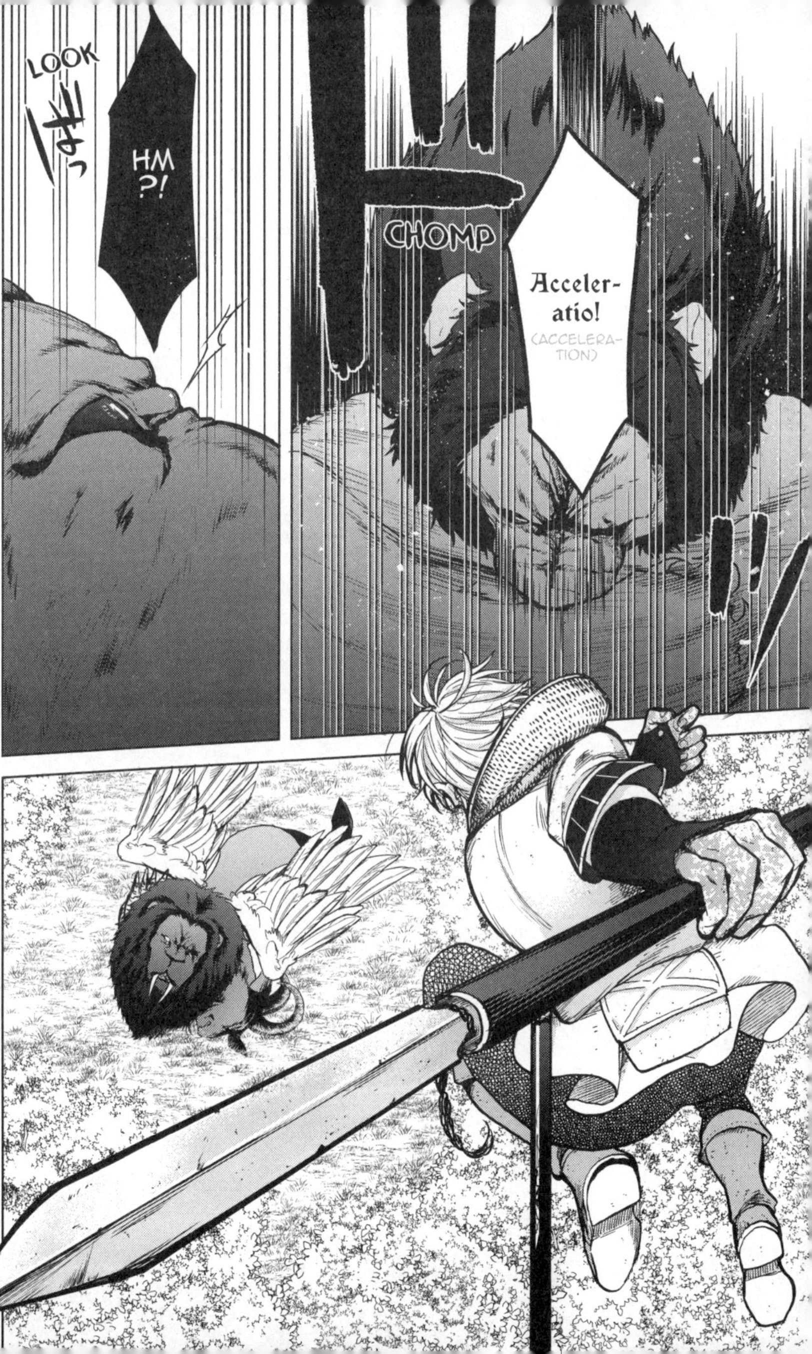
CHOMP
Acceler-atio!
(ACCELERA-TION)
LOOK
HM ?!

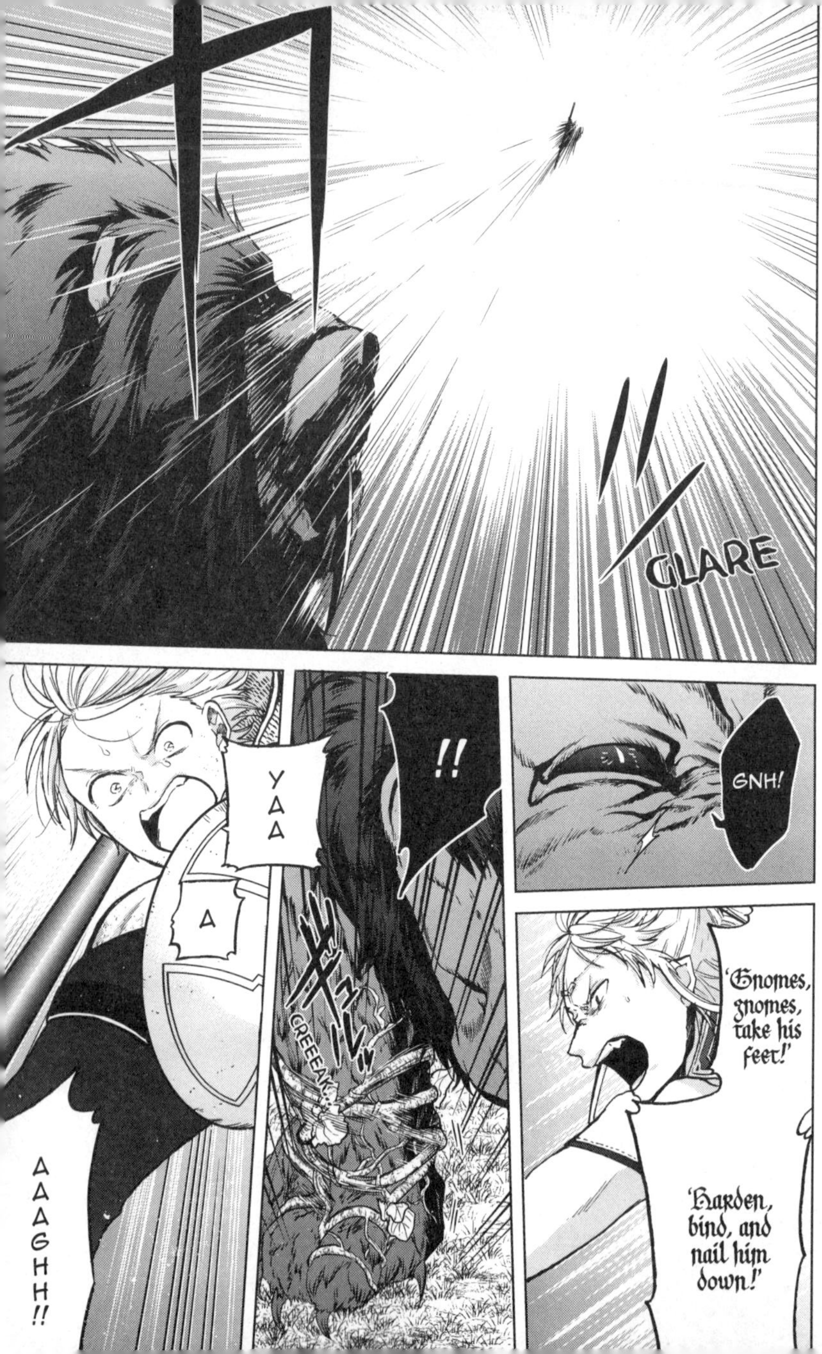
GLARE
GNH!
'Gnomes, gnomes, take his feet!'
'Harden, bind, and nail him down!'
!!
CREEEAK...
YAA
A
AAAGHH!!

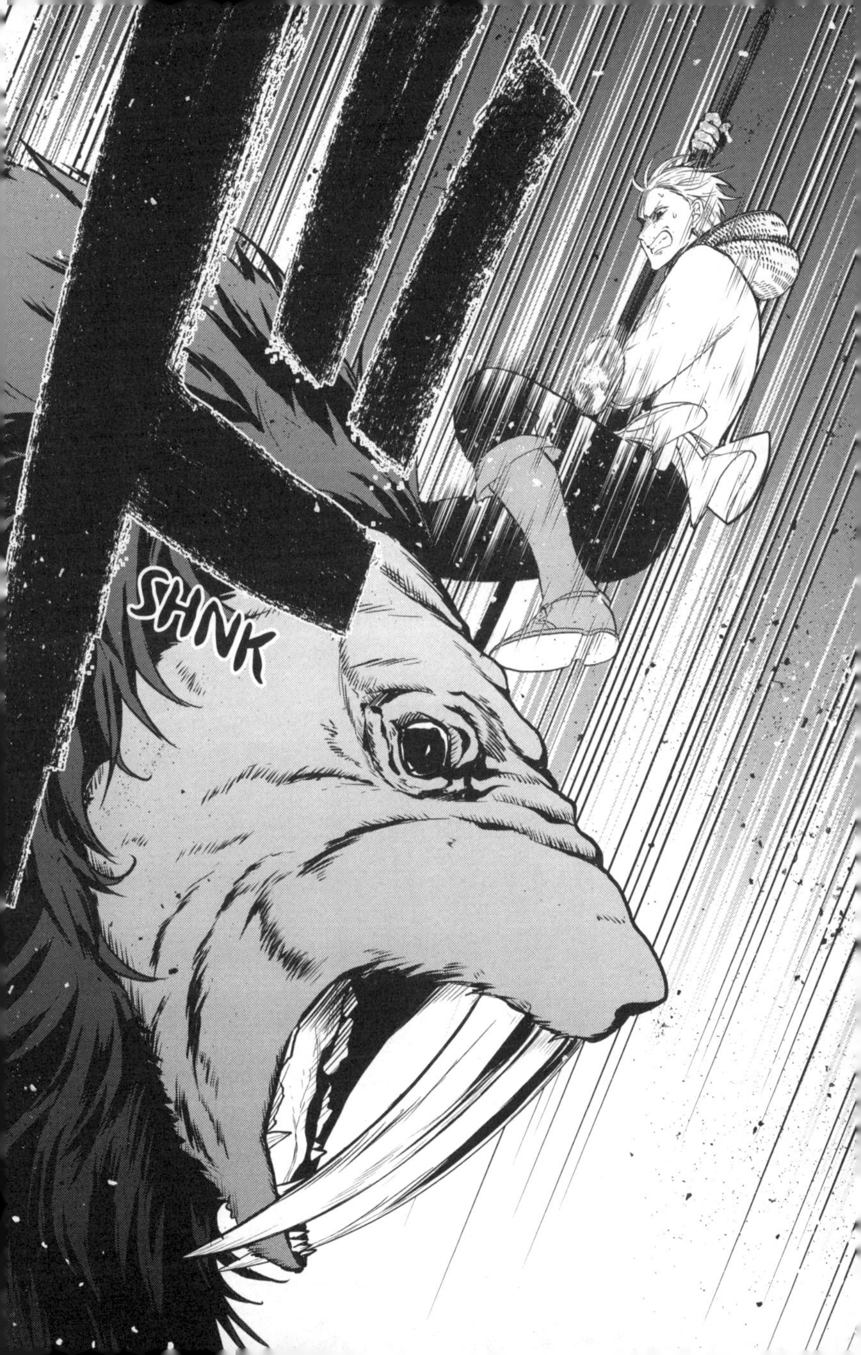
SHNK

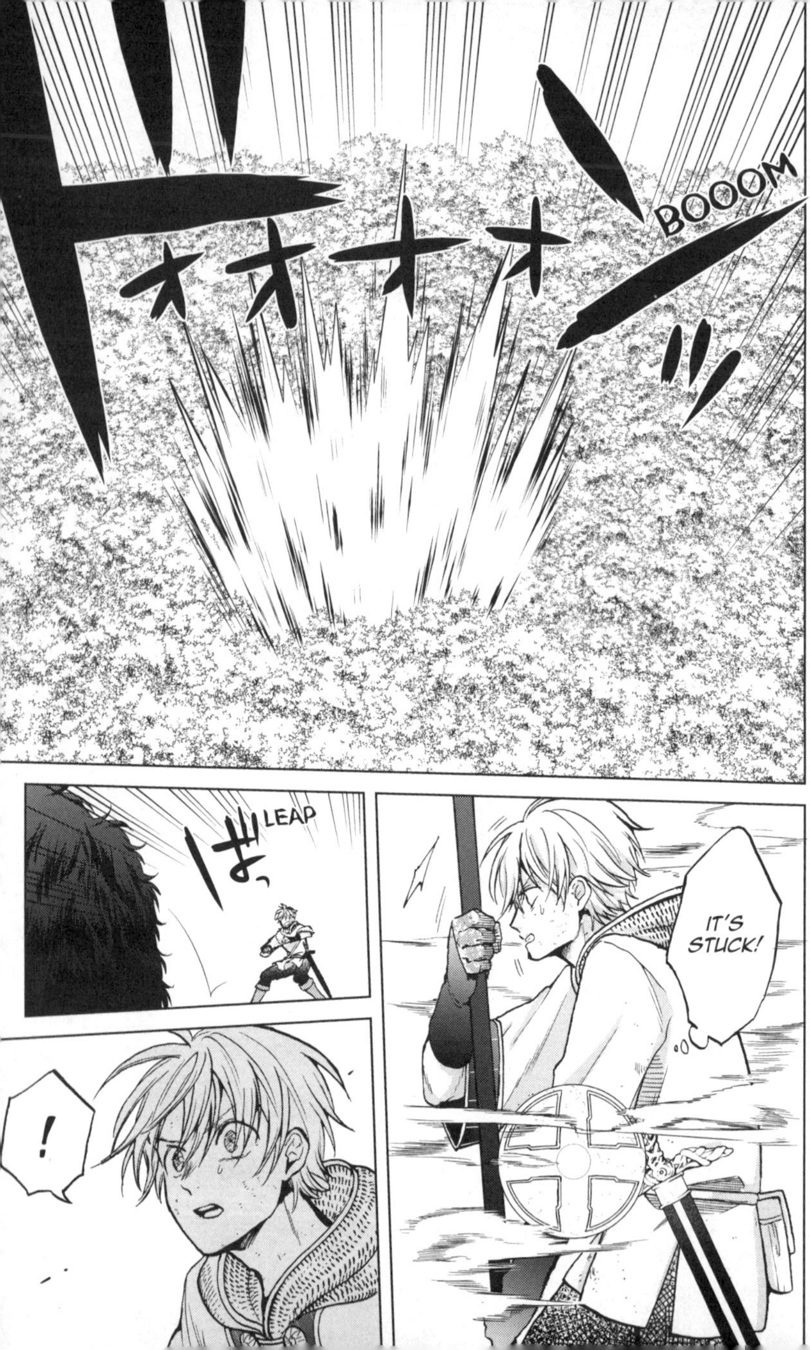
BOOOM
IT'S STUCK!
LEAP
!

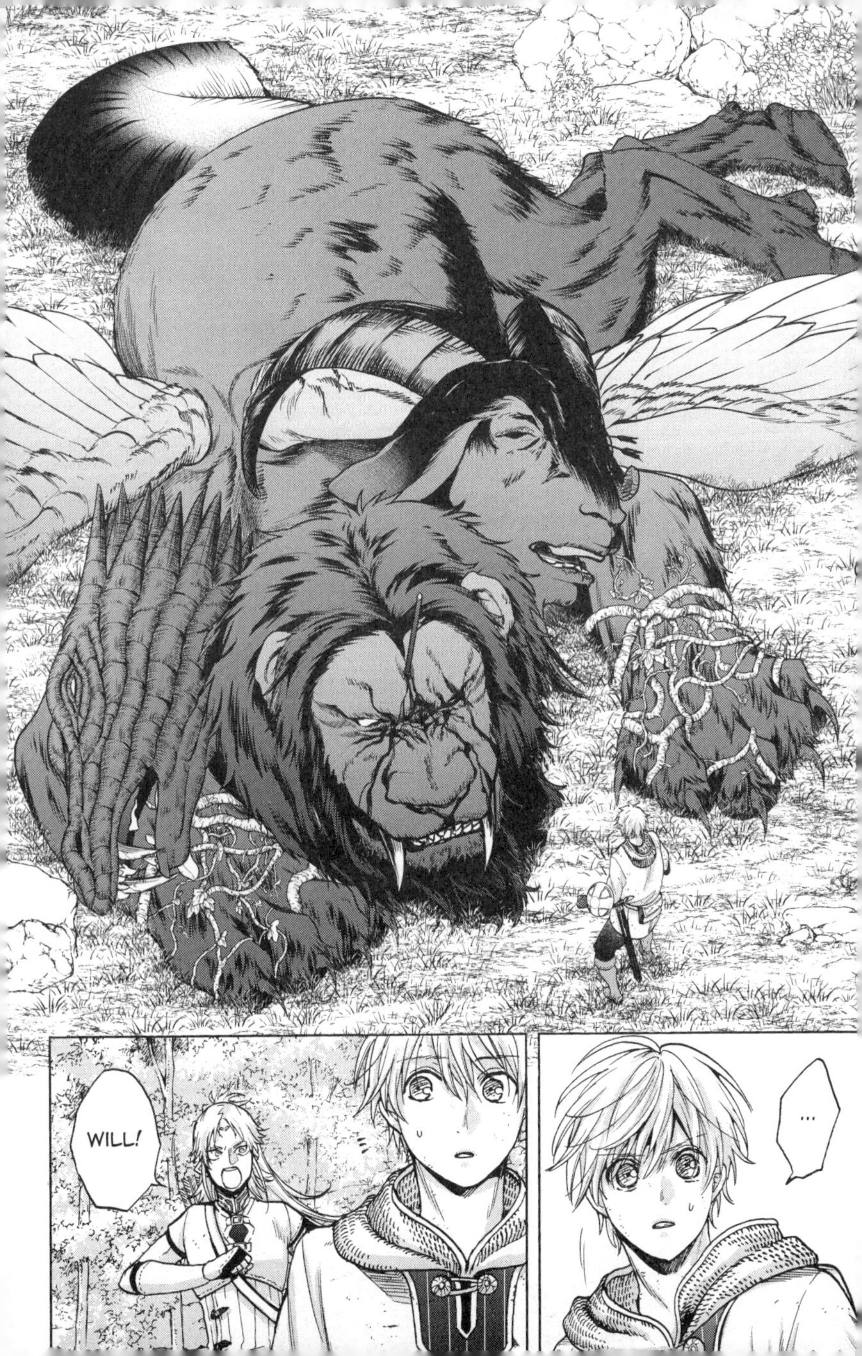
...
WILL!

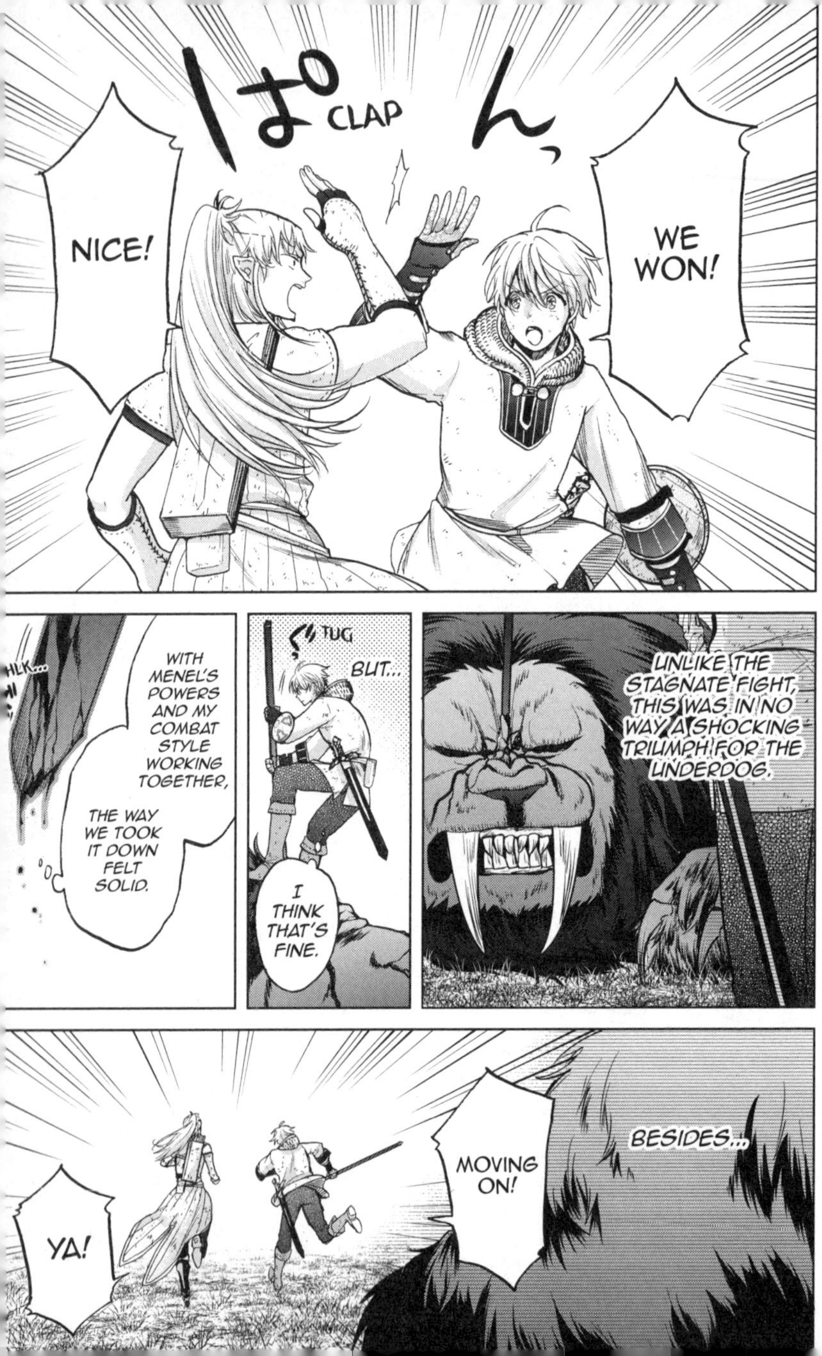
ぽん
CLAP
WE WON!
NICE!
UNLIKE THE STAGNATE FIGHT, THIS WAS IN NO WAY A SHOCKING TRIUMPH FOR THE UNDERDOG.
TUG
BUT...
I THINK THAT'S FINE.
WITH MENEL'S POWERS AND MY COMBAT STYLE WORKING TOGETHER,
THE WAY WE TOOK IT DOWN FELT SOLID.
BESIDES...
MOVING ON!
YA!

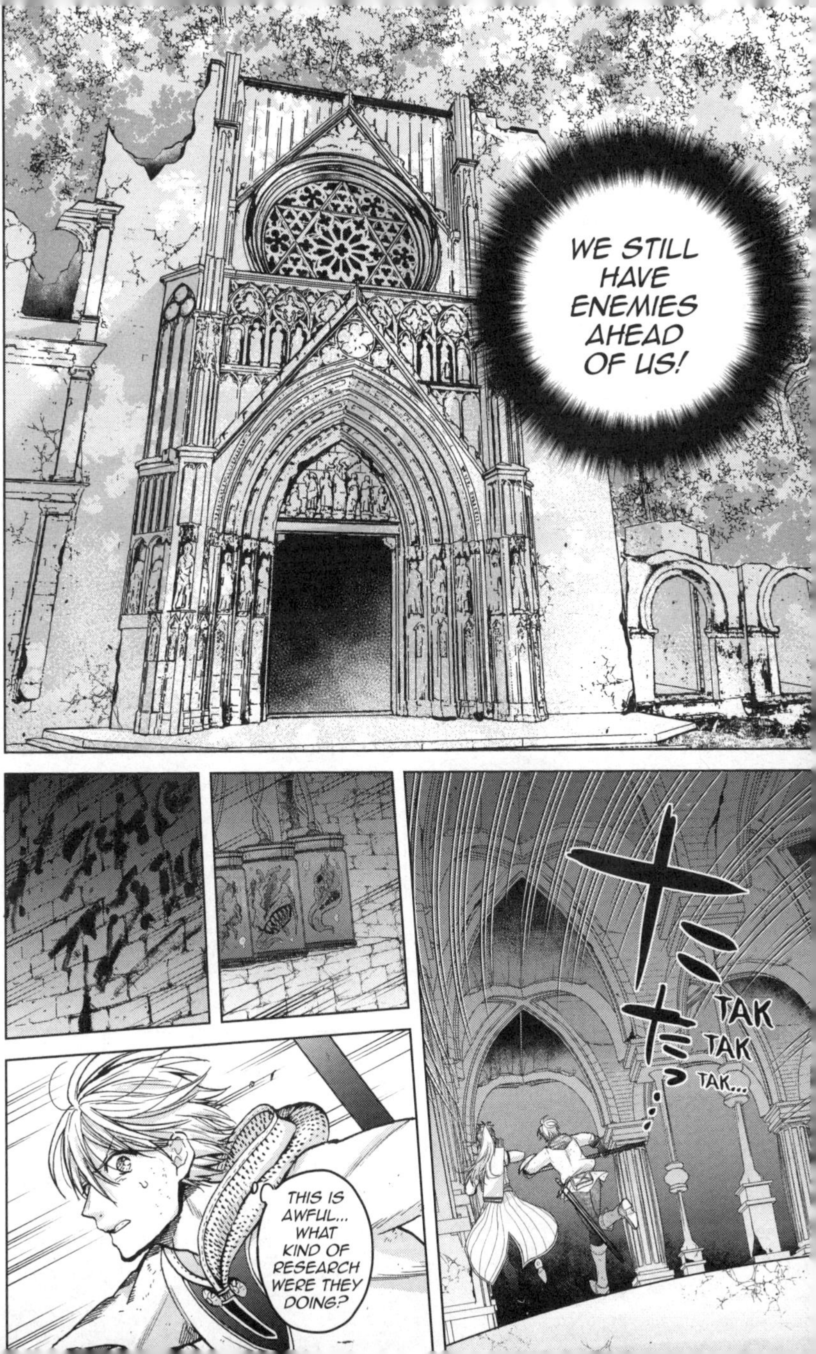
WE STILL HAVE ENEMIES AHEAD OF US!
TAK
TAK
TAK...
THIS IS AWFUL... WHAT KIND OF RESEARCH WERE THEY DOING?

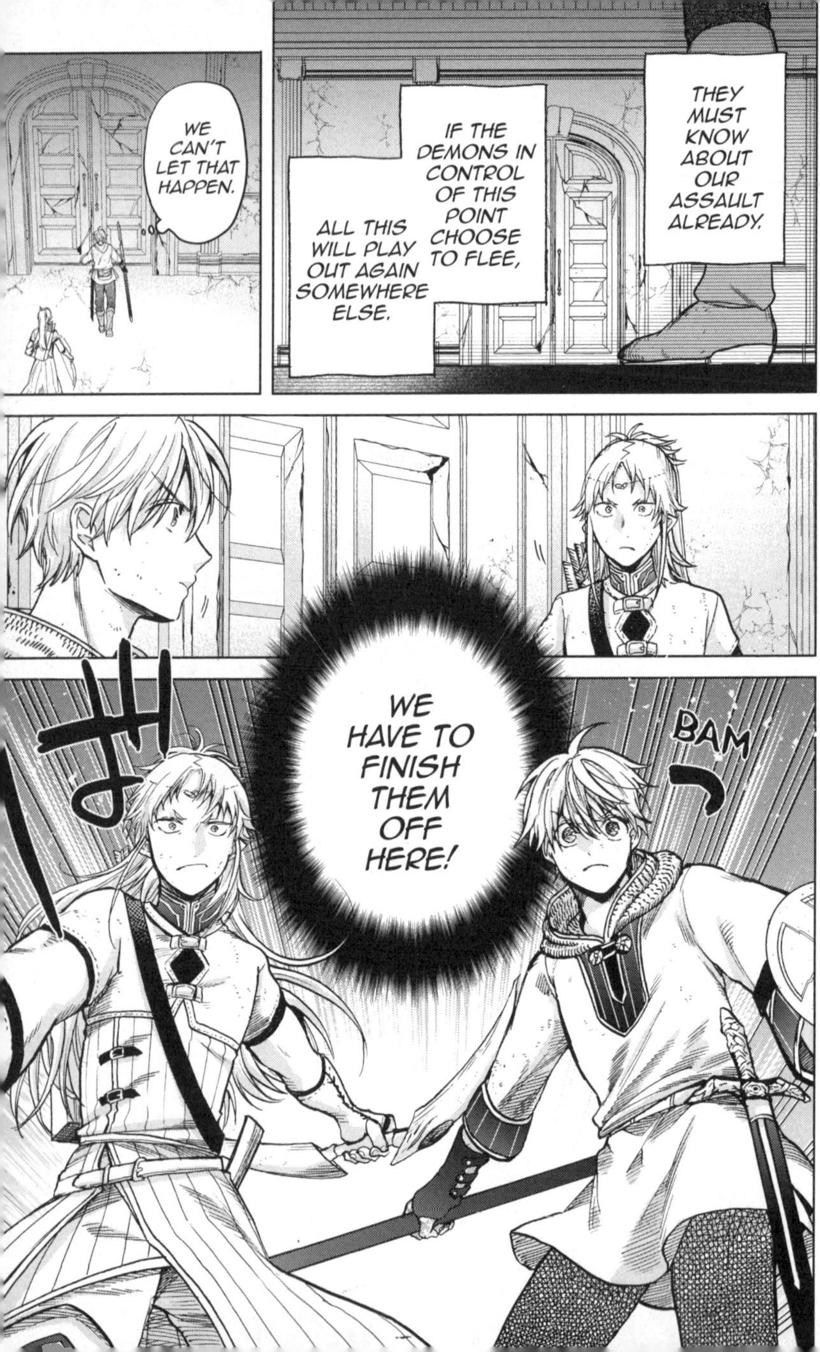
THEY MUST KNOW ABOUT OUR ASSAULT ALREADY.
IF THE DEMONS IN CONTROL OF THIS POINT CHOOSE TO FLEE,
ALL THIS WILL PLAY OUT AGAIN SOMEWHERE ELSE.
WE CAN'T LET THAT HAPPEN.
BAM
WE HAVE TO FINISH THEM OFF HERE!

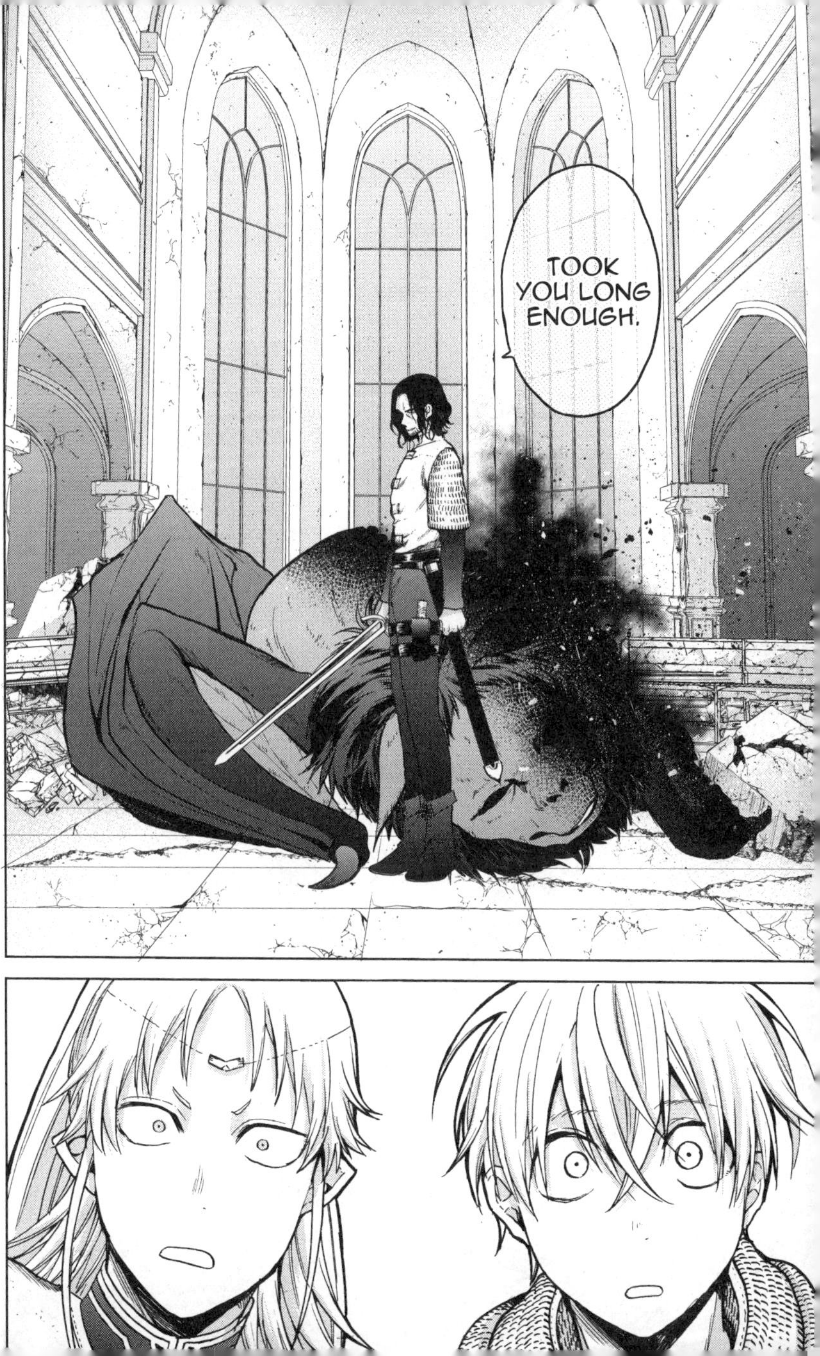
TOOK YOU LONG ENOUGH.

NOD

YOU OWE ME TEN GOLD COINS.

REYSTOV?

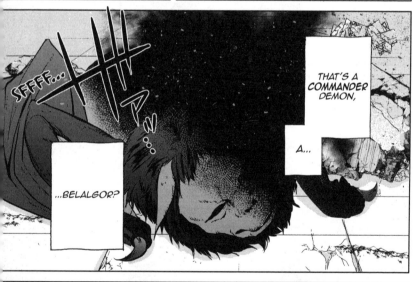

SFFFF...

...BELALGOR?

THAT'S A COMMANDER DEMON,

A...

UM...

YOU...

IN SHORT,

SO...

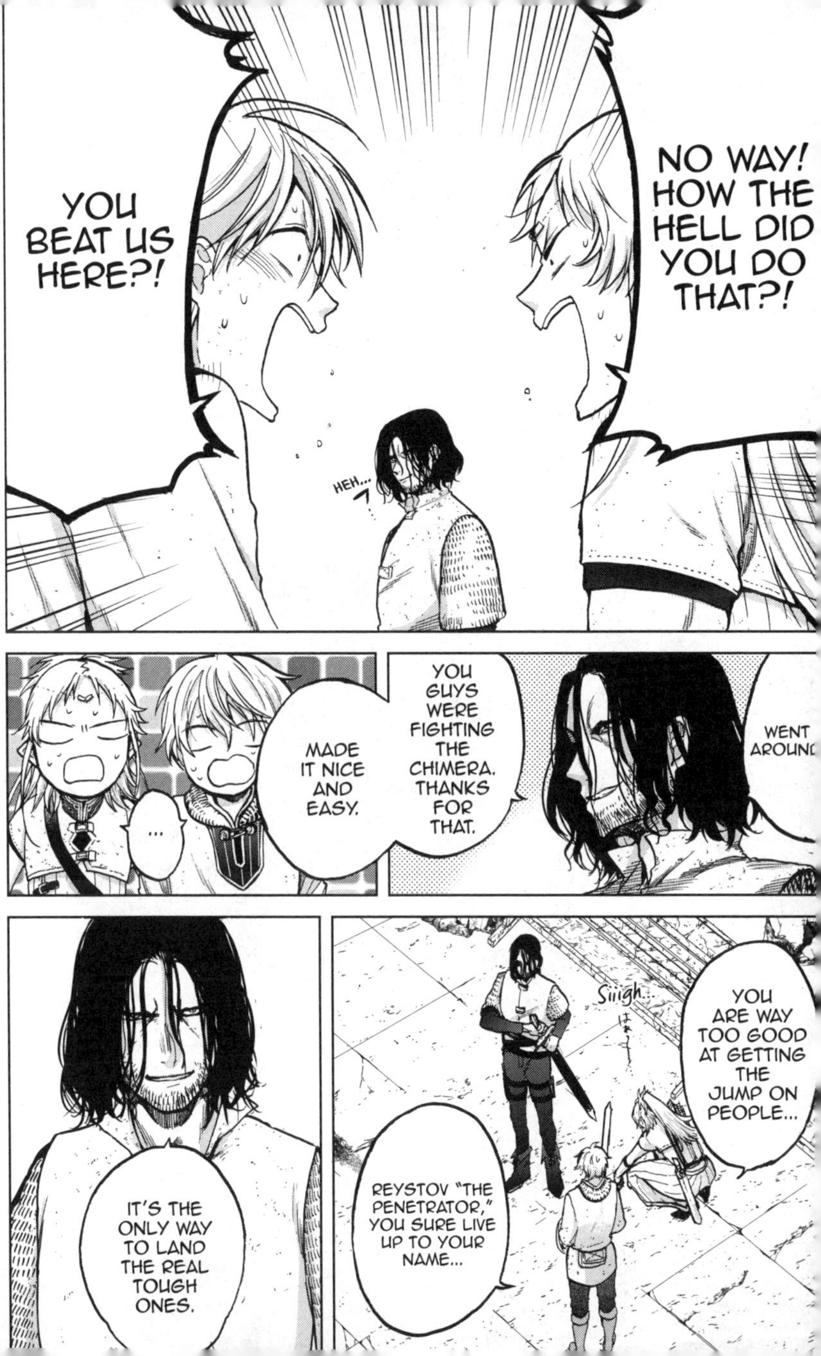
NO WAY! HOW THE HELL DID YOU DO THAT?!
YOU BEAT US HERE?!
HEH...
WENT AROUN
YOU GUYS WERE FIGHTING THE CHIMERA. THANKS FOR THAT.
MADE IT NICE AND EASY.
...
YOU ARE WAY TOO GOOD AT GETTING THE JUMP ON PEOPLE...
Siiigh...
REYSTOV "THE PENETRATOR," YOU SURE LIVE UP TO YOUR NAME...
IT'S THE ONLY WAY TO LAND THE REAL TOUGH ONES.

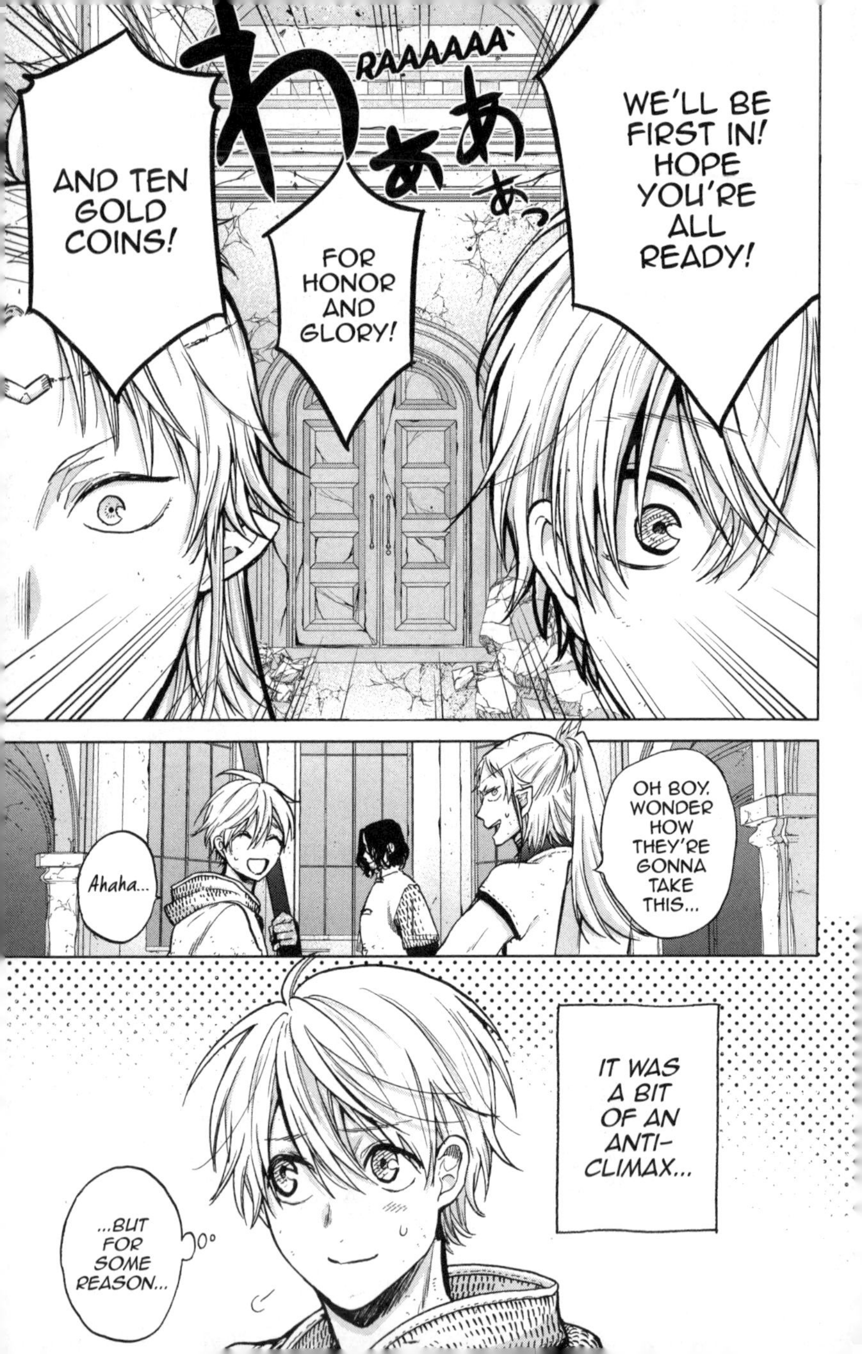
WE'LL BE FIRST IN! HOPE YOU'RE ALL READY!
わぁぁぁっ
RAAAAAA
FOR HONOR AND GLORY!
AND TEN GOLD COINS!
OH BOY. WONDER HOW THEY'RE GONNA TAKE THIS...
Ahaha...
IT WAS A BIT OF AN ANTI-CLIMAX...
...BUT FOR SOME REASON...

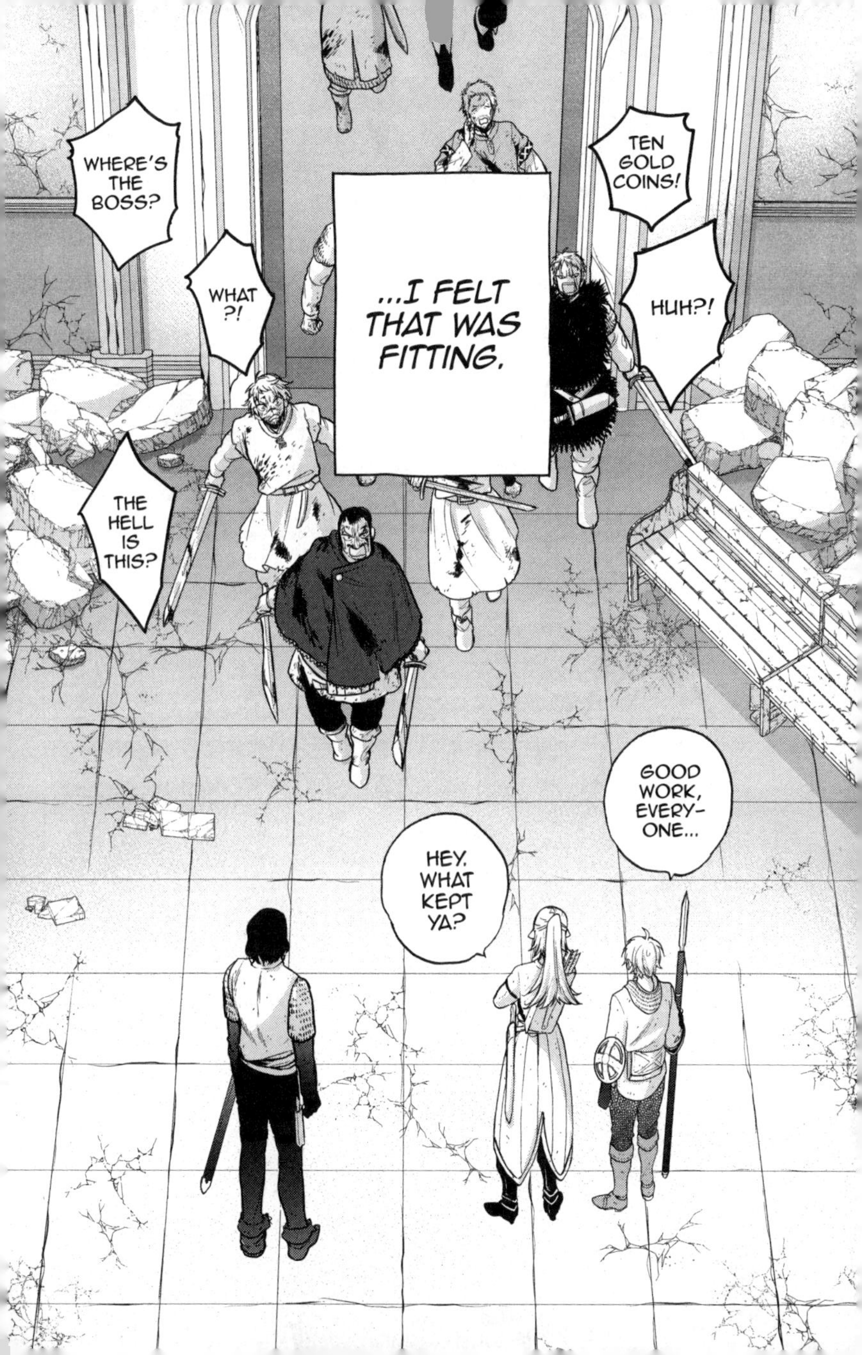
TEN GOLD COINS!
WHERE'S THE BOSS?
HUH?!
...I FELT THAT WAS FITTING.
WHAT?!
THE HELL IS THIS?
GOOD WORK, EVERY-ONE...
HEY, WHAT KEPT YA?

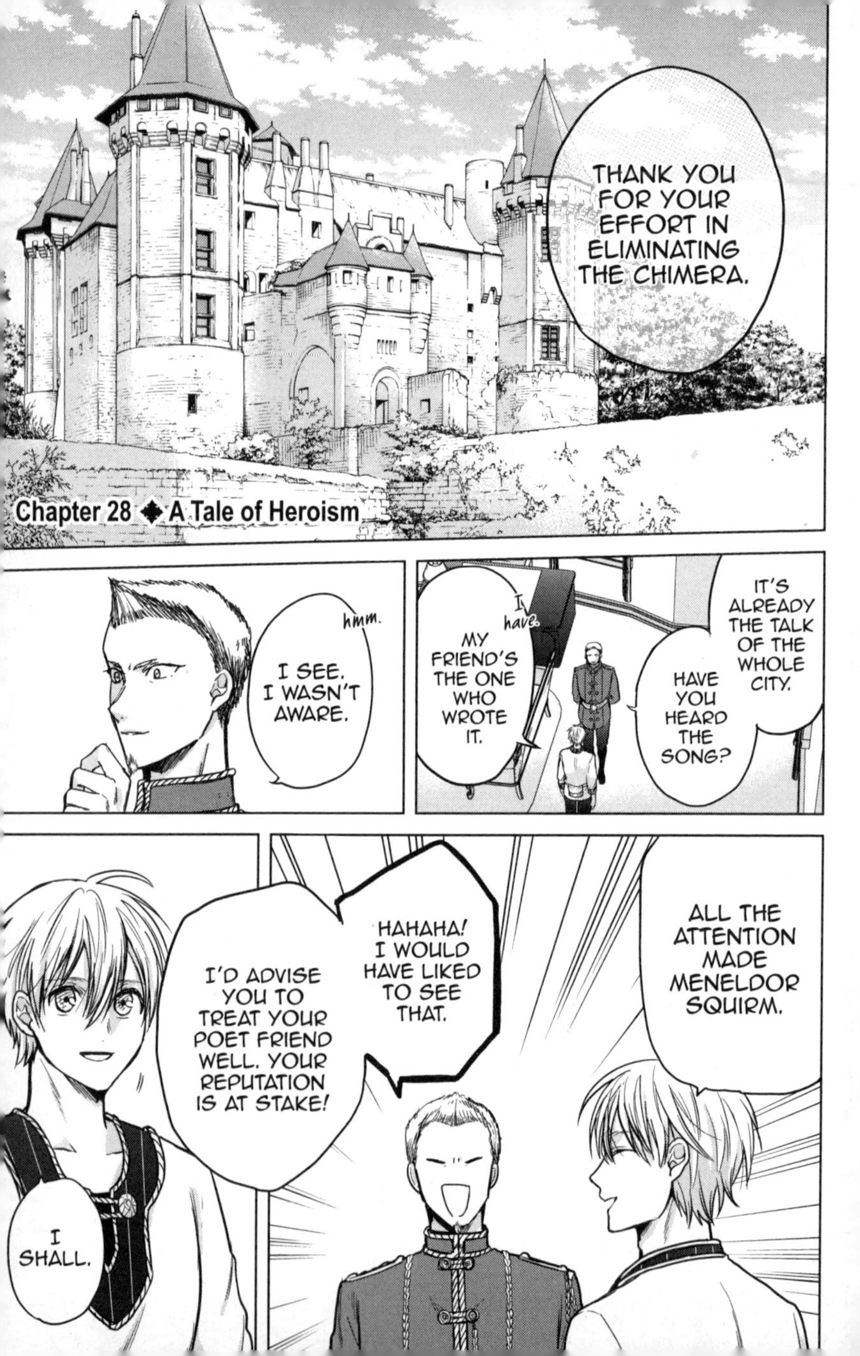
THANK YOU FOR YOUR EFFORT IN ELIMINATING THE CHIMERA.
Chapter 28 ◆ A Tale of Heroism
IT'S ALREADY THE TALK OF THE WHOLE CITY.
HAVE YOU HEARD THE SONG?
I have.
MY FRIEND'S THE ONE WHO WROTE IT.
hmm.
I SEE. I WASN'T AWARE.
ALL THE ATTENTION MADE MENELDOR SQUIRM.
HAHAHA! I WOULD HAVE LIKED TO SEE THAT.
I'D ADVISE YOU TO TREAT YOUR POET FRIEND WELL. YOUR REPUTATION IS AT STAKE!
I SHALL.

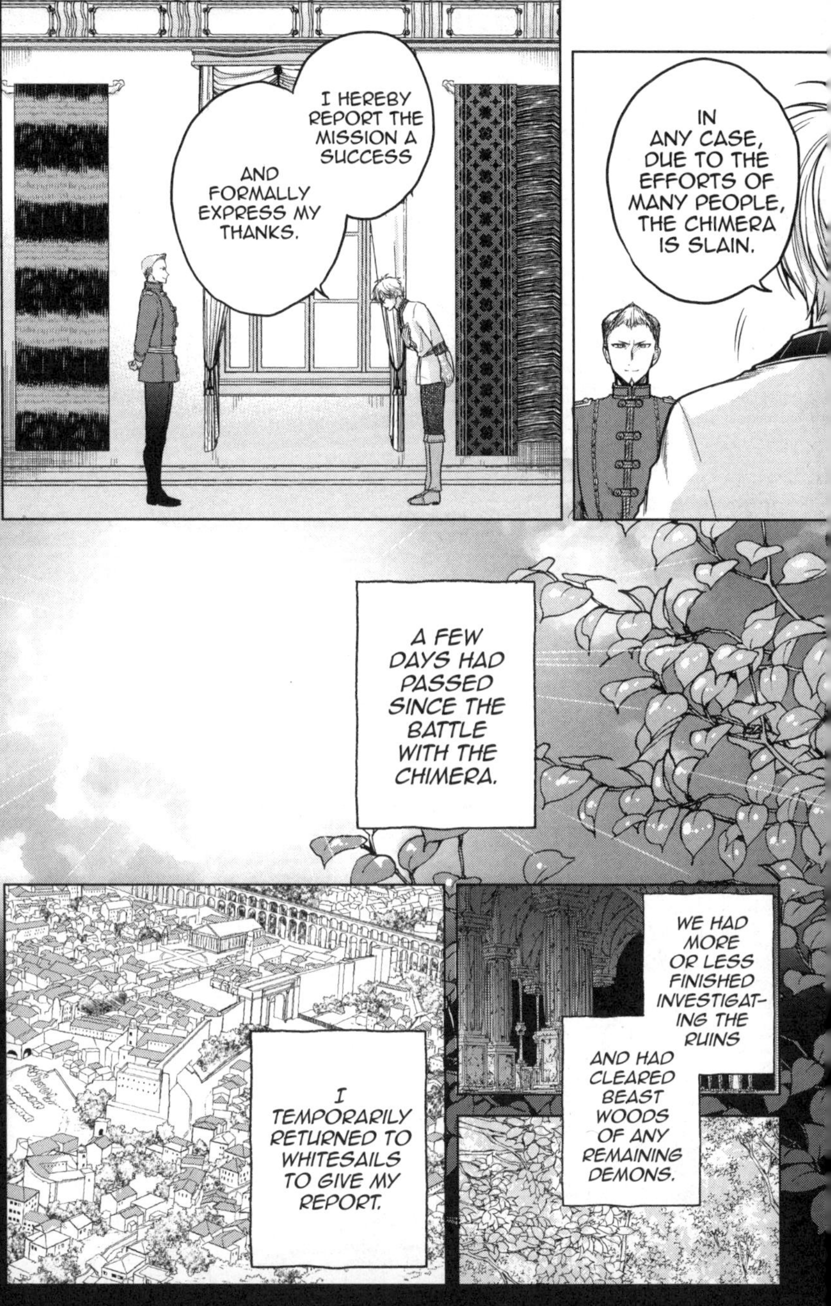
IN ANY CASE, DUE TO THE EFFORTS OF MANY PEOPLE, THE CHIMERA IS SLAIN.
I HEREBY REPORT THE MISSION A SUCCESS
AND FORMALLY EXPRESS MY THANKS.
A FEW DAYS HAD PASSED SINCE THE BATTLE WITH THE CHIMERA.
WE HAD MORE OR LESS FINISHED INVESTIGAT-ING THE RUINS
AND HAD CLEARED BEAST WOODS OF ANY REMAINING DEMONS.
I TEMPORARILY RETURNED TO WHITESAILS TO GIVE MY REPORT.

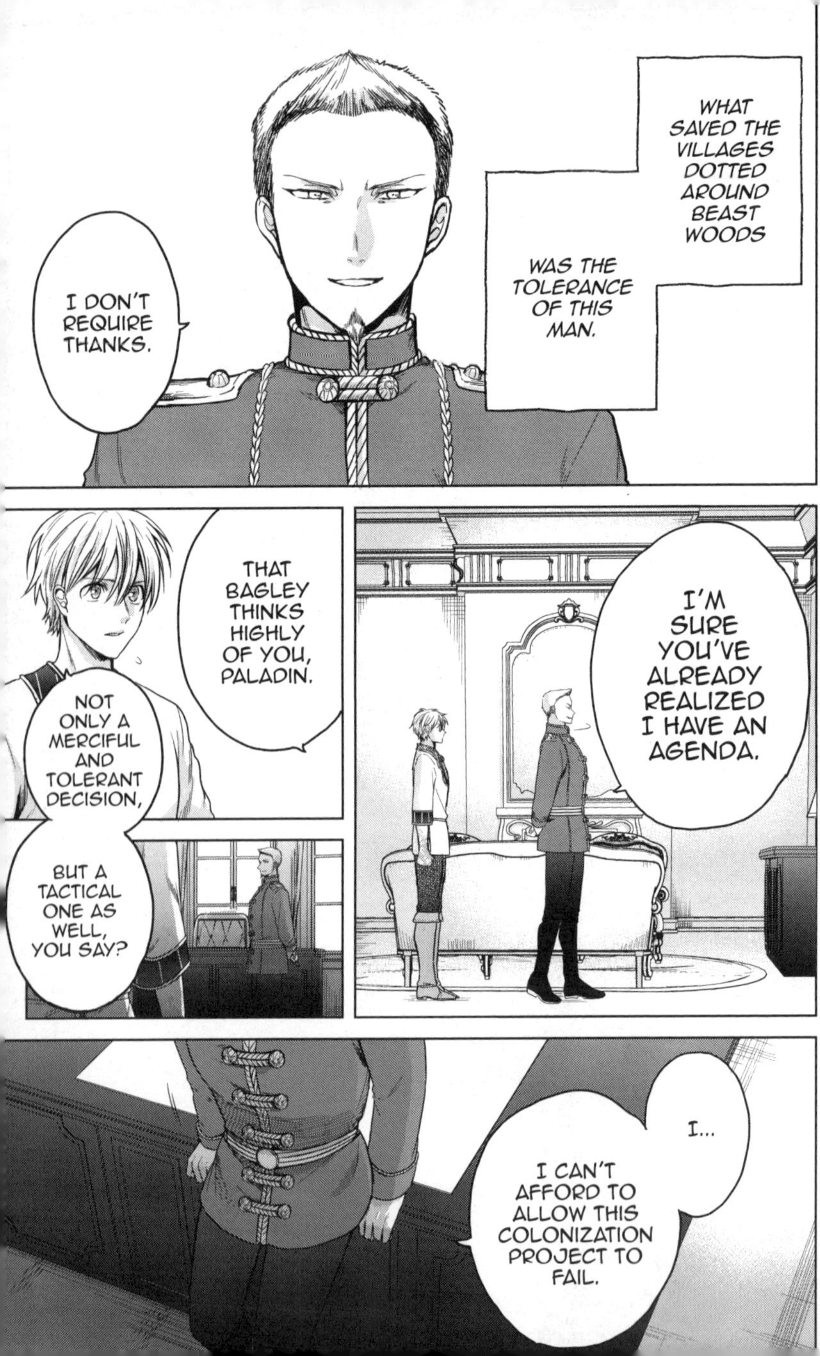
WHAT SAVED THE VILLAGES DOTTED AROUND BEAST WOODS
WAS THE TOLERANCE OF THIS MAN.
I DON'T REQUIRE THANKS.
I'M SURE YOU'VE ALREADY REALIZED I HAVE AN AGENDA.
THAT BAGLEY THINKS HIGHLY OF YOU, PALADIN.
NOT ONLY A MERCIFUL AND TOLERANT DECISION,
BUT A TACTICAL ONE AS WELL, YOU SAY?
I...
I CAN'T AFFORD TO ALLOW THIS COLONIZATION PROJECT TO FAIL.

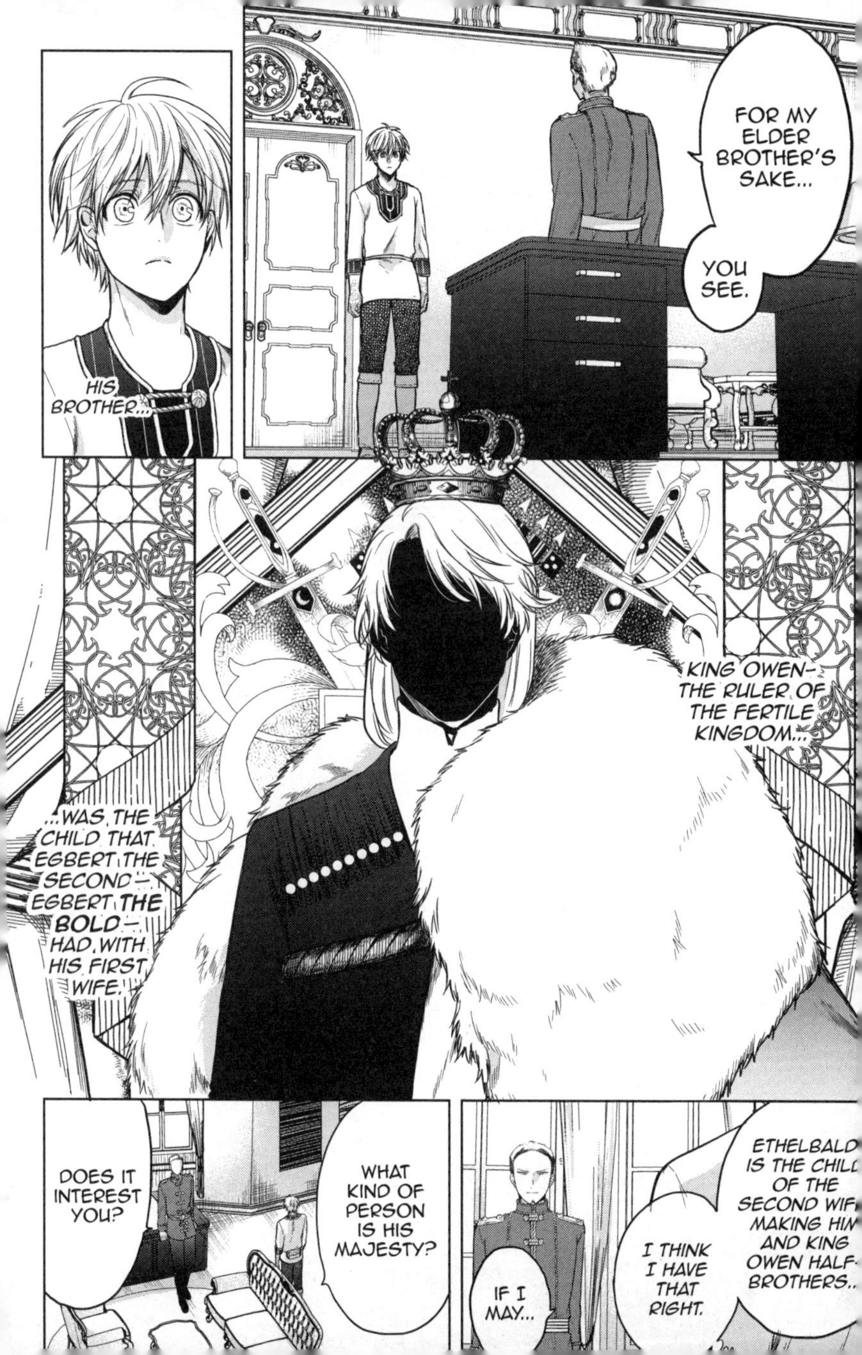
FOR MY ELDER BROTHER'S SAKE...
YOU SEE.
HIS BROTHER...
KING OWEN- THE RULER OF THE FERTILE KINGDOM...
...WAS THE CHILD THAT EGBERT THE SECOND— EGBERT THE BOLD— HAD WITH HIS FIRST WIFE.
ETHELBALD IS THE CHILD OF THE SECOND WIF MAKING HIM AND KING OWEN HALF-BROTHERS..
I THINK I HAVE THAT RIGHT.
IF I MAY...
WHAT KIND OF PERSON IS HIS MAJESTY?
DOES IT INTEREST YOU?

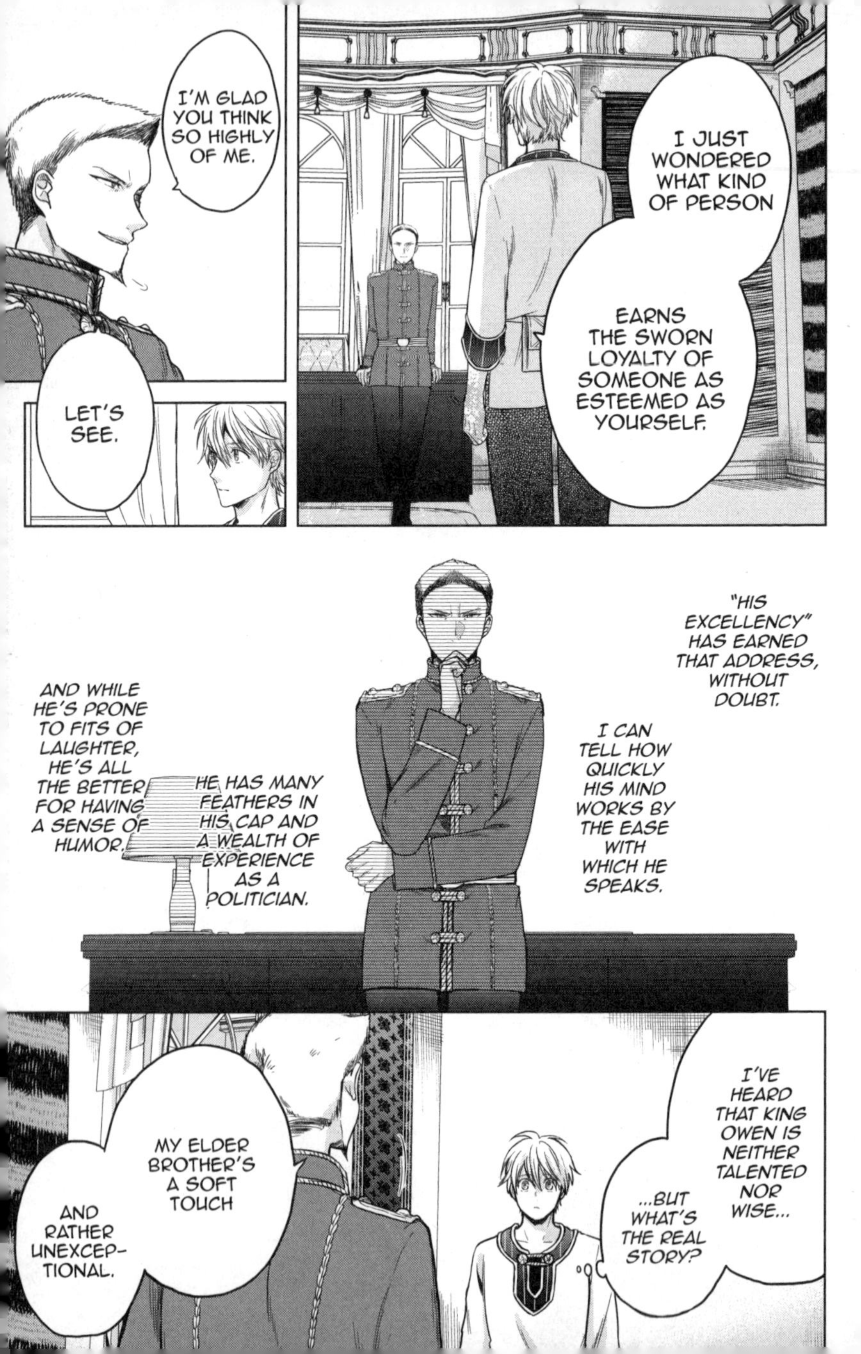
I JUST WONDERED WHAT KIND OF PERSON
EARNS THE SWORN LOYALTY OF SOMEONE AS ESTEEMED AS YOURSELF.
I'M GLAD YOU THINK SO HIGHLY OF ME.
LET'S SEE.
"HIS EXCELLENCY" HAS EARNED THAT ADDRESS, WITHOUT DOUBT.
I CAN TELL HOW QUICKLY HIS MIND WORKS BY THE EASE WITH WHICH HE SPEAKS.
HE HAS MANY FEATHERS IN HIS CAP AND A WEALTH OF EXPERIENCE AS A POLITICIAN.
AND WHILE HE'S PRONE TO FITS OF LAUGHTER, HE'S ALL THE BETTER FOR HAVING A SENSE OF HUMOR.
I'VE HEARD THAT KING OWEN IS NEITHER TALENTED NOR WISE...
...BUT WHAT'S THE REAL STORY?
MY ELDER BROTHER'S A SOFT TOUCH
AND RATHER UNEXCEPTIONAL.

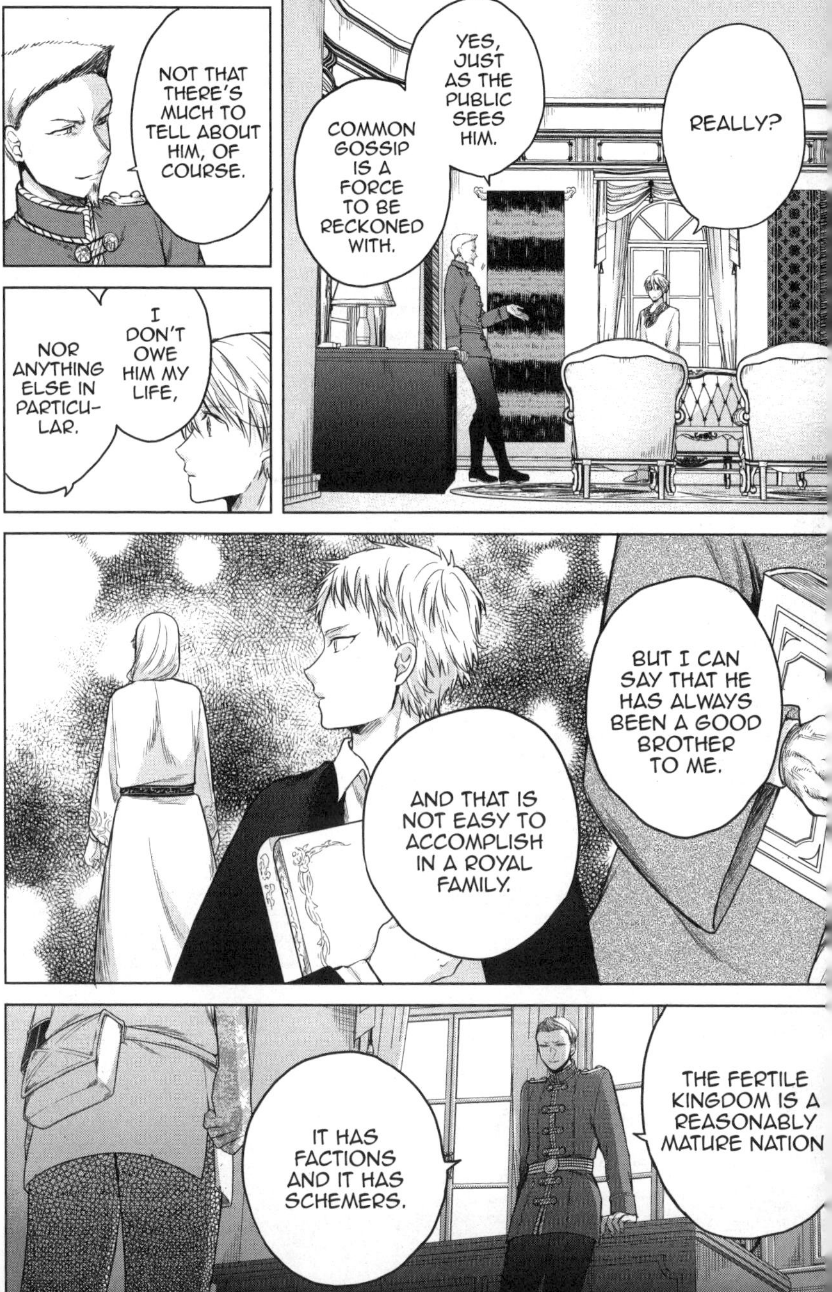
REALLY?
YES, JUST AS THE PUBLIC SEES HIM.
COMMON GOSSIP IS A FORCE TO BE RECKONED WITH.
NOT THAT THERE'S MUCH TO TELL ABOUT HIM, OF COURSE.
I DON'T OWE HIM MY LIFE,
NOR ANYTHING ELSE IN PARTICU-LAR.
BUT I CAN SAY THAT HE HAS ALWAYS BEEN A GOOD BROTHER TO ME.
AND THAT IS NOT EASY TO ACCOMPLISH IN A ROYAL FAMILY.
THE FERTILE KINGDOM IS A REASONABLY MATURE NATION
IT HAS FACTIONS AND IT HAS SCHEMERS.

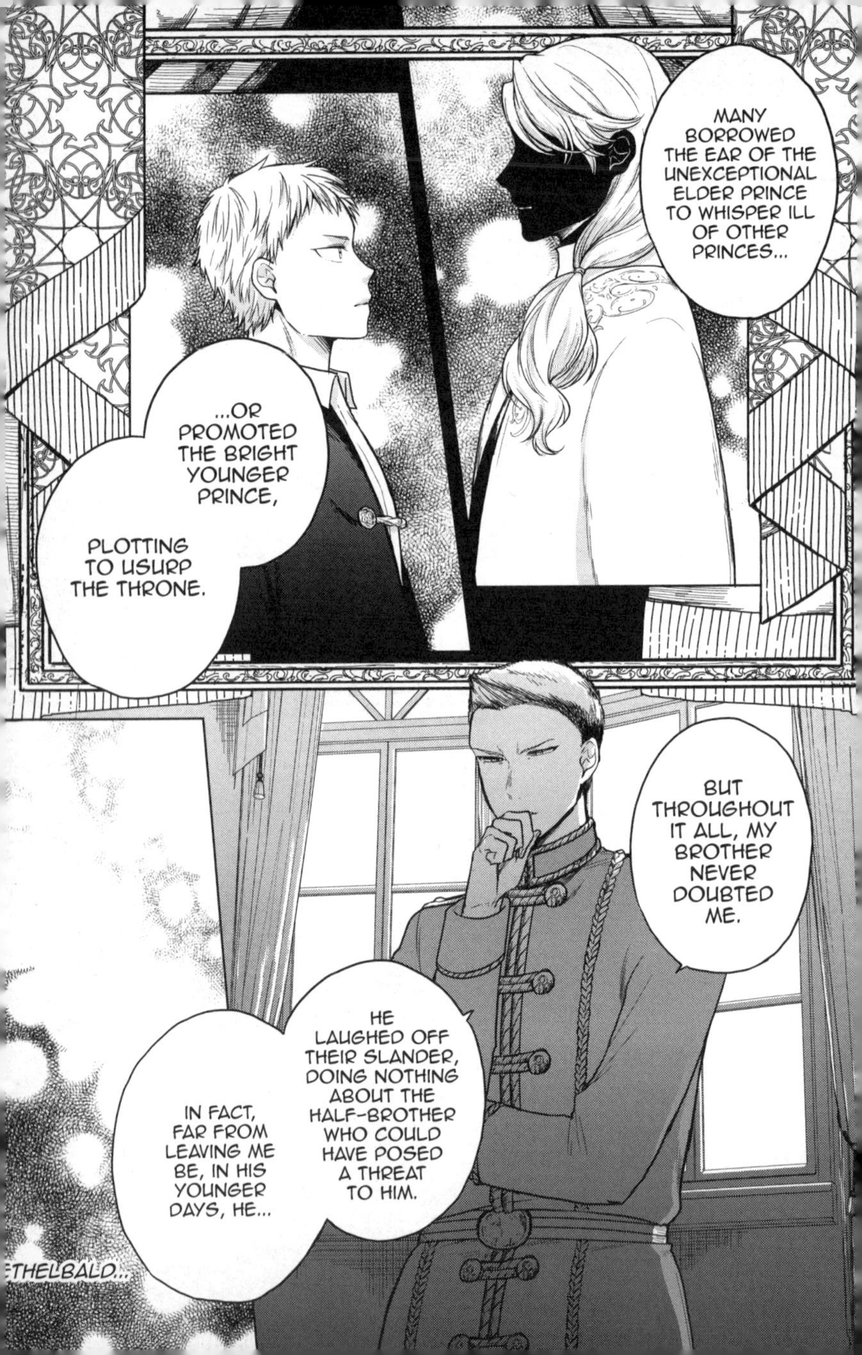
MANY BORROWED THE EAR OF THE UNEXCEPTIONAL ELDER PRINCE TO WHISPER ILL OF OTHER PRINCES...
...OR PROMOTED THE BRIGHT YOUNGER PRINCE,
PLOTTING TO USURP THE THRONE.
BUT THROUGHOUT IT ALL, MY BROTHER NEVER DOUBTED ME.
HE LAUGHED OFF THEIR SLANDER, DOING NOTHING ABOUT THE HALF-BROTHER WHO COULD HAVE POSED A THREAT TO HIM.
IN FACT, FAR FROM LEAVING ME BE, IN HIS YOUNGER DAYS, HE...
ETHELBALD...

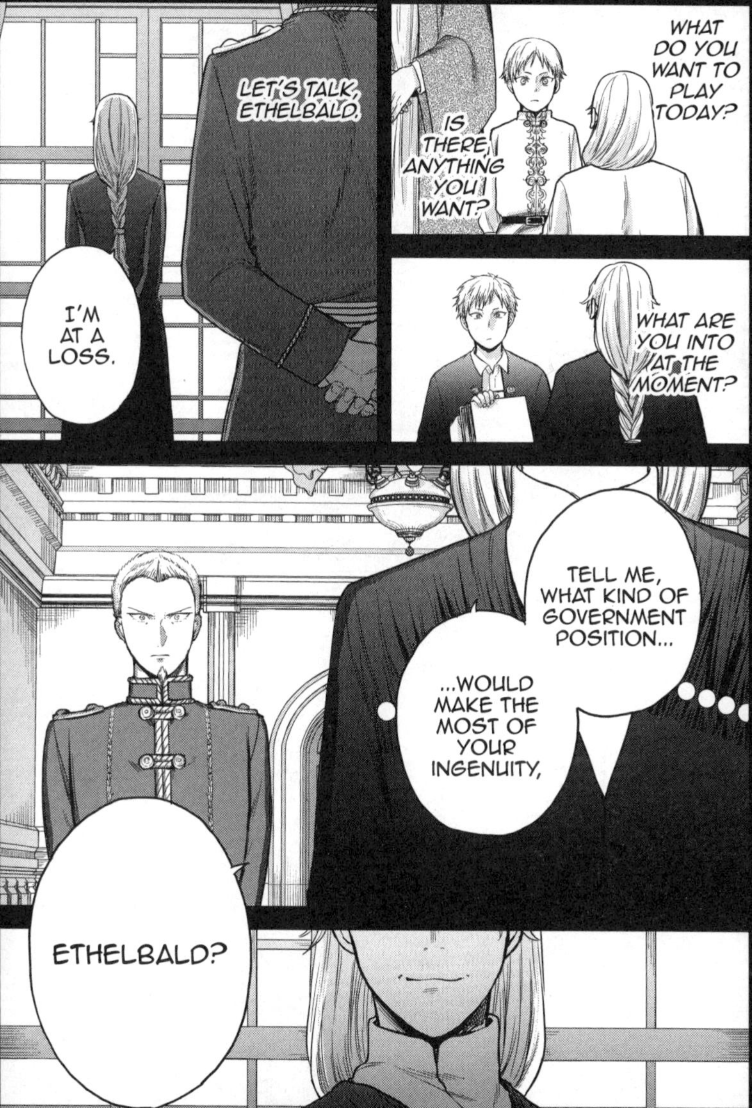
WHAT DO YOU WANT TO PLAY TODAY?
IS THERE ANYTHING YOU WANT?
WHAT ARE YOU INTO AT THE MOMENT?
LET'S TALK, ETHELBALD.
I'M AT A LOSS.
TELL ME, WHAT KIND OF GOVERNMENT POSITION...
...WOULD MAKE THE MOST OF YOUR INGENUITY,
ETHELBALD?

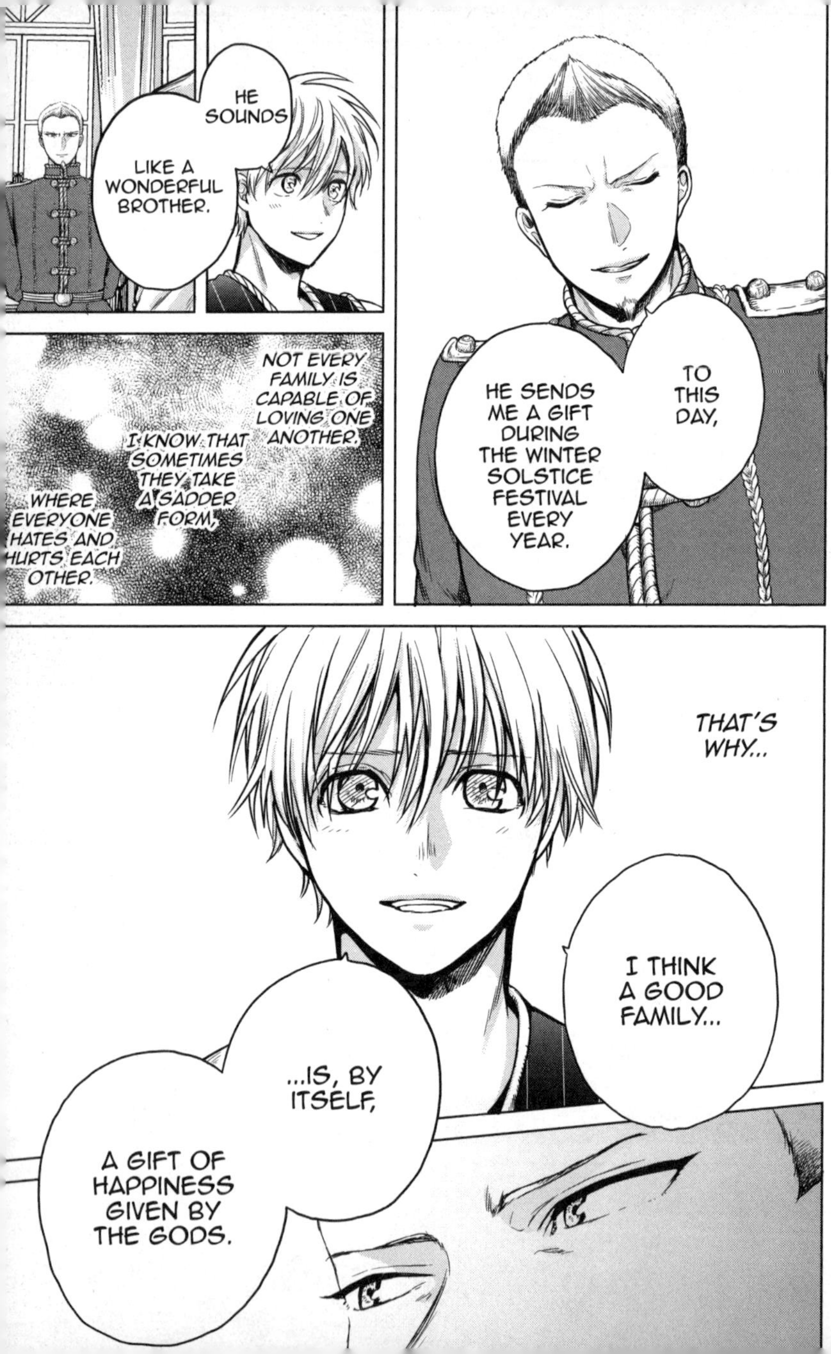
TO THIS DAY,
HE SENDS ME A GIFT DURING THE WINTER SOLSTICE FESTIVAL EVERY YEAR.
HE SOUNDS
LIKE A WONDERFUL BROTHER.
NOT EVERY FAMILY IS CAPABLE OF LOVING ONE ANOTHER.
I KNOW THAT SOMETIMES THEY TAKE A SADDER FORM,
WHERE EVERYONE HATES AND HURTS EACH OTHER.
THAT'S WHY...
I THINK A GOOD FAMILY...
...IS, BY ITSELF,
A GIFT OF HAPPINESS GIVEN BY THE GODS.

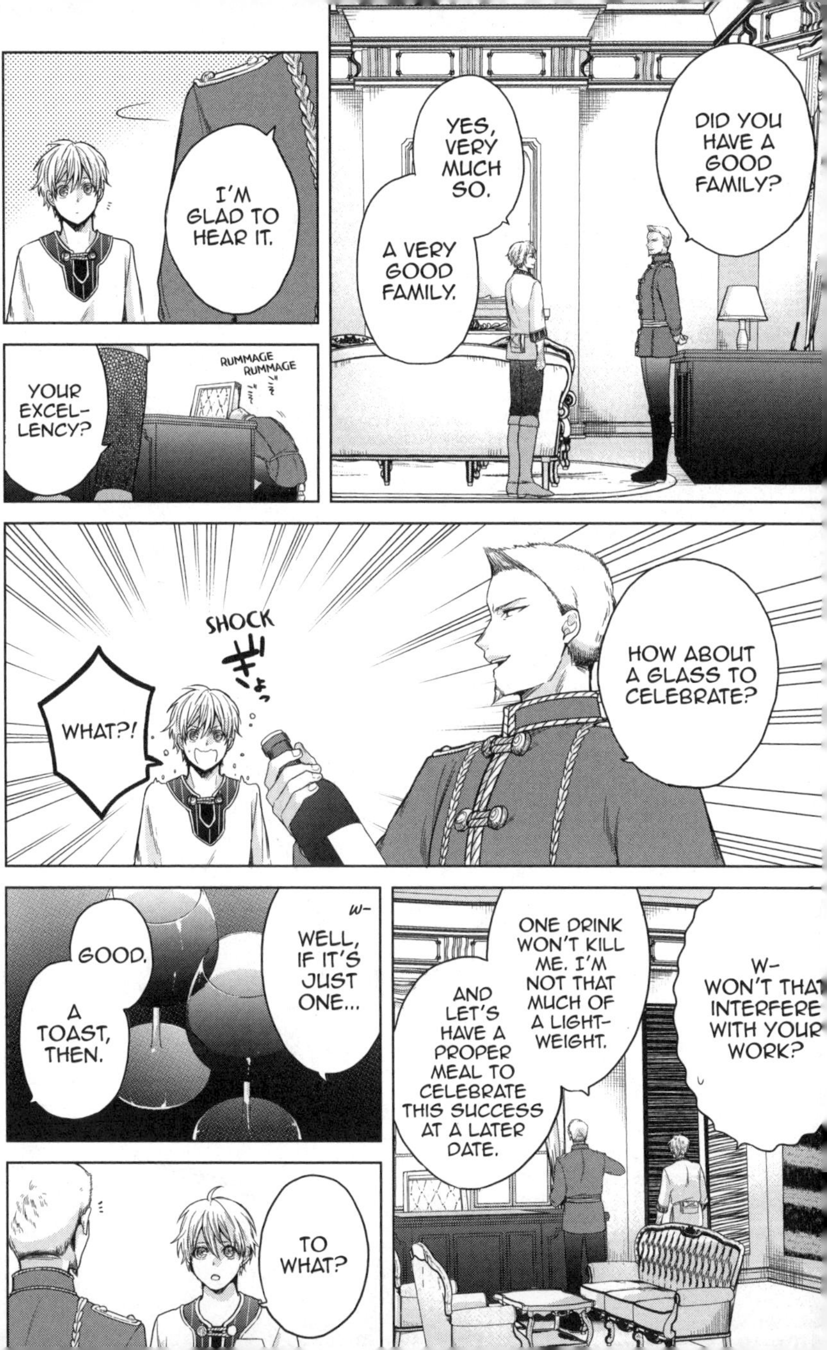
DID YOU HAVE A GOOD FAMILY?
YES, VERY MUCH SO.
A VERY GOOD FAMILY.
I'M GLAD TO HEAR IT.
RUMMAGE RUMMAGE
YOUR EXCEL-LENCY?
HOW ABOUT A GLASS TO CELEBRATE?
SHOCK
WHAT?!
W- WON'T THAT INTERFERE WITH YOUR WORK?
ONE DRINK WON'T KILL ME. I'M NOT THAT MUCH OF A LIGHT-WEIGHT.
AND LET'S HAVE A PROPER MEAL TO CELEBRATE THIS SUCCESS AT A LATER DATE.
W-
WELL, IF IT'S JUST ONE...
GOOD.
A TOAST, THEN.
TO WHAT?

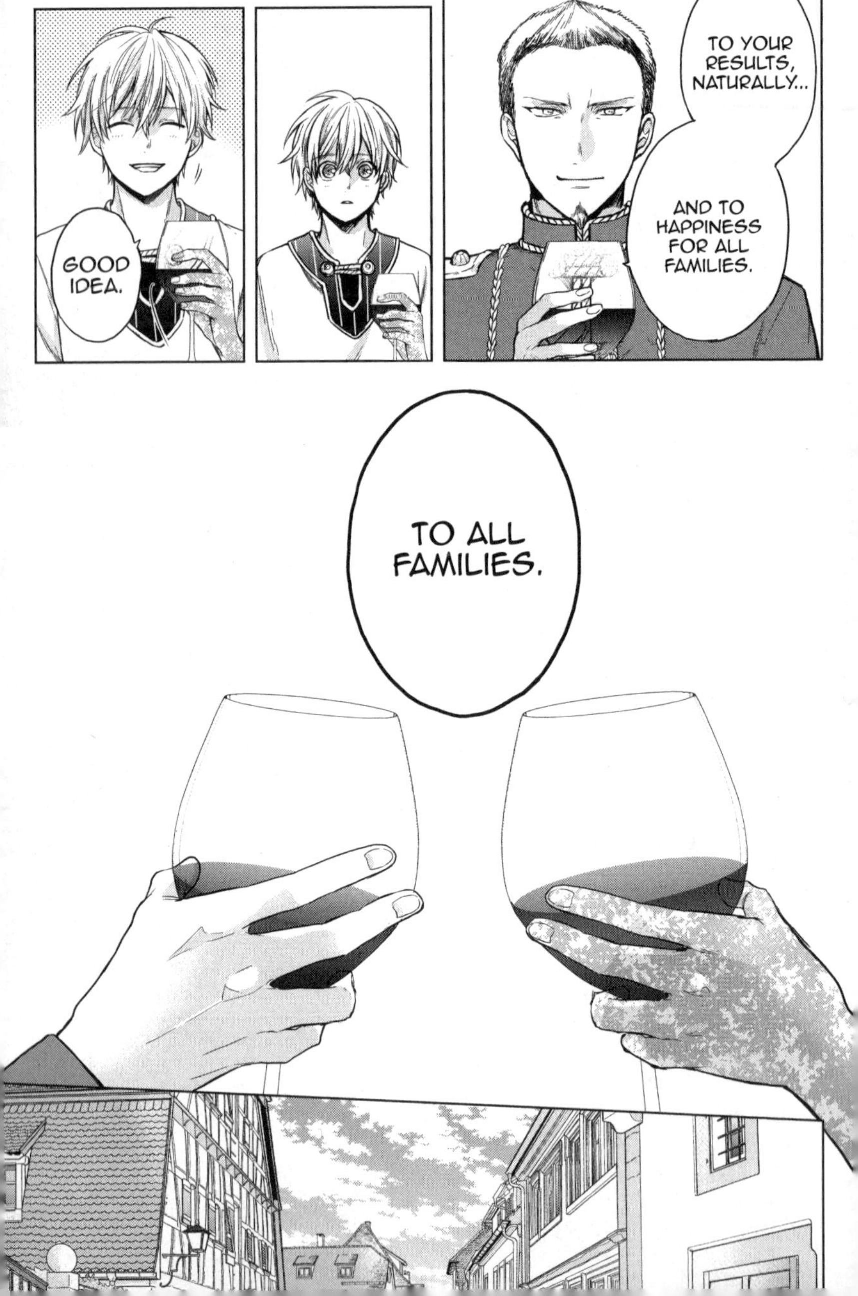
TO YOUR RESULTS, NATURALLY...
AND TO HAPPINESS FOR ALL FAMILIES.
GOOD IDEA.
TO ALL FAMILIES.

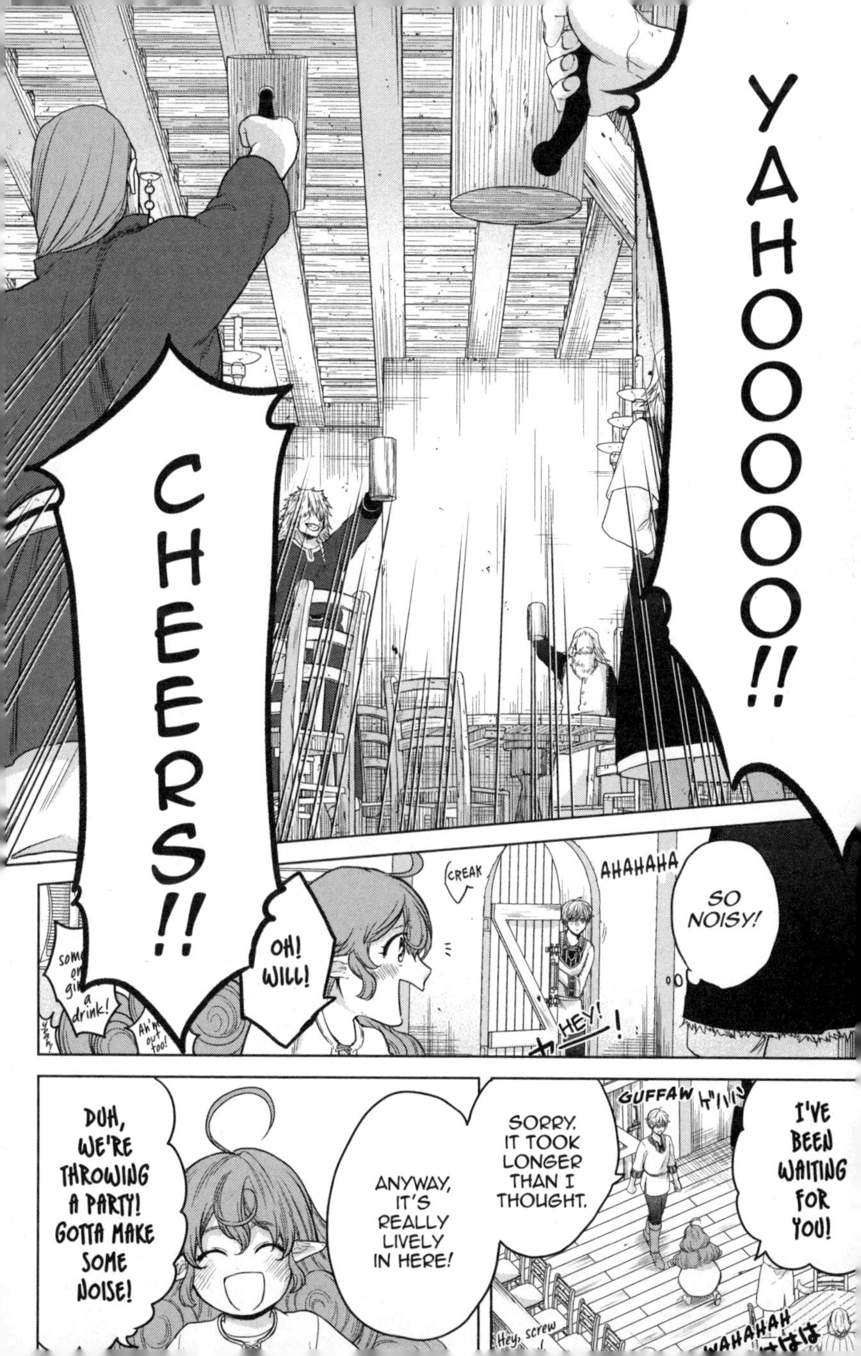

YAHOOOOO!!
CHEERS!!
SO NOISY!
AHAHAHA
CREAK
HEY!
OH! WILL!
a drink!
Ah'm out too!
GUFFAW
I'VE BEEN WAITING FOR YOU!
SORRY. IT TOOK LONGER THAN I THOUGHT.
WAHAHAH
Hey, screw
ANYWAY, IT'S REALLY LIVELY IN HERE!
DUH, WE'RE THROWING A PARTY! GOTTA MAKE SOME NOISE!

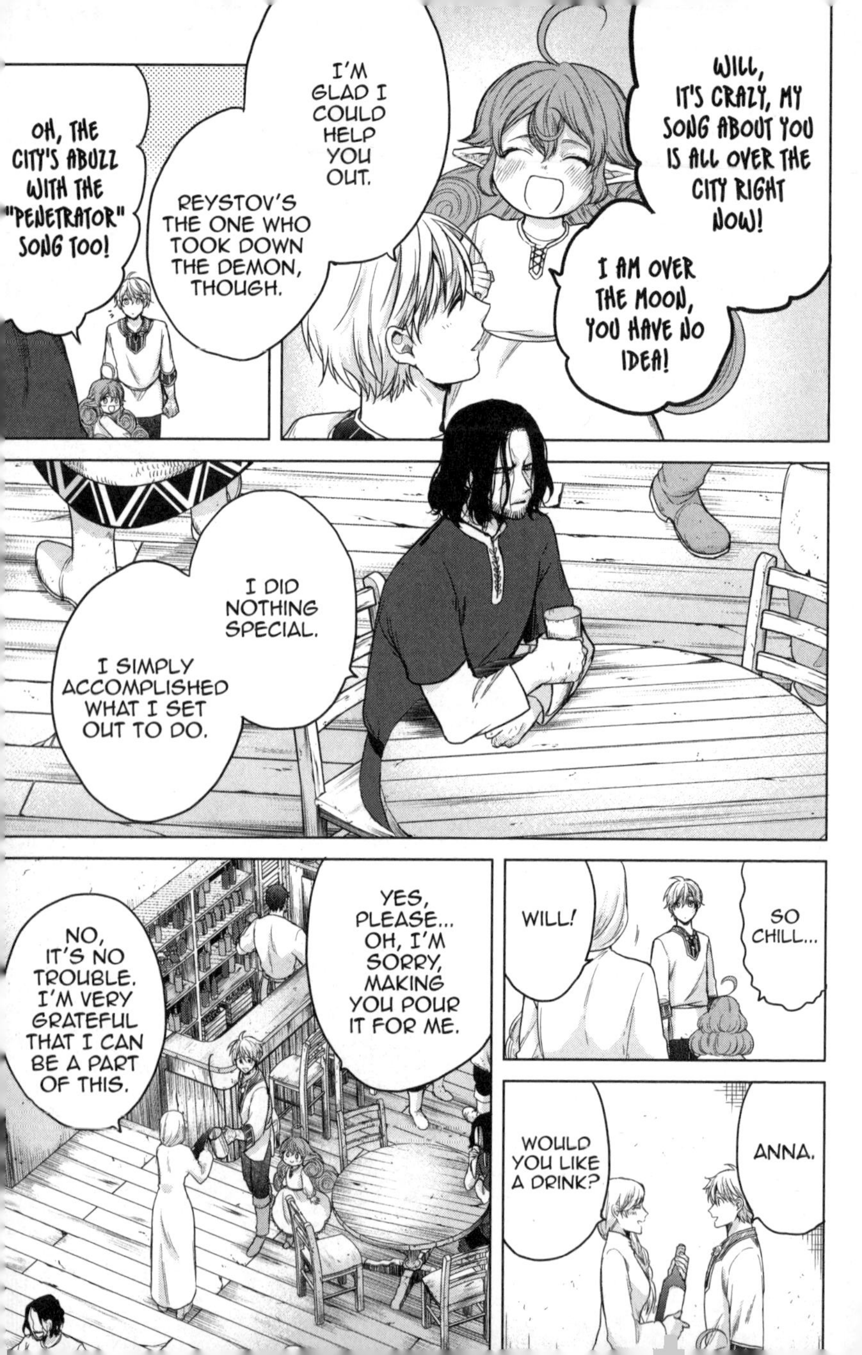
WILL, IT'S CRAZY, MY SONG ABOUT YOU IS ALL OVER THE CITY RIGHT NOW!
I AM OVER THE MOON, YOU HAVE NO IDEA!
I'M GLAD I COULD HELP YOU OUT.
REYSTOV'S THE ONE WHO TOOK DOWN THE DEMON, THOUGH.
OH, THE CITY'S ABUZZ WITH THE "PENETRATOR" SONG TOO!
I DID NOTHING SPECIAL.
I SIMPLY ACCOMPLISHED WHAT I SET OUT TO DO.
SO CHILL...
WILL!
ANNA.
WOULD YOU LIKE A DRINK?
YES, PLEASE... OH, I'M SORRY, MAKING YOU POUR IT FOR ME.
NO, IT'S NO TROUBLE. I'M VERY GRATEFUL THAT I CAN BE A PART OF THIS.

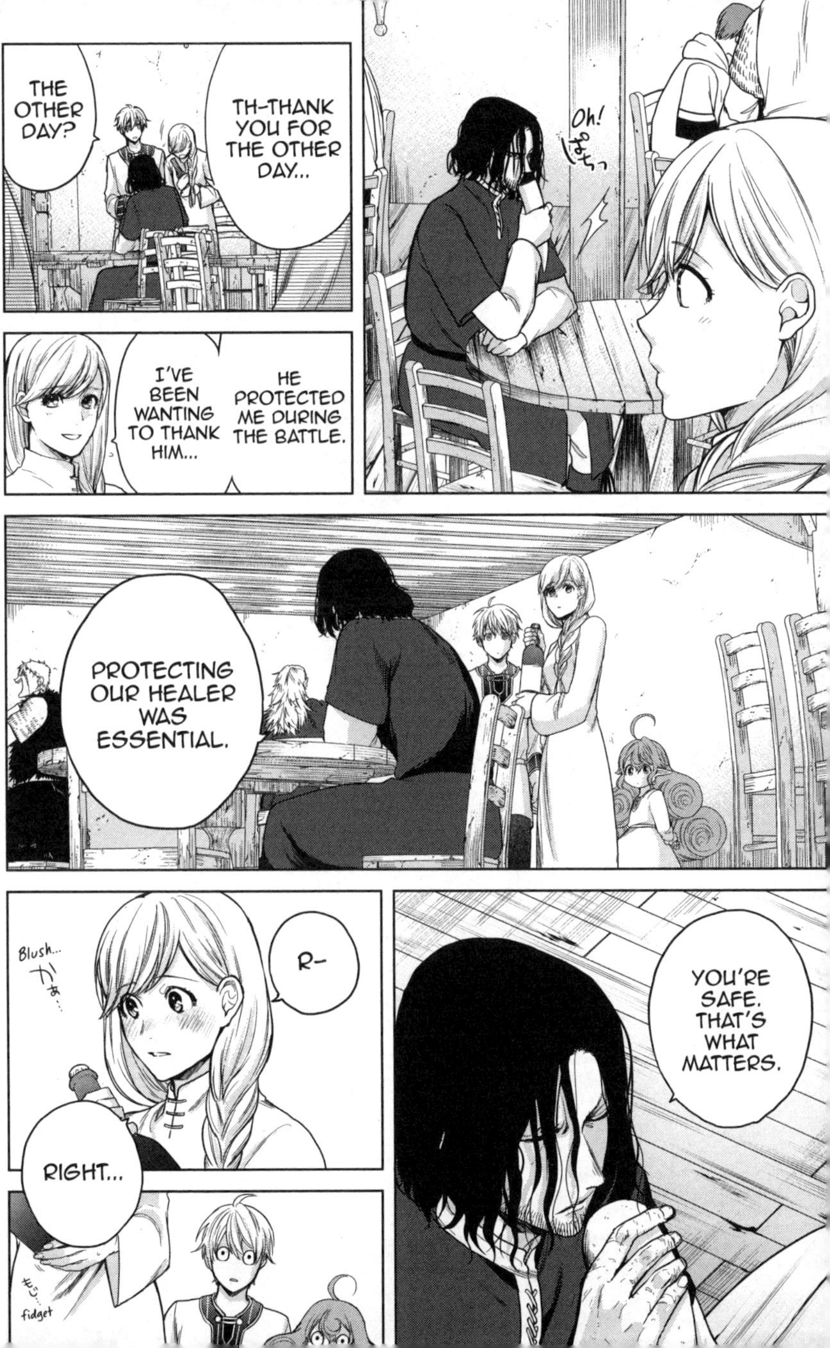
Oh!
ぱちっ
TH-THANK YOU FOR THE OTHER DAY...
THE OTHER DAY?
HE PROTECTED ME DURING THE BATTLE.
I'VE BEEN WANTING TO THANK HIM...
PROTECTING OUR HEALER WAS ESSENTIAL.
YOU'RE SAFE. THAT'S WHAT MATTERS.
R-
Blush... かぁ...
RIGHT...
もじ... fidget

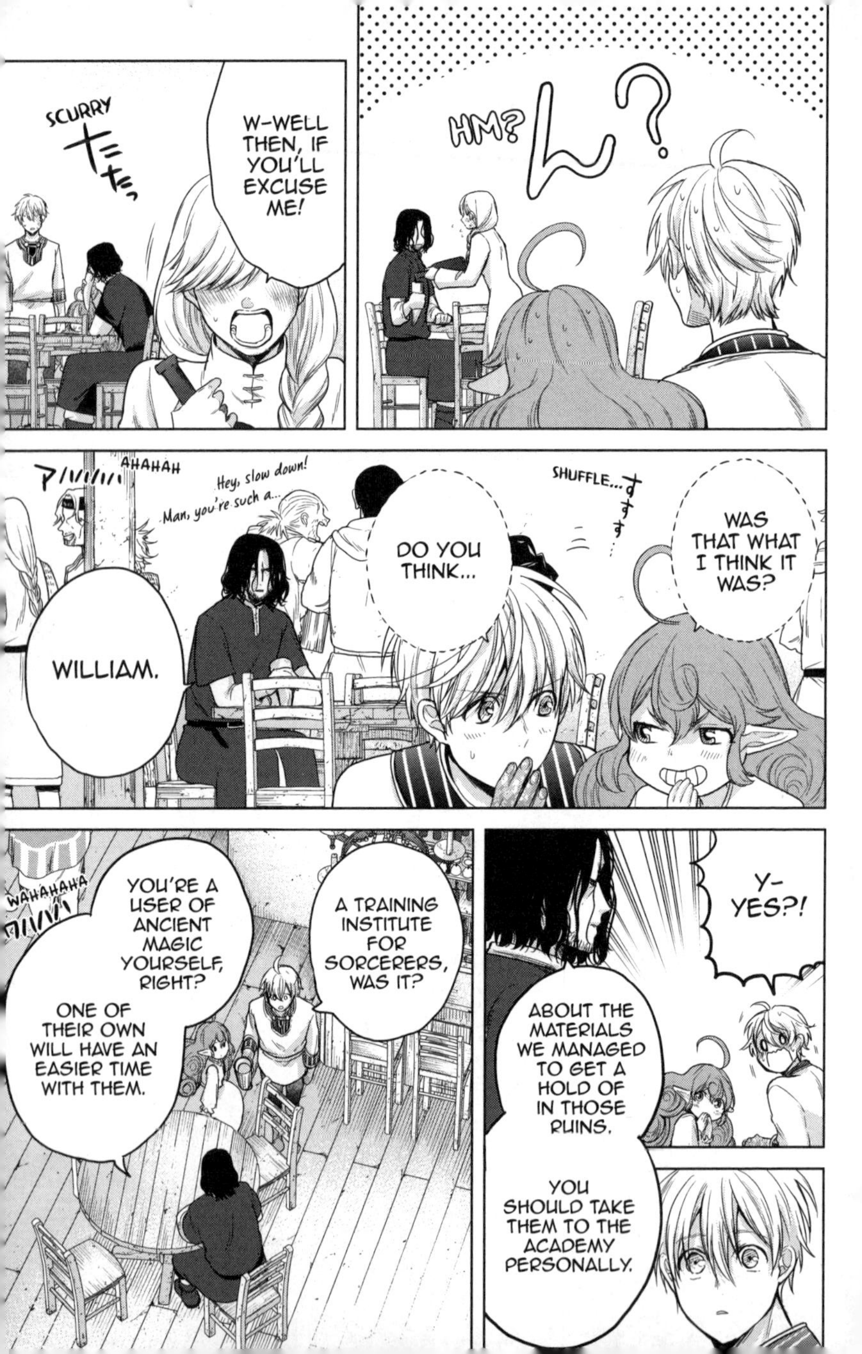
HM?
ん?
W-WELL THEN, IF YOU'LL EXCUSE ME!
SCURRY
たたっ
WAS THAT WHAT I THINK IT WAS?
SHUFFLE...
すすす
DO YOU THINK...
Hey, slow down!
Man, you're such a...
AHAHAH
アハハハハ
WILLIAM.
Y-YES?!
ABOUT THE MATERIALS WE MANAGED TO GET A HOLD OF IN THOSE RUINS.
YOU SHOULD TAKE THEM TO THE ACADEMY PERSONALLY.
A TRAINING INSTITUTE FOR SORCERERS, WAS IT?
YOU'RE A USER OF ANCIENT MAGIC YOURSELF, RIGHT?
ONE OF THEIR OWN WILL HAVE AN EASIER TIME WITH THEM.
WAHAHAHA
ワハハハ

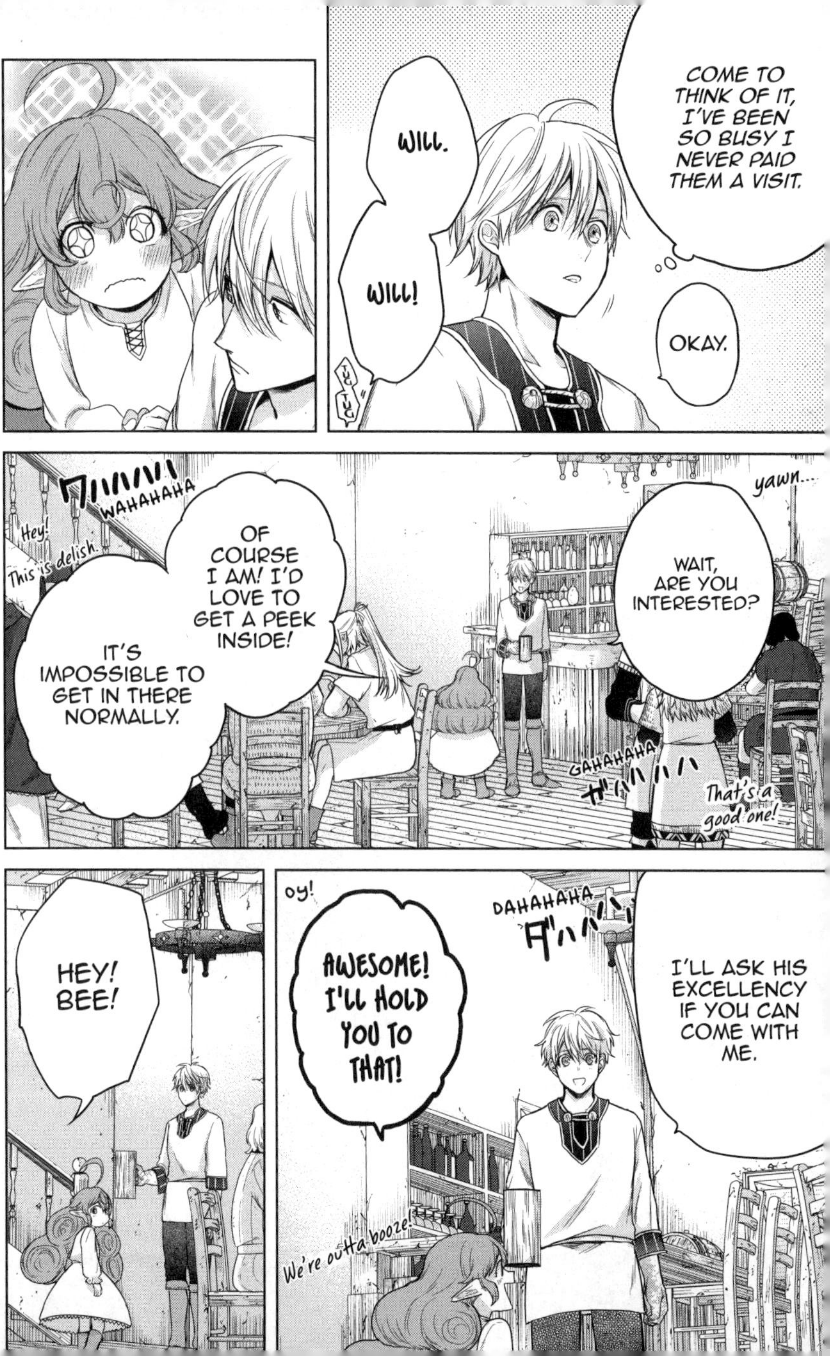
COME TO THINK OF IT, I'VE BEEN SO BUSY I NEVER PAID THEM A VISIT.
OKAY.
WILL.
WILL!
TUG TUG
yawn...
WAIT, ARE YOU INTERESTED?
OF COURSE I AM! I'D LOVE TO GET A PEEK INSIDE!
IT'S IMPOSSIBLE TO GET IN THERE NORMALLY.
WAHAHAHA
Hey! This is delish.
GAHAHAHA
That's a good one!
I'LL ASK HIS EXCELLENCY IF YOU CAN COME WITH ME.
DAHAHAHA
oy!
AWESOME! I'LL HOLD YOU TO THAT!
We're outta booze!
HEY! BEE!

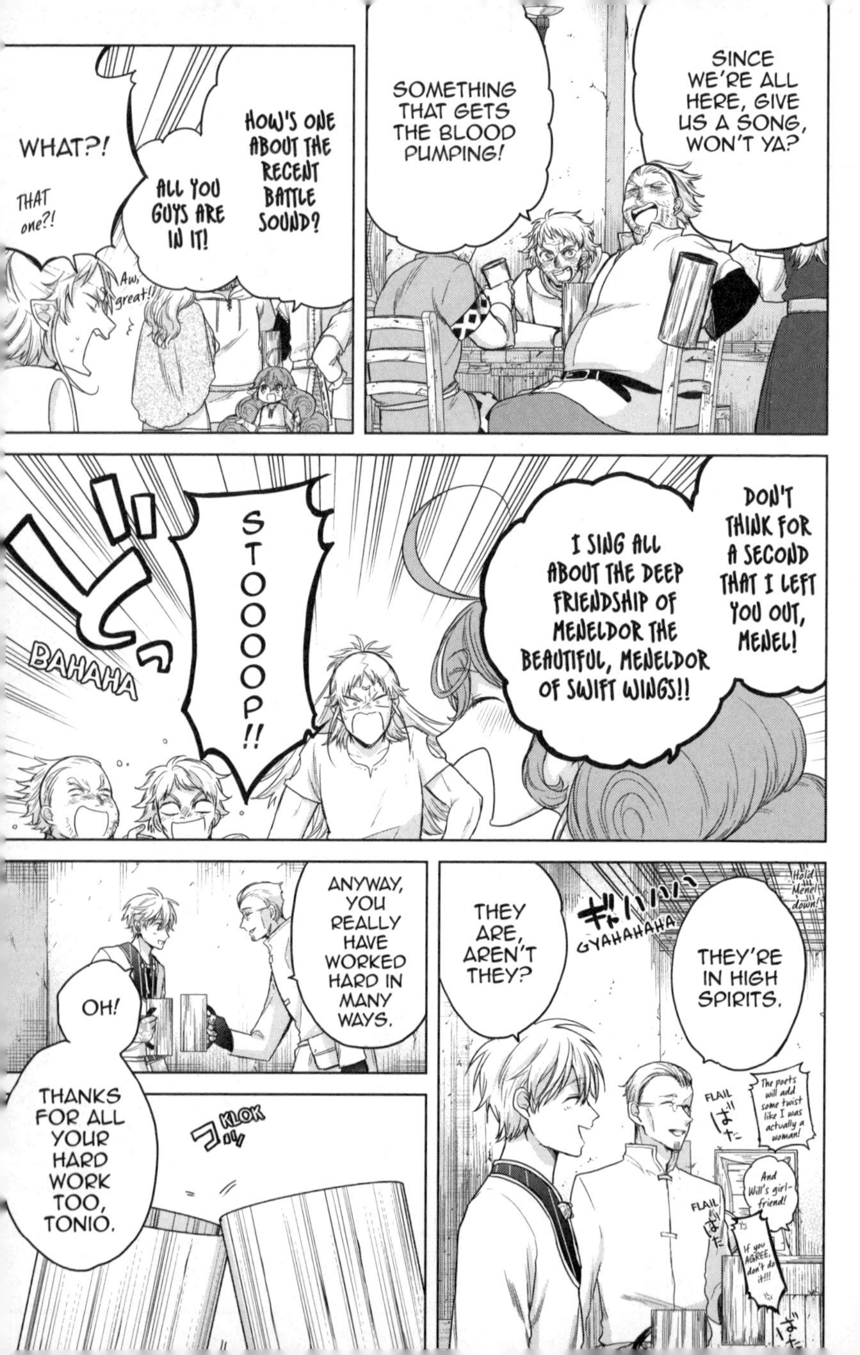

SINCE WE'RE ALL HERE, GIVE US A SONG, WON'T YA?
SOMETHING THAT GETS THE BLOOD PUMPING!
HOW'S ONE ABOUT THE RECENT BATTLE SOUND?
ALL YOU GUYS ARE IN IT!
WHAT?!
THAT one?!
Aw, great!
DON'T THINK FOR A SECOND THAT I LEFT YOU OUT, MENEL!
I SING ALL ABOUT THE DEEP FRIENDSHIP OF MENELDOR THE BEAUTIFUL, MENELDOR OF SWIFT WINGS!!
STOOOOOP!!
BAHAHA
Hold Menel down!
GYAHAHAHA
THEY'RE IN HIGH SPIRITS.
THEY ARE, AREN'T THEY?
FLAIL
The poets will add some twist like I was actually a woman!
And Will's girlfriend!
FLAIL
If you AGREE, don't do it!!!
ANYWAY, YOU REALLY HAVE WORKED HARD IN MANY WAYS.
OH!
THANKS FOR ALL YOUR HARD WORK TOO, TONIO.
KLOK

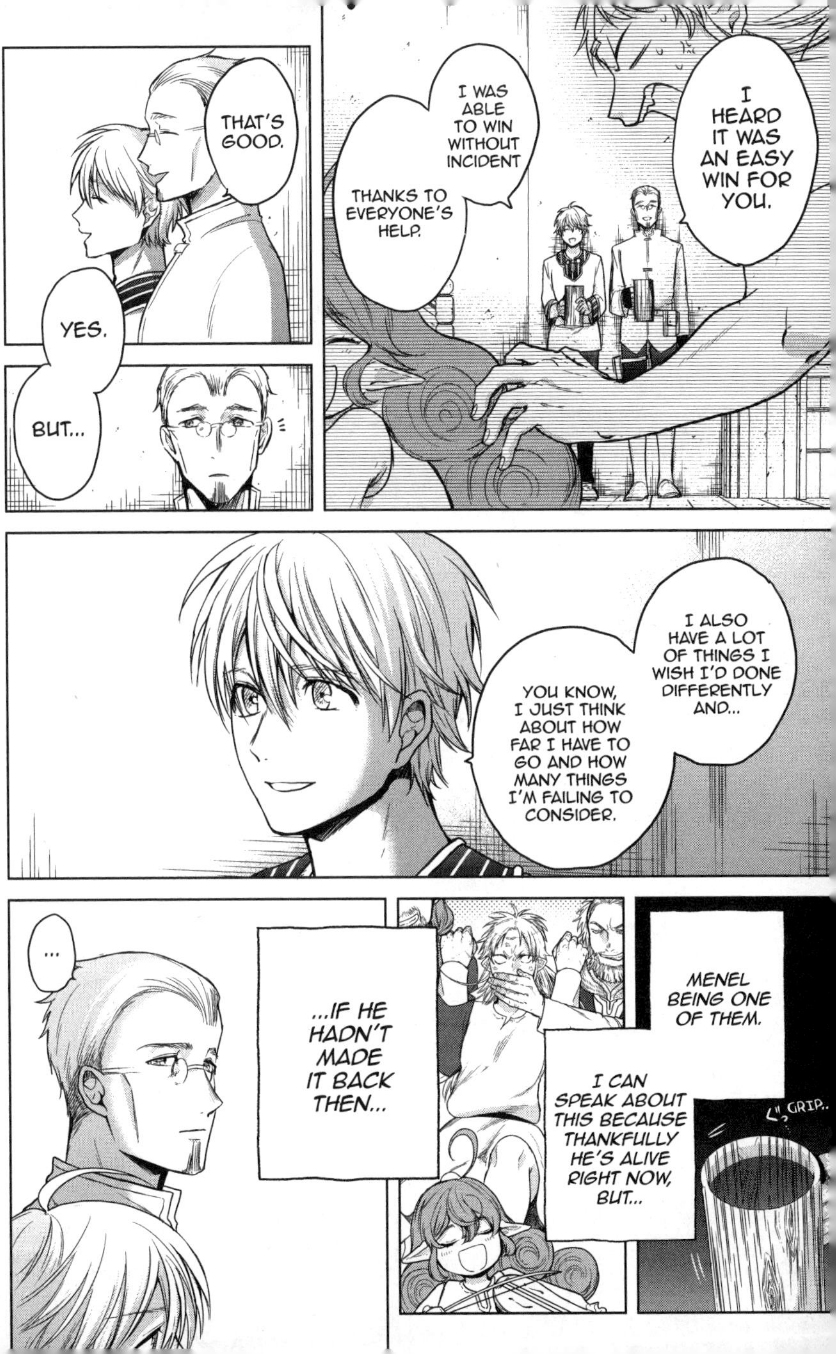
I HEARD IT WAS AN EASY WIN FOR YOU.
I WAS ABLE TO WIN WITHOUT INCIDENT
THANKS TO EVERYONE'S HELP.
THAT'S GOOD.
YES.
BUT...
I ALSO HAVE A LOT OF THINGS I WISH I'D DONE DIFFERENTLY AND...
YOU KNOW, I JUST THINK ABOUT HOW FAR I HAVE TO GO AND HOW MANY THINGS I'M FAILING TO CONSIDER.
MENEL BEING ONE OF THEM.
GRIP..
I CAN SPEAK ABOUT THIS BECAUSE THANKFULLY HE'S ALIVE RIGHT NOW, BUT...
...IF HE HADN'T MADE IT BACK THEN...
...

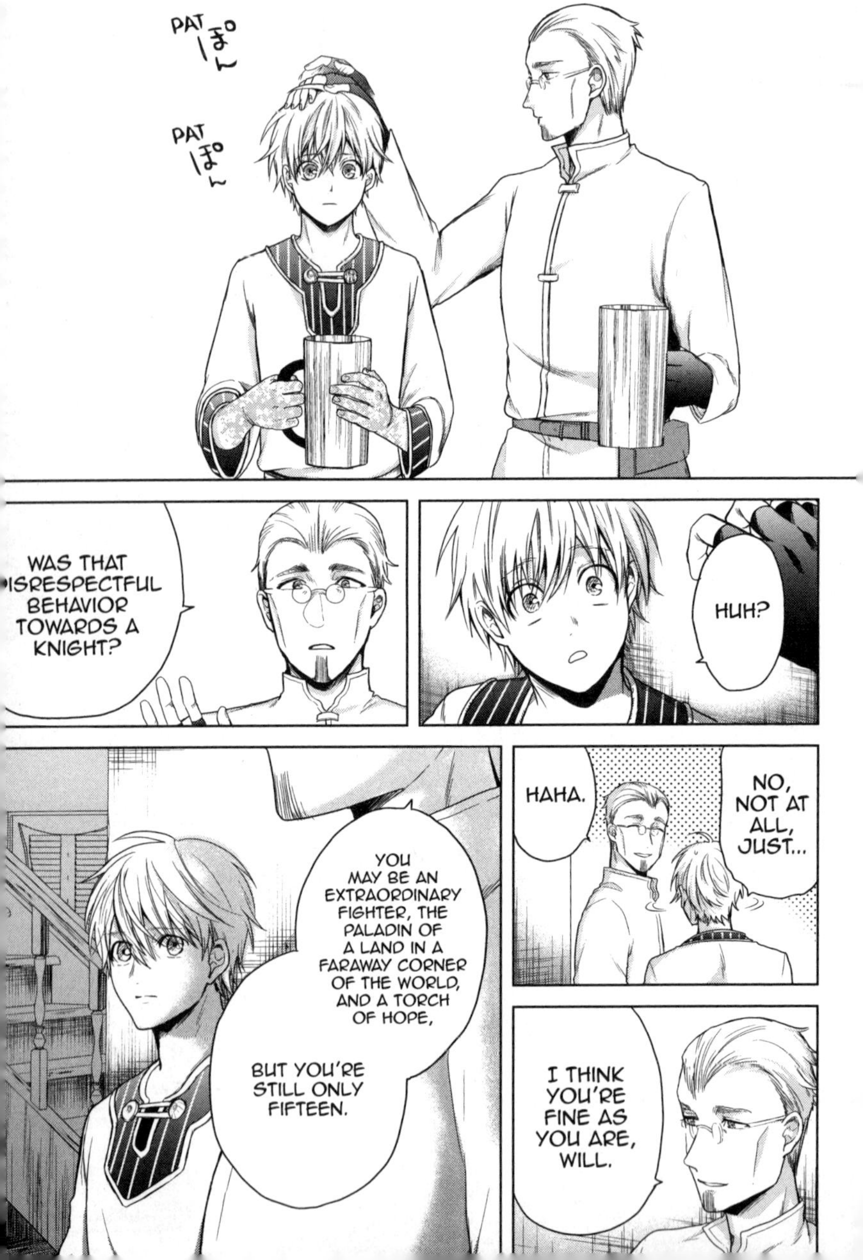
PAT ぽん
PAT ぽん
HUH?
WAS THAT ISRESPECTFUL BEHAVIOR TOWARDS A KNIGHT?
NO, NOT AT ALL, JUST...
HAHA.
I THINK YOU'RE FINE AS YOU ARE, WILL.
YOU MAY BE AN EXTRAORDINARY FIGHTER, THE PALADIN OF A LAND IN A FARAWAY CORNER OF THE WORLD, AND A TORCH OF HOPE,
BUT YOU'RE STILL ONLY FIFTEEN.

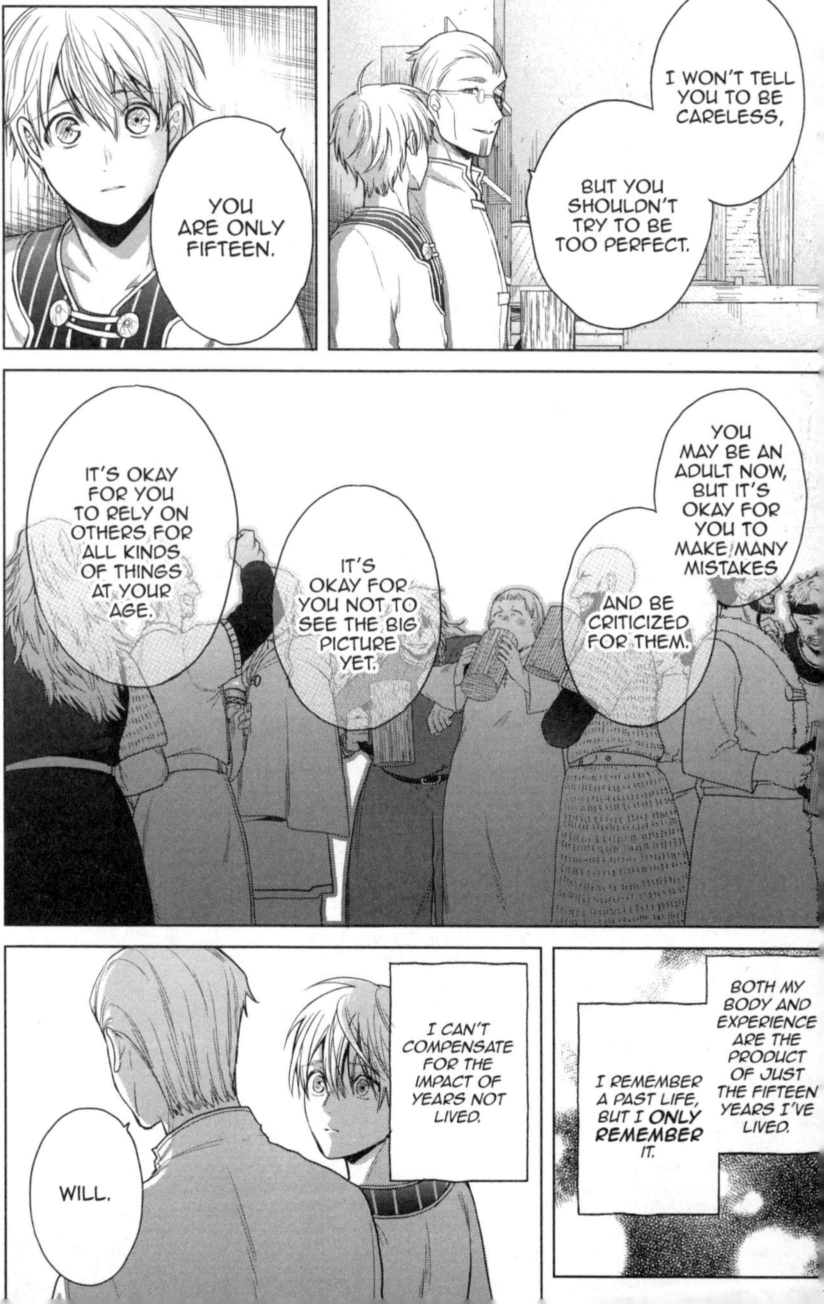
I WON'T TELL YOU TO BE CARELESS,
BUT YOU SHOULDN'T TRY TO BE TOO PERFECT.
YOU ARE ONLY FIFTEEN.
YOU MAY BE AN ADULT NOW, BUT IT'S OKAY FOR YOU TO MAKE MANY MISTAKES
AND BE CRITICIZED FOR THEM.
IT'S OKAY FOR YOU NOT TO SEE THE BIG PICTURE YET.
IT'S OKAY FOR YOU TO RELY ON OTHERS FOR ALL KINDS OF THINGS AT YOUR AGE.
BOTH MY BODY AND EXPERIENCE ARE THE PRODUCT OF JUST THE FIFTEEN YEARS I'VE LIVED.
I REMEMBER A PAST LIFE, BUT I **ONLY REMEMBER** IT.
I CAN'T COMPENSATE FOR THE IMPACT OF YEARS NOT LIVED.
WILL.

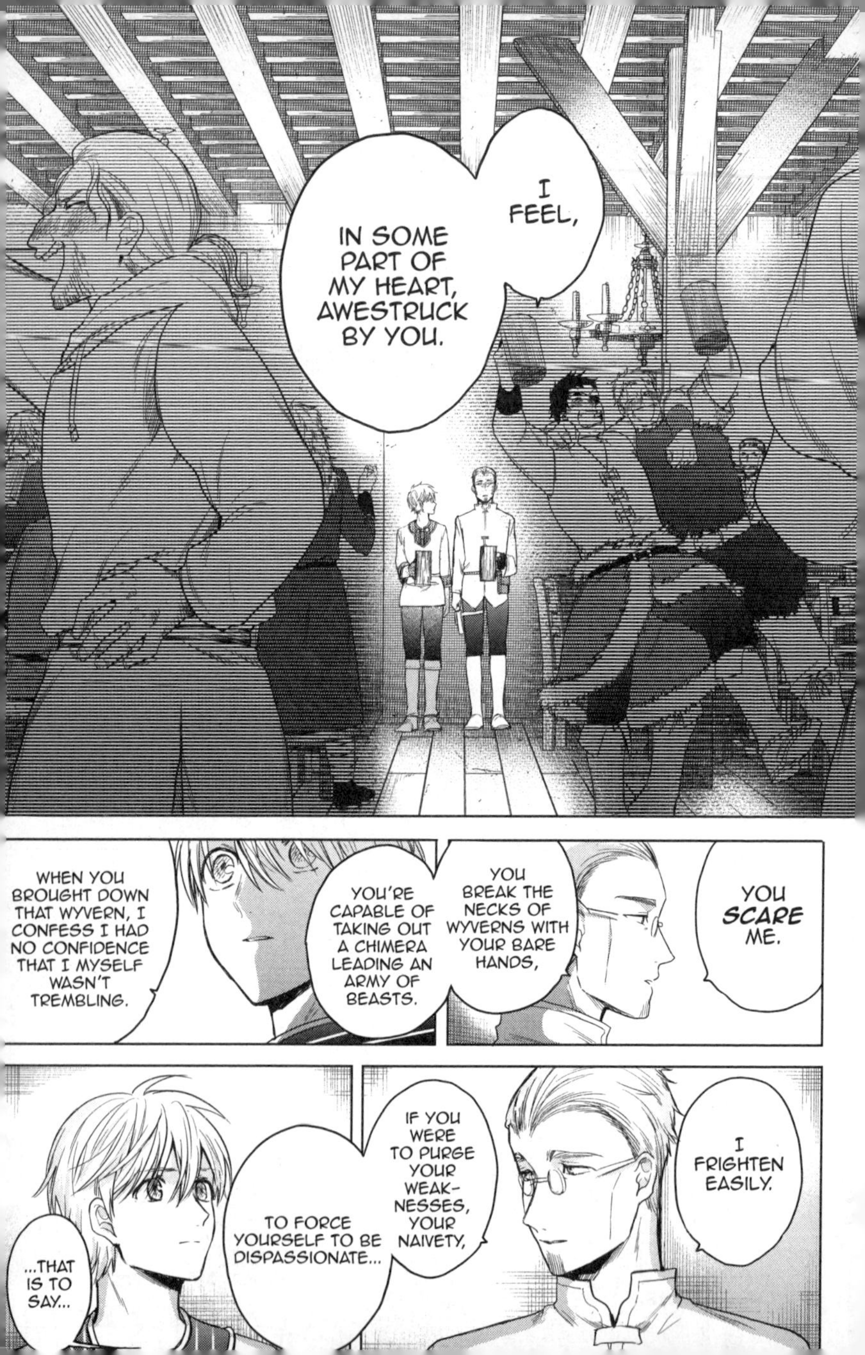
I FEEL,
IN SOME PART OF MY HEART, AWESTRUCK BY YOU.
YOU *SCARE* ME.
YOU BREAK THE NECKS OF WYVERNS WITH YOUR BARE HANDS,
YOU'RE CAPABLE OF TAKING OUT A CHIMERA LEADING AN ARMY OF BEASTS.
WHEN YOU BROUGHT DOWN THAT WYVERN, I CONFESS I HAD NO CONFIDENCE THAT I MYSELF WASN'T TREMBLING.
I FRIGHTEN EASILY.
IF YOU WERE TO PURGE YOUR WEAK-NESSES, YOUR NAIVETY,
TO FORCE YOURSELF TO BE DISPASSIONATE...
...THAT IS TO SAY...

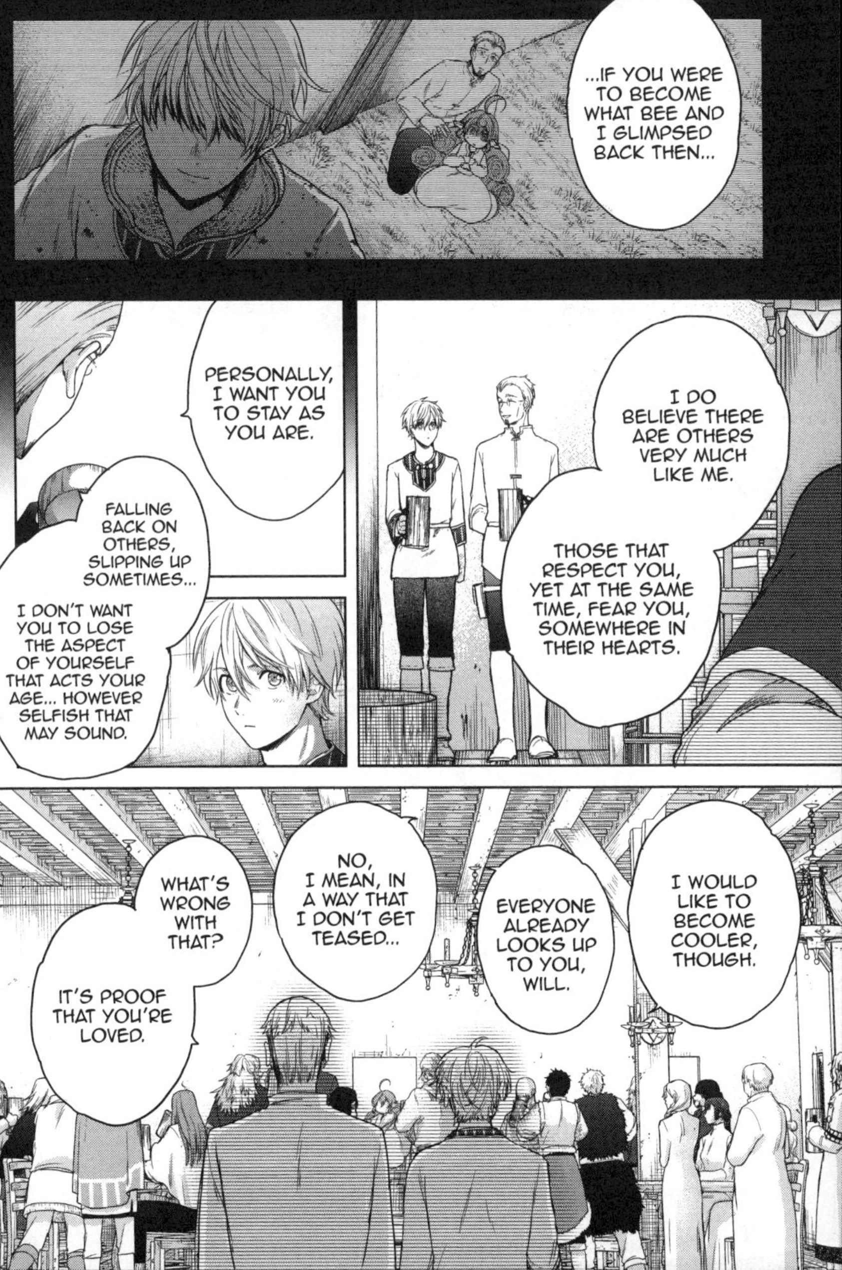
...IF YOU WERE TO BECOME WHAT BEE AND I GLIMPSED BACK THEN...
I DO BELIEVE THERE ARE OTHERS VERY MUCH LIKE ME.
THOSE THAT RESPECT YOU, YET AT THE SAME TIME, FEAR YOU, SOMEWHERE IN THEIR HEARTS.
PERSONALLY, I WANT YOU TO STAY AS YOU ARE.
FALLING BACK ON OTHERS, SLIPPING UP SOMETIMES...
I DON'T WANT YOU TO LOSE THE ASPECT OF YOURSELF THAT ACTS YOUR AGE... HOWEVER SELFISH THAT MAY SOUND.
I WOULD LIKE TO BECOME COOLER, THOUGH.
EVERYONE ALREADY LOOKS UP TO YOU, WILL.
NO, I MEAN, IN A WAY THAT I DON'T GET TEASED...
WHAT'S WRONG WITH THAT?
IT'S PROOF THAT YOU'RE LOVED.

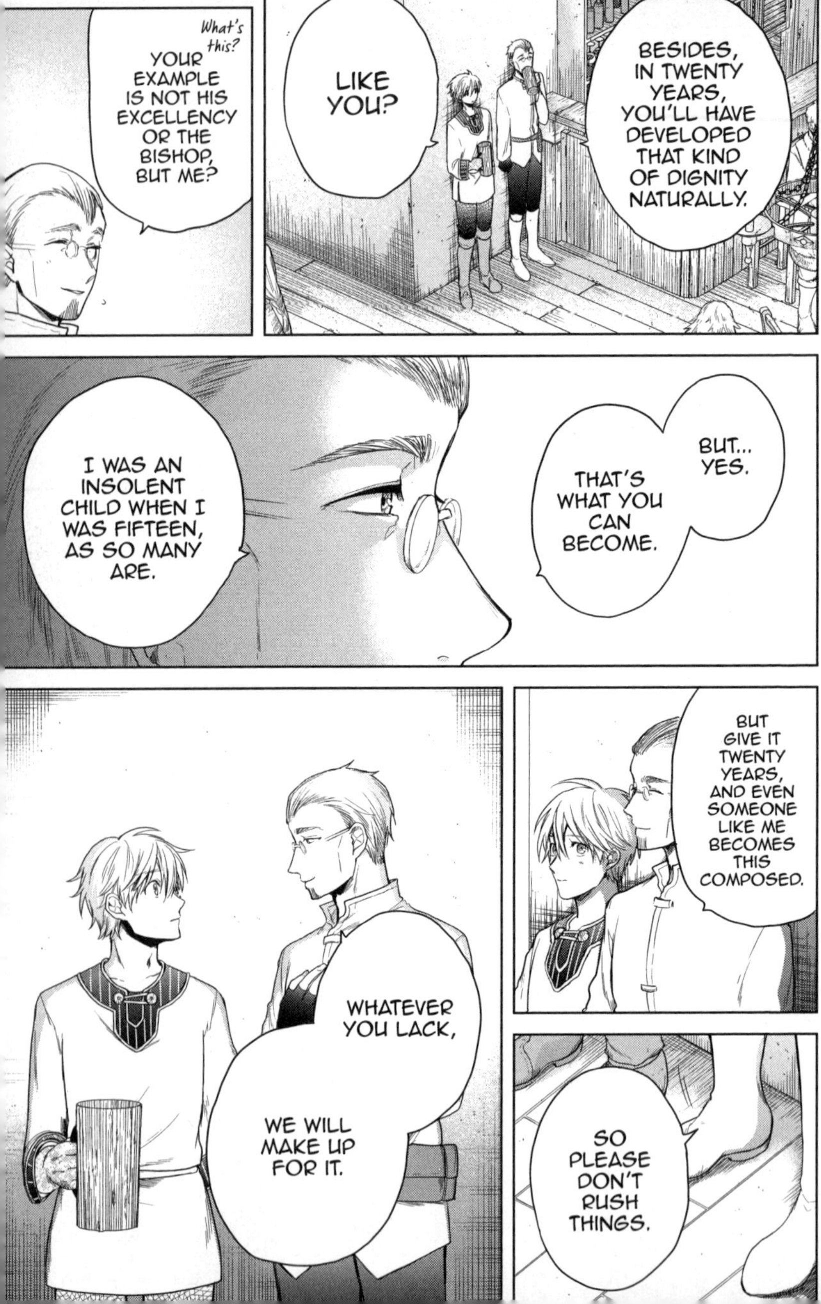
BESIDES, IN TWENTY YEARS, YOU'LL HAVE DEVELOPED THAT KIND OF DIGNITY NATURALLY.
LIKE YOU?
What's this?
YOUR EXAMPLE IS NOT HIS EXCELLENCY OR THE BISHOP, BUT ME?
BUT... YES.
THAT'S WHAT YOU CAN BECOME.
I WAS AN INSOLENT CHILD WHEN I WAS FIFTEEN, AS SO MANY ARE.
BUT GIVE IT TWENTY YEARS, AND EVEN SOMEONE LIKE ME BECOMES THIS COMPOSED.
SO PLEASE DON'T RUSH THINGS.
WHATEVER YOU LACK,
WE WILL MAKE UP FOR IT.

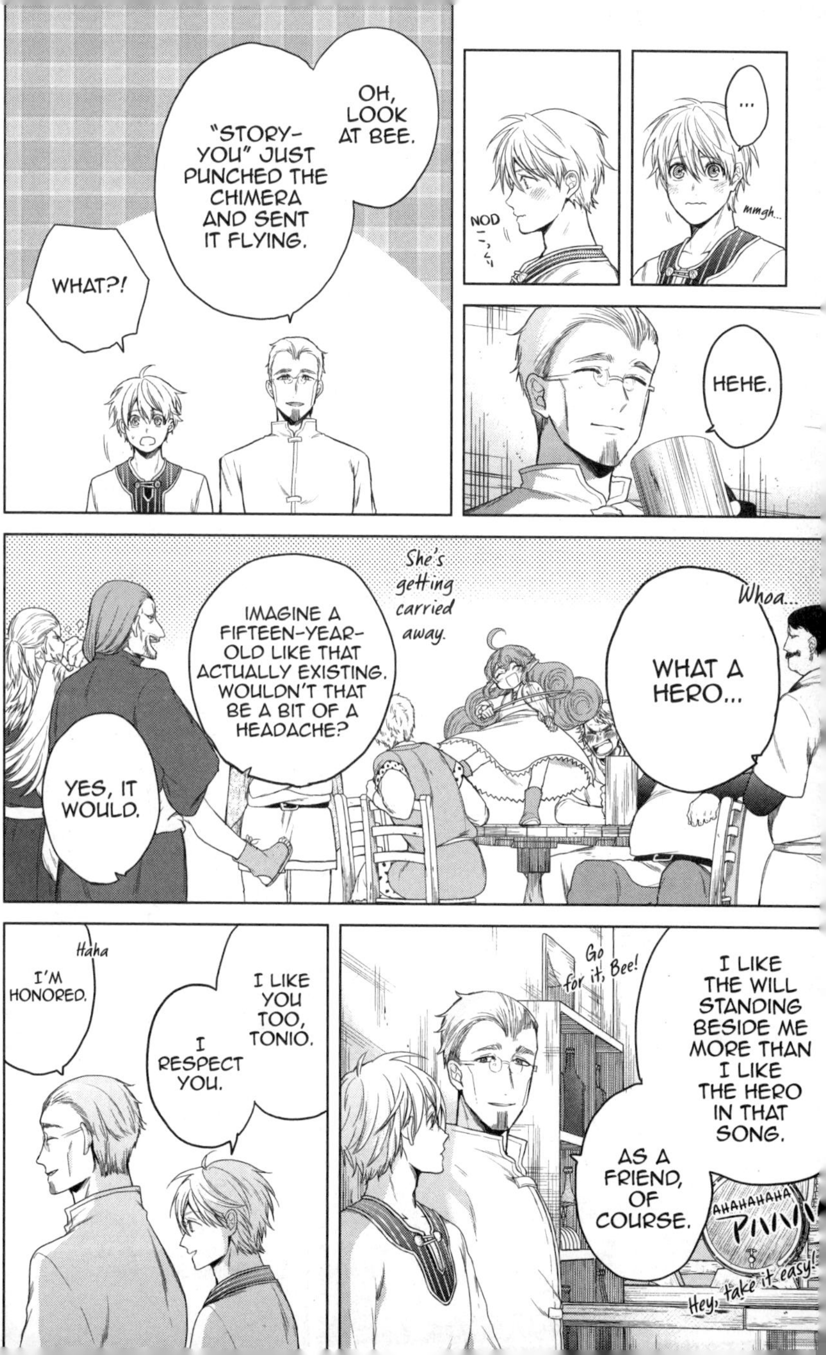
...
mmgh...
NOD
HEHE.
OH, LOOK AT BEE.
"STORY-YOU" JUST PUNCHED THE CHIMERA AND SENT IT FLYING.
WHAT?!
Whoa...
WHAT A HERO...
She's getting carried away.
IMAGINE A FIFTEEN-YEAR-OLD LIKE THAT ACTUALLY EXISTING. WOULDN'T THAT BE A BIT OF A HEADACHE?
YES, IT WOULD.
Go for it, Bee!
I LIKE THE WILL STANDING BESIDE ME MORE THAN I LIKE THE HERO IN THAT SONG.
AS A FRIEND, OF COURSE.
AHAHAHAHA
Hey, take it easy!
I LIKE YOU TOO, TONIO.
I RESPECT YOU.
Haha
I'M HONORED.

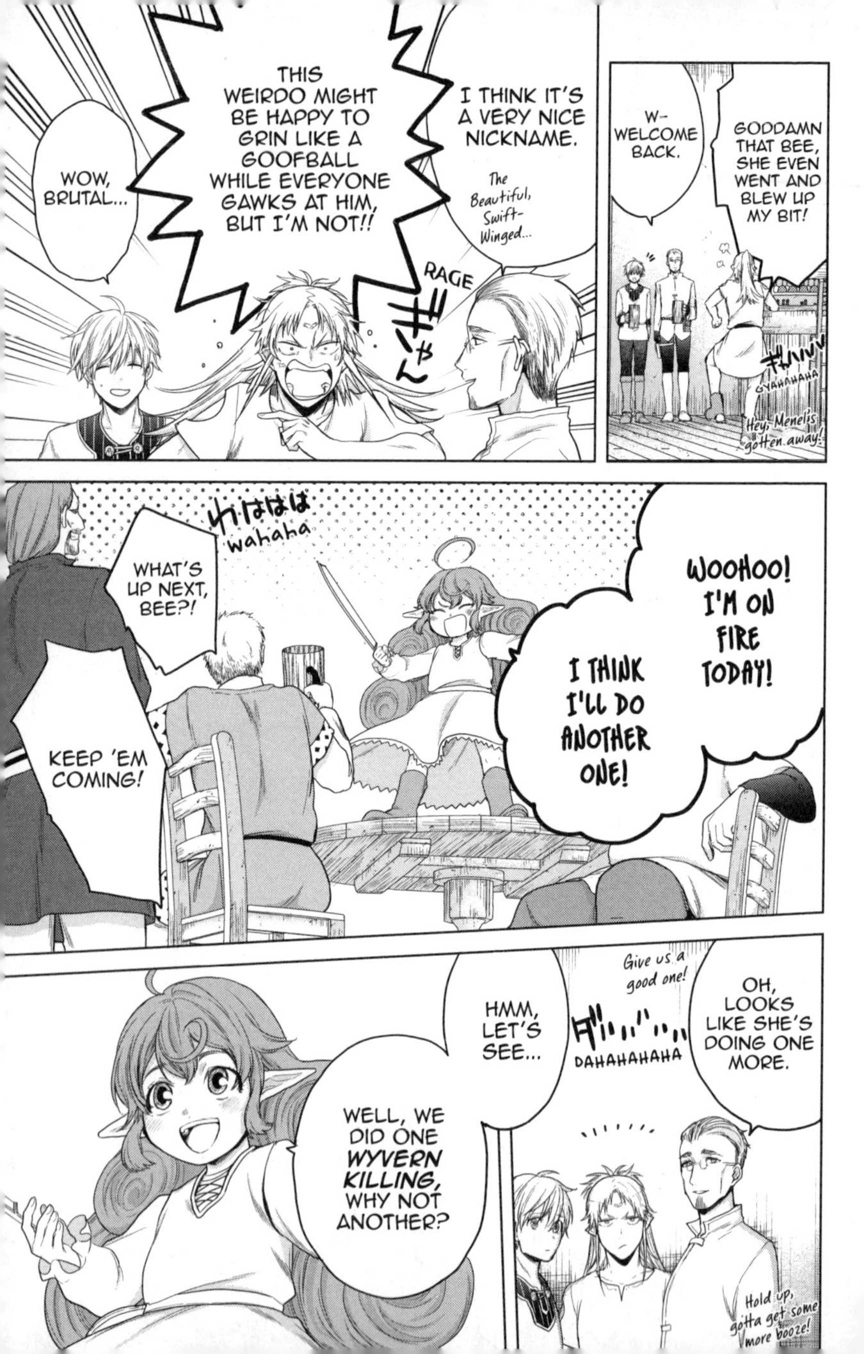
GODDAMN THAT BEE, SHE EVEN WENT AND BLEW UP MY BIT!
W-WELCOME BACK.
GYAHAHAHA
Hey, Menel's gotten away!
I THINK IT'S A VERY NICE NICKNAME.
The Beautiful, Swift-Winged...
THIS WEIRDO MIGHT BE HAPPY TO GRIN LIKE A GOOFBALL WHILE EVERYONE GAWKS AT HIM, BUT I'M NOT!!
ぎゃん
RAGE
WOW, BRUTAL...
WOOHOO! I'M ON FIRE TODAY!
I THINK I'LL DO ANOTHER ONE!
わははは
wahaha
WHAT'S UP NEXT, BEE?!
KEEP 'EM COMING!
OH, LOOKS LIKE SHE'S DOING ONE MORE.
Give us a good one!
DAHAHAHAHA
HMM, LET'S SEE...
WELL, WE DID ONE WYVERN KILLING, WHY NOT ANOTHER?
Hold up, gotta get some more booze!

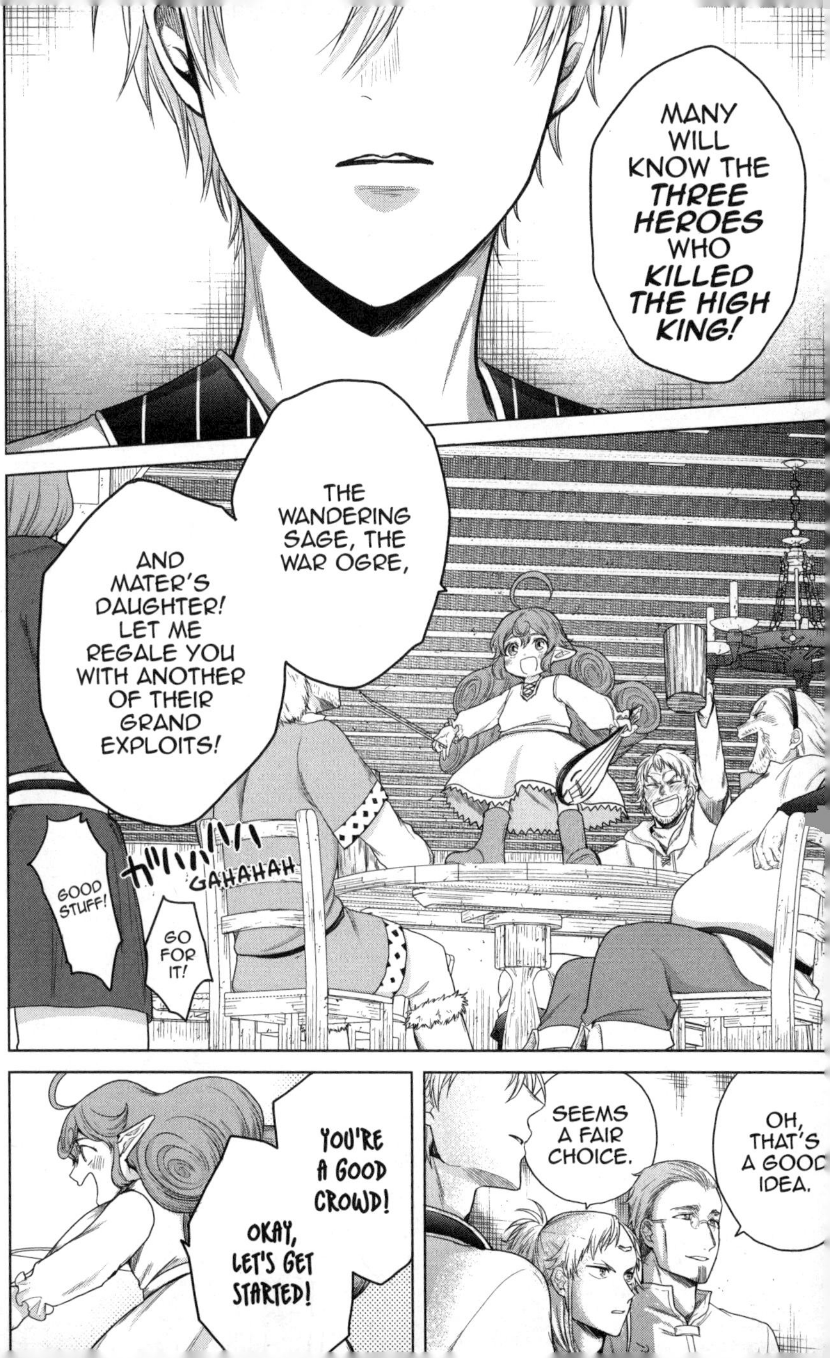
MANY WILL KNOW THE THREE HEROES WHO KILLED THE HIGH KING!
THE WANDERING SAGE, THE WAR OGRE,
AND MATER'S DAUGHTER! LET ME REGALE YOU WITH ANOTHER OF THEIR GRAND EXPLOITS!
GAHAHAH
GO FOR IT!
GOOD STUFF!
OH, THAT'S A GOOD IDEA.
SEEMS A FAIR CHOICE.
YOU'RE A GOOD CROWD!
OKAY, LET'S GET STARTED!

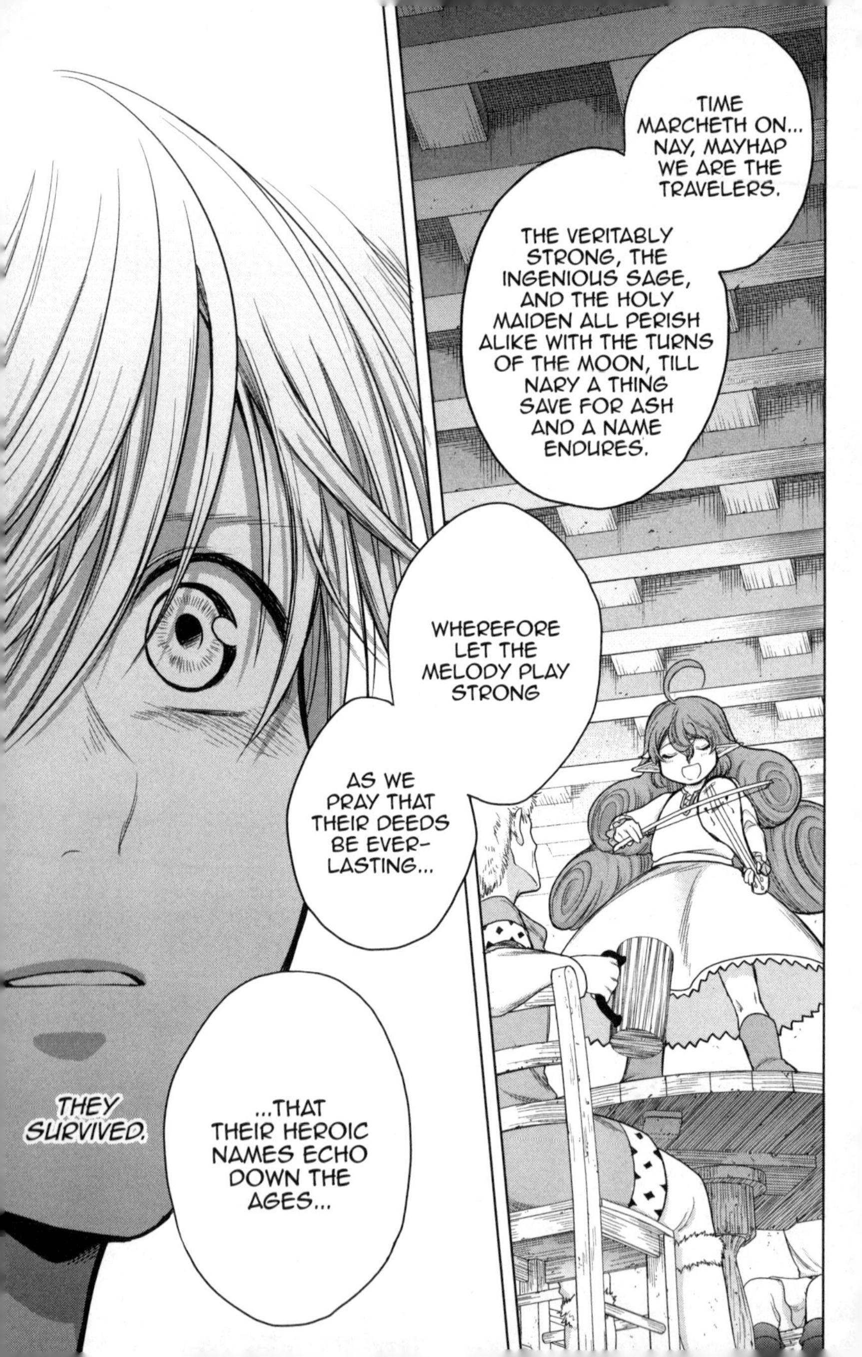
TIME MARCHETH ON... NAY, MAYHAP WE ARE THE TRAVELERS.
THE VERITABLY STRONG, THE INGENIOUS SAGE, AND THE HOLY MAIDEN ALL PERISH ALIKE WITH THE TURNS OF THE MOON, TILL NARY A THING SAVE FOR ASH AND A NAME ENDURES.
WHEREFORE LET THE MELODY PLAY STRONG
AS WE PRAY THAT THEIR DEEDS BE EVER-LASTING...
...THAT THEIR HEROIC NAMES ECHO DOWN THE AGES...
THEY SURVIVED.

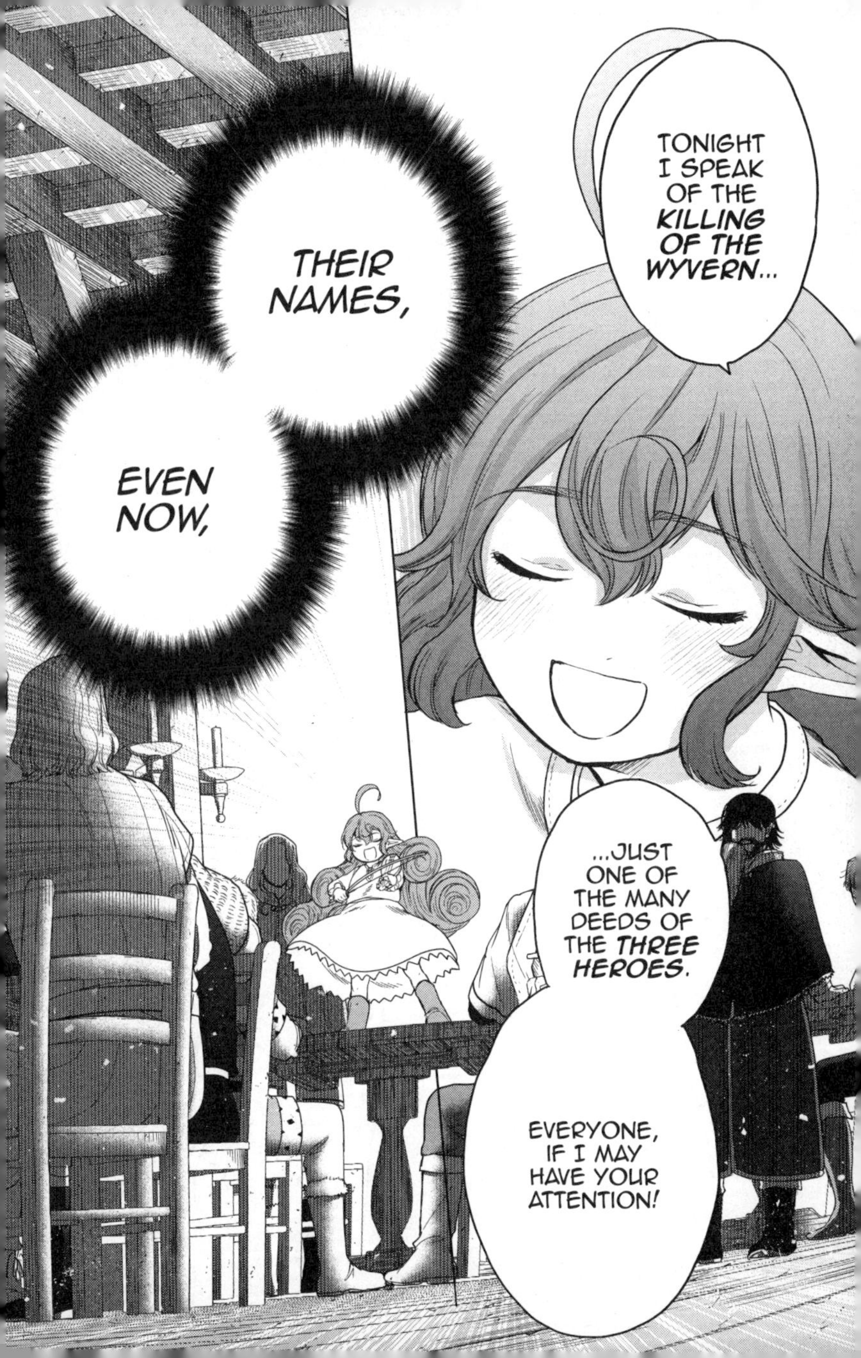
TONIGHT I SPEAK OF THE KILLING OF THE WYVERN...
THEIR NAMES,
EVEN NOW,
...JUST ONE OF THE MANY DEEDS OF THE THREE HEROES.
EVERYONE, IF I MAY HAVE YOUR ATTENTION!

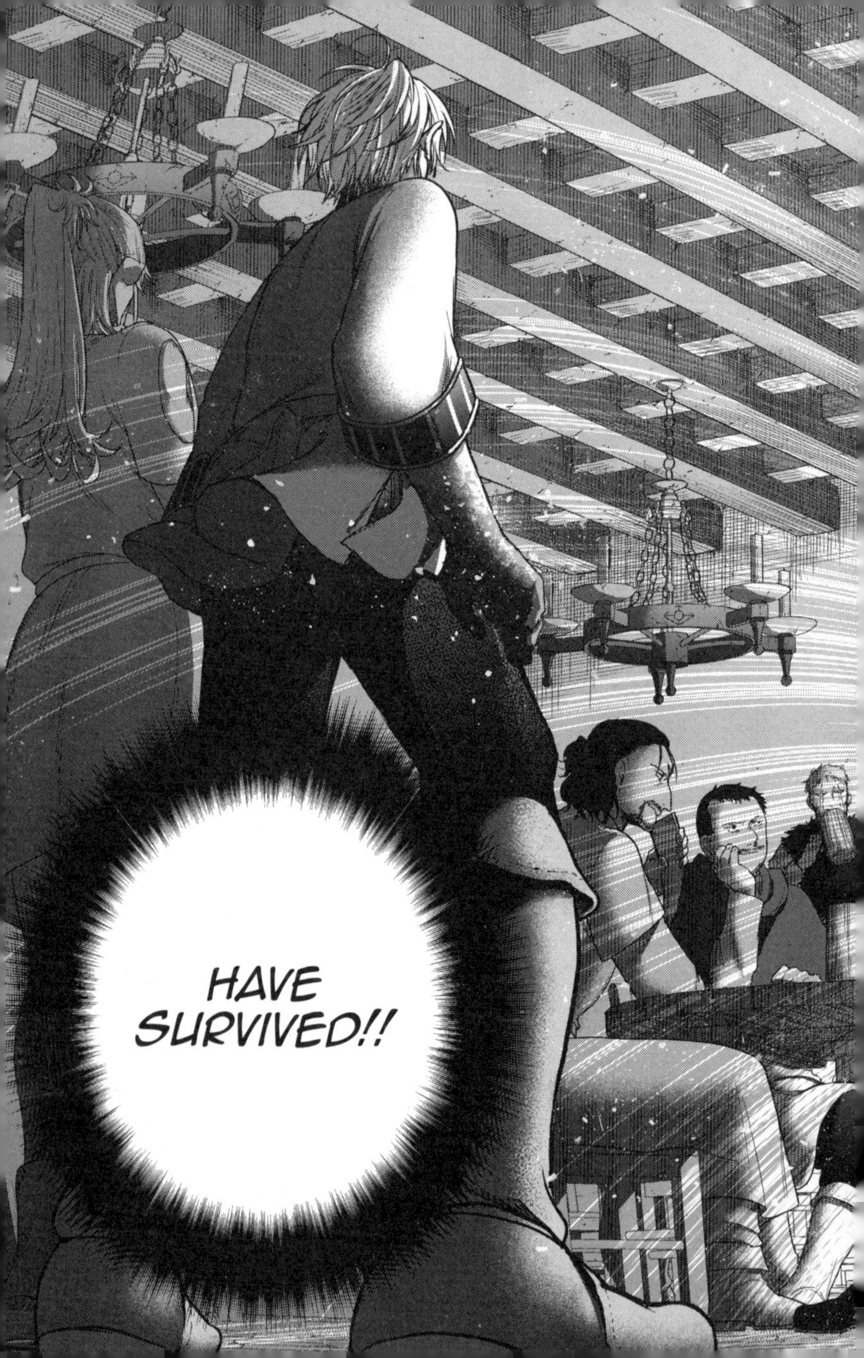
HAVE SURVIVED!!

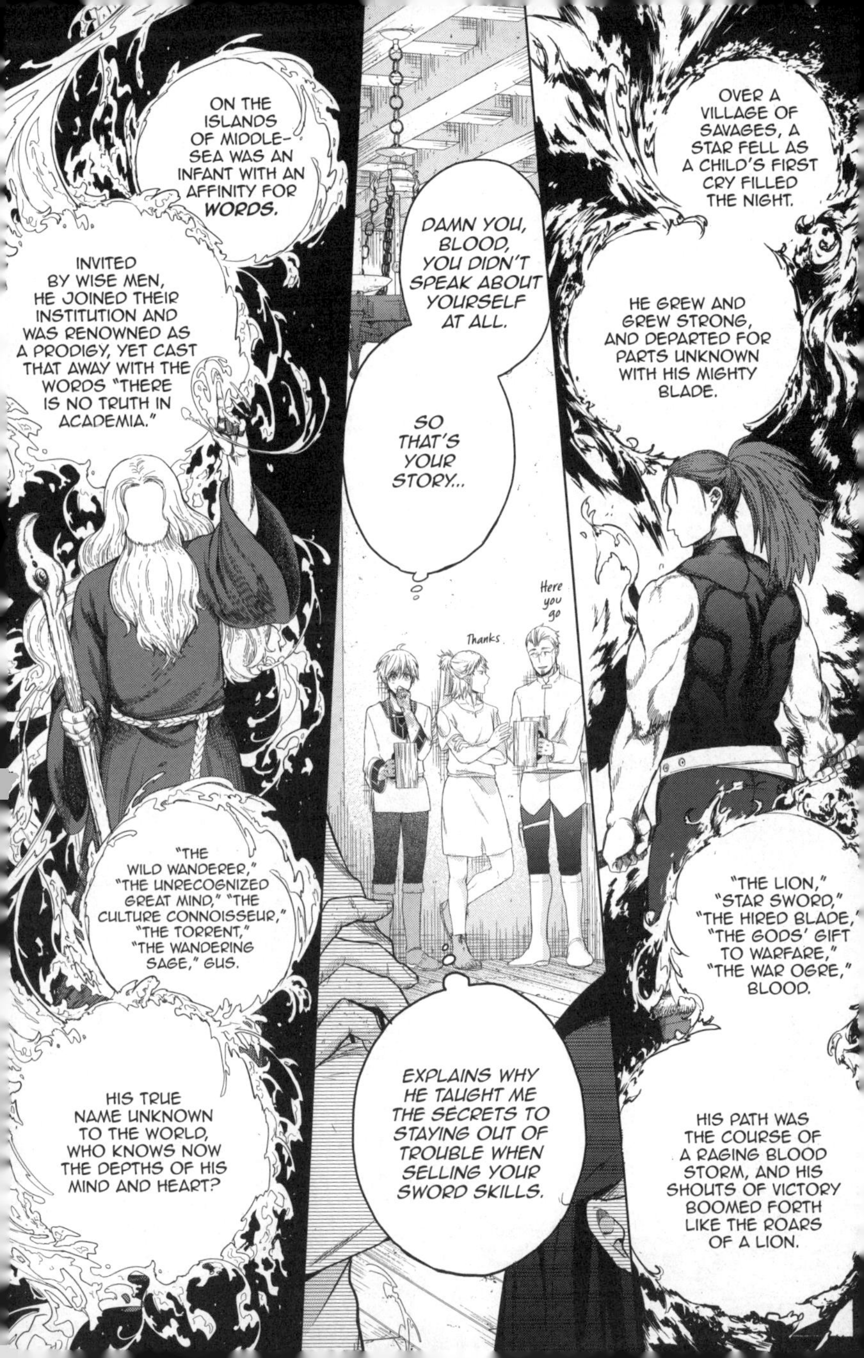
OVER A VILLAGE OF SAVAGES, A STAR FELL AS A CHILD'S FIRST CRY FILLED THE NIGHT.
HE GREW AND GREW STRONG, AND DEPARTED FOR PARTS UNKNOWN WITH HIS MIGHTY BLADE.
"THE LION," "STAR SWORD," "THE HIRED BLADE," "THE GODS' GIFT TO WARFARE," "THE WAR OGRE," BLOOD.
HIS PATH WAS THE COURSE OF A RAGING BLOOD STORM, AND HIS SHOUTS OF VICTORY BOOMED FORTH LIKE THE ROARS OF A LION.
DAMN YOU, BLOOD, YOU DIDN'T SPEAK ABOUT YOURSELF AT ALL.
SO THAT'S YOUR STORY...
Here you go
Thanks
EXPLAINS WHY HE TAUGHT ME THE SECRETS TO STAYING OUT OF TROUBLE WHEN SELLING YOUR SWORD SKILLS.
ON THE ISLANDS OF MIDDLE-SEA WAS AN INFANT WITH AN AFFINITY FOR WORDS.
INVITED BY WISE MEN, HE JOINED THEIR INSTITUTION AND WAS RENOWNED AS A PRODIGY, YET CAST THAT AWAY WITH THE WORDS "THERE IS NO TRUTH IN ACADEMIA."
"THE WILD WANDERER," "THE UNRECOGNIZED GREAT MIND," "THE CULTURE CONNOISSEUR," "THE TORRENT," "THE WANDERING SAGE," GUS.
HIS TRUE NAME UNKNOWN TO THE WORLD, WHO KNOWS NOW THE DEPTHS OF HIS MIND AND HEART?

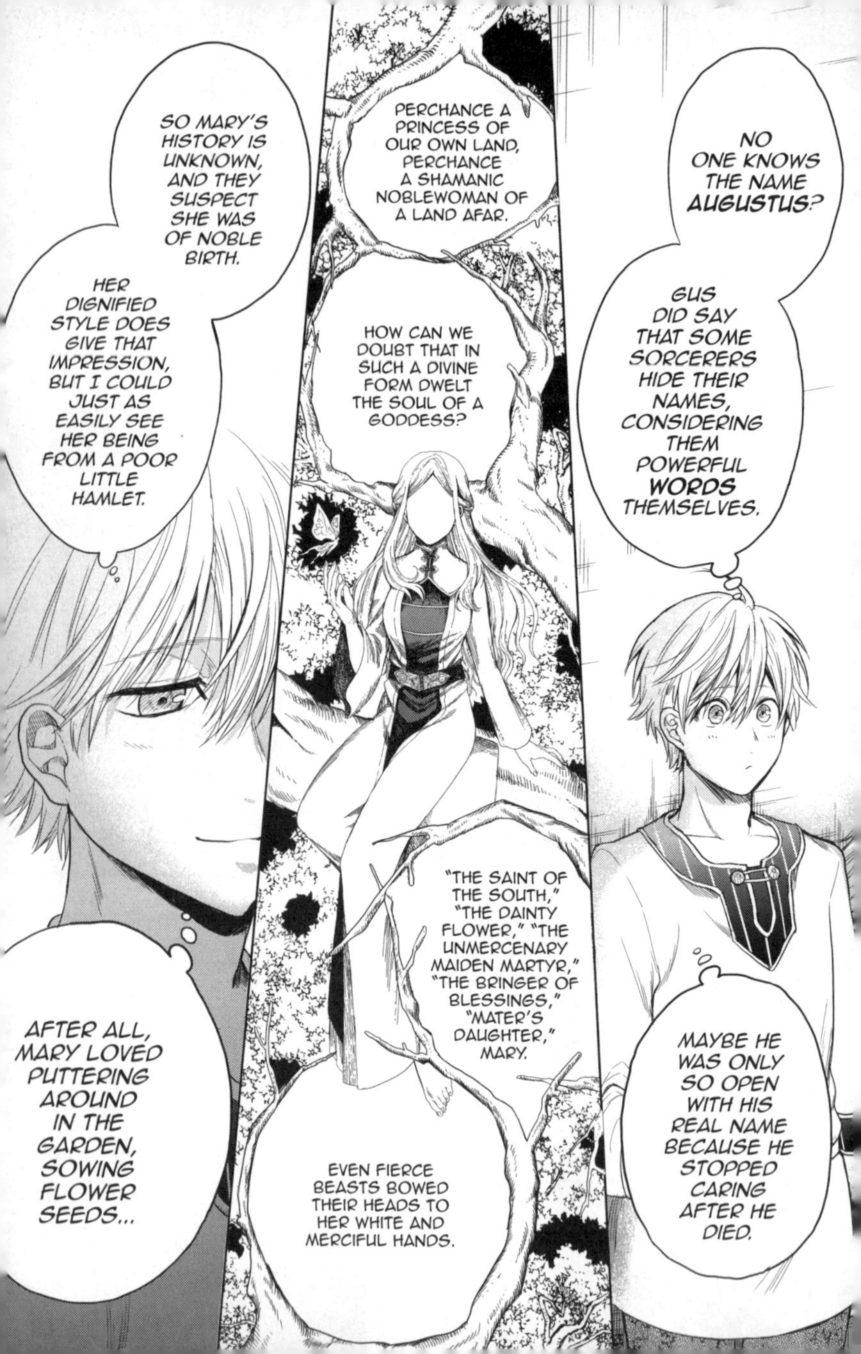
NO ONE KNOWS THE NAME **AUGUSTUS**?
GUS DID SAY THAT SOME SORCERERS HIDE THEIR NAMES, CONSIDERING THEM POWERFUL **WORDS** THEMSELVES.
MAYBE HE WAS ONLY SO OPEN WITH HIS REAL NAME BECAUSE HE STOPPED CARING AFTER HE DIED.
PERCHANCE A PRINCESS OF OUR OWN LAND, PERCHANCE A SHAMANIC NOBLEWOMAN OF A LAND AFAR.
HOW CAN WE DOUBT THAT IN SUCH A DIVINE FORM DWELT THE SOUL OF A GODDESS?
"THE SAINT OF THE SOUTH," "THE DAINTY FLOWER," "THE UNMERCENARY MAIDEN MARTYR," "THE BRINGER OF BLESSINGS," "MATER'S DAUGHTER," MARY.
EVEN FIERCE BEASTS BOWED THEIR HEADS TO HER WHITE AND MERCIFUL HANDS.
SO MARY'S HISTORY IS UNKNOWN, AND THEY SUSPECT SHE WAS OF NOBLE BIRTH.
HER DIGNIFIED STYLE DOES GIVE THAT IMPRESSION, BUT I COULD JUST AS EASILY SEE HER BEING FROM A POOR LITTLE HAMLET.
AFTER ALL, MARY LOVED PUTTERING AROUND IN THE GARDEN, SOWING FLOWER SEEDS...

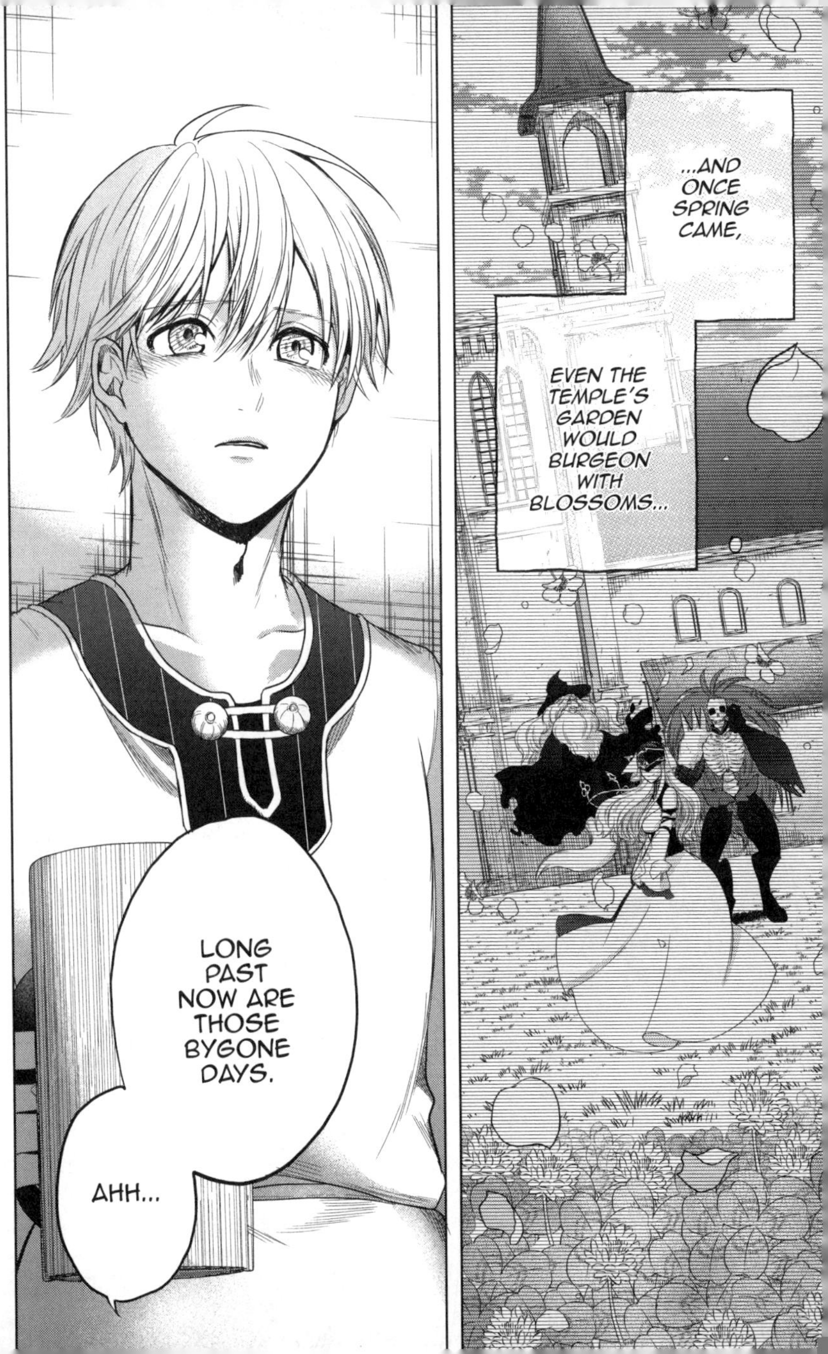
...AND ONCE SPRING CAME,
EVEN THE TEMPLE'S GARDEN WOULD BURGEON WITH BLOSSOMS...
LONG PAST NOW ARE THOSE BYGONE DAYS.
AHH...

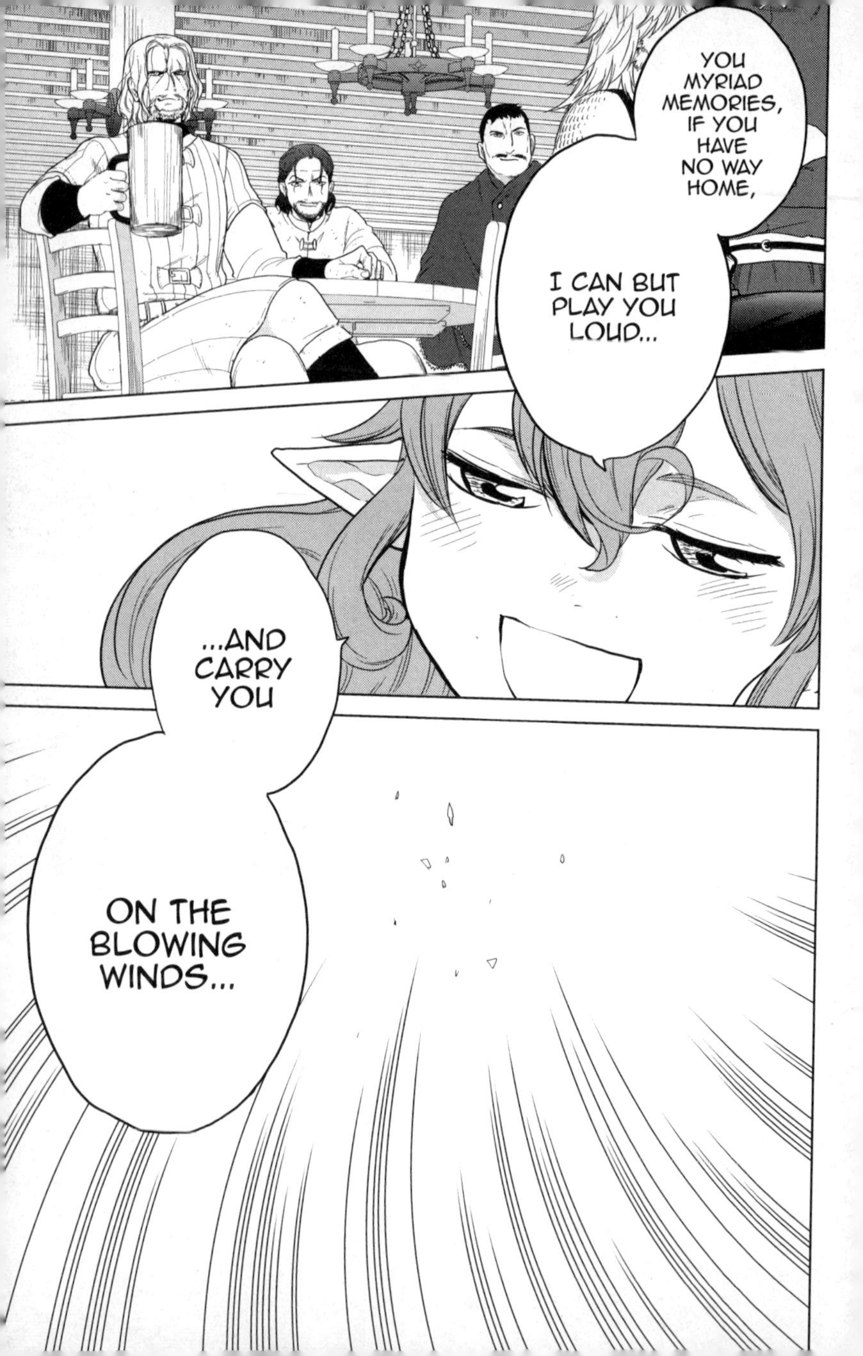
YOU MYRIAD MEMORIES, IF YOU HAVE NO WAY HOME,
I CAN BUT PLAY YOU LOUD...
...AND CARRY YOU
ON THE BLOWING WINDS...

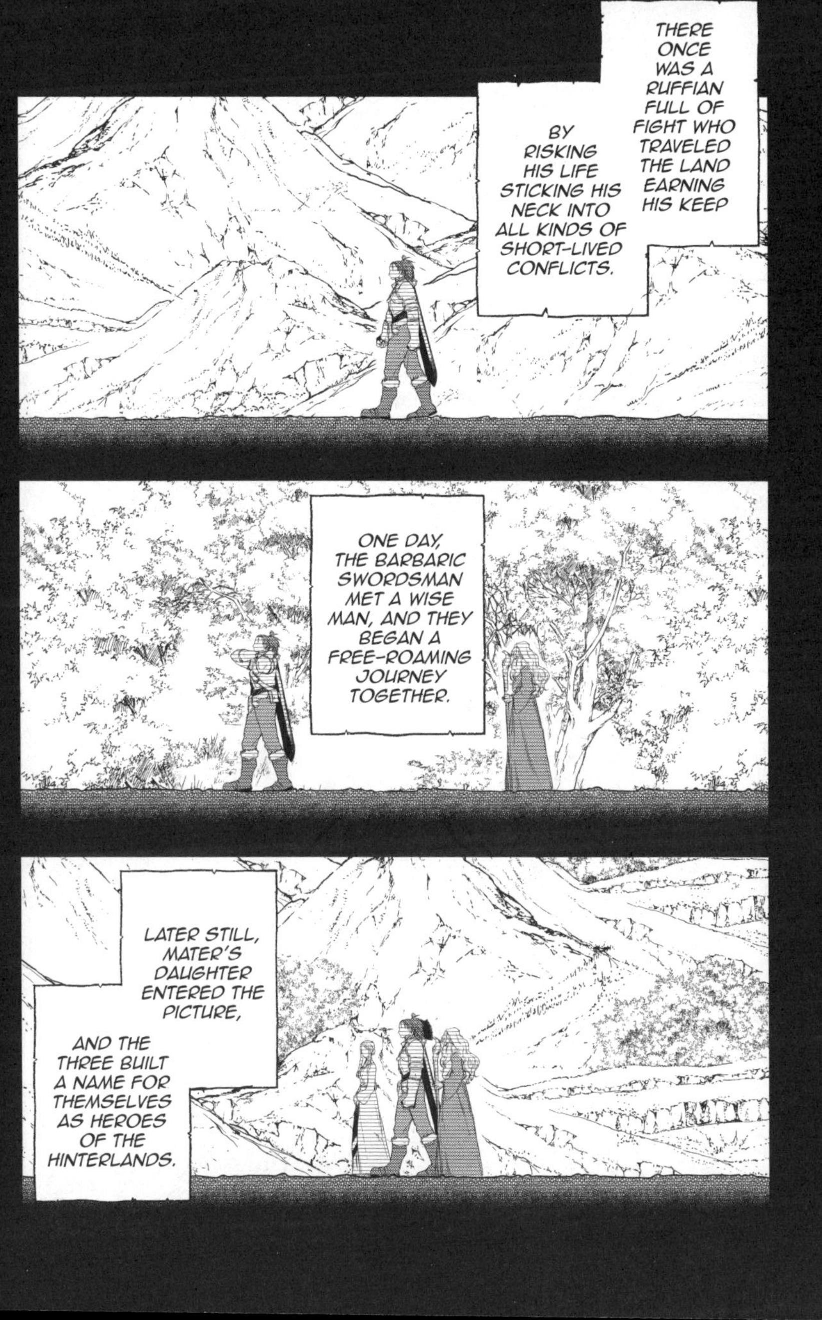
THERE ONCE WAS A RUFFIAN FULL OF FIGHT WHO TRAVELED THE LAND EARNING HIS KEEP
BY RISKING HIS LIFE STICKING HIS NECK INTO ALL KINDS OF SHORT-LIVED CONFLICTS.
ONE DAY, THE BARBARIC SWORDSMAN MET A WISE MAN, AND THEY BEGAN A FREE-ROAMING JOURNEY TOGETHER.
LATER STILL, MATER'S DAUGHTER ENTERED THE PICTURE,
AND THE THREE BUILT A NAME FOR THEMSELVES AS HEROES OF THE HINTERLANDS.

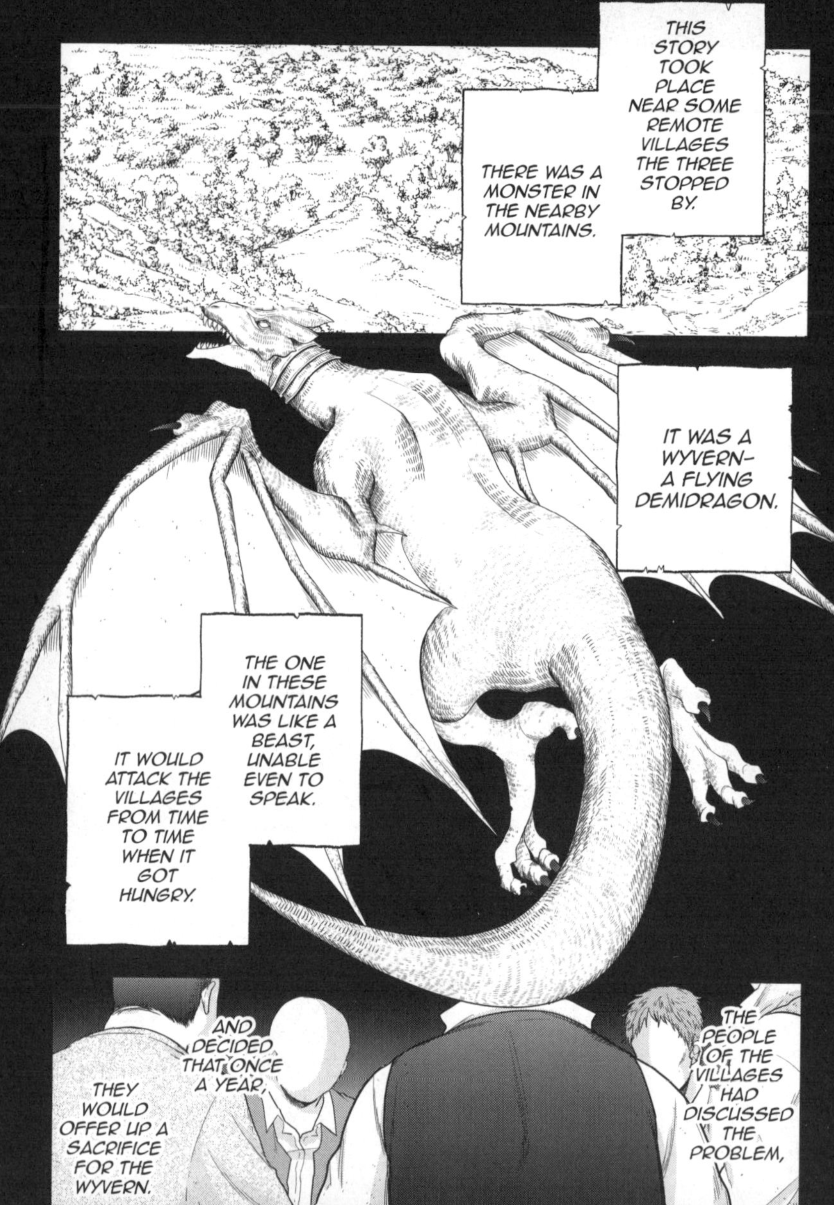
THIS STORY TOOK PLACE NEAR SOME REMOTE VILLAGES THE THREE STOPPED BY.
THERE WAS A MONSTER IN THE NEARBY MOUNTAINS.
IT WAS A WYVERN—A FLYING DEMIDRAGON.
THE ONE IN THESE MOUNTAINS WAS LIKE A BEAST, UNABLE EVEN TO SPEAK.
IT WOULD ATTACK THE VILLAGES FROM TIME TO TIME WHEN IT GOT HUNGRY.
THE PEOPLE OF THE VILLAGES HAD DISCUSSED THE PROBLEM,
AND DECIDED THAT ONCE A YEAR,
THEY WOULD OFFER UP A SACRIFICE FOR THE WYVERN.

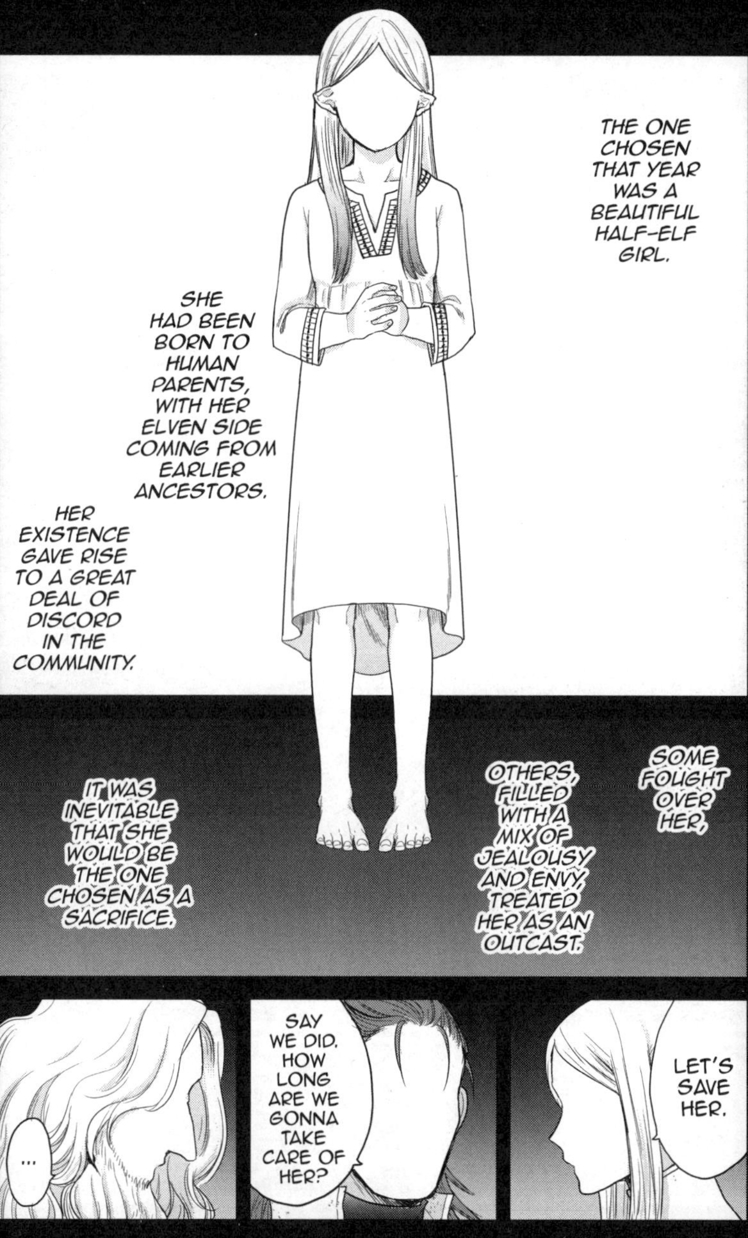
THE ONE CHOSEN THAT YEAR WAS A BEAUTIFUL HALF-ELF GIRL.
SHE HAD BEEN BORN TO HUMAN PARENTS, WITH HER ELVEN SIDE COMING FROM EARLIER ANCESTORS.
HER EXISTENCE GAVE RISE TO A GREAT DEAL OF DISCORD IN THE COMMUNITY.
SOME FOUGHT OVER HER,
OTHERS, FILLED WITH A MIX OF JEALOUSY AND ENVY, TREATED HER AS AN OUTCAST.
IT WAS INEVITABLE THAT SHE WOULD BE THE ONE CHOSEN AS A SACRIFICE.
LET'S SAVE HER.
SAY WE DID. HOW LONG ARE WE GONNA TAKE CARE OF HER?
...

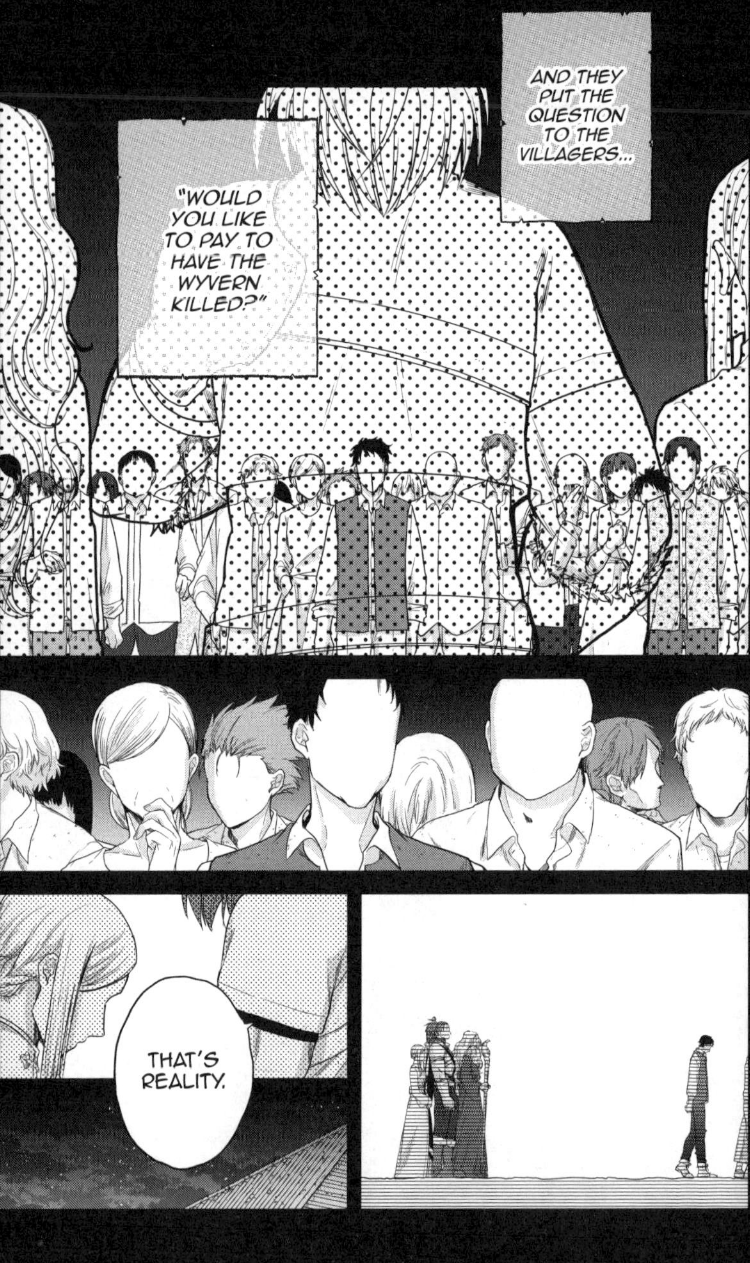
AND THEY PUT THE QUESTION TO THE VILLAGERS...
"WOULD YOU LIKE TO PAY TO HAVE THE WYVERN KILLED?"
THAT'S REALITY.

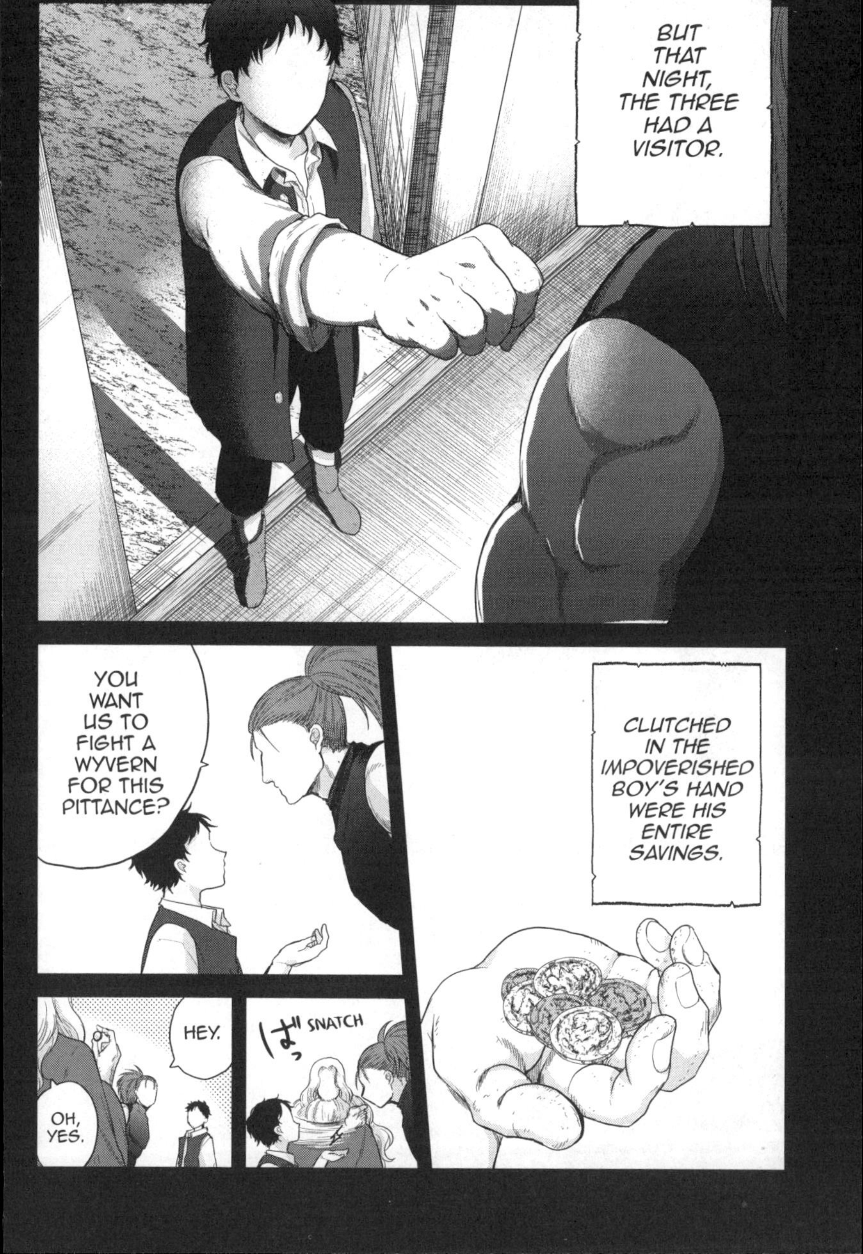
BUT THAT NIGHT, THE THREE HAD A VISITOR.
CLUTCHED IN THE IMPOVERISHED BOY'S HAND WERE HIS ENTIRE SAVINGS.
YOU WANT US TO FIGHT A WYVERN FOR THIS PITTANCE?
ぱっ
SNATCH
HEY.
OH, YES.

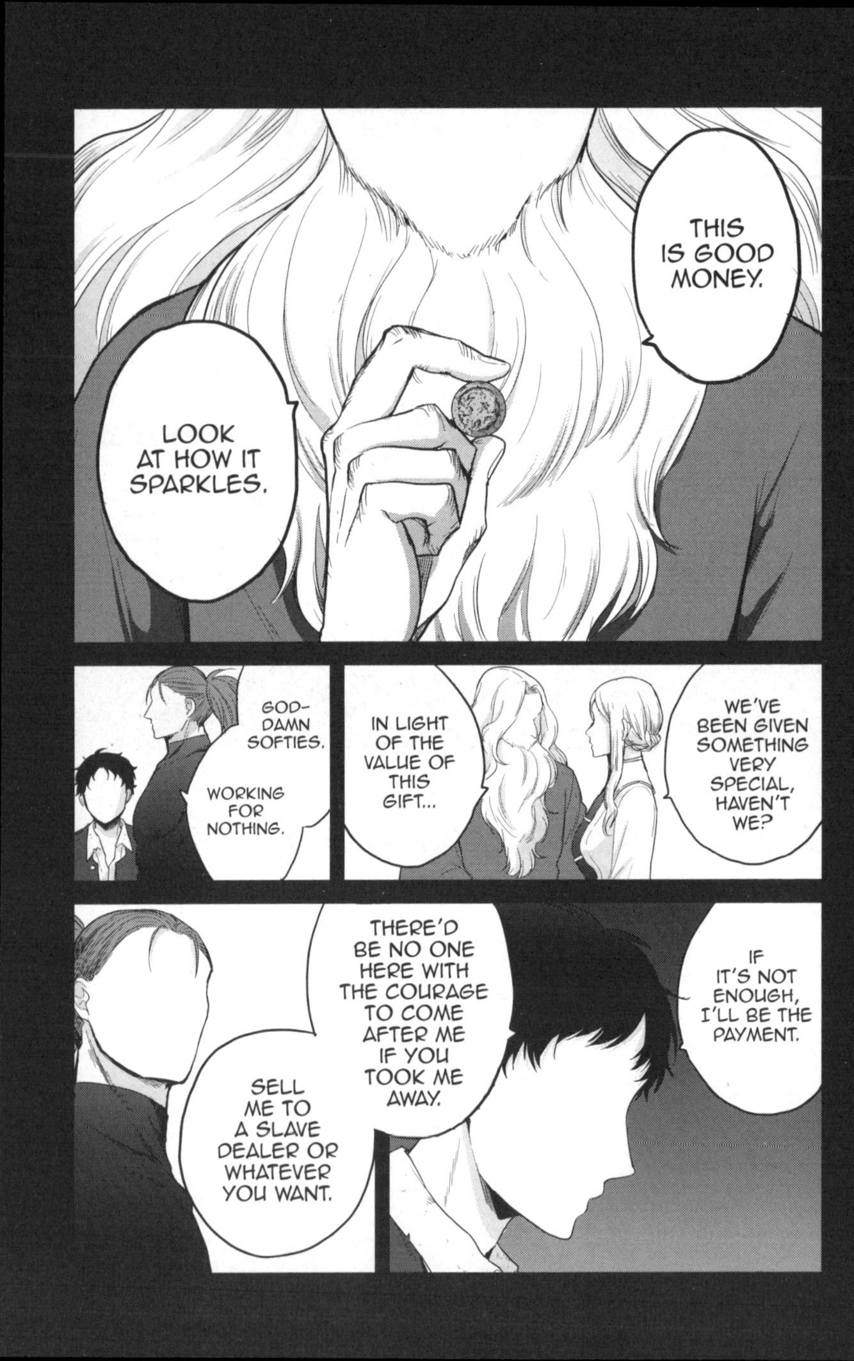
THIS IS GOOD MONEY.
LOOK AT HOW IT SPARKLES.
WE'VE BEEN GIVEN SOMETHING VERY SPECIAL, HAVEN'T WE?
IN LIGHT OF THE VALUE OF THIS GIFT...
GOD-DAMN SOFTIES.
WORKING FOR NOTHING.
IF IT'S NOT ENOUGH, I'LL BE THE PAYMENT.
THERE'D BE NO ONE HERE WITH THE COURAGE TO COME AFTER ME IF YOU TOOK ME AWAY.
SELL ME TO A SLAVE DEALER OR WHATEVER YOU WANT.

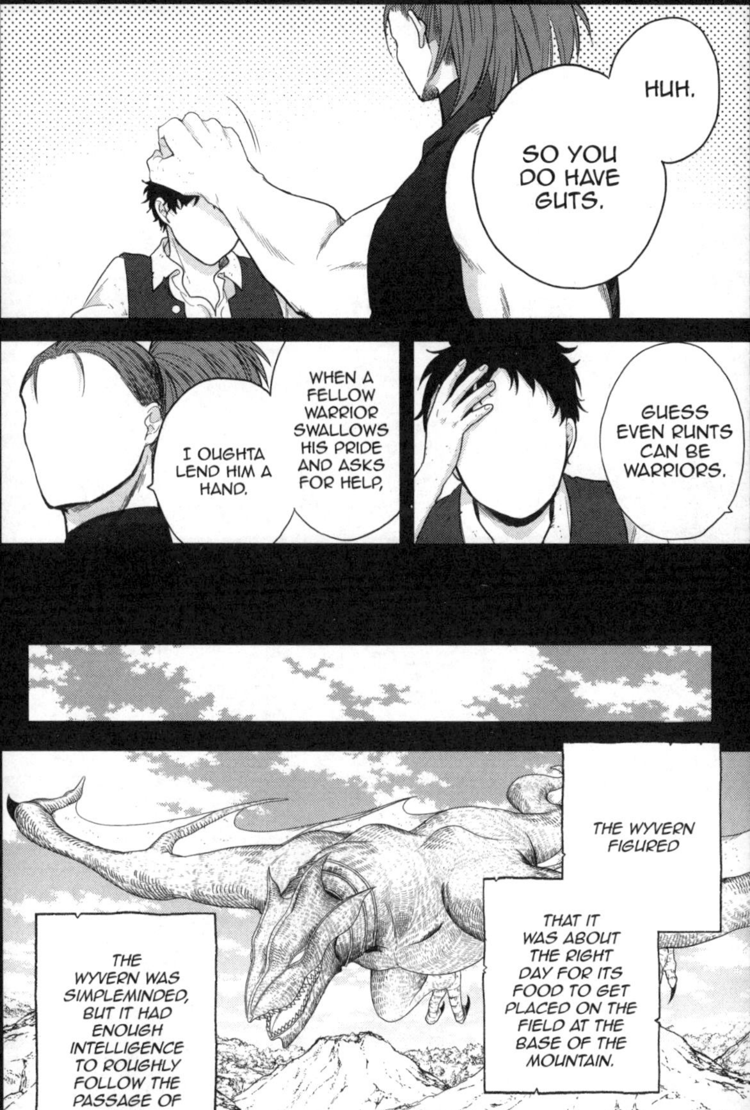
HUH.
SO YOU DO HAVE GUTS.
GUESS EVEN RUNTS CAN BE WARRIORS.
WHEN A FELLOW WARRIOR SWALLOWS HIS PRIDE AND ASKS FOR HELP,
I OUGHTA LEND HIM A HAND.
THE WYVERN FIGURED
THAT IT WAS ABOUT THE RIGHT DAY FOR ITS FOOD TO GET PLACED ON THE FIELD AT THE BASE OF THE MOUNTAIN.
THE WYVERN WAS SIMPLEMINDED, BUT IT HAD ENOUGH INTELLIGENCE TO ROUGHLY FOLLOW THE PASSAGE OF TIME.

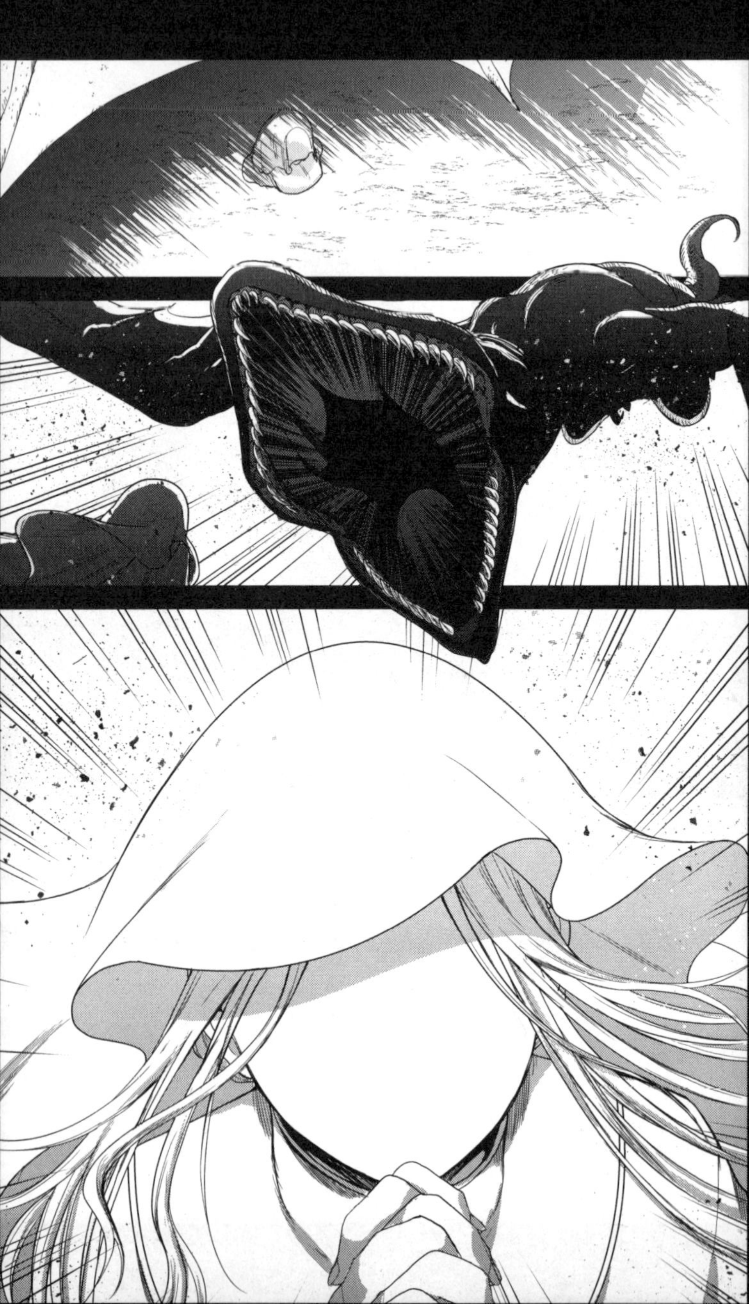

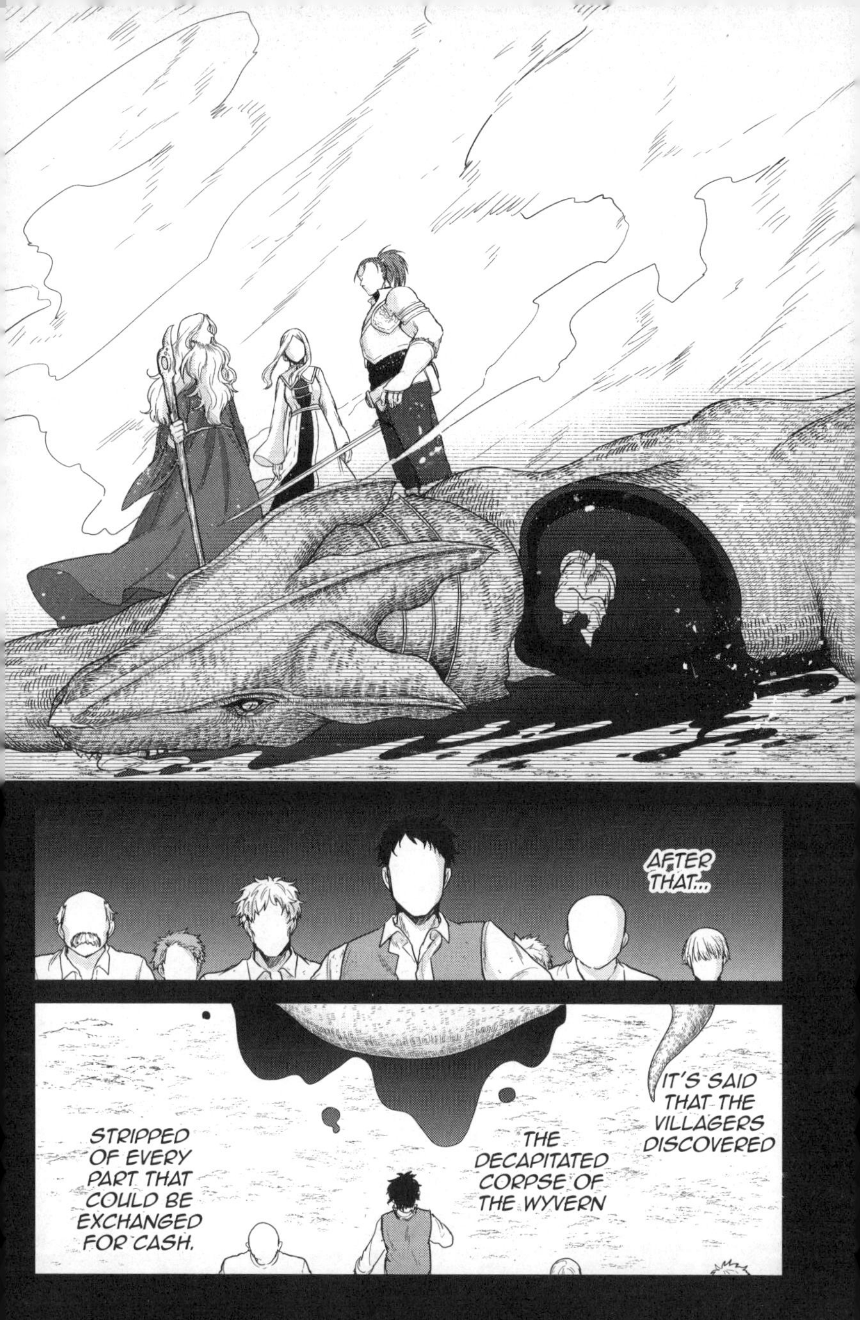
AFTER THAT...
IT'S SAID THAT THE VILLAGERS DISCOVERED
THE DECAPITATED CORPSE OF THE WYVERN
STRIPPED OF EVERY PART THAT COULD BE EXCHANGED FOR CASH.

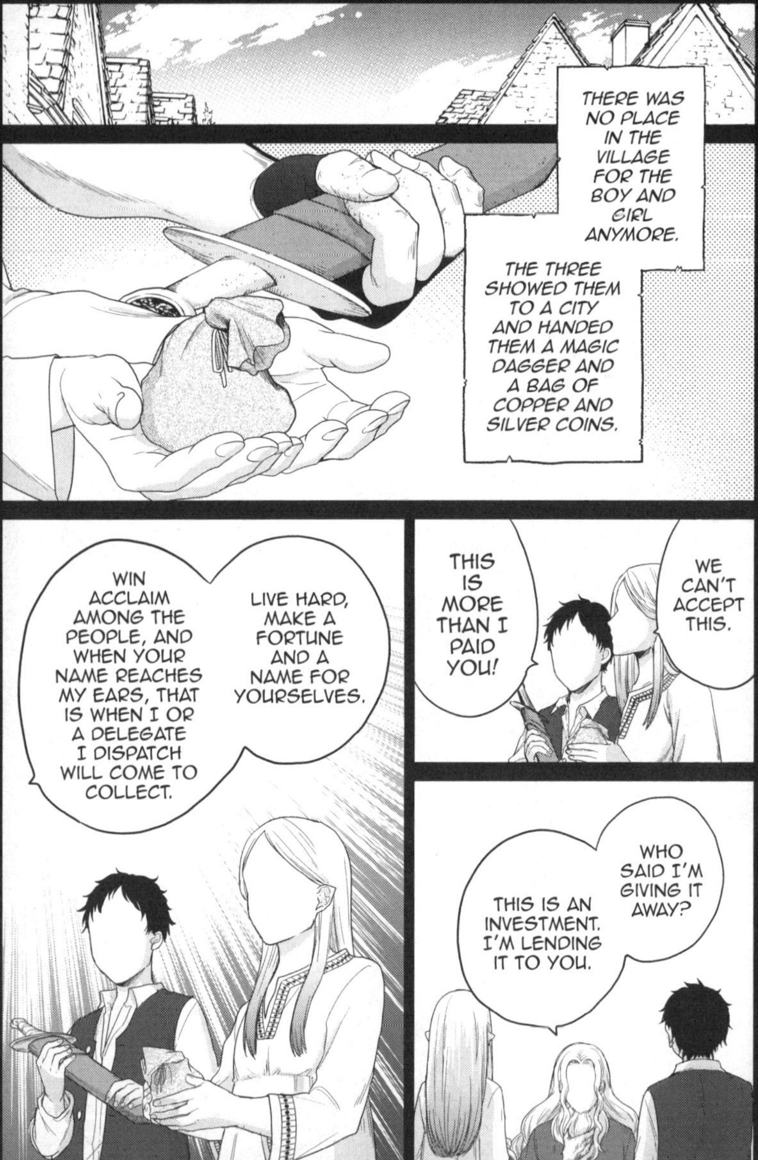
THERE WAS NO PLACE IN THE VILLAGE FOR THE BOY AND GIRL ANYMORE.
THE THREE SHOWED THEM TO A CITY AND HANDED THEM A MAGIC DAGGER AND A BAG OF COPPER AND SILVER COINS.
WE CAN'T ACCEPT THIS.
THIS IS MORE THAN I PAID YOU!
WHO SAID I'M GIVING IT AWAY?
THIS IS AN INVESTMENT. I'M LENDING IT TO YOU.
LIVE HARD, MAKE A FORTUNE AND A NAME FOR YOURSELVES.
WIN ACCLAIM AMONG THE PEOPLE, AND WHEN YOUR NAME REACHES MY EARS, THAT IS WHEN I OR A DELEGATE I DISPATCH WILL COME TO COLLECT.

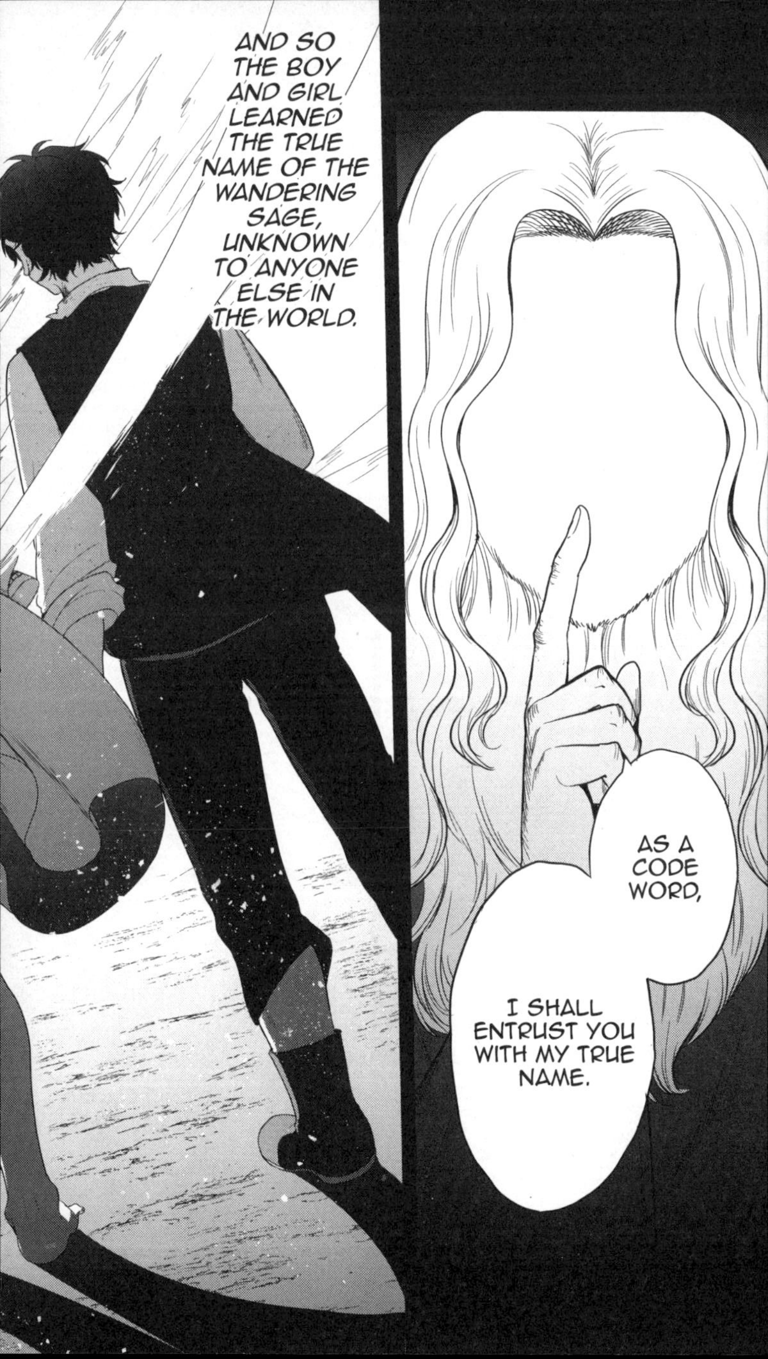
AS A CODE WORD,
I SHALL ENTRUST YOU WITH MY TRUE NAME.
AND SO THE BOY AND GIRL LEARNED THE TRUE NAME OF THE WANDERING SAGE, UNKNOWN TO ANYONE ELSE IN THE WORLD.

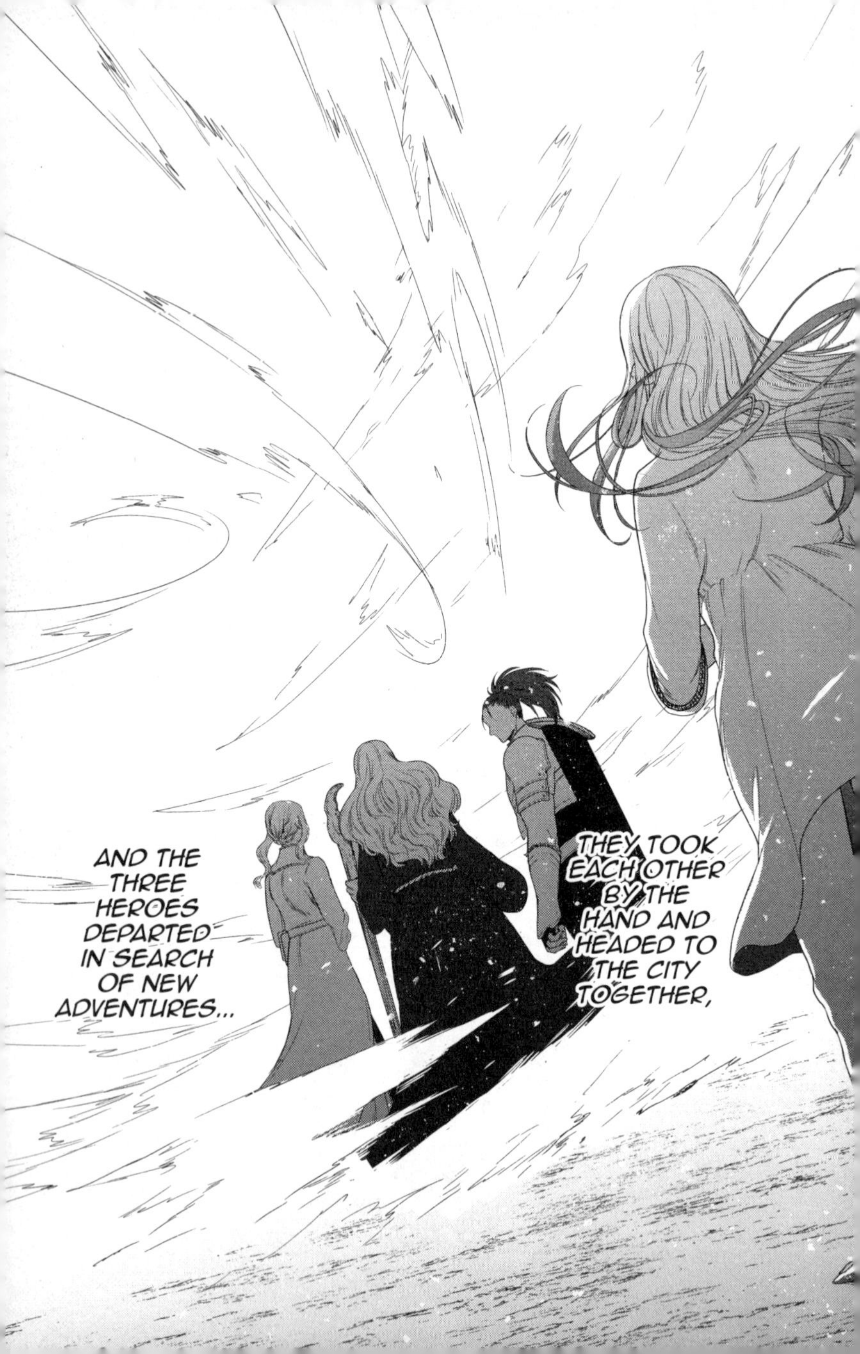
THEY TOOK EACH OTHER BY THE HAND AND HEADED TO THE CITY TOGETHER,
AND THE THREE HEROES DEPARTED IN SEARCH OF NEW ADVENTURES...

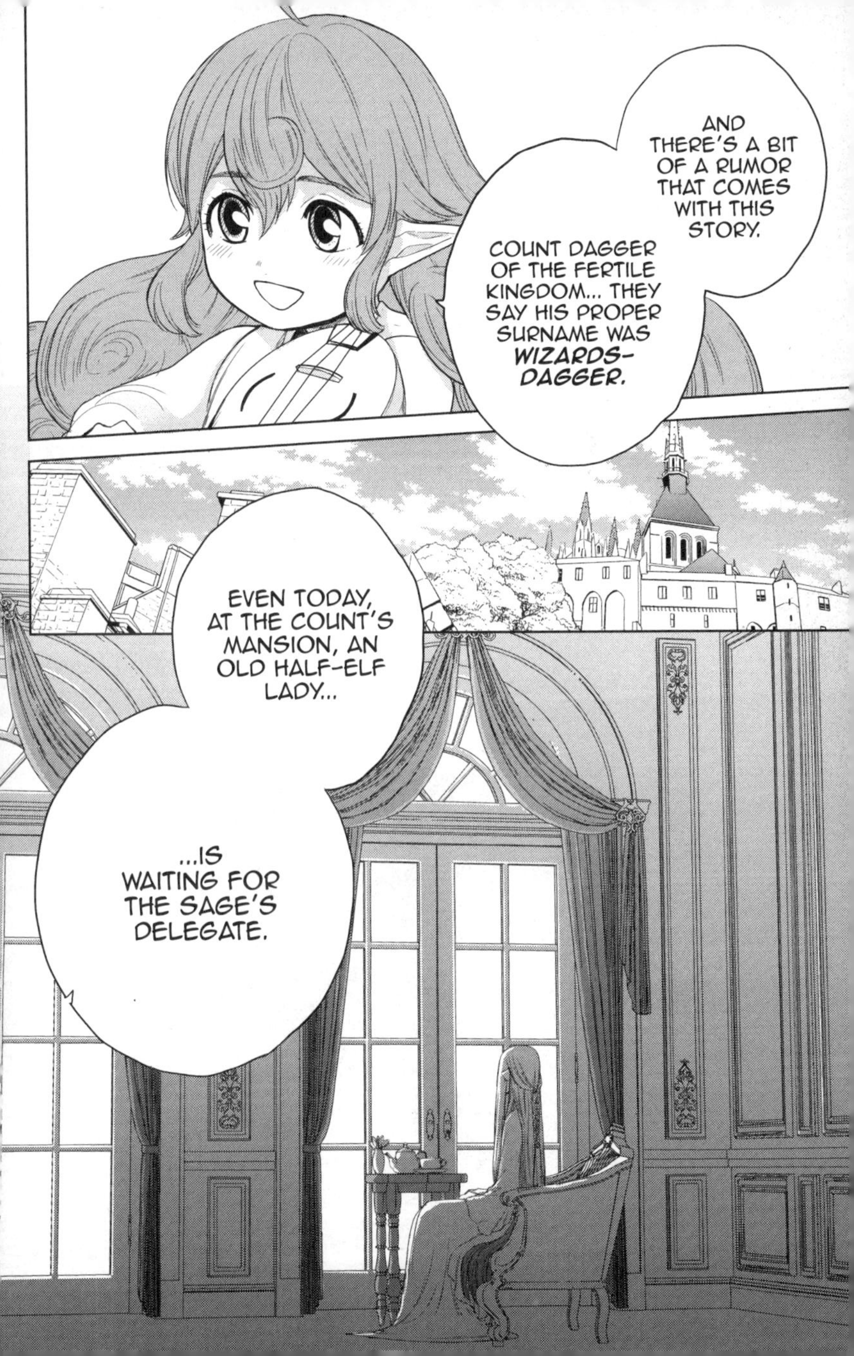
AND THERE'S A BIT OF A RUMOR THAT COMES WITH THIS STORY.
COUNT DAGGER OF THE FERTILE KINGDOM... THEY SAY HIS PROPER SURNAME WAS WIZARDS-DAGGER.
EVEN TODAY, AT THE COUNT'S MANSION, AN OLD HALF-ELF LADY...
...IS WAITING FOR THE SAGE'S DELEGATE.

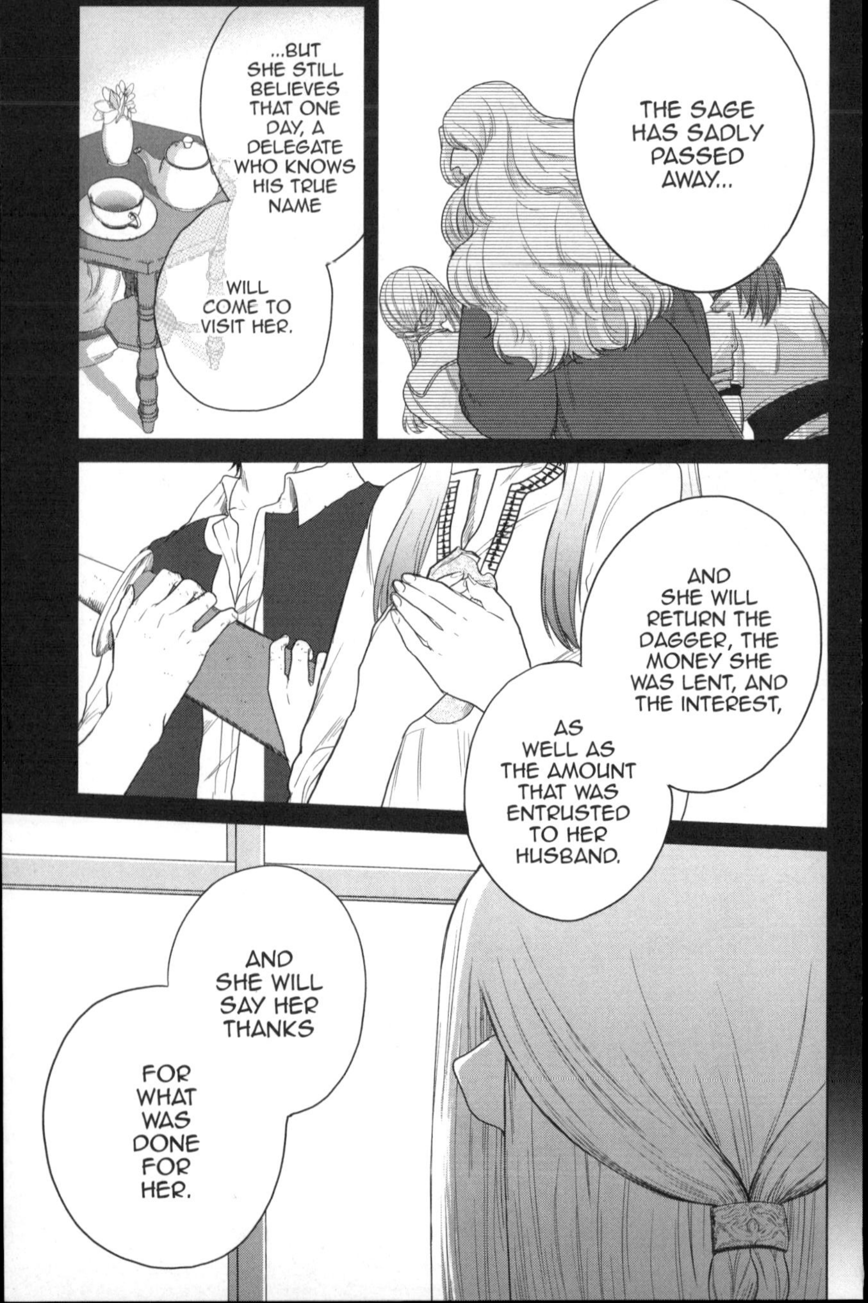
THE SAGE HAS SADLY PASSED AWAY...
...BUT SHE STILL BELIEVES THAT ONE DAY, A DELEGATE WHO KNOWS HIS TRUE NAME
WILL COME TO VISIT HER.
AND SHE WILL RETURN THE DAGGER, THE MONEY SHE WAS LENT, AND THE INTEREST,
AS WELL AS THE AMOUNT THAT WAS ENTRUSTED TO HER HUSBAND.
AND SHE WILL SAY HER THANKS
FOR WHAT WAS DONE FOR HER.

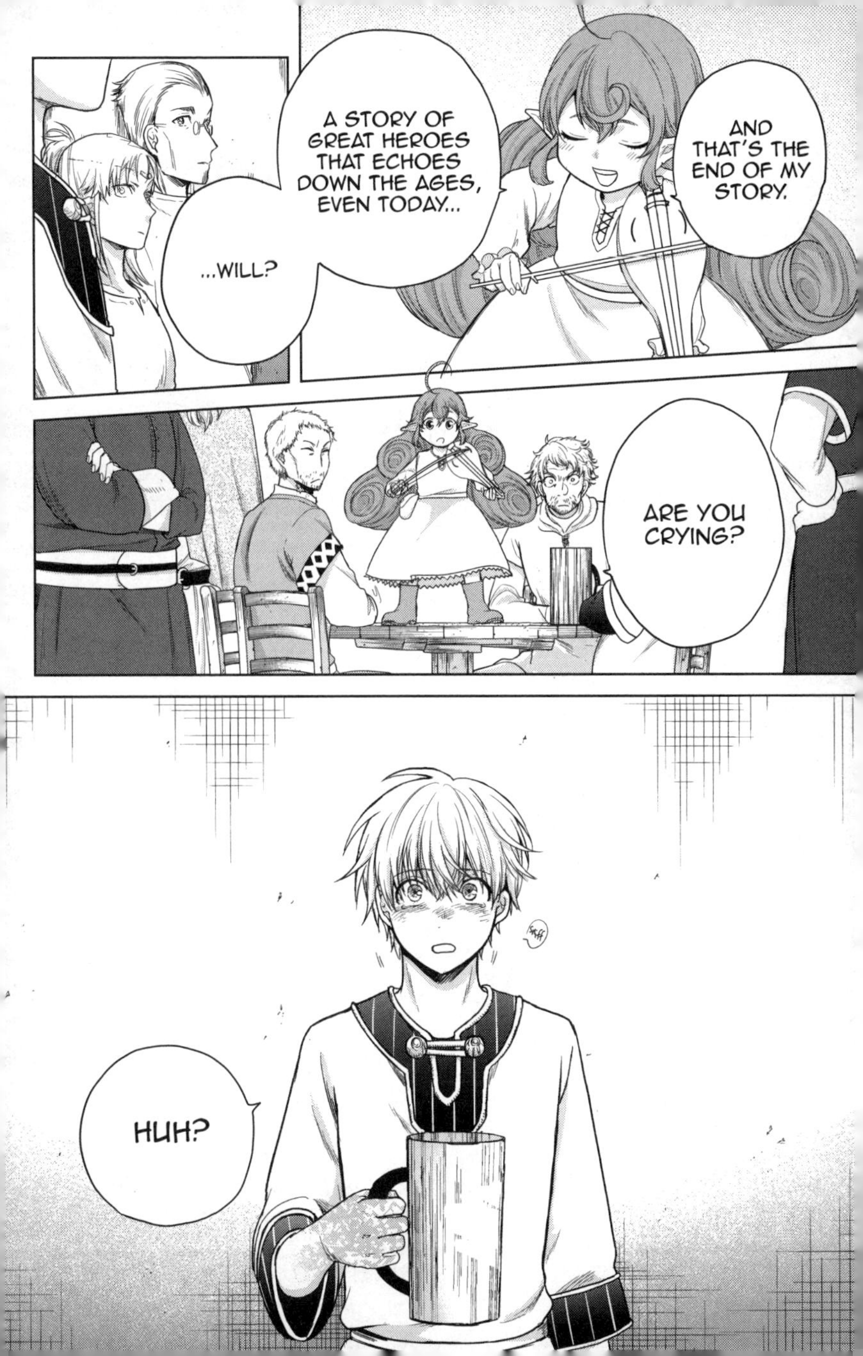
AND THAT'S THE END OF MY STORY.
A STORY OF GREAT HEROES THAT ECHOES DOWN THE AGES, EVEN TODAY...
...WILL?
ARE YOU CRYING?
Sniff
HUH?

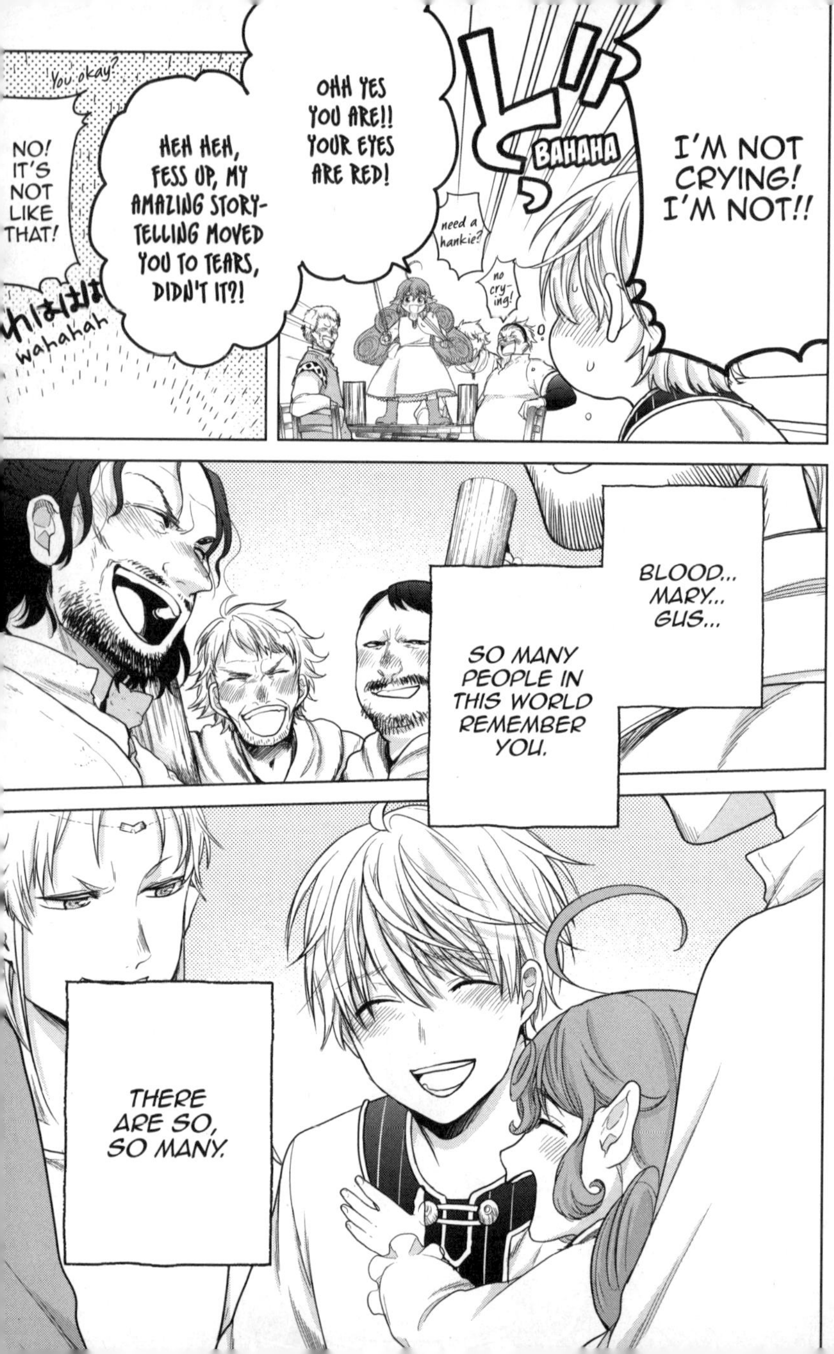
I'M NOT CRYING! I'M NOT!!
BAHAHA
OHH YES YOU ARE!! YOUR EYES ARE RED!
HEH HEH, FESS UP, MY AMAZING STORY-TELLING MOVED YOU TO TEARS, DIDN'T IT?!
need a hankie?
no cry-ing!
You okay?
NO! IT'S NOT LIKE THAT!
わははは
wahahah
BLOOD... MARY... GUS...
SO MANY PEOPLE IN THIS WORLD REMEMBER YOU.
THERE ARE SO, SO MANY.

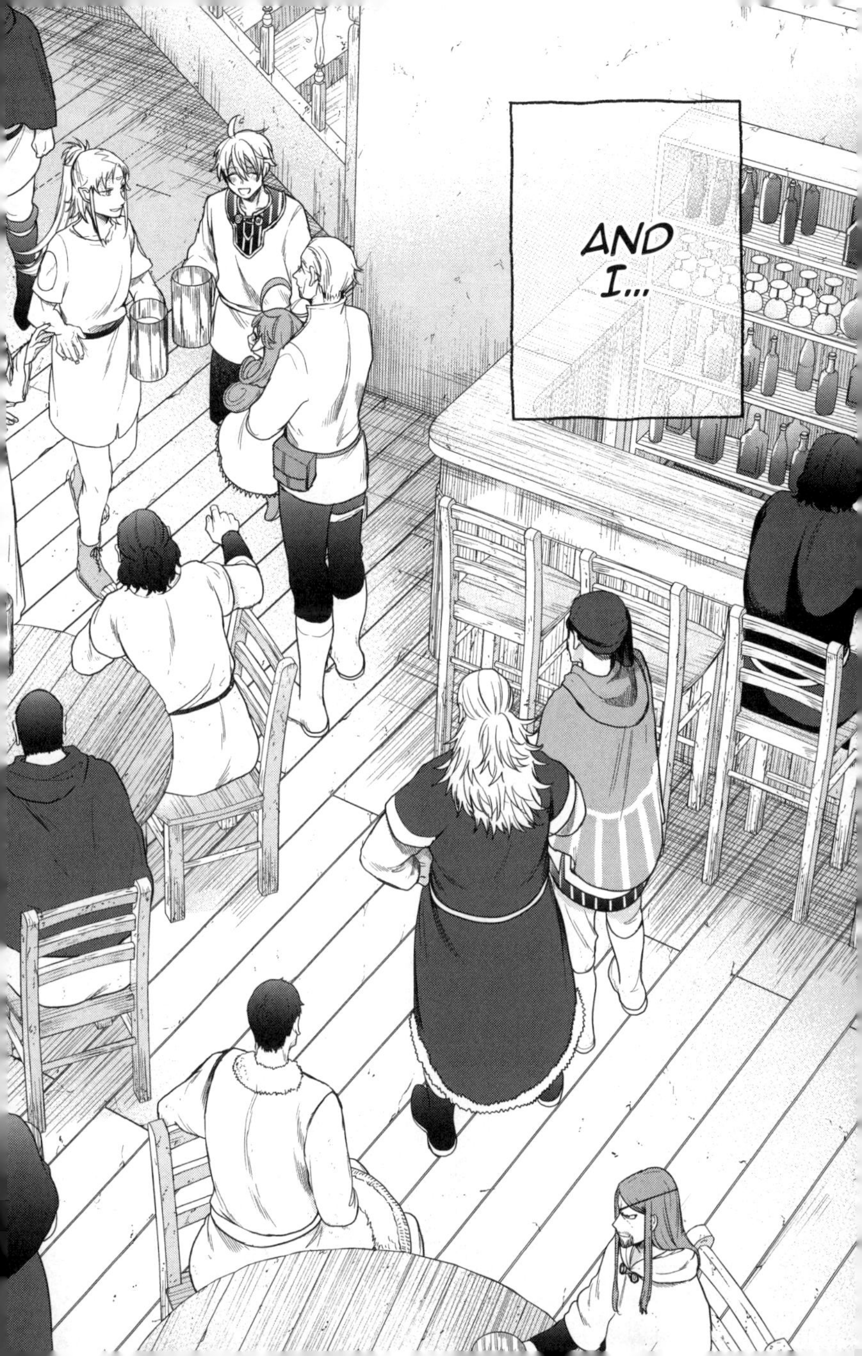
AND I...

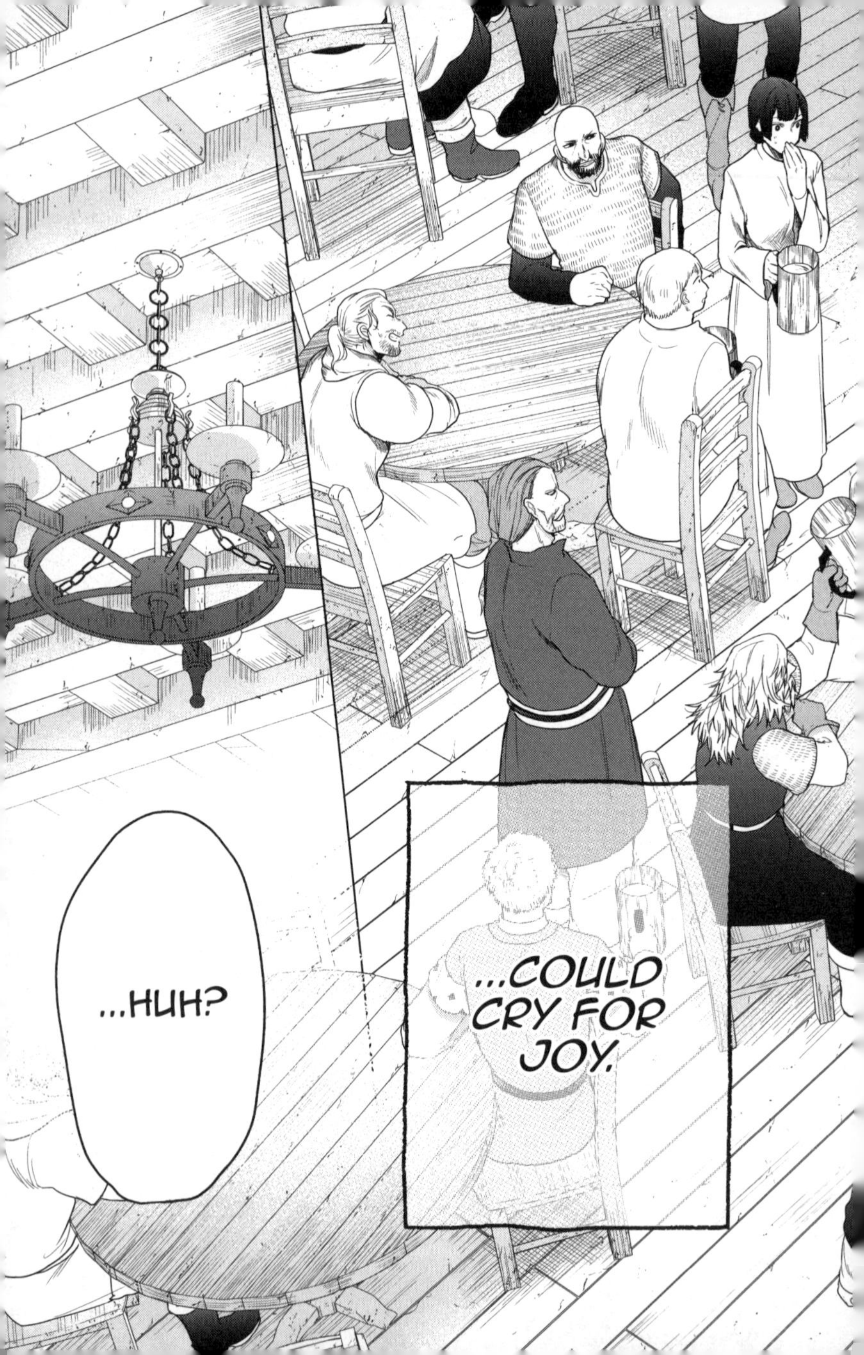
...COULD CRY FOR JOY.
...HUH?

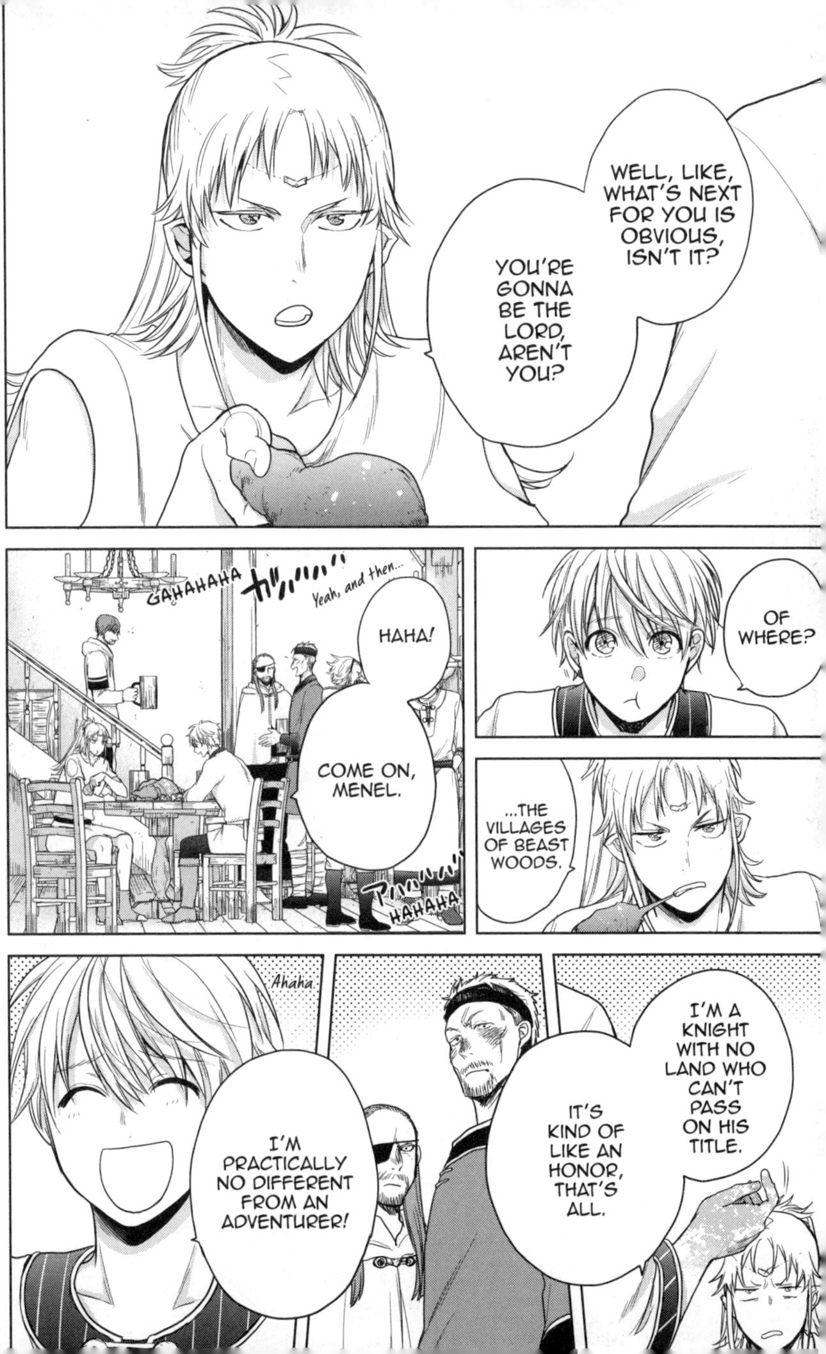
WELL, LIKE, WHAT'S NEXT FOR YOU IS OBVIOUS, ISN'T IT?
YOU'RE GONNA BE THE LORD, AREN'T YOU?
OF WHERE?
...THE VILLAGES OF BEAST WOODS.
GAHAHAHA
Yeah, and then...
HAHA!
COME ON, MENEL.
HAHAHA
I'M A KNIGHT WITH NO LAND WHO CAN'T PASS ON HIS TITLE.
IT'S KIND OF LIKE AN HONOR, THAT'S ALL.
Ahaha.
I'M PRACTICALLY NO DIFFERENT FROM AN ADVENTURER!

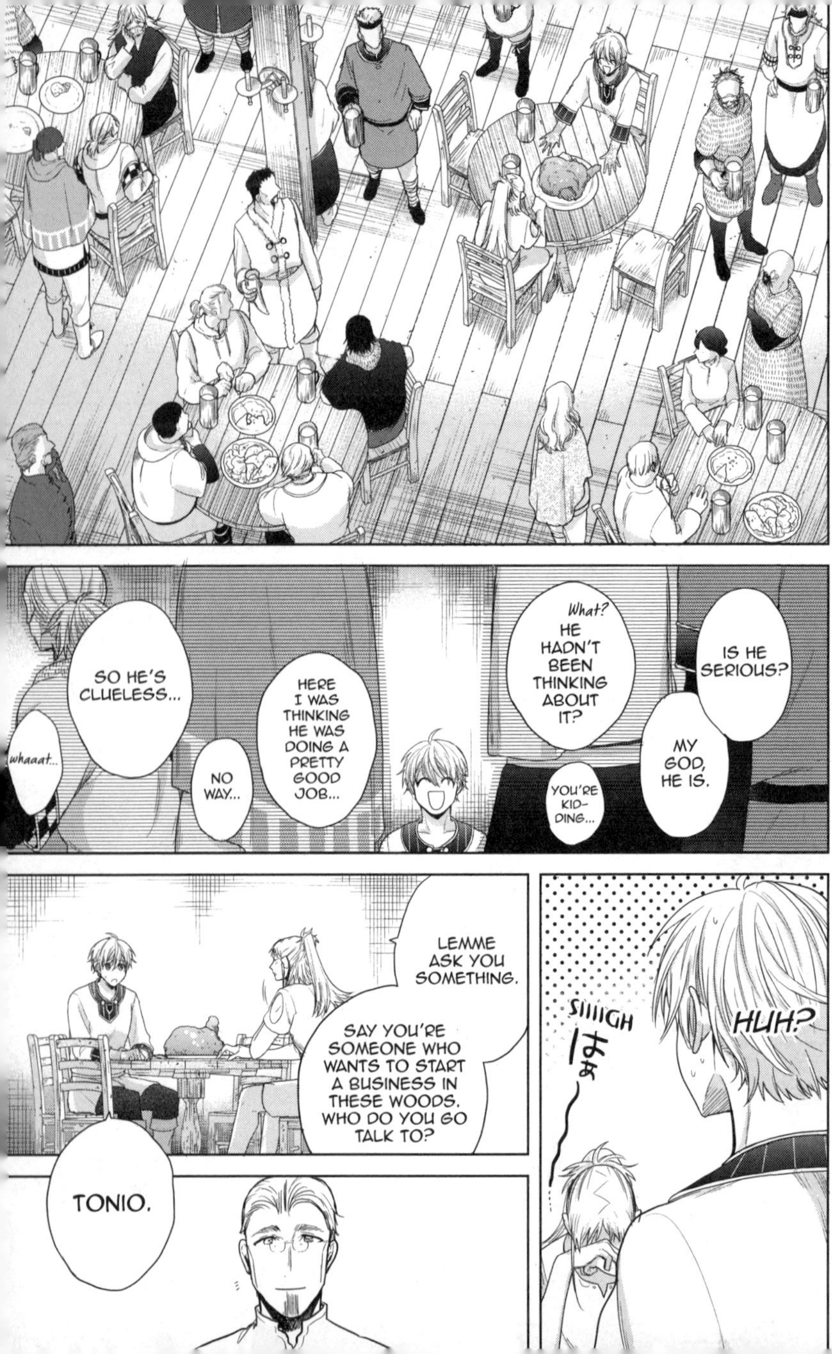
IS HE SERIOUS?
MY GOD, HE IS.
What? HE HADN'T BEEN THINKING ABOUT IT?
YOU'RE KID-DING...
HERE I WAS THINKING HE WAS DOING A PRETTY GOOD JOB...
NO WAY...
SO HE'S CLUELESS...
whaaat...
HUH?
SIIIGH
はぁ〜
LEMME ASK YOU SOMETHING.
SAY YOU'RE SOMEONE WHO WANTS TO START A BUSINESS IN THESE WOODS. WHO DO YOU GO TALK TO?
TONIO.

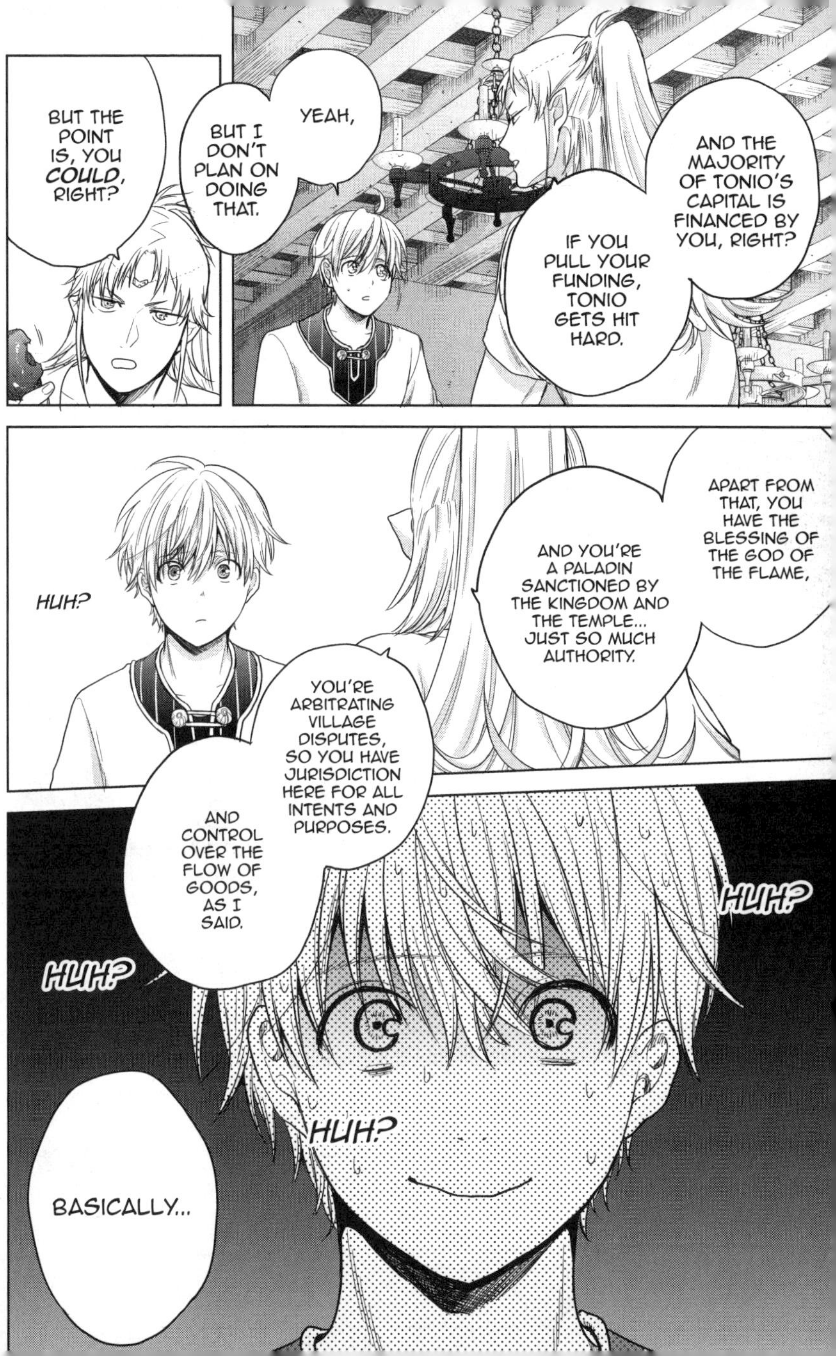
AND THE MAJORITY OF TONIO'S CAPITAL IS FINANCED BY YOU, RIGHT?
IF YOU PULL YOUR FUNDING, TONIO GETS HIT HARD.
YEAH,
BUT I DON'T PLAN ON DOING THAT.
BUT THE POINT IS, YOU COULD, RIGHT?
APART FROM THAT, YOU HAVE THE BLESSING OF THE GOD OF THE FLAME,
AND YOU'RE A PALADIN SANCTIONED BY THE KINGDOM AND THE TEMPLE... JUST SO MUCH AUTHORITY.
YOU'RE ARBITRATING VILLAGE DISPUTES, SO YOU HAVE JURISDICTION HERE FOR ALL INTENTS AND PURPOSES.
HUH?
AND CONTROL OVER THE FLOW OF GOODS, AS I SAID.
HUH?
HUH?
HUH?
BASICALLY...

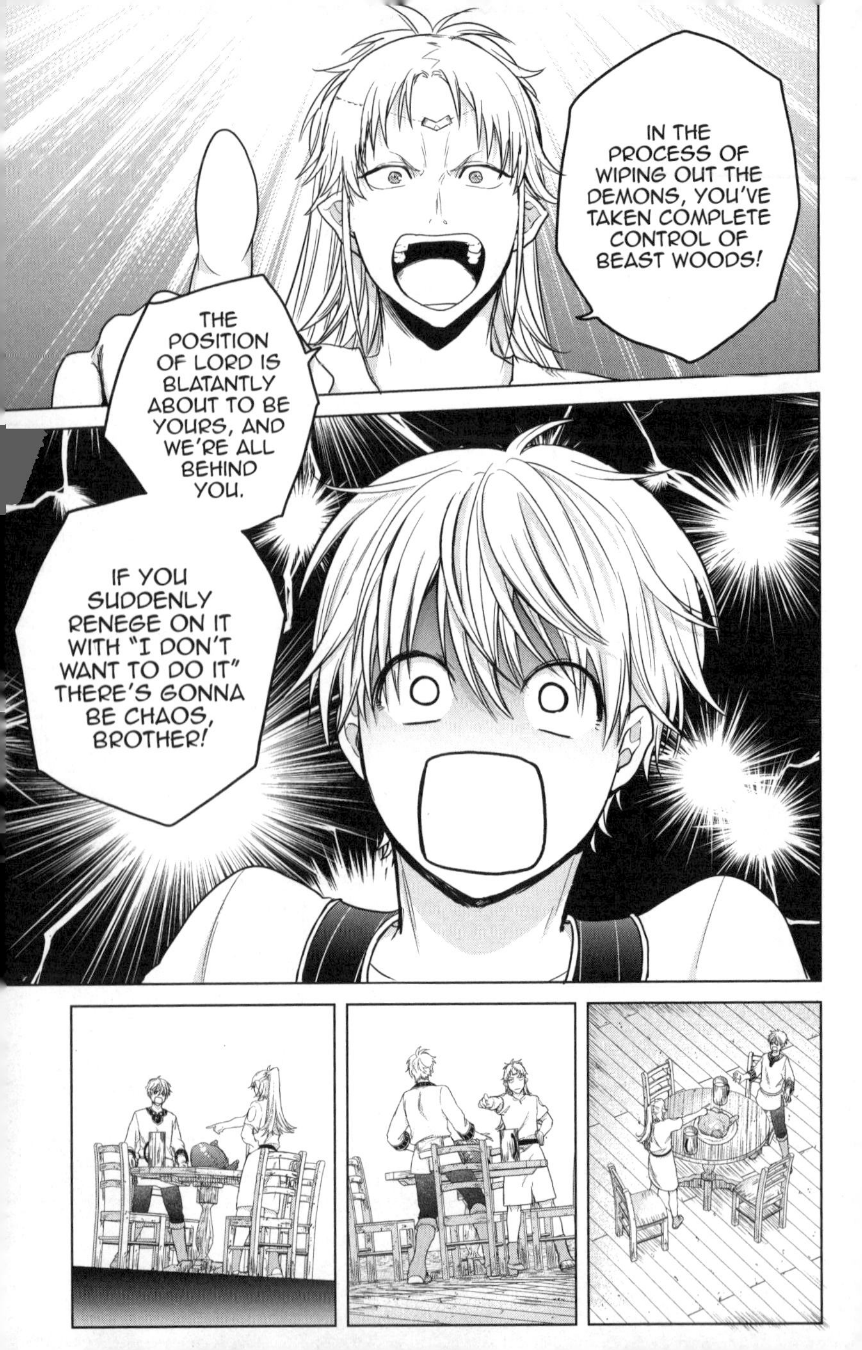
IN THE PROCESS OF WIPING OUT THE DEMONS, YOU'VE TAKEN COMPLETE CONTROL OF BEAST WOODS!
THE POSITION OF LORD IS BLATANTLY ABOUT TO BE YOURS, AND WE'RE ALL BEHIND YOU.
IF YOU SUDDENLY RENEGE ON IT WITH "I DON'T WANT TO DO IT" THERE'S GONNA BE CHAOS, BROTHER!

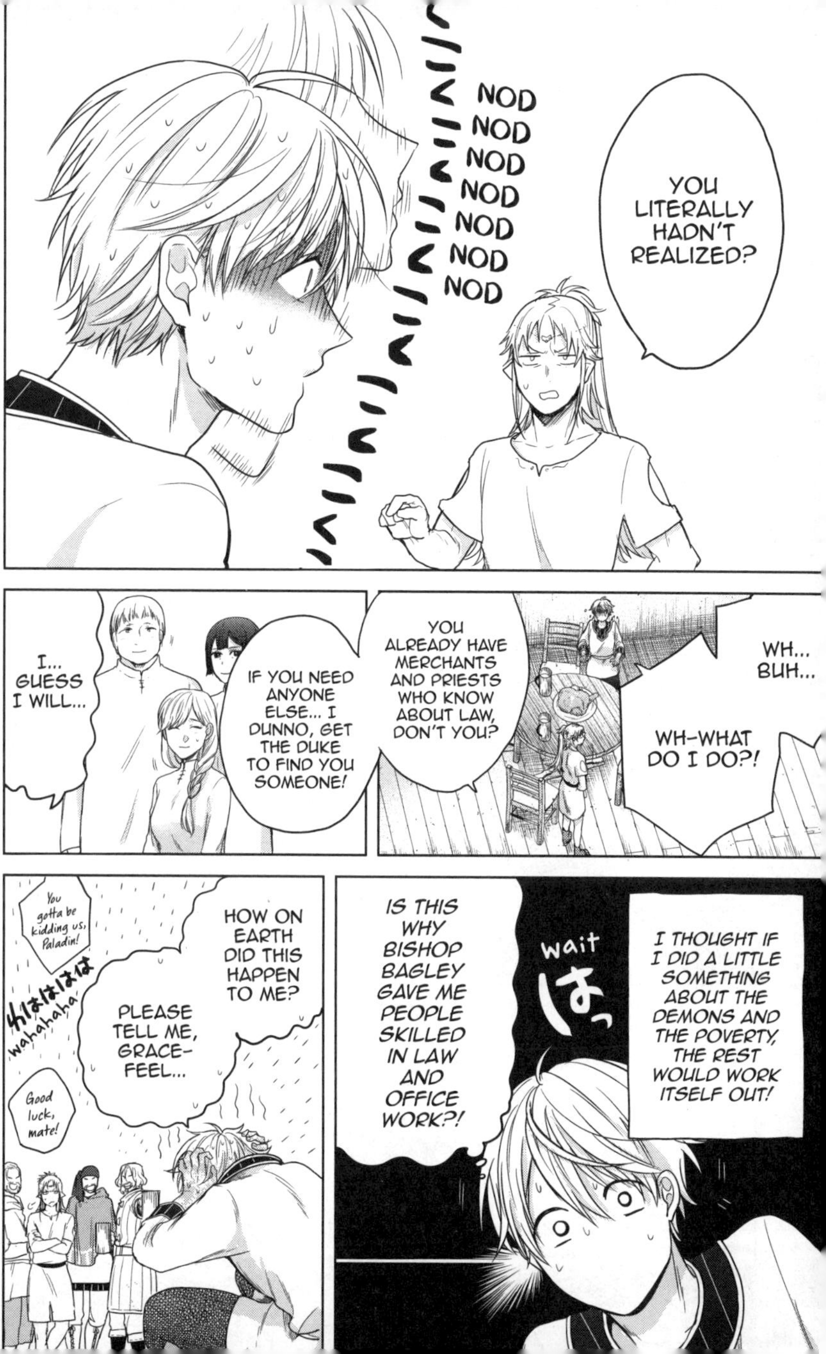
YOU LITERALLY HADN'T REALIZED?
NOD NOD NOD NOD NOD NOD NOD
WH... BUH...
WH-WHAT DO I DO?!
YOU ALREADY HAVE MERCHANTS AND PRIESTS WHO KNOW ABOUT LAW, DON'T YOU?
IF YOU NEED ANYONE ELSE... I DUNNO, GET THE DUKE TO FIND YOU SOMEONE!
I... GUESS I WILL...
I THOUGHT IF I DID A LITTLE SOMETHING ABOUT THE DEMONS AND THE POVERTY, THE REST WOULD WORK ITSELF OUT!
wait
はっ
IS THIS WHY BISHOP BAGLEY GAVE ME PEOPLE SKILLED IN LAW AND OFFICE WORK?!
HOW ON EARTH DID THIS HAPPEN TO ME?
PLEASE TELL ME, GRACE-FEEL...
You gotta be kidding us, Paladin!
わははははは
wahahaha
Good luck, mate!

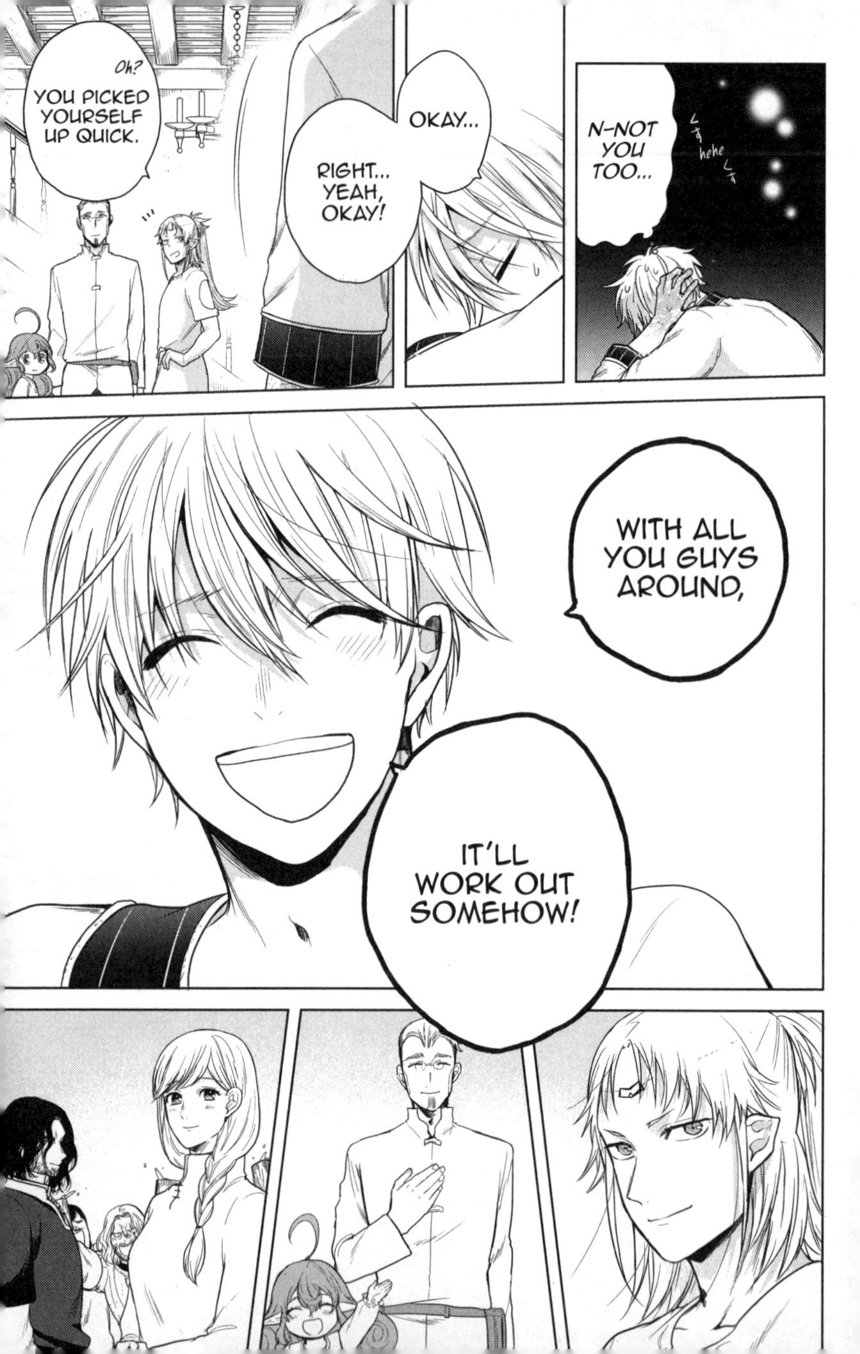
N-NOT YOU TOO...
くす hehe くす
OKAY...
RIGHT... YEAH, OKAY!
Oh?
YOU PICKED YOURSELF UP QUICK.
WITH ALL YOU GUYS AROUND,
IT'LL WORK OUT SOMEHOW!

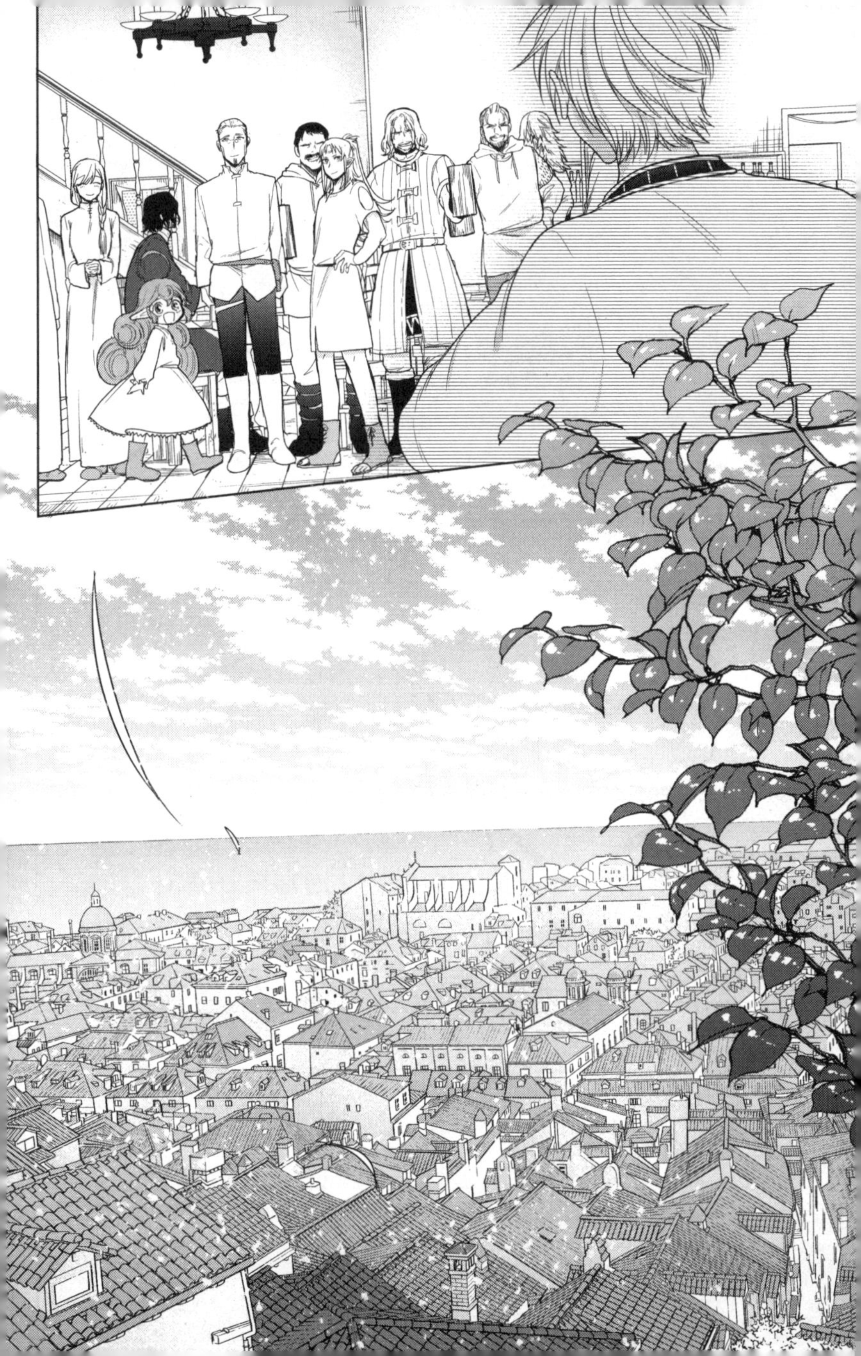

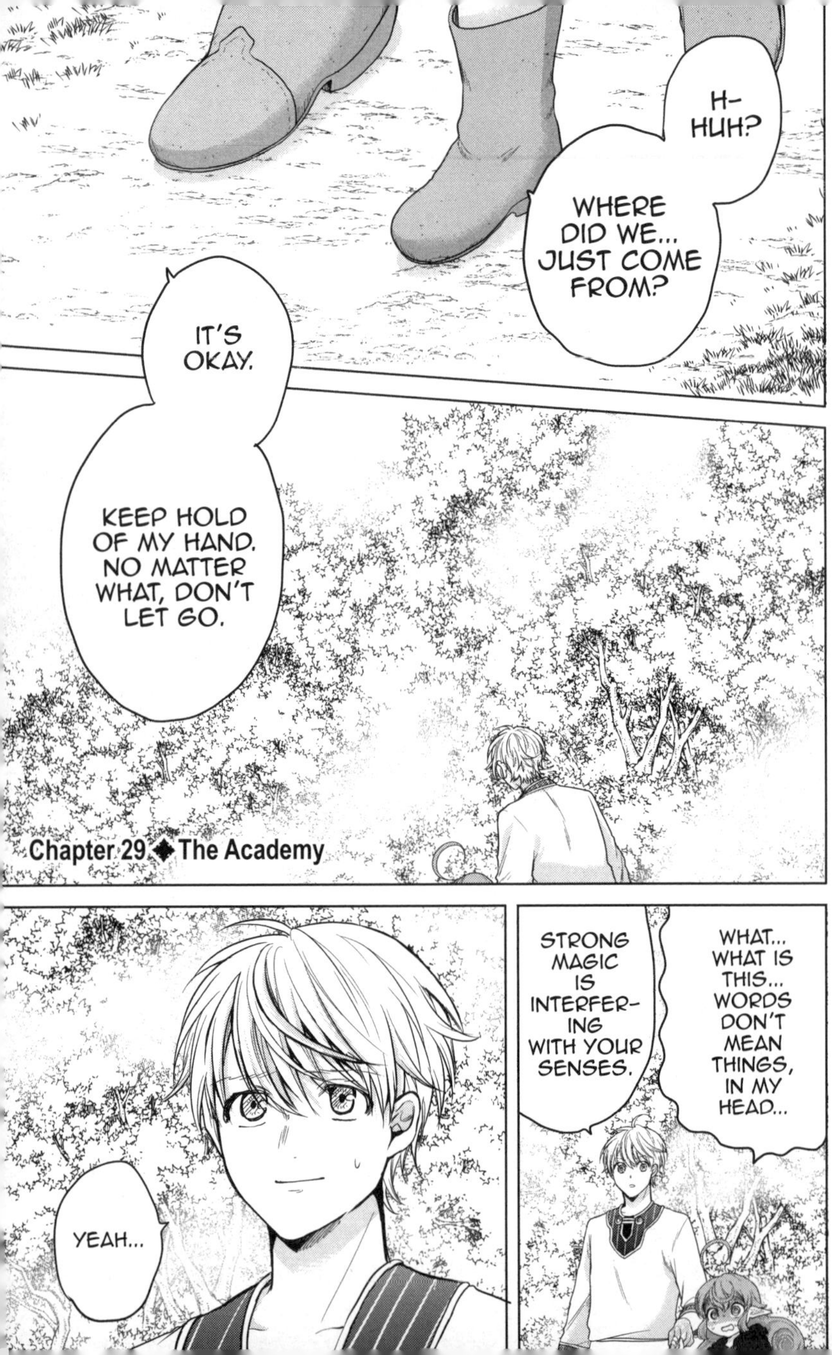
H-HUH?
WHERE DID WE... JUST COME FROM?
IT'S OKAY.
KEEP HOLD OF MY HAND. NO MATTER WHAT, DON'T LET GO.
Chapter 29 ◆ The Academy
WHAT... WHAT IS THIS... WORDS DON'T MEAN THINGS, IN MY HEAD...
STRONG MAGIC IS INTERFER-ING WITH YOUR SENSES.
YEAH...

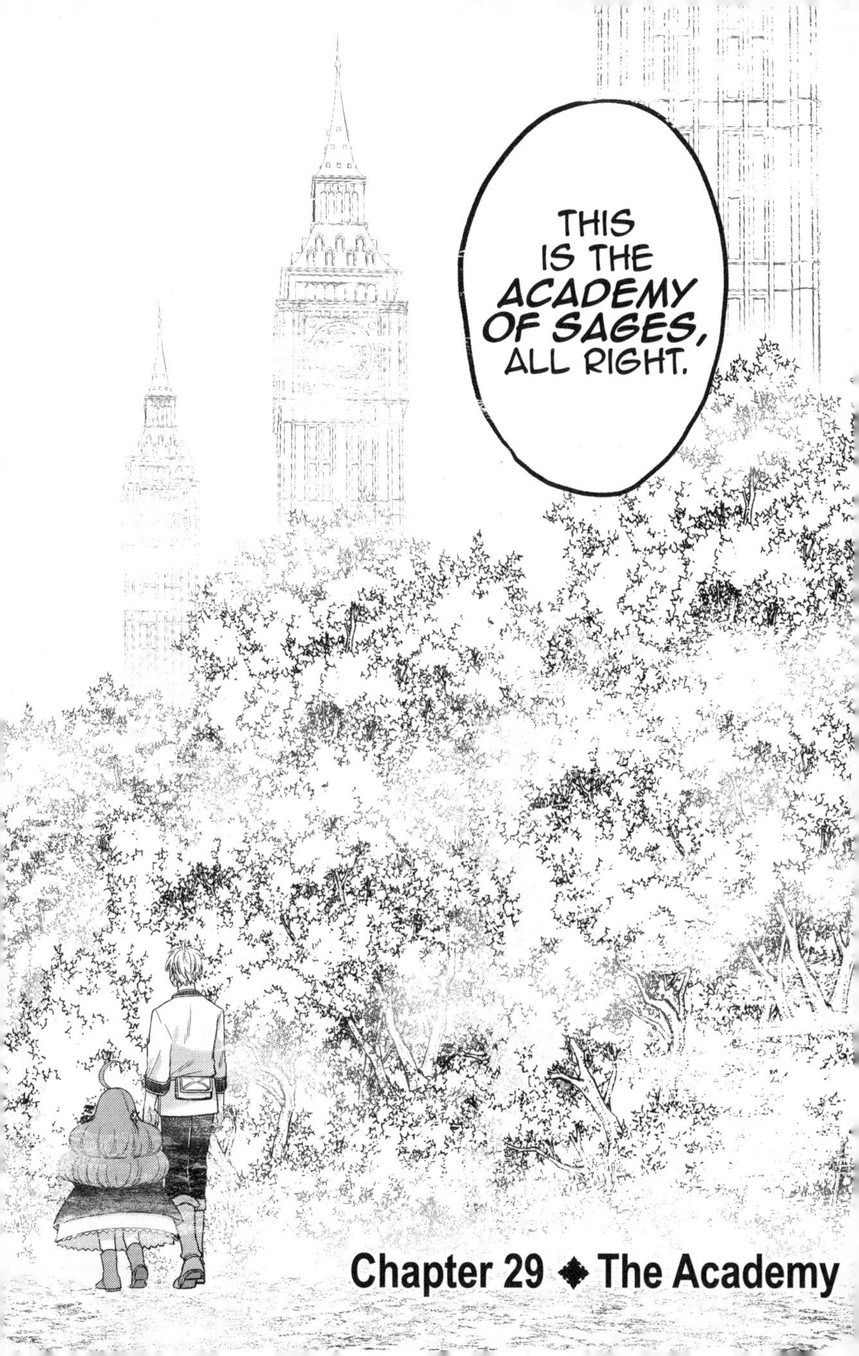
THIS IS THE *ACADEMY OF SAGES,* ALL RIGHT.
Chapter 29 ◆ The Academy

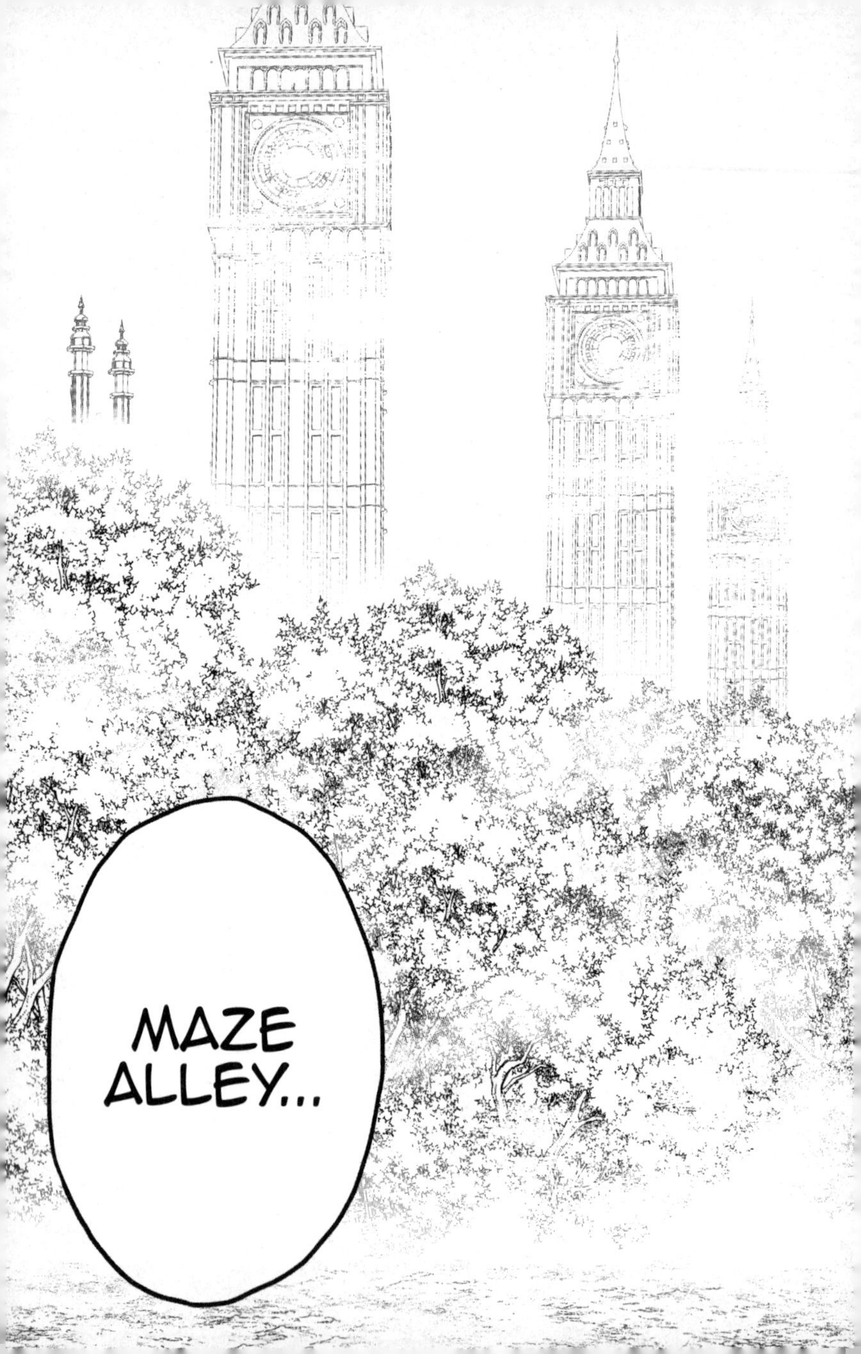
MAZE ALLEY...

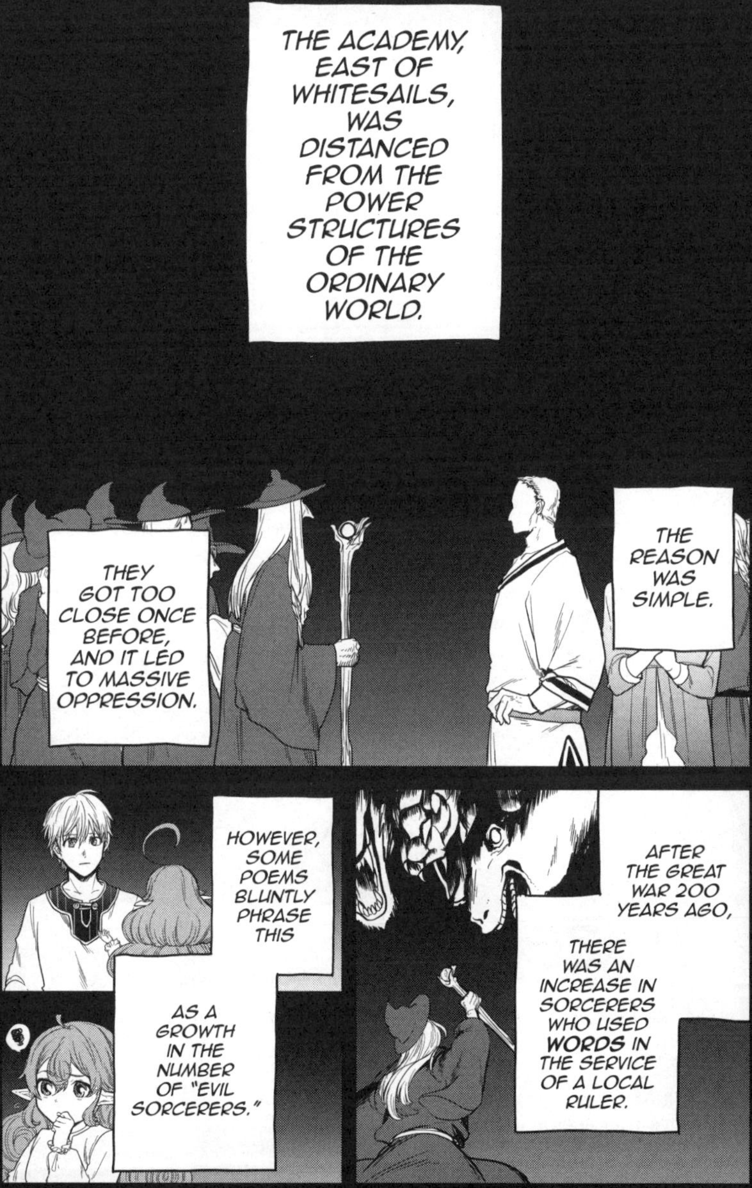
THE ACADEMY, EAST OF WHITESAILS, WAS DISTANCED FROM THE POWER STRUCTURES OF THE ORDINARY WORLD.
THE REASON WAS SIMPLE.
THEY GOT TOO CLOSE ONCE BEFORE, AND IT LED TO MASSIVE OPPRESSION.
AFTER THE GREAT WAR 200 YEARS AGO,
THERE WAS AN INCREASE IN SORCERERS WHO USED **WORDS** IN THE SERVICE OF A LOCAL RULER.
HOWEVER, SOME POEMS BLUNTLY PHRASE THIS
AS A GROWTH IN THE NUMBER OF "EVIL SORCERERS."

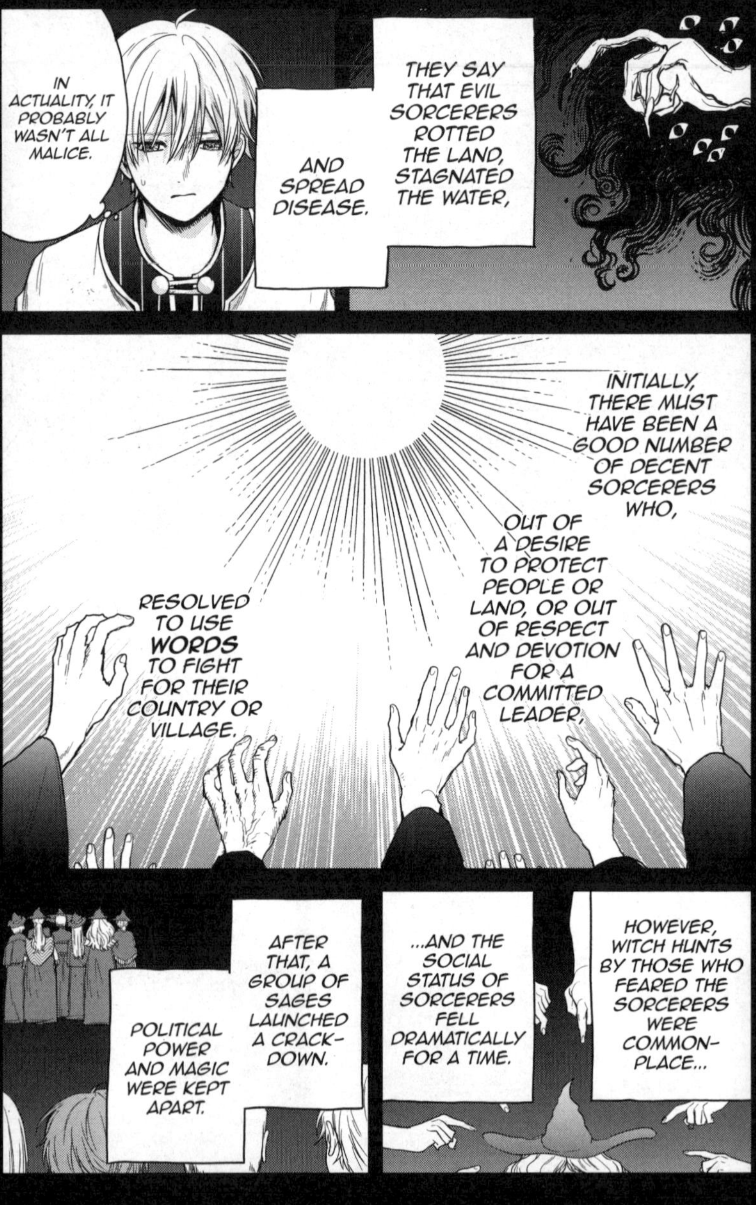
THEY SAY THAT EVIL SORCERERS ROTTED THE LAND, STAGNATED THE WATER,
AND SPREAD DISEASE.
IN ACTUALITY, IT PROBABLY WASN'T ALL MALICE.
INITIALLY, THERE MUST HAVE BEEN A GOOD NUMBER OF DECENT SORCERERS WHO,
OUT OF A DESIRE TO PROTECT PEOPLE OR LAND, OR OUT OF RESPECT AND DEVOTION FOR A COMMITTED LEADER,
RESOLVED TO USE **WORDS** TO FIGHT FOR THEIR COUNTRY OR VILLAGE.
HOWEVER, WITCH HUNTS BY THOSE WHO FEARED THE SORCERERS WERE COMMON-PLACE...
...AND THE SOCIAL STATUS OF SORCERERS FELL DRAMATICALLY FOR A TIME.
AFTER THAT, A GROUP OF SAGES LAUNCHED A CRACK-DOWN.
POLITICAL POWER AND MAGIC WERE KEPT APART.

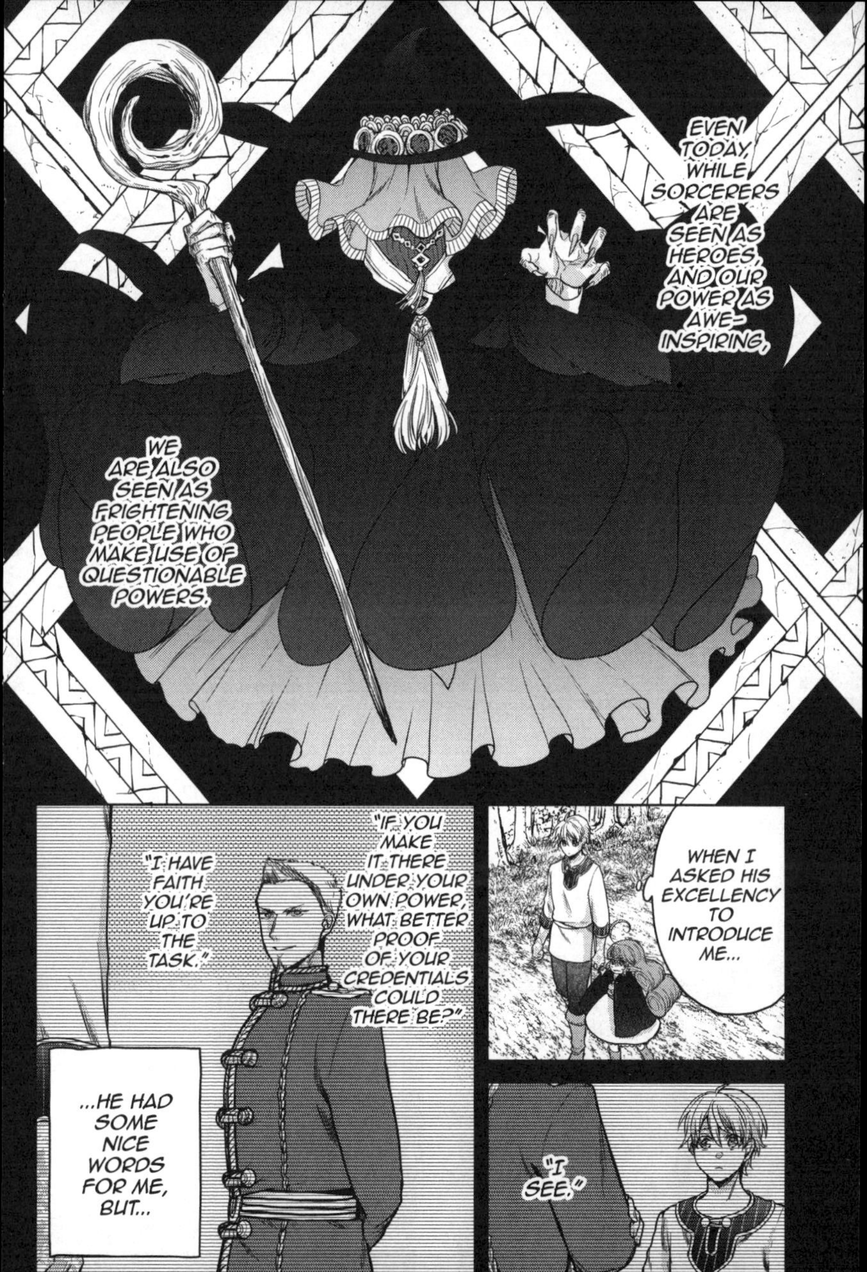
EVEN TODAY, WHILE SORCERERS ARE SEEN AS HEROES, AND OUR POWER AS AWE-INSPIRING,
WE ARE ALSO SEEN AS FRIGHTENING PEOPLE WHO MAKE USE OF QUESTIONABLE POWERS.
WHEN I ASKED HIS EXCELLENCY TO INTRODUCE ME...
"I SEE."
"IF YOU MAKE IT THERE UNDER YOUR OWN POWER, WHAT BETTER PROOF OF YOUR CREDENTIALS COULD THERE BE?"
"I HAVE FAITH YOU'RE UP TO THE TASK."
...HE HAD SOME NICE WORDS FOR ME, BUT...

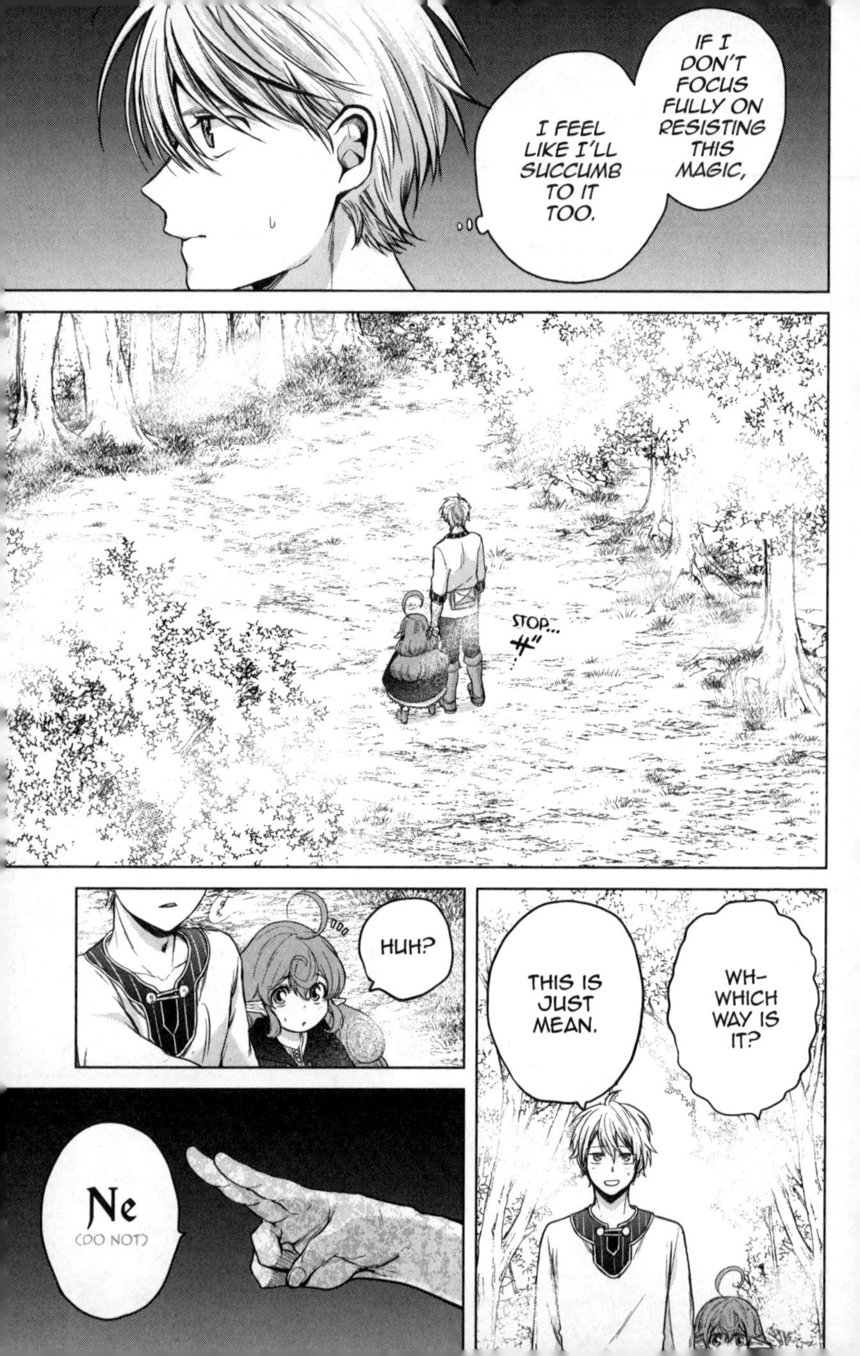
IF I DON'T FOCUS FULLY ON RESISTING THIS MAGIC,
I FEEL LIKE I'LL SUCCUMB TO IT TOO.
STOP...
WH- WHICH WAY IS IT?
THIS IS JUST MEAN.
HUH?
Ne
(DO NOT)

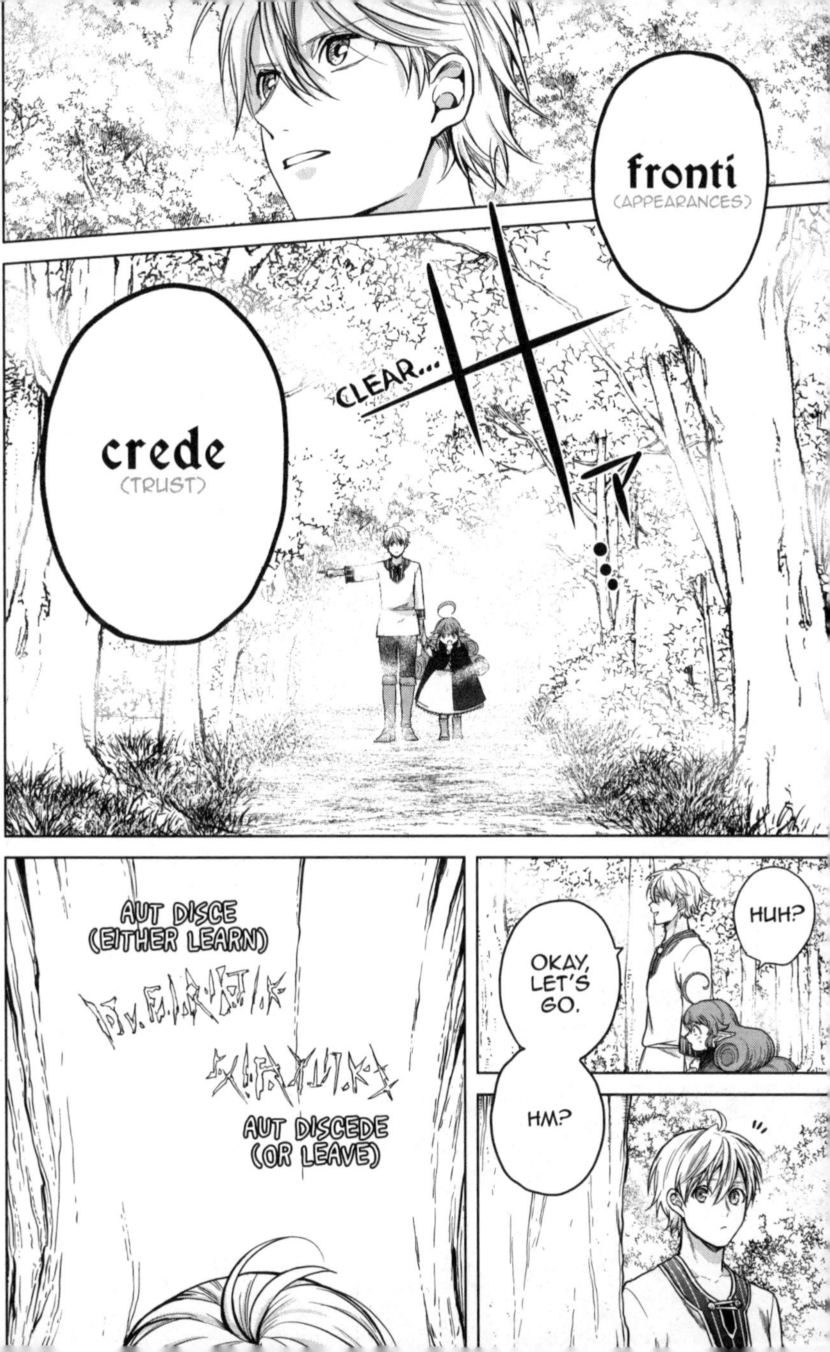
fronti
(APPEARANCES)
CLEAR...
crede
(TRUST)
HUH?
OKAY, LET'S GO.
HM?
AUT DISCE
(EITHER LEARN)
AUT DISCEDE
(OR LEAVE)

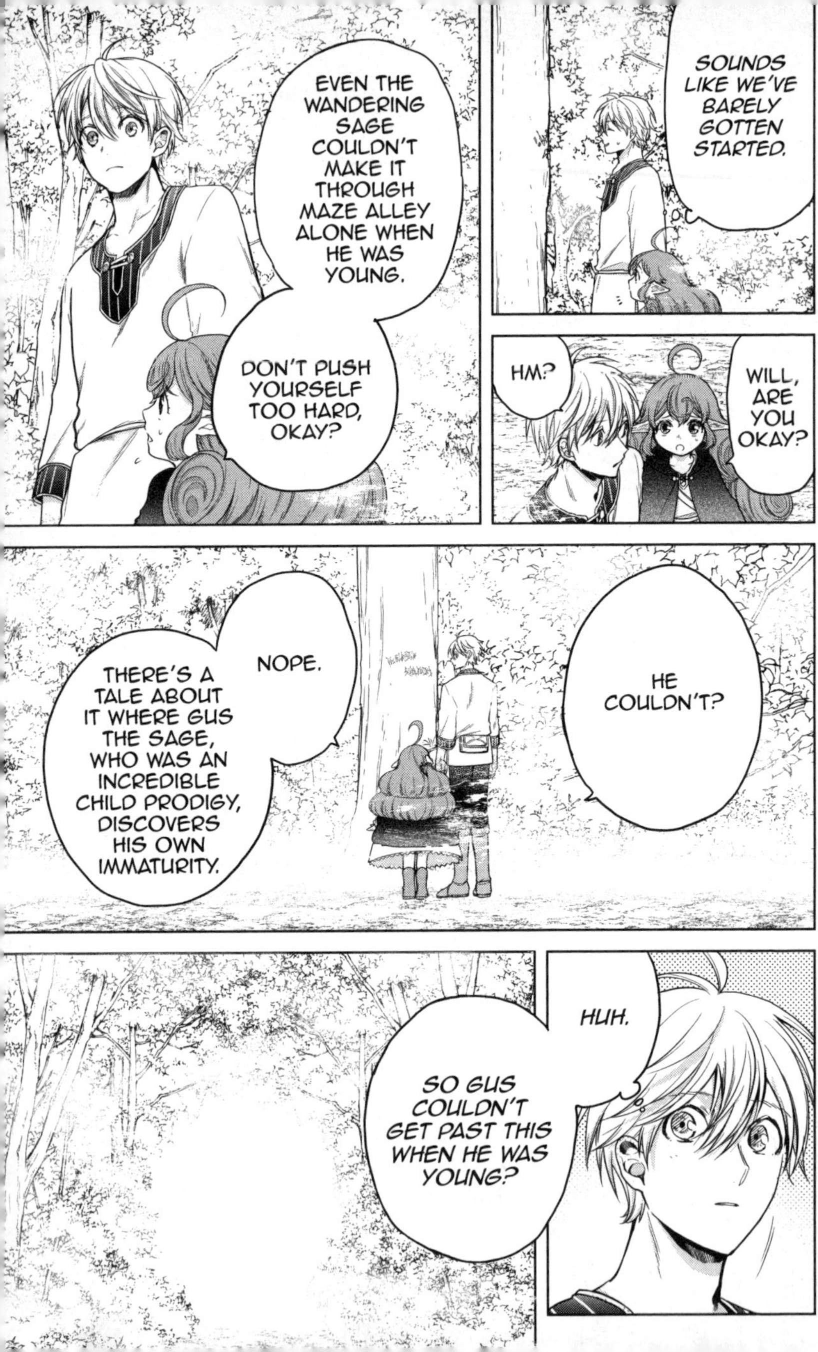
SOUNDS LIKE WE'VE BARELY GOTTEN STARTED.
WILL, ARE YOU OKAY?
HM?
EVEN THE WANDERING SAGE COULDN'T MAKE IT THROUGH MAZE ALLEY ALONE WHEN HE WAS YOUNG.
DON'T PUSH YOURSELF TOO HARD, OKAY?
HE COULDN'T?
NOPE.
THERE'S A TALE ABOUT IT WHERE GUS THE SAGE, WHO WAS AN INCREDIBLE CHILD PRODIGY, DISCOVERS HIS OWN IMMATURITY.
HUH.
SO GUS COULDN'T GET PAST THIS WHEN HE WAS YOUNG?

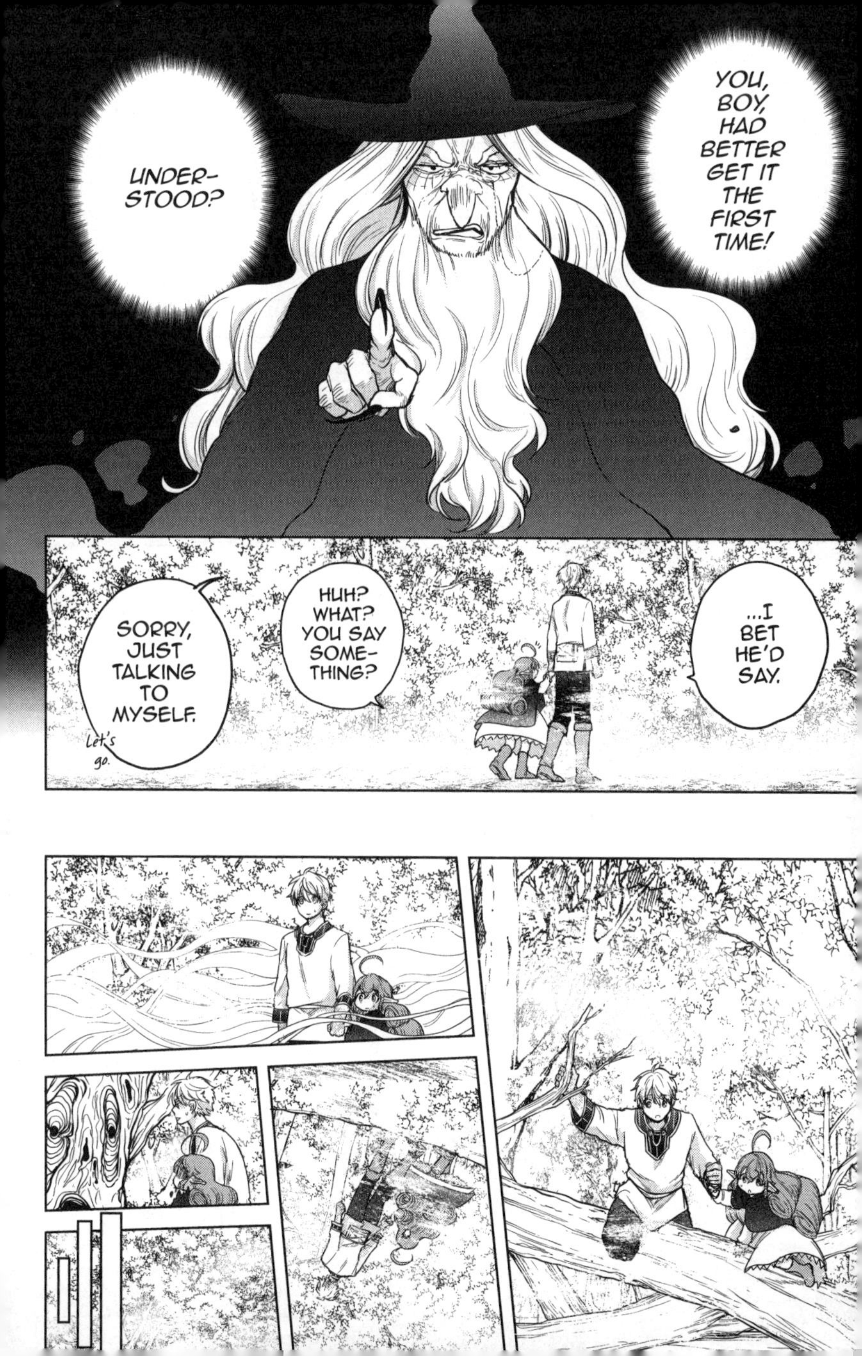
YOU, BOY, HAD BETTER GET IT THE FIRST TIME!
UNDER-STOOD?
...I BET HE'D SAY.
HUH? WHAT? YOU SAY SOME-THING?
SORRY, JUST TALKING TO MYSELF.
Let's go.

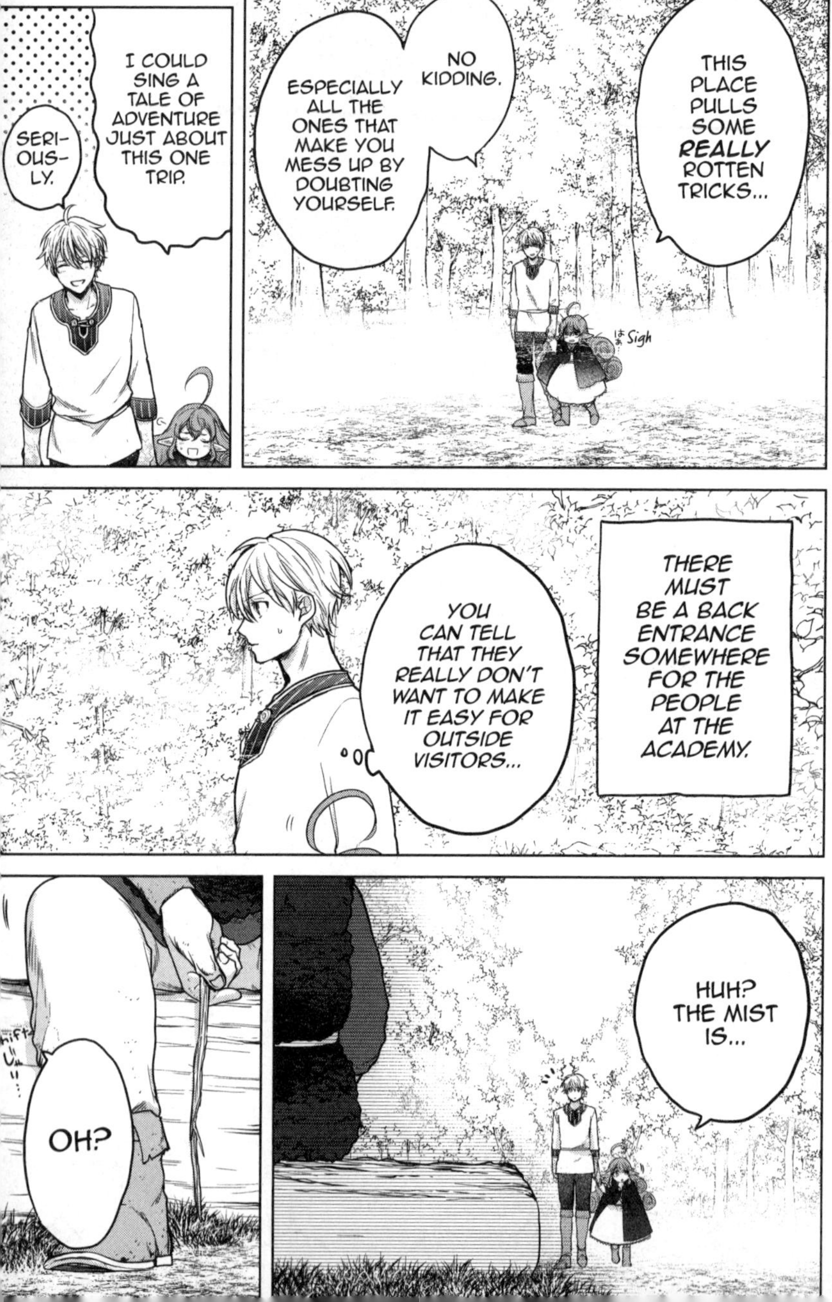
THIS PLACE PULLS SOME *REALLY* ROTTEN TRICKS...
NO KIDDING.
ESPECIALLY ALL THE ONES THAT MAKE YOU MESS UP BY DOUBTING YOURSELF.
はぁ Sigh
I COULD SING A TALE OF ADVENTURE JUST ABOUT THIS ONE TRIP.
SERI-OUS-LY.
THERE MUST BE A BACK ENTRANCE SOMEWHERE FOR THE PEOPLE AT THE ACADEMY.
YOU CAN TELL THAT THEY REALLY DON'T WANT TO MAKE IT EASY FOR OUTSIDE VISITORS...
HUH? THE MIST IS...
OH?

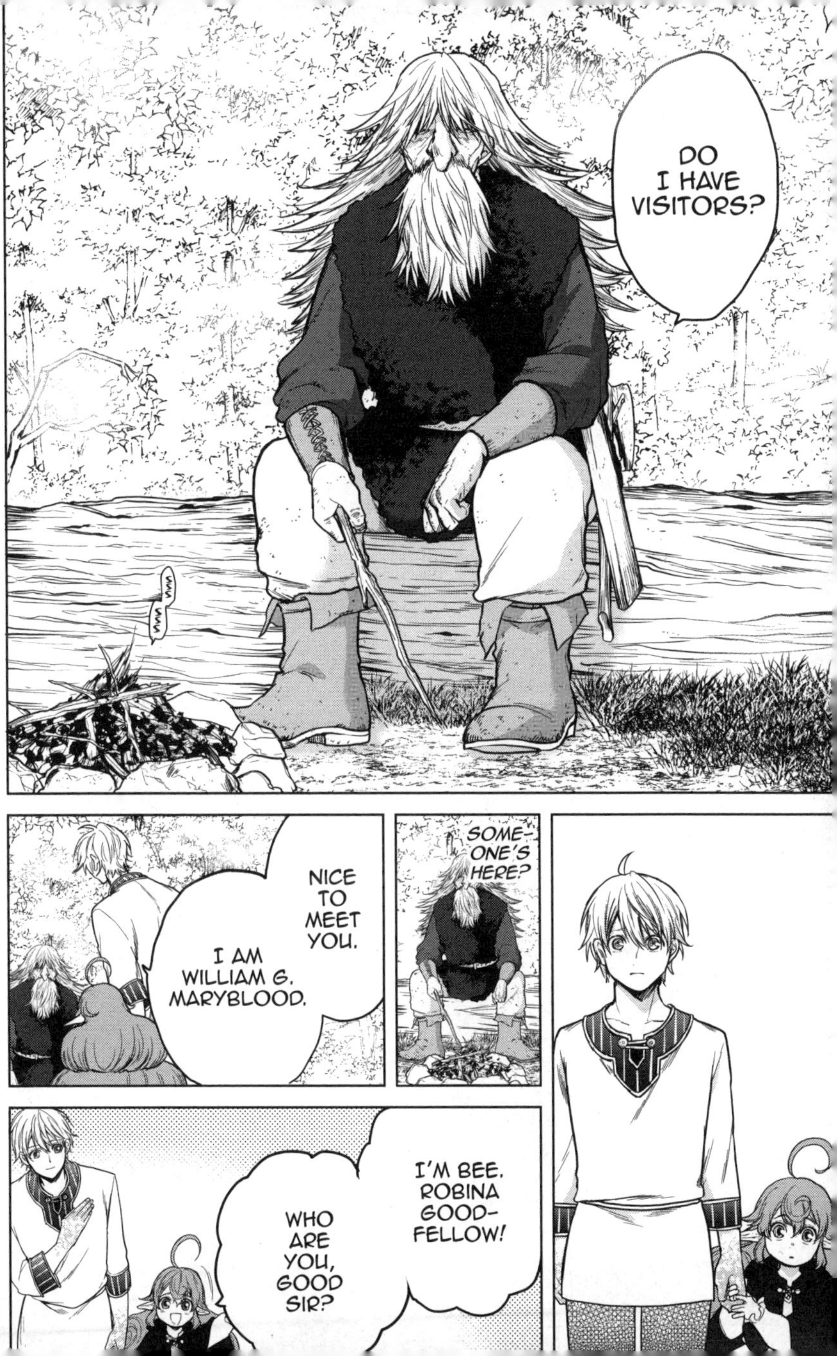
DO I HAVE VISITORS?
SOME-ONE'S HERE?
NICE TO MEET YOU.
I AM WILLIAM G. MARYBLOOD.
I'M BEE. ROBINA GOOD-FELLOW!
WHO ARE YOU, GOOD SIR?

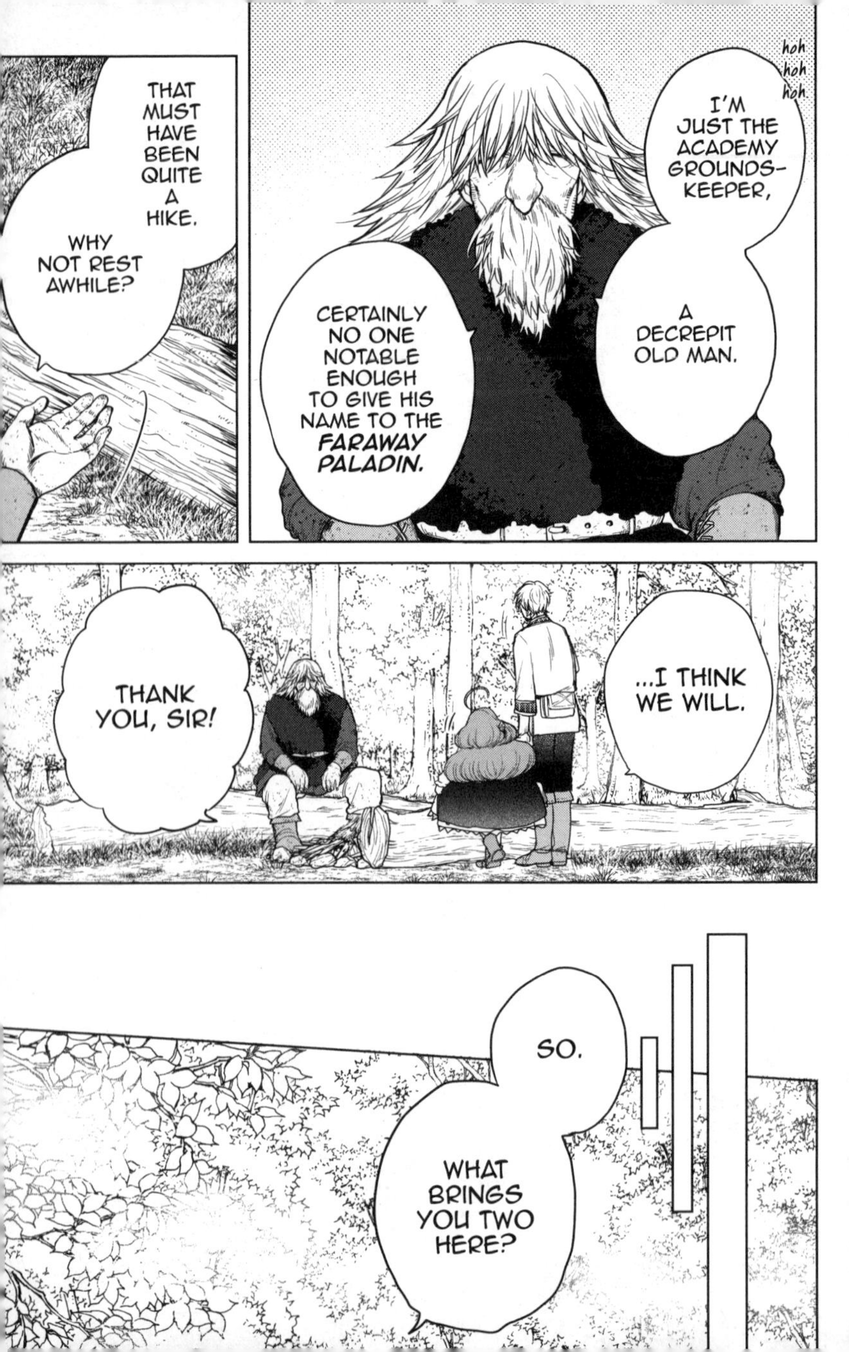
hoh hoh hoh
I'M JUST THE ACADEMY GROUNDS-KEEPER,
A DECREPIT OLD MAN.
CERTAINLY NO ONE NOTABLE ENOUGH TO GIVE HIS NAME TO THE *FARAWAY PALADIN*.
THAT MUST HAVE BEEN QUITE A HIKE.
WHY NOT REST AWHILE?
...I THINK WE WILL.
THANK YOU, SIR!
SO.
WHAT BRINGS YOU TWO HERE?

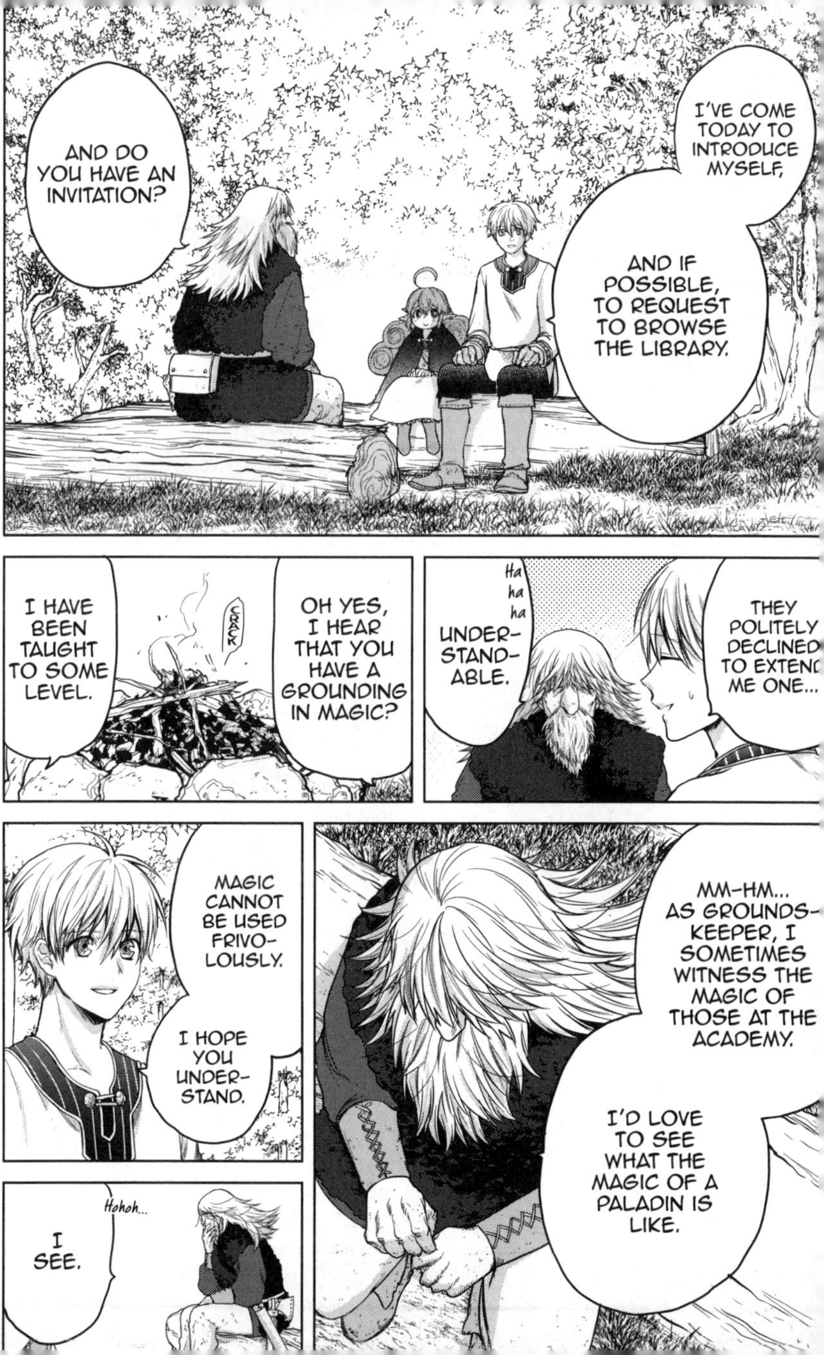
I'VE COME TODAY TO INTRODUCE MYSELF,
AND IF POSSIBLE, TO REQUEST TO BROWSE THE LIBRARY.
AND DO YOU HAVE AN INVITATION?
THEY POLITELY DECLINED TO EXTEND ME ONE...
Ha ha ha
UNDER-STAND-ABLE.
OH YES, I HEAR THAT YOU HAVE A GROUNDING IN MAGIC?
CRACK
I HAVE BEEN TAUGHT TO SOME LEVEL.
MM-HM... AS GROUNDS-KEEPER, I SOMETIMES WITNESS THE MAGIC OF THOSE AT THE ACADEMY.
I'D LOVE TO SEE WHAT THE MAGIC OF A PALADIN IS LIKE.
MAGIC CANNOT BE USED FRIVO-LOUSLY.
I HOPE YOU UNDER-STAND.
Hohoh...
I SEE.

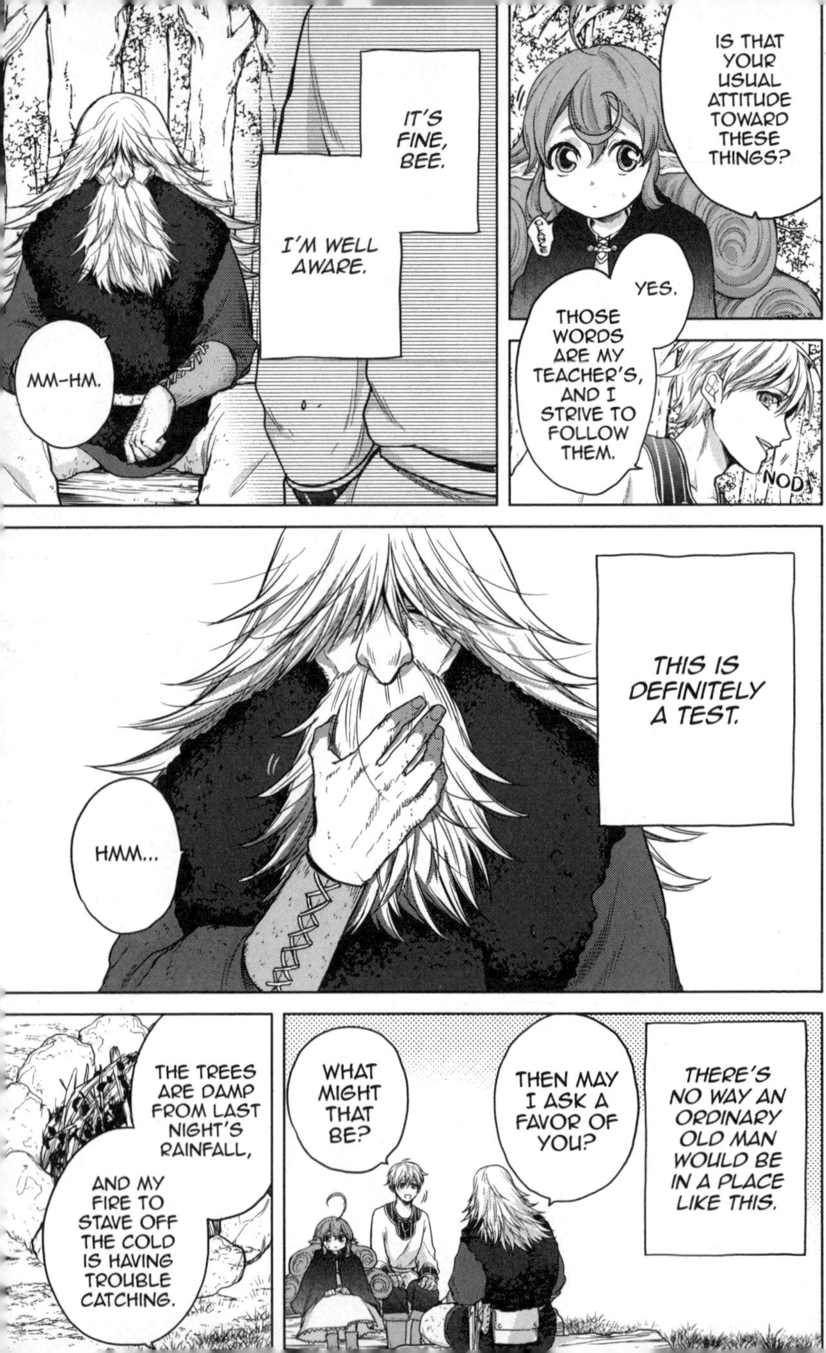
IS THAT YOUR USUAL ATTITUDE TOWARD THESE THINGS?
YES.
THOSE WORDS ARE MY TEACHER'S, AND I STRIVE TO FOLLOW THEM.
NOD
IT'S FINE, BEE.
I'M WELL AWARE.
MM-HM.
THIS IS DEFINITELY A TEST.
HMM...
THERE'S NO WAY AN ORDINARY OLD MAN WOULD BE IN A PLACE LIKE THIS.
THEN MAY I ASK A FAVOR OF YOU?
WHAT MIGHT THAT BE?
THE TREES ARE DAMP FROM LAST NIGHT'S RAINFALL,
AND MY FIRE TO STAVE OFF THE COLD IS HAVING TROUBLE CATCHING.

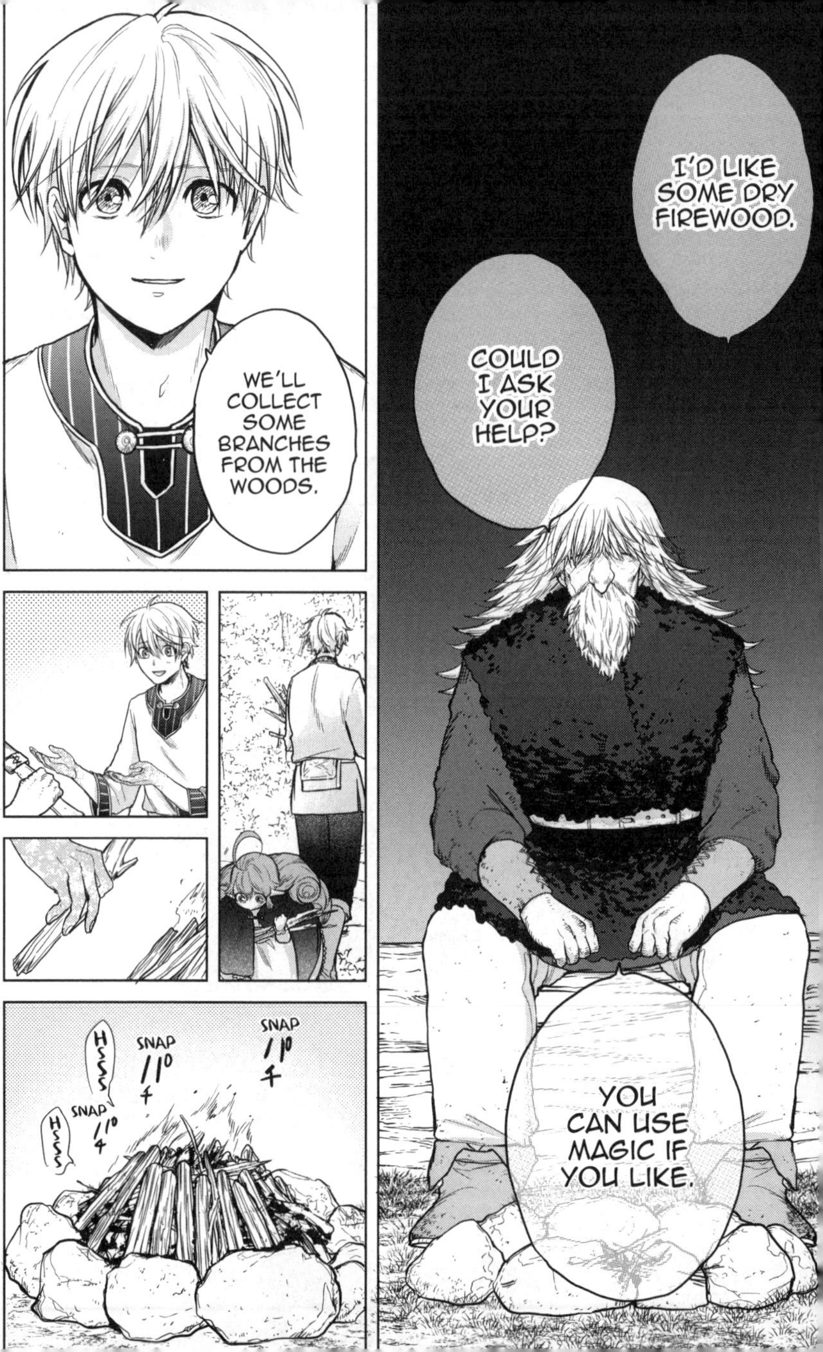
I'D LIKE SOME DRY FIREWOOD.
COULD I ASK YOUR HELP?
YOU CAN USE MAGIC IF YOU LIKE.
WE'LL COLLECT SOME BRANCHES FROM THE WOODS.
SNAP
SNAP
HSSS
SNAP
HSSS

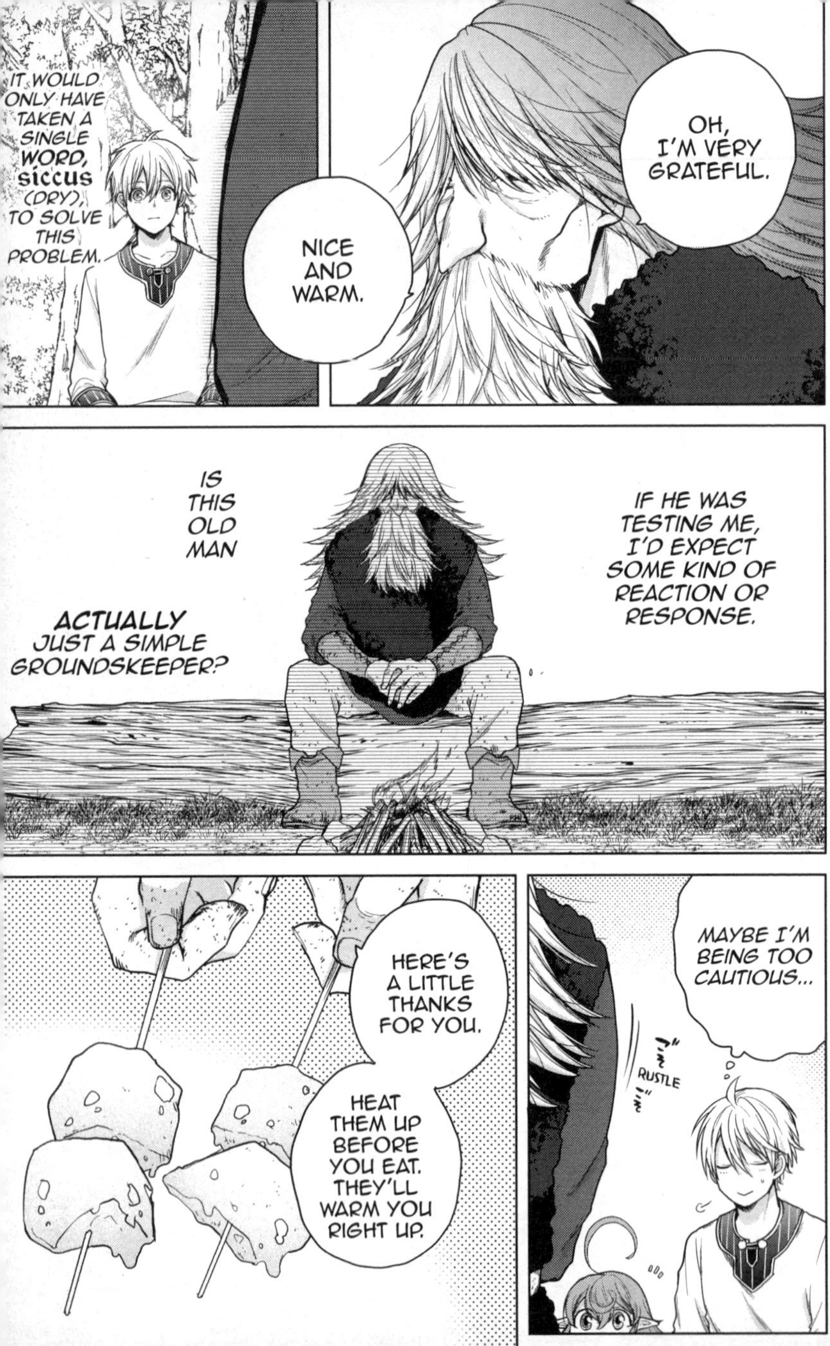
OH, I'M VERY GRATEFUL.
NICE AND WARM.
IT WOULD ONLY HAVE TAKEN A SINGLE WORD, siccus (DRY), TO SOLVE THIS PROBLEM.
IF HE WAS TESTING ME, I'D EXPECT SOME KIND OF REACTION OR RESPONSE.
IS THIS OLD MAN
ACTUALLY JUST A SIMPLE GROUNDSKEEPER?
MAYBE I'M BEING TOO CAUTIOUS...
RUSTLE
HERE'S A LITTLE THANKS FOR YOU.
HEAT THEM UP BEFORE YOU EAT. THEY'LL WARM YOU RIGHT UP.

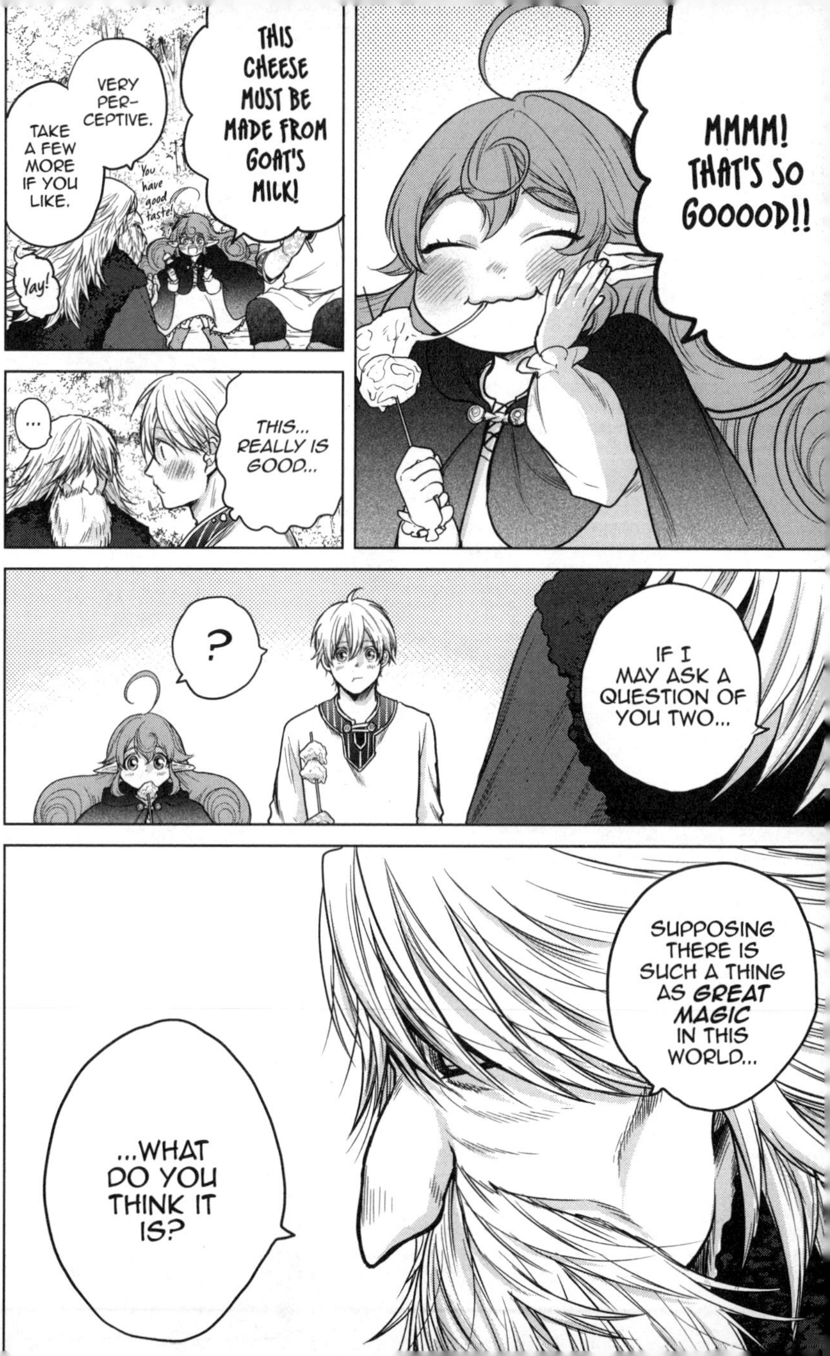
MMMM! THAT'S SO GOOOOD!!
THIS CHEESE MUST BE MADE FROM GOAT'S MILK!
VERY PER-CEPTIVE.
You have good taste!
TAKE A FEW MORE IF YOU LIKE.
Yay!
THIS... REALLY IS GOOD...
...
IF I MAY ASK A QUESTION OF YOU TWO...
?
SUPPOSING THERE IS SUCH A THING AS GREAT MAGIC IN THIS WORLD...
...WHAT DO YOU THINK IT IS?

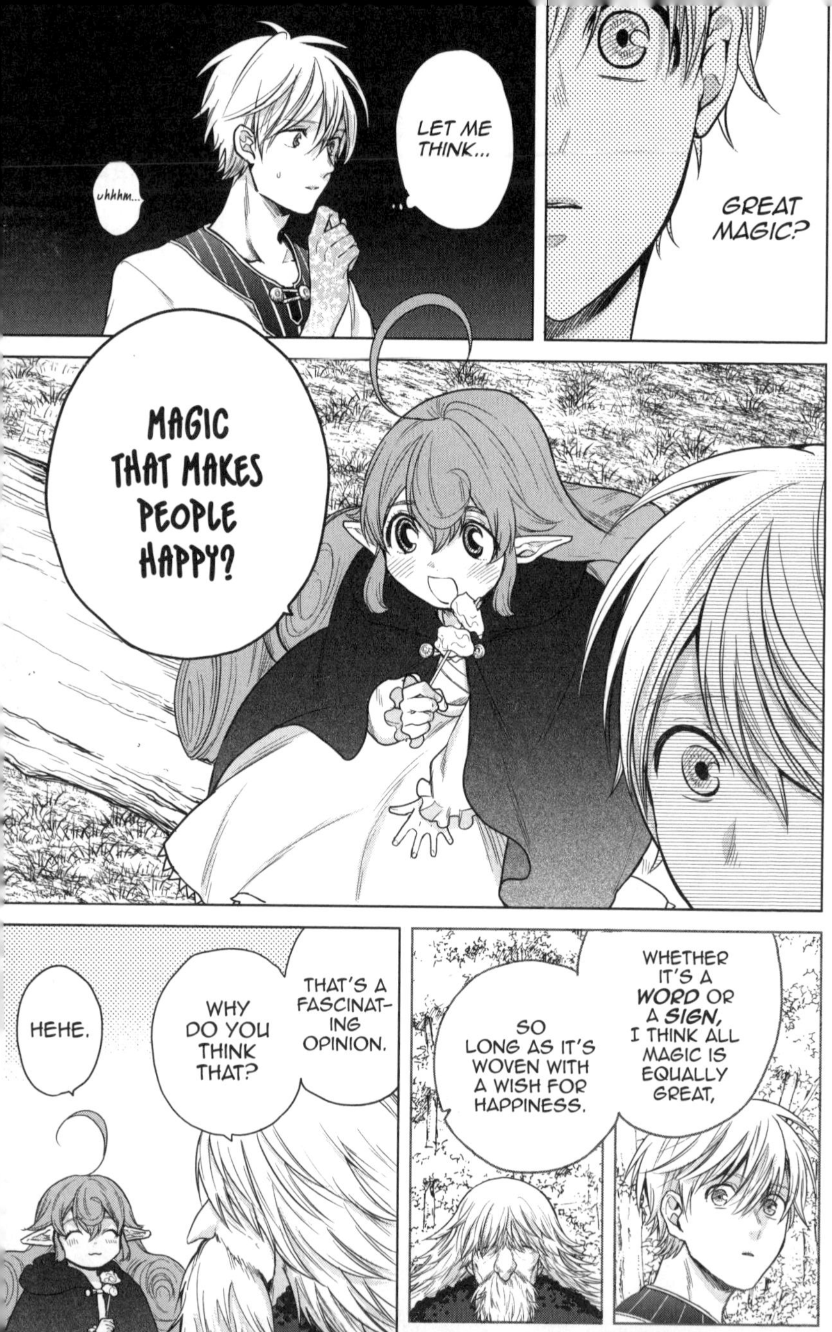
GREAT MAGIC?
LET ME THINK...
uhhhm...
MAGIC THAT MAKES PEOPLE HAPPY?
WHETHER IT'S A *WORD* OR A *SIGN*, I THINK ALL MAGIC IS EQUALLY GREAT,
SO LONG AS IT'S WOVEN WITH A WISH FOR HAPPINESS.
THAT'S A FASCINATING OPINION.
WHY DO YOU THINK THAT?
HEHE.

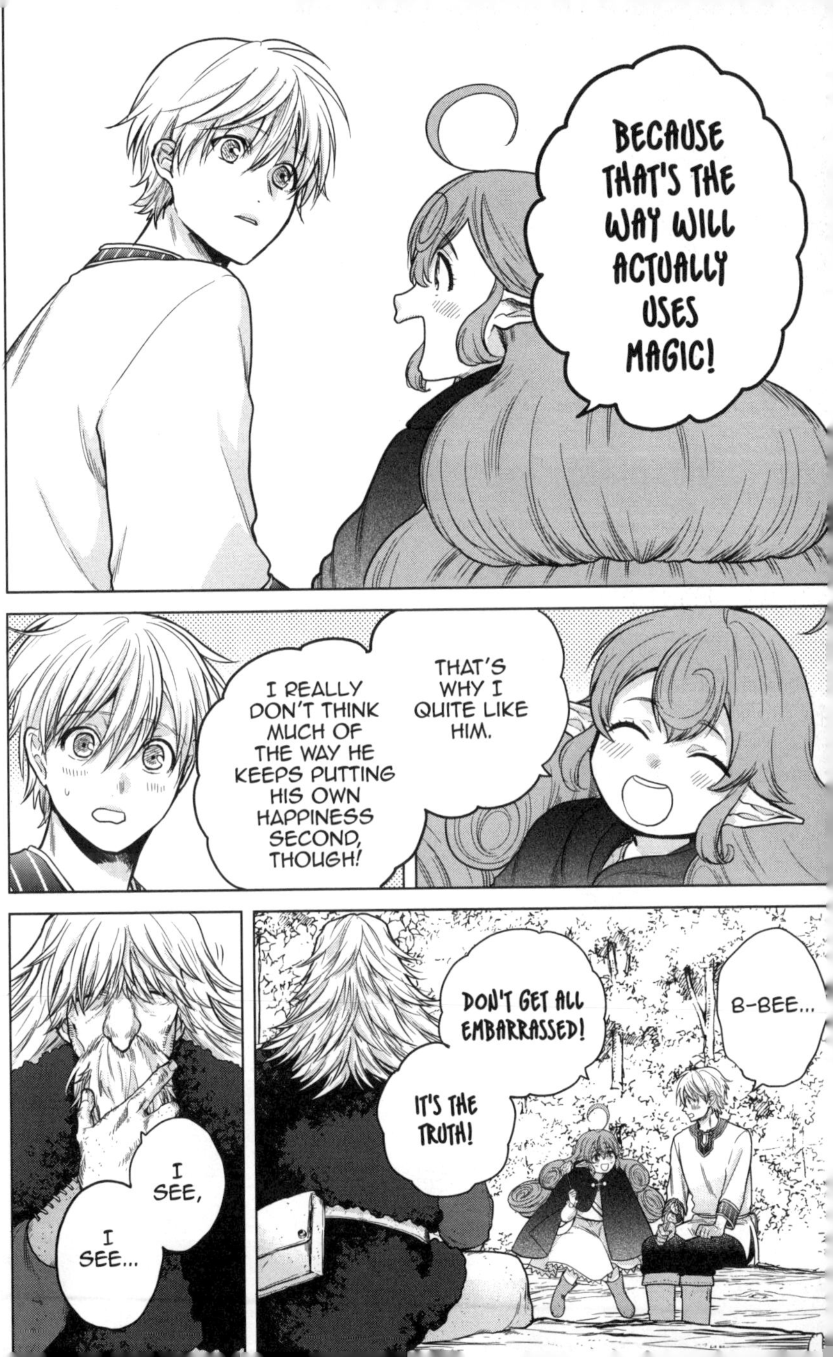
BECAUSE THAT'S THE WAY WILL ACTUALLY USES MAGIC!
THAT'S WHY I QUITE LIKE HIM.
I REALLY DON'T THINK MUCH OF THE WAY HE KEEPS PUTTING HIS OWN HAPPINESS SECOND, THOUGH!
B-BEE...
DON'T GET ALL EMBARRASSED!
IT'S THE TRUTH!
I SEE,
I SEE...

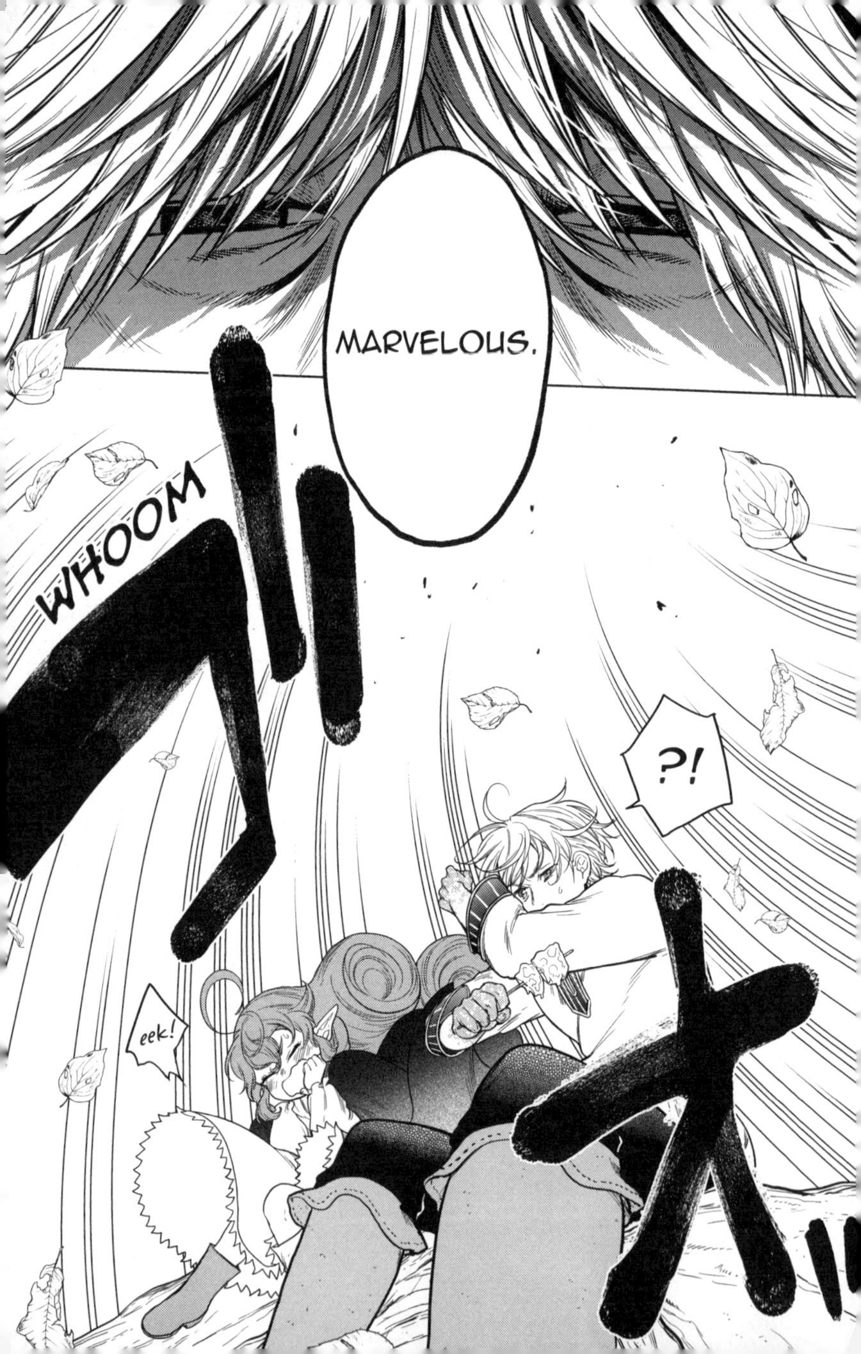
MARVELOUS.
WHOOM
?!
eek!

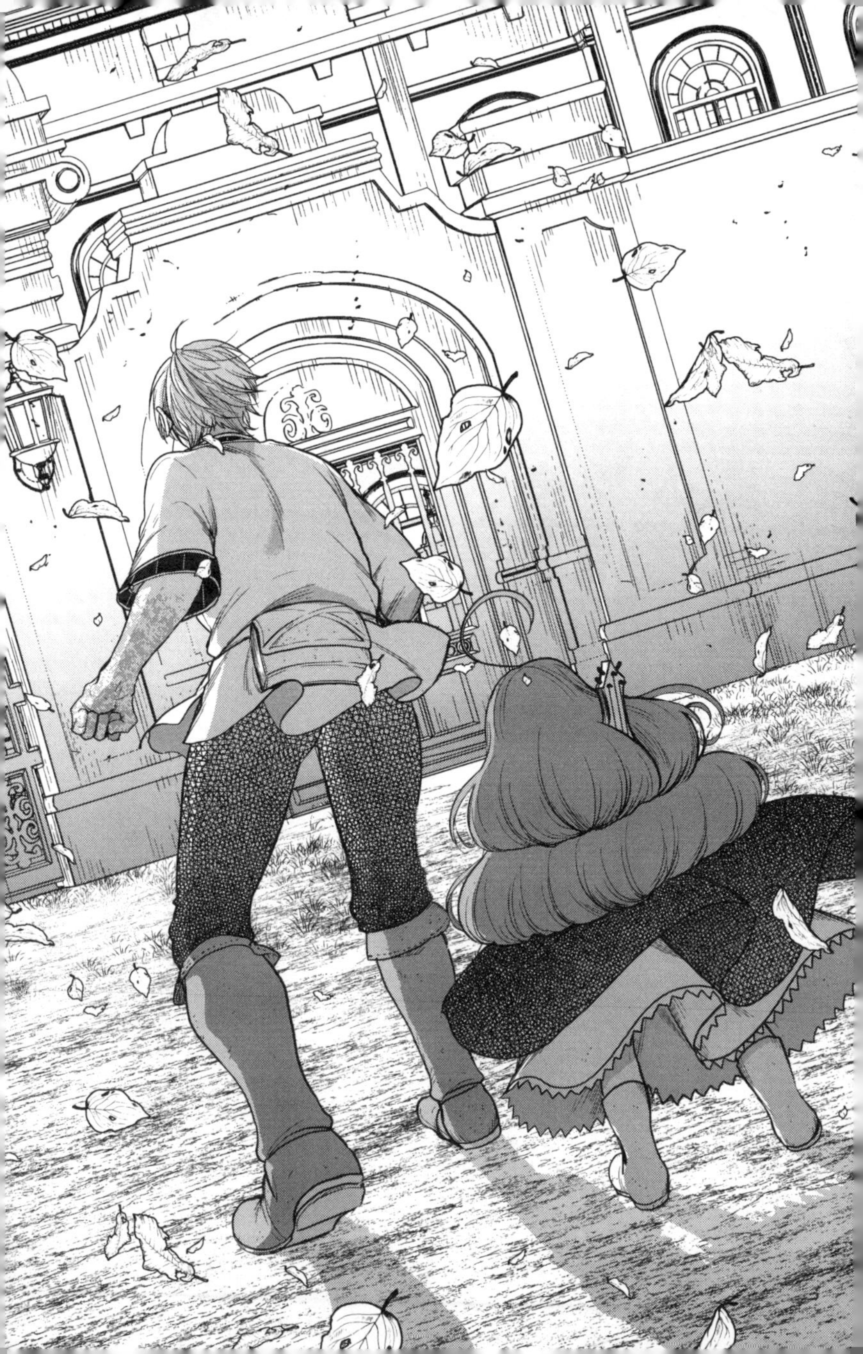

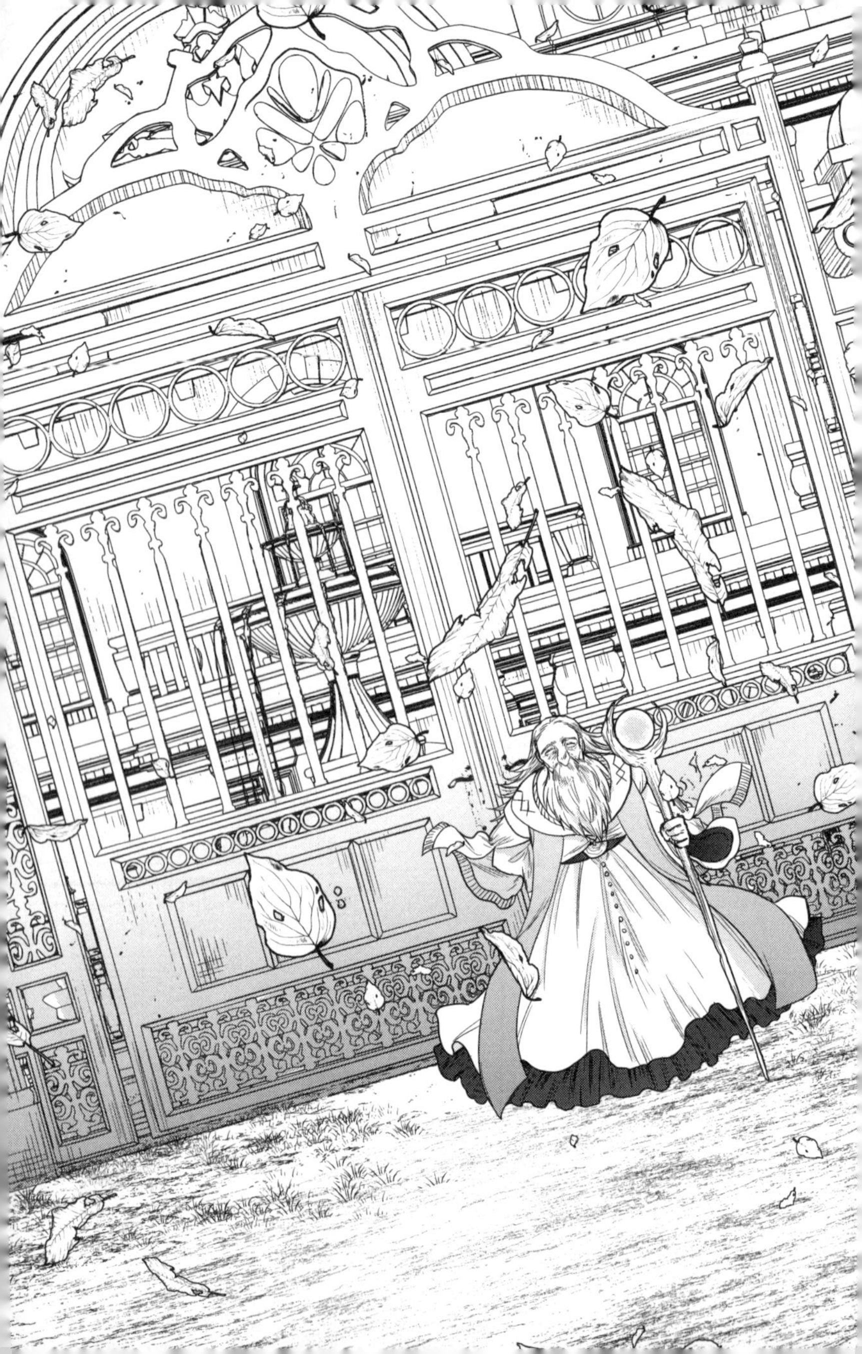

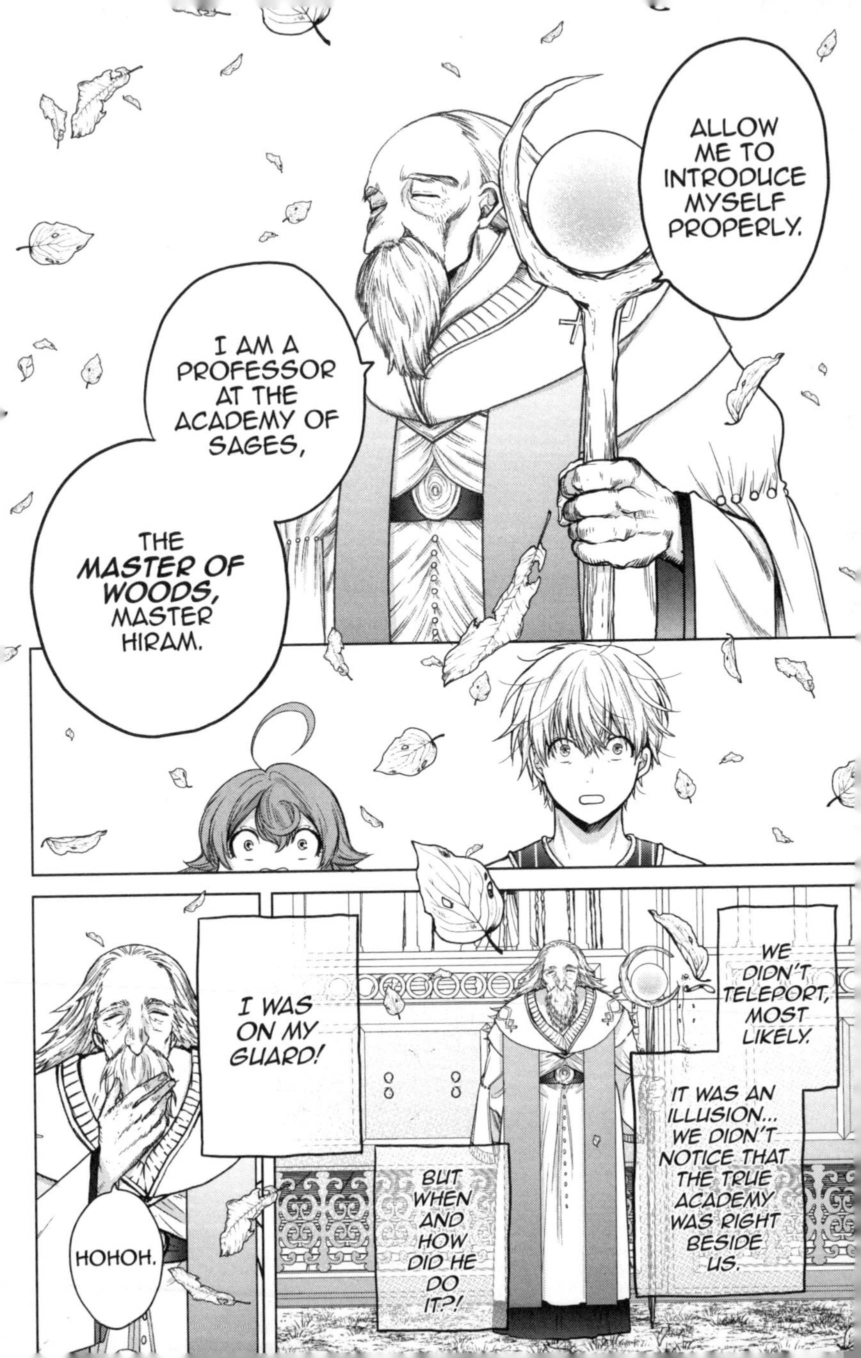
ALLOW ME TO INTRODUCE MYSELF PROPERLY.
I AM A PROFESSOR AT THE ACADEMY OF SAGES,
THE *MASTER OF WOODS,* MASTER HIRAM.
WE DIDN'T TELEPORT, MOST LIKELY.
IT WAS AN ILLUSION... WE DIDN'T NOTICE THAT THE TRUE ACADEMY WAS RIGHT BESIDE US.
BUT WHEN AND HOW DID HE DO IT?!
I WAS ON MY GUARD!
HOHOH.

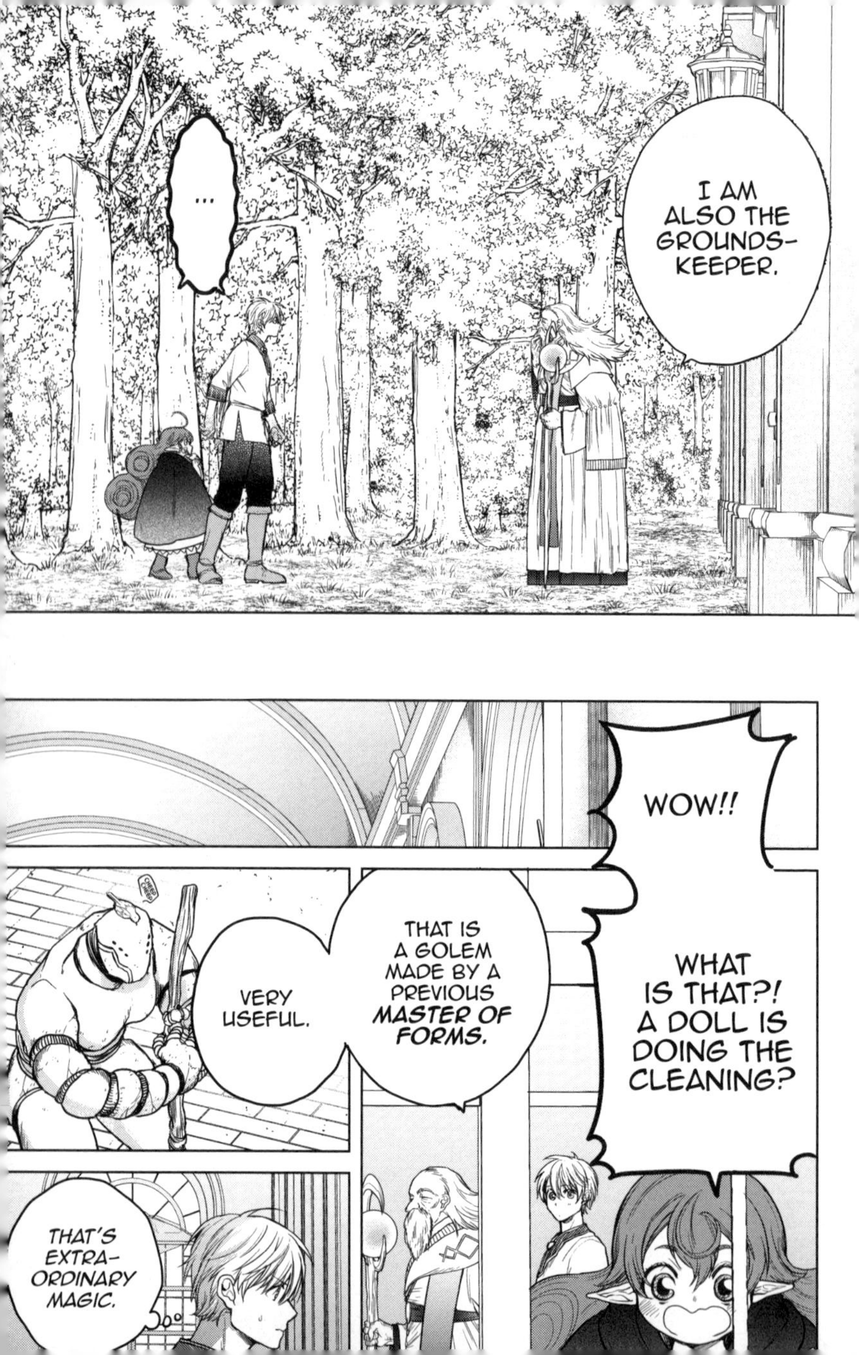
I AM ALSO THE GROUNDS-KEEPER.
...
WOW!!
WHAT IS THAT?! A DOLL IS DOING THE CLEANING?
THAT IS A GOLEM MADE BY A PREVIOUS *MASTER OF FORMS.*
VERY USEFUL.
THAT'S EXTRA-ORDINARY MAGIC.

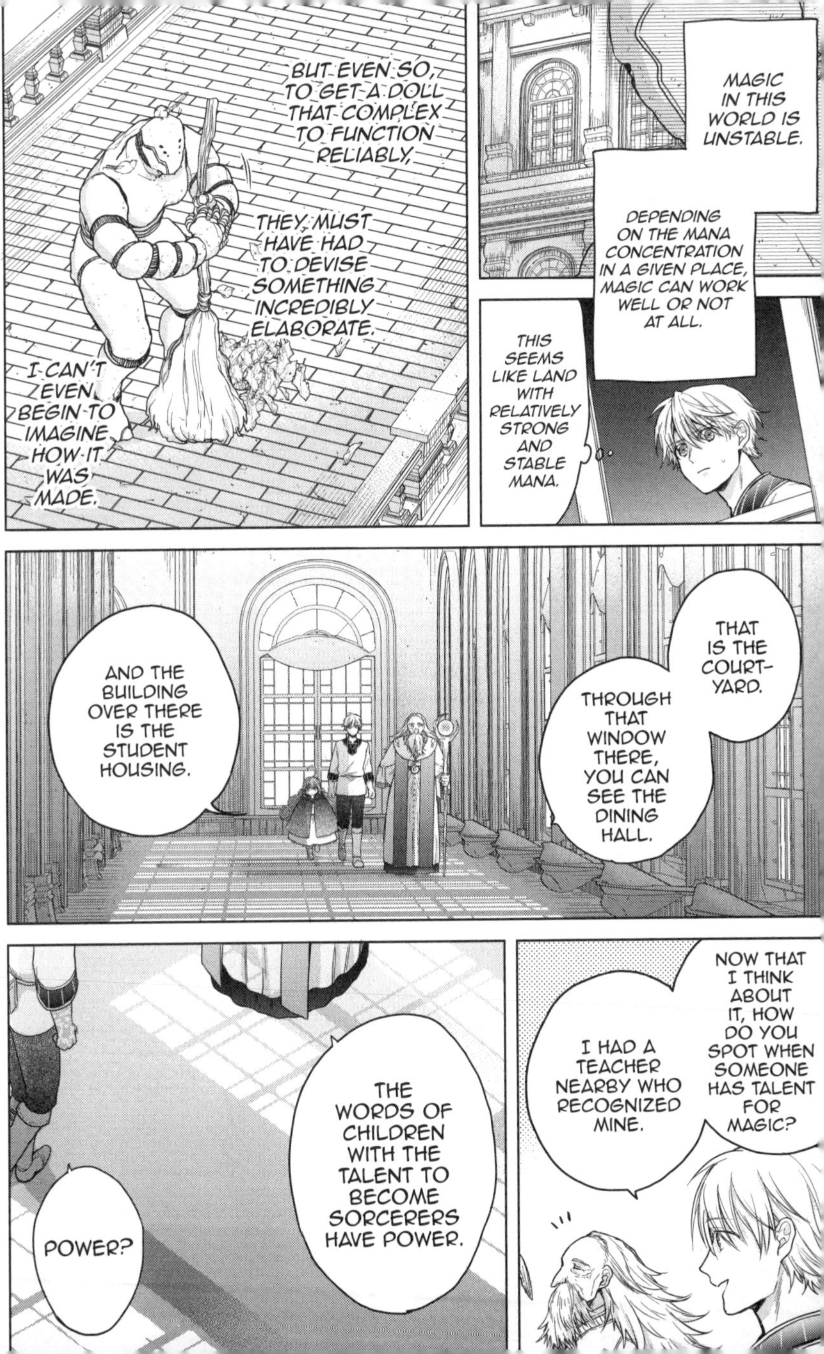
MAGIC IN THIS WORLD IS UNSTABLE.
DEPENDING ON THE MANA CONCENTRATION IN A GIVEN PLACE, MAGIC CAN WORK WELL OR NOT AT ALL.
THIS SEEMS LIKE LAND WITH RELATIVELY STRONG AND STABLE MANA.
BUT EVEN SO, TO GET A DOLL THAT COMPLEX TO FUNCTION RELIABLY,
THEY MUST HAVE HAD TO DEVISE SOMETHING INCREDIBLY ELABORATE.
I CAN'T EVEN BEGIN TO IMAGINE HOW IT WAS MADE.
THAT IS THE COURTYARD.
THROUGH THAT WINDOW THERE, YOU CAN SEE THE DINING HALL.
AND THE BUILDING OVER THERE IS THE STUDENT HOUSING.
NOW THAT I THINK ABOUT IT, HOW DO YOU SPOT WHEN SOMEONE HAS TALENT FOR MAGIC?
I HAD A TEACHER NEARBY WHO RECOGNIZED MINE.
THE WORDS OF CHILDREN WITH THE TALENT TO BECOME SORCERERS HAVE POWER.
POWER?

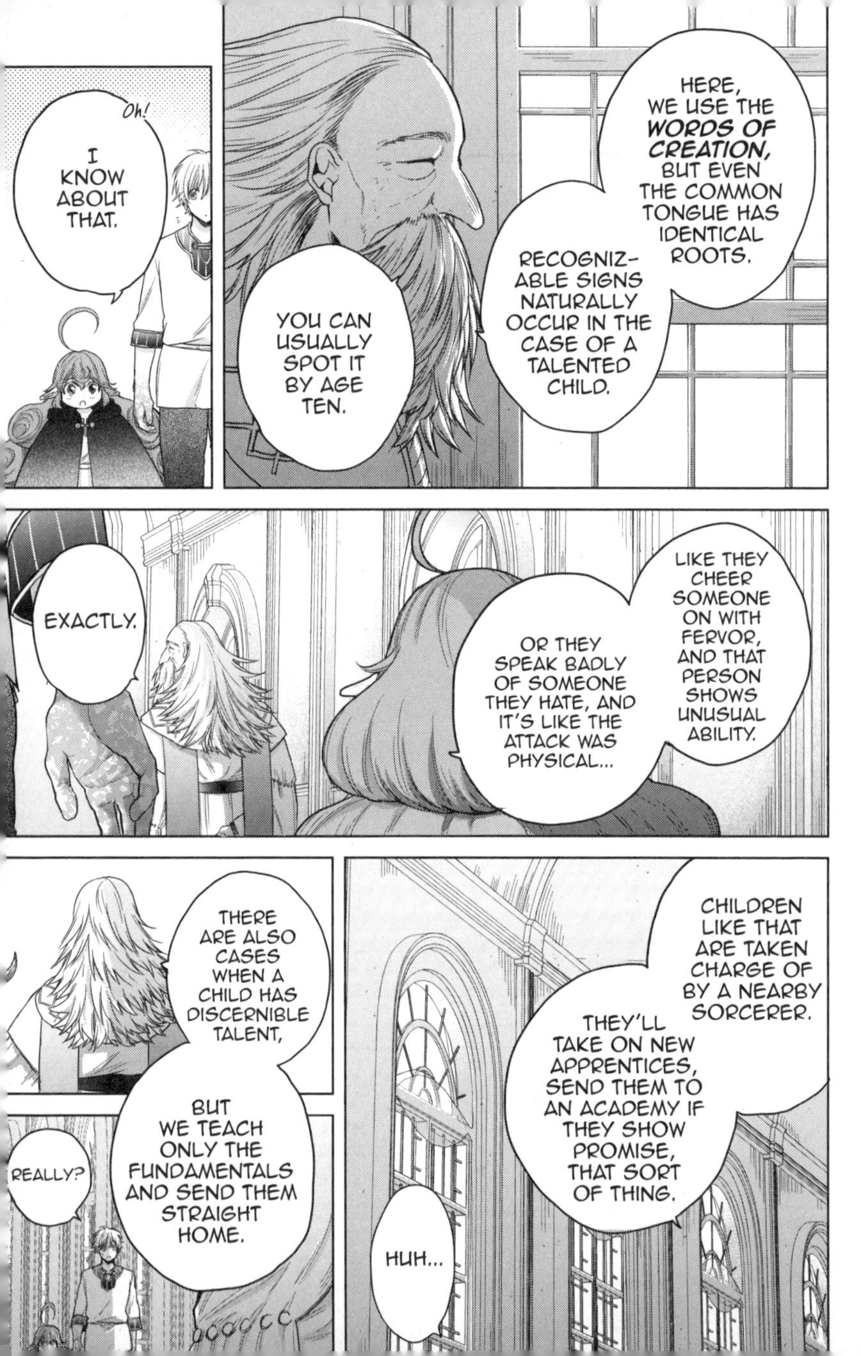
HERE, WE USE THE ***WORDS OF CREATION,*** BUT EVEN THE COMMON TONGUE HAS IDENTICAL ROOTS.
RECOGNIZ-ABLE SIGNS NATURALLY OCCUR IN THE CASE OF A TALENTED CHILD.
YOU CAN USUALLY SPOT IT BY AGE TEN.
Oh!
I KNOW ABOUT THAT.
LIKE THEY CHEER SOMEONE ON WITH FERVOR, AND THAT PERSON SHOWS UNUSUAL ABILITY.
OR THEY SPEAK BADLY OF SOMEONE THEY HATE, AND IT'S LIKE THE ATTACK WAS PHYSICAL...
EXACTLY.
CHILDREN LIKE THAT ARE TAKEN CHARGE OF BY A NEARBY SORCERER.
THEY'LL TAKE ON NEW APPRENTICES, SEND THEM TO AN ACADEMY IF THEY SHOW PROMISE, THAT SORT OF THING.
HUH...
THERE ARE ALSO CASES WHEN A CHILD HAS DISCERNIBLE TALENT,
BUT WE TEACH ONLY THE FUNDAMENTALS AND SEND THEM STRAIGHT HOME.
REALLY?

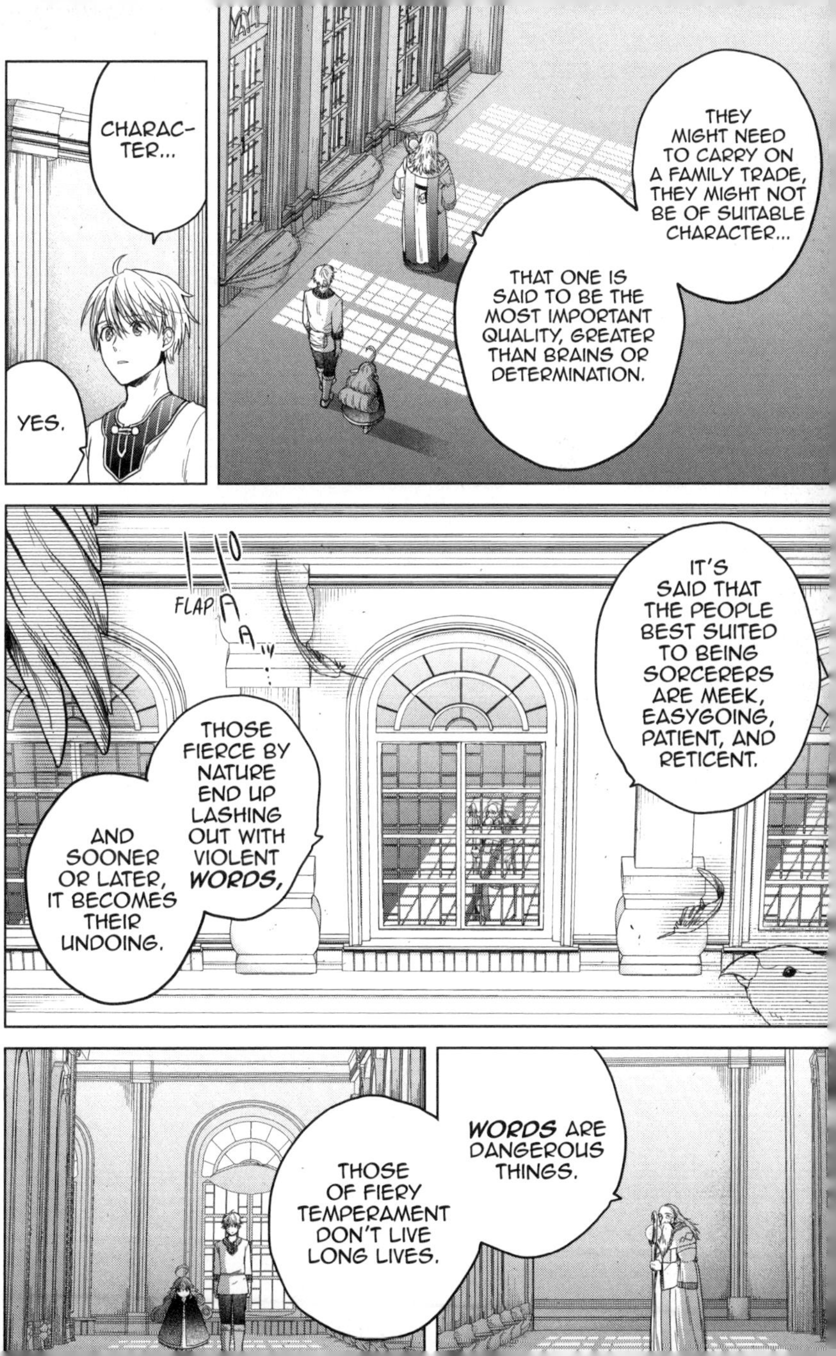
THEY MIGHT NEED TO CARRY ON A FAMILY TRADE, THEY MIGHT NOT BE OF SUITABLE CHARACTER...
THAT ONE IS SAID TO BE THE MOST IMPORTANT QUALITY, GREATER THAN BRAINS OR DETERMINATION.
CHARAC-TER...
YES.
IT'S SAID THAT THE PEOPLE BEST SUITED TO BEING SORCERERS ARE MEEK, EASYGOING, PATIENT, AND RETICENT.
FLAP
THOSE FIERCE BY NATURE END UP LASHING OUT WITH VIOLENT WORDS,
AND SOONER OR LATER, IT BECOMES THEIR UNDOING.
WORDS ARE DANGEROUS THINGS.
THOSE OF FIERY TEMPERAMENT DON'T LIVE LONG LIVES.

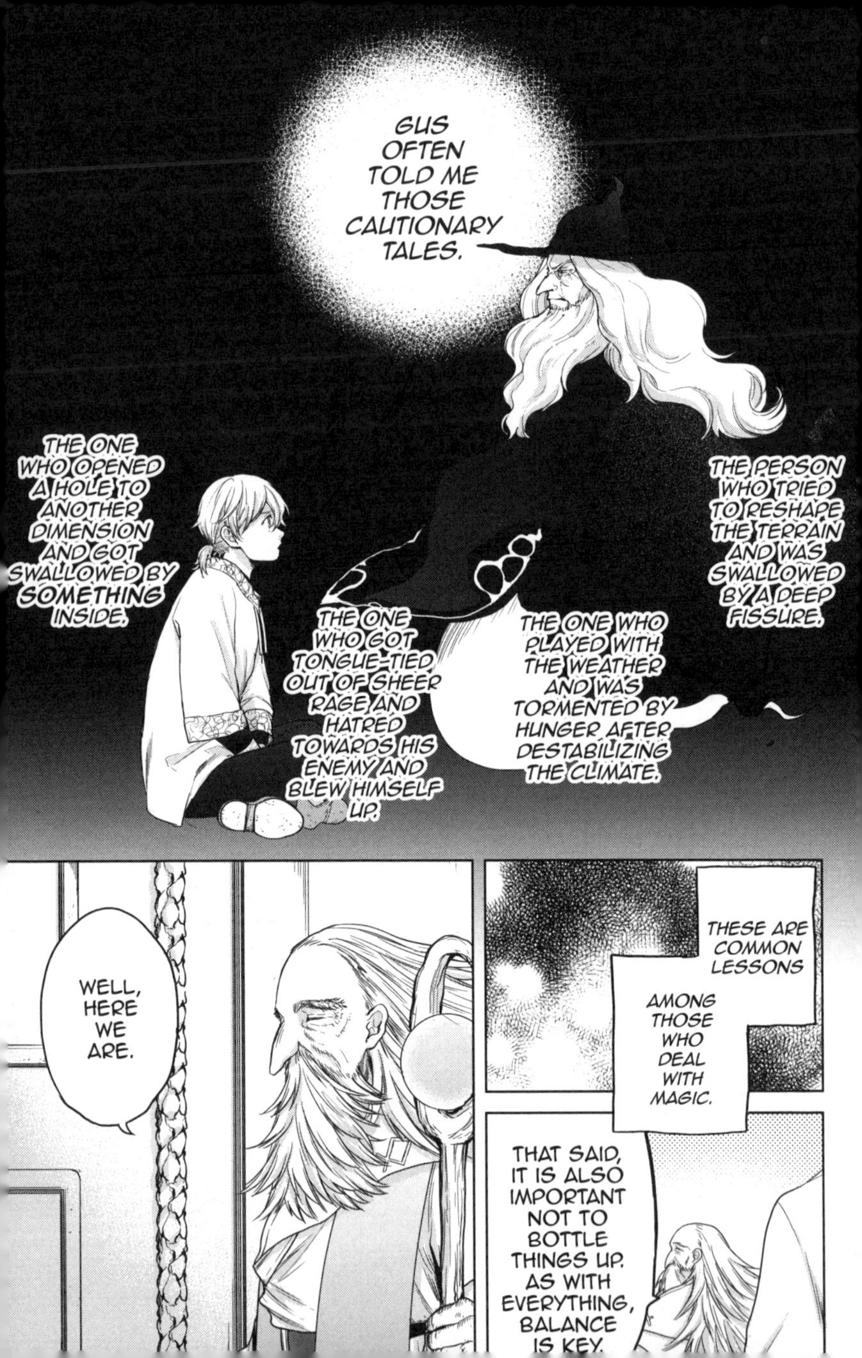
GUS OFTEN TOLD ME THOSE CAUTIONARY TALES.
THE PERSON WHO TRIED TO RESHAPE THE TERRAIN AND WAS SWALLOWED BY A DEEP FISSURE.
THE ONE WHO PLAYED WITH THE WEATHER AND WAS TORMENTED BY HUNGER AFTER DESTABILIZING THE CLIMATE.
THE ONE WHO GOT TONGUE-TIED OUT OF SHEER RAGE AND HATRED TOWARDS HIS ENEMY AND BLEW HIMSELF UP.
THE ONE WHO OPENED A HOLE TO ANOTHER DIMENSION AND GOT SWALLOWED BY SOMETHING INSIDE.
THESE ARE COMMON LESSONS
AMONG THOSE WHO DEAL WITH MAGIC.
THAT SAID, IT IS ALSO IMPORTANT NOT TO BOTTLE THINGS UP. AS WITH EVERYTHING, BALANCE IS KEY.
WELL, HERE WE ARE.

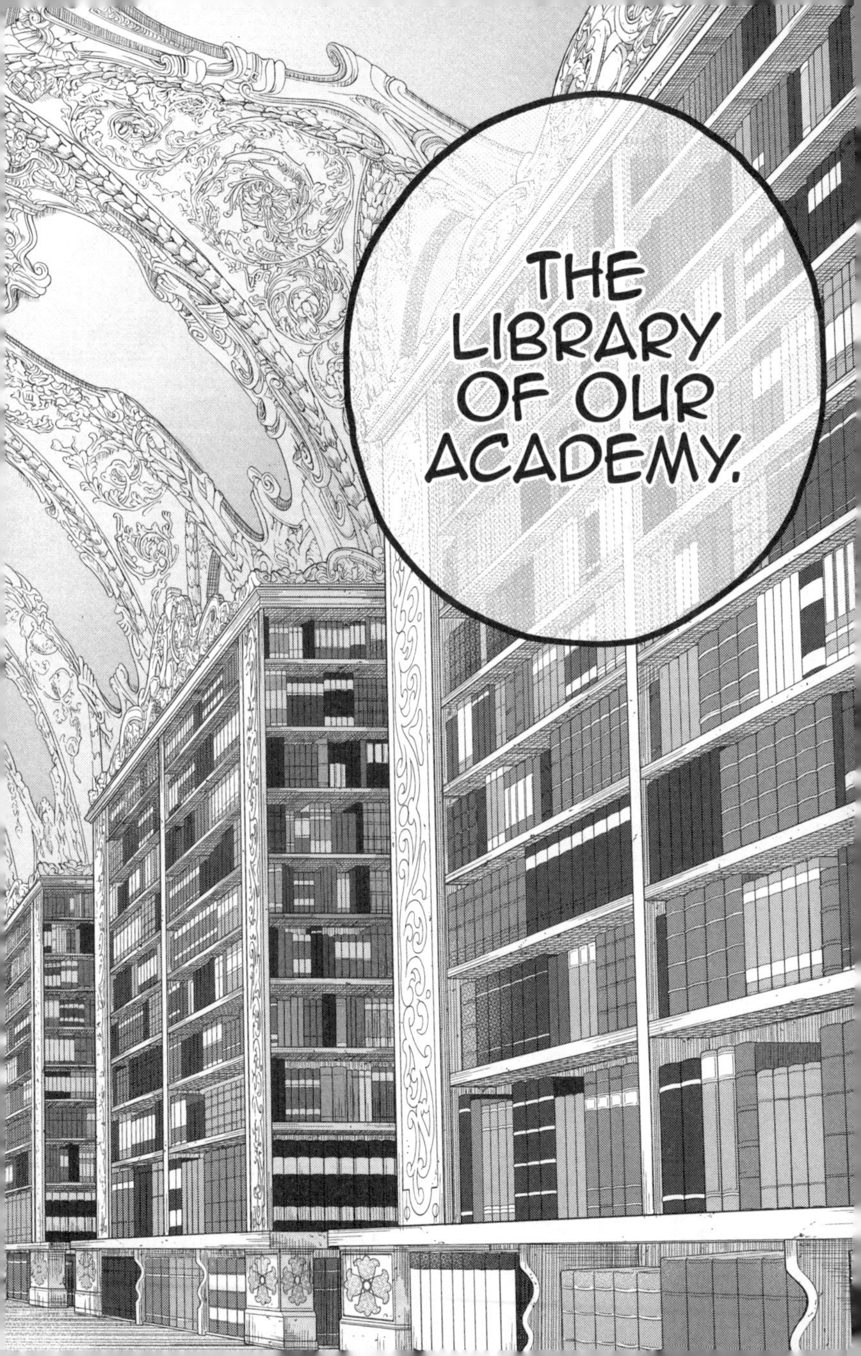
THE LIBRARY OF OUR ACADEMY.

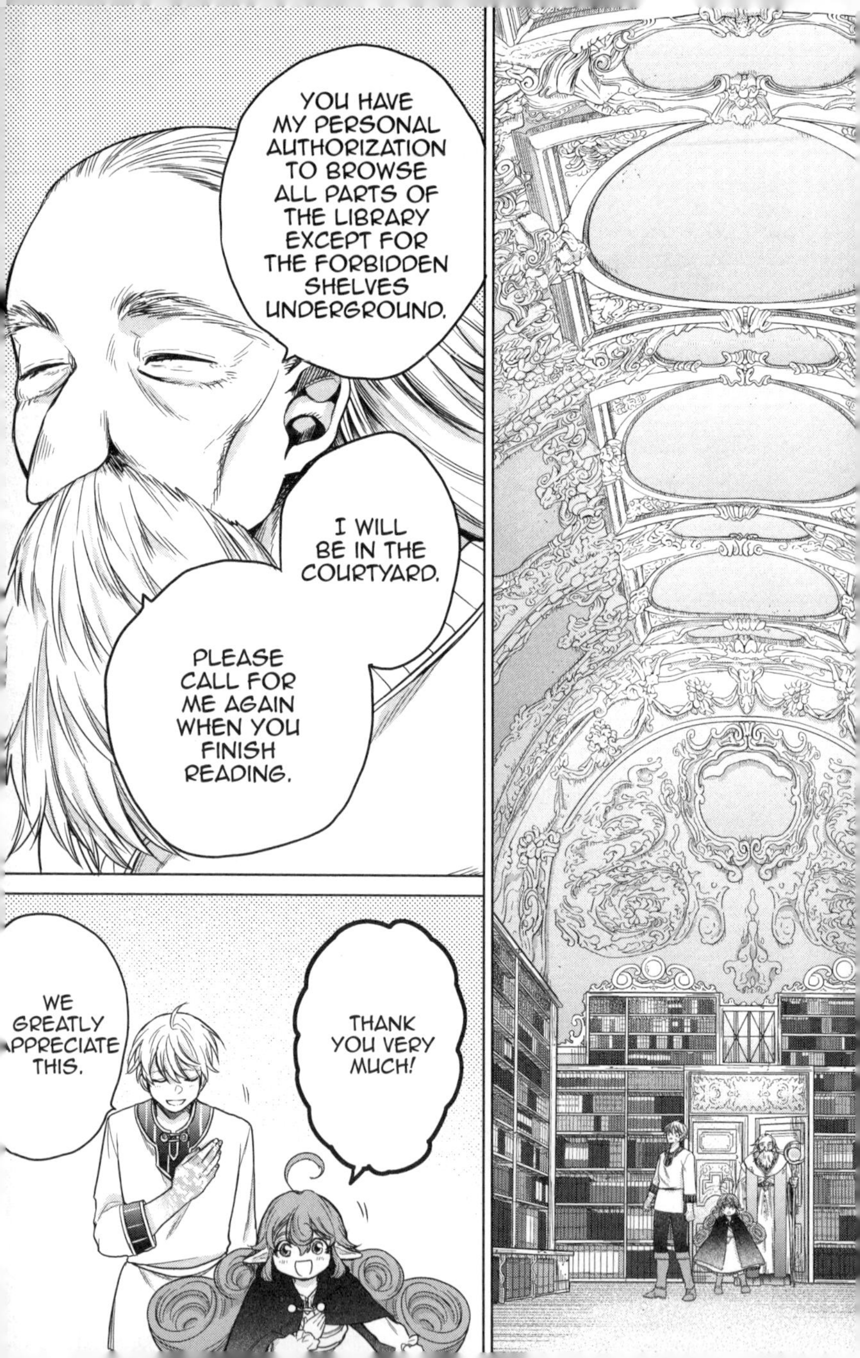
YOU HAVE MY PERSONAL AUTHORIZATION TO BROWSE ALL PARTS OF THE LIBRARY EXCEPT FOR THE FORBIDDEN SHELVES UNDERGROUND.
I WILL BE IN THE COURTYARD.
PLEASE CALL FOR ME AGAIN WHEN YOU FINISH READING.
THANK YOU VERY MUCH!
WE GREATLY APPRECIATE THIS.

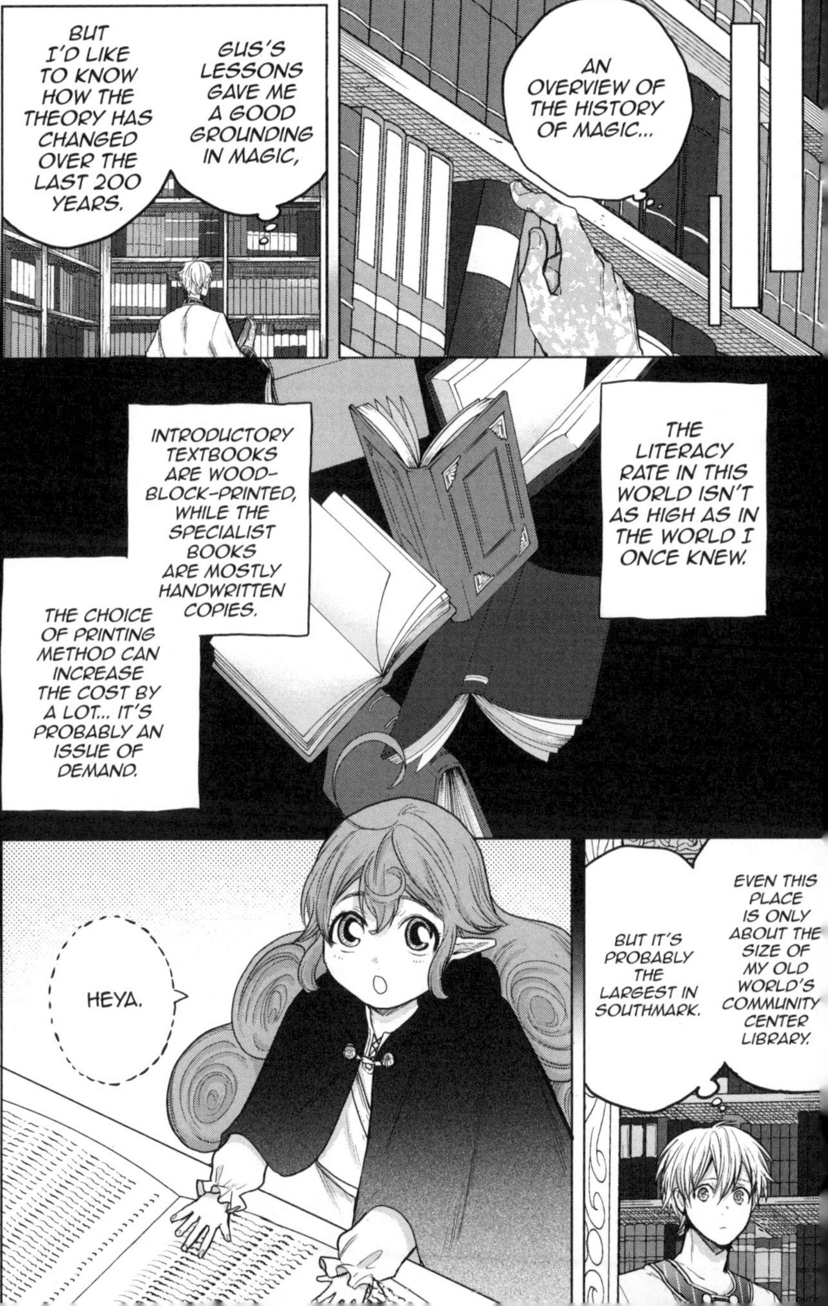
AN OVERVIEW OF THE HISTORY OF MAGIC...
GUS'S LESSONS GAVE ME A GOOD GROUNDING IN MAGIC,
BUT I'D LIKE TO KNOW HOW THE THEORY HAS CHANGED OVER THE LAST 200 YEARS.
THE LITERACY RATE IN THIS WORLD ISN'T AS HIGH AS IN THE WORLD I ONCE KNEW.
INTRODUCTORY TEXTBOOKS ARE WOOD-BLOCK-PRINTED, WHILE THE SPECIALIST BOOKS ARE MOSTLY HANDWRITTEN COPIES.
THE CHOICE OF PRINTING METHOD CAN INCREASE THE COST BY A LOT... IT'S PROBABLY AN ISSUE OF DEMAND.
EVEN THIS PLACE IS ONLY ABOUT THE SIZE OF MY OLD WORLD'S COMMUNITY CENTER LIBRARY.
BUT IT'S PROBABLY THE LARGEST IN SOUTHMARK.
HEYA.

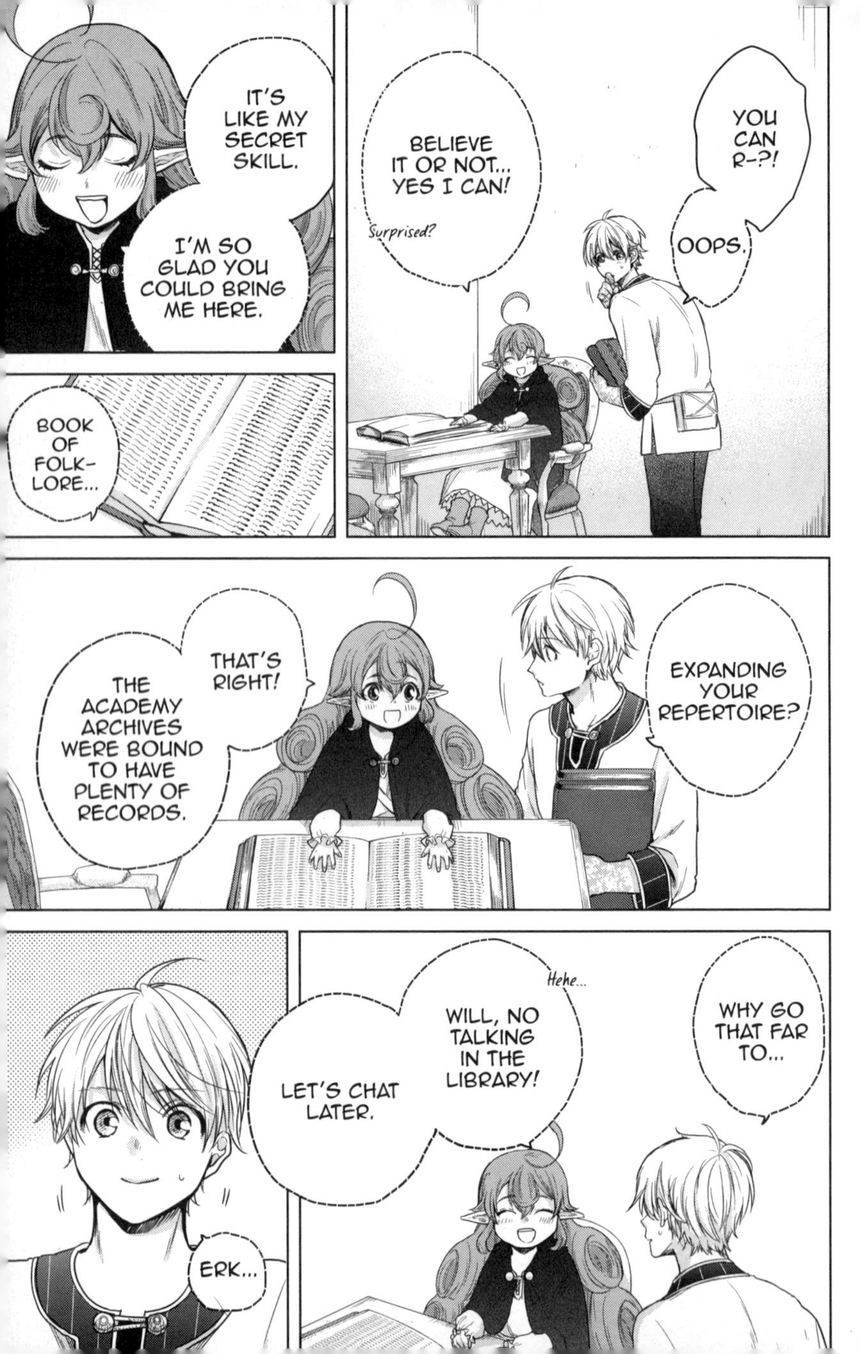
YOU CAN R-?!
OOPS.
BELIEVE IT OR NOT... YES I CAN!
Surprised?
IT'S LIKE MY SECRET SKILL.
I'M SO GLAD YOU COULD BRING ME HERE.
BOOK OF FOLK-LORE...
EXPANDING YOUR REPERTOIRE?
THAT'S RIGHT!
THE ACADEMY ARCHIVES WERE BOUND TO HAVE PLENTY OF RECORDS.
WHY GO THAT FAR TO...
Hehe...
WILL, NO TALKING IN THE LIBRARY!
LET'S CHAT LATER.
ERK...

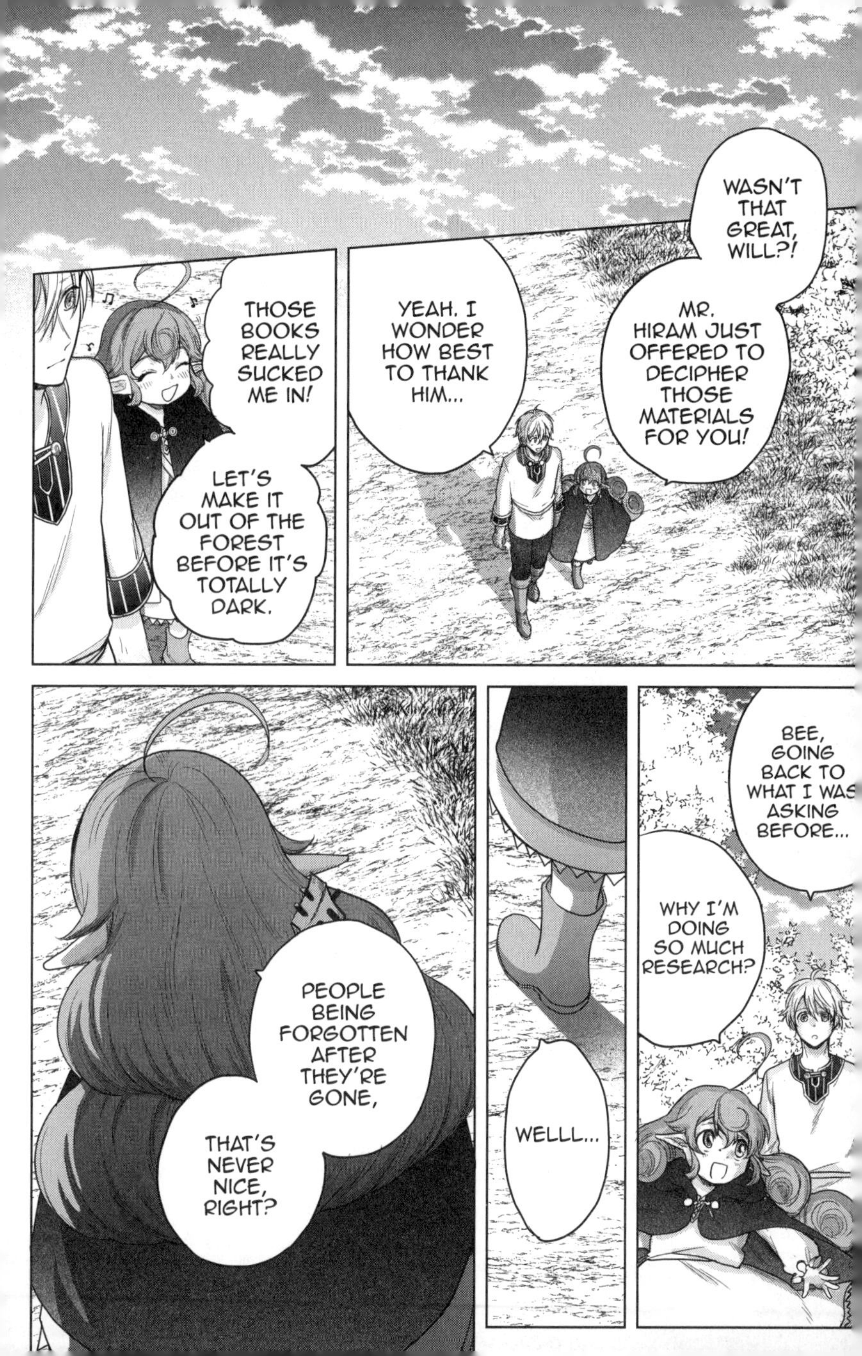
WASN'T THAT GREAT, WILL?!
MR. HIRAM JUST OFFERED TO DECIPHER THOSE MATERIALS FOR YOU!
YEAH. I WONDER HOW BEST TO THANK HIM...
THOSE BOOKS REALLY SUCKED ME IN!
LET'S MAKE IT OUT OF THE FOREST BEFORE IT'S TOTALLY DARK.
BEE, GOING BACK TO WHAT I WAS ASKING BEFORE...
WHY I'M DOING SO MUCH RESEARCH?
WELLL...
PEOPLE BEING FORGOTTEN AFTER THEY'RE GONE,
THAT'S NEVER NICE, RIGHT?

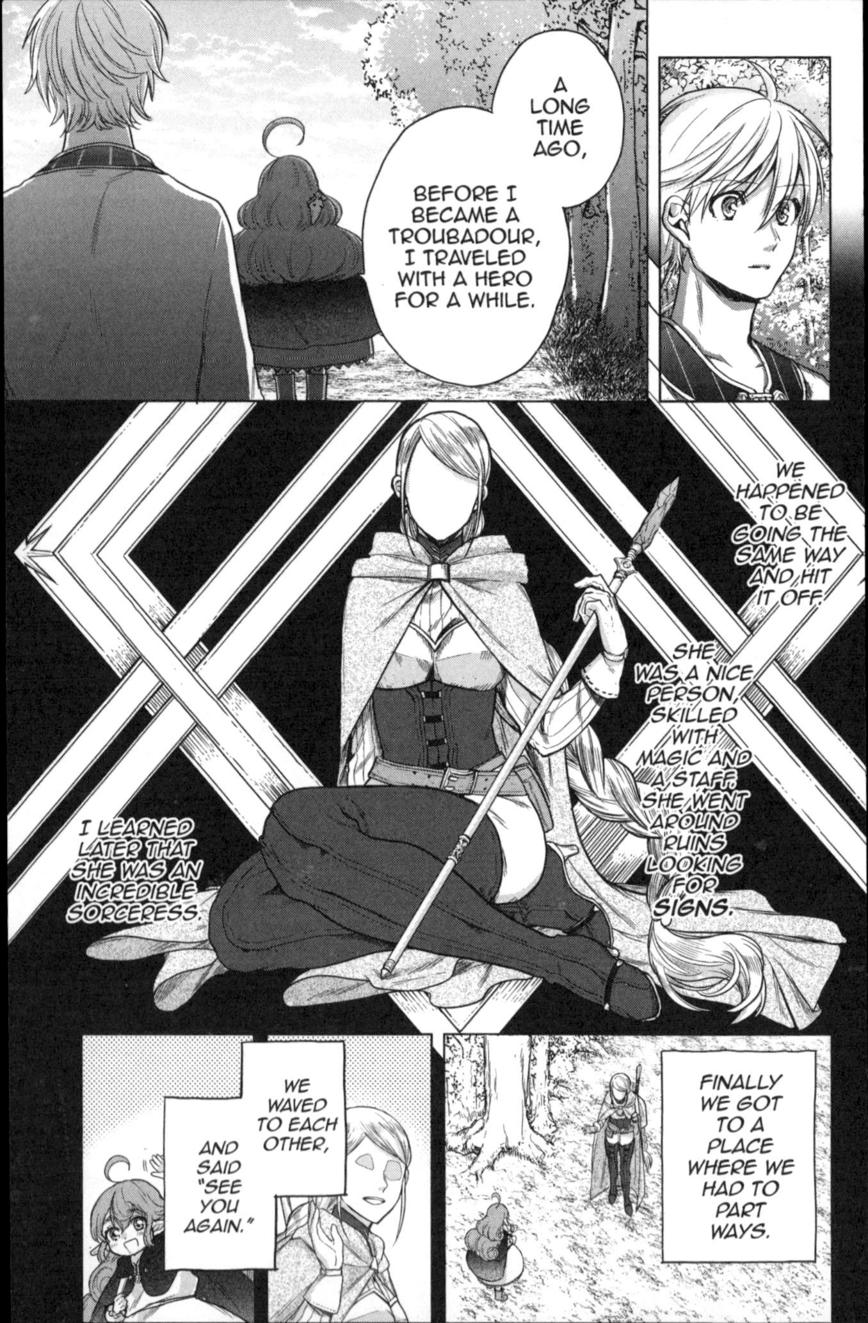
A LONG TIME AGO,
BEFORE I BECAME A TROUBADOUR, I TRAVELED WITH A HERO FOR A WHILE.
WE HAPPENED TO BE GOING THE SAME WAY AND HIT IT OFF.
SHE WAS A NICE PERSON, SKILLED WITH MAGIC AND A STAFF. SHE WENT AROUND RUINS LOOKING FOR SIGNS.
I LEARNED LATER THAT SHE WAS AN INCREDIBLE SORCERESS.
FINALLY WE GOT TO A PLACE WHERE WE HAD TO PART WAYS.
WE WAVED TO EACH OTHER,
AND SAID "SEE YOU AGAIN."

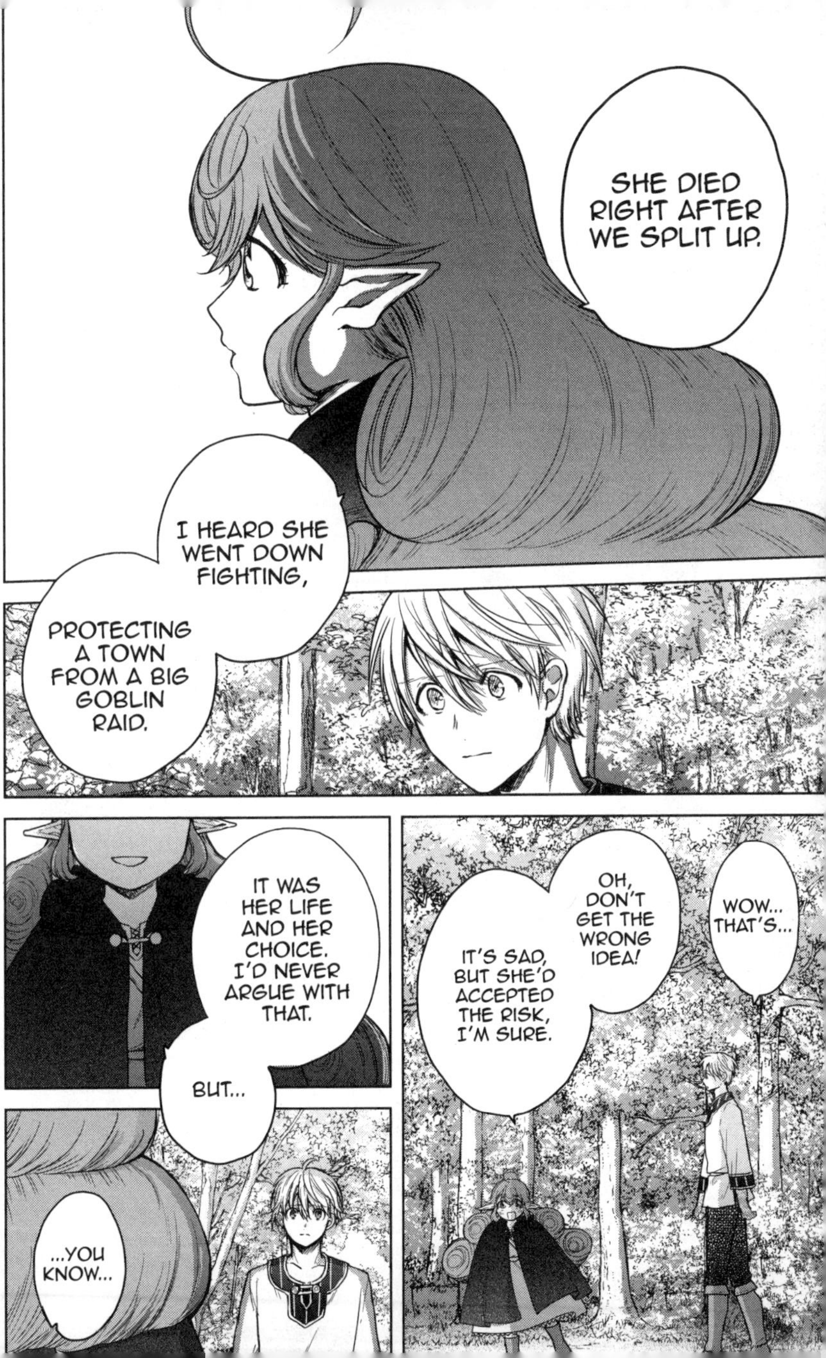
SHE DIED RIGHT AFTER WE SPLIT UP.
I HEARD SHE WENT DOWN FIGHTING,
PROTECTING A TOWN FROM A BIG GOBLIN RAID.
WOW... THAT'S...
OH, DON'T GET THE WRONG IDEA!
IT'S SAD, BUT SHE'D ACCEPTED THE RISK, I'M SURE.
IT WAS HER LIFE AND HER CHOICE. I'D NEVER ARGUE WITH THAT.
BUT...
...YOU KNOW...

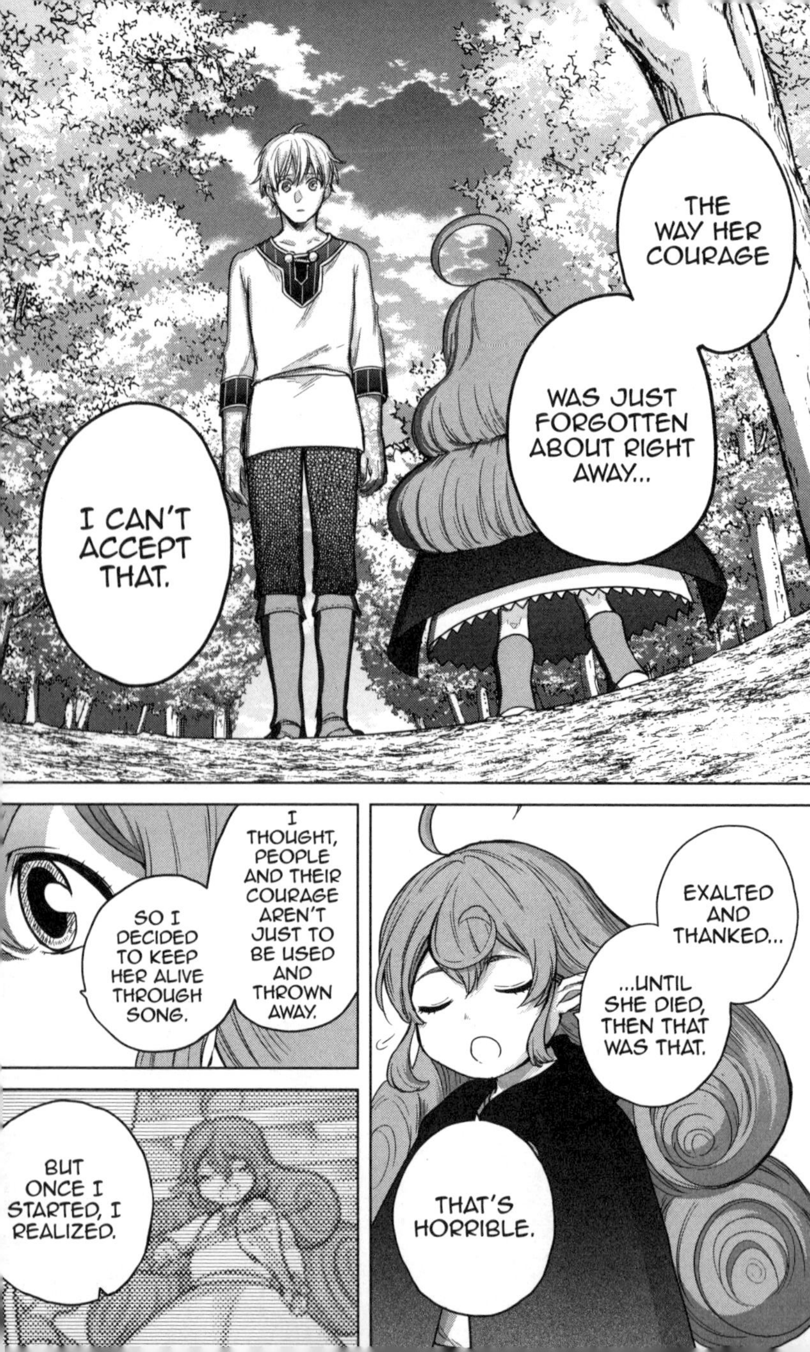
THE WAY HER COURAGE
WAS JUST FORGOTTEN ABOUT RIGHT AWAY...
I CAN'T ACCEPT THAT.
EXALTED AND THANKED...
...UNTIL SHE DIED, THEN THAT WAS THAT.
THAT'S HORRIBLE.
I THOUGHT, PEOPLE AND THEIR COURAGE AREN'T JUST TO BE USED AND THROWN AWAY.
SO I DECIDED TO KEEP HER ALIVE THROUGH SONG.
BUT ONCE I STARTED, I REALIZED.

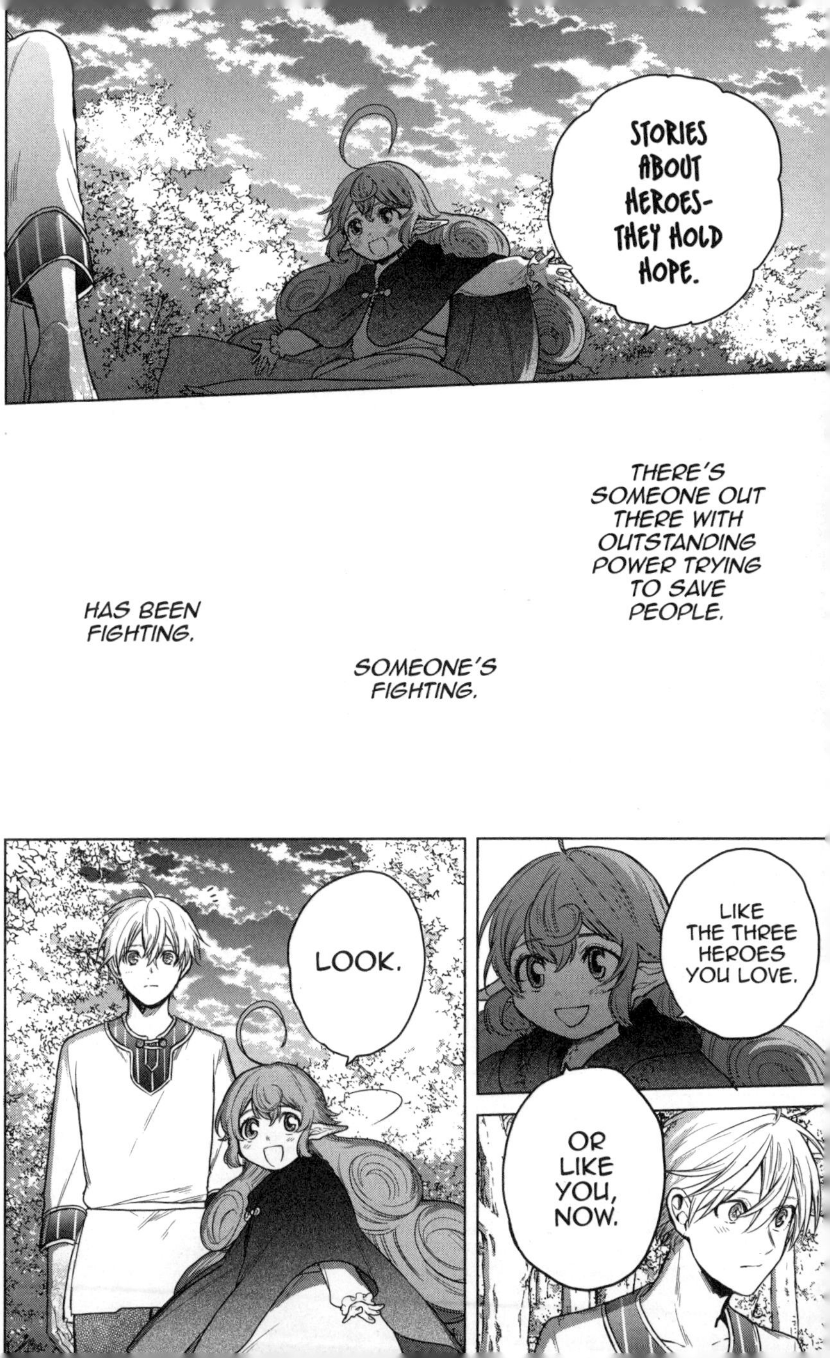
STORIES ABOUT HEROES- THEY HOLD HOPE.
THERE'S SOMEONE OUT THERE WITH OUTSTANDING POWER TRYING TO SAVE PEOPLE.
SOMEONE'S FIGHTING.
HAS BEEN FIGHTING.
LIKE THE THREE HEROES YOU LOVE.
OR LIKE YOU, NOW.
LOOK.

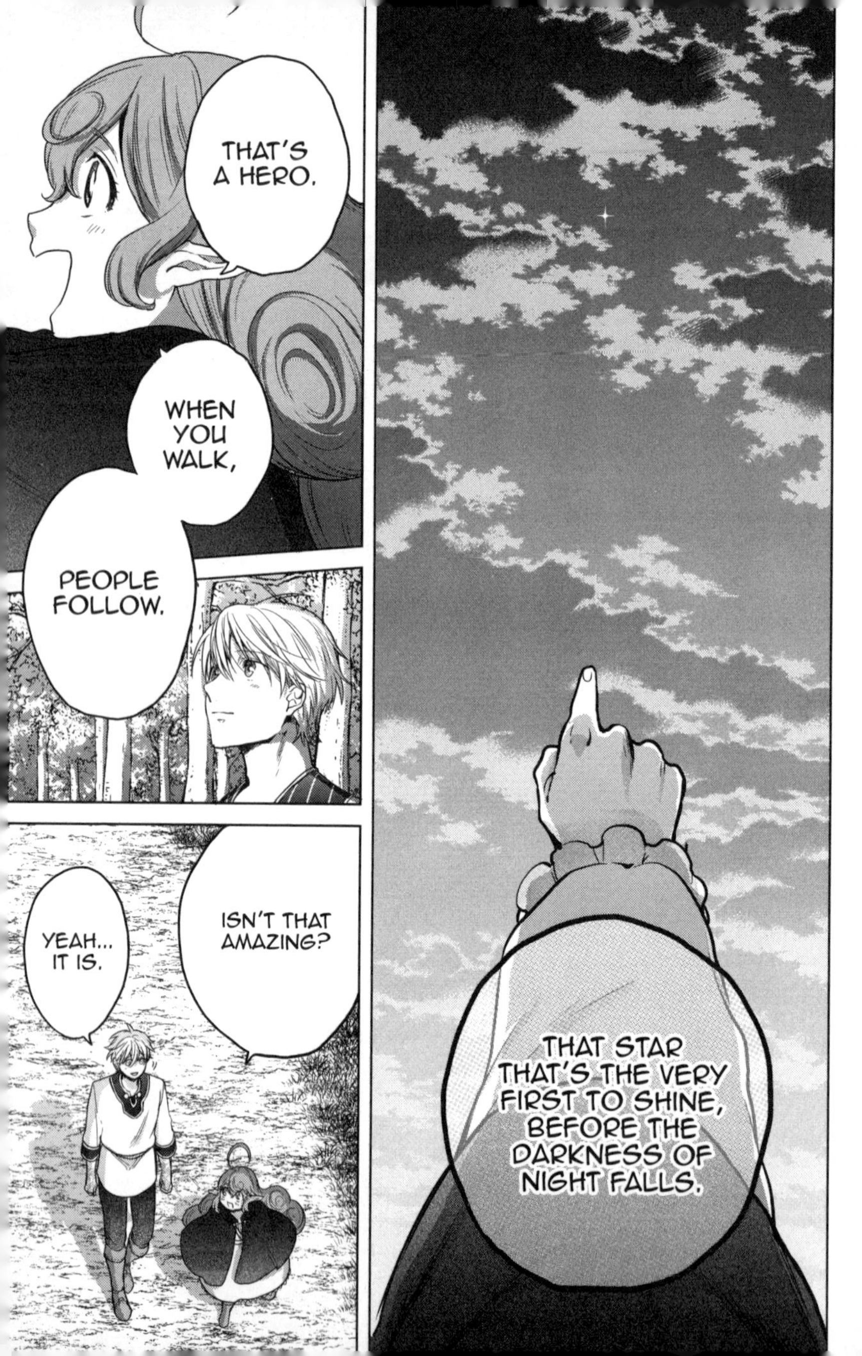
THAT STAR THAT'S THE VERY FIRST TO SHINE, BEFORE THE DARKNESS OF NIGHT FALLS.
THAT'S A HERO.
WHEN YOU WALK,
PEOPLE FOLLOW.
ISN'T THAT AMAZING?
YEAH... IT IS.

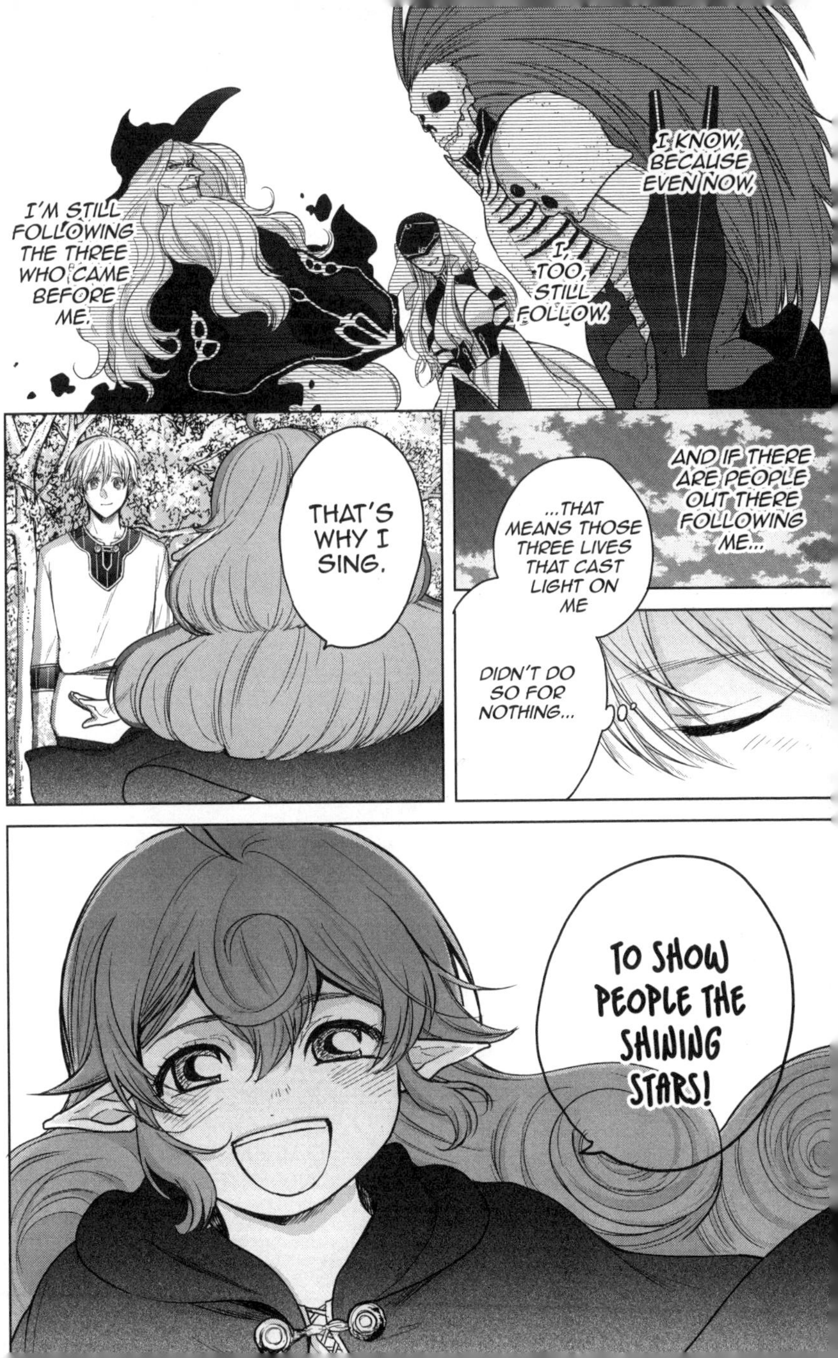
I KNOW, BECAUSE EVEN NOW,
I, TOO, STILL FOLLOW.
I'M STILL FOLLOWING THE THREE WHO CAME BEFORE ME.
AND IF THERE ARE PEOPLE OUT THERE FOLLOWING ME...
...THAT MEANS THOSE THREE LIVES THAT CAST LIGHT ON ME
DIDN'T DO SO FOR NOTHING...
THAT'S WHY I SING.
TO SHOW PEOPLE THE SHINING STARS!

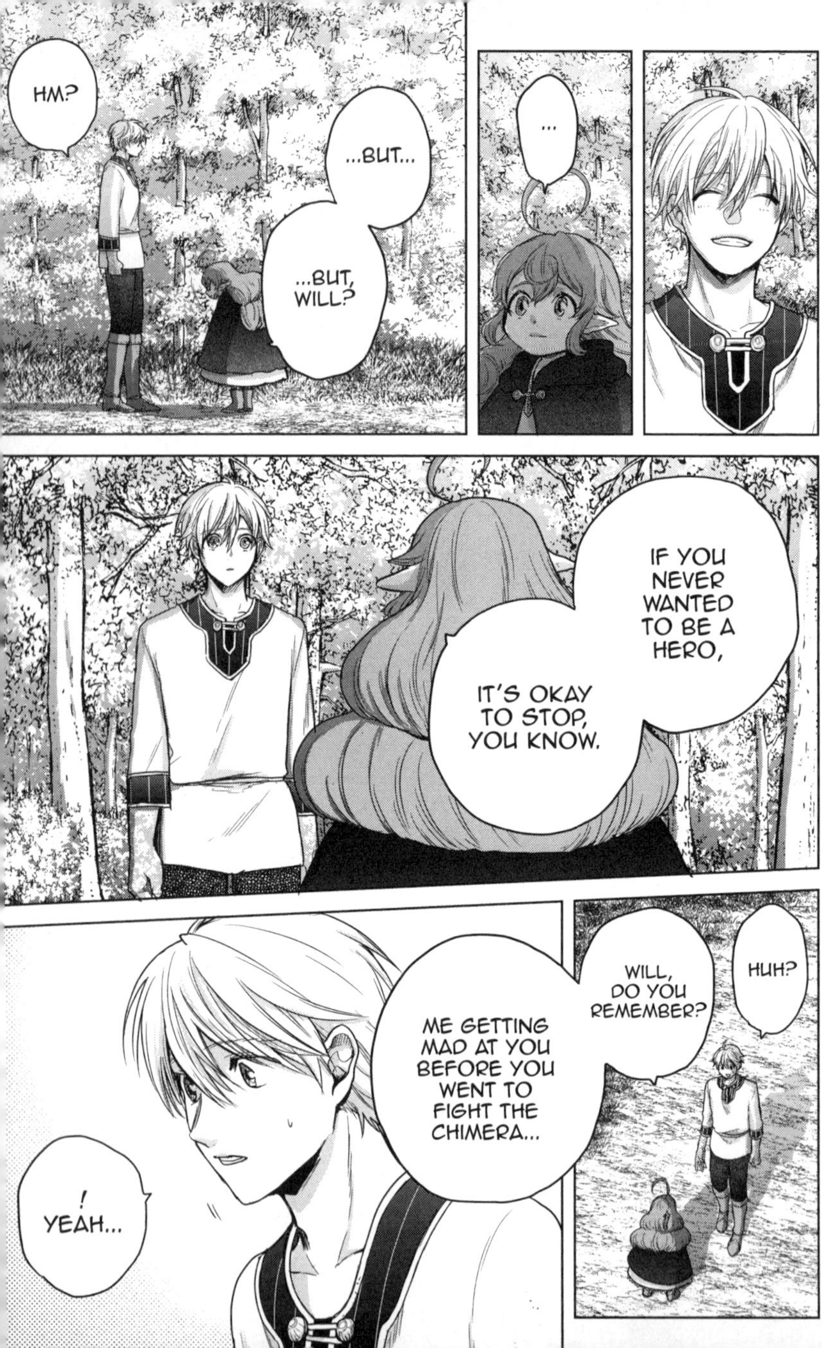
...
...BUT...
HM?
...BUT, WILL?
IF YOU NEVER WANTED TO BE A HERO,
IT'S OKAY TO STOP, YOU KNOW.
HUH?
WILL, DO YOU REMEMBER?
ME GETTING MAD AT YOU BEFORE YOU WENT TO FIGHT THE CHIMERA...
! YEAH...

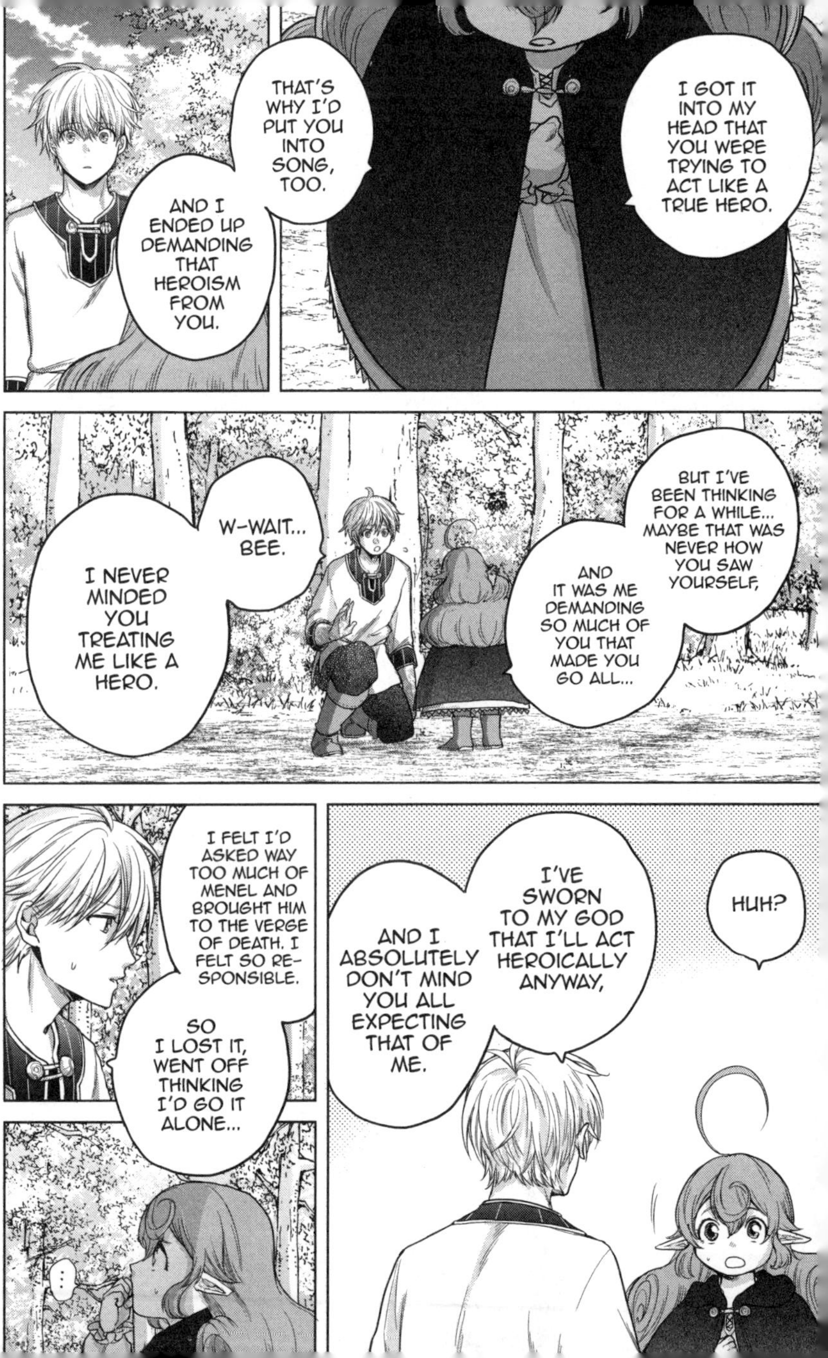
I GOT IT INTO MY HEAD THAT YOU WERE TRYING TO ACT LIKE A TRUE HERO.
THAT'S WHY I'D PUT YOU INTO SONG, TOO.
AND I ENDED UP DEMANDING THAT HEROISM FROM YOU.
BUT I'VE BEEN THINKING FOR A WHILE... MAYBE THAT WAS NEVER HOW YOU SAW YOURSELF,
AND IT WAS ME DEMANDING SO MUCH OF YOU THAT MADE YOU GO ALL...
W-WAIT... BEE.
I NEVER MINDED YOU TREATING ME LIKE A HERO.
HUH?
I'VE SWORN TO MY GOD THAT I'LL ACT HEROICALLY ANYWAY,
AND I ABSOLUTELY DON'T MIND YOU ALL EXPECTING THAT OF ME.
I FELT I'D ASKED WAY TOO MUCH OF MENEL AND BROUGHT HIM TO THE VERGE OF DEATH. I FELT SO RE-SPONSIBLE.
SO I LOST IT, WENT OFF THINKING I'D GO IT ALONE...
...

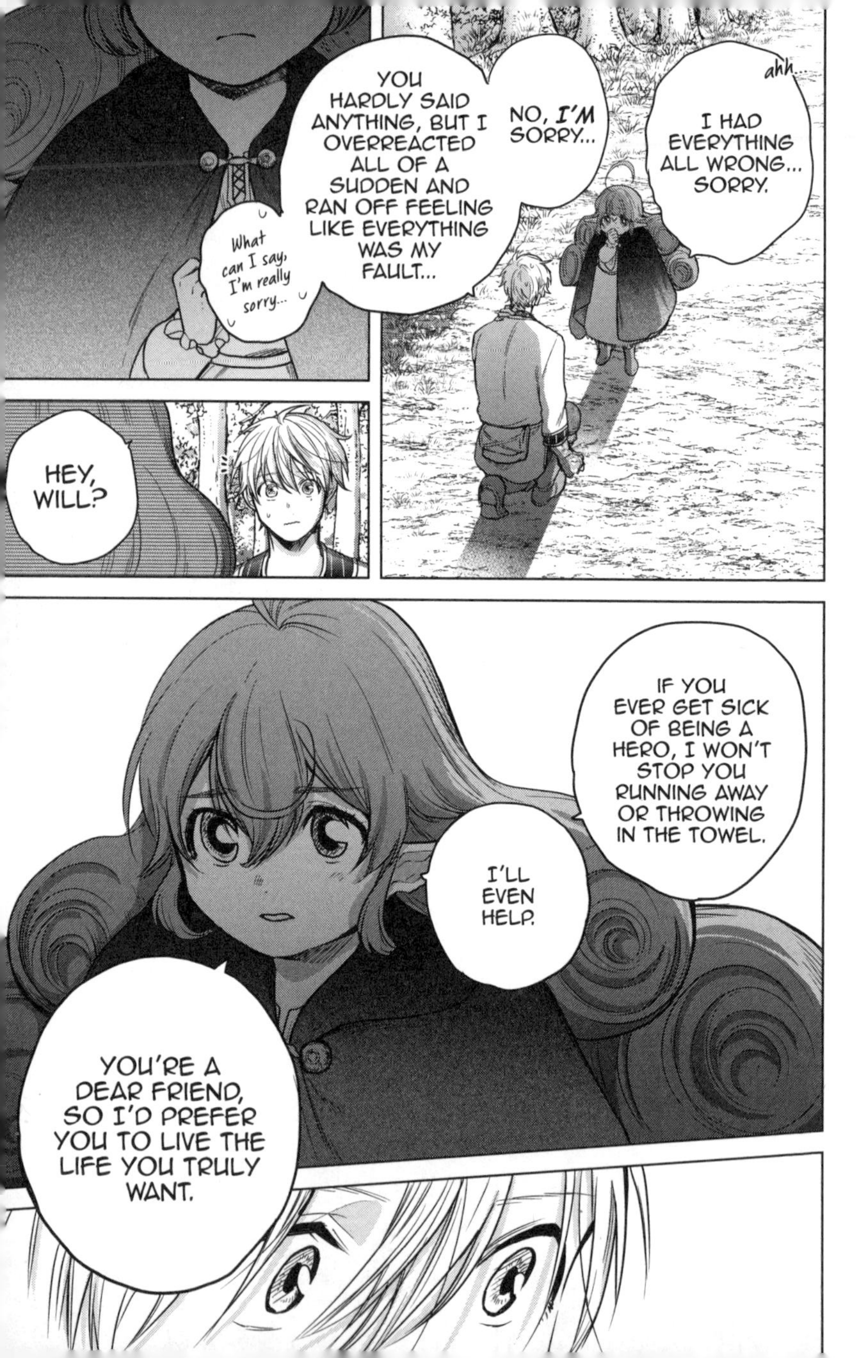
ahh...
I HAD EVERYTHING ALL WRONG... SORRY.
NO, *I'M* SORRY...
YOU HARDLY SAID ANYTHING, BUT I OVERREACTED ALL OF A SUDDEN AND RAN OFF FEELING LIKE EVERYTHING WAS MY FAULT...
What can I say, I'm really sorry...
HEY, WILL?
IF YOU EVER GET SICK OF BEING A HERO, I WON'T STOP YOU RUNNING AWAY OR THROWING IN THE TOWEL.
I'LL EVEN HELP.
YOU'RE A DEAR FRIEND, SO I'D PREFER YOU TO LIVE THE LIFE YOU TRULY WANT.

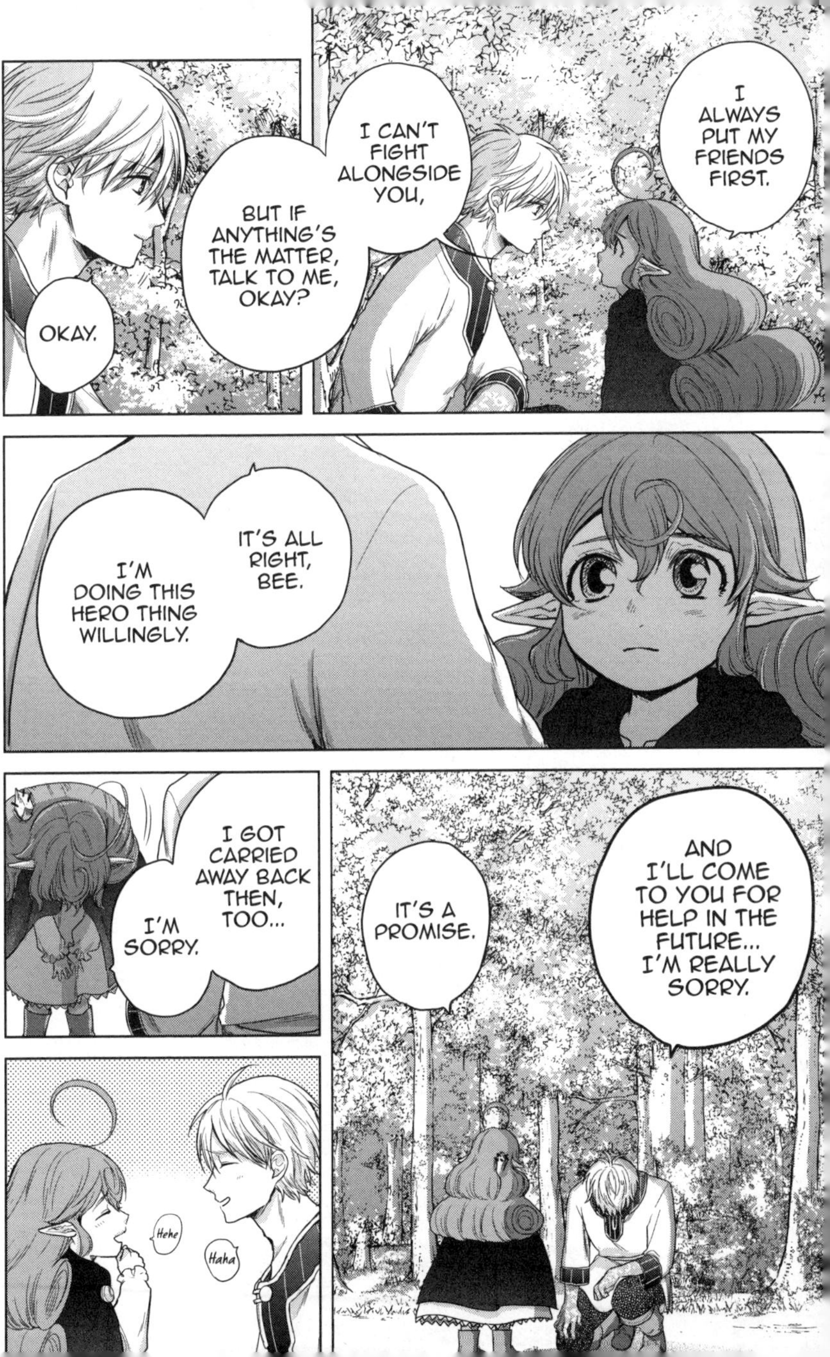
I ALWAYS PUT MY FRIENDS FIRST.
I CAN'T FIGHT ALONGSIDE YOU,
BUT IF ANYTHING'S THE MATTER, TALK TO ME, OKAY?
OKAY.
IT'S ALL RIGHT, BEE.
I'M DOING THIS HERO THING WILLINGLY.
AND I'LL COME TO YOU FOR HELP IN THE FUTURE... I'M REALLY SORRY.
IT'S A PROMISE.
I GOT CARRIED AWAY BACK THEN, TOO...
I'M SORRY.
Hehe
Haha

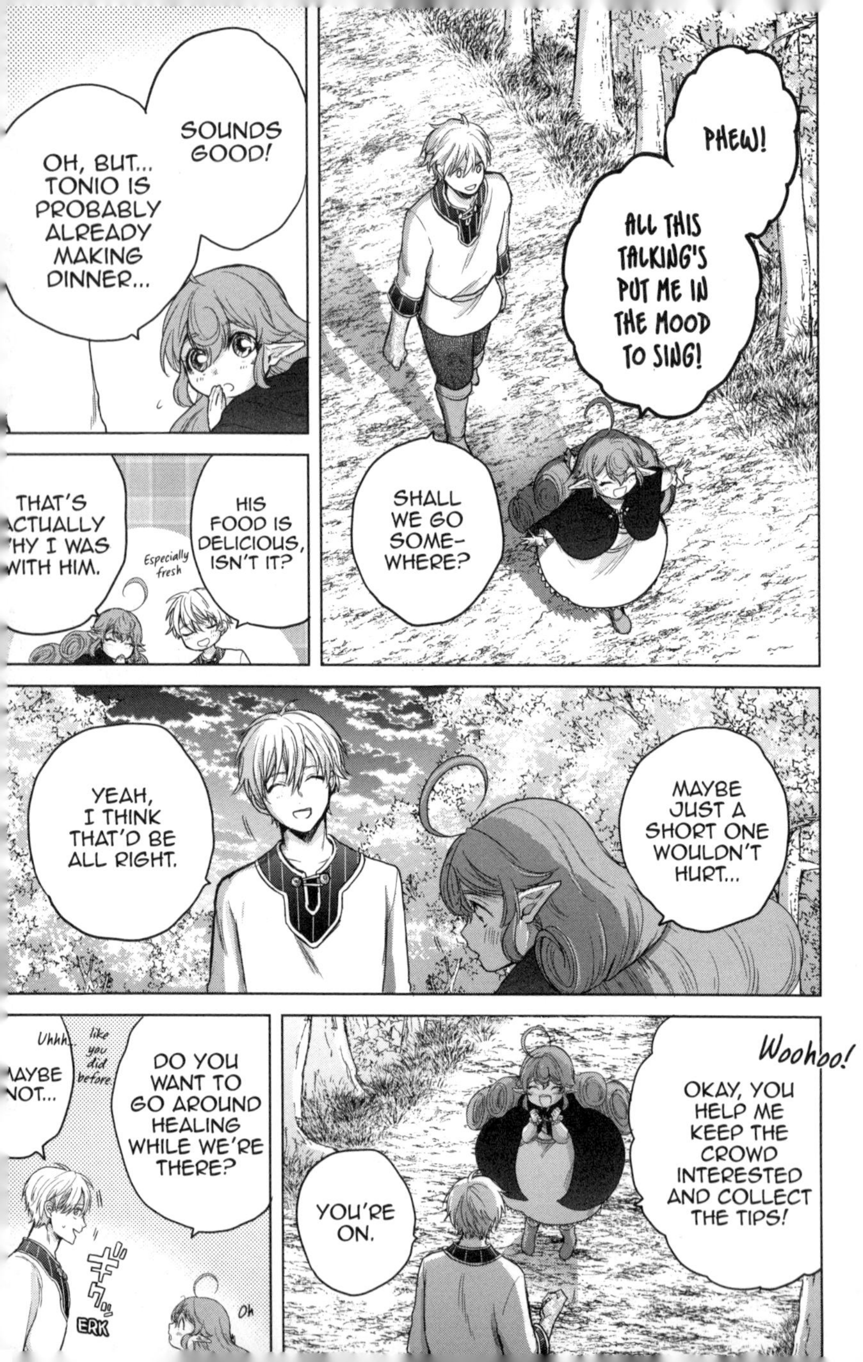
PHEW!
ALL THIS TALKING'S PUT ME IN THE MOOD TO SING!
SHALL WE GO SOME-WHERE?
SOUNDS GOOD!
OH, BUT... TONIO IS PROBABLY ALREADY MAKING DINNER...
HIS FOOD IS DELICIOUS, ISN'T IT?
Especially fresh
THAT'S ACTUALLY WHY I WAS WITH HIM.
MAYBE JUST A SHORT ONE WOULDN'T HURT...
YEAH, I THINK THAT'D BE ALL RIGHT.
Woohoo!
OKAY, YOU HELP ME KEEP THE CROWD INTERESTED AND COLLECT THE TIPS!
YOU'RE ON.
DO YOU WANT TO GO AROUND HEALING WHILE WE'RE THERE?
like you did before
ERK
Oh
Uhhh...
MAYBE NOT...

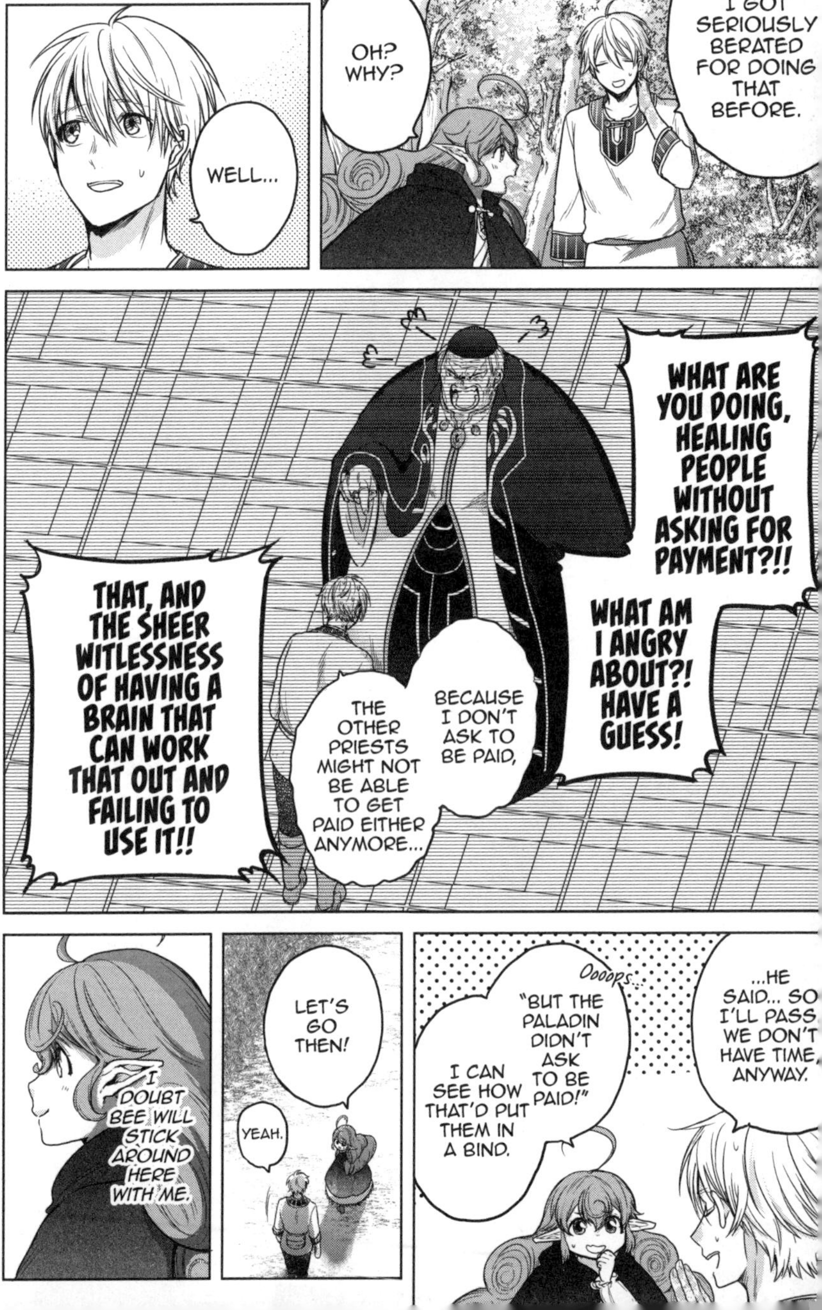
I GOT SERIOUSLY BERATED FOR DOING THAT BEFORE.
OH? WHY?
WELL...
WHAT ARE YOU DOING, HEALING PEOPLE WITHOUT ASKING FOR PAYMENT?!!
WHAT AM I ANGRY ABOUT?! HAVE A GUESS!
BECAUSE I DON'T ASK TO BE PAID,
THE OTHER PRIESTS MIGHT NOT BE ABLE TO GET PAID EITHER ANYMORE...
THAT, AND THE SHEER WITLESSNESS OF HAVING A BRAIN THAT CAN WORK THAT OUT AND FAILING TO USE IT!!
...HE SAID... SO I'LL PASS. WE DON'T HAVE TIME, ANYWAY.
Oooops...
"BUT THE PALADIN DIDN'T ASK TO BE PAID!"
I CAN SEE HOW THAT'D PUT THEM IN A BIND.
LET'S GO THEN!
YEAH.
I DOUBT BEE WILL STICK AROUND HERE WITH ME.

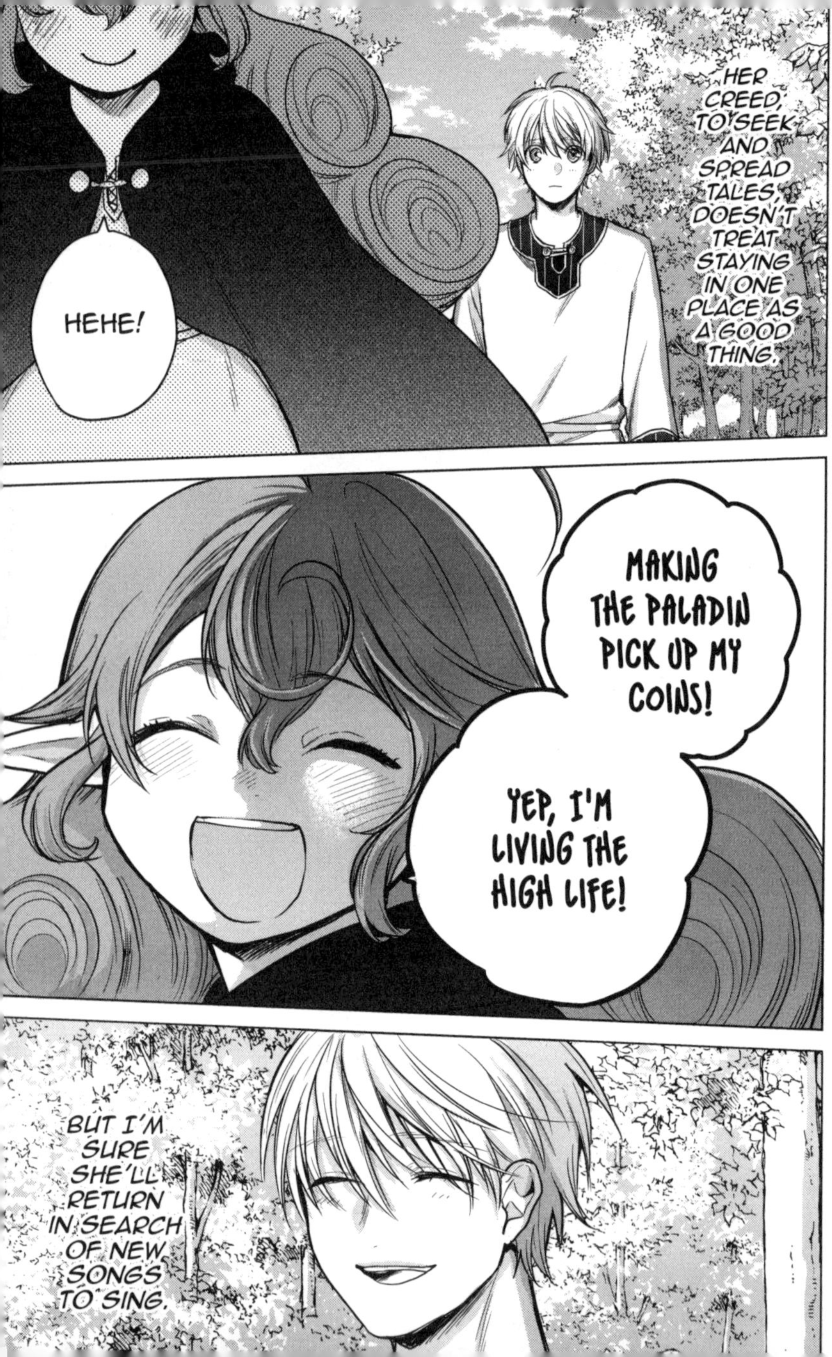
HER CREED, TO SEEK AND SPREAD TALES, DOESN'T TREAT STAYING IN ONE PLACE AS A GOOD THING.
HEHE!
MAKING THE PALADIN PICK UP MY COINS!
YEP, I'M LIVING THE HIGH LIFE!
BUT I'M SURE SHE'LL RETURN IN SEARCH OF NEW SONGS TO SING.

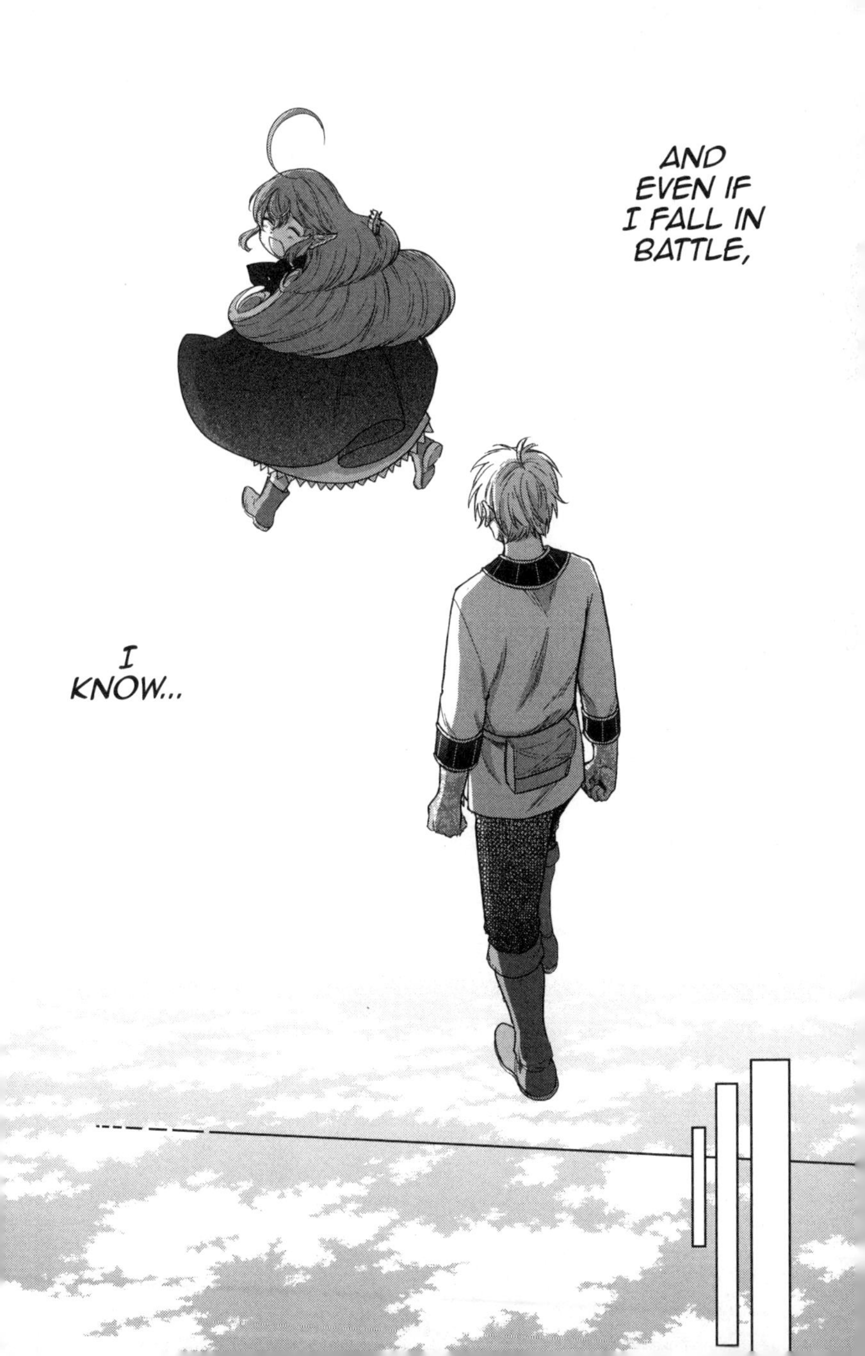
AND EVEN IF I FALL IN BATTLE,
I KNOW...

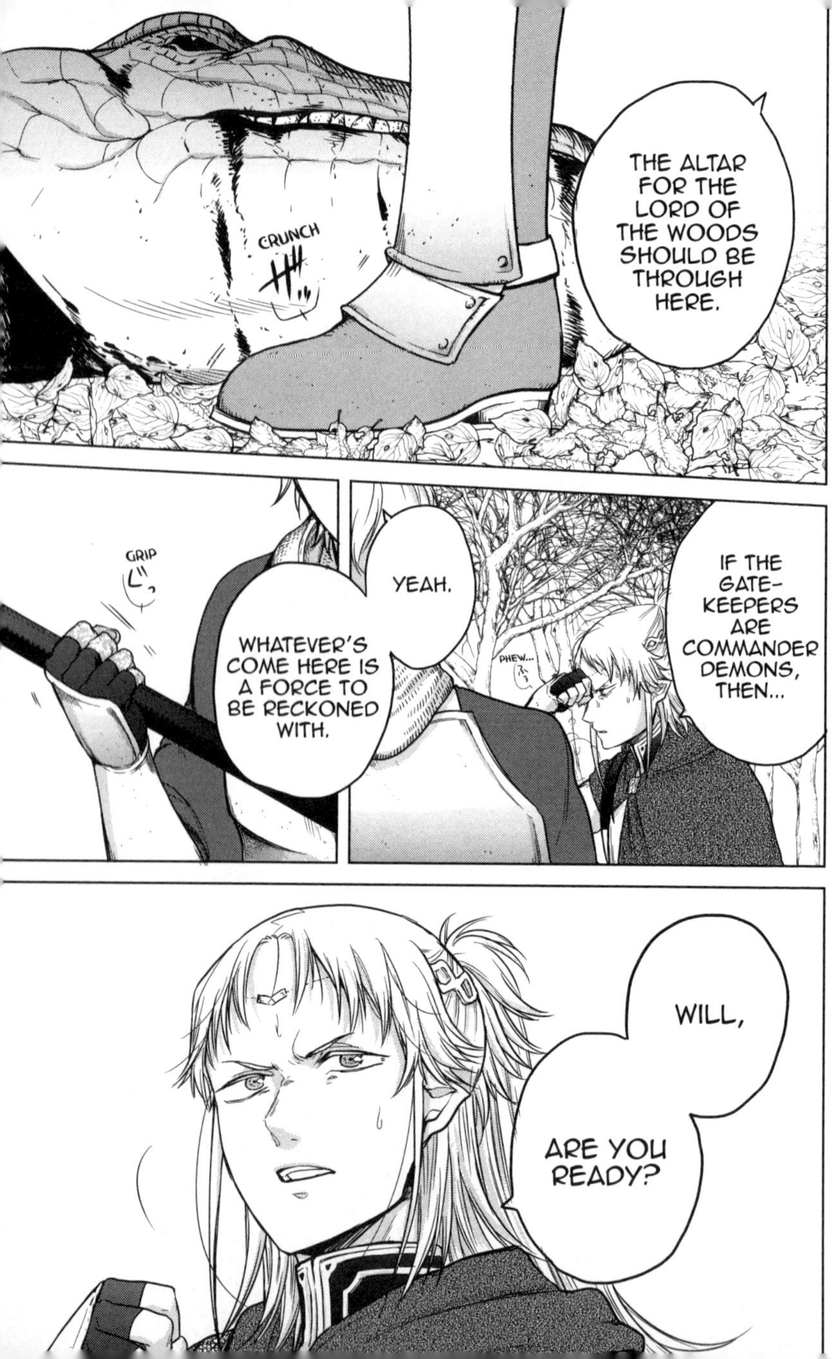
THE ALTAR FOR THE LORD OF THE WOODS SHOULD BE THROUGH HERE.
CRUNCH
IF THE GATE-KEEPERS ARE COMMANDER DEMONS, THEN...
PHEW...
YEAH.
WHATEVER'S COME HERE IS A FORCE TO BE RECKONED WITH.
GRIP
WILL,
ARE YOU READY?

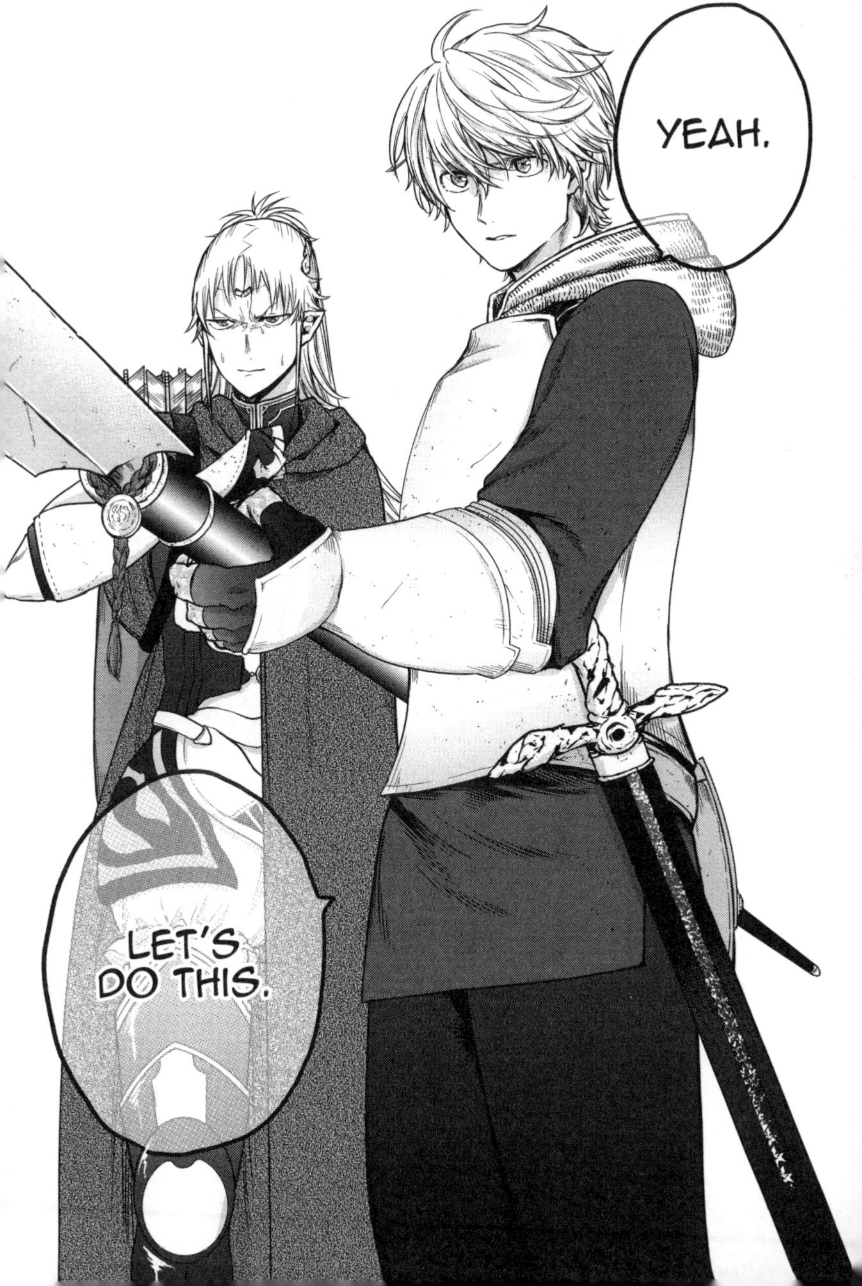
YEAH.
LET'S DO THIS.

Chapter 30 ◆ Torch Port

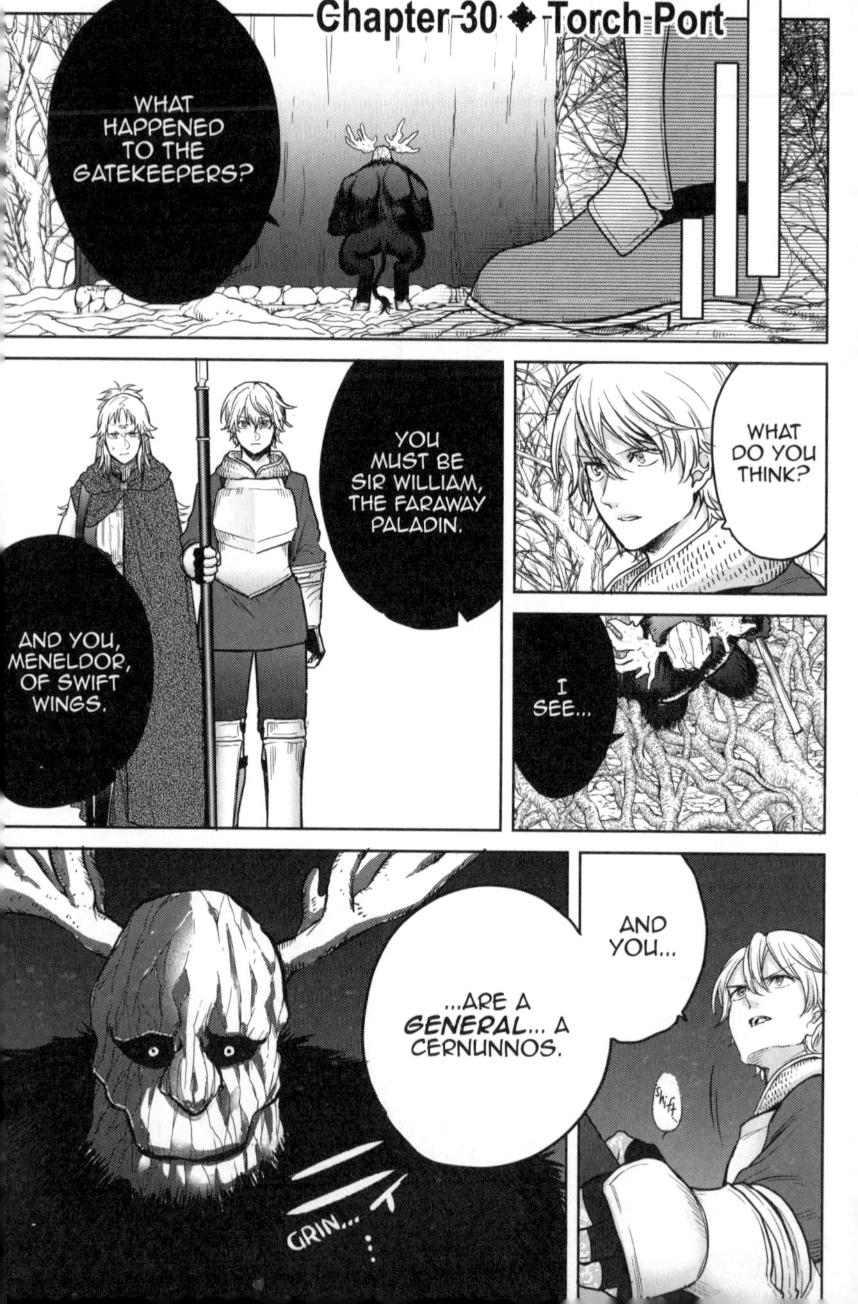
WHAT HAPPENED TO THE GATEKEEPERS?
WHAT DO YOU THINK?
I SEE...
YOU MUST BE SIR WILLIAM, THE FARAWAY PALADIN.
AND YOU, MENELDOR, OF SWIFT WINGS.
AND YOU...
...ARE A **GENERAL**... A CERNUNNOS.
shift...
GRIN...

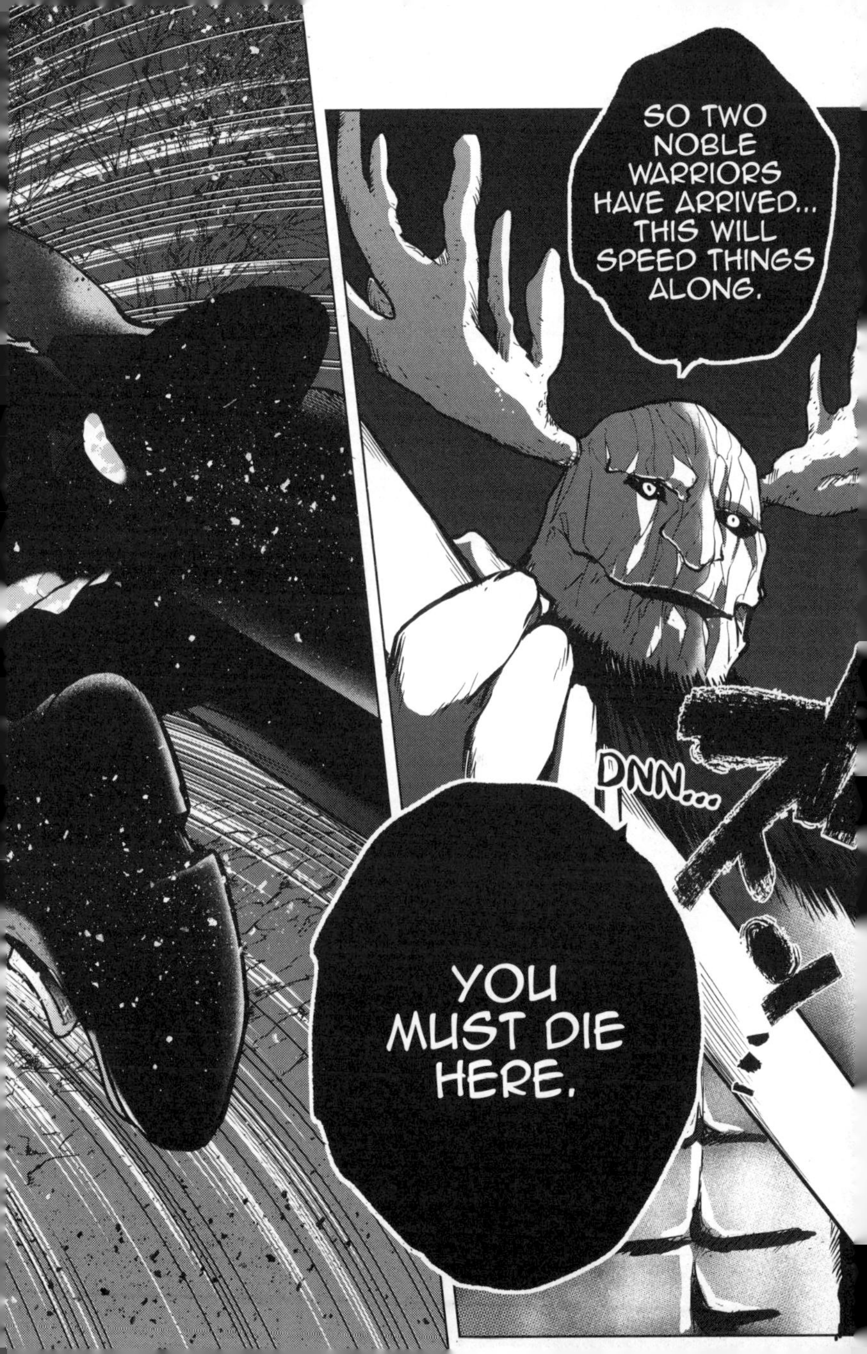
SO TWO NOBLE WARRIORS HAVE ARRIVED... THIS WILL SPEED THINGS ALONG.
DNN...
YOU MUST DIE HERE.

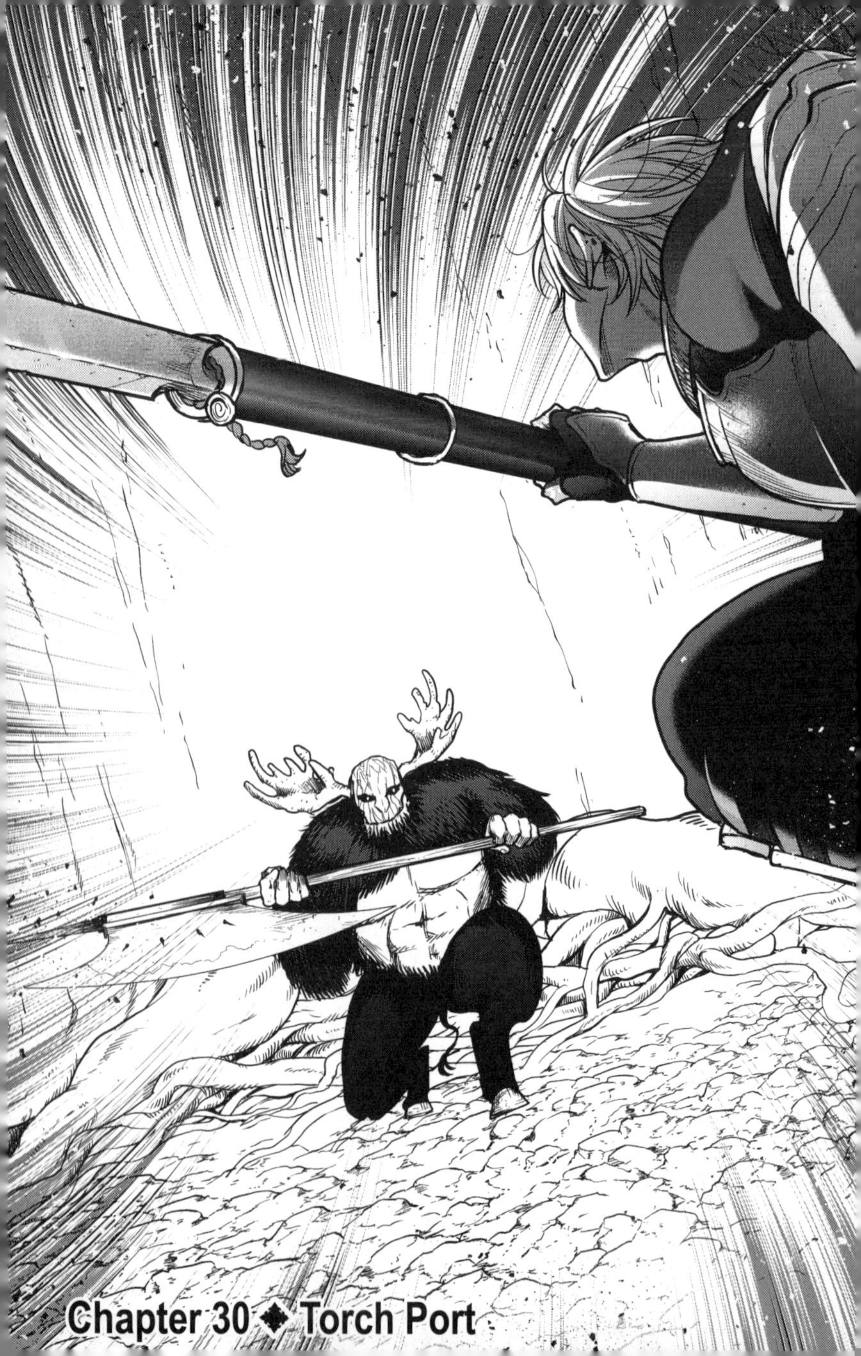

Chapter 30 ◆ Torch Port

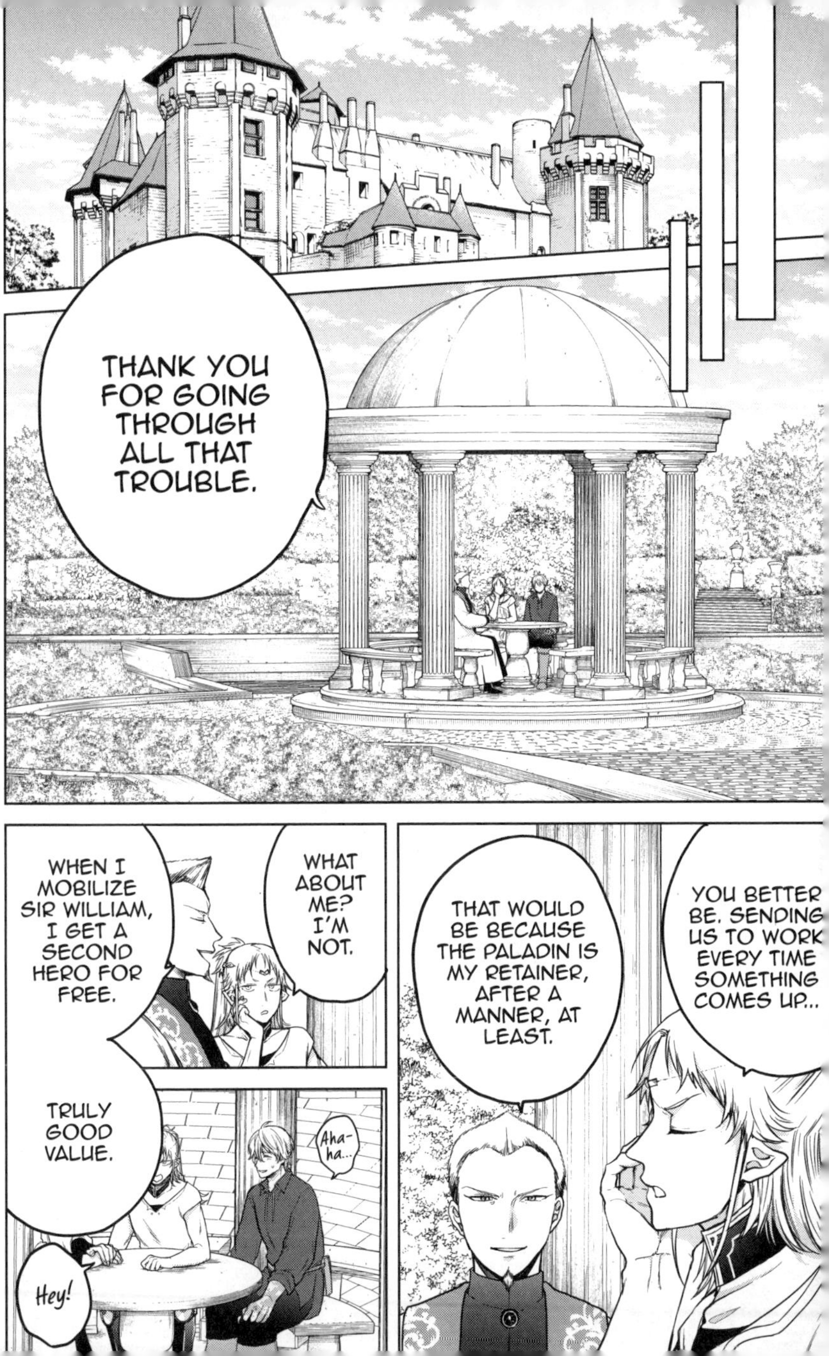
THANK YOU FOR GOING THROUGH ALL THAT TROUBLE.
YOU BETTER BE. SENDING US TO WORK EVERY TIME SOMETHING COMES UP...
THAT WOULD BE BECAUSE THE PALADIN IS MY RETAINER, AFTER A MANNER, AT LEAST.
WHAT ABOUT ME? I'M NOT.
WHEN I MOBILIZE SIR WILLIAM, I GET A SECOND HERO FOR FREE.
Aha-ha...
TRULY GOOD VALUE.
Hey!

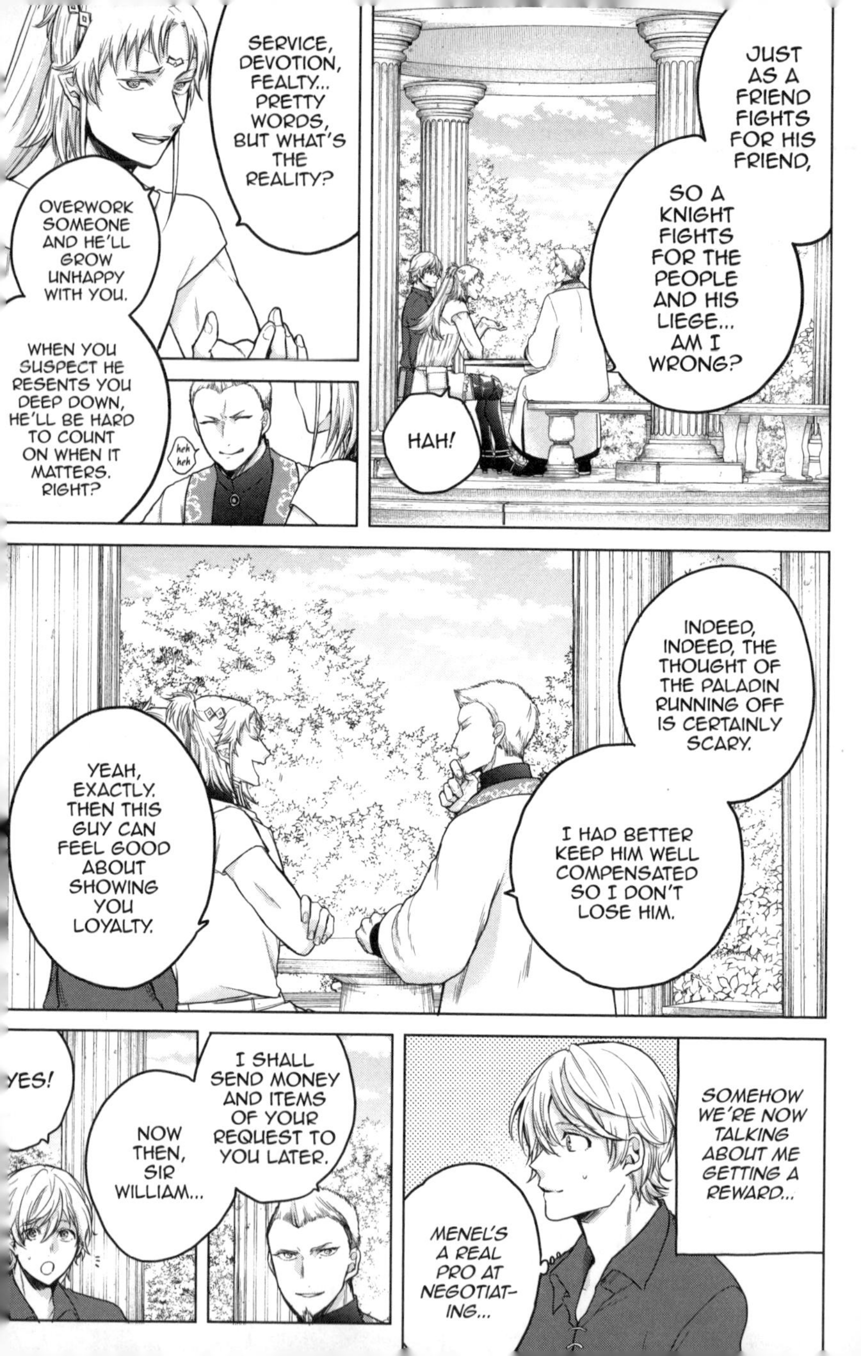
JUST AS A FRIEND FIGHTS FOR HIS FRIEND,
SO A KNIGHT FIGHTS FOR THE PEOPLE AND HIS LIEGE... AM I WRONG?
HAH!
SERVICE, DEVOTION, FEALTY... PRETTY WORDS, BUT WHAT'S THE REALITY?
OVERWORK SOMEONE AND HE'LL GROW UNHAPPY WITH YOU.
WHEN YOU SUSPECT HE RESENTS YOU DEEP DOWN, HE'LL BE HARD TO COUNT ON WHEN IT MATTERS. RIGHT?
heh heh
INDEED, INDEED, THE THOUGHT OF THE PALADIN RUNNING OFF IS CERTAINLY SCARY.
I HAD BETTER KEEP HIM WELL COMPENSATED SO I DON'T LOSE HIM.
YEAH, EXACTLY. THEN THIS GUY CAN FEEL GOOD ABOUT SHOWING YOU LOYALTY.
SOMEHOW WE'RE NOW TALKING ABOUT ME GETTING A REWARD...
MENEL'S A REAL PRO AT NEGOTIAT-ING...
I SHALL SEND MONEY AND ITEMS OF YOUR REQUEST TO YOU LATER.
NOW THEN, SIR WILLIAM...
YES!

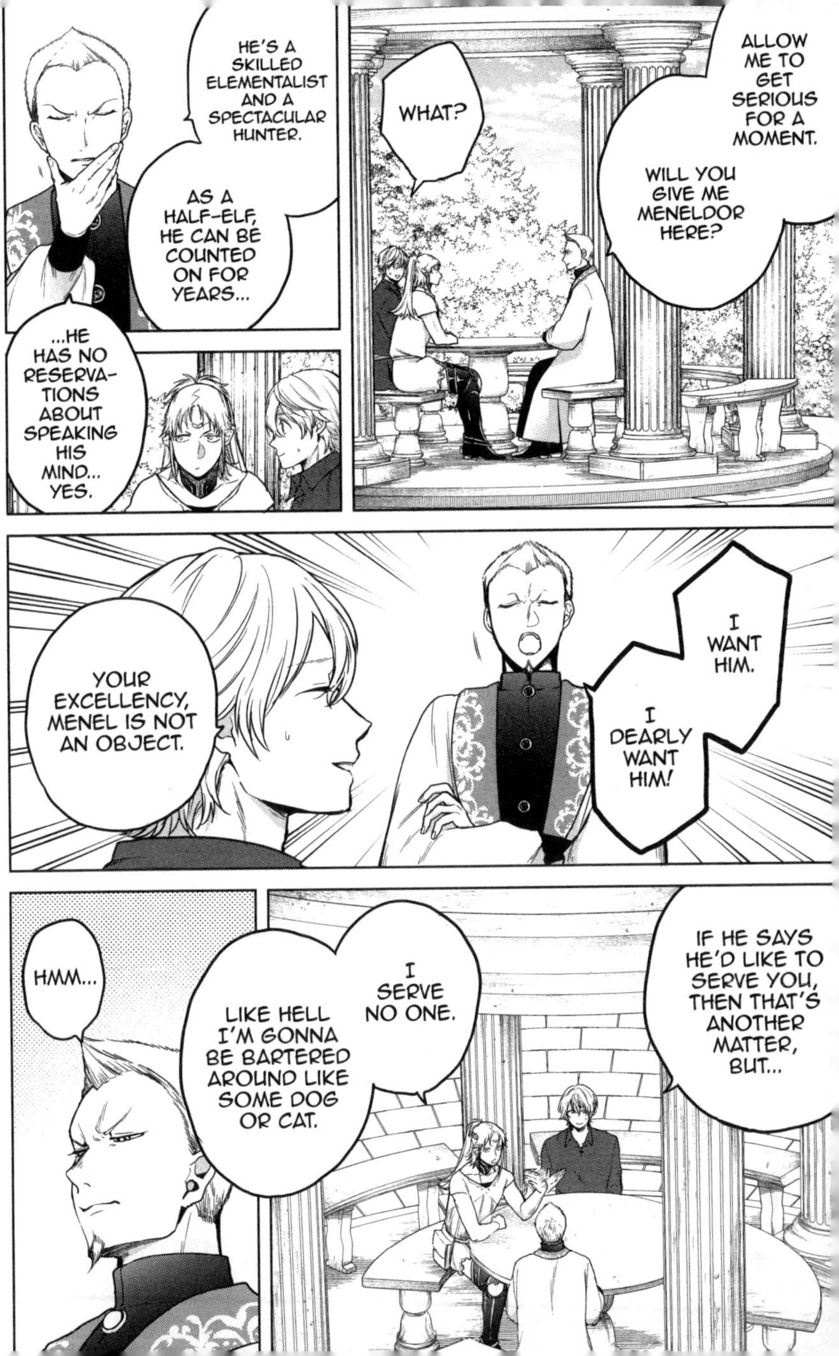
ALLOW ME TO GET SERIOUS FOR A MOMENT.
WILL YOU GIVE ME MENELDOR HERE?
WHAT?
HE'S A SKILLED ELEMENTALIST AND A SPECTACULAR HUNTER.
AS A HALF-ELF, HE CAN BE COUNTED ON FOR YEARS...
...HE HAS NO RESERVATIONS ABOUT SPEAKING HIS MIND... YES.
I WANT HIM.
I DEARLY WANT HIM!
YOUR EXCELLENCY, MENEL IS NOT AN OBJECT.
IF HE SAYS HE'D LIKE TO SERVE YOU, THEN THAT'S ANOTHER MATTER, BUT...
I SERVE NO ONE.
LIKE HELL I'M GONNA BE BARTERED AROUND LIKE SOME DOG OR CAT.
HMM...

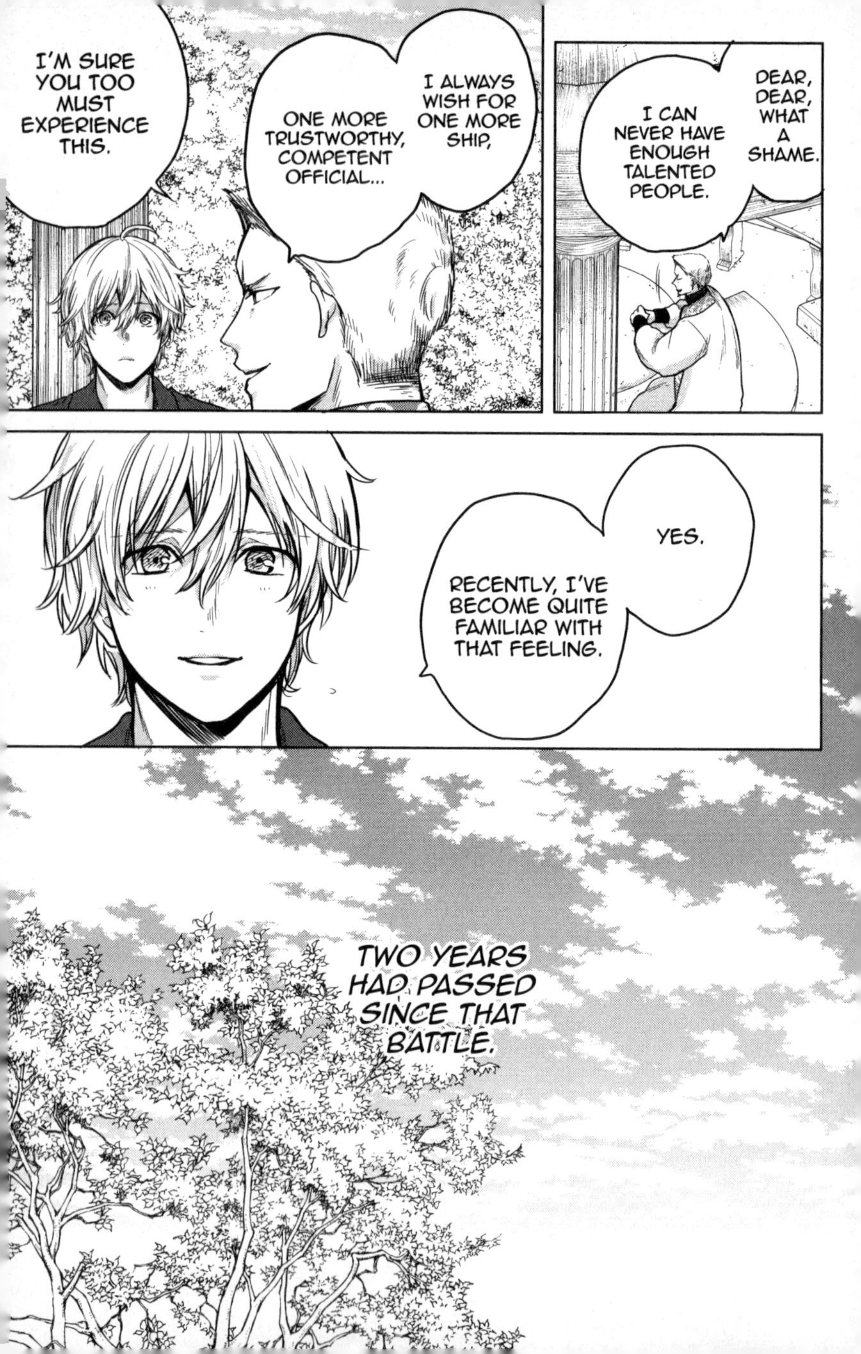
DEAR, DEAR, WHAT A SHAME.
I CAN NEVER HAVE ENOUGH TALENTED PEOPLE.
I ALWAYS WISH FOR ONE MORE SHIP,
ONE MORE TRUSTWORTHY, COMPETENT OFFICIAL...
I'M SURE YOU TOO MUST EXPERIENCE THIS.
YES.
RECENTLY, I'VE BECOME QUITE FAMILIAR WITH THAT FEELING.
TWO YEARS HAD PASSED SINCE THAT BATTLE.

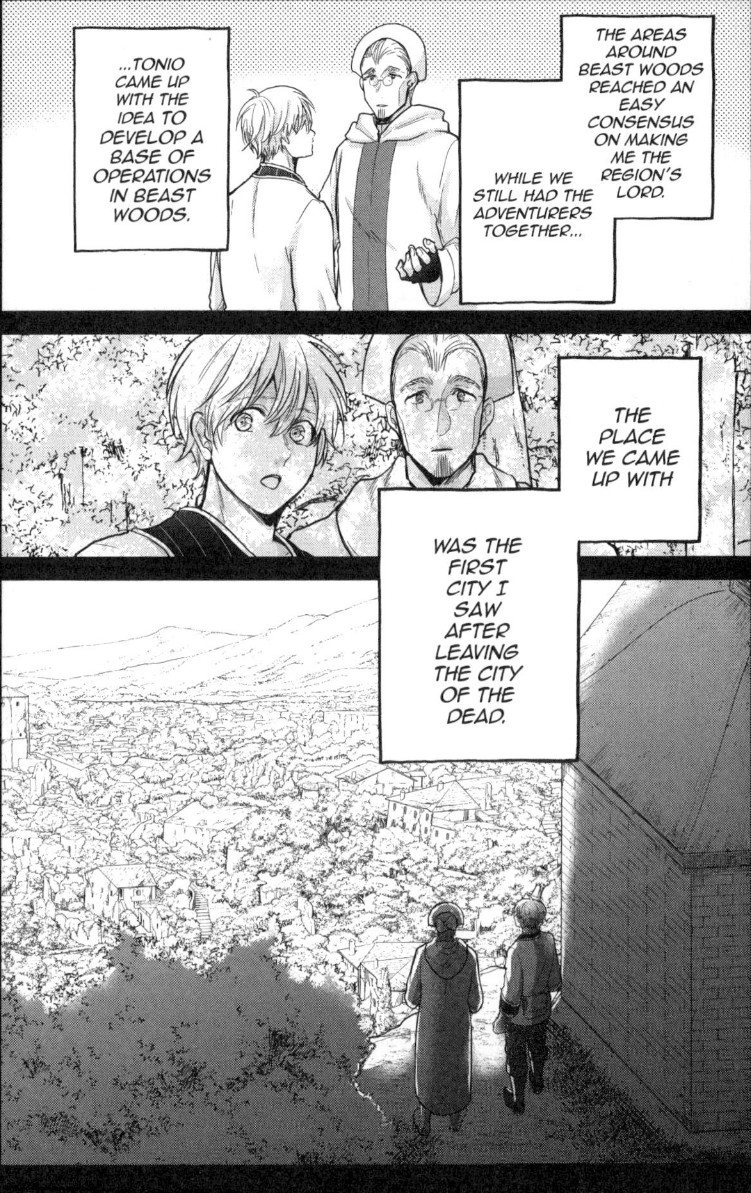
THE AREAS AROUND BEAST WOODS REACHED AN EASY CONSENSUS ON MAKING ME THE REGION'S LORD.
WHILE WE STILL HAD THE ADVENTURERS TOGETHER...
...TONIO CAME UP WITH THE IDEA TO DEVELOP A BASE OF OPERATIONS IN BEAST WOODS.
THE PLACE WE CAME UP WITH
WAS THE FIRST CITY I SAW AFTER LEAVING THE CITY OF THE DEAD.

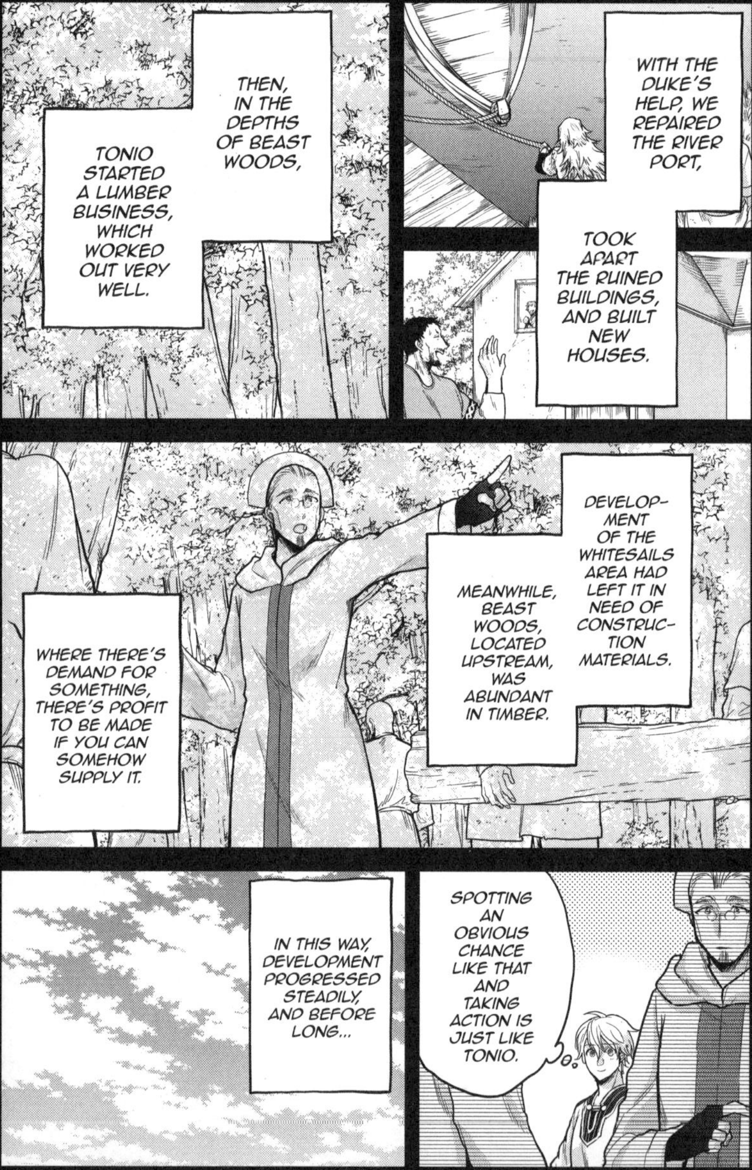
WITH THE DUKE'S HELP, WE REPAIRED THE RIVER PORT,
TOOK APART THE RUINED BUILDINGS, AND BUILT NEW HOUSES.
THEN, IN THE DEPTHS OF BEAST WOODS,
TONIO STARTED A LUMBER BUSINESS, WHICH WORKED OUT VERY WELL.
DEVELOP-MENT OF THE WHITESAILS AREA HAD LEFT IT IN NEED OF CONSTRUC-TION MATERIALS.
MEANWHILE, BEAST WOODS, LOCATED UPSTREAM, WAS ABUNDANT IN TIMBER.
WHERE THERE'S DEMAND FOR SOMETHING, THERE'S PROFIT TO BE MADE IF YOU CAN SOMEHOW SUPPLY IT.
SPOTTING AN OBVIOUS CHANCE LIKE THAT AND TAKING ACTION IS JUST LIKE TONIO.
IN THIS WAY, DEVELOPMENT PROGRESSED STEADILY, AND BEFORE LONG...

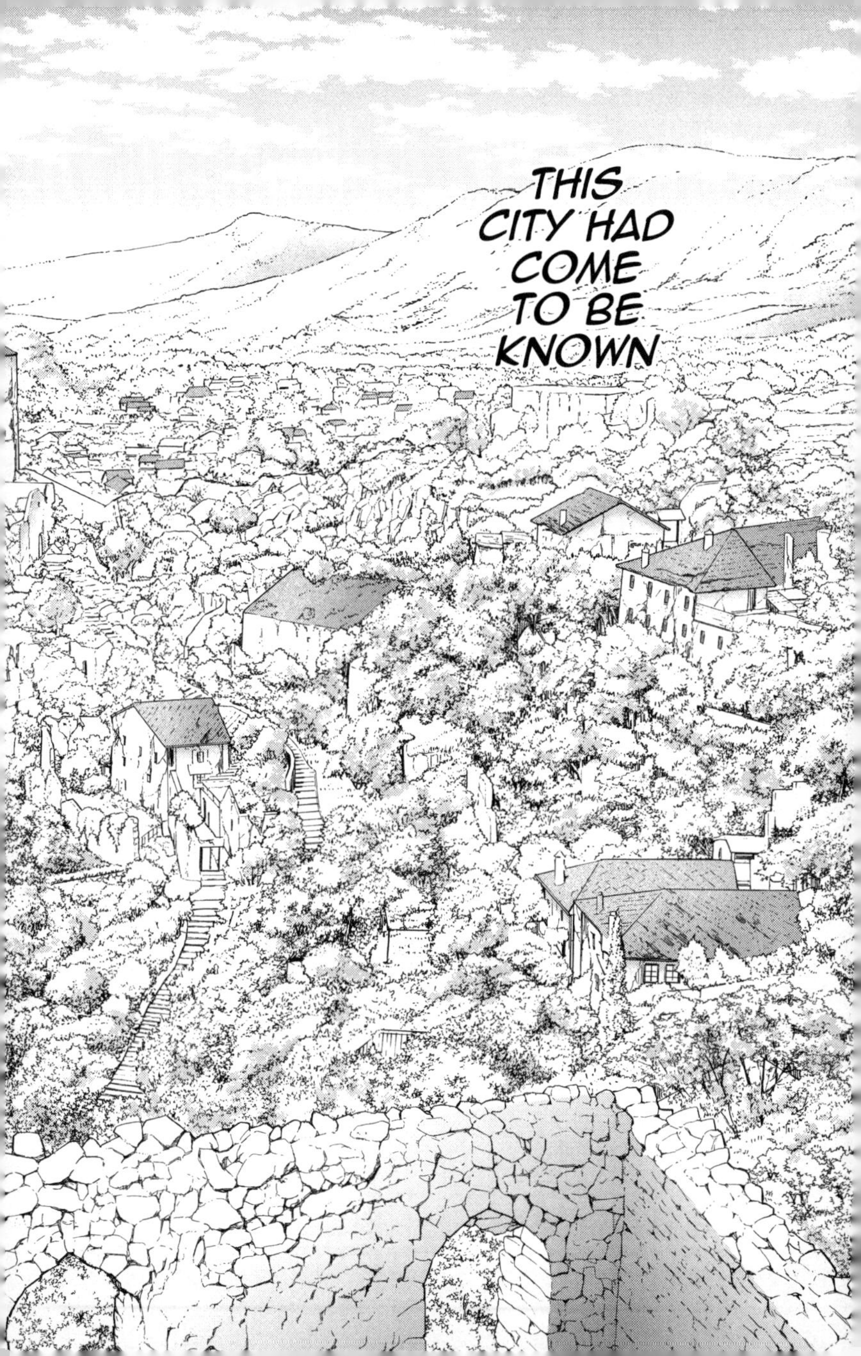
THIS CITY HAD COME TO BE KNOWN

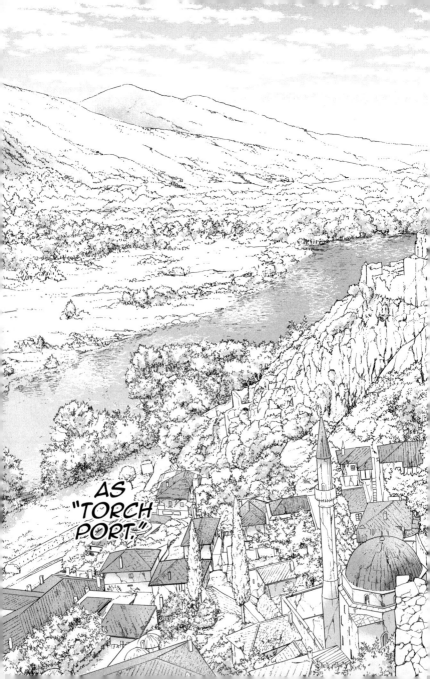

AS "TORCH PORT."

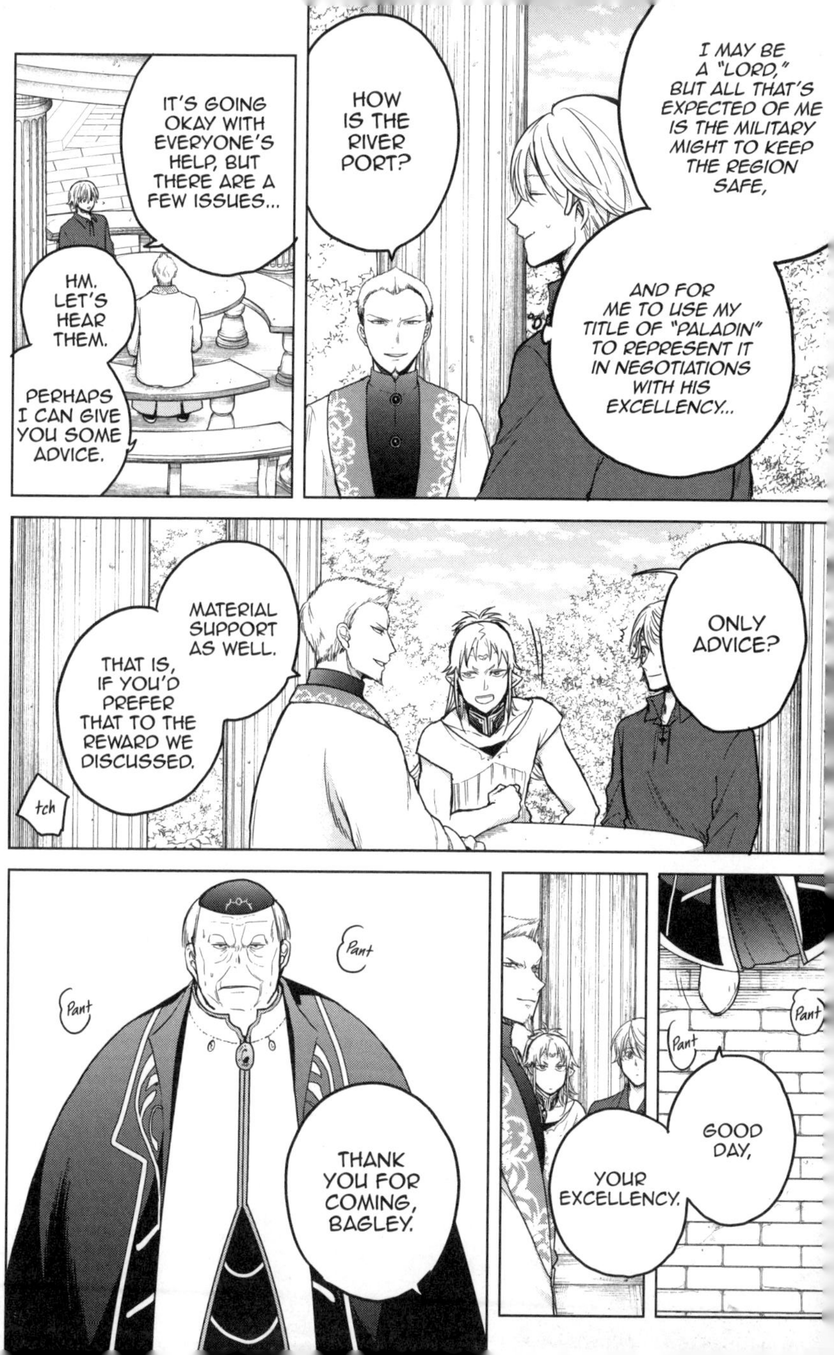
I MAY BE A "LORD," BUT ALL THAT'S EXPECTED OF ME IS THE MILITARY MIGHT TO KEEP THE REGION SAFE,
AND FOR ME TO USE MY TITLE OF "PALADIN" TO REPRESENT IT IN NEGOTIATIONS WITH HIS EXCELLENCY...
HOW IS THE RIVER PORT?
IT'S GOING OKAY WITH EVERYONE'S HELP, BUT THERE ARE A FEW ISSUES...
HM. LET'S HEAR THEM.
PERHAPS I CAN GIVE YOU SOME ADVICE.
ONLY ADVICE?
MATERIAL SUPPORT AS WELL.
THAT IS, IF YOU'D PREFER THAT TO THE REWARD WE DISCUSSED.
tch
Pant
Pant
GOOD DAY,
YOUR EXCELLENCY.
Pant
Pant
THANK YOU FOR COMING, BAGLEY.

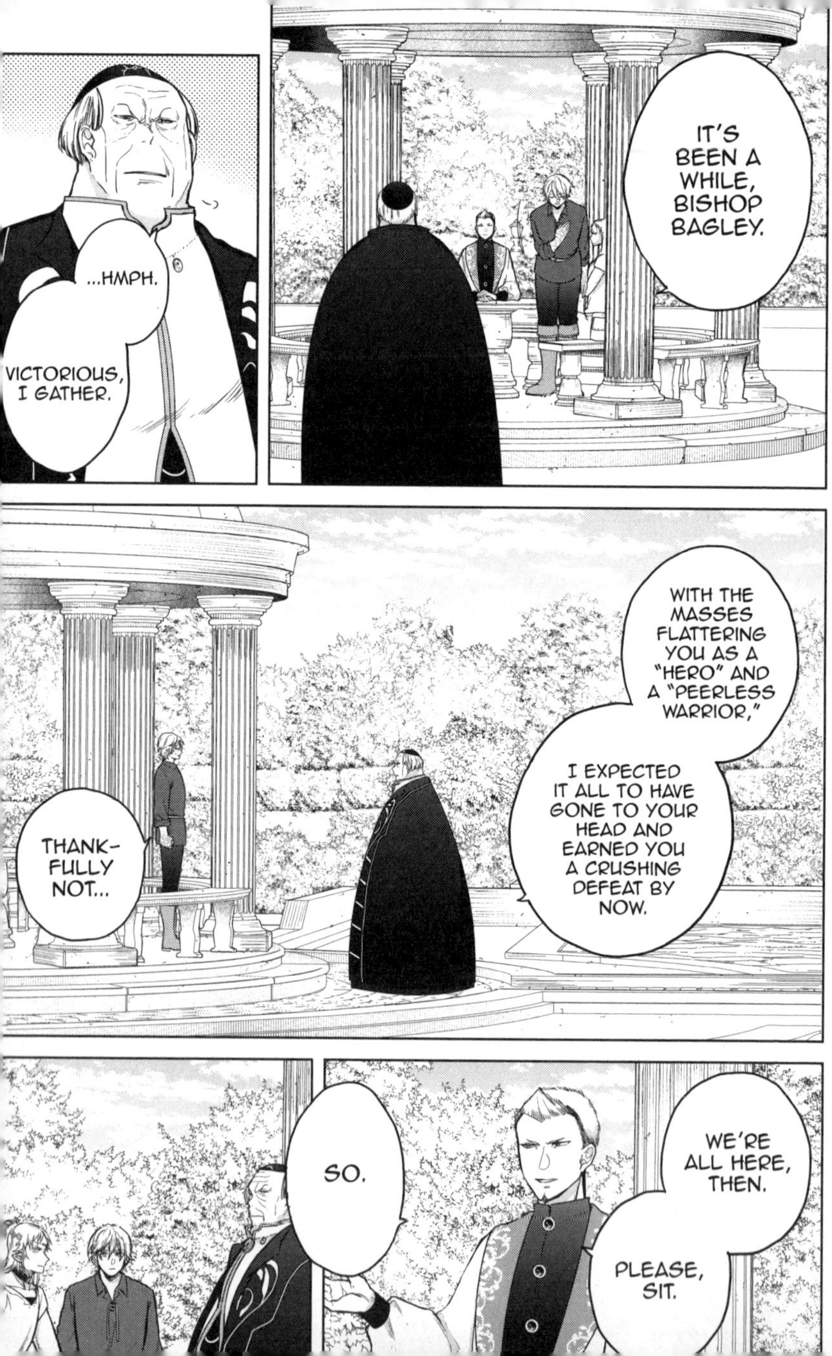
IT'S BEEN A WHILE, BISHOP BAGLEY.
...HMPH.
VICTORIOUS, I GATHER.
WITH THE MASSES FLATTERING YOU AS A "HERO" AND A "PEERLESS WARRIOR,"
I EXPECTED IT ALL TO HAVE GONE TO YOUR HEAD AND EARNED YOU A CRUSHING DEFEAT BY NOW.
THANK-FULLY NOT...
WE'RE ALL HERE, THEN.
PLEASE, SIT.
SO.

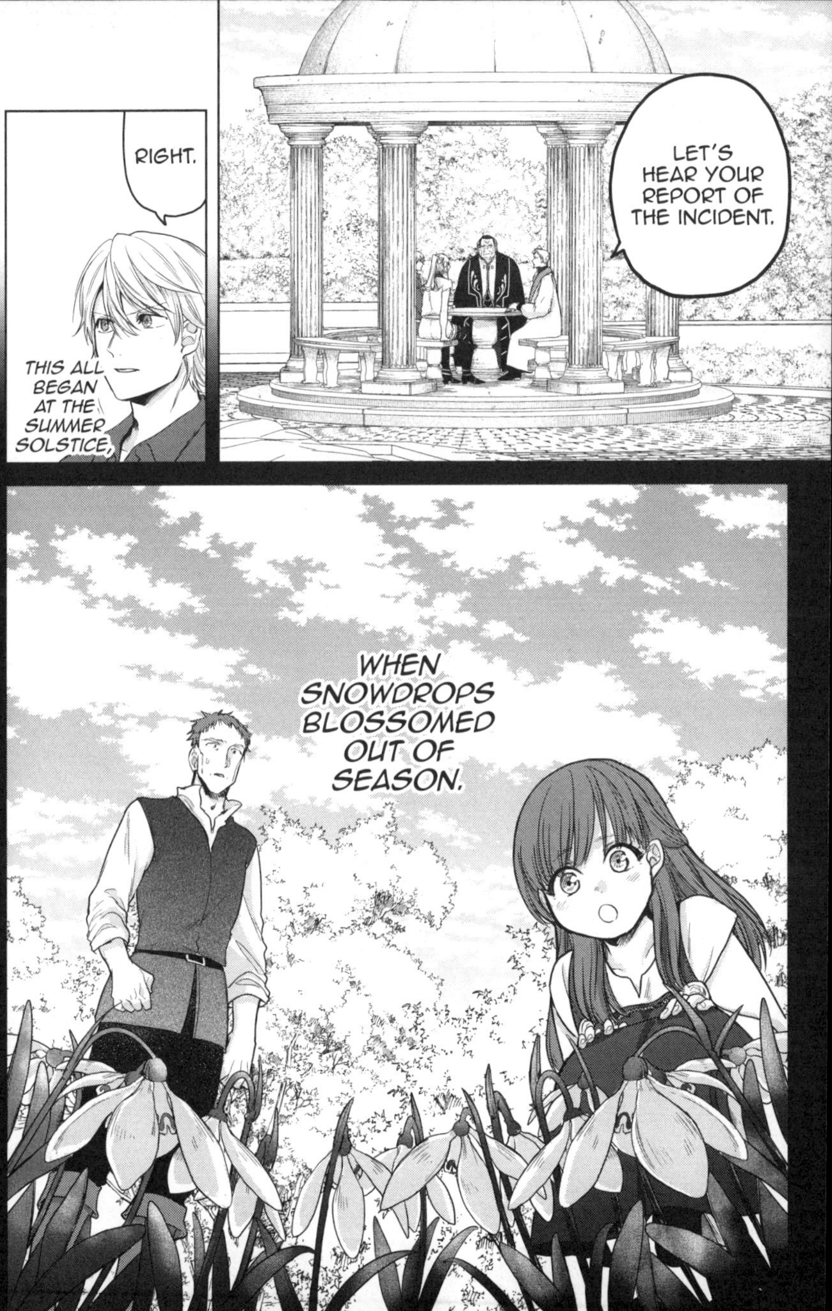
LET'S HEAR YOUR REPORT OF THE INCIDENT.
RIGHT.
THIS ALL BEGAN AT THE SUMMER SOLSTICE,
WHEN SNOWDROPS BLOSSOMED OUT OF SEASON.

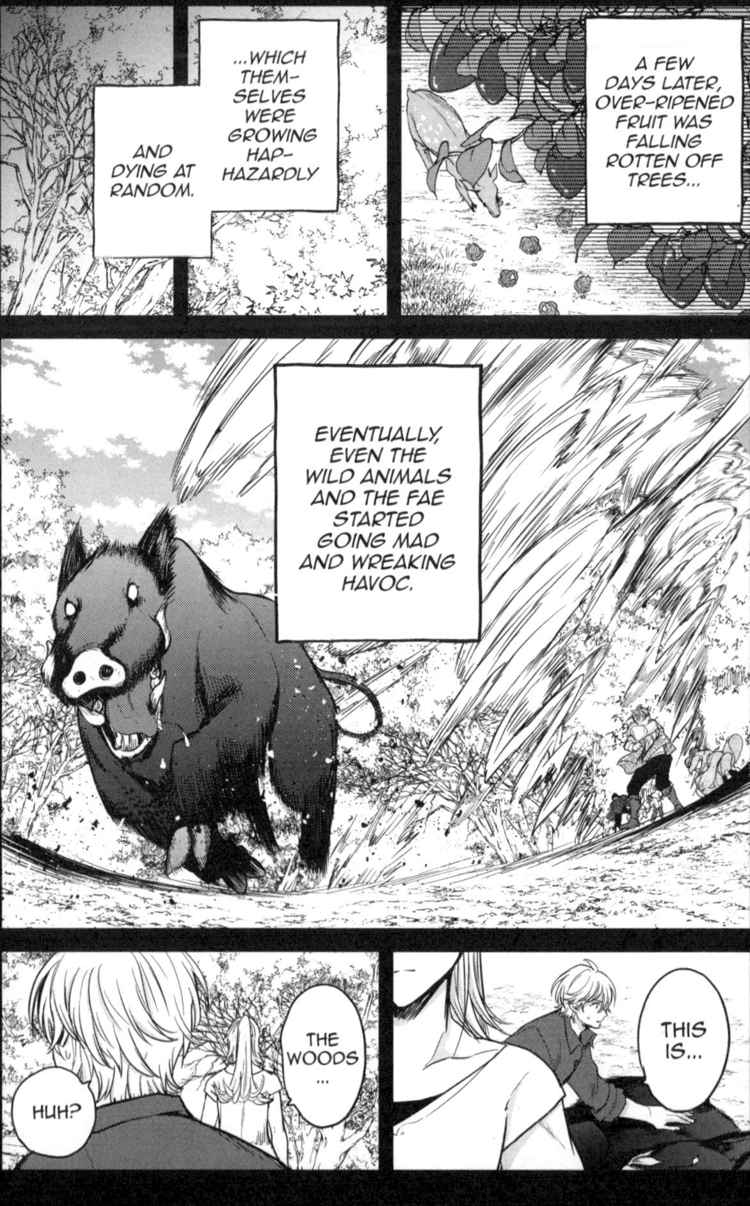
A FEW DAYS LATER, OVER-RIPENED FRUIT WAS FALLING ROTTEN OFF TREES...
...WHICH THEMSELVES WERE GROWING HAPHAZARDLY
AND DYING AT RANDOM.
EVENTUALLY, EVEN THE WILD ANIMALS AND THE FAE STARTED GOING MAD AND WREAKING HAVOC.
THIS IS...
THE WOODS ...
HUH?

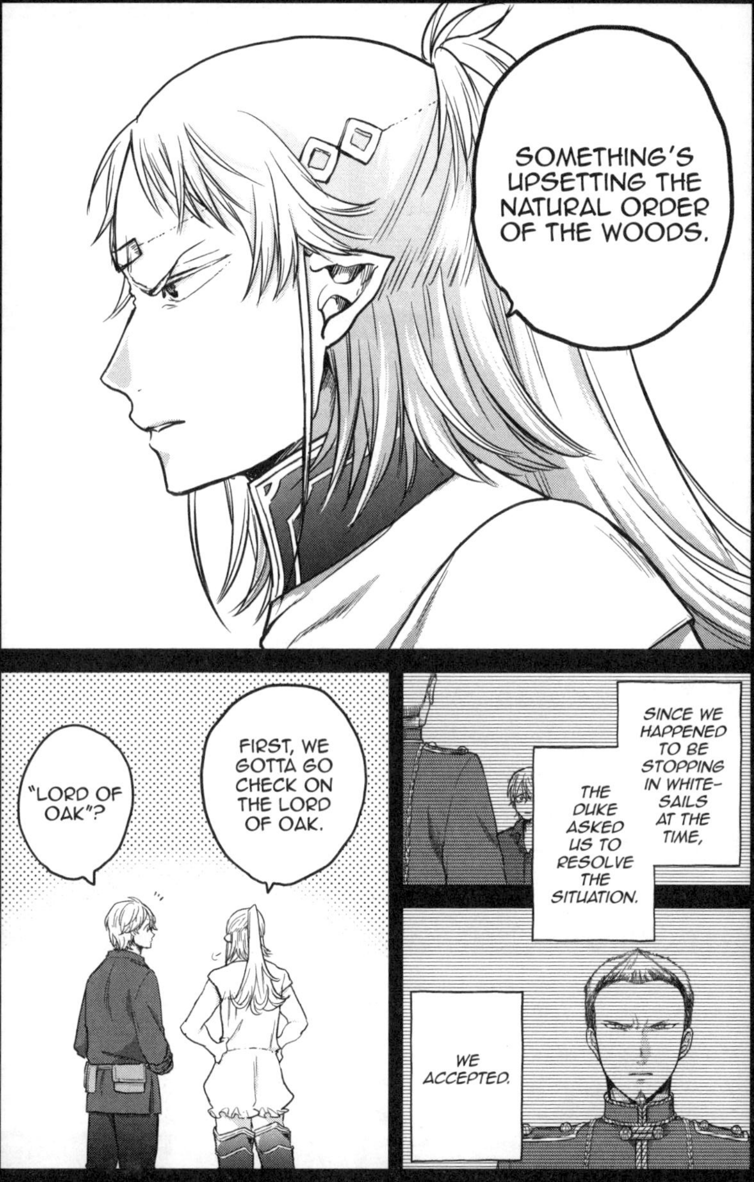
SOMETHING'S UPSETTING THE NATURAL ORDER OF THE WOODS.
SINCE WE HAPPENED TO BE STOPPING IN WHITE-SAILS AT THE TIME,
THE DUKE ASKED US TO RESOLVE THE SITUATION.
WE ACCEPTED.
FIRST, WE GOTTA GO CHECK ON THE LORD OF OAK.
"LORD OF OAK"?

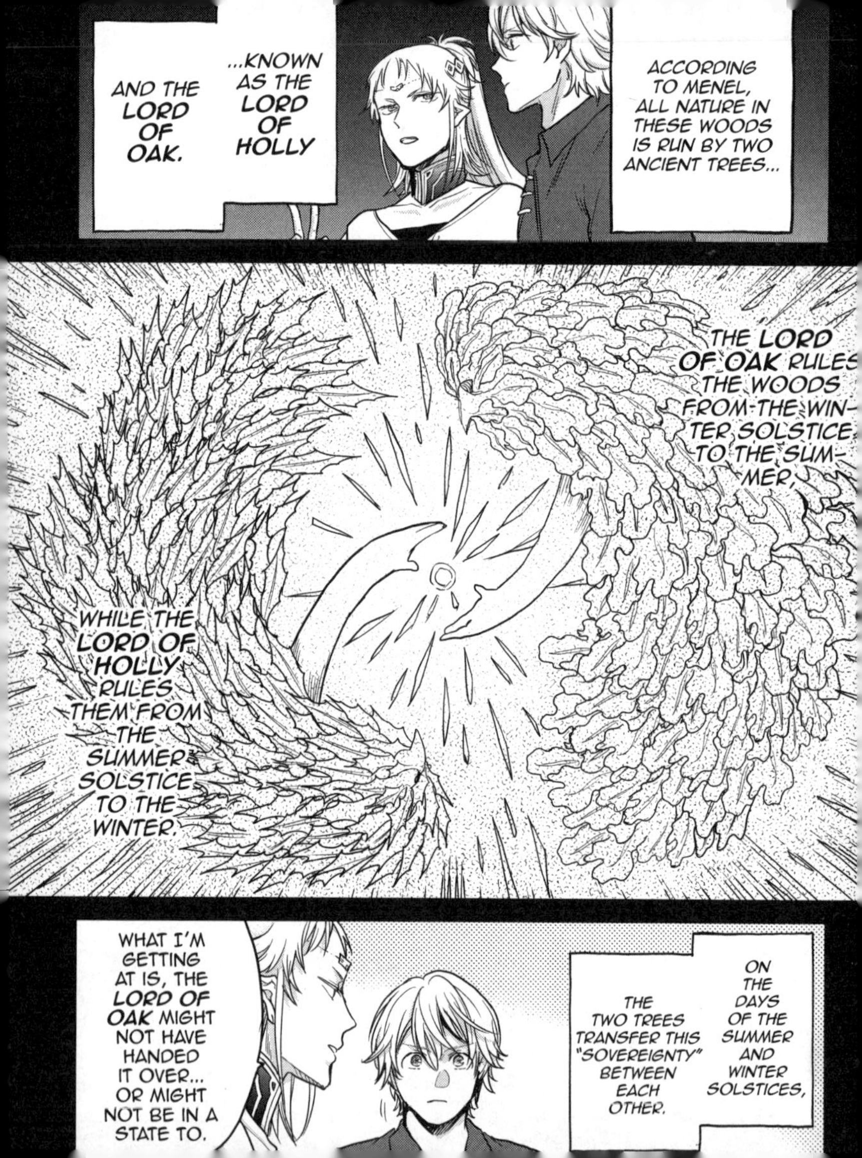
ACCORDING TO MENEL, ALL NATURE IN THESE WOODS IS RUN BY TWO ANCIENT TREES...
...KNOWN AS THE LORD OF HOLLY
AND THE LORD OF OAK.
THE LORD OF OAK RULES THE WOODS FROM THE WINTER SOLSTICE TO THE SUMMER,
WHILE THE LORD OF HOLLY RULES THEM FROM THE SUMMER SOLSTICE TO THE WINTER.
ON THE DAYS OF THE SUMMER AND WINTER SOLSTICES,
THE TWO TREES TRANSFER THIS "SOVEREIGNTY" BETWEEN EACH OTHER.
WHAT I'M GETTING AT IS, THE LORD OF OAK MIGHT NOT HAVE HANDED IT OVER... OR MIGHT NOT BE IN A STATE TO.

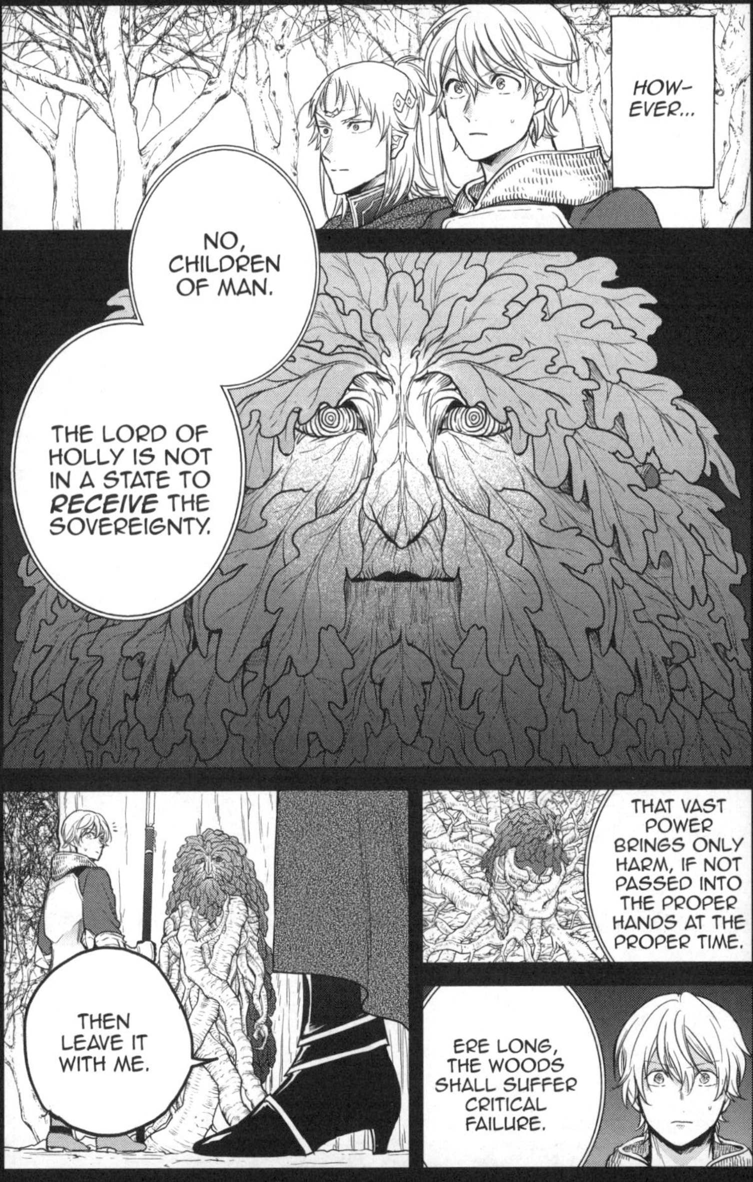
HOW-EVER...
NO, CHILDREN OF MAN.
THE LORD OF HOLLY IS NOT IN A STATE TO *RECEIVE* THE SOVEREIGNTY.
THAT VAST POWER BRINGS ONLY HARM, IF NOT PASSED INTO THE PROPER HANDS AT THE PROPER TIME.
ERE LONG, THE WOODS SHALL SUFFER CRITICAL FAILURE.
THEN LEAVE IT WITH ME.

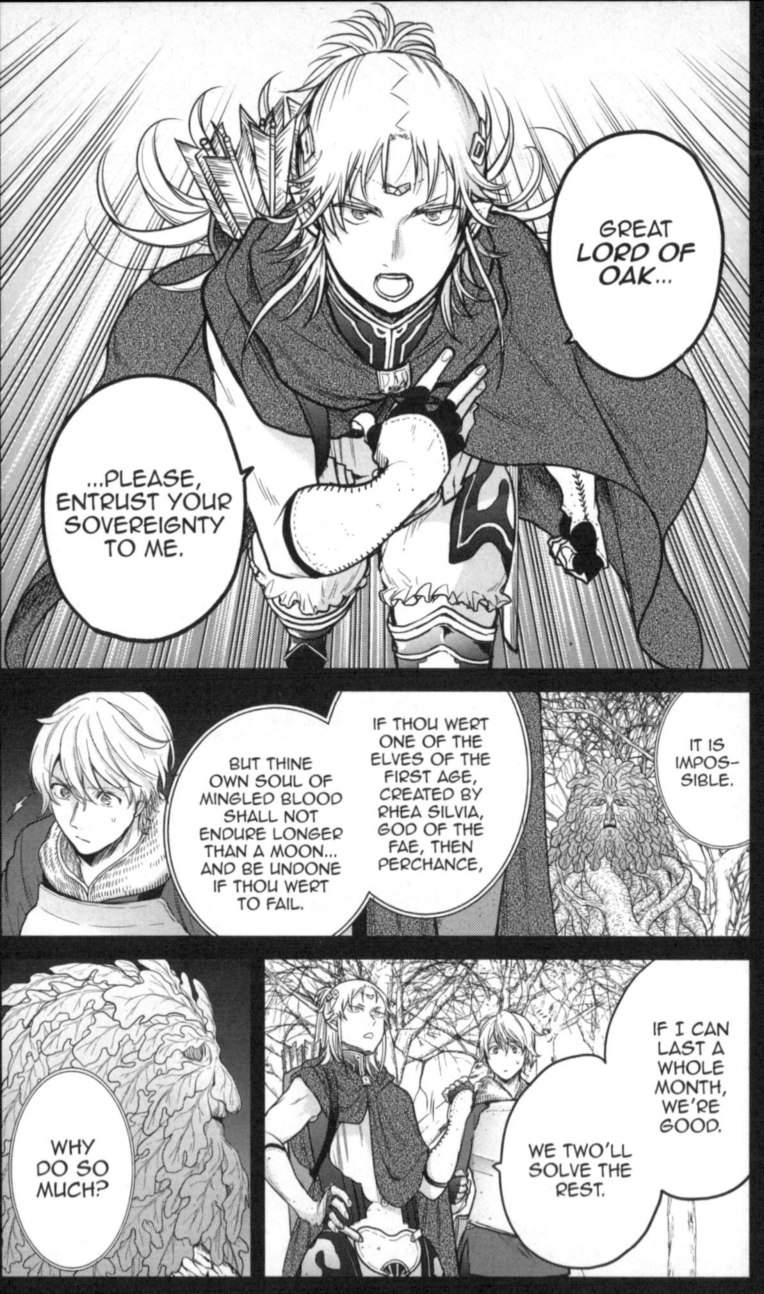
GREAT LORD OF OAK...
...PLEASE, ENTRUST YOUR SOVEREIGNTY TO ME.
IT IS IMPOSSIBLE.
IF THOU WERT ONE OF THE ELVES OF THE FIRST AGE, CREATED BY RHEA SILVIA, GOD OF THE FAE, THEN PERCHANCE,
BUT THINE OWN SOUL OF MINGLED BLOOD SHALL NOT ENDURE LONGER THAN A MOON... AND BE UNDONE IF THOU WERT TO FAIL.
IF I CAN LAST A WHOLE MONTH, WE'RE GOOD.
WE TWO'LL SOLVE THE REST.
WHY DO SO MUCH?

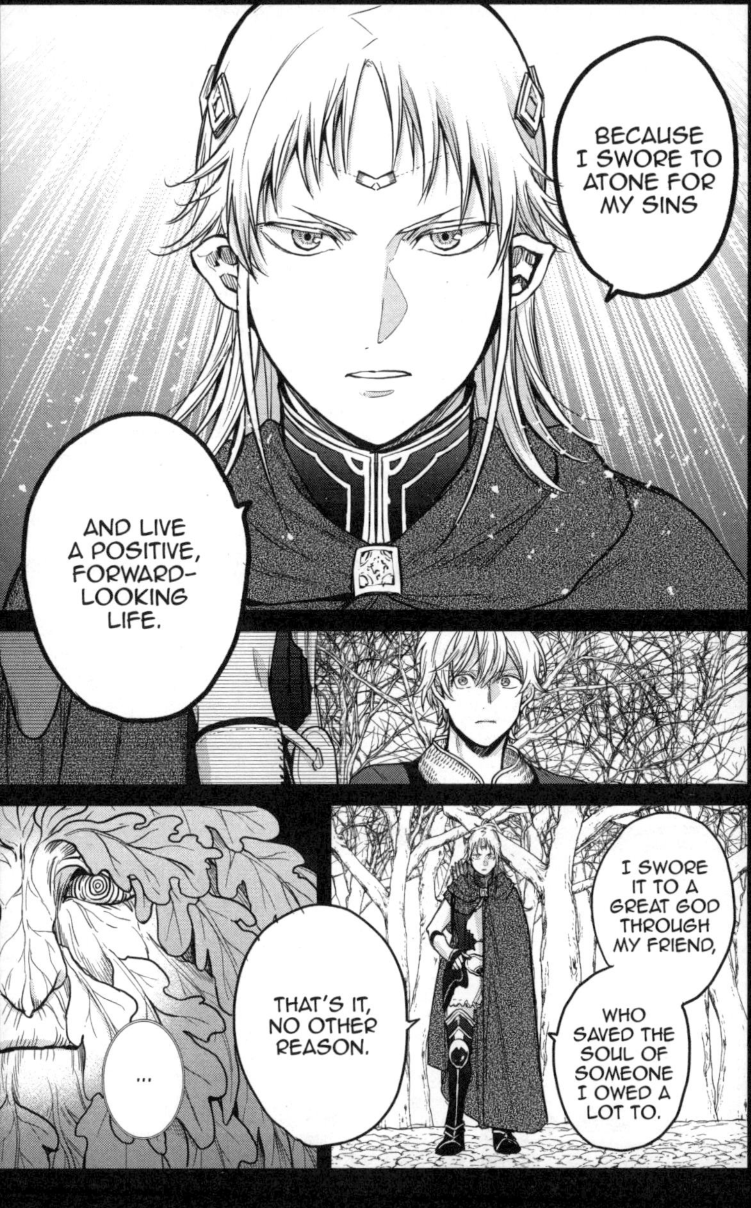
BECAUSE I SWORE TO ATONE FOR MY SINS
AND LIVE A POSITIVE, FORWARD-LOOKING LIFE.
I SWORE IT TO A GREAT GOD THROUGH MY FRIEND,
WHO SAVED THE SOUL OF SOMEONE I OWED A LOT TO.
THAT'S IT, NO OTHER REASON.
...

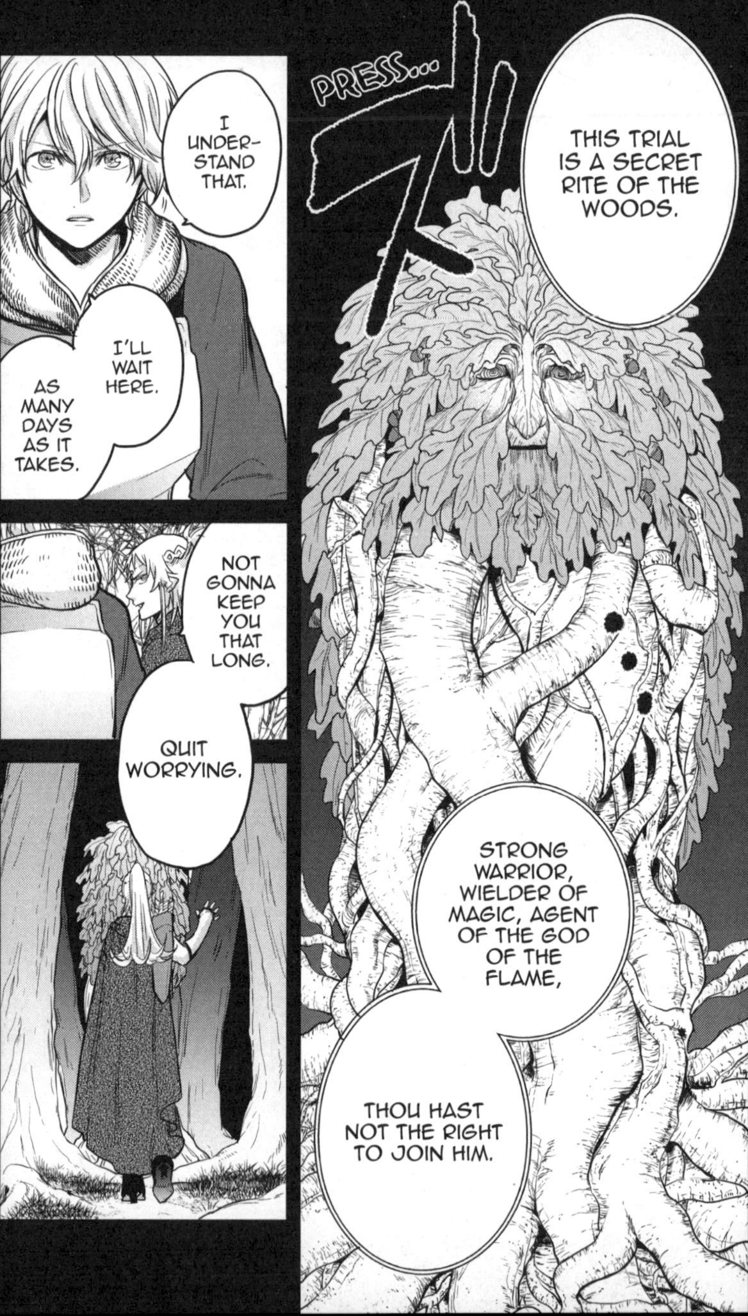
PRESS...
THIS TRIAL IS A SECRET RITE OF THE WOODS.
STRONG WARRIOR, WIELDER OF MAGIC, AGENT OF THE GOD OF THE FLAME,
THOU HAST NOT THE RIGHT TO JOIN HIM.
I UNDERSTAND THAT.
I'LL WAIT HERE.
AS MANY DAYS AS IT TAKES.
NOT GONNA KEEP YOU THAT LONG.
QUIT WORRYING.

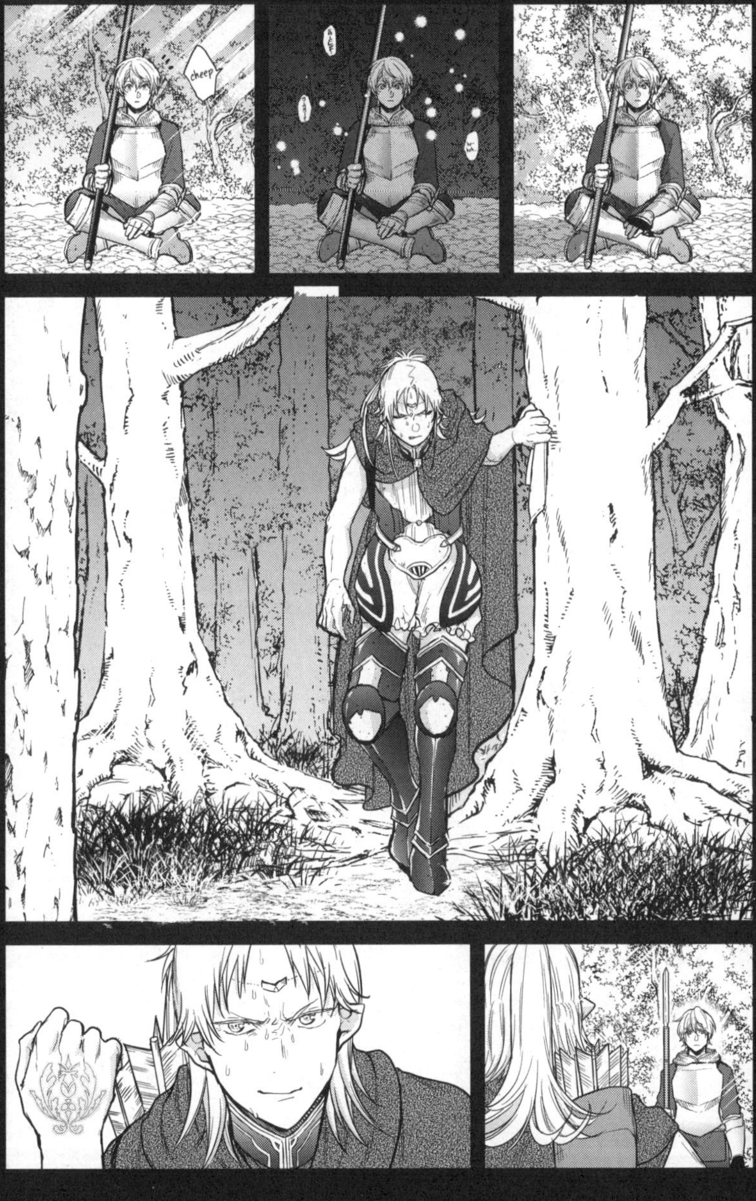
cheep

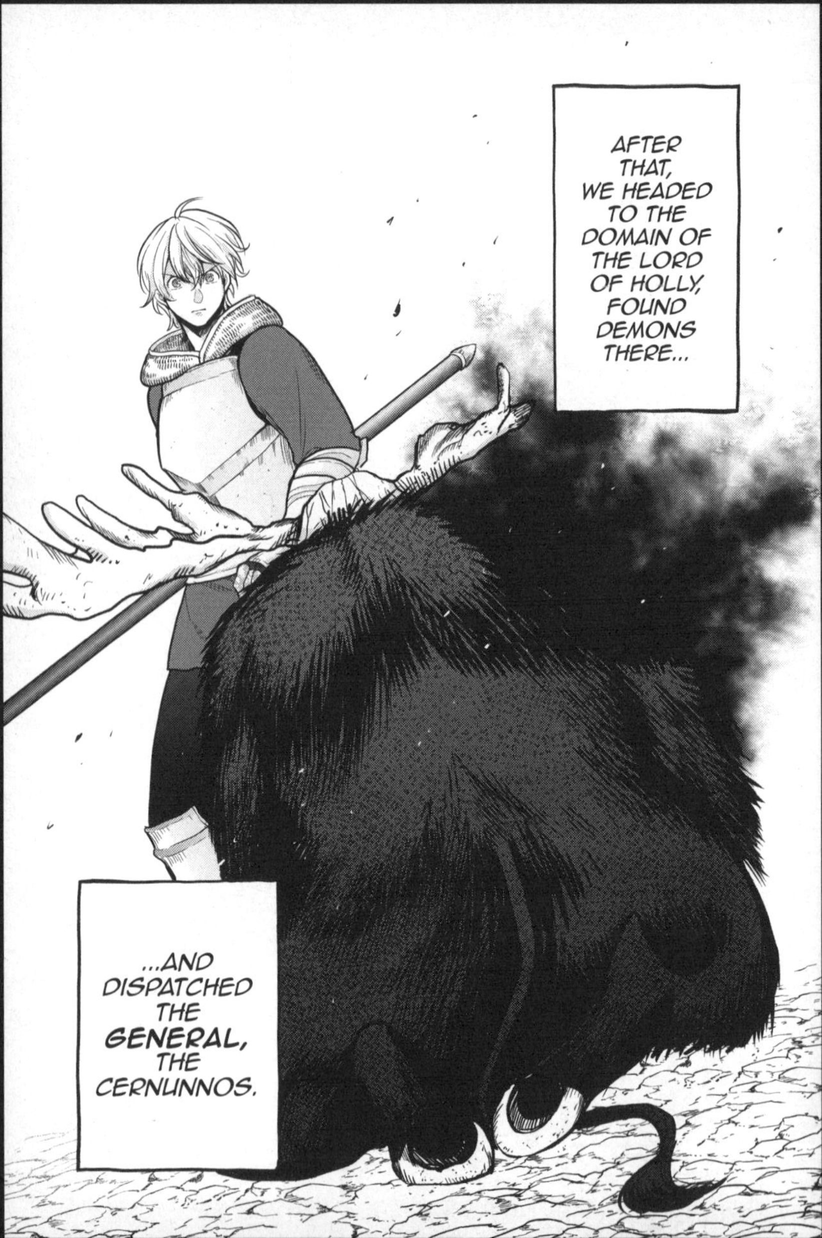
AFTER THAT, WE HEADED TO THE DOMAIN OF THE LORD OF HOLLY, FOUND DEMONS THERE...
...AND DISPATCHED THE GENERAL, THE CERNUNNOS.

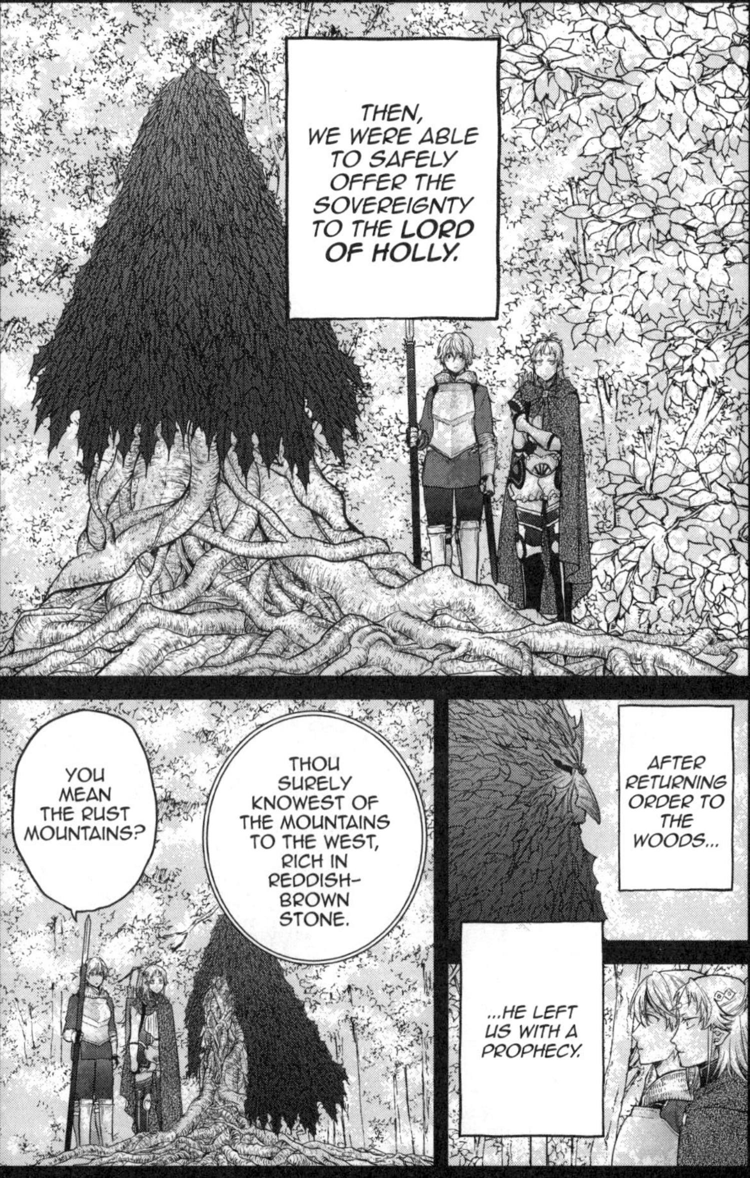
THEN, WE WERE ABLE TO SAFELY OFFER THE SOVEREIGNTY TO THE LORD OF HOLLY.
AFTER RETURNING ORDER TO THE WOODS...
...HE LEFT US WITH A PROPHECY.
THOU SURELY KNOWEST OF THE MOUNTAINS TO THE WEST, RICH IN REDDISH-BROWN STONE.
YOU MEAN THE RUST MOUNTAINS?

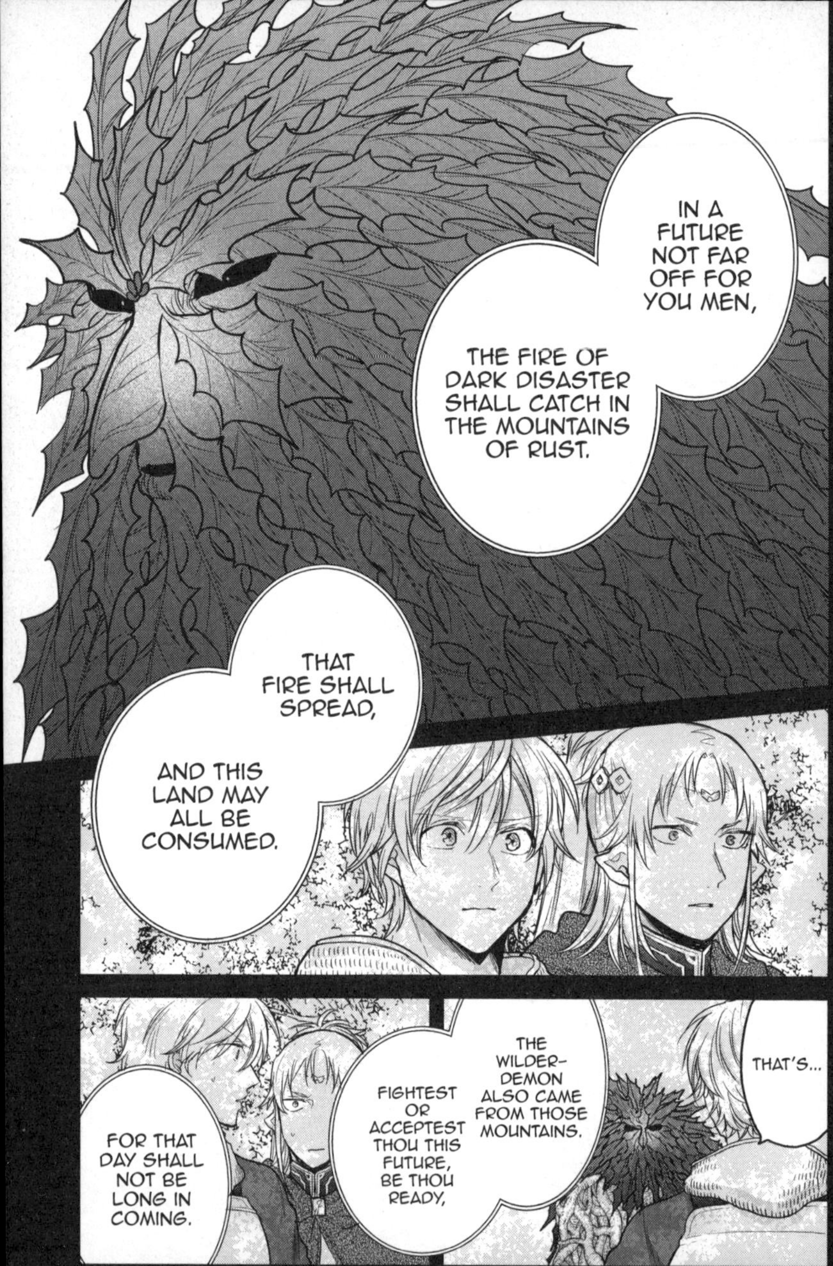
IN A FUTURE NOT FAR OFF FOR YOU MEN,
THE FIRE OF DARK DISASTER SHALL CATCH IN THE MOUNTAINS OF RUST.
THAT FIRE SHALL SPREAD,
AND THIS LAND MAY ALL BE CONSUMED.
THAT'S...
THE WILDER-DEMON ALSO CAME FROM THOSE MOUNTAINS.
FIGHTEST OR ACCEPTEST THOU THIS FUTURE, BE THOU READY,
FOR THAT DAY SHALL NOT BE LONG IN COMING.

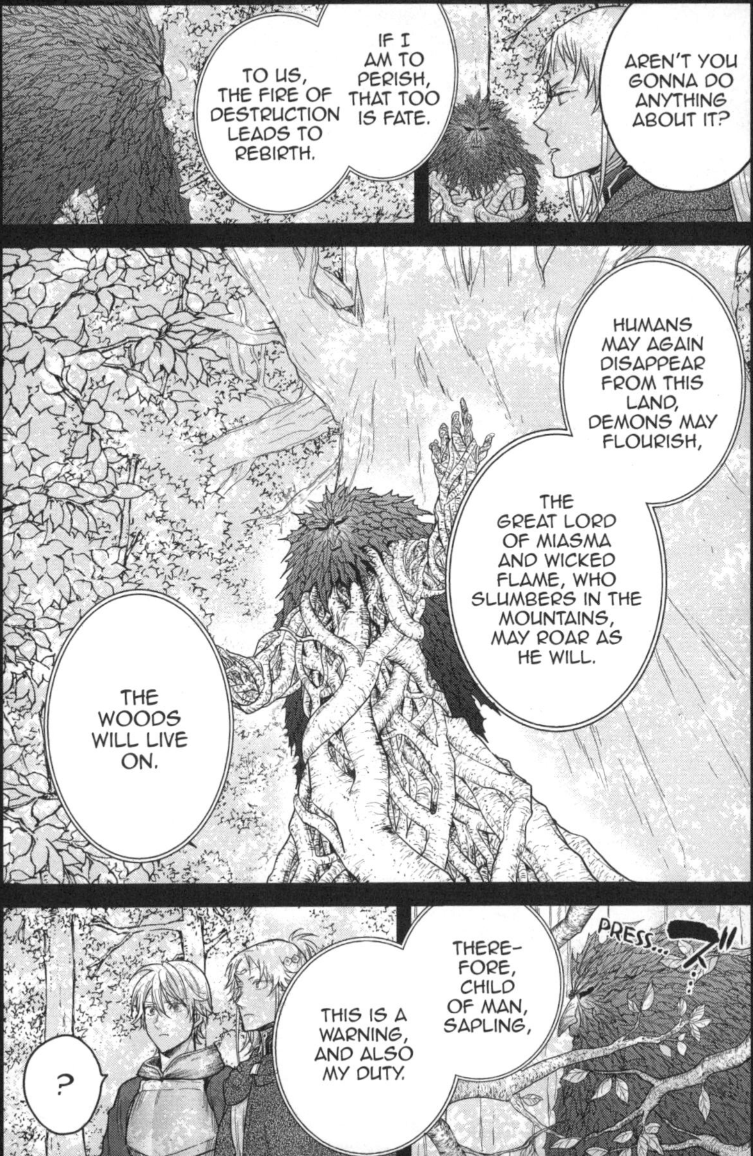
AREN'T YOU GONNA DO ANYTHING ABOUT IT?
IF I AM TO PERISH, THAT TOO IS FATE.
TO US, THE FIRE OF DESTRUCTION LEADS TO REBIRTH.
HUMANS MAY AGAIN DISAPPEAR FROM THIS LAND, DEMONS MAY FLOURISH,
THE GREAT LORD OF MIASMA AND WICKED FLAME, WHO SLUMBERS IN THE MOUNTAINS, MAY ROAR AS HE WILL.
THE WOODS WILL LIVE ON.
PRESS...
THERE-FORE, CHILD OF MAN, SAPLING,
THIS IS A WARNING, AND ALSO MY DUTY.
?

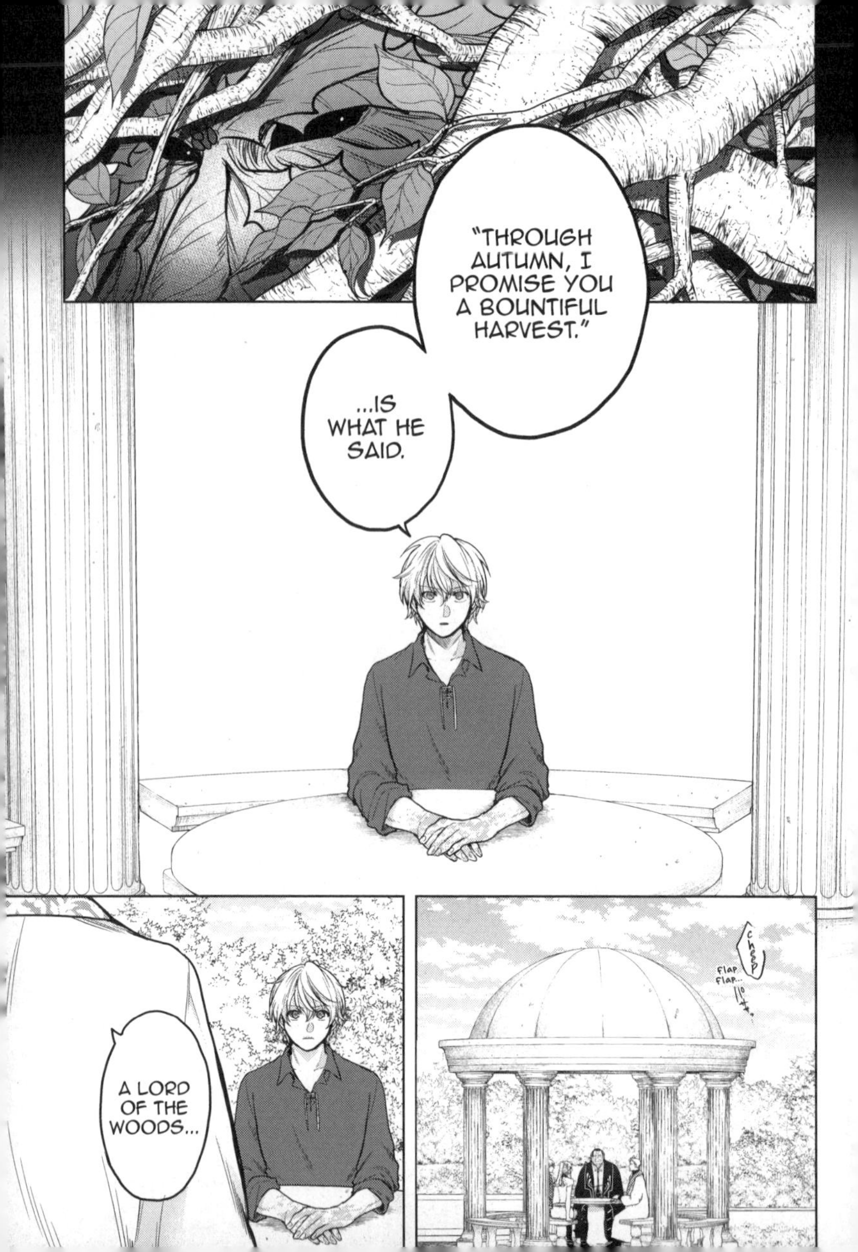
"THROUGH AUTUMN, I PROMISE YOU A BOUNTIFUL HARVEST."
...IS WHAT HE SAID.
cheep
Flap Flap...
A LORD OF THE WOODS...

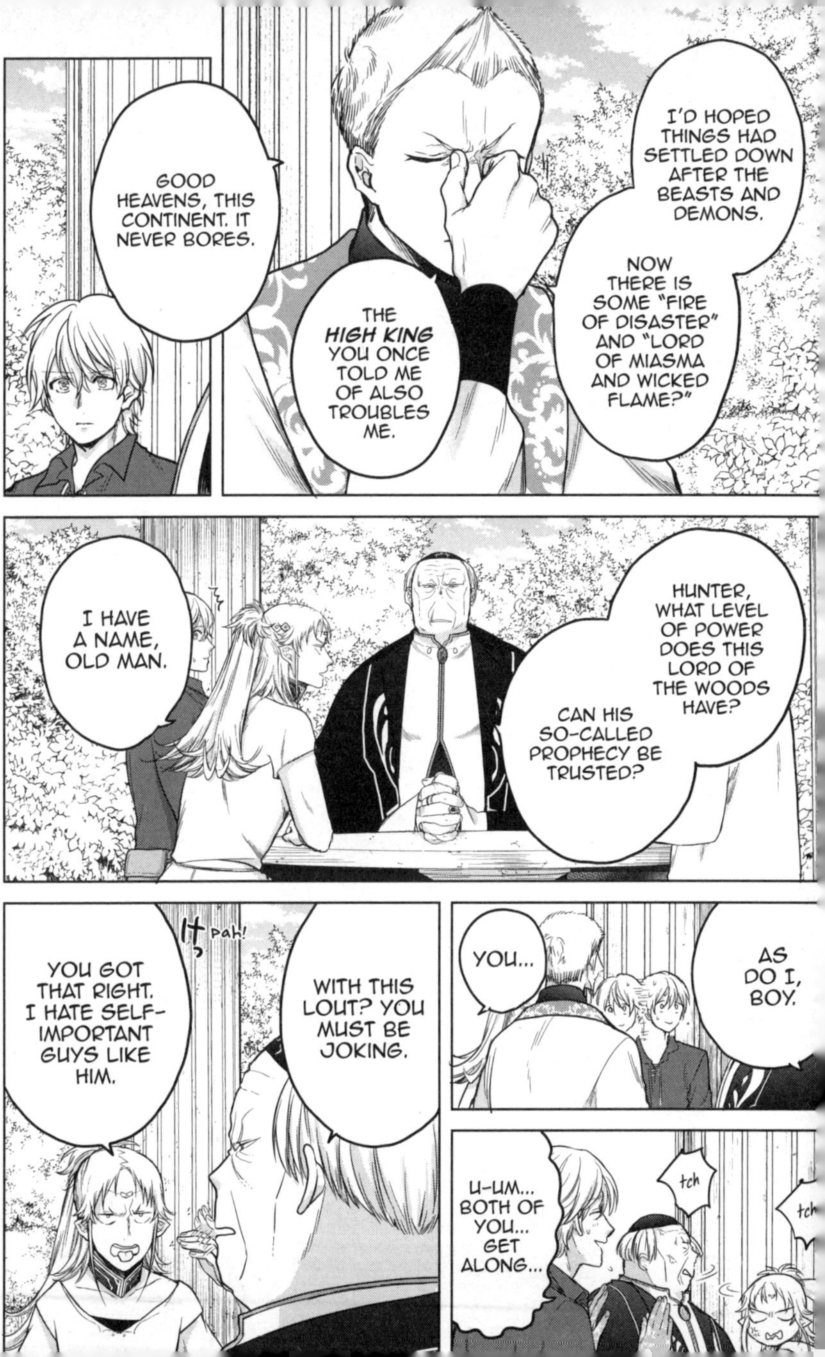
I'D HOPED THINGS HAD SETTLED DOWN AFTER THE BEASTS AND DEMONS.
NOW THERE IS SOME "FIRE OF DISASTER" AND "LORD OF MIASMA AND WICKED FLAME?"
THE *HIGH KING* YOU ONCE TOLD ME OF ALSO TROUBLES ME.
GOOD HEAVENS, THIS CONTINENT. IT NEVER BORES.
HUNTER, WHAT LEVEL OF POWER DOES THIS LORD OF THE WOODS HAVE?
CAN HIS SO-CALLED PROPHECY BE TRUSTED?
I HAVE A NAME, OLD MAN.
AS DO I, BOY.
YOU...
tch
tch
U-UM... BOTH OF YOU... GET ALONG...
WITH THIS LOUT? YOU MUST BE JOKING.
け pah!
YOU GOT THAT RIGHT. I HATE SELF-IMPORTANT GUYS LIKE HIM.

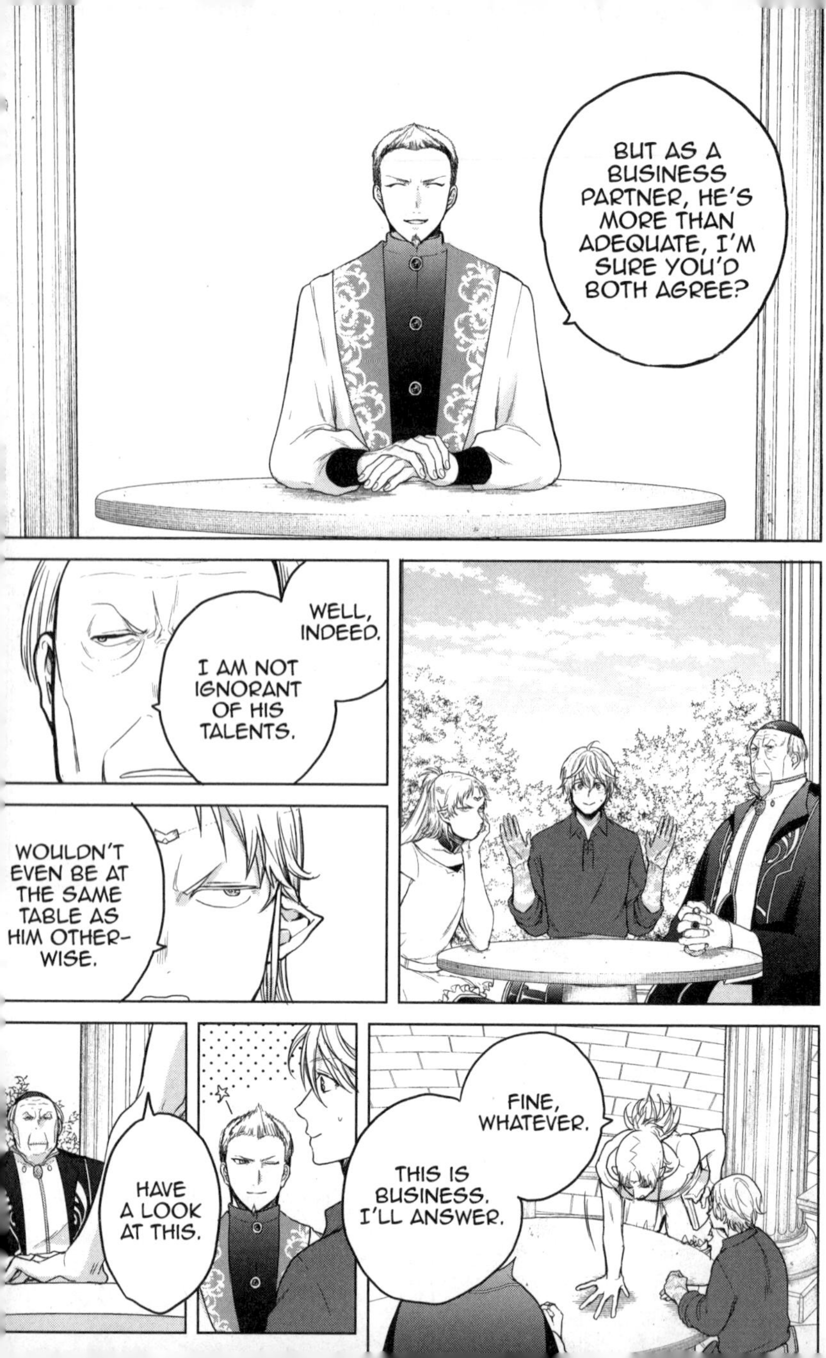
BUT AS A BUSINESS PARTNER, HE'S MORE THAN ADEQUATE, I'M SURE YOU'D BOTH AGREE?
WELL, INDEED.
I AM NOT IGNORANT OF HIS TALENTS.
WOULDN'T EVEN BE AT THE SAME TABLE AS HIM OTHER-WISE.
FINE, WHATEVER.
THIS IS BUSINESS. I'LL ANSWER.
HAVE A LOOK AT THIS.

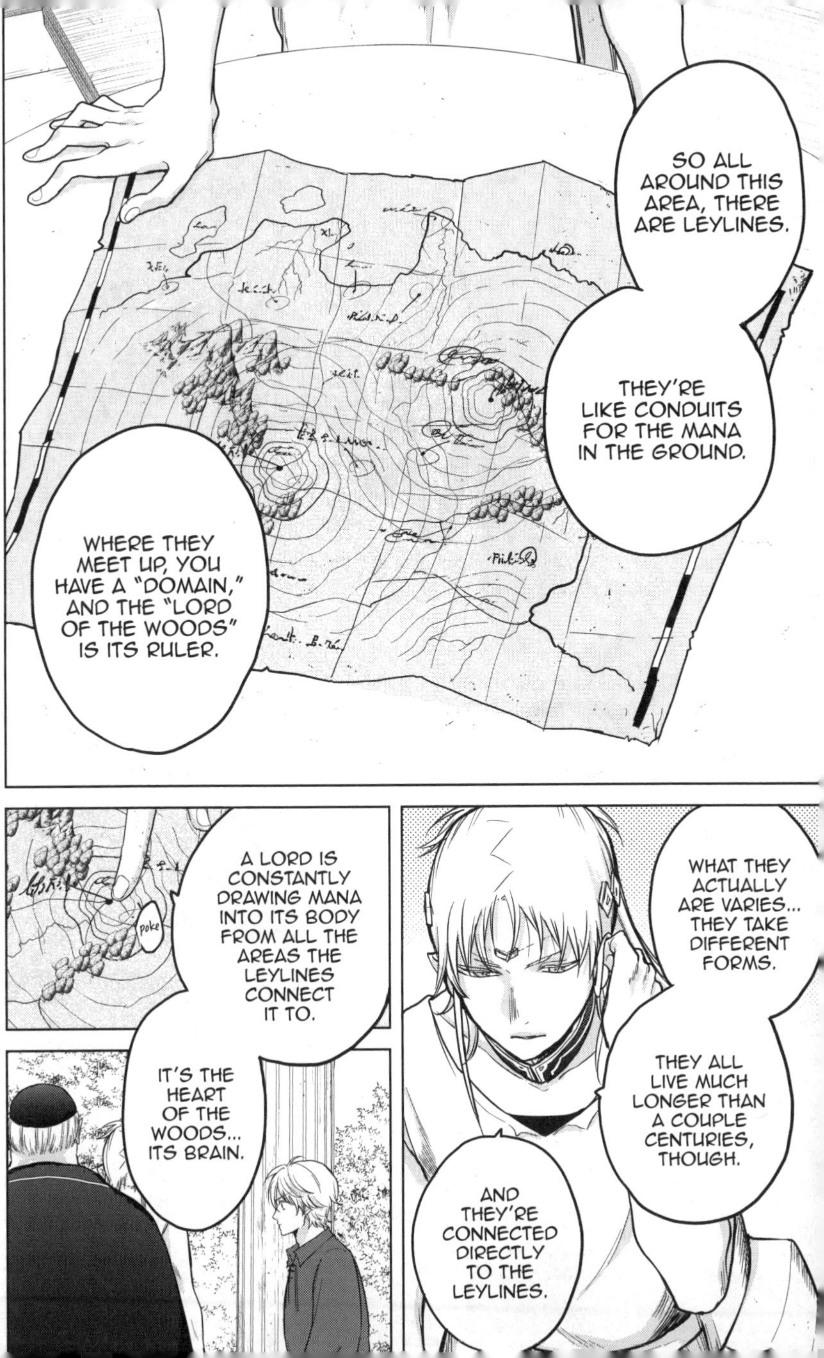
SO ALL AROUND THIS AREA, THERE ARE LEYLINES.
THEY'RE LIKE CONDUITS FOR THE MANA IN THE GROUND.
WHERE THEY MEET UP, YOU HAVE A "DOMAIN," AND THE "LORD OF THE WOODS" IS ITS RULER.
WHAT THEY ACTUALLY ARE VARIES... THEY TAKE DIFFERENT FORMS.
THEY ALL LIVE MUCH LONGER THAN A COUPLE CENTURIES, THOUGH.
AND THEY'RE CONNECTED DIRECTLY TO THE LEYLINES.
A LORD IS CONSTANTLY DRAWING MANA INTO ITS BODY FROM ALL THE AREAS THE LEYLINES CONNECT IT TO.
Poke
IT'S THE HEART OF THE WOODS... ITS BRAIN.

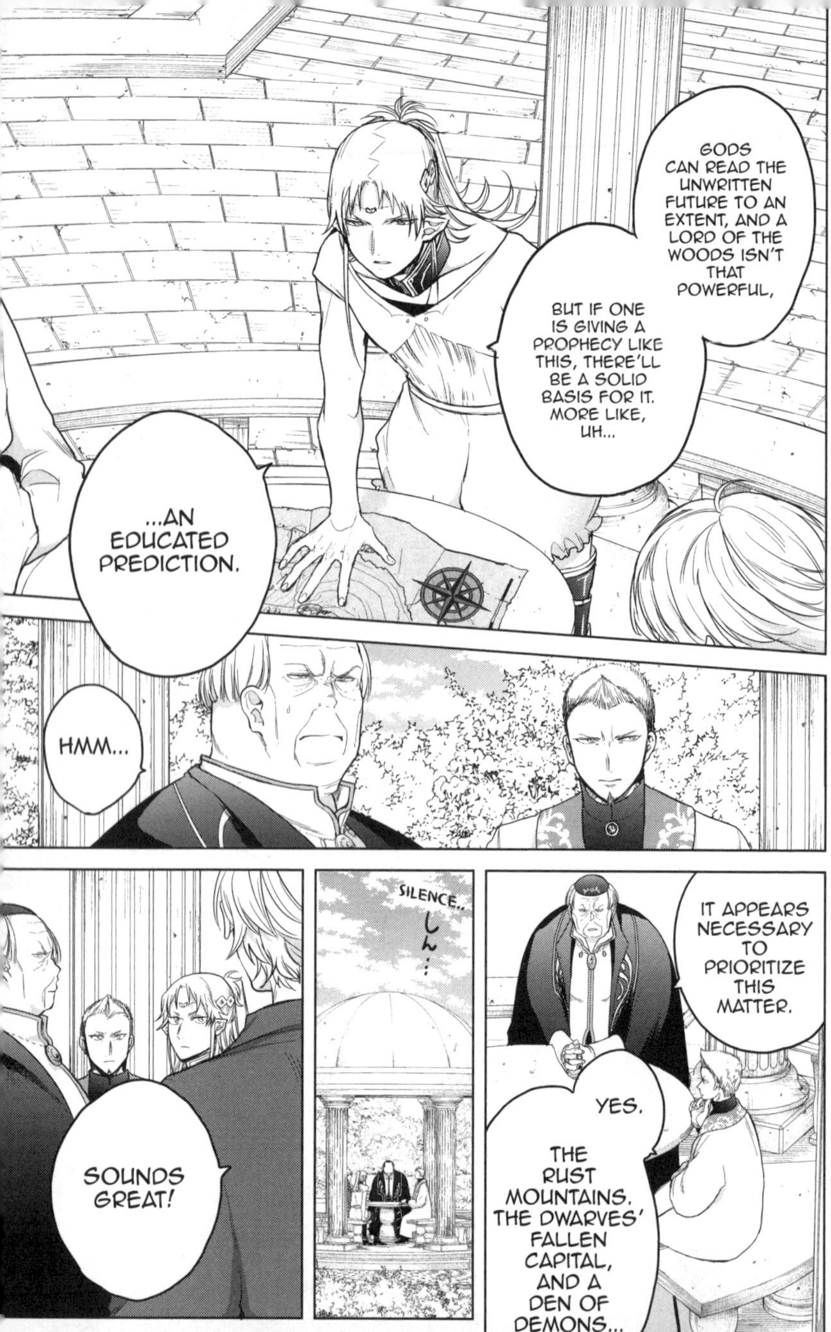
GODS CAN READ THE UNWRITTEN FUTURE TO AN EXTENT, AND A LORD OF THE WOODS ISN'T THAT POWERFUL,
BUT IF ONE IS GIVING A PROPHECY LIKE THIS, THERE'LL BE A SOLID BASIS FOR IT. MORE LIKE, UH...
...AN EDUCATED PREDICTION.
HMM...
IT APPEARS NECESSARY TO PRIORITIZE THIS MATTER.
YES.
THE RUST MOUNTAINS. THE DWARVES' FALLEN CAPITAL, AND A DEN OF DEMONS...
SILENCE...
しん…
SOUNDS GREAT!

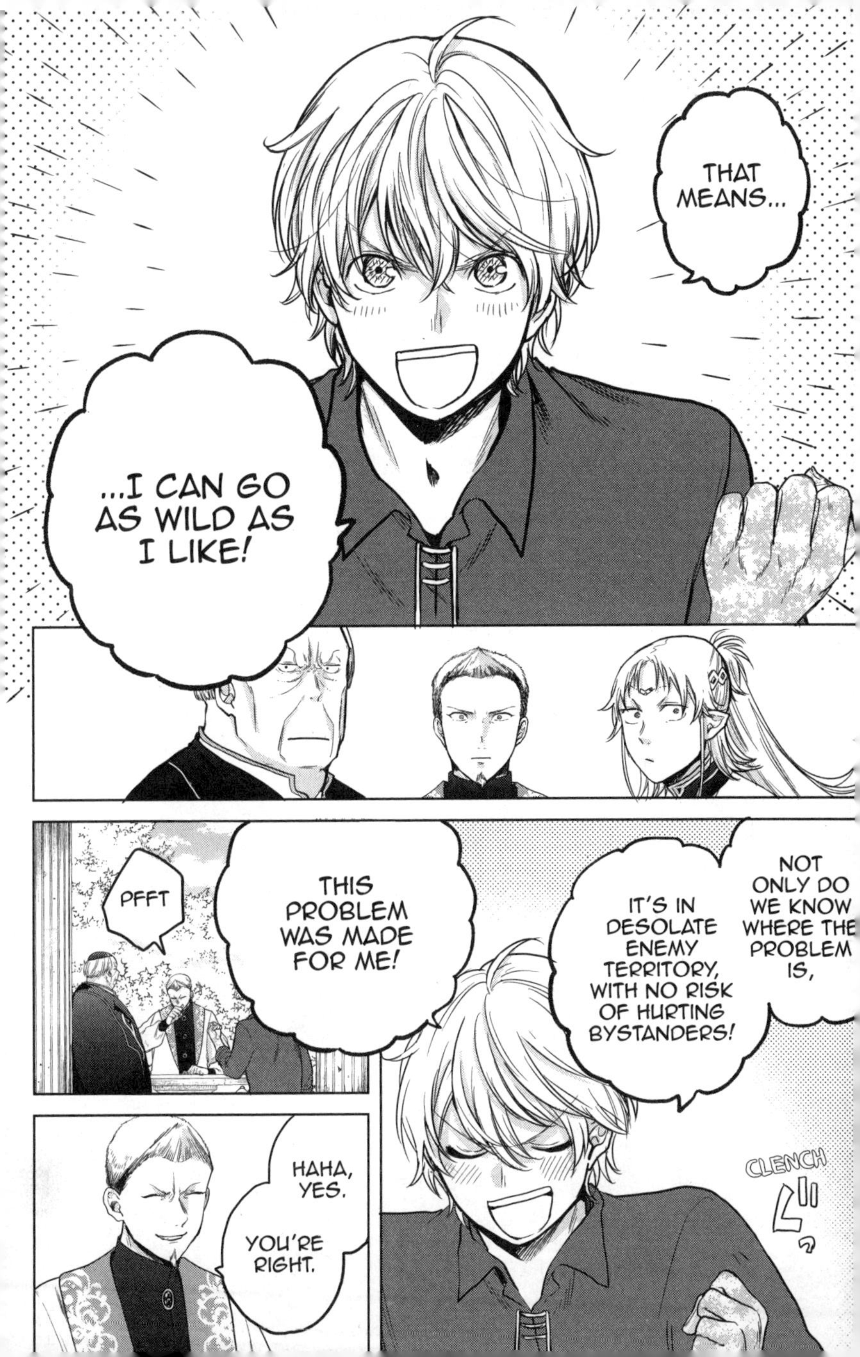
THAT MEANS...
...I CAN GO AS WILD AS I LIKE!
NOT ONLY DO WE KNOW WHERE THE PROBLEM IS,
IT'S IN DESOLATE ENEMY TERRITORY, WITH NO RISK OF HURTING BYSTANDERS!
THIS PROBLEM WAS MADE FOR ME!
CLENCH
PFFT
HAHA, YES.
YOU'RE RIGHT.

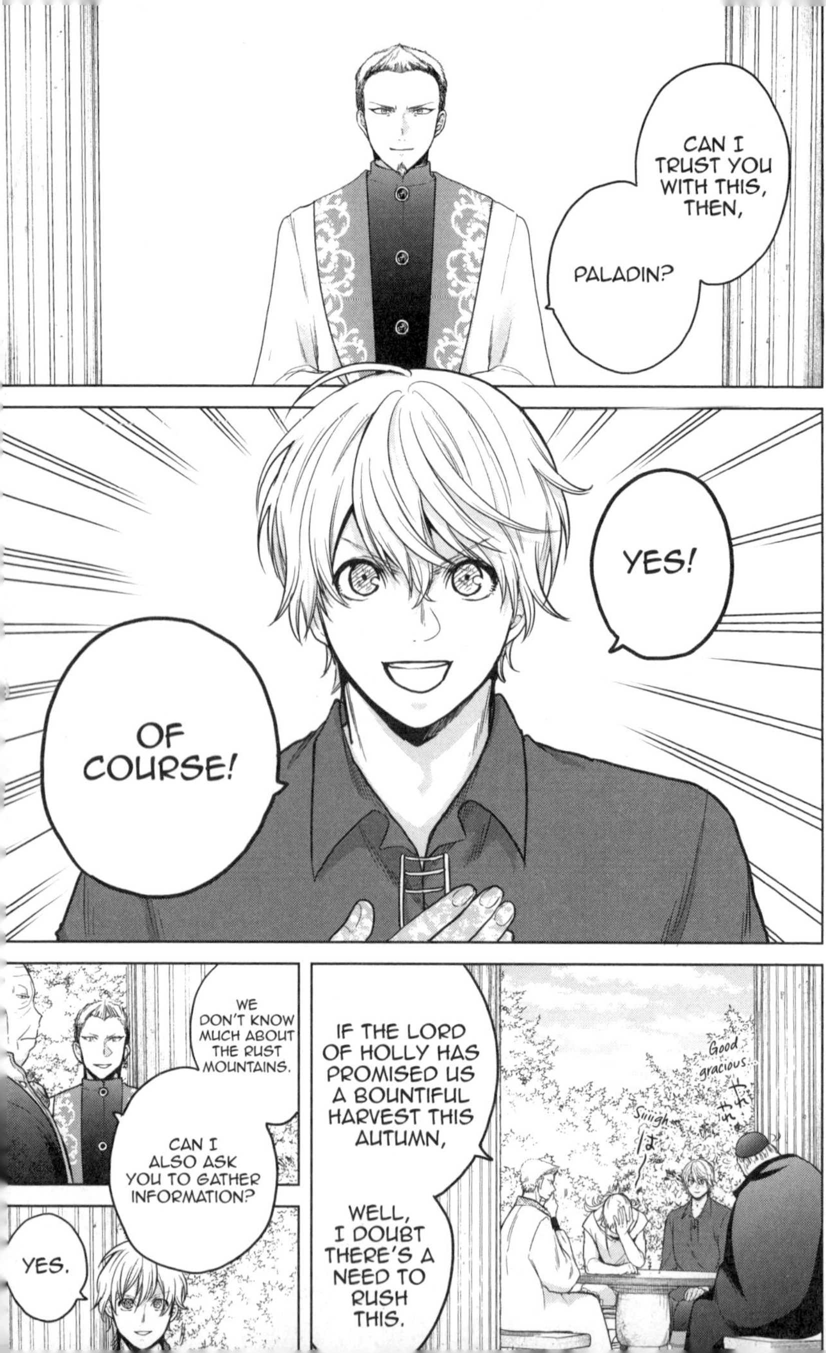
CAN I TRUST YOU WITH THIS, THEN,
PALADIN?
YES!
OF COURSE!
Good gracious...
Siiiigh
IF THE LORD OF HOLLY HAS PROMISED US A BOUNTIFUL HARVEST THIS AUTUMN,
WELL, I DOUBT THERE'S A NEED TO RUSH THIS.
WE DON'T KNOW MUCH ABOUT THE RUST MOUNTAINS.
CAN I ALSO ASK YOU TO GATHER INFORMATION?
YES.

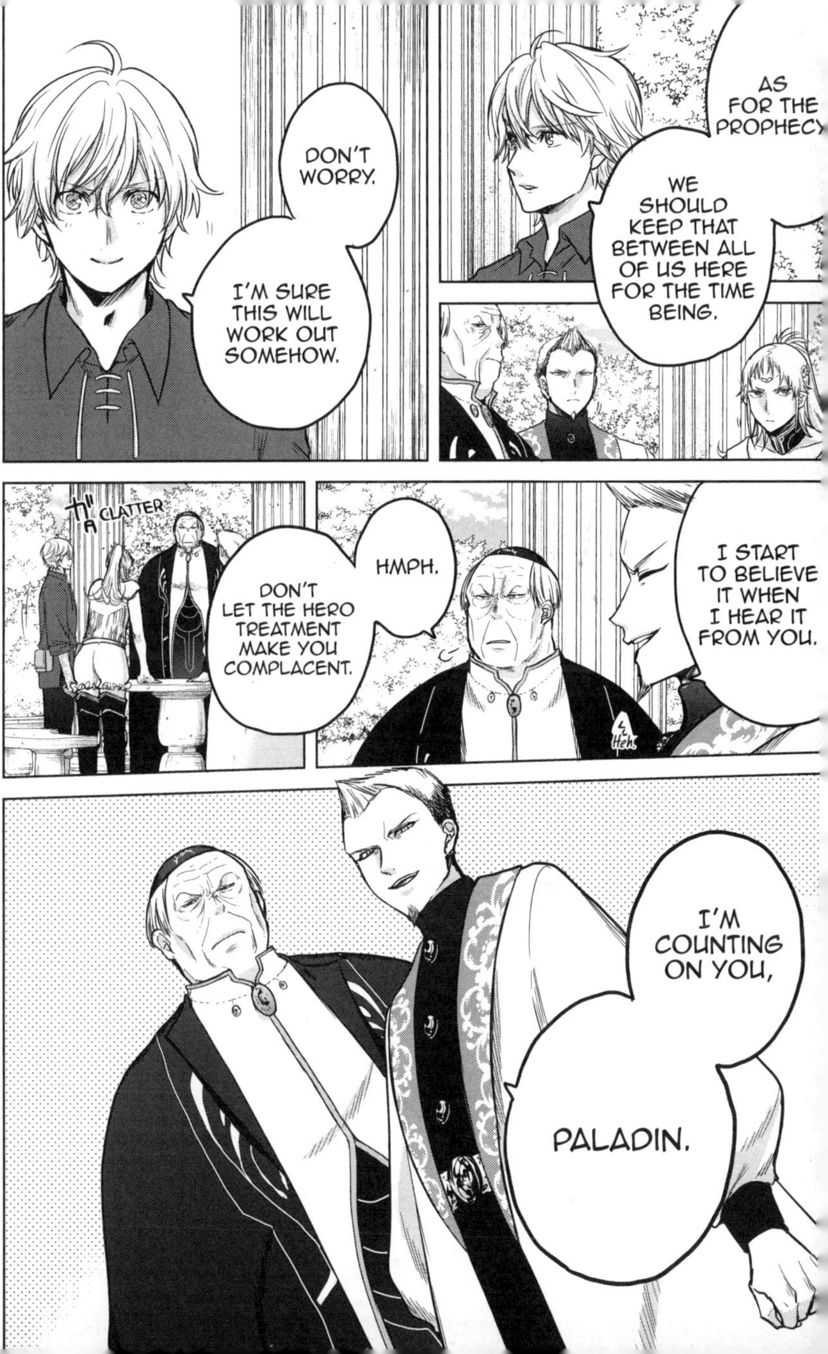
AS FOR THE PROPHECY
WE SHOULD KEEP THAT BETWEEN ALL OF US HERE FOR THE TIME BEING.
DON'T WORRY.
I'M SURE THIS WILL WORK OUT SOMEHOW.
I START TO BELIEVE IT WHEN I HEAR IT FROM YOU.
Heh
HMPH.
DON'T LET THE HERO TREATMENT MAKE YOU COMPLACENT.
ガ CLATTER
I'M COUNTING ON YOU,
PALADIN.

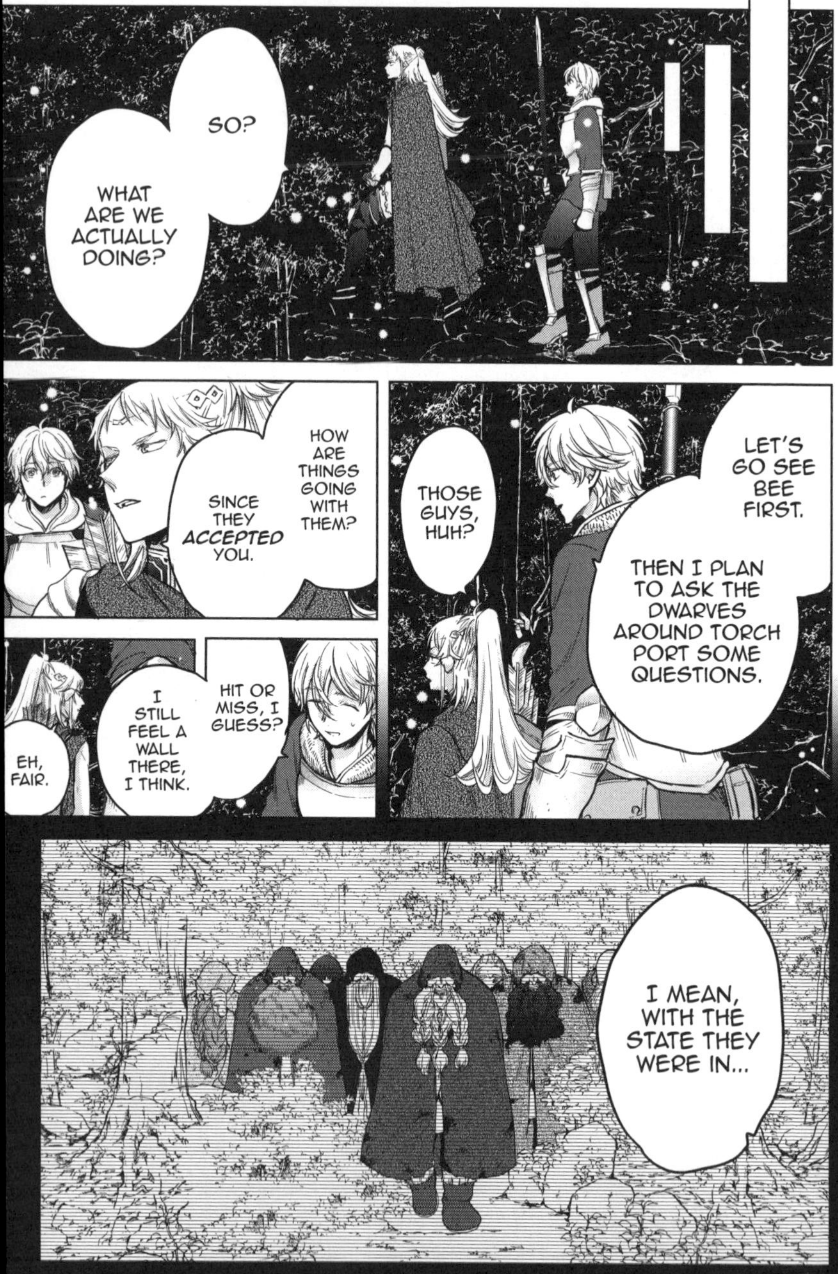
SO?
WHAT ARE WE ACTUALLY DOING?
LET'S GO SEE BEE FIRST.
THEN I PLAN TO ASK THE DWARVES AROUND TORCH PORT SOME QUESTIONS.
THOSE GUYS, HUH?
HOW ARE THINGS GOING WITH THEM?
SINCE THEY *ACCEPTED* YOU.
HIT OR MISS, I GUESS?
I STILL FEEL A WALL THERE, I THINK.
EH, FAIR.
I MEAN, WITH THE STATE THEY WERE IN...

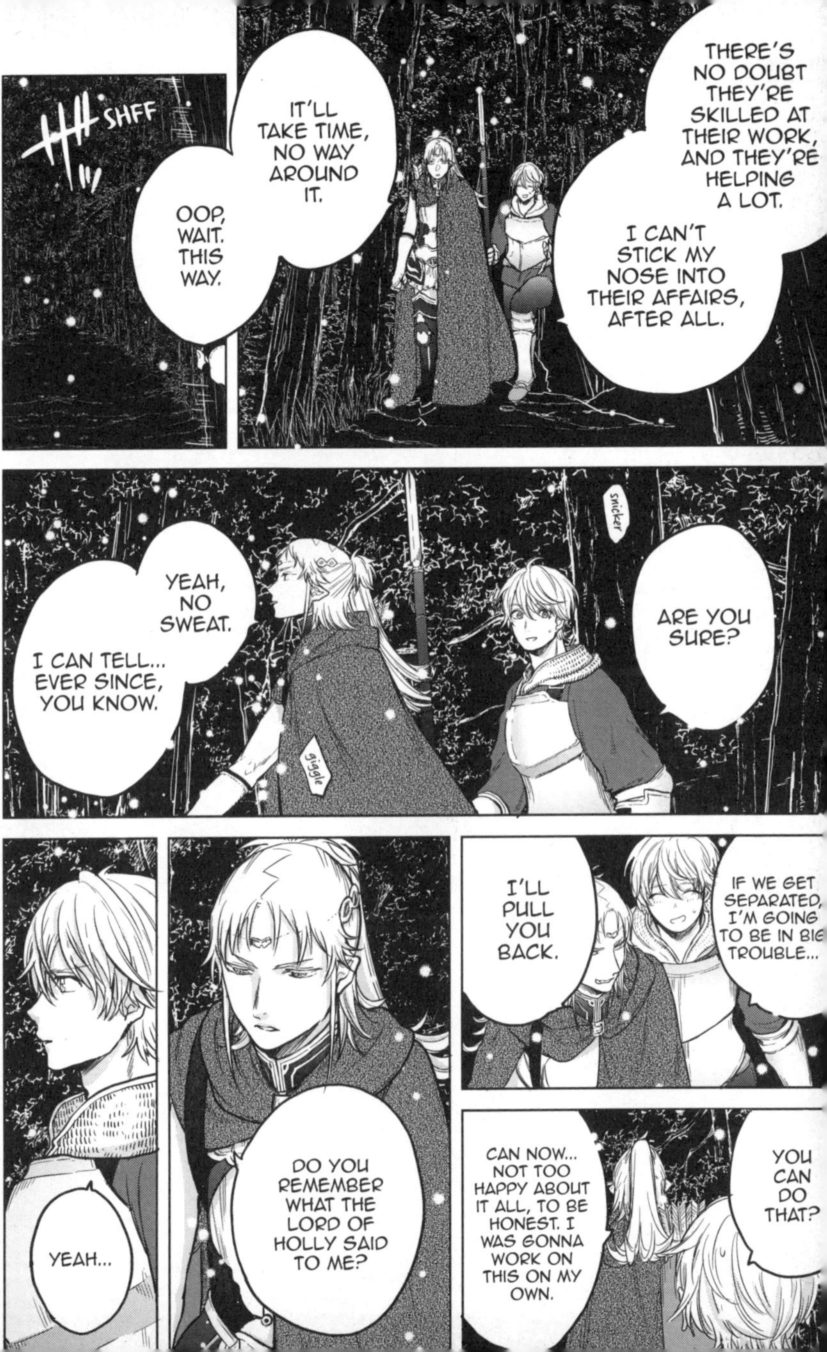
THERE'S NO DOUBT THEY'RE SKILLED AT THEIR WORK, AND THEY'RE HELPING A LOT.
I CAN'T STICK MY NOSE INTO THEIR AFFAIRS, AFTER ALL.
IT'LL TAKE TIME, NO WAY AROUND IT.
SHFF
OOP, WAIT. THIS WAY.
snicker
ARE YOU SURE?
YEAH, NO SWEAT.
I CAN TELL... EVER SINCE, YOU KNOW.
giggle
IF WE GET SEPARATED, I'M GOING TO BE IN BIG TROUBLE...
I'LL PULL YOU BACK.
YOU CAN DO THAT?
CAN NOW... NOT TOO HAPPY ABOUT IT ALL, TO BE HONEST. I WAS GONNA WORK ON THIS ON MY OWN.
DO YOU REMEMBER WHAT THE LORD OF HOLLY SAID TO ME?
YEAH...

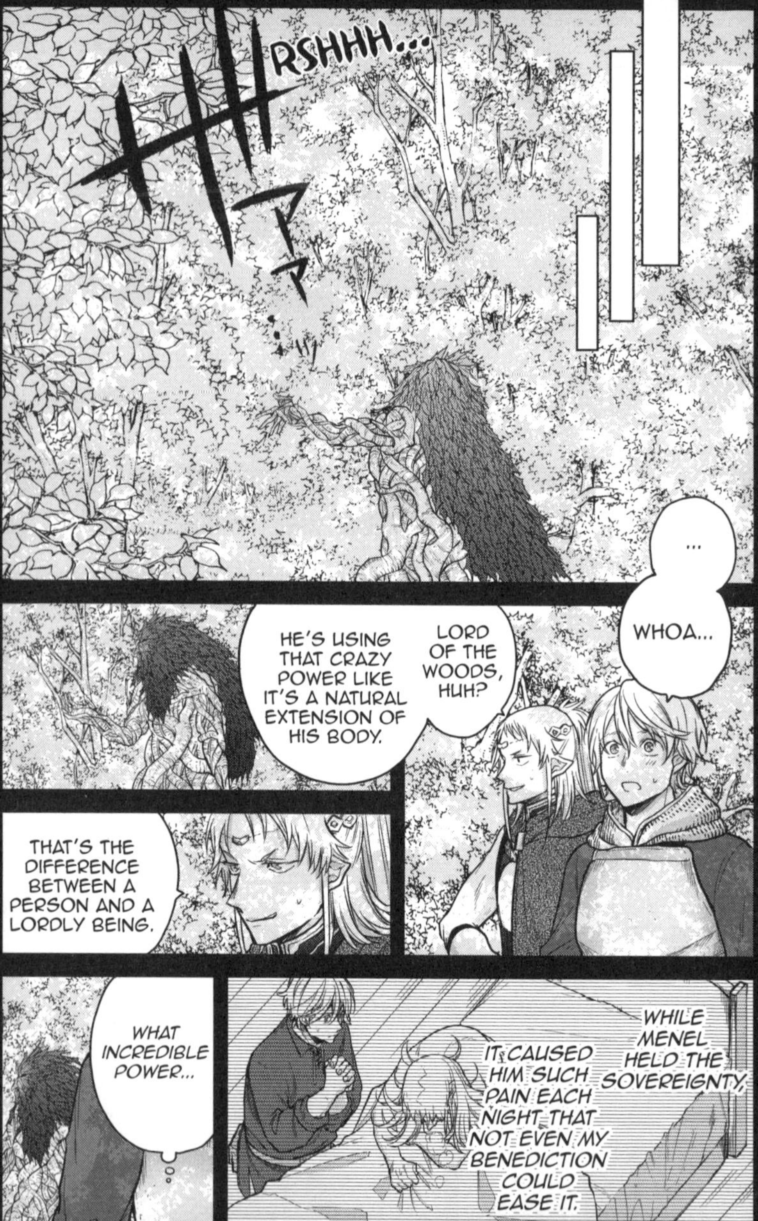
RSHHH...
...
WHOA...
LORD OF THE WOODS, HUH?
HE'S USING THAT CRAZY POWER LIKE IT'S A NATURAL EXTENSION OF HIS BODY.
THAT'S THE DIFFERENCE BETWEEN A PERSON AND A LORDLY BEING.
WHILE MENEL HELD THE SOVEREIGNTY,
IT CAUSED HIM SUCH PAIN EACH NIGHT THAT NOT EVEN MY BENEDICTION COULD EASE IT.
WHAT INCREDIBLE POWER...

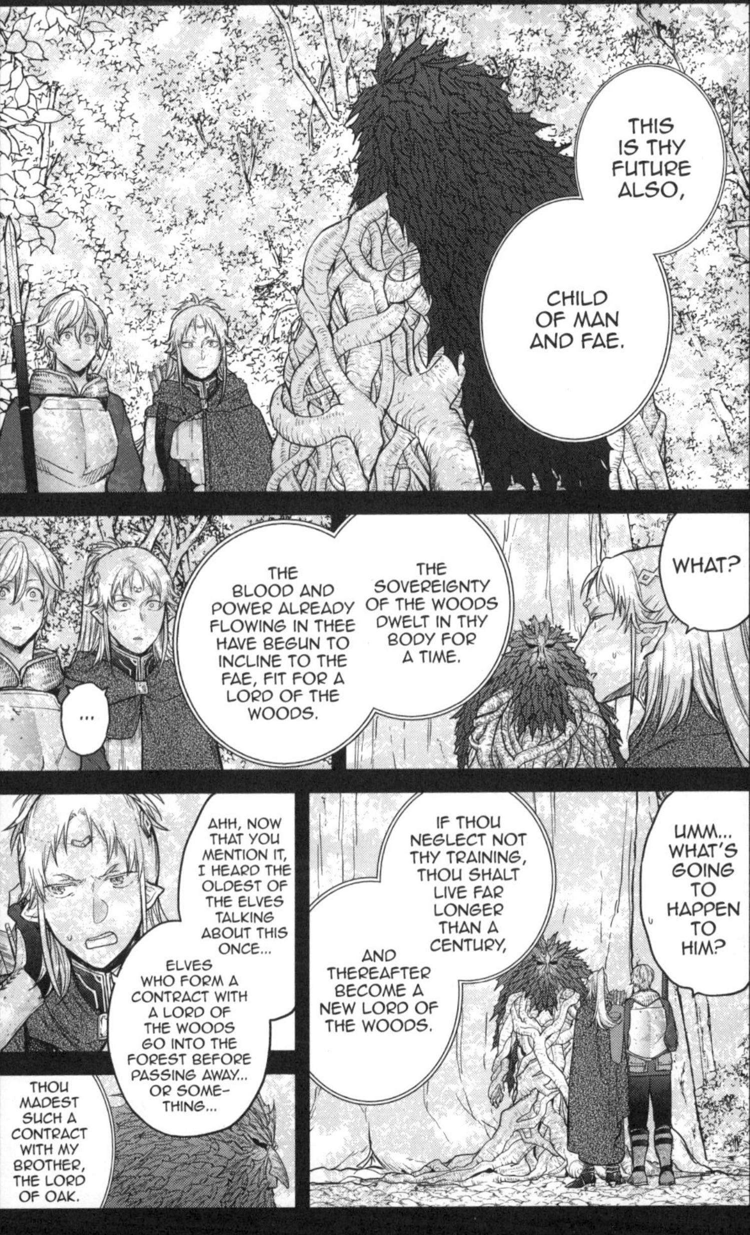
THIS IS THY FUTURE ALSO,
CHILD OF MAN AND FAE.
WHAT?
THE SOVEREIGNTY OF THE WOODS DWELT IN THY BODY FOR A TIME.
THE BLOOD AND POWER ALREADY FLOWING IN THEE HAVE BEGUN TO INCLINE TO THE FAE, FIT FOR A LORD OF THE WOODS.
...
UMM... WHAT'S GOING TO HAPPEN TO HIM?
IF THOU NEGLECT NOT THY TRAINING, THOU SHALT LIVE FAR LONGER THAN A CENTURY,
AND THEREAFTER BECOME A NEW LORD OF THE WOODS.
AHH, NOW THAT YOU MENTION IT, I HEARD THE OLDEST OF THE ELVES TALKING ABOUT THIS ONCE...
ELVES WHO FORM A CONTRACT WITH A LORD OF THE WOODS GO INTO THE FOREST BEFORE PASSING AWAY... OR SOME-THING...
THOU MADEST SUCH A CONTRACT WITH MY BROTHER, THE LORD OF OAK.

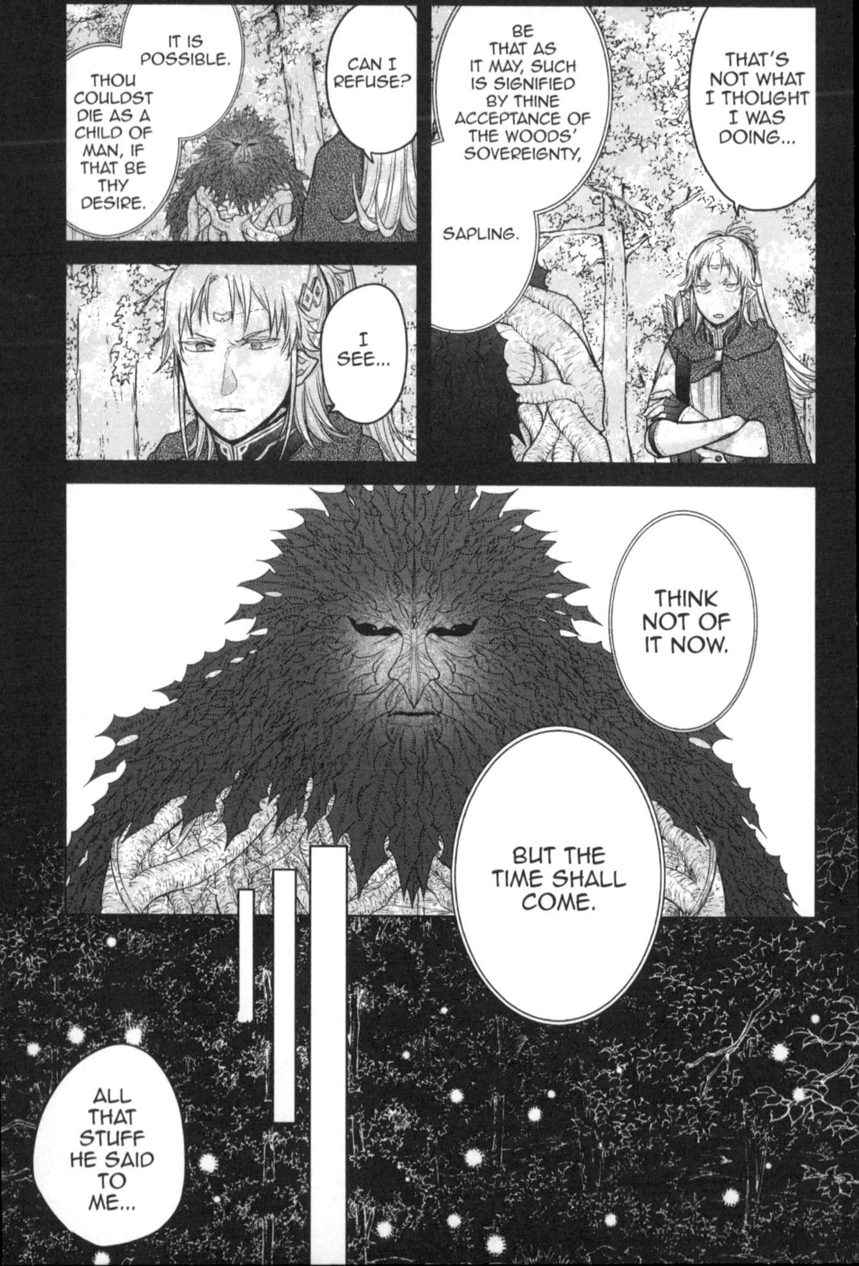
THAT'S NOT WHAT I THOUGHT I WAS DOING...
BE THAT AS IT MAY, SUCH IS SIGNIFIED BY THINE ACCEPTANCE OF THE WOODS' SOVEREIGNTY,
SAPLING.
CAN I REFUSE?
IT IS POSSIBLE.
THOU COULDST DIE AS A CHILD OF MAN, IF THAT BE THY DESIRE.
I SEE...
THINK NOT OF IT NOW.
BUT THE TIME SHALL COME.
ALL THAT STUFF HE SAID TO ME...

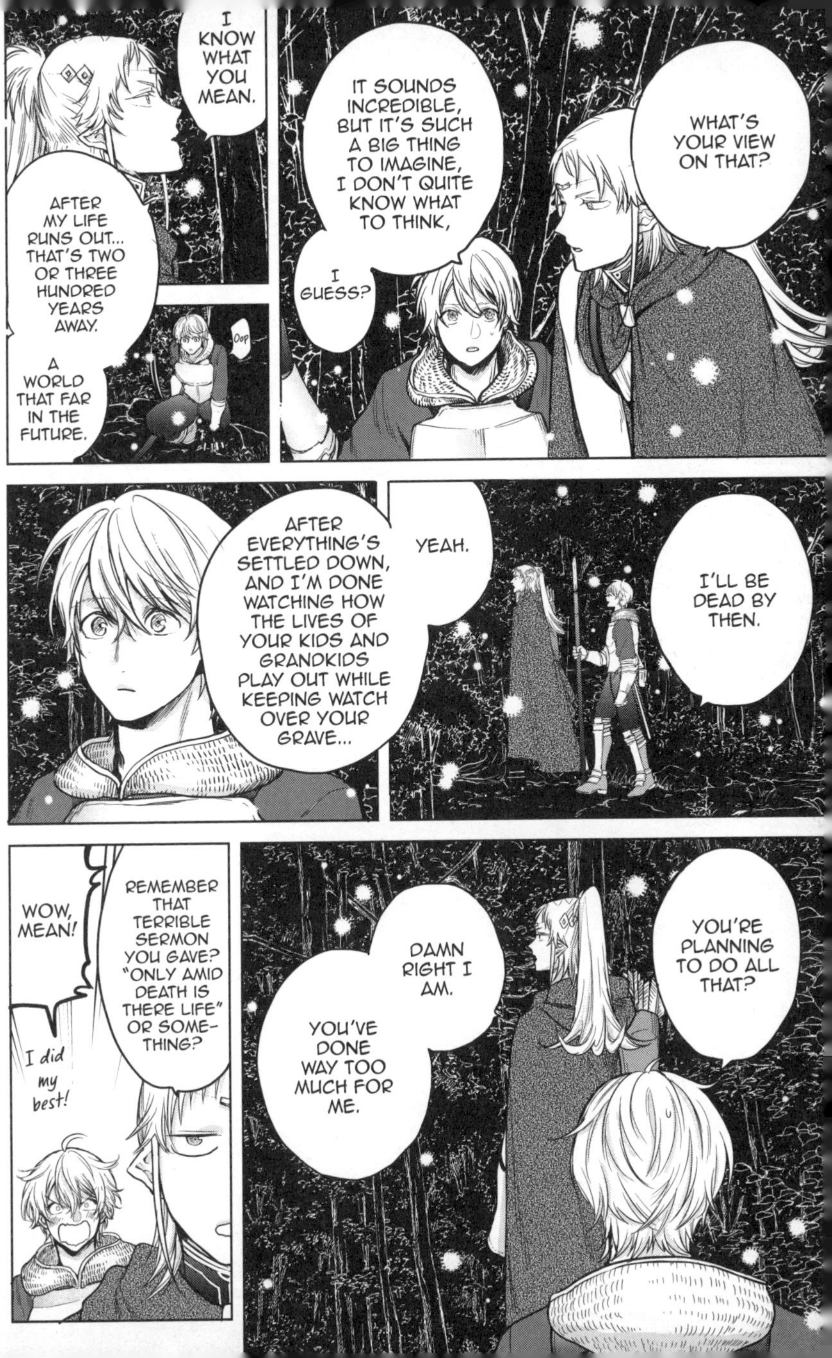
WHAT'S YOUR VIEW ON THAT?
IT SOUNDS INCREDIBLE, BUT IT'S SUCH A BIG THING TO IMAGINE, I DON'T QUITE KNOW WHAT TO THINK,
I GUESS?
I KNOW WHAT YOU MEAN.
AFTER MY LIFE RUNS OUT... THAT'S TWO OR THREE HUNDRED YEARS AWAY.
Oop
A WORLD THAT FAR IN THE FUTURE.
I'LL BE DEAD BY THEN.
YEAH.
AFTER EVERYTHING'S SETTLED DOWN, AND I'M DONE WATCHING HOW THE LIVES OF YOUR KIDS AND GRANDKIDS PLAY OUT WHILE KEEPING WATCH OVER YOUR GRAVE...
YOU'RE PLANNING TO DO ALL THAT?
DAMN RIGHT I AM.
YOU'VE DONE WAY TOO MUCH FOR ME.
REMEMBER THAT TERRIBLE SERMON YOU GAVE? "ONLY AMID DEATH IS THERE LIFE" OR SOME-THING?
WOW, MEAN!
I did my best!

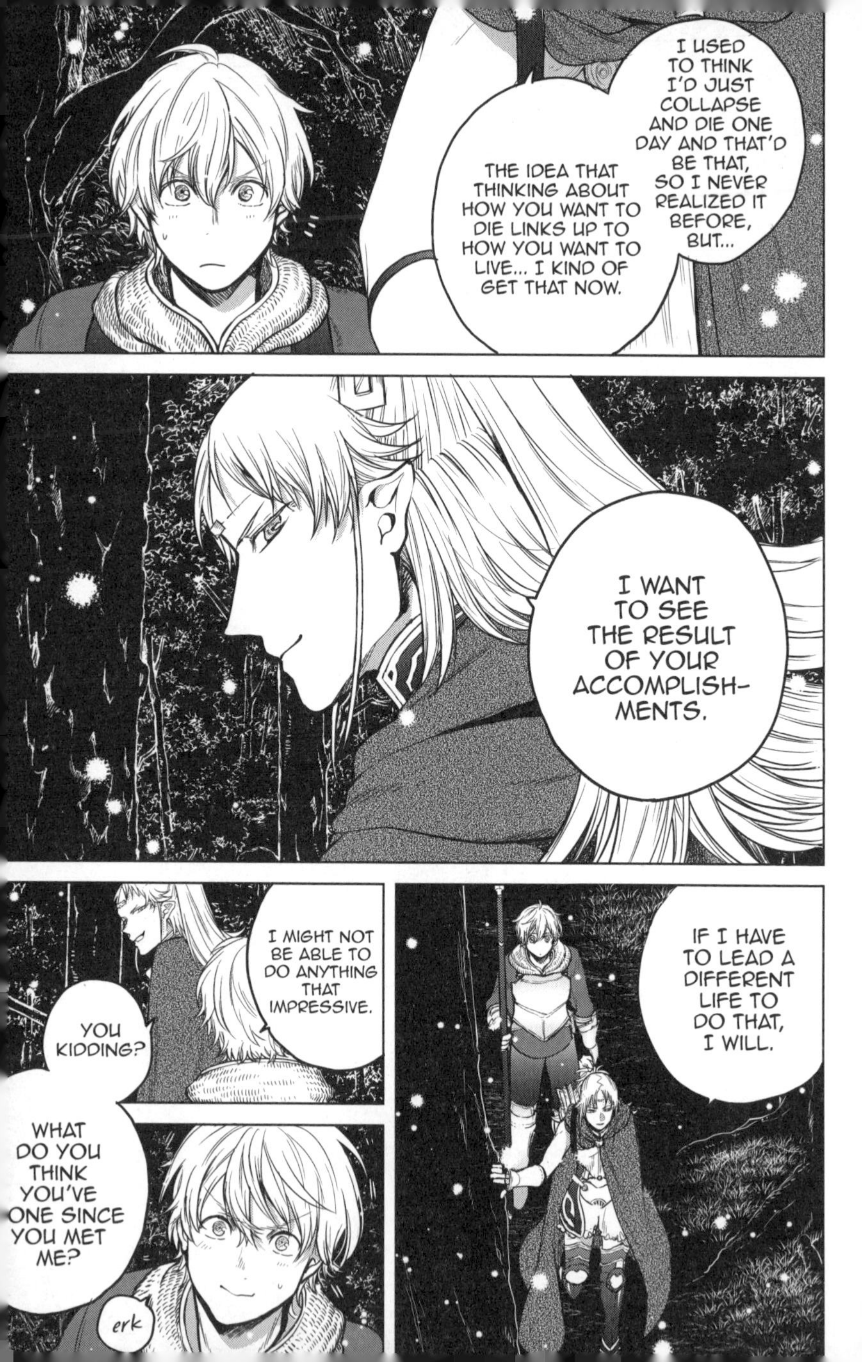
I USED TO THINK I'D JUST COLLAPSE AND DIE ONE DAY AND THAT'D BE THAT, SO I NEVER REALIZED IT BEFORE, BUT...
THE IDEA THAT THINKING ABOUT HOW YOU WANT TO DIE LINKS UP TO HOW YOU WANT TO LIVE... I KIND OF GET THAT NOW.
I WANT TO SEE THE RESULT OF YOUR ACCOMPLISH-MENTS.
IF I HAVE TO LEAD A DIFFERENT LIFE TO DO THAT, I WILL.
I MIGHT NOT BE ABLE TO DO ANYTHING THAT IMPRESSIVE.
YOU KIDDING?
WHAT DO YOU THINK YOU'VE ONE SINCE YOU MET ME?
erk

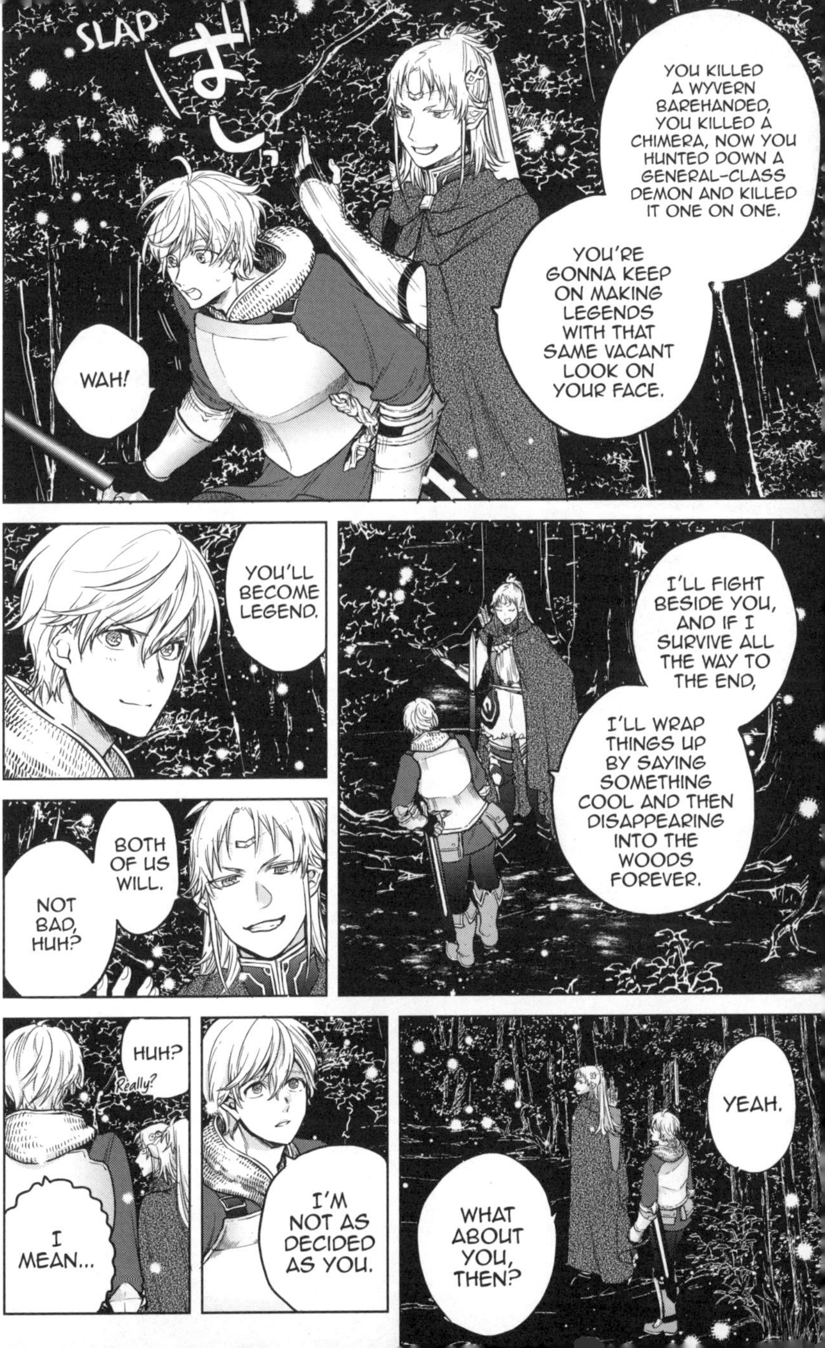

YOU KILLED A WYVERN BAREHANDED, YOU KILLED A CHIMERA, NOW YOU HUNTED DOWN A GENERAL-CLASS DEMON AND KILLED IT ONE ON ONE.
YOU'RE GONNA KEEP ON MAKING LEGENDS WITH THAT SAME VACANT LOOK ON YOUR FACE.
SLAP
WAH!
I'LL FIGHT BESIDE YOU, AND IF I SURVIVE ALL THE WAY TO THE END,
I'LL WRAP THINGS UP BY SAYING SOMETHING COOL AND THEN DISAPPEARING INTO THE WOODS FOREVER.
YOU'LL BECOME LEGEND.
BOTH OF US WILL.
NOT BAD, HUH?
YEAH.
WHAT ABOUT YOU, THEN?
I'M NOT AS DECIDED AS YOU.
HUH?
Really?
I MEAN...

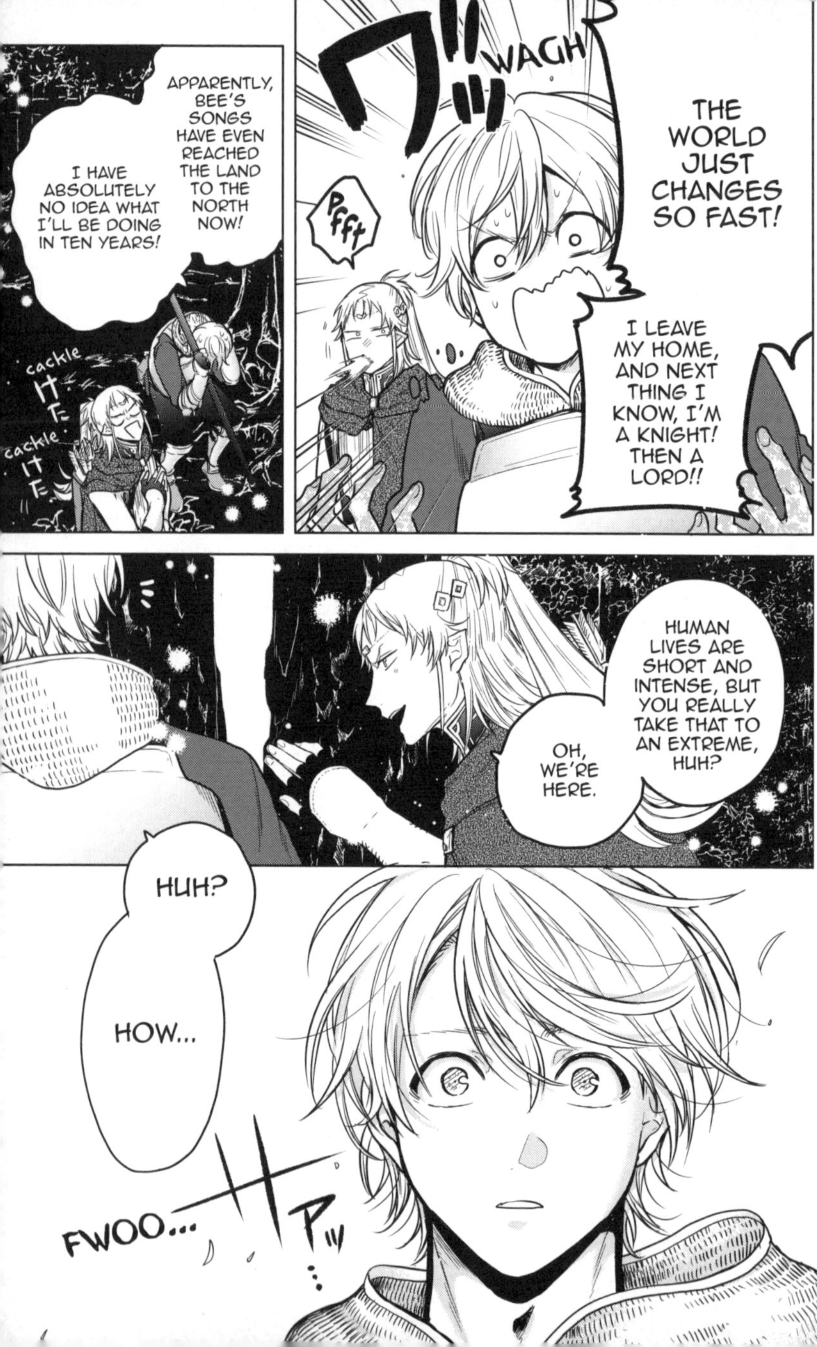
WAGH
THE WORLD JUST CHANGES SO FAST!
I LEAVE MY HOME, AND NEXT THING I KNOW, I'M A KNIGHT! THEN A LORD!!
Pffft
APPARENTLY, BEE'S SONGS HAVE EVEN REACHED THE LAND TO THE NORTH NOW!
I HAVE ABSOLUTELY NO IDEA WHAT I'LL BE DOING IN TEN YEARS!
cackle
cackle
HUMAN LIVES ARE SHORT AND INTENSE, BUT YOU REALLY TAKE THAT TO AN EXTREME, HUH?
OH, WE'RE HERE.
HUH?
HOW...
FWOO...

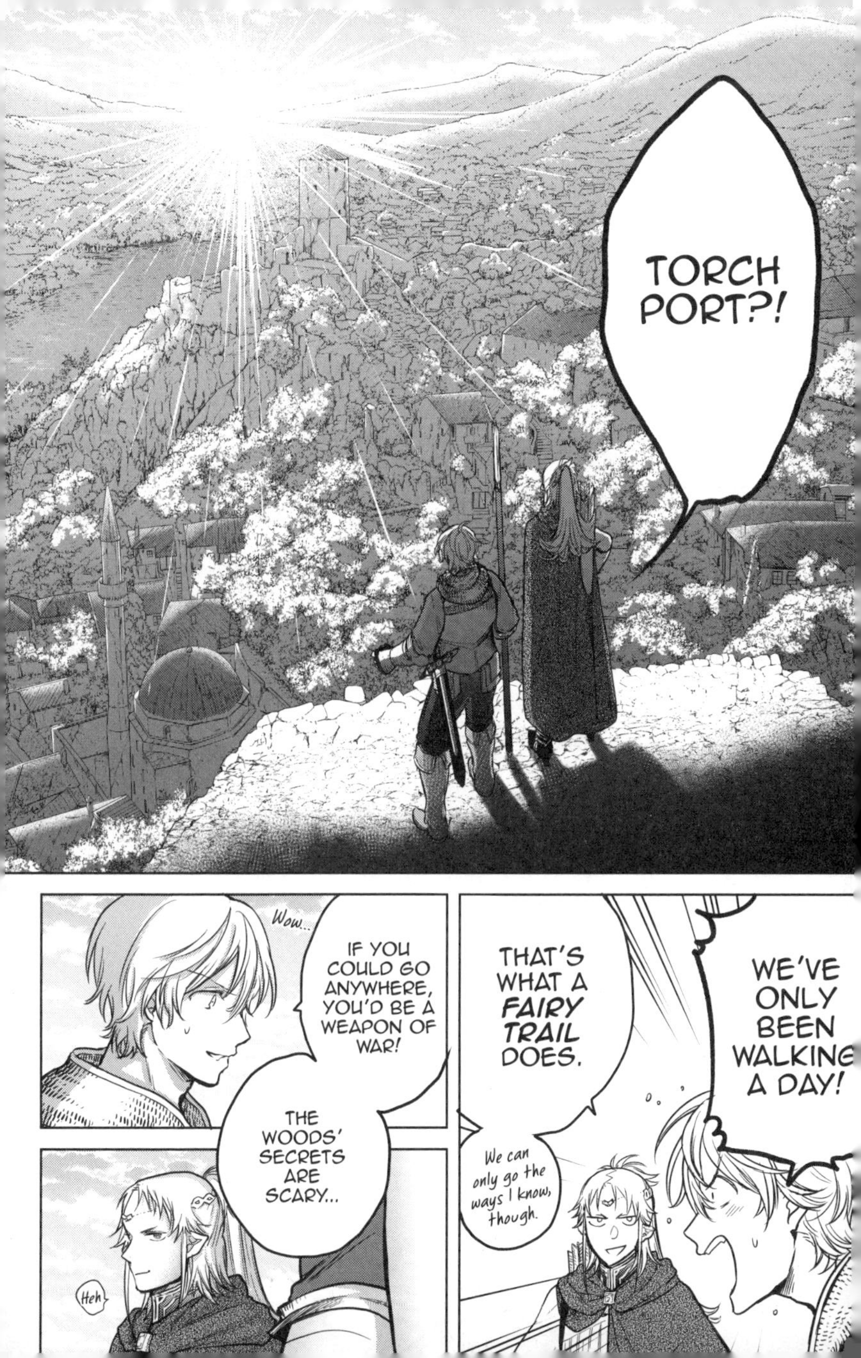
TORCH PORT?!
WE'VE ONLY BEEN WALKING A DAY!
THAT'S WHAT A FAIRY TRAIL DOES.
We can only go the ways I know, though.
Wow...
IF YOU COULD GO ANYWHERE, YOU'D BE A WEAPON OF WAR!
THE WOODS' SECRETS ARE SCARY...
Heh

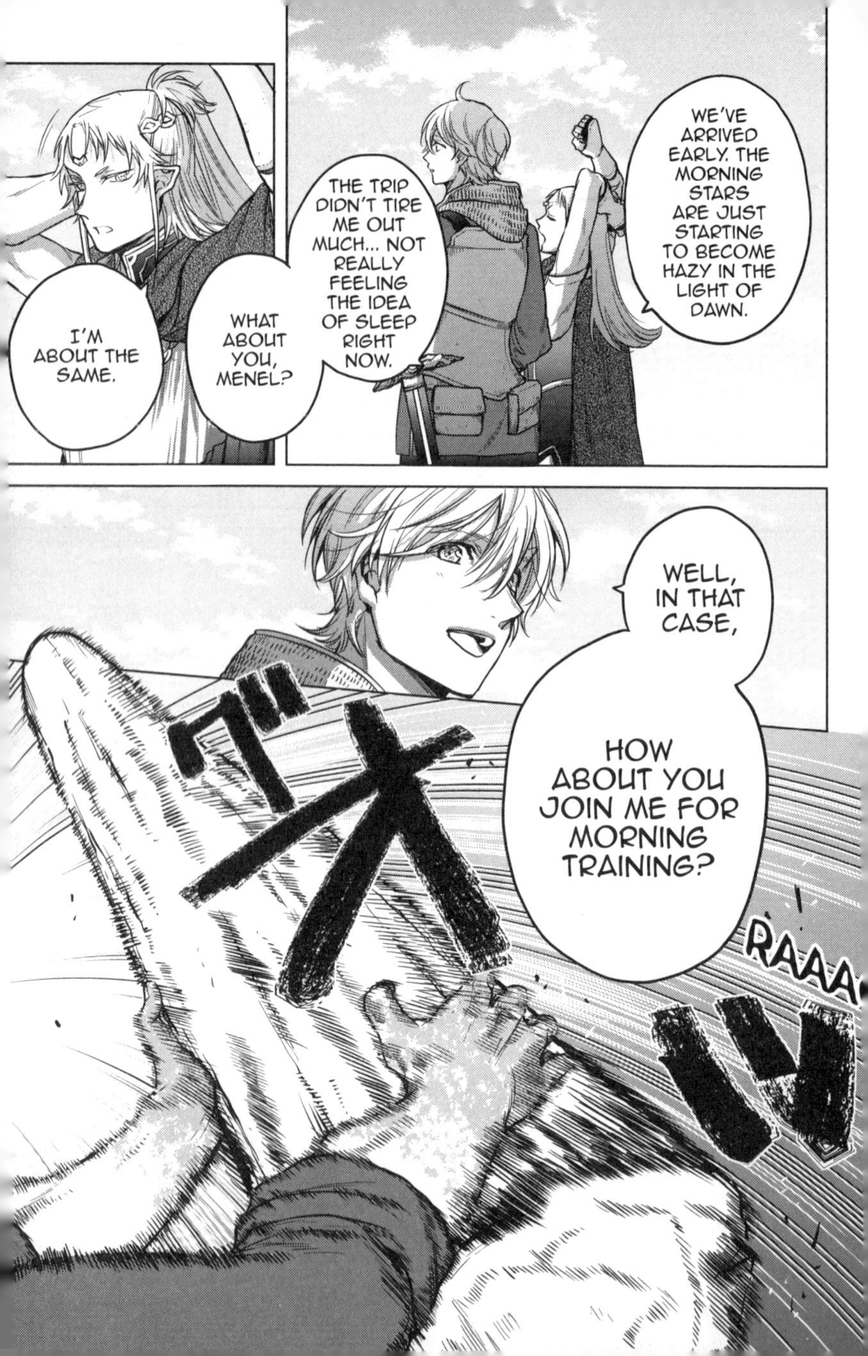

WE'VE ARRIVED EARLY. THE MORNING STARS ARE JUST STARTING TO BECOME HAZY IN THE LIGHT OF DAWN.
THE TRIP DIDN'T TIRE ME OUT MUCH... NOT REALLY FEELING THE IDEA OF SLEEP RIGHT NOW.
WHAT ABOUT YOU, MENEL?
I'M ABOUT THE SAME.
WELL, IN THAT CASE,
HOW ABOUT YOU JOIN ME FOR MORNING TRAINING?
RAAA

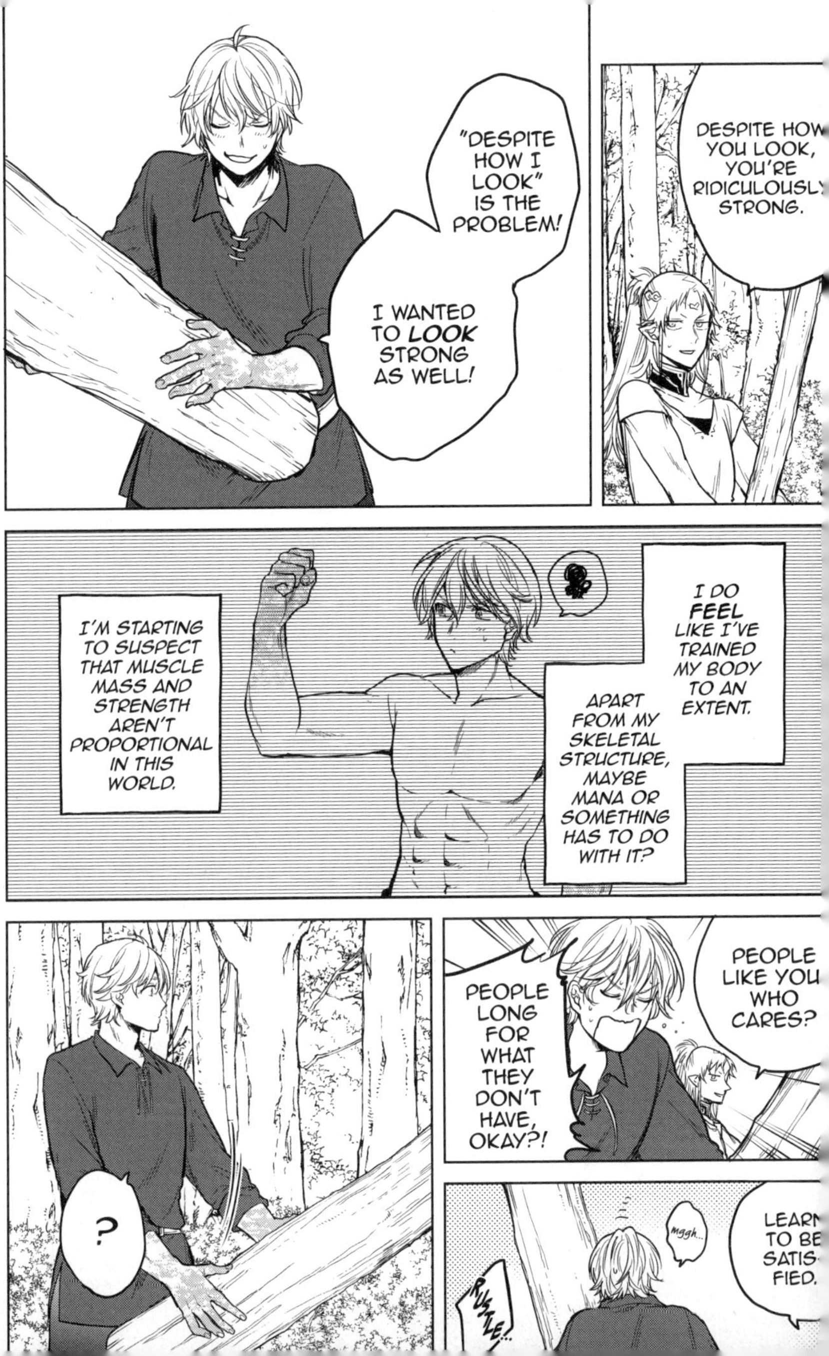
DESPITE HOW YOU LOOK, YOU'RE RIDICULOUSLY STRONG.
"DESPITE HOW I LOOK" IS THE PROBLEM!
I WANTED TO *LOOK* STRONG AS WELL!
I DO *FEEL* LIKE I'VE TRAINED MY BODY TO AN EXTENT.
APART FROM MY SKELETAL STRUCTURE, MAYBE MANA OR SOMETHING HAS TO DO WITH IT?
I'M STARTING TO SUSPECT THAT MUSCLE MASS AND STRENGTH AREN'T PROPORTIONAL IN THIS WORLD.
PEOPLE LIKE YOU WHO CARES?
PEOPLE LONG FOR WHAT THEY DON'T HAVE, OKAY?!
LEARN TO BE SATIS-FIED.
mggh...
RUSTLE...
?

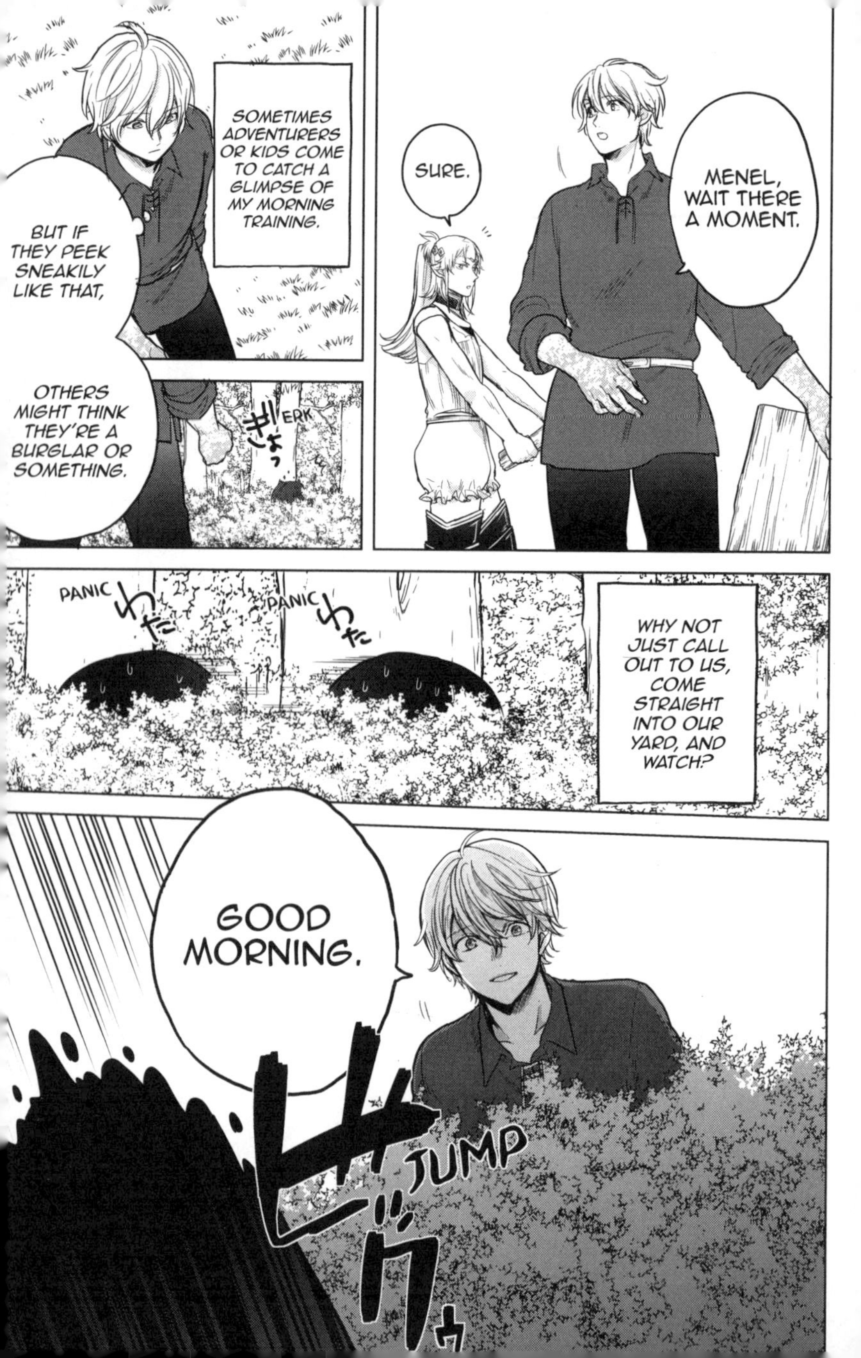

MENEL, WAIT THERE A MOMENT.
SURE.
SOMETIMES ADVENTURERS OR KIDS COME TO CATCH A GLIMPSE OF MY MORNING TRAINING.
BUT IF THEY PEEK SNEAKILY LIKE THAT,
OTHERS MIGHT THINK THEY'RE A BURGLAR OR SOMETHING.
ERK
WHY NOT JUST CALL OUT TO US, COME STRAIGHT INTO OUR YARD, AND WATCH?
PANIC
わた
PANIC
わた
GOOD MORNING.
JUMP
ビクゥ

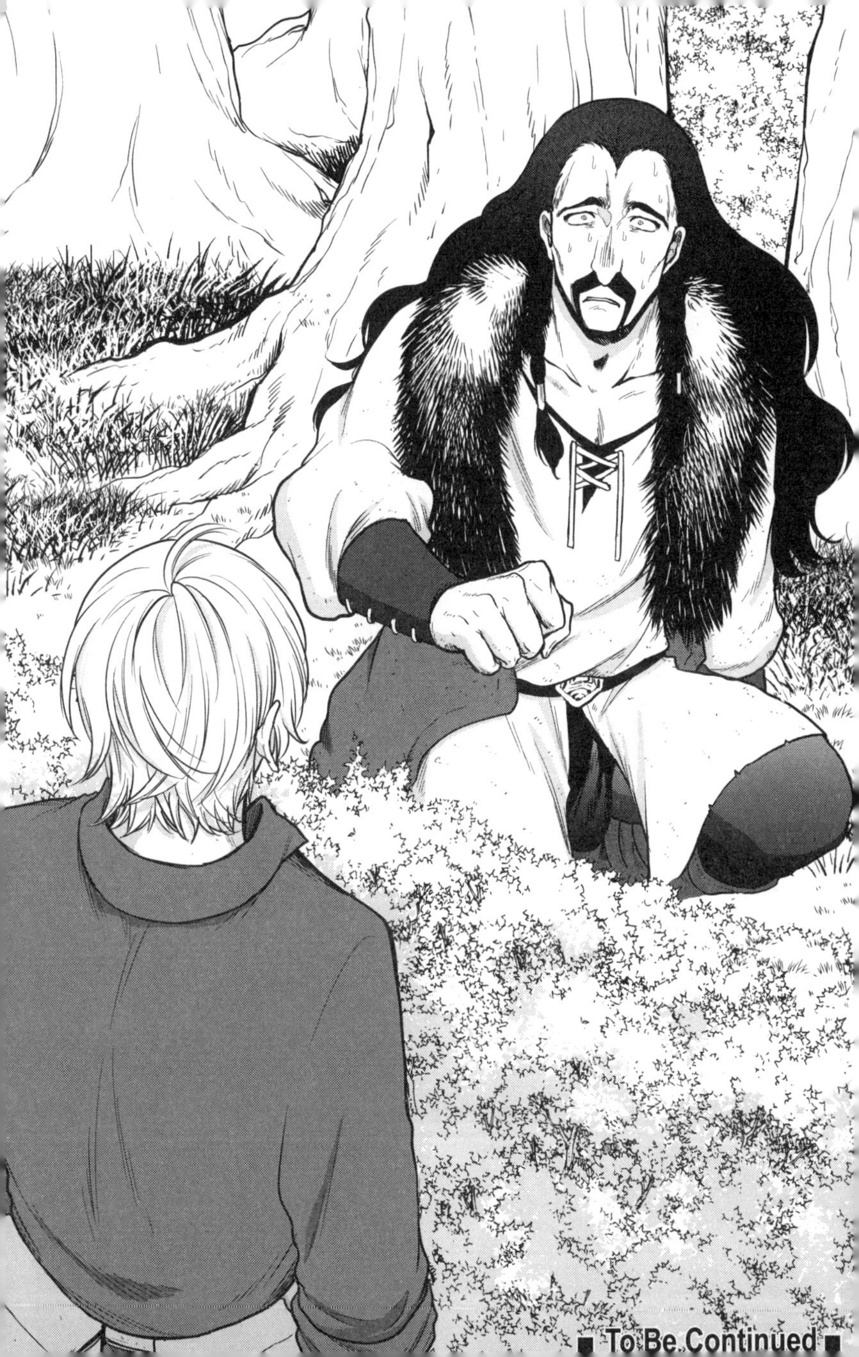
To Be Continued

Afterword

Manga artist: Mutsumi Okubashi

Volume six! This turned into a volume stuffed with content, from battles to daily life to magic. I'm very honored to be able to draw the new adventures of Will, now two years older at 17. I'll roll up my sleeves again and give it my best shot!

Original work: Kanata Yanagino

I fell ill and by the time I recovered, I found myself in the manga's sixth volume. It's impossible for me to fully express my gratitude to Okubashi-sensei. I'll be doing my best to chase after you!

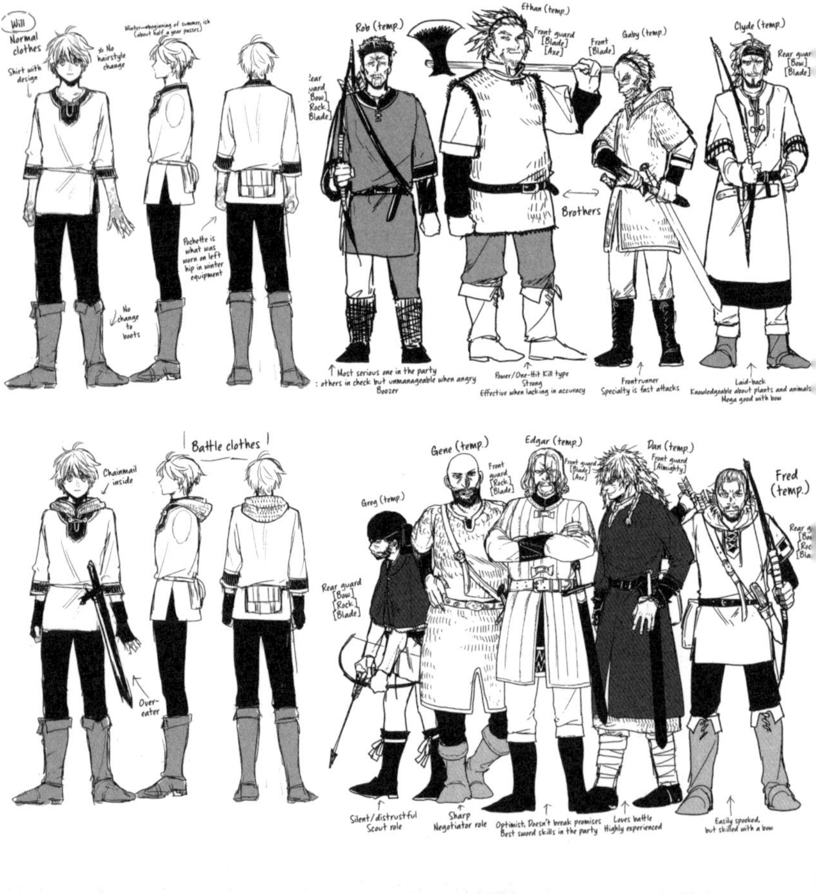

Will
Normal clothes
Shirt with design
No hairstyle change
Winter—beginning of summer, ish (about half a year passes)
Pochette is what was worn on left hip in winter equipment
No change to boots
Rob (temp.)
Rear guard [Bow] [Rock] [Blade]
Most serious one in the party
: others in check but unmanageable when angry
Boozer
Ethan (temp.)
Front guard [Blade] [Axe]
Power/One-Hit Kill type
Strong
Effective when lacking in accuracy
Brothers
Gaby (temp.)
Front [Blade]
Frontrunner
Specialty is fast attacks
Clyde (temp.)
Rear guard [Bow] [Blade]
Laid-back
Knowledgeable about plants and animals
Mega good with bow
Battle clothes
Chainmail inside
Over-eater
Greg (temp.)
Rear guard [Bow] [Rock] [Blade]
Silent/distrustful
Scout role
Gene (temp.)
Front guard [Rock] [Blade]
Sharp
Negotiator role
Edgar (temp.)
Front guard [Blade] [Axe]
Optimist. Doesn't break promises
Best sword skills in the party
Dan (temp.)
Front guard [Almighty]
Loves battle
Highly experienced
Fred (temp.)
Easily spooked, but skilled with a bow

THE FARAWAY PALADIN (MANGA) OMNIBUS 3
by Kanata Yanagino (story) and Mutsumi Okubashi (artwork)
Original character designs by Kususaga Rin

Originally Published as THE FARAWAY PALADIN (MANGA) VOLUMES 5 & 6

Translated by James Rushton
Edited by Sasha McGlynn
Lettered by Brandon Bovia

First published in Japan in 2020 by OVERLAP Inc., Tokyo.
Publication rights for this English edition arranged through OVERLAP Inc., Tokyo.

Find more books like this one at www.j-novel.club!

Managing Director: Samuel Pinansky
Manga Line Manager: J. Collis
Managing Editor: Jan Mitsuko Cash
Managing Translator: Kristi Fernandez
QA Manager: Hannah N. Carter
Marketing Manager: Stephanie Hii

ISBN: 978-1-7183-5932-1
First Printing: July 2022
Printed in Korea
10 9 8 7 6 5 4 3 2 1

THE FARAWAY PALADIN
Manga: MUTSUMI OKUBASHI
Original Work: KANATA YANAGINO
Character Design: KUSUSAGA RIN
MANGA OMNIBUS 4 ON SALE OCTOBER 2022

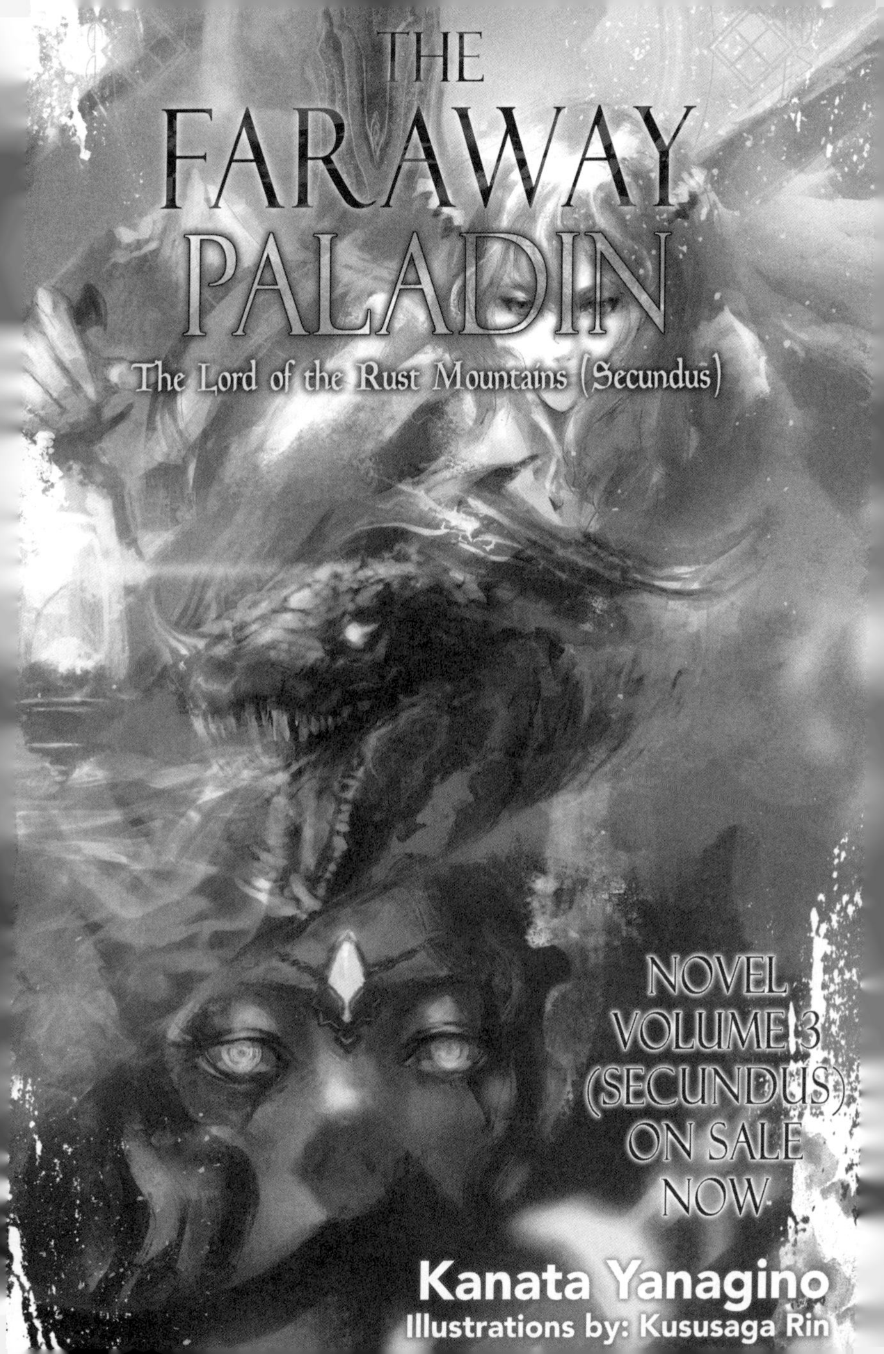
THE FARAWAY PALADIN
The Lord of the Rust Mountains (Secundus)
NOVEL VOLUME 3 (SECUNDUS) ON SALE NOW
Kanata Yanagino
Illustrations by: Kususaga Rin

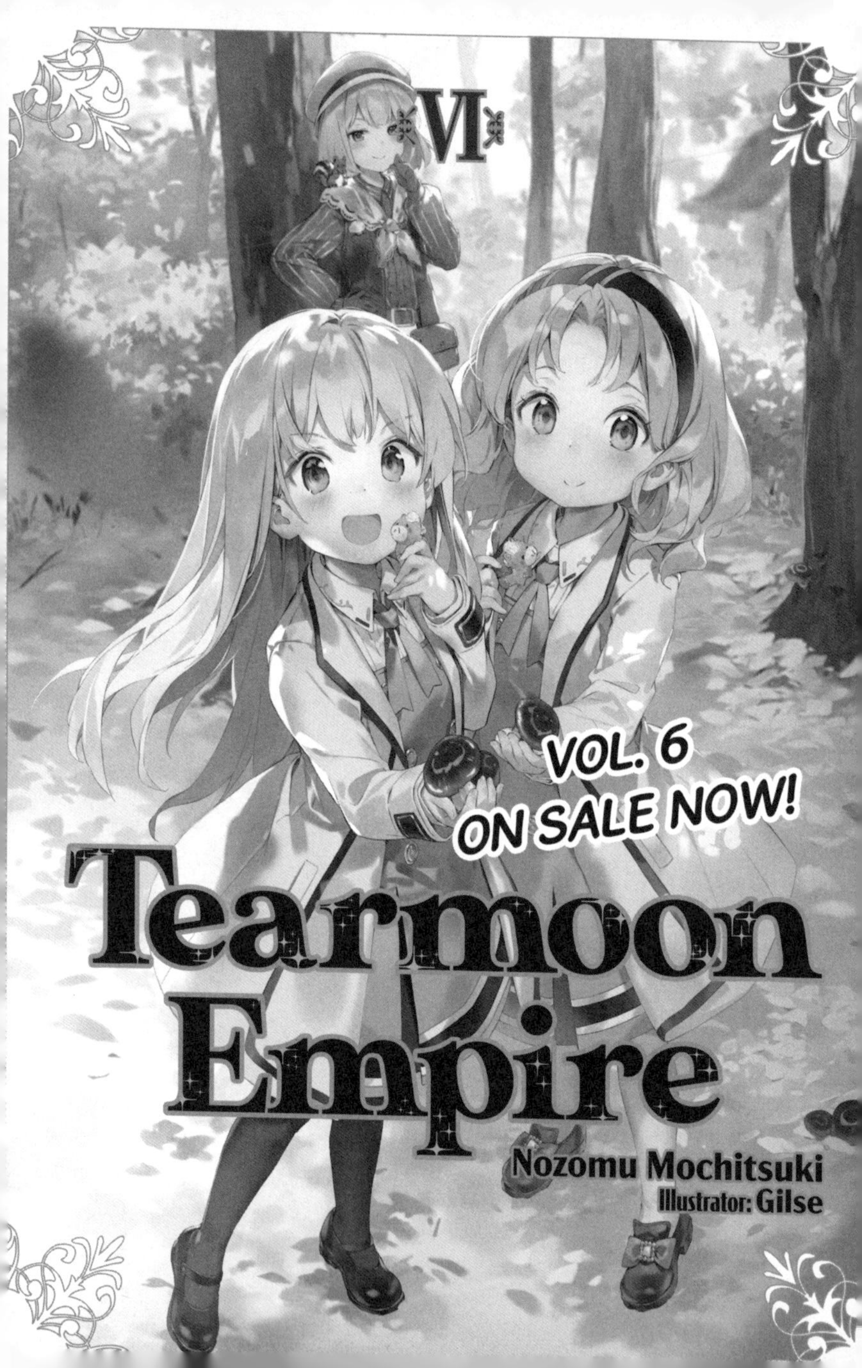
VI
VOL. 6
ON SALE NOW!
Tearmoon Empire
Nozomu Mochitsuki
Illustrator: Gilse

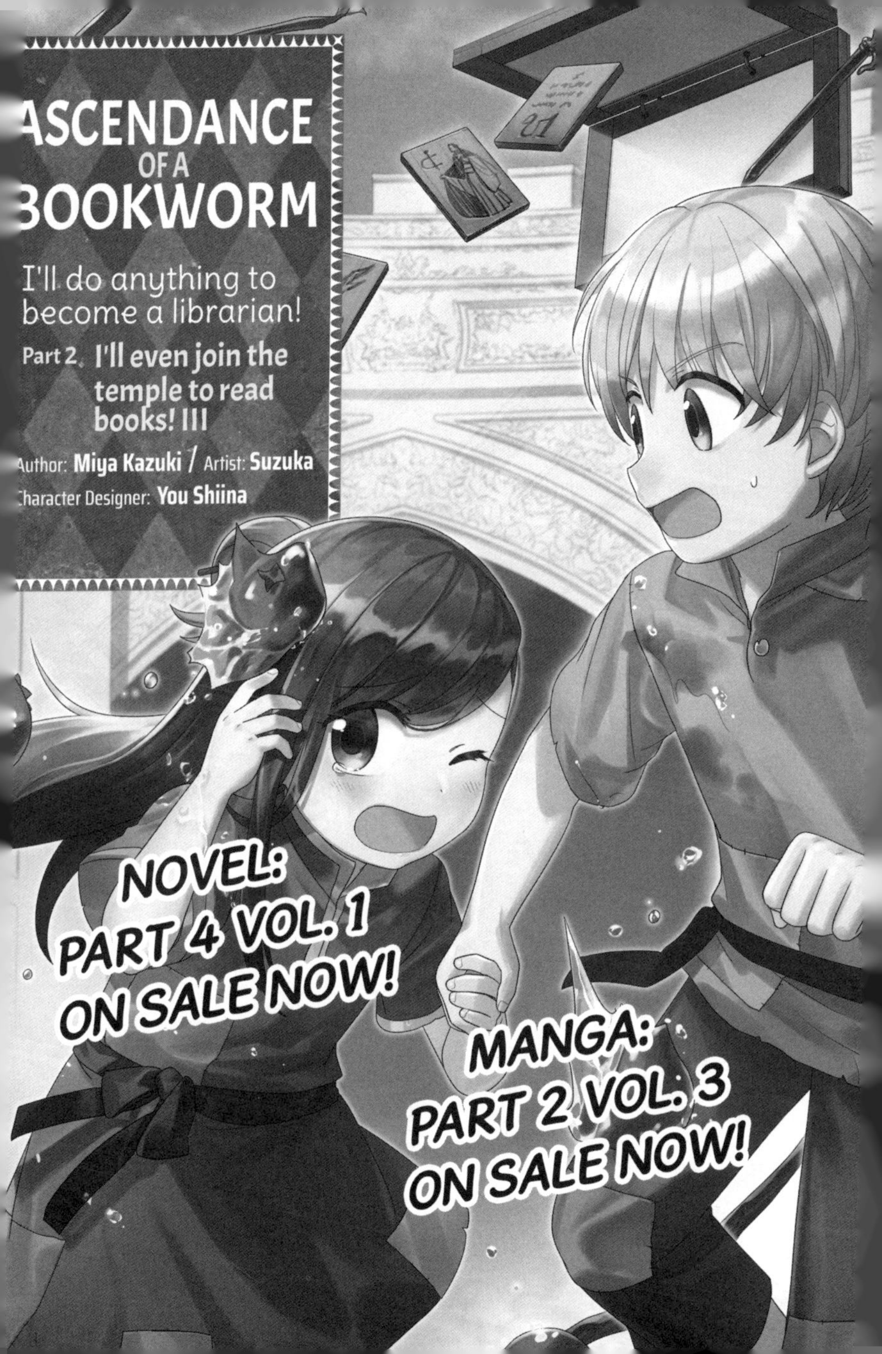
ASCENDANCE
OF A
BOOKWORM
I'll do anything to become a librarian!
Part 2 I'll even join the temple to read books! III
Author: Miya Kazuki / Artist: Suzuka
Character Designer: You Shiina
NOVEL:
PART 4 VOL. 1
ON SALE NOW!
MANGA:
PART 2 VOL. 3
ON SALE NOW!

J

Lat

Altina the Sword Princess
Amagi Brilliant Park
Animeta!**
The Apothecary Diaries
An Archdemon's Dilemma: How to Love Your Elf Bride*
Are You Okay With a Slightly Older Girlfriend?
Arifureta: From Commonplace to World's Strongest
Arifureta Zero
Ascendance of a Bookworm*
Banner of the Stars
Bibliophile Princess*
Black Summoner*
The Bloodline
By the Grace of the Gods
Campfire Cooking in Another World with My Absurd Skill*
Can Someone Please Explain What's Going On?!
Chillin' in Another World with Level 2 Super Cheat Powers
The Combat Baker and Automaton Waitress
Cooking with Wild Game*
Culinary Chronicles of the Court Flower
Dahlia in Bloom: Crafting a Fresh Start with Magical Tools
Deathbound Duke's Daughter
Demon Lord, Retry!*
Der Werwolf: The Annals of Veight*
Dragon Daddy Diaries: A Girl Grows to Greatness
Dungeon Busters
The Emperor's Lady-in-Waiting Is Wanted as a Bride*
Endo and Kobayashi Live! The Latest on Tsundere Villainess Lieselotte
The Faraway Paladin*
Full Metal Panic!
Full Clearing Another World under a Goddess with Zero Believers*
Fushi no Kami: Rebuilding Civilization Starts With a Village
Goodbye Otherworld, See You Tomorrow
The Great Cleric
The Greatest Magicmaster's Retirement Plan
Girls Kingdom
Grimgar of Fantasy and Ash
Hell Mode
Her Majesty's Swarm
Holmes of Kyoto
How a Realist Hero Rebuilt the Kingdom*
How NOT to Summon a Demon Lord
I Shall Survive Using Potions!*
I'll Never Set Foot in That House Again!
The Ideal Sponger Life
If It's for My Daughter, I'd Even Defeat a Demon Lord
In Another World With My Smartphone
Infinite Dendrogram*
Invaders of the Rokujouma!?
Jessica Bannister
JK Haru is a Sex Worker in Another World
John Sinclair: Demon Hunter
A Late-Start Tamer's Laid-Back Life
Lazy Dungeon Master
A Lily Blooms in Another World
Maddrax
The Magic in this Other World is Too Far Behind!*
The Magician Who Rose From Failure
Mapping: The Trash-Tier Skill That Got Me Into a Top-Tier Party*
Marginal Operation**
The Master of Ragnarok & Blesser of Einherjar*
Min-Maxing My TRPG Build in Another World
Monster Tamer
My Daughter Left the Nest and Returned an S-Rank Adventurer
My Friend's Little Sister Has It In for Me!
My Instant Death Ability is So Overpowered, No One in This Other World Stands a Chance Against Me!*
My Next Life as a Villainess: All Routes Lead to Doom!
Otherside Picnic
Outbreak Company
Perry Rhodan NEO
Private Tutor to the Duke's Daughter
Reborn to Master the Blade: From Hero-King to Extraordinary Squire ♀*
Record of Wortenia War*
Reincarnated as the Piggy Duke: This Time I'm Gonna Tell Her How I Feel!
The Reincarnated Princess Spends Another Day Skipping Story Routes
Seirei Gensouki: Spirit Chronicles*
Sexiled: My Sexist Party Leader Kicked Me Out, So I Teamed Up With a Mythical Sorceress!
She's the Cutest... But We're Just Friends!
The Sidekick Never Gets the Girl, Let Alone the Protag's Sister!
Slayers
The Sorcerer's Receptionist
Sorcerous Stabber Orphen*
Sweet Reincarnation**
The Tales of Marielle Clarac*
Tearmoon Empire
Teogonia
The Underdog of the Eight Greater Tribes
The Unwanted Undead Adventurer*
Villainess: Reloaded! Blowing Away Bad Ends with Modern Weapons*
Welcome to Japan, Ms. Elf!*
The White Cat's Revenge as Plotted from the Dragon King's Lap
A Wild Last Boss Appeared!
The World's Least Interesting Master Swordsman

...and more!
* Novel and Manga Editions
** Manga Only
Keep an eye out at j-novel.club for further new title announcements!